2007 SUPPLEMENT

CIVIL PROCEDURE

RULES, STATUTES, AND RECENT DEVELOPMENTS

by

THOMAS D. ROWE, JR.
Elvin R. Latty Professor of Law
Duke University School of Law

SUZANNA SHERRY
Herman O. Loewenstein Professor of Law
Vanderbilt University Law School

JAY TIDMARSH
Professor of Law
Notre Dame Law School

NEW YORK, NEW YORK
FOUNDATION PRESS
2007

395 Hudson Street
New York, NY 10014
Phone Toll Free 1–877–888–1330
Fax (212) 367–6799
foundation–press.com
Printed in the United States of America

ISBN 978–1–59941–305–1

TEXT IS PRINTED ON 10% POST
CONSUMER RECYCLED PAPER

TABLE OF CONTENTS

DEVELOPMENTS AND CLARIFICATIONS

AUTHORS' NOTE

On April 30, 2007, the Supreme Court promulgated an extensively revised version of the Federal Rules of Civil Procedure. Unless Congress passes legislation to keep these rules from taking effect, which seems very unlikely, the revised Federal Rules of Civil Procedure will become effective on December 1, 2007, during the middle of your first year of law school. With the exception of the new Rule 5.2 and some very minor "style/substance" fixes, these amendments to the Federal Rules of Civil Procedure are meant to be only stylistic. For a number of years, the Supreme Court and various committees within the federal judiciary have been engaged in a project to make the rules used in federal courts nationwide more readable and user-friendly. The latest set of rules to be revised is the Federal Rules of Civil Procedure.

Although the stylistic changes are intended only to make the rules clearer and more accessible, they change much of the language of the present Federal Rules. You will probably notice two types of changes. First, the Rules are broken into more sections, subsections, and sub-subsections. As a result, although each Federal Rule retains its original number, the sections, subsections, and sub-subsections of that Rule will often have a different title, number, or designation. As you read the cases in the casebook, which have all been decided under the present or earlier Federal Rules, you will sometimes need to identify the new provision containing the same Rule. Second, the new Rules use various clarifying techniques such as active voice and replacing longer noun-and-preposition-laden phrases with shorter gerunds. An example of both types of change is the present Rule 16(c)(1), which you can compare with the pending Rule 16(c)(2)(A). Another good example of breaking into subsections for clarity and ease of reference is Rule 14(a), a ten-sentence, single-paragraph monster in its present form that will now have six subsections with descriptive catchlines, with one subsection having four sub-subsections.

This Supplement includes both the present Rules (starting *infra* p. 71) and the pending Rules (starting *infra* p. 401). During the transitional period and even beyond (when we will sometimes need to match up pre- and post-2007 provisions), all of us need to be conversant with both sets of Rules.

CHAPTER TWO: PLEADING

Page 44: In the last two years the Supreme Court has become more active in the area of policing pleadings. In 2005, the Supreme Court for the first time encountered a pleading that failed to meet the requirements of Rule 8(a). Dura Pharms., Inc. v. Broudo, 544 U.S. 336 (2005). In *Dura Pharmaceuticals*, the plaintiffs alleged that they had bought stock in the defendant after the defendant had made false claims about a new asthma drug that it was developing. The price of the stock fell when the defendant failed to meet earnings expectations. Several months later, the price again fell on the day that the defendant announced that the Food and Drug Administration had not approved the new asthma drug, but then rebounded in the following week to its level before the FDA announcement. The plaintiffs' theory was that they could prove their loss simply by showing that their purchase price was inflated because of the misrepresentation. The Court first rejected the view that such a claim established a violation of federal securities laws, which require that the shareholders' losses be caused by the defendant's fraudulent behavior. Although a misrepresentation might result in an inflated purchase price, that fact does not mean that the misrepresentation caused shareholders' losses — which might instead have resulted from market forces other than the misrepresentation. Next, the Court found that the complaint, which pleaded only enough facts to show that the price of the stock was inflated due to fraud, did not provide adequate notice of the causal connection between the defendant's wrong and the plaintiffs' loss.

In 2007, the Supreme Court decided four cases whose implications will be sorted out in the years to come. First, in Jones v. Bock, 549 U.S. —, 127 S. Ct. 910 (2007), inmates sued prison officials under 42 U.S.C. § 1983 for violating their civil rights. Under the federal Prison Litigation Reform Act, inmates must first exhaust any grievance procedures available within the prison before filing suit, and federal courts must try to screen out frivolous complaints. Pursuant to this law, the Court of Appeals for the Sixth Circuit imposed three requirements on inmates: They needed to plead the fact of exhaustion in their complaints, they were able to sue only those prison officials named in the grievance, and their filing of a mixture of exhausted and unexhausted claims resulted in dismissal of the entire complaint, not just the unexhausted claims. The Supreme Court rejected each of the three limitations. In rejecting the first requirement, the Court made these observations:

> Federal Rule of Civil Procedure 8(a) requires simply a "short and plain statement of the claim" in a complaint, while Rule 8(c) identifies a nonexhaustive list of affirmative defenses that must be pleaded in response. . . . [The inmates] assert that courts typically regard exhaustion as an affirmative defense in other contexts, and respondents do not seriously dispute the general proposition. . . .This is strong evidence that the usual practice should be followed, and the usual

practice under the Federal Rules is to regard exhaustion as an affirmative defense.

> In a series of recent cases, we have explained that courts should generally not depart from the usual practice under the Federal Rules on the basis of perceived policy concerns. Thus, in Leatherman v. Tarrant County Narcotics Intelligence and Coordination Unit, 507 U.S. 163 (1993), we unanimously reversed the court of appeals for imposing a heightened pleading standard in § 1983 suits against municipalities. . . .
>
> In Swierkiewicz v. Sorema N.A., 534 U.S. 506 (2002), we unanimously reversed the court of appeals for requiring employment discrimination plaintiffs to specifically allege the elements of a prima facie case of discrimination. We explained that "the Federal Rules do not contain a heightened pleading standard for employment discrimination suits," and a "requirement of greater specificity for particular claims" must be obtained by amending the Federal Rules. And just last Term, in Hill v. McDonough, 547 U.S. —, 126 S.Ct. 2096, (2006), we unanimously rejected a proposal that § 1983 suits challenging a method of execution must identify an acceptable alternative: "Specific pleading requirements are mandated by the Federal Rules of Civil Procedure, and not, as a general rule, through case-by-case determinations of the federal courts." . . .
>
> . . . We understand the reasons behind the decisions of some lower courts to impose a pleading requirement on plaintiffs in this context, but that effort cannot fairly be viewed as an interpretation of the PLRA. "Whatever temptations the statesmanship of policy-making might wisely suggest," the judge's job is to construe the statute — not to make it better. . . . Given that the PLRA does not itself require plaintiffs to plead exhaustion, such a result "must be obtained by the process of amending the Federal Rules, and not by judicial interpretation."

Second, in Bell Atlantic Corp. v. Twombly, 550 U.S. —, 127 S. Ct. 1955 (2007) (*infra* p. 25), the Court seems to have swung back in the direction of *Dura Pharmaceuticals*. *Bell Atlantic* involved an antitrust complaint filed by consumers against some of the largest regional phone companies (such as SBC, Verizon, and Qwest) that provide local phone service. The claim was that, despite a 1996 law that tried to break down the local-service monopolies that each carrier enjoyed within its regions, the defendants had essentially maintained their monopolistic positions by agreeing among themselves both to render difficult the entry of other competitors into the local telephone market and not to enter each other's local markets. Under the relevant antitrust law, the plaintiffs needed to prove at trial that the defendants had actually conspired with each other to maintain their market positions; simply engaging in the same behavior without agreeing to do so is lawful. The plaintiffs had no direct evidence of an illegal agreement. As a result, their complaint contained allegations taken from newspaper articles and reports that described both the barriers to entry that each of the defendants had erected and the failure of the companies to compete in each other's territories. The complaint then concluded with this allegation:

> In the absence of any meaningful competition between the [defendants] in one another's markets, and in light of the parallel course of conduct that each engaged in to prevent competition from [other companies] within their respective local telephone and/or high speed internet services markets and the other facts and market circumstances alleged above, Plaintiffs allege upon information and belief that Defendants have entered into a contract, combination or conspiracy to prevent competitive entry in their respective local telephone and/or high speed internet services markets and have agreed not to compete with one another and otherwise allocated customers and markets to one another.

The Supreme Court held that, in the absence of further factual allegations demonstrating an unlawful agreement, the complaint failed to state a claim; thus, it affirmed dismissal of the case. It ruled that "a conclusory allegation of agreement at some unidentified point does not supply facts adequate to show illegality." In the course of the decision, the Court emphasized that the behavior alleged by the plaintiff had a benign and legal alternative explanation, that antitrust litigation is very expensive, and that the "no set of facts" standard of Conley v. Gibson, 355 U.S. 41 (1957) (Casebook p. 58) should be put into "retirement." The Court distinguished *Swierkiewicz* on the ground that while the court of appeals in *Swierkiewicz* had imposed a "heightened pleading requirement" by "insisting that Swierkiewicz allege 'specific facts,'" the *Twombly* holding did "not require heightened fact pleading of specifics, but only enough facts to state a claim to relief that is plausible on its face." The plaintiffs had not, however, "nudged their claims across the line from conceivable to plausible." Justice Stevens, joined by Justice Ginsburg, filed a vigorous dissent arguing that the Court's holding in fact imposed a heightened pleading standard.

Third, in Erickson v. Pardus, 551 U.S. —, 127 S. Ct. 2197 (2007) (per curiam) (*infra* p. 35), the Court arguably veered back toward a more liberal construction of pleadings. *Erickson* involved a decision by prison officials to suspend medical treatment of an inmate for 18 months because the inmate allegedly was taking illegal drugs. The inmate's complaint alleged the prison officials had "removed [him] from [his] hepatitis C treatment" in violation of department protocol, "thus endangering [his] life." The court of appeals upheld a dismissal of the case, arguing that the complaint had failed to state facts, as opposed to a single "conclusory" statement, showing that his health would be jeopardized by the 18-month delay. The Supreme Court reversed, holding that the allegation was sufficient. Without any extended discussion, the Court cited both *Bell Atlantic* and *Conley v. Gibson* — but only for the proposition that a complaint must give fair notice of the claim and the grounds on which it rests.

Finally, in Tellabs, Inc. v. Makor Issues & Rights, Ltd., 551 U.S. —, 2007 WL 1773208 (2007), the Court interpreted the Private Securities Litigation Reform Act of 1995 (PSLRA), which explicitly imposes a higher pleading standard for private class-action complaints alleging securities fraud: Plaintiffs must "state with particularity facts giving rise to a strong inference" of intent to defraud. The Court held that "[t]o qualify as 'strong'

. . . an inference [of intent to defraud] must be more than merely plausible or reasonable — it must be cogent and at least as compelling as any opposing inference of nonfraudulent intent." The Court thus distinguished between "plausible" claims and claims sufficient to satisfy the PSLRA's more stringent pleading requirement. While drawing on other cases dealing with ordinary as opposed to heightened federal pleading standards, the Court did not cite *Bell Atlantic*, which had first imposed the requirement that ordinary pleadings be "plausible."

Page 47, Note 7: In Wilkinson v. Wells Fargo Bank MN, 2007 WL 1414888 (E.D. Wis. May 9, 2007), the district court dismissed a case in part because the complaint was too long and therefore failed to meet the "short and plain" requirement of Rule 8(a)(2). The case involved a creditor's decision to foreclose on the plaintiff's home when the plaintiff's account allegedly became delinquent; the plaintiff disputed the delinquency, but the creditor allegedly refused to respond to his claim. The plaintiff, who was proceeding without a lawyer, filed a "massive, nearly incomprehensible [complaint] of roughly 200 pages." The district court observed that, "[t]o the extent the complaint is comprehensible," it appeared to assert claims under federal debt-collection and mail-fraud statutes, as well as "two seemingly non-existent Wisconsin laws." The opinion stated that ["i]t is not the duty of the court or the defendants to sift through a massive filing in an attempt to discern a 'short and plain statement of the claim.' For this reason, courts routinely dismiss complaints on the ground that they are unintelligible." The court also found that a number of the claims lacked legal merit.

Page 57: Williams v. Advertising Sex LLC, 231 F.R.D. 483 (N.D. W. Va. 2005), followed *Rio* and authorized e-mail service under Rule 4(f)(3) on three Australian defendants. The defendants operated a pornographic Web site, and were among the 59 defendants sued for posting a graphic video that falsely claimed to involve the plaintiff, a former Miss West Virginia. The defendants were even dodgier than Rio International, successfully avoiding 13 efforts at personal service and another effort by international registered mail. Among the factors cited by the court in authorizing e-mail service were the defendants' sophistication in e-commerce and the failure of Australia to sign the Hague Convention on the Service Abroad of Judicial and Extrajudicial Documents. Unlike *Rio*, it is not clear that the defendants had actual notice of the lawsuit. In light of Australia's failure to sign the Hague Convention and the defendants' slipperiness, it also is not clear how the plaintiff intended to enforce a judgment in Australia.

Also following *Rio* is Philip Morris USA Inc. v. Veles Ltd, 2007 WL 725412 (S.D.N.Y. Mar. 12, 2007), in which the court authorized service by fax and e-mail on online sellers of cigarettes. Efforts to locate and serve the defendants took the plaintiff around the world, from Singapore to Russia, Dominica, and Moldova — all without success. In its motion to permit service by fax and e-mail, the plaintiff showed that service under either Rule 4(f)(1) or Rule 4(f)(2) was an inadequate option.

Page 60: In Bell Atlantic Corp. v. Twombly, 550 U.S. —, 127 S. Ct.1955 (2007) (*infra* p. 25), discussed *supra* pp. 3-4 (Note for Page 44), the Supreme

Court stated that the "no set of facts" standard announced in Conley v. Gibson, 355 U.S. 41 (1957) (Casebook p. 58) "has been questioned, criticized, and explained away long enough," and therefore put the standard into "retirement." The "no set of facts" standard relates to substantive insufficiency, but *Bell Atlantic* emphasized the complaint's failure to allege sufficient facts to demonstrate unlawful behavior and began its analysis with *Conley*'s "fair notice" standard for formal insufficiency.

Dura Pharmaceuticals, Inc. v. Broudo, 544 U.S. 336 (2005), discussed *supra* p. 2 (Note for Page 44), also shows the slipperiness between formal and substantive insufficiency. Although the opinion speaks of the failure of the complaint to give adequate notice of a viable legal theory (a question of formal insufficiency), the case might be better understood to hold that a legal theory that was adequately pleaded failed to state a claim (a question of substantive insufficiency).

Page 61: The Second Circuit reversed the district court's 12(b)(6) dismissal of *Pelman*. *See* Pelman v. McDonald's Corp., 396 F.3d 508 (2d Cir. 2005). The Court of Appeals held the complaint sufficient primarily because New York's consumer-protection statute does not require proof that plaintiffs relied on defendant's alleged misrepresentations, but only that the defendant's statements were objectively misleading or deceptive. Plaintiffs in *Pelman* had adequately alleged deceptive and misleading statements. On remand, the district court granted in part the defendant's motion for a more definite statement under Rule 12(e). *See* Pelman v. McDonald's Corp., 396 F.Supp.2d 439 (S.D.N.Y. 2005). It then declined to dismiss the amended complaint. *See* Pelman v. McDonald's Corp., 452 F.Supp.2d 320 (S.D.N.Y. 2006) (finding sufficient allegations of defendant's awareness of allegedly deceptive nutritional schemes and of injuries suffered by each plaintiff).

Pages 67-70: In Day v. McDonough, 547 U.S. 198 (2006), the Supreme Court addressed the issue of a defendant's failure to raise the statute of limitations as an affirmative defense. The failure arose because of a simple miscalculation of time, which the defendant failed to notice. The Court held that absent a defendant's deliberate waiver of the statute-of-limitations defense, the federal court was permitted to overlook the defendant's error and dismiss the case *sua sponte* (on the court's own initiative). *Day* may or may not have much precedential value in ordinary civil cases, because it involved a petition for a writ of habeas corpus. Habeas is a specialized legal procedure for prisoners who seek federal review of their criminal convictions. According to Fed. R. Civ. P. 81(a)(2) (*infra* p. 277), the Federal Rules of Civil Procedure apply in habeas proceedings unless they are altered by specific rules governing habeas. What makes *Day* unusual, and therefore difficult to interpret, is that ordinarily when the Court departs from the Federal Rules of Civil Procedure in habeas cases, it points to a specific inconsistency between the Rule at issue and the habeas statutes, rules, or historical practice. As the dissent pointed out, the majority in *Day* found no such inconsistency. The dissenters thought that a straightforward application of the forfeiture rule for unpleaded Rule 8(c) affirmative defenses barred the majority's reliance on the statute of limitations. The majority instead relied on the similarity between the statute of limitations and other affirmative defenses that *are* part of the habeas statutes, rules, or historical practice, and that courts are able to raise on their own even when the defendant neglects to do so. So the holding in *Day* might (or might not) be limited to habeas corpus.

What all the Justices agreed on, however, is that even if the district court had not dismissed the case *sua sponte*, the judge was permitted to point out the error to the defendant, who could then move for leave to amend the answer under Fed. R. Civ. P. 15(a) in order to assert the statute-of-limitations defense. As discussed in the casebook at pp. 70-73, that motion is in most cases freely granted.

In Jones v. Bock, 549 U.S. —, 127 S. Ct. 910 (2007), discussed *supra* pp. 2-3 (Note for Page 44), the Supreme Court held that an inmate's failure to exhaust administrative remedies is an affirmative defense that a defendant should plead under Rule 8(c).

Pages 74-76: The Supreme Court interpreted the "same conduct, transaction, or occurrence" language of Rule 15(c)(2) narrowly in Mayle v. Felix, 545 U.S. 644 (2005):

> The majority of Circuits . . . allow relation back only when the claims added by amendment arise from the same core facts as the timely filed claims, and not when the new claims depend upon events separate in "both time and type" from the originally raised episodes. . . .
>
> . . . Rule 15(c)(2) relaxes, but does not obliterate, the statute of limitations; hence relation back depends on the existence of a common "core of operative facts" uniting the original and newly asserted claims.

Pages 82-85: The First Circuit has explicitly disagreed with the Second Circuit's interpretation of Rule 11 in *Pennie & Edmonds*. *See* Young v. City of Providence, 404 F.3d 33, 39-40 (1st Cir. 2005). In *Young*, the court held that the same standard applies regardless of whether the imposition of sanctions is the result of another party's motion or a *sua sponte* inquiry by the court. In either case, sanctions can be imposed for "falsity and serious carelessness" — the court's description of objective unreasonableness — even in the absence of subjective bad faith. This ruling means that the last sentence in Note 1 on page 85 of the casebook is incorrect: The issue is no longer "undecided" in other circuits. And now that there is a circuit split, the chances increase that the Supreme Court will decide the question. *See also* Jenkins v. Methodist Hosps. of Dallas, Inc., 478 F.3d 255 (5th Cir. 2007) (citing *Young* favorably and applying an objective standard to counsel sanctioned *sua sponte*, but not directly rejecting *Pennie & Edmonds*).

CHAPTER THREE: DISCOVERY

Page 106: In the sixth line from the bottom of the page, "and within 120 days of filing the complaint" should be "and within 120 days after any defendant has been served."

Pages 118-27: On December 1, 2006, important amendments to Rules 16, 26, 33, 34, 37, and 45 went into effect. The amendments deal with the increasingly vexatious problem of disclosure and discovery of electronically stored information ("e-discovery"). Here we summarize reasons for the changes and key aspects of the amendments.

E-discovery problems are not entirely novel; kindred issues have arisen for decades with discovery of paper documents, and e-discovery has been and to a considerable extent will remain governed by the general disclosure and discovery rules — sometimes with judicial interpretations to adapt those rules to new circumstances. *See, e.g.*, Zubulake v. UBS Warburg LLC, 217 F.R.D. 309 (S.D.N.Y. 2003) (Casebook p. 118). But e-discovery can greatly intensify some problems or present novel twists. Although computer searching for relevant information can sometimes be easy, the sheer volume of electronically stored files and their organization for purposes other than litigation can make discovery difficult and expensive — perhaps increasing pressure to settle to avoid the discovery costs. Converting data on disaster-recovery tapes to active form can be disruptive to regular operations; "litigation holds" forbidding the destruction, alteration, or overwriting of such materials can escalate costs for tapes and storage, especially for large, often-sued companies. Inadvertent waivers of possible privilege claims from producing documents may be harder to avoid with massive e-discovery than with hard copy.

At the same time, parties may find it harder to prove legitimate claims or defenses without getting at sometimes hard-to-find electronically stored information, and concern for inadvertent or deliberate destruction of possibly relevant evidence is genuine. Finally, some district courts had begun to adopt their own local e-discovery rules; federal rulemakers were concerned that proliferation of local rules could lead to entrenchment that would make uniform national rulemaking harder ("We're happy with the way we're doing it here, so please leave us alone.").

The 2006 amendments sometimes give special treatment to e-discovery; sometimes, however, the amendments clarify that the existing rules apply to e-discovery, or make changes to the discovery process not limited to e-discovery but prompted at least in part by experience with it. The two most controversial aspects, both involving special treatment for e-discovery, are: (1) to add a new Rule 26(b)(2)(B), which permits a party not to produce relevant and otherwise discoverable electronically stored information on the ground that it is from a source identified as "not reasonably accessible because of undue burden or cost," and (2) to add a new Rule 37(f) limiting sanctions for loss of discoverable information through "routine, good-faith operation of an electronic information system."

Examples of the types of electronically stored information for which the Rule 26(b)(2)(B) "two-tier" approach might permit a responding party to claim that it was "not reasonably accessible" are deleted items, disaster-recovery tapes, and "legacy" data that can be accessed only with earlier technology no longer in use. This approach may be less significant than it first appears, because the ground for asserting that data are "not reasonably accessible" must be "undue burden or cost" — and excessive "burden or expense" is already a ground for limiting discovery under existing Rule 26(b)(2)(iii). On a motion to compel or for a protective order, the requested party must satisfy the court that its assertion is justified. Even if the court so finds, it may still order discovery from the "not reasonably accessible" sources "if the requesting party shows good cause." In ordering such discovery, the court may impose conditions including cost-sharing or cost-shifting.

Most controversial is Rule 37(f)'s "safe-harbor" feature, which forbids, absent "exceptional circumstances," sanctions for the loss of discoverable information through "routine, good-faith operation of an electronic information system" such as a record retention/destruction program. This provision is a compromise. Some, especially the defense bar, feared that sanctions (such as an adverse-inference instruction to the jury) could follow too readily from legitimate operation of systems designed to save expense by destroying old records; others, mostly the plaintiffs' bar, saw danger of systems being tweaked to "routinely" destroy possibly damaging information. The likeliest source of litigation under Rule 37(f) may be a party's failure to change or suspend routine operation of the system when the party is obligated (by, say, court order or party agreement) to preserve information. The Advisory Committee Note to Rule 37(f) indicates that such a failure can be reason to find a lack of good faith. The new rule by itself creates no obligations respecting pre-litigation conduct, although a statute, a regulation, common law, or a rule of professional responsibility may impose a duty to preserve information.

Briefly, the three other main aspects of the e-discovery amendments are:

- Changes to Rule 26(f) on the parties' planning conference and Rule 16(b) on scheduling orders to deal with planning for disclosure and discovery. The amendments add e-discovery matters (such as form of production) to existing lists of what the parties are to discuss in their planning conference and to include in their discovery plan, and what the court may include in its scheduling order. They also add to the existing lists other items such as preserving discoverable information, which applies to — but is not limited to — e-discovery.
- Addition of Rule 26(b)(5)(B) to deal with situations in which a party who has produced *any* form of information (including but not limited to electronically stored data) thinks that it has produced information for which it can nonetheless claim a privilege or protection — such as attorney-client or work-product. Under the Rule, the producing party notifies the receiving party, who has two options: either return, sequester, or destroy the material — subject to a possible later ruling on whether the material was privileged or protected and whether a waiver has taken place — or present the material to the court under seal for a ruling on the claim. The producing party must preserve the information until the claim is resolved. This amendment deals solely with the process of seeking

to recapture produced material; it does not affect whether a privilege or protection applies or whether waiver has occurred.

- Alterations in Rules 33 and 34 to deal with producing information in response to interrogatories and requests for production and inspection:
  - » To Rule 33(d), which extends a responding party's option to produce business records (instead of providing answers) in response to interrogatories to electronically stored information. The rule already requires that, for the responder to use this option, the burden of deriving the requested answer from the records must be substantially the same for both parties.
  - » To Rule 34(a)(1), which makes explicit that electronically stored information, like information in other forms, is subject to requests for production and inspection.
  - » To Rule 34(b), which both permits a requesting party to specify the form or forms in which e-data must be produced and allows a responding party to object to those form or forms and state the form or forms it will use. Absent such a specification, amended Rule 34(b) — subject to change by the parties' agreement or court order — requires production of e-data either in a form or forms in which they are "ordinarily maintained," or in a form or forms "reasonably usable" by the requester.

Finally, with respect to the seven cost-shifting factors mentioned in *Zubulake*, you might wish to look at the Committee Note for the 2006 Amendment to Rule 26(b)(2). The Note also lists seven factors relevant to the decision whether to require a party to search for and produce e-discovery. *See infra* p. 186. The list of factors significantly overlaps with, but is distinct from, the *Zubulake* list. For a case that refuses to shift the costs of searching a disaster-recovery tape and analyzes the relationship between the *Zubulake* factors and the Committee Note's factors, see Semsroth v. City of Wichita, 239 F.R.D. 630 (D. Kan. 2006).

Pages 147-52: For a sanctions case that would make a great sitcom episode if it were not true, see Recinos-Recinos v. Express Forestry, Inc., 2006 WL 2349459 (E.D. La. Aug. 11, 2006). A group of migrant employees sued their employer, who had allegedly failed to pay them the wages they were due under federal law. The defendant always seemed to have another reason why it could not produce some of the employees' time records and pay stubs, but then kept finding more records as the plaintiffs moved to compel and the court put on the heat. The defendant claimed, among other things, that many of its computer files had been overwritten, and that many of its paper records had been destroyed in Hurricane Katrina. The problem with the latter claim was that the defendant's headquarters was in Arkansas, and "[b]y defendants' own admission, nearing the height of the Atlantic hurricane season, they transferred *all* of their only copies of critical employment records to a beach house on the Gulf Coast . . . after having been placed on notice as to the importance of these documents by plaintiff's lawsuit." The court ordered the defendant to pay more than $36,000 as a sanction.

CHAPTER FOUR: CASE MANAGEMENT, SETTLEMENT, AND ALTERNATIVE DISPUTE RESOLUTION

Pages 176 and 188: The casebook can be read to suggest that a pretrial conference is mandatory under Rule 16. In fact, although such a conference is almost always held, it is not mandatory under the Rule.

Pages 215-16 (carryover paragraph): The decision pattern in state and federal courts is becoming more mixed than the cases cited in the casebook may imply. *See, e.g.*, Kristian v. Comcast Corp., 446 F.3d 25 (1st Cir. 2006) (in context of antitrust claims, striking down prohibitions against treble damages, attorney fees, and class processing in consumer arbitration agreement; distinguishing cases upholding some of these provisions in other legal contexts); Discover Bank v. Superior Court, 113 P. 3d 1100, 1103 (Cal. 2005) ("[W]e conclude that, at least under some circumstances, the law in California is that class action waivers in consumer contracts of adhesion are unenforceable, whether the consumer is being asked to waive the right to class action litigation or the right to classwide arbitration. We further conclude that the [Federal Arbitration Act does not preempt] California law in this respect.").

CHAPTER FIVE: JUDGE AND JURY

Pages 248-58: In Scott v. Harris, 550 U.S. —, 127 S. Ct. 1769 (2007) (*infra* p. 37), the Supreme Court reversed a judgment in which a court of appeals had affirmed a district court's refusal to grant a motion for summary judgment. The issue involved the reasonableness of the force used by a police officer to stop a car that was speeding away from the police. The officer's maneuver caused the plaintiff's car to crash and left him a quadriplegic. The officer argued that the maneuver was reasonable in light of the danger that the speeding car posed to motorists and pedestrians; the plaintiff argued that he had his car under control, and that his driving never put anyone at serious risk. Both the district court and the court of appeals thought that a jury should resolve the factual dispute. After reviewing a videotape of the chase, the Court held, over a dissent by Justice Stevens, that no reasonable jury could find that the force used was improper, and that the officer was entitled to summary judgment. To view the videotape, go to http://www.supremecourtus.gov/opinions/video/scott_v_harris.rmvb.

Page 267: An amendment that became effective on December 1, 2006, revised Rule 50(a). *See infra* p. 12 (Note for Pages 271-81). The operative test for granting the motion remains the same.

Page 268 (Note 5): McSherry v. City of Long Beach 423 F.3d 1015 (9th Cir. 2005), reversed a district court's grant of a Rule 50(a) motion that the defendants made at the very beginning of the case, even before the opening statements to the jury. The court reserved the possibility that such a motion might be granted if made *after* opening statements and before the admission of any evidence if it was then obvious that the opposing party could not prevail. *McSherry* noted, without approving, a recent trend among some courts of appeals to reverse judgments as a matter of law that were entered before a party had finished presenting all of its evidence and rested its case. *See* Echeverria v. Chevron USA Inc., 391 F.3d 607, 611 (5th Cir. 2004) (describing other cases as holding that "a party has not been fully heard until he has submitted all of his evidence and closed his case"). *Echeverria* seems inconsistent with the 1991 amendment to Rule 50(a), which switched the timing on a Rule 50(a) motion from the end of an opponent's case to any time after an opponent has been "fully heard" on a dispositive issue. A fair reading of the cases *Echeverria* cites suggests that *Echeverria* might have overread them; even though the cases indicate that a Rule 50(a) motion should rarely be granted before the close of a party's case, they still appear to permit a court to grant Rule 50(a) motion made before an opponent has rested.

Pages 271-81: A number of developments concerning renewed motions for judgment as a matter of law merit mention. First, an amendment that became effective on December 1, 2006, removed a major trap for the unwary in Rule 50(b). As we describe on pp. 271-72 of the casebook, traditionally a party could not renew a motion for judgment as a matter of law under Rule 50(b) unless the party made a motion for judgment as a matter of law under Rule 50(a) "at the close of all the evidence"; with very limited exceptions, a Rule 50(a) motion made earlier in the trial did not count. The amendment removed that timing requirement, so that a Rule 50(a) motion made at any time during the trial now preserves a party's right to renew the motion after trial.

Second, Unitherm Food Sys., Inc. v. Swift-Eckrich, Inc., 546 U.S. 394 (2006) (*infra* p. 41), dealt with the interplay of Rules 50(a), 50(b), and 59. In *Unitherm*, the plaintiff proceeded to trial on an antitrust claim. The district court denied the defendant's motion for judgment as a matter of law under Rule 50(a). The defendant lost, and inexplicably neither renewed the motion for judgment under Rule 50(b) nor asked for a new trial under Rule 59. On appeal, the defendant argued that the court improperly denied the Rule 50(a) motion. Under the law of the relevant circuit, a party whose Rule 50(a) motion was improperly denied but who failed to renew that motion under Rule 50(b) was not entitled to the entry of judgment in his or her favor, but could nonetheless receive a new trial. The appellate court determined that the defendant's Rule 50(a) motion should have been granted, and therefore ordered a new trial. The Supreme Court reversed, holding that the defendant's failure to renew the motion for judgment as a matter of law under Rule 50(b) or to ask for a new trial under Rule 59 deprived the appellate court of the power to order a new trial.

Third, in the course of the opinion, *Unitherm* casts some doubt on the reasoning and result of one of the cases cited in Note b.iii on page 273 of the casebook. As we mention, courts of appeals have disagreed about what effect, if any, the failure to renew a motion for judgment as a matter of law under Rule 50(b) has on the ability of a court to grant a motion for new trial under Rule 59 because the verdict was against the weight of the evidence. On one view, represented by the *Oliveras* case cited in the casebook, the two motions are distinct, and the failure to move under Rule 50(b) has no effect on an "against the weight" motion under Rule 59. On another view, represented by *Yohannon*, the failure to file a Rule 50(b) motion bars any "against the weight" motion under Rule 59. There is also a third, intermediate position not mentioned in the casebook, represented by Greenleaf v. Garlock, Inc., 174 F.3d 352 (3d Cir.1999): The failure to renew a motion for judgment as a matter of law under Rule 50(b) bars a motion for a new trial under Rule 59 that is premised on the legal insufficiency of the evidence, but not any Rule 59 motion that is premised on any other "against the weight" argument. *Unitherm* was addressing a different issue from the one debated in *Oliveras*, *Yohannon*, and *Greenleaf*. Nonetheless, in somewhat loose language certain to provoke further discussion, *Unitherm* observed:

> . . . Here, respondent does not seek to pursue on appeal the precise claim it raised in its Rule 50(a) motion before the District Court — namely, its entitlement to judgment as a matter of law. Rather, it seeks a new trial based on the legal insufficiency of the evidence. But if . . . a litigant that has failed to file a Rule 50(b) motion is foreclosed from seeking the relief it sought in its Rule 50(a) motion — *i.e.*, the entry of judgment — then surely respondent is foreclosed from seeking a new trial, relief it did not and could not seek in its preverdict motion. . . .
>
> The text of Rule 50(b) confirms that respondent's preverdict Rule 50(a) motion did not present the District Court with the option of ordering a new trial. That text provides that a district court may only order a new trial on the basis of issues raised in a preverdict Rule 50(a) motion when "ruling on a renewed motion" under Rule 50(b). Accordingly, even if the District Court was inclined to grant a new trial on the basis of arguments raised in respondent's preverdict motion, it was without the power to do so under Rule 50(b) absent a postverdict motion pursuant to that Rule.

Pages 284-91: The Supreme Court reaffirmed that a Rule 60(b) motion should be granted only in "extraordinary circumstances" in Gonzalez v. Crosby, 545 U.S. 524 (2005).

CHAPTER SIX: APPEALS

Page 300: Rule 50(b) was amended, effective December 1, 2006, to eliminate the requirement of a motion for judgment as a matter of law at the close of all the evidence, as long as the party seeking to renew a motion for judgment as a matter of law made a proper Rule 50(a) motion at some point during the trial. *See supra* p. 12 (Note for Pages 271-81).

CHAPTER NINE: PERSONAL JURISDICTION AND VENUE

Page 463: The en banc Ninth Circuit dismissed *Gator.com* as moot after the parties settled. *See* Gator.com Corp. v. L.L. Bean, Inc., 398 F.3d 1125 (9th Cir. 2005). The effect of the dismissal is that the state of the law in the Ninth Circuit remains as if the panel had never decided *Gator.com*.

Pages 483-90: The Supreme Court recently applied *Mullane* to find notice inadequate. In Jones v. Flowers, 547 U.S. 220 (2006) (*infra* p. 45), the state had sent a notice of tax delinquency to Jones via certified mail addressed to him at the delinquent property, but the letter was returned unclaimed. Despite this knowledge that its attempt to notify Jones had failed, the state sold the property to Flowers. Although certified mail might satisfy due process in the abstract, the Court reiterated that in previous cases it had "required the government to consider unique information about an intended recipient regardless of whether a statutory scheme is reasonably calculated to provide notice in the ordinary case." The Court analogized the situation to one in which "the Commissioner prepared a stack of letters to mail to delinquent taxpayers, handed them to the postman, and then watched as the departing postman accidentally dropped the letters down a storm drain." It held that the state's inaction after the initial letter was returned was not "not what someone 'desirous of actually informing' Jones would do; such a person would take further reasonable steps if any were available."

Page 495: The *Gherebi* decision described in the next-to-last Note on this page of the casebook was summarily vacated by the Supreme Court for consideration in light of another decision, after which the Ninth Circuit upheld federal jurisdiction but transferred the case to the United States District Court for the District of Columbia. *See* Bush v. Gherebi, 542 U.S. 952 (2004) (vacating and remanding for further consideration in light of Rumsfeld v. Padilla, 542 U.S. 426 (2004)); Gherebi v. Bush, 374 F.3d 727 (9th Cir. 2004) (after remand, upholding federal jurisdiction but ordering transfer of venue).

CHAPTER TEN: SUBJECT MATTER JURISDICTION

Pages 516-29: The Supreme Court revisited the issue of embedded federal questions in Grable & Sons Metal Prods., Inc. v. Darue Eng'g & Mfg., 545 U.S. 308 (2005) (*infra* p. 52). The case involved a state quiet-title action removed from state court. The embedded federal-law issue on which resolution of the state-law claim would turn was whether an IRS tax-seizure notice was inadequately served on Grable, thus invalidating the later tax sale to Darue. The Court held that the lack of a private federal right of action does not necessarily preclude federal jurisdiction over an embedded federal question as long as the state-law claim "necessarily raise[s] a stated federal issue, actually disputed and substantial, which a federal forum may entertain without disturbing any congressionally approved balance of federal and state judicial responsibilities," thus settling the dispute mentioned in Note 5 on page 528 of the casebook. The Court held that *Merrell Dow* had not created any bright-line test for jurisdiction over embedded federal questions, but had rather "specifically retained the contextual enquiry that had been *Smith*'s hallmark for over 60 years." The Court unanimously concluded that the federal tax policy issue embedded in the state property claim was — unlike the FDCA question in *Merrell Dow* — a substantial federal question that was unlikely to attract "a horde of original filings and removal cases" and thus would not disturb the congressionally approved balance. The Court did not cite *Moore* at all.

More recently, the Supreme Court distinguished *Grable* in Empire HealthChoice Assurance, Inc. v. McVeigh, 547 U.S. —, 126 S. Ct. 2121 (2006). In *Empire HealthChoice*, an insurer who contracted with the federal government to cover federal employees filed a subrogation claim to recover previously disbursed benefits, which it alleged had been recovered by the beneficiary in a state-court tort suit. While a federal statute governed the relationship between the insurer and the government, and also preempted state law on coverage and benefits, the statute said nothing about subrogation and did not expressly confer federal jurisdiction over such claims. Among other arguments, the insurer contended that the suit was within federal question jurisdiction under *Grable* because federal law was a "necessary element" of the insurer's claim for relief. The majority rejected that argument, concluding that the case did "not fit within the special and small category" defined by *Grable*:

> This case is poles apart from *Grable*. The dispute there centered on the action of a federal agency (IRS) and its compatibility with a federal statute, the question qualified as "substantial," and its resolution was both dispositive of the case and would be controlling in numerous other cases. Here, the reimbursement claim was triggered, not by the action of any federal department, agency, or service, but by the settlement of a personal-injury action launched in state court, and the bottom-line practical issue is the share of that settlement properly payable to Empire.
>
> *Grable* presented a nearly "pure issue of law," one "that could be settled once and for all and thereafter would govern numerous tax sale cases." In contrast, Empire's reimbursement claim . . . is fact-bound and situation-specific.

Pages 529-543: A recent Supreme Court case reinvigorated discussion of an issue not mentioned in the casebook. Under the "domestic relations" and "probate" exceptions to federal jurisdiction, federal courts may not hear cases about such matters as divorce, custody, or the administration of a will, even if the requirements of federal jurisdiction are otherwise met. Many lower courts had expanded the exceptions to preclude jurisdiction in cases that touched on any aspect of family law or estate law. The Court clarified these exceptions in Marshall v. Marshall, 547 U.S. 293 (2006), which limited the probate exception to cases that involve the "probate or annulment of a will and the administration of a decedent's estate," or that endeavor "to dispose of property that is in the custody of a state probate court." The Court indicated that the domestic relations exception is similarly narrow. Justice Stevens, concurring, would have eliminated the probate exception entirely.

The case involved an attempt by former *Playboy* Playmate Anna Nicole Smith (Vickie Marshall) to obtain a share of her deceased husband's multi-billion-dollar estate. In the course of federal bankruptcy proceedings, she filed a state-law tort claim against her stepson, accusing him of tampering with his father's efforts to leave her a part of the estate. The Court held that this tort claim did not fit within the probate exception to federal jurisdiction and could therefore be heard in federal court (which, at the trial level, had awarded her almost $90 million) rather than in probate court in Texas (where she had lost). The Court hinted without deciding that the probate and domestic-relations exceptions may extend beyond the diversity context in which they have been generally applied; it based its decision on the ground that the appellate decision below stretched the probate exception so far beyond its proper narrow bounds that it was unnecessary to decide whether the exception extended beyond diversity cases to bankruptcy jurisdiction.

Page 530: Congress enacted an important minimal diversity statute as part of the Class Action Fairness Act (CAFA), Pub. L. No. 109-2, § 4, 119 Stat. 4, codified at 28 U.S.C. § 1332(d) (2005). This supplement discusses CAFA in more detail *infra* pp. 17-23.

Page 537 (Note 3): In Wachovia Bank, N.A. v. Schmidt, 546 U.S. 303 (2006), the Supreme Court held that a national bank, which is a corporation chartered not by any state but by the federal government, is a citizen only of the state in which it has its main office.

Pages 541-42 (Note 2): The Supreme Court further refined its jurisprudence on punitive damages in Philip Morris USA v. Williams, 549 U.S. —, 127 S. Ct. 1057 (2007), although it did not add anything to the numerical analysis.

Pages 552-58: The Supreme Court finally settled the circuit split on whether § 1367 overrules *Clark* and *Zahn* in Exxon Mobil Corp. v. Allapattah Servs., Inc., 545 U.S. 546 (2005) (*infra* p. 58). In *Allapattah*, the Court concluded that the statute is unambiguous on its face in permitting jurisdiction when one plaintiff meets the amount-in-controversy requirement and others do not, resolving the circuit split in favor of the Seventh Circuit's reading in *Stromberg Metal Works*. The five-Justice majority carefully distinguished the situation in which one plaintiff is not diverse from the defendant: In that case, the "[i]ncomplete diversity destroys original jurisdiction with respect to all claims, so there is nothing to which supplemental jurisdiction can adhere."

Page 563: The Supreme Court held that a defendant who removes a case to federal court has no obligation to "negate the existence of a potential codefendant whose presence in the action would destroy diversity." Lincoln Prop. Co. v. Roche, 546 U.S. 81 (2005). As the Court noted, "[i]t was not incumbent on [the removing defendant] to propose as additional defendants persons the [plaintiffs], as masters of their complaint, permissively might have joined."

Page 564 (Note 5): In Osborn v. Haley, 549 U.S. —, 127 S. Ct. 881 (2007), the Supreme Court held that § 1447(d) did not bar an appeal of a remand order in the specific context of a federal statute that permitted removal by federal officials sued in state court on tort claims. Later in the same Term, the Court distinguished *Osborn*, in Powerex Corp. v. Reliant Energy Servs., Inc., 551 U.S. —, 127 S. Ct. 2411 (2007). In *Powerex*, the district court had jurisdiction only if the removing defendant was entitled to sovereign immunity. Once it concluded that the defendant was not so entitled, the district court remanded for lack of subject matter jurisdiction. Without reaching the merits of the sovereign immunity question, the Supreme Court held that § 1447(d) precluded appeal of the remand order.

Page 564 (Note 6): *See also* Martin v. Franklin Capital Corp., 546 U.S. 132 (2005) (authority under 28 U.S.C. § 1447(c) to award "just costs and any actual expenses, including attorney fees," in connection with remand should not be exercised with presumption in favor of award but depending on whether there was "objectively reasonable basis" for removal despite remand).

CHAPTER TWELVE: CLASS ACTIONS

Pages 654-59: In 2005 Congress enacted the Class Action Fairness Act (CAFA), Pub. L. No. 109-2, 119 Stat. 4 (2005). CAFA significantly changed the subject matter jurisdiction of federal courts over class actions, and made it easier for federal courts to hear class actions both as an original matter and on removal jurisdiction. *See* 28 U.S.C. §§ 1332(d), 1453. CAFA creates a complex set of jurisdictional rules whose interpretive intricacies will occupy courts for years to come.

Because CAFA, together with Exxon Mobil Corp. v. Allapattah Servs., Inc., 545 U.S. 546 (2005) (*infra* p. 58), significantly changes the law as it stood when the casebook was published, we suggest substituting the following for subsection C.2 (Subject Matter Jurisdiction), pp. 654-59:

---

2. Subject Matter Jurisdiction

As we have seen, federal courts obtain subject matter jurisdiction over most civil cases under either the federal question or the diversity grant. The jurisdictional rules that we studied ("well-pleaded complaint" and "arising under" for federal questions, and "complete diversity" and usually "no aggregation of the amount in controversy of multiple plaintiffs" for diversity) are clear in the main. Supplemental jurisdiction complicates matters a bit, especially because of some textual ambiguities in 28 U.S.C. § 1367(b). Nonetheless, in simple litigation involving only a few parties, the rules are generally easy to apply. Do class actions change these rules?

For cases arising under federal question jurisdiction, the answer is "no": The rules for federal question jurisdiction operate the same regardless of whether the claim involves a single plaintiff or a class. A federal claim must appear on the face of the well-pleaded class complaint.

For diversity cases, however, the situation is more complicated. Recall than, in an ordinary diversity case, *each* plaintiff had to be of different citizenship from *each* defendant, and (with a few exceptions) *each* plaintiff needed to claim at least the requisite amount in controversy (now set at $75,000.01). In a class action, must each member of the class be of different citizenship from the opposing parties? Must each member of the class have more than $75,000 at stake? If so, then many state-law class actions will never find their way into federal court.

The answer to these questions proceeds in three historical phases. The first established the ground rules that held sway until the passage of the supplemental jurisdictional statute, 28 U.S.C. § 1367, in 1990. In Supreme Tribe of Ben-Hur v. Cauble, 255 U.S. 356 (1921), the Supreme Court held that diversity of citizenship in a class action is determined by comparing the citizenship of the *class representatives* to the citizenship of the parties opposing the class. This holding constitutes a modest breach of the usual rule of complete diversity. The citizenship of the absent class members is ignored; even if some *class members* have the same citizenship as some of the opposing parties, diversity jurisdiction under § 1332 exists as long as the named class members are fully diverse from the defendants. In class actions with members from many states, *Ben-Hur* gives the class counsel great power to create or destroy diversity jurisdiction by picking class representatives with the appropriate citizenship.

In Snyder v. Harris, 394 U.S. 332 (1969), the Court turned its attention to the amount-in-controversy requirement. *Snyder* rejected the effort of a group of class plaintiffs to aggregate their individual claims to satisfy the amount in controversy for original jurisdiction. None of the 4,000 class members had the requisite amount in controversy, but added together, their claims exceeded $1.2 million. *Snyder* left open one question: Might the amount-in-controversy requirement be satisfied if the class representatives, but not all of the class members, had claims exceeding the requirement? Zahn v. International Paper Co., 414 U.S. 291 (1973), answered the question negatively: The claim of each and every class member needed to meet the amount-in-controversy requirement. Thus, the incomplete diversity of class members was ignored for diversity jurisdiction, but the inadequacy of the amount of each class member's claims was not. The rules may not have been entirely consistent, but there they were.

So things stood until the passage of § 1367. We have already examined one important textual ambiguity in § 1367(b): Whether Congress's failure to mention *plaintiffs* joined under Rule 20(a) allows, in contravention to the traditional rules, the joinder of additional Rule 20 plaintiffs who destroy complete diversity or have less than the necessary amount in controversy. *See* Casebook pp. 552-58; *supra* p. 16 (Note for Pages 552-58), *infra* p. 58. Notice that, as with Rule 20 plaintiffs, § 1367(b) fails to mention Rule 23 at all. Does this omission mean that Congress overruled *Zahn* and allowed federal jurisdiction over diversity class actions as long as at least one class member has more than $75,000 at stake, and the claims of other class members formed part of the same case or controversy under § 1367(a)? (*Snyder,* which concerned original rather than supplemental jurisdiction, is unaffected by § 1367.) Does the omission mean that Congress expanded the *Ben-Hur* rule, so that federal jurisdiction over diversity class actions exists as long as one class representative *or* a single absent class member is of diverse citizenship from one party opposing the class?

During the second historical phase, from 1990 until 2005, courts grappled with these questions, and divided almost evenly on the answer. The matter finally came to rest in Exxon Mobil Corp. v. Allapattah Servs., Inc., 545 U.S. 546 (2005) (*infra* p. 58). The Court held that Congress's failure to mention Rule 23 in § 1367(b) means that federal courts have jurisdiction over the claims of class members who fail to meet the amount-in-controversy requirements as long as those claims form part of the same case or controversy as the claims of members who satisfy the requirement. "We hold that § 1367 by its plain text overruled . . . *Zahn* and authorized supplemental jurisdiction over all claims by diverse parties arising out of the same Article III case or controversy."

The third phase slightly overlaps the second, and begins with the passage of the Class Action Fairness Act (CAFA), Pub. L. No. 109-2, 119 Stat. 4 (2005). Responding to the perception that state-court class actions were leading to unfairly generous awards injuring American business interests, Congress gave federal courts considerably more original and removal jurisdiction over class actions. The result was one of the most complex jurisdictional grants ever enacted by Congress — so complicated that interpretive questions will likely occupy the courts for at least a decade. At this point, we can sketch only the basic outlines of the statute.

Original Jurisdiction. Begin with what CAFA does not cover:

- Except to the extent that it might provide an additional basis for jurisdiction, it does not affect class actions that plead a federal question. It is a diversity class-action statute. 28 U.S.C. § 1332(d)(2).
- It does not apply to diversity-based class actions with fewer than 100 members. *Id.* § 1332(d)(5)(B).
- It does not apply to diversity-based class actions in which the court could probably not grant relief against government officials or entities in any event. *Id.* § 1332(d)(5)(A).
- It does not apply to diversity-based class actions involving shareholder claims against a corporation's management, or certain claims alleging state-law securities fraud. *Id.*, § 1332(d)(9). Federal

jurisdiction over state-law securities-fraud class actions is already covered in other provisions of the United States Code.

For the second and third exclusions, as well as for shareholder claims, federal jurisdiction could presumably still be obtained under the traditional rules, as modified by § 1367. In dicta, *Exxon Mobil* indicates that CAFA is not the exclusive means for establishing federal jurisdiction of a diversity-based class action.

Next, examine the initial breadth of the jurisdiction CAFA provides for included class actions. Federal jurisdiction exists as long as (1) *any* plaintiff class member has citizenship different from *any* defendant (i.e., minimal diversity), and (2) the aggregate amount in controversy of all the class members exceeds $5 million. 28 U.S.C. § 1332(d)(2), (d)(6). These requirements are considerably different from those that apply in ordinary diversity cases, which require complete diversity (no plaintiff may have the same citizenship as any defendant) and an amount-in-controversy rule that requires each plaintiff to have more than $75,000 at stake. They are also different from the *Ben-Hur/Snyder* regime, even as modified by § 1367. Take, for example, a consumer-fraud class action involving 1,000,000 citizens of California and one citizen of New York suing a New York issuer of credit cards. Each California plaintiff has a $5 claim under a California consumer-protection statute, and the New York plaintiff has an $80,000 claim under the same statute. Because no class member who is diverse from the defendant has a claim exceeding $75,000, a federal court has no original jurisdiction over the case, and therefore cannot use supplemental jurisdiction to add other claims to the case. CAFA provides jurisdiction: At least one class plaintiff has citizenship different from the defendant, and the aggregated total of the claims exceeds $5 million.

In a complex set of provisions driven by concerns for federalism, Congress also tried to carve out certain state-law class actions that were truly local in nature, and to allow state courts to continue to hear them. Roughly, Congress divided class actions into three types: cases in which one-third or fewer of the class members were from the state in which the class action was filed, cases in which greater than one-third and less than two-thirds of the class members were from the forum state, and cases in which greater than two-thirds or more of the class members were from the forum state. In the first category, federal courts have original jurisdiction *simpliciter*. In the second category, Congress gave federal courts *discretion* to decline jurisdiction when the "primary defendants" are also citizens of the forum state. CAFA provides a list of six factors intended to guide a court's discretion in deciding whether to retain or decline jurisdiction. 28 U.S.C. § 1367(d)(3)(A)-(F). We encountered the idea of a discretionary refusal to exercise jurisdiction in United Mine Workers of America v. Gibbs, 383 U.S. 715 (1966) (Casebook p. 544), whose factors were codified, perhaps with some modifications, in 28 U.S.C. § 1367(c) (Casebook p. 558, Note 6). Although the idea here is similar, be careful: The six factors listed in § 1332(d)(3) bear only a modest relation to the four factors listed in § 1367(c), and the legislative history of CAFA suggests that the six factors should not be interpreted to frustrate CAFA's goal of providing broad federal jurisdiction over state-law class actions.

The third type of class action, in which two-thirds or more of the class members are from the forum state, involves different considerations. Here, CAFA *requires* a federal court to decline jurisdiction when either:

- two-thirds or more of the class plaintiffs *and* the "primary defendants" are citizens of the forum state, 28 U.S.C. § 1332(d)(4)(B); or
- more than two-thirds of the class plaintiffs are citizens of the forum state, at least one defendant from whom "significant relief" is sought and whose conduct "forms a significant basis" for the plaintiffs' claims is also a citizen of the forum state, and no other class action has made the same or similar claims against a defendant in the prior three years, *id.* § 1332(d)(4)(A).

Although Congress employs it on rare occasion in specific statutory schemes, we have not previously encountered in this book the idea of a mandatory refusal to exercise otherwise available subject matter jurisdiction.

Removal Jurisdiction. CAFA creates original, but not exclusive, federal jurisdiction. Hence, plaintiffs might file CAFA-covered class actions in state court. Therefore, CAFA establishes a removal process that changes — only for class actions covered by § 1332(d) — a number of the usual rules for removal. As we learned in Chapter Ten, under those rules, all defendants must join in the removal notice, removal must occur within thirty days after the case first become removable, state-law claims cannot be removed more than one year after they are filed even if they first become removable then, and the decision of a federal court to remand a removed case is not ordinarily appealable while decisions to deny remand are appealable only after the case is over. 28 U.S.C. §§ 1441, 1446, 1447. CAFA's new removal rule, 28 U.S.C. § 1453, does not change the thirty-day rule for seeking removal, but does change the remaining removal requirements to make removal of class actions easier. Only one defendant needs to seek removal; other defendants need not consent to removal. *Id.* § 1453(b). A case can be removed even after the one-year limit that applies in other diversity cases; thus, if a plaintiff first seeks class treatment of a case three years after it is filed, it is still removable within the next thirty days. *Id.* A party can petition the court of appeals for permission to file an appeal from an order granting or denying a motion to remand a class action; if the court of appeals accepts the appeal, it is put on a very short leash, and must typically decide the appeal within sixty days. *Id.* § 1453(c).

Relationship between Traditional Class Actions and CAFA-Covered Class Actions. In *Exxon Mobil*, the Court noted that the passage of CAFA did not affect the question of how to interpret § 1367, nor did it moot the § 1367 question before the Court. The Court was right on both counts. But the reality is that the new jurisdictional provisions of §§ 1332(d) and 1453 effectively, if not legally, moot the traditional jurisdictional rules, as modified by § 1367, in all but a small set of class actions. (Principally, this set includes class actions with fewer than 100 class members or less than $5 million in aggregate claim value; the traditional rules might also be relevant when either § 1332(d)(3) permits or §1332(d)(4) requires a federal court to decline jurisdiction.) By switching from complete to minimal diversity and from the each-plaintiff to the aggregate-to-defendant method of calculating the amount in controversy, CAFA will bring many more class actions into federal court than the traditional rules ever permitted. Whether jurisdictional rules should vary so markedly in ordinary and complex litigation is a complicated subject whose full answer requires study beyond this introductory book, but the variance should suggest the historical contingency, and therefore the mutability, of the complete-diversity and each-plaintiff amount-in-controversy rules of the diversity grant. The same is true of the removal provisions that CAFA changes.

Early Developments in the Case Law. CAFA is a complex statute with enough interpretive questions to occupy federal courts for years to come. The earliest cases typically addressed the question of CAFA's applicability to class actions commenced before CAFA's effective date; defendants seeking removal to federal court argued, with mixed success, that the addition of new claims or new parties, or the deletion of claims or parties, in a state-court class action originally commenced before CAFA's effective date amounted to a "commencement" of the case after CAFA's effective date.

In the last year, courts have begun to interpret language at the heart of CAFA. One threshold issue that has arisen involves the question of which party bears the burden of proving the federal court's jurisdiction. (Certain jurisdictional issues, such as the percentage of in-state class members and the "primacy" of some of the defendants, are factual in nature.) The courts seem to be coalescing around the traditional burden-of-proof rule for federal jurisdiction: The party seeking to invoke the federal court's jurisdiction bears the burden of proof. But some courts have held that the burden of proof switches when it comes time to argue for the court's discretionary refusal to entertain the case. A second issue that has arisen involves the interpretation of the discretionary and mandatory refusals to exercise jurisdiction contained in §§ 1332(d)(3) and (d)(4). For cases sorting through one or both of these issues, see Evans v. Walter Indus., Inc., 449 F.3d 1149 (11th Cir. 2006); Serrano v. 180 Connect, Inc., 478 F.3d 1018 (9th Cir. 2007); Lowdermilk v. U.S. Bank Nat'l Ass'n, 479 F.3d 994 (9th Cir. 2007); Preston v. Tenet Healthsystem Mem'l Med. Ctr., Inc., 485 F.3d 793 (5th Cir. 2007); and Preston v. Tenet Healthsystem Mem'l Med. Ctr., Inc., 485 F.3d 804 (5th Cir. 2007). The two *Preston* cases especially interesting. They involved two class actions that arose out of injuries and deaths allegedly suffered at medical facilities in the wake of Hurricane Katrina. Applying the standards of §§ 1332(d)(3) and (d)(4), the court of appeals held that one of the class actions should remain in federal court, and the other should be remanded to state court. *See also* Lowery v. Alabama Power Co., 483 F.3d 1184 (11th Cir. 2007) (interpreting CAFA's "mass action" provision in § 1332(d)(11)).

Page 684: The Class Action Fairness Act (CAFA), Pub. L. No. 109-2, 119 Stat. 4 (Feb. 18, 2005), affects the settlement of federal class actions in several ways. First, the legislation creates certain disincentives for parties to engage in what are often called "coupon settlements," in which class members allegedly economically or physically injured by the defendant's behavior receive a coupon that allows to the plaintiffs to receive a discount on other products or services of the defendant. Although such settlements are rare and not necessarily without value, they obtained the status of urban legend, with the claim being that such settlements enriched the plaintiffs' lawyers, let defendants off the hook for next to nothing, and left the class members holding the bag. CAFA limits the attorneys' fees awardable to class counsel in coupon settlements. 28 U.S.C. § 1712.

CAFA also contains provisions that affects all class-action settlements in federal court. Responding to an infamous (although apparently *sui generis*) settlement in which some supposedly prevailing class members ended up worse off after the settlement because of small recoveries and large attorneys' fees, CAFA establishes a "net benefit" rule: Class members cannot be required to pay fees to class counsel unless the settlement's combination of monetary and injunctive relief is a net benefit to the class members. 28 U.S.C. § 1713. Next, in a curious provision that does not appear to relate to any known instance or pattern of unfairness, some class members cannot receive more benefits than others simply because they are geographically closer to the courthouse. 28 U.S.C. § 1714.

Finally, CAFA requires the parties to notify the "appropriate" federal or state official within ten days of reaching a settlement. 28 U.S.C. § 1715(b). The court must then wait at least ninety days after notification to approve the settlement. § 1715(d). Although the relevant official is not required to do anything after receiving notice of the settlement, the purposes of the notification requirement are to allow the relevant official to ensure that the settlement does not frustrate the government's enforcement objectives and to give the official an opportunity to protect the interests of class members if the settlement appears inadequate. The "appropriate" official varies with the nature of the case; as a default, the official is the relevant state or federal Attorney General, but in some cases another official is appropriate. *See* § 1715(a), -(c).

RECENT SUPREME COURT CASES

BELL ATLANTIC CORP. v. TWOMBLY

550 U.S. —, 127 S. Ct. 1955 (2007)

■ JUSTICE SOUTER delivered the opinion of the Court.

Liability under § 1 of the Sherman Act, 15 U.S.C. § 1, requires a "contract, combination . . ., or conspiracy, in restraint of trade or commerce." The question in this putative class action is whether a § 1 complaint can survive a motion to dismiss when it alleges that major telecommunications providers engaged in certain parallel conduct unfavorable to competition, absent some factual context suggesting agreement, as distinct from identical, independent action. We hold that such a complaint should be dismissed.

I

The upshot of the 1984 divestiture of the American Telephone & Telegraph Company's (AT&T) local telephone business was a system of regional service monopolies (variously called "Regional Bell Operating Companies," "Baby Bells," or "Incumbent Local Exchange Carriers" (ILECs)), and a separate, competitive market for long-distance service from which the ILECs were excluded. [In 1996, Congress enacted the Telecommunications Act of 1996 (1996 Act), which withdrew the local monopolies enjoyed by the ILECs. A critical provision in the 1996 Act required each ILEC to share its network with competitors, known as "competitive local exchange carriers" (CLECs). The ILECs vigorously litigated the scope of this obligation during the ensuing decade.]

Respondents William Twombly and Lawrence Marcus (hereinafter plaintiffs) represent a putative class consisting of all "subscribers of local telephone and/or high speed internet services . . . from February 8, 1996 to present." In this action against petitioners, a group of ILECs, plaintiffs seek treble damages and declaratory and injunctive relief for claimed violations of § 1 of the Sherman Act . . . .

The complaint alleges that the ILECs conspired to restrain trade in two ways . . . . Plaintiffs say, first, that the ILECs "engaged in parallel conduct" in their respective service areas to inhibit the growth of upstart CLECs. . . .

Second, the complaint charges agreements by the ILECs to refrain from competing against one another. . . .

[The complaint included these allegations, which we quote verbatim:

39. . . . [T]he [ILECs] have refrained from engaging in meaningful head-to-head competition in each other's markets. . . .

40. The failure of the [ILECs] to compete with one another would be anomalous in the absence of an agreement among the [ILECs] not to compete with one another in view of the fact that in significant respects, the territories that they service are non-contiguous. As reflected in Exhibit A hereto, SBC serves most of the State of Connecticut even though Verizon rather than SBC serves the surrounding states. SBC serves California and Nevada, even though Qwest serves the other surrounding states. . . . The failure of the [ILECs] that serve the surrounding territories to make significant attempts to compete in the surrounded territories is strongly suggestive of conspiracy, since the service of such surrounded territories presents the [ILECs] serving surrounding territories with an especially attractive business opportunity that such [ILECs] have not meaningfully pursued.

42. On October 31, 2002, Richard Notebaert[,] the former Chief Executive Officer of Ameritech, who sold the company to Defendant SBC in 1999 and who currently serves as the Chief Executive Officer of Defendant Qwest, was quoted in a *Chicago Tribune* article as saying it would be fundamentally wrong to compete in the SBC/Ameritech territory, adding "it might be a good way to turn a quick dollar but that doesn't make it right." . . .

46. The [ILECs] do indeed communicate amongst themselves through a myriad of organizations . . . .

47. Defendants have engaged in parallel conduct in order to prevent competition in their respective local telephone and/or high speed internet services markets. "They have refused to open their markets by dragging their feet in allowing competitors to interconnect, refusing to negotiate in good faith, litigating every nook and cranny of the law, and avoiding head-to-head competition like the plague." Consumer Federation of America, Lessons From 1996 Telecommunications Act: Deregulation Before Meaningful Competition Spells Consumer Disaster, February 2001, p. 1. Defendants also have engaged and continue to engage in unanimity of action by committing one or more of the following wrongful acts in furtherance of a common anticompetitive objective to prevent competition from [CLECs] in the their respective local telephone and/or high speed internet services markets: [Here the complaint listed 12 courses of action in which the defendants either discriminated against the CLECs in the provision of services or the quality of service, or otherwise used their monopoly power to maintain a competitive advantage.] . . .

51. In the absence of any meaningful competition between the [ILECs] in one another's markets, and in light of the parallel course of

conduct that each engaged in to prevent competition from CLECs within their respective local telephone and/or high speed internet services markets and the other facts and market circumstances alleged above, Plaintiffs allege upon information and belief that Defendants have entered into a contract, combination or conspiracy to prevent competitive entry in their respective local telephone and/or high speed internet services markets and have agreed not to compete with one another and otherwise allocated customers and markets to one another.]

The United States District Court for the Southern District of New York dismissed the complaint for failure to state a claim upon which relief can be granted. The District Court acknowledged that "plaintiffs may allege a conspiracy by citing instances of parallel business behavior that suggest an agreement," but emphasized that "while '[c]ircumstantial evidence of consciously parallel behavior may have made heavy inroads into the traditional judicial attitude toward conspiracy[, . . .] "conscious parallelism" has not yet read conspiracy out of the Sherman Act entirely.'" . . .

The Court of Appeals for the Second Circuit reversed . . . . Although the Court of Appeals took the view that plaintiffs must plead facts that "include conspiracy among the realm of 'plausible' possibilities in order to survive a motion to dismiss," it then said that "to rule that allegations of parallel anticompetitive conduct fail to support a plausible conspiracy claim, a court would have to conclude that there is no set of facts that would permit a plaintiff to demonstrate that the particular parallelism asserted was the product of collusion rather than coincidence."

We granted certiorari to address the proper standard for pleading an antitrust conspiracy through allegations of parallel conduct, and now reverse.

II

A

Because § 1 of the Sherman Act "does not prohibit [all] unreasonable restraints of trade . . . but only restraints effected by a contract, combination, or conspiracy," "[t]he crucial question" is whether the challenged anticompetitive conduct "stem[s] from independent decision or from an agreement, tacit or express." While a showing of parallel "business behavior is admissible circumstantial evidence from which the fact finder may infer agreement," it falls short of "conclusively establish[ing] agreement or . . . itself constitut[ing] a Sherman Act offense." Even "conscious parallelism," a common reaction of "firms in a concentrated market [that] recogniz[e] their shared economic interests and their interdependence with respect to price and output decisions" is "not in itself unlawful." . . .

Accordingly, we have previously hedged against false inferences from identical behavior at a number of points in the trial sequence. An antitrust conspiracy plaintiff with evidence showing nothing beyond parallel conduct is not entitled to a directed verdict; proof of a § 1 conspiracy must include evidence tending to exclude the possibility of independent action; and at the summary judgment stage a § 1 plaintiff's offer of conspiracy evidence must tend to rule out the possibility that the defendants were acting independently.

B

This case presents the antecedent question of what a plaintiff must plead in order to state a claim under § 1 of the Sherman Act. Federal Rule of Civil Procedure 8(a)(2) requires only "a short and plain statement of the claim showing that the pleader is entitled to relief," in order to "give the defendant fair notice of what the . . . claim is and the grounds upon which it rests," Conley v. Gibson, 355 U.S. 41, 47 (1957). While a complaint attacked by a Rule 12(b)(6) motion to dismiss does not need detailed factual allegations, a plaintiff's obligation to provide the "grounds" of his "entitle[ment] to relief" requires more than labels and conclusions, and a formulaic recitation of the elements of a cause of action will not do. Factual allegations must be enough to raise a right to relief above the speculative level,[3] on the assumption that all the allegations in the complaint are true (even if doubtful in fact), *see, e.g.*, Swierkiewicz v. Sorema N. A., 534 U.S. 506, 508, n. 1 (2002).

In applying these general standards to a § 1 claim, we hold that stating such a claim requires a complaint with enough factual matter (taken as true) to suggest that an agreement was made. Asking for plausible grounds to infer an agreement does not impose a probability requirement at the pleading stage; it simply calls for enough fact to raise a reasonable expectation that discovery will reveal evidence of illegal agreement.[4] And, of course, a well-pleaded complaint may proceed even if it strikes a savvy judge that actual proof of those facts is improbable, and "that a recovery is very remote and unlikely." In identifying facts that are suggestive enough to render a § 1 conspiracy plausible, we have the benefit of the prior rulings and considered views of leading commentators . . . that lawful parallel conduct fails to bespeak unlawful agreement. It makes sense to say, therefore, that an allegation of parallel conduct and a bare assertion of conspiracy will not suffice. Without more, parallel conduct does not suggest

3. The dissent greatly oversimplifies matters by suggesting that the Federal Rules somehow dispensed with the pleading of facts altogether. While, for most types of cases, the Federal Rules eliminated the cumbersome requirement that a claimant "set out *in detail* the facts upon which he bases his claim," Conley v. Gibson, 355 U.S. 41, 47 (1957) (emphasis added), Rule 8(a)(2) still requires a "showing," rather than a blanket assertion, of entitlement to relief. Without some factual allegation in the complaint, it is hard to see how a claimant could satisfy the requirement of providing not only "fair notice" of the nature of the claim, but also "grounds" on which the claim rests.

4. Commentators have offered several examples of parallel conduct allegations that would state a § 1 claim under this standard. . . . The parties in this case agree that "complex and historically unprecedented changes in pricing structure made at the very same time by multiple competitors, and made for no other discernible reason" would support a plausible inference of conspiracy.

conspiracy, and a conclusory allegation of agreement at some unidentified point does not supply facts adequate to show illegality. Hence, when allegations of parallel conduct are set out in order to make a § 1 claim, they must be placed in a context that raises a suggestion of a preceding agreement, not merely parallel conduct that could just as well be independent action.

The need at the pleading stage for allegations plausibly suggesting (not merely consistent with) agreement reflects the threshold requirement of Rule 8(a)(2) that the "plain statement" possess enough heft to "sho[w] that the pleader is entitled to relief." A statement of parallel conduct, even conduct consciously undertaken, needs some setting suggesting the agreement necessary to make out a § 1 claim; without that further circumstance pointing toward a meeting of the minds, an account of a defendant's commercial efforts stays in neutral territory. An allegation of parallel conduct is thus much like a naked assertion of conspiracy in a § 1 complaint: it gets the complaint close to stating a claim, but without some further factual enhancement it stops short of the line between possibility and plausibility of "entitle[ment] to relief."

. . . So, when the allegations in a complaint, however true, could not raise a claim of entitlement to relief, "'this basic deficiency should . . . be exposed at the point of minimum expenditure of time and money by the parties and the court.'"

Thus, it is one thing to be cautious before dismissing an antitrust complaint in advance of discovery, but quite another to forget that proceeding to antitrust discovery can be expensive. . . . "[A] district court must retain the power to insist upon some specificity in pleading before allowing a potentially massive factual controversy to proceed." *See also* MANUAL FOR COMPLEX LITIGATION, FOURTH, § 30, p. 519 (2004) (describing extensive scope of discovery in antitrust cases). That potential expense is obvious enough in the present case: plaintiffs represent a putative class of at least 90 percent of all subscribers to local telephone or high-speed Internet service in the continental United States, in an action against America's largest telecommunications firms (with many thousands of employees generating reams and gigabytes of business records) for unspecified (if any) instances of antitrust violations that allegedly occurred over a period of seven years.

It is no answer to say that a claim just shy of a plausible entitlement to relief can, if groundless, be weeded out early in the discovery process through "careful case management," given the common lament that the success of judicial supervision in checking discovery abuse has been on the modest side. And it is self-evident that the problem of discovery abuse cannot be solved by "careful scrutiny of evidence at the summary judgment stage," much less "lucid instructions to juries"; the threat of discovery expense will push cost-conscious defendants to settle even anemic cases before reaching those proceedings. Probably, then, it is only by taking care to require allegations that reach the level suggesting conspiracy that we can hope to avoid the potentially enormous expense of discovery in cases with no "'reasonably founded hope that the [discovery] process will reveal relevant evidence'" to support a § 1 claim.

Plaintiffs do not, of course, dispute the requirement of plausibility and the need for something more than merely parallel behavior . . ., and their main argument against the plausibility standard at the pleading stage is its ostensible conflict with an early statement of ours construing Rule 8. Justice Black's opinion for the Court in *Conley v. Gibson* spoke not only of the need for fair notice of the grounds for entitlement to relief but of "the accepted rule that a complaint should not be dismissed for failure to state a claim unless it appears beyond doubt that the plaintiff can prove no set of facts in support of his claim which would entitle him to relief." This "no set of facts" language can be read in isolation as saying that any statement revealing the theory of the claim will suffice unless its factual impossibility may be shown from the face of the pleadings; and the Court of Appeals appears to have read *Conley* in some such way when formulating its understanding of the proper pleading standard.

On such a focused and literal reading of *Conley*'s "no set of facts," a wholly conclusory statement of claim would survive a motion to dismiss whenever the pleadings left open the possibility that a plaintiff might later establish some "set of [undisclosed] facts" to support recovery. So here, the Court of Appeals specifically found the prospect of unearthing direct evidence of conspiracy sufficient to preclude dismissal, even though the complaint does not set forth a single fact in a context that suggests an agreement. It seems fair to say that this approach to pleading would dispense with any showing of a "'reasonably founded hope'" that a plaintiff would be able to make a case; Mr. Micawber's optimism would be enough.

Seeing this, a good many judges and commentators have balked at taking the literal terms of the *Conley* passage as a pleading standard.

. . . *Conley*'s "no set of facts" language has been questioned, criticized, and explained away long enough. To be fair to the *Conley* Court, the passage should be understood in light of the opinion's preceding summary of the complaint's concrete allegations, which the Court quite reasonably understood as amply stating a claim for relief. But the passage so often quoted fails to mention this understanding on the part of the Court, and after puzzling the profession for 50 years, this famous observation has earned its retirement. The phrase is best forgotten as an incomplete, negative gloss on an accepted pleading standard: once a claim has been stated adequately, it may be supported by showing any set of facts consistent with the allegations in the complaint. *Conley*, then, described the breadth of opportunity to prove what an adequate complaint claims, not the minimum standard of adequate pleading to govern a complaint's survival.

III

When we look for plausibility in this complaint, we agree with the District Court that plaintiffs' claim of conspiracy in restraint of trade comes up short. To begin with, the complaint leaves no doubt that plaintiffs rest their § 1 claim on descriptions of parallel conduct and not on any independent allegation of actual agreement among the ILECs. Although in form a few stray statements speak directly of agreement, on fair reading these are merely legal conclusions resting on the prior allegations. . . .[10] The nub of the complaint, then, is the ILECs' parallel behavior, consisting of steps to keep the CLECs out and manifest disinterest in becoming CLECs themselves, and its sufficiency turns on the suggestions raised by this conduct when viewed in light of common economic experience.

We think that nothing contained in the complaint invests either the action or inaction alleged with a plausible suggestion of conspiracy. As to the ILECs' supposed agreement to disobey the 1996 Act and thwart the CLECs' attempts to compete, we agree with the District Court that nothing in the complaint intimates that the resistance to the upstarts was anything more than the natural, unilateral reaction of each ILEC intent on keeping its regional dominance. The 1996 Act did more than just subject the ILECs to competition; it obliged them to subsidize their competitors with their own equipment at wholesale rates. The economic incentive to resist was powerful, but resisting competition is routine market conduct . . . .

Plaintiffs' second conspiracy theory rests on the competitive reticence among the ILECs themselves in the wake of the 1996 Act . . . .

But [this behavior] was not suggestive of conspiracy, not if history teaches anything. In a traditionally unregulated industry with low barriers to entry, sparse competition among large firms dominating separate geographical segments of the market could very well signify illegal agreement, but here we have an obvious alternative explanation. In the decade preceding the 1996 Act and well before that, monopoly was the norm in telecommunications, not the exception. The ILECs were born in that world, doubtless liked the world the way it was, and surely knew the adage about him who lives by the sword. Hence, a natural explanation for the noncompetition alleged is that the former Government-sanctioned monopolists were sitting tight, expecting their neighbors to do the same thing. . . .

10. If the complaint had not explained that the claim of agreement rested on the parallel conduct described, we doubt that the complaint's references to an agreement among the ILECs would have given the notice required by Rule 8. Apart from identifying a seven-year span in which the § 1 violations were supposed to have occurred (*i.e.*, "[b]eginning at least as early as February 6, 1996, and continuing to the present"), the pleadings mentioned no specific time, place, or person involved in the alleged conspiracies. This lack of notice contrasts sharply with the model form for pleading negligence, Form 9, which the dissent says exemplifies the kind of "bare allegation" that survives a motion to dismiss. Whereas the model form alleges that the defendant struck the plaintiff with his car while plaintiff was crossing a particular highway at a specified date and time, the complaint here furnishes no clue as to which of the four ILECs (much less which of their employees) supposedly agreed, or when and where the illicit agreement took place. A defendant wishing to prepare an answer in the simple fact pattern laid out in Form 9 would know what to answer; a defendant seeking to respond to plaintiffs' conclusory allegations in the § 1 context would have little idea where to begin.

. . . We agree with the District Court's assessment that antitrust conspiracy was not suggested by the facts adduced under either theory of the complaint, which thus fails to state a valid § 1 claim.[14]

Plaintiffs say that our analysis runs counter to Swierkiewicz v. Sorema N. A., 534 U.S. 506, 508 (2002) . . . . Even though *Swierkiewicz*'s pleadings "detailed the events leading to his termination, provided relevant dates, and included the ages and nationalities of at least some of the relevant persons involved with his termination," the Court of Appeals dismissed his complaint for failing to allege certain additional facts that Swierkiewicz would need at the trial stage to support his claim in the absence of direct evidence of discrimination. We reversed on the ground that the Court of Appeals had impermissibly applied what amounted to a heightened pleading requirement by insisting that Swierkiewicz allege "specific facts" beyond those necessary to state his claim and the grounds showing entitlement to relief.

Here, in contrast, we do not require heightened fact pleading of specifics, but only enough facts to state a claim to relief that is plausible on its face. Because the plaintiffs here have not nudged their claims across the line from conceivable to plausible, their complaint must be dismissed.

* * * * *

The judgment of the Court of Appeals for the Second Circuit is reversed, and the cause is remanded for further proceedings consistent with this opinion.

It is so ordered.

■ JUSTICE STEVENS, with whom JUSTICE GINSBURG joins. . ., dissenting. . . .

Under rules of procedure that have been well settled . . ., a judge ruling on a defendant's motion to dismiss a complaint, "must accept as true all of the factual allegations contained in the complaint." Swierkiewicz v. Sorema N. A., 534 U.S. 506, 508, n.1 (2002). But instead of requiring knowledgeable executives such as Notebaert to respond to these allegations by way of sworn depositions or other limited discovery — and indeed without so much as requiring petitioners to file an answer denying that they entered into any agreement — the majority permits immediate dismissal based on the assurances of company lawyers that nothing untoward was afoot. . . .

14. In reaching this conclusion, we do not apply any "heightened" pleading standard, nor do we seek to broaden the scope of Federal Rule of Civil Procedure 9, which can only be accomplished "'by the process of amending the Federal Rules, and not by judicial interpretation.'" Swierkiewicz v. Sorema N. A., 534 U.S. 506, 515 (2002) (quoting Leatherman v. Tarrant County Narcotics Intelligence and Coordination Unit, 507 U.S. 163, 168 (1993)). On certain subjects understood to raise a high risk of abusive litigation, a plaintiff must state factual allegations with greater particularity than Rule 8 requires. Fed. Rules Civ. Proc. 9(b)-(c). Here, our concern is not that the allegations in the complaint were insufficiently "particular[ized]"; rather, the complaint warranted dismissal because it failed in toto to render plaintiffs' entitlement to relief plausible.

The Court and petitioners' legal team are no doubt correct that the parallel conduct alleged is consistent with the absence of any contract, combination, or conspiracy. But that conduct is also entirely consistent with the *presence* of the illegal agreement alleged in the complaint. And the charge that petitioners "agreed not to compete with one another" is not just one of a "a few stray statements"; it is an allegation describing unlawful conduct. As such, the Federal Rules of Civil Procedure, our longstanding precedent, and sound practice mandate that the District Court at least require some sort of response from petitioners before dismissing the case.

Two practical concerns presumably explain the Court's dramatic departure from settled procedural law. Private antitrust litigation can be enormously expensive, and there is a risk that jurors may mistakenly conclude that evidence of parallel conduct has proved that the parties acted pursuant to an agreement when they in fact merely made similar independent decisions. Those concerns merit careful case management, including strict control of discovery, careful scrutiny of evidence at the summary judgment stage, and lucid instructions to juries; they do not, however, justify the dismissal of an adequately pleaded complaint without even requiring the defendants to file answers denying a charge that they in fact engaged in collective decisionmaking. More importantly, they do not justify an interpretation of Federal Rule of Civil Procedure 12(b)(6) that seems to be driven by the majority's appraisal of the plausibility of the ultimate factual allegation rather than its legal sufficiency. . . .

Rule 8(a)(2) . . . did not come about by happenstance and its language is not inadvertent. The English experience with Byzantine special pleading rules — illustrated by the hypertechnical Hilary rules of 1834 — made obvious the appeal of a pleading standard that was easy for the common litigant to understand and sufficed to put the defendant on notice as to the nature of the claim against him and the relief sought. Stateside, David Dudley Field developed the highly influential New York Code of 1848, which required "[a] statement of the facts constituting the cause of action, in ordinary and concise language, without repetition, and in such a manner as to enable a person of common understanding to know what is intended." Substantially similar language appeared in the Federal Equity Rules adopted in 1912.

A difficulty arose, however, in that the Field Code and its progeny required a plaintiff to plead "facts" rather than "conclusions," a distinction that proved far easier to say than to apply. . . .

Under the relaxed pleading standards of the Federal Rules, the idea was not to keep litigants out of court but rather to keep them in. The merits of a claim would be sorted out during a flexible pretrial process and, as appropriate, through the crucible of trial. Charles E. Clark, the "principal draftsman" of the Federal Rules, put it thus:

> "Experience has shown . . . that we cannot expect the proof of the case to be made through the pleadings, and that such proof is really not their function. We can expect a general statement distinguishing the case

> from all others, so that the manner and form of trial and remedy expected are clear, and so that a permanent judgment will result." . . .

The pleading paradigm under the New Federal Rules was well illustrated by the inclusion in the appendix of Form 9, a complaint for negligence. . . . The asserted ground for relief — namely, the defendant's negligent driving — would have been called a "'conclusion of law'" under the code pleading of old. But that bare allegation suffices under a system that "restrict[s] the pleadings to the task of general notice-giving and invest[s] the deposition-discovery process with a vital role in the preparation for trial." . . .

It is in the context of this history that *Conley v. Gibson* must be understood. . . .

Consistent with the design of the Federal Rules, *Conley*'s "no set of facts" formulation permits outright dismissal only when proceeding to discovery or beyond would be futile. Once it is clear that a plaintiff has stated a claim that, if true, would entitle him to relief, matters of proof are appropriately relegated to other stages of the trial process. Today, however, in its explanation of a decision to dismiss a complaint that it regards as a fishing expedition, the Court scraps *Conley*'s "no set of facts" language. Concluding that the phrase has been "questioned, criticized, and explained away long enough," Court dismisses it as careless composition.

If *Conley*'s "no set of facts" language is to be interred, let it not be without a eulogy. That exact language, which the majority says has "puzzl[ed] the profession for 50 years," has been cited as authority in a dozen opinions of this Court and four separate writings. In not one of those 16 opinions was the language "questioned," "criticized," or "explained away." Indeed, today's opinion is the first by any Member of this Court to express any doubt as to the adequacy of the *Conley* formulation. Taking their cues from the federal courts, 26 States and the District of Columbia utilize as their standard for dismissal of a complaint the very language the majority repudiates: whether it appears "beyond doubt" that "no set of facts" in support of the claim would entitle the plaintiff to relief.

Petitioners have not requested that the *Conley* formulation be retired . . . . I would not rewrite the Nation's civil procedure textbooks and call into doubt the pleading rules of most of its States without far more informed deliberation as to the costs of doing so. Congress has established a process — a rulemaking process — for revisions of that order. *See* 28 U.S.C. §§ 2072-2074. . . .

In this [case,] the Court succumbs to the temptation that previous Courts have steadfastly resisted. While the majority assures us that it is not applying any "heightened" pleading standard, . . . I have a difficult time understanding its opinion any other way.

ERICKSON v. PARDUS

551 U.S. —, 127 S. Ct. 2197 (2007)

■ PER CURIAM.

Imprisoned by the State of Colorado and alleging violations of his Eighth and Fourteenth Amendment protections against cruel and unusual punishment, William Erickson, the petitioner in this Court, filed suit against prison officials in the United States District Court for the District of Colorado. He alleged that a liver condition resulting from hepatitis C required a treatment program that officials had commenced but then wrongfully terminated, with life-threatening consequences. Deeming these allegations, and others to be noted, to be "conclusory," the Court of Appeals for the Tenth Circuit affirmed the District Court's dismissal of petitioner's complaint. The holding departs in so stark a manner from the pleading standard mandated by the Federal Rules of Civil Procedure that we grant review. We vacate the court's judgment and remand the case for further consideration.

Petitioner was incarcerated in the Limon Correctional Facility in Limon, Colorado, where respondents Barry Pardus and Dr. Anita Bloor were working as prison officials. [According to the complaint and its attachments, the petitioner contracted hepatitis C, which required him to undergo a year-long protocol of self-administered injections of medication. One of the syringes that the petitioner (and others) used went missing. When prison officials later found the syringe, they believed that it had been used for the injection of illegal drugs. Because the use of illegal drugs damaged the liver and thwarted the purpose of the treatment, Dr. Bloor removed the petitioner from his hepatitis C treatment for a period of 18 months — a 12-month waiting period followed by a 6-month drug-education class. The complaint alleged that Dr. Bloor had "removed [him] from [his] hepatitis C treatment" in violation of department protocol, "thus endangering [his] life." Subsequently, the petitioner filed a motion seeking expedited review of his case. In this motion he stated that "furtherance of this disease can cause irreversible damage to [his] liver and possible death," that "numerous inmates" in the prison had died of Hepatitis C, and that he was "in imminent danger" himself "due to [the Department's] refusal to treat him."]

Respondents answered these filings with a motion to dismiss. The Magistrate Judge recommended . . . that the District Court dismiss the complaint on the ground it failed to allege Dr. Bloor's actions had caused petitioner "substantial harm." The District Court issued a short order indicating its agreement with the Magistrate Judge and dismissing the complaint.

The Court of Appeals affirmed. . . . Acknowledging decisions by courts that have found Eighth Amendment violations when delays in medical treatment have involved "life-threatening situations and instances in which it is apparent that delay would exacerbate the prisoner's medical problems" (and that have, moreover, indicated the Eighth Amendment "protects against future harm to an inmate"), the court nevertheless found petitioner's complaint deficient: Petitioner had, according to the court, failed to "allege that as a result of the discontinuance of the treatment itself shortly after it began or the interruption of treatment for approximately eighteen months he suffered any harm, let alone substantial harm, [other] than what he already faced from the Hepatitis C itself." . . .

. . . It was error for the Court of Appeals to conclude that the allegations in question, concerning harm caused petitioner by the termination of his medication, were too conclusory to establish for pleading purposes that petitioner had suffered "a cognizable independent harm" as a result of his removal from the hepatitis C treatment program.

Federal Rule of Civil Procedure 8(a)(2) requires only "a short and plain statement of the claim showing that the pleader is entitled to relief." Specific facts are not necessary; the statement need only "'give the defendant fair notice of what the . . . claim is and the grounds upon which it rests.'" Bell Atlantic Corp. v. Twombly, 550 U. S. —, — (2007) (quoting Conley v. Gibson, 355 U. S. 41, 47 (1957)). In addition, when ruling on a defendant's motion to dismiss, a judge must accept as true all of the factual allegations contained in the complaint.

The complaint stated that Dr. Bloor's decision to remove petitioner from his prescribed hepatitis C medication was "endangering [his] life." It alleged this medication was withheld "shortly after" petitioner had commenced a treatment program that would take one year, that he was "still in need of treatment for this disease," and that the prison officials were in the meantime refusing to provide treatment. This alone was enough to satisfy Rule 8(a)(2). Petitioner, in addition, bolstered his claim by making more specific allegations in documents attached to the complaint and in later filings.

The Court of Appeals' departure from the liberal pleading standards set forth by Rule 8(a)(2) is even more pronounced in this particular case because petitioner has been proceeding, from the litigation's outset, without counsel. A document filed pro se is "to be liberally construed," and "a pro se complaint, however inartfully pleaded, must be held to less stringent standards than formal pleadings drafted by lawyers." *Cf.* Fed. Rule Civ. Proc. 8(f) ("All pleadings shall be so construed as to do substantial justice").

. . . Certiorari and leave to proceed in forma pauperis are granted, the judgment of the Court of Appeals is vacated, and the case is remanded for further proceedings consistent with this opinion.

It is so ordered.

■ JUSTICE SCALIA would deny the petition for a writ of certiorari.

■ [The dissenting opinion of JUSTICE THOMAS is omitted.]

SCOTT v. HARRIS

550 U.S. —, 127 S. Ct. 1769 (2007)

■ Justice SCALIA delivered the opinion of the Court.

We consider whether a law enforcement official can, consistent with the Fourth Amendment, attempt to stop a fleeing motorist from continuing his public-endangering flight by ramming the motorist's car from behind. Put another way: Can an officer take actions that place a fleeing motorist at risk of serious injury or death in order to stop the motorist's flight from endangering the lives of innocent bystanders?

I

In March 2001, a Georgia county deputy clocked respondent's vehicle traveling at 73 miles per hour on a road with a 55-mile-per-hour speed limit. The deputy activated his blue flashing lights indicating that respondent should pull over. Instead, respondent sped away, initiating a chase down what is in most portions a two-lane road, at speeds exceeding 85 miles per hour. . . . Petitioner, Deputy Timothy Scott, heard the radio communication and joined the pursuit along with other officers. . . .

. . . Scott took over as the lead pursuit vehicle. Six minutes and nearly 10 miles after the chase had begun, Scott decided to attempt to terminate the episode by employing a "Precision Intervention Technique ('PIT') maneuver, which causes the fleeing vehicle to spin to a stop." Having radioed his supervisor for permission, Scott was told to "'[g]o ahead and take him out.'" Instead, Scott applied his push bumper to the rear of respondent's vehicle. As a result, respondent lost control of his vehicle, which left the roadway, ran down an embankment, overturned, and crashed. Respondent was badly injured and was rendered a quadriplegic. [Scott stated that he decided not to employ the PIT maneuver because he was "concerned that the vehicles were moving too quickly to safely execute the maneuver."]

Respondent filed suit against Deputy Scott and others under 42 U.S.C. § 1983, alleging, *inter alia*, a violation of his federal constitutional rights, viz. use of excessive force resulting in an unreasonable seizure under the Fourth Amendment. In response, Scott filed a motion for summary judgment based on an assertion of qualified immunity. The District Court denied the motion, finding that "there are material issues of fact on which the issue of qualified immunity turns which present sufficient disagreement to require submission to a jury." On interlocutory appeal, the United States Court of Appeals for the Eleventh Circuit affirmed the District Court's decision . . . . Taking respondent's view of the facts as given, the Court of Appeals concluded that Scott's actions could constitute "deadly force" . . ., and that the use of such force in this context "would violate [respondent's] constitutional right to be free from excessive force during a seizure. Accordingly, a reasonable jury could find that Scott violated [respondent's] Fourth Amendment rights." . . . We granted certiorari, and now reverse. . . .

III

A

The first step in assessing the constitutionality of Scott's actions is to determine the relevant facts. As this case was decided on summary judgment, there have not yet been factual findings by a judge or jury, and respondent's version of events (unsurprisingly) differs substantially from Scott's version. When things are in such a posture, courts are required to view the facts and draw reasonable inferences "in the light most favorable to the party opposing the [summary judgment] motion." In qualified immunity cases, this usually means adopting (as the Court of Appeals did here) the plaintiff's version of the facts.

There is, however, an added wrinkle in this case: existence in the record of a videotape capturing the events in question. There are no allegations or indications that this videotape was doctored or altered in any way, nor any contention that what it depicts differs from what actually happened. The videotape quite clearly contradicts the version of the story told by respondent and adopted by the Court of Appeals.[5] For example, the Court of Appeals adopted respondent's assertions that, during the chase, "there was little, if any, actual threat to pedestrians or other motorists, as the roads were mostly empty and [respondent] remained in control of his vehicle." Indeed, reading the lower court's opinion, one gets the impression that respondent, rather than fleeing from police, was attempting to pass his driving test:

> "[T]aking the facts from the non-movant's viewpoint, [respondent] remained in control of his vehicle, slowed for turns and intersections, and typically used his indicators for turns. He did not run any motorists off the road. . . . Significantly, by the time . . . Scott rammed [respondent], the motorway had been cleared of motorists and pedestrians allegedly because of police blockades of the nearby intersections."

The videotape tells quite a different story. There we see respondent's vehicle racing down narrow, two-lane roads in the dead of night at speeds that are shockingly fast. We see it swerve around more than a dozen other cars, cross the double-yellow line, and force cars traveling in both directions

5. JUSTICE STEVENS suggests that our reaction to the videotape is somehow idiosyncratic, and seems to believe we are misrepresenting its contents. *See post* (dissenting opinion) ("In sum, the factual statements by the Court of Appeals quoted by the Court . . . were entirely accurate"). We are happy to allow the videotape to speak for itself. *See* Record 36, Exh. A, available at http:// www. supremecourtus. gov/ opinions/ video/ scott_ v_ harris. rmvb and in Clerk of Court's case file.

to their respective shoulders to avoid being hit.[6] We see it run multiple red lights and travel for considerable periods of time in the occasional center left-turn-only lane, chased by numerous police cars forced to engage in the same hazardous maneuvers just to keep up. Far from being the cautious and controlled driver the lower court depicts, what we see on the video more closely resembles a Hollywood-style car chase of the most frightening sort, placing police officers and innocent bystanders alike at great risk of serious injury.[7]

At the summary judgment stage, facts must be viewed in the light most favorable to the nonmoving party only if there is a "genuine" dispute as to those facts. As we have emphasized, "[w]hen the moving party has carried its burden under Rule 56(c), its opponent must do more than simply show that there is some metaphysical doubt as to the material facts . . . . Where the record taken as a whole could not lead a rational trier of fact to find for the nonmoving party, there is no 'genuine issue for trial.'" Matsushita Elec. Industrial Co. v. Zenith Radio Corp., 475 U.S. 574, 586-587 (1986). "[T]he mere existence of some alleged factual dispute between the parties will not defeat an otherwise properly supported motion for summary judgment; the requirement is that there be no genuine issue of material fact." Anderson v. Liberty Lobby, Inc., 477 U.S. 242, 247-248 (1986). When opposing parties tell two different stories, one of which is blatantly contradicted by the record, so that no reasonable jury could believe it, a court should not adopt that version of the facts for purposes of ruling on a motion for summary judgment.

That was the case here with regard to the factual issue whether respondent was driving in such fashion as to endanger human life. Respondent's version of events is so utterly discredited by the record that no reasonable jury could have believed him. The Court of Appeals should not have relied on such visible fiction; it should have viewed the facts in the light depicted by the videotape.

B

Judging the matter on that basis, we think it is quite clear that Deputy Scott did not violate the Fourth Amendment. . . .

The car chase that respondent initiated in this case posed a substantial

6. JUSTICE STEVENS hypothesizes that these cars "had already pulled to the side of the road or were driving along the shoulder because they heard the police sirens or saw the flashing lights," so that "[a] jury could certainly conclude that those motorists were exposed to no greater risk than persons who take the same action in response to a speeding ambulance." It is not our experience that ambulances and fire engines careen down two-lane roads at 85-plus miles per hour, with an unmarked scout car out in front of them. . . .

7. This is not to say that each and every factual statement made by the Court of Appeals is inaccurate. For example, the videotape validates the court's statement that when Scott rammed respondent's vehicle it was not threatening any other vehicles or pedestrians. (Undoubtedly Scott waited for the road to be clear before executing his maneuver.)

and immediate risk of serious physical injury to others; no reasonable jury could conclude otherwise. Scott's attempt to terminate the chase by forcing respondent off the road was reasonable, and Scott is entitled to summary judgment. The Court of Appeals' decision to the contrary is reversed.

It is so ordered.

■ [The concurring opinion of JUSTICE GINSBURG is omitted.]

■ JUSTICE BREYER, concurring.

. . . Because watching the video footage of the car chase made a difference to my own view of the case, I suggest that the interested reader take advantage of the link in the Court's opinion, and watch it. Having done so, I do not believe a reasonable jury could, in this instance, find that Officer Timothy Scott (who joined the chase late in the day and did not know the specific reason why the respondent was being pursued) acted in violation of the Constitution. . . .

■ JUSTICE STEVENS, dissenting.

Relying on a *de novo* review of a videotape of a portion of a nighttime chase on a lightly traveled road in Georgia where no pedestrians or other "bystanders" were present, buttressed by uninformed speculation about the possible consequences of discontinuing the chase, eight of the jurors on this Court reach a verdict that differs from the views of the judges on both the District Court and the Court of Appeals who are surely more familiar with the hazards of driving on Georgia roads than we are. . . .

My colleagues on the jury saw respondent "swerve around more than a dozen other cars," and "force cars traveling in both directions to their respective shoulders," but they apparently discounted the possibility that those cars were already out of the pursuit's path as a result of hearing the sirens. Even if that were not so, passing a slower vehicle on a two-lane road always involves some degree of swerving and is not especially dangerous if there are no cars coming from the opposite direction. At no point during the chase did respondent pull into the opposite lane other than to pass a car in front of him; he did the latter no more than five times and, on most of those occasions, used his turn signal. On none of these occasions was there a car traveling in the opposite direction. In fact, at one point, when respondent found himself behind a car in his own lane and there were cars traveling in the other direction, he slowed and waited for the cars traveling in the other direction to pass before overtaking the car in front of him while using his turn signal to do so. This is hardly the stuff of Hollywood. To the contrary, the video does not reveal any incidents that could even be remotely characterized as "close calls." . . .

If two groups of judges can disagree so vehemently about the nature of the pursuit and the circumstances surrounding that pursuit, it seems eminently likely that a reasonable juror could disagree with this Court's characterization of events. Moreover, it is certainly possible that "a jury could conclude that Scott unreasonably used deadly force to seize Harris by ramming him off the road under the instant circumstances." . . .

UNITHERM FOOD SYSTEMS, INC. v. SWIFT-ECKRICH, INC.

546 U.S. 394 (2006)

■ JUSTICE THOMAS delivered the opinion of the Court

Ordinarily, a party in a civil jury trial that believes the evidence is legally insufficient to support an adverse jury verdict will seek a judgment as a matter of law by filing a motion pursuant to Federal Rule of Civil Procedure 50(a) before submission of the case to the jury, and then (if the Rule 50(a) motion is not granted and the jury subsequently decides against that party) a motion pursuant to Rule 50(b). In this case, however, the respondent filed a Rule 50(a) motion before the verdict, but did not file a Rule 50(b) motion after the verdict. Nor did respondent request a new trial under Rule 59. The Court of Appeals nevertheless proceeded to review the sufficiency of the evidence and, upon a finding that the evidence was insufficient, remanded the case for a new trial. Because our cases addressing the requirements of Rule 50 compel a contrary result, we reverse.

I

[The case arose out of a patent dispute in which ConAgra claimed that Unitherm, one of its competitors, was infringing on one of its patents. Unitherm sought a declaratory judgment that the patent was invalid, and further claimed that ConAgra's accusations constituted an antitrust violation. ConAgra counterclaimed for patent infringement. In an earlier ruling, the district concluded that the patent was invalid, so that only Unitherm's antitrust claim remained for trial.] Prior to the court's submission of the case to the jury, ConAgra moved for a directed verdict under Rule 50(a) based on legal insufficiency of the evidence. The District Court denied that motion. The jury returned a verdict for Unitherm, and ConAgra neither renewed its motion for judgment as a matter of law pursuant to Rule 50(b), nor moved for a new trial on antitrust liability pursuant to Rule 59.

On appeal . . ., ConAgra maintained that there was insufficient evidence to sustain the jury's [antitrust] verdict. . . . Under Tenth Circuit law, a party that has failed to file a postverdict motion challenging the sufficiency of the evidence may nonetheless raise such a claim on appeal, so long as that party filed a Rule 50(a) motion prior to submission of the case to the jury. Cummings v. General Motors Corp., 365 F.3d 944, 950-951 (2004). Notably, the only available relief in such a circumstance is a new trial.

Freed to examine the sufficiency of the evidence, the [court of appeals] concluded that, although Unitherm had presented sufficient evidence to support a determination that ConAgra had attempted to enforce a patent that it had obtained through fraud . . ., Unitherm had failed to present evidence sufficient to support the remaining elements of its antitrust claim. Accordingly, it vacated the jury's judgment in favor of Unitherm and remanded for a new trial. We granted certiorari, and now reverse.

II

Federal Rule of Civil Procedure 50 sets forth the procedural requirements for challenging the sufficiency of the evidence in a civil jury trial and establishes two stages for such challenges — prior to submission of the case to the jury, and after the verdict and entry of judgment. Rule 50(a) allows a party to challenge the sufficiency of the evidence prior to submission of the case to the jury, and authorizes the District Court to grant such motions at the court's discretion . . . .

Rule 50(b), by contrast, sets forth the procedural requirements for renewing a sufficiency of the evidence challenge after the jury verdict and entry of judgment. . . .

This Court has addressed the implications of a party's failure to file a postverdict motion under Rule 50(b) on several occasions and in a variety of procedural contexts. This Court has concluded that, "[i]n the absence of such a motion" an "appellate court [is] without power to direct the District Court to enter judgment contrary to the one it had permitted to stand." Cone v. West Virginia Pulp & Paper Co., 330 U.S. 212, 218 (1947). This Court has similarly concluded that a party's failure to file a Rule 50(b) motion deprives the appellate court of the power to order the entry of judgment in favor of that party where the district court directed the jury's verdict, and where the district court expressly reserved a party's preverdict motion for a directed verdict and then denied that motion after the verdict was returned. A postverdict motion is necessary because "[d]etermination of whether a new trial should be granted or a judgment entered under Rule 50(b) calls for the judgment in the first instance of the judge who saw and heard the witnesses and has the feel of the case which no appellate printed transcript can impart."[3] Moreover, the "requirement of a timely application for judgment after verdict is not an idle motion" because it "is . . . an essential part of the rule, firmly grounded in principles of fairness."

The foregoing authorities lead us to reverse the judgment below. Respondent correctly points out that these authorities address whether an

3. Neither Neely v. Martin K. Eby Constr. Co., 386 U.S. 317 (1967), nor Weisgram v. Marley Co., 528 U.S. 440 (2000), undermine[s] our judgment about the benefit of postverdict input from the district court. In those cases this Court determined that an appellate court may, in certain circumstances, direct the entry of judgment when it reverses the district court's denial of a Rule 50(b) motion. But in such circumstances the district court will have had an opportunity to consider the propriety of entering judgment or ordering a new trial by virtue of the postverdict motion. Moreover, these cases reiterate the value of the district court's input, cautioning the courts of appeals to be "'constantly alert' to 'the trial judge's first-hand knowledge of witnesses, testimony, and issues.'"

appellate court may enter judgment in the absence of a postverdict motion, as opposed to whether an appellate court may order a new trial . . . . But this distinction is immaterial. This Court's observations about the necessity of a postverdict motion under Rule 50(b), and the benefits of the district court's input at that stage, apply with equal force whether a party is seeking judgment as a matter of law or simply a new trial. In *Cone*, this Court concluded that, because Rule 50(b) permits the district court to exercise its discretion to choose between ordering a new trial and entering judgment, its "appraisal of the bona fides of the claims asserted by the litigants is of great value in reaching a conclusion as to whether a *new trial* should be granted." 330 U.S. at 216 (emphasis added). Similarly, this Court has determined that a party may only pursue on appeal a particular avenue of relief available under Rule 50(b), namely the entry of judgment or a new trial, when that party has complied with the Rule's filing requirements by requesting that particular relief below. . . .

Despite the straightforward language employed in *Cone* [and other cases], respondent maintains that those cases dictate affirmance here, because in each of those cases the litigants secured a new trial. But in each of those cases the appellants moved for a new trial postverdict in the District Court, and did not seek to establish their entitlement to a new trial solely on the basis of a denied Rule 50(a) motion. Accordingly, these outcomes merely underscore our holding today — a party is not entitled to pursue a new trial on appeal unless that party makes an appropriate postverdict motion in the district court.

Our determination that respondent's failure to comply with Rule 50(b) forecloses its challenge to the sufficiency of the evidence is further validated by the purported basis of respondent's appeal, namely the District Court's denial of respondent's preverdict Rule 50(a) motion. As an initial matter, *Cone* [and other cases] unequivocally establish that the precise subject matter of a party's Rule 50(a) motion — namely, its entitlement to judgment as a matter of law — cannot be appealed unless that motion is renewed pursuant to Rule 50(b). Here, respondent does not seek to pursue on appeal the precise claim it raised in its Rule 50(a) motion before the District Court — namely, its entitlement to judgment as a matter of law. Rather, it seeks a new trial based on the legal insufficiency of the evidence. But if, as in *Cone* [and other cases], a litigant that has failed to file a Rule 50(b) motion is foreclosed from seeking the relief it sought in its Rule 50(a) motion — *i.e.*, the entry of judgment — then surely respondent is foreclosed from seeking a new trial, relief it did not and could not seek in its preverdict motion. In short, respondent never sought a new trial before the District Court, and thus forfeited its right to do so on appeal.

The text of Rule 50(b) confirms that respondent's preverdict Rule 50(a) motion did not present the District Court with the option of ordering a new trial. That text provides that a district court may only order a new trial on the basis of issues raised in a preverdict Rule 50(a) motion when "ruling on a renewed motion" under Rule 50(b). Accordingly, even if the District Court was inclined to grant a new trial on the basis of arguments raised in respondent's preverdict motion, it was without the power to do so under Rule 50(b) absent a postverdict motion pursuant to that Rule. Consequently, the Court of Appeals was similarly powerless.

Similarly, the text and application of Rule 50(a) support our determination that respondent may not challenge the sufficiency of the evidence on appeal on the basis of the District Court's denial of its Rule 50(a) motion. The Rule provides that "the court *may* determine" that "there is no legally sufficient evidentiary basis for a reasonable jury to find for [a] party on [a given] issue," and "*may* grant a motion for judgment as a matter of law against that party . . . ." (Emphasis added.) Thus, while a district court is permitted to enter judgment as a matter of law when it concludes that the evidence is legally insufficient, it is not required to do so. To the contrary, the district courts are, if anything, encouraged to submit the case to the jury, rather than granting such motions. . . . Thus, the District Court's denial of respondent's preverdict motion cannot form the basis of respondent's appeal, because the denial of that motion was not error. It was merely an exercise of the District Court's discretion, in accordance with the text of the Rule and the accepted practice of permitting the jury to make an initial judgment about the sufficiency of the evidence. The only error here was counsel's failure to file a postverdict motion pursuant to Rule 50(b).

* * * * *

For the foregoing reasons, we hold that since respondent failed to renew its preverdict motion as specified in Rule 50(b), there was no basis for review of respondent's sufficiency of the evidence challenge in the Court of Appeals. The judgment of the Court of Appeals is reversed.

It is so ordered.

■ JUSTICE STEVENS, with whom JUSTICE KENNEDY joins, dissenting.

Murphy's law applies to trial lawyers as well as pilots. Even an expert will occasionally blunder. . . . This is not a case, in my view, in which the authority of the appellate court is limited by an explicit statute or controlling rule. The spirit of the Federal Rules of Civil Procedure favors preservation of a court's power to avoid manifestly unjust results in exceptional cases. . . .

* * * * * * *

JONES v. FLOWERS

547 U.S. 220 (2006)

■ CHIEF JUSTICE ROBERTS delivered the opinion of the Court.

Before a State may take property and sell it for unpaid taxes, the Due Process Clause of the Fourteenth Amendment requires the government to provide the owner "notice and opportunity for hearing appropriate to the nature of the case." Mullane v. Central Hanover Bank & Trust Co., 339 U.S. 306, 313 (1950). We granted certiorari to determine whether, when notice of a tax sale is mailed to the owner and returned undelivered, the government must take additional reasonable steps to provide notice before taking the owner's property.

I

In 1967, petitioner Gary Jones purchased a house at 717 North Bryan Street in Little Rock, Arkansas. He lived in the house with his wife until they separated in 1993. Jones then moved into an apartment in Little Rock, and his wife continued to live in the North Bryan Street house. Jones paid his mortgage each month for 30 years, and the mortgage company paid Jones' property taxes. After Jones paid off his mortgage in 1997, the property taxes went unpaid, and the property was certified as delinquent.

In April 2000, respondent Mark Wilcox, the Commissioner of State Lands (Commissioner), attempted to notify Jones of his tax delinquency, and his right to redeem the property, by mailing a certified letter to Jones at the North Bryan Street address. The packet of information stated that unless Jones redeemed the property, it would be subject to public sale two years later on April 17, 2002. Nobody was home to sign for the letter, and nobody appeared at the post office to retrieve the letter within the next 15 days. The post office returned the unopened packet to the Commissioner marked "'unclaimed.'"

Two years later, and just a few weeks before the public sale, the Commissioner published a notice of public sale in the Arkansas Democrat Gazette. No bids were submitted, which permitted the State to negotiate a private sale of the property. Several months later, respondent Linda Flowers submitted a purchase offer. The Commissioner mailed another certified letter to Jones at the North Bryan Street address, attempting to notify him that his house would be sold to Flowers if he did not pay his taxes. Like the first letter, the second was also returned to the Commissioner marked "unclaimed." Flowers purchased the house, which the parties stipulated in the trial court had a fair market value of $80,000, for $21,042.15. Immediately after the 30-day period for postsale redemption passed, Flowers had an unlawful detainer notice delivered to the property.

The notice was served on Jones' daughter, who contacted Jones and notified him of the tax sale.

Jones filed a lawsuit in Arkansas state court against the Commissioner and Flowers, alleging that the Commissioner's failure to provide notice of the tax sale and of Jones' right to redeem resulted in the taking of his property without due process. The Commissioner and Flowers moved for summary judgment on the ground that the two unclaimed letters sent by the Commissioner were a constitutionally adequate attempt at notice, and Jones filed a cross-motion for summary judgment. The trial court granted summary judgment in favor of the Commissioner and Flowers. It concluded that the Arkansas tax sale statute, which set forth the notice procedure followed by the Commissioner, complied with constitutional due process requirements.

Jones appealed, and the Arkansas Supreme Court affirmed the trial court's judgment. 198 S.W.3d 520 (2004). The court noted our precedent stating that due process does not require actual notice, *see* Dusenbery v. United States, 534 U.S. 161, 170 (2002), and it held that attempting to provide notice by certified mail satisfied due process in the circumstances presented.

We granted certiorari to resolve a conflict among the Circuits and State Supreme Courts concerning whether the Due Process Clause requires the government to take additional reasonable steps to notify a property owner when notice of a tax sale is returned undelivered. . . . We hold that when mailed notice of a tax sale is returned unclaimed, the State must take additional reasonable steps to attempt to provide notice to the property owner before selling his property, if it is practicable to do so. Under the circumstances presented here, additional reasonable steps were available to the State. We therefore reverse the judgment of the Arkansas Supreme Court.

II

A

Due process does not require that a property owner receive actual notice before the government may take his property. *Dusenbery*, *supra*, at 170. Rather, we have stated that due process requires the government to provide "notice reasonably calculated, under all the circumstances, to apprise interested parties of the pendency of the action and afford them an opportunity to present their objections." *Mullane,* 339 U.S. at 314. The Commissioner argues that once the State provided notice reasonably calculated to apprise Jones of the impending tax sale by mailing him a certified letter, due process was satisfied. The Arkansas statutory scheme is reasonably calculated to provide notice, the Commissioner continues, because it provides for notice by certified mail to an address that the property owner is responsible for keeping up to date. The Commissioner notes this Court's ample precedent condoning notice by mail, *see, e.g.*,

Dusenbery, *supra*, at 169; Tulsa Professional Collection Services, Inc. v. Pope, 485 U.S. 478, 490 (1988); Mennonite Bd. of Missions v. Adams, 462 U.S. 791, 798 (1983); *Mullane*, *supra*, at 318-319, and adds that the Arkansas scheme exceeds constitutional requirements by requiring the Commissioner to use certified mail.

It is true that this Court has deemed notice constitutionally sufficient if it was reasonably calculated to reach the intended recipient when sent. *See, e.g.*, *Dusenbery*, *supra*, at 168-169; *Mullane,* 339 U.S., at 314. In each of these cases, the government attempted to provide notice and heard nothing back indicating that anything had gone awry, and we stated that "[t]he reasonableness and hence the constitutional validity of [the] chosen method may be defended on the ground that it is in itself reasonably certain to inform those affected." *Id.*, at 315; *see also Dusenbery*, *supra*, at 170. But we have never addressed whether due process entails further responsibility when the government becomes aware prior to the taking that its attempt at notice has failed. That is a new wrinkle, and we have explained that the "notice required will vary with circumstances and conditions." Walker v. City of Hutchinson, 352 U.S. 112, 115 (1956). The question presented is whether such knowledge on the government's part is a "circumstance and condition" that varies the "notice required."

The Courts of Appeals and State Supreme Courts have addressed this question on frequent occasions, and most have decided that when the government learns its attempt at notice has failed, due process requires the government to do something more before real property may be sold in a tax sale. . . . Many States already require in their statutes that the government do more than simply mail notice to delinquent owners, either at the outset or as a followup measure if initial mailed notice is ineffective.

In *Mullane,* we stated that "when notice is a person's due . . . [t]he means employed must be such as one desirous of actually informing the absentee might reasonably adopt to accomplish it," 339 U.S., at 315, and that assessing the adequacy of a particular form of notice requires balancing the "interest of the State" against "the individual interest sought to be protected by the Fourteenth Amendment," *id.*, at 314. . . .

We do not think that a person who actually desired to inform a real property owner of an impending tax sale of a house he owns would do nothing when a certified letter sent to the owner is returned unclaimed. If the Commissioner prepared a stack of letters to mail to delinquent taxpayers, handed them to the postman, and then watched as the departing postman accidentally dropped the letters down a storm drain, one would certainly expect the Commissioner's office to prepare a new stack of letters and send them again. No one "desirous of actually informing" the owners would simply shrug his shoulders as the letters disappeared and say "I tried." Failure to follow up would be unreasonable, despite the fact that the letters were reasonably calculated to reach their intended recipients when delivered to the postman.

By the same token, when a letter is returned by the post office, the sender will ordinarily attempt to resend it, if it is practicable to do so. This is especially true when, as here, the subject matter of the letter concerns such an important and irreversible prospect as the loss of a house. Although the State may have made a reasonable calculation of how to reach Jones, it had good reason to suspect when the notice was returned that Jones was "no better off than if the notice had never been sent." Deciding to take no further action is not what someone "desirous of actually informing" Jones would do; such a person would take further reasonable steps if any were available.

In prior cases, we have required the government to consider unique information about an intended recipient regardless of whether a statutory scheme is reasonably calculated to provide notice in the ordinary case. In Robinson v. Hanrahan, 409 U.S. 38 (1972), we held that notice of forfeiture proceedings sent to a vehicle owner's home address was inadequate when the State knew that the property owner was in prison. 409 U.S., at 40. In Covey v. Town of Somers, 351 U.S. 141 (1956), we held that notice of foreclosure by mailing, posting, and publication was inadequate when town officials knew that the property owner was incompetent and without a guardian's protection. *Id.*, at 146-147. . . .

It is certainly true, as the Commissioner and Solicitor General contend, that the failure of notice in a specific case does not establish the inadequacy of the attempted notice; in that sense, the constitutionality of a particular procedure for notice is assessed *ex ante,* rather than *post hoc*. But if a feature of the State's chosen procedure is that it promptly provides additional information to the government about the effectiveness of notice, it does not contravene the *ex ante* principle to consider what the government does with that information in assessing the adequacy of the chosen procedure. After all, the State knew *ex ante* that it would promptly learn whether its effort to effect notice through certified mail had succeeded. It would not be inconsistent with the approach the Court has taken in notice cases to ask, with respect to a procedure under which telephone calls were placed to owners, what the State did when no one answered. Asking what the State does when a notice letter is returned unclaimed is not substantively different. . . .

Finally, the Commissioner reminds us of a statement from *Mullane* that the State can assume an owner leaves his property in the hands of one who will inform him if his interest is in jeopardy. 339 U.S., at 316. But in this passage, Justice Jackson writes of ". . . attachment of a chattel[,] or entry upon real estate in the name of law" — such "seiz[ures]" of property, he concluded, "may reasonably be expected to come promptly to the owner's attention." *Ibid.* An occupant, however, is not charged with acting as the owner's agent in all respects, and it is quite a leap from Justice Jackson's examples to conclude that it is an obligation of tenancy to follow up with certified mail of unknown content addressed to the owner. In fact, the State makes it impossible for the occupant to learn why the Commissioner is writing the owner, because an occupant cannot call for a certified letter without first obtaining the owner's signature. For all the occupant knows, the Commissioner of State Lands might write to certain residents about a variety of matters he finds important, such as state parks or highway construction; it would by no means be obvious to an occupant observing a certified mail slip from the Commissioner that the owner is in danger of losing his property. In any event, there is no record evidence that notices of attempted delivery were left at 717 North Bryan Street.

Mr. Jones should have been more diligent with respect to his property, no question. People must pay their taxes, and the government may hold citizens accountable for tax delinquency by taking their property. But before forcing a citizen to satisfy his debt by forfeiting his property, due process requires the government to provide adequate notice of the impending taking. U.S. Const., Amdt. 14; *Mennonite, supra*, at 799.

B

In response to the returned form suggesting that Jones had not received notice that he was about to lose his property, the State did — nothing. For the reasons stated, we conclude the State should have taken additional reasonable steps to notify Jones, if practicable to do so. The question remains whether there were any such available steps. While "[i]t is not our responsibility to prescribe the form of service that the [government] should adopt," Greene v. Lindsey, 456 U.S. 444, 455, n.9 (1982), if there were no reasonable additional steps the government could have taken upon return of the unclaimed notice letter, it cannot be faulted for doing nothing.

We think there were several reasonable steps the State could have taken. What steps are reasonable in response to new information depends upon what the new information reveals. The return of the certified letter marked "unclaimed" meant either that Jones still lived at 717 North Bryan Street, but was not home when the postman called and did not retrieve the letter at the post office, or that Jones no longer resided at that address. One reasonable step primarily addressed to the former possibility would be for the State to resend the notice by regular mail, so that a signature was not required. The Commissioner says that use of certified mail makes actual notice more likely, because requiring the recipient's signature protects against misdelivery. But that is only true, of course, when someone is home to sign for the letter, or to inform the mail carrier that he has arrived at the wrong address. Otherwise, "[c]ertified mail is dispatched and handled in transit as ordinary mail," United States Postal Service, Domestic Mail Manual § 503.3.2.1 (Mar. 16, 2006), and the use of certified mail might make actual notice less likely in some cases — the letter cannot be left like regular mail to be examined at the end of the day, and it can only be retrieved from the post office for a specified period of time. Following up with regular mail might also increase the chances of actual notice to Jones if — as it turned out — he had moved. Even occupants who ignored certified mail notice slips addressed to the owner (if any had been left) might scrawl the owner's new address on the notice packet and leave it for the postman to retrieve, or notify Jones directly.

Other reasonable followup measures, directed at the possibility that Jones had moved as well as that he had simply not retrieved the certified letter, would have been to post notice on the front door, or to address otherwise undeliverable mail to "occupant." Most States that explicitly outline additional procedures in their tax sale statutes require just such steps. . . .

The Solicitor General argues that requiring further effort when the government learns that notice was not delivered will cause the government to favor modes of providing notice that do not generate additional information — for example, starting (and stopping) with regular mail instead of certified mail. We find this unlikely, as we have no doubt that the government repeatedly finds itself being asked to prove that notice was sent and received. Using certified mail provides the State with documentation of personal delivery and protection against false claims that notice was never received. That added security, however, comes at a price — the State also learns when notice has *not* been received. We conclude that, under the circumstances presented, the State cannot simply ignore that information in proceeding to take and sell the owner's property — any more than it could ignore the information that the owner in *Robinson* was in jail, or that the owner in *Covey* was incompetent.

Though the Commissioner argues that followup measures are not constitutionally required, he reminds us that the State did make some attempt to follow up with Jones by publishing notice in the newspaper a few weeks before the public sale. Several decades ago, this Court observed that "[c]hance alone" brings a person's attention to "an advertisement in small type inserted in the back pages of a newspaper," *Mullane,* 339 U.S., at 315, and that notice by publication is adequate only where "it is not reasonably possible or practicable to give more adequate warning," *id.*, at 317. Following up by publication was not constitutionally adequate under the circumstances presented here because, as we have explained, it was possible and practicable to give Jones more adequate warning of the impending tax sale. . . .

* * * * *

There is no reason to suppose that the State will ever be less than fully zealous in its efforts to secure the tax revenue it needs. The same cannot be said for the State's efforts to ensure that its citizens receive proper notice before the State takes action against them. In this case, the State is exerting extraordinary power against a property owner — taking and selling a house he owns. It is not too much to insist that the State do a bit more to attempt to let him know about it when the notice letter addressed to him is returned unclaimed.

The Commissioner's effort to provide notice to Jones of an impending tax sale of his house was insufficient to satisfy due process given the circumstances of this case. The judgment of the Arkansas Supreme Court is reversed, and the case is remanded for proceedings not inconsistent with this opinion.

It is so ordered.

■ JUSTICE ALITO took no part in the consideration or decision of this case.

■ [The dissenting opinion of JUSTICE THOMAS, with whom JUSTICE SCALIA and JUSTICE KENNEDY joined, is omitted.]

* * * * * * *

GRABLE & SONS METAL PRODUCTS, INC. v. DARUE ENGINEERING & MANUFACTURING

545 U.S. 308 (2005)

■ JUSTICE SOUTER delivered the opinion for a unanimous Court.

The question is whether want of a federal cause of action to try claims of title to land obtained at a federal tax sale precludes removal to federal court of a state action with non-diverse parties raising a disputed issue of federal title law. We answer no, and hold that the national interest in providing a federal forum for federal tax litigation is sufficiently substantial to support the exercise of federal question jurisdiction over the disputed issue on removal, which would not distort any division of labor between the state and federal courts, provided or assumed by Congress.

I

In 1994, the Internal Revenue Service seized Michigan real property belonging to petitioner Grable & Sons Metal Products, Inc., to satisfy Grable's federal tax delinquency. Title 26 U.S.C. § 6335 required the IRS to give notice of the seizure, and there is no dispute that Grable received actual notice by certified mail before the IRS sold the property to respondent Darue Engineering & Manufacturing. Although Grable also received notice of the sale itself, it did not exercise its statutory right to redeem the property within 180 days of the sale, and after that period had passed, the Government gave Darue a quitclaim deed.

Five years later, Grable brought a quiet title action in state court, claiming that Darue's record title was invalid because the IRS had failed to notify Grable of its seizure of the property in the exact manner required by § 6335(a), which provides that written notice must be "given by the Secretary to the owner of the property [or] left at his usual place of abode or business." Grable said that the statute required personal service, not service by certified mail.

Darue removed the case to Federal District Court as presenting a federal question, because the claim of title depended on the interpretation of the notice statute in the federal tax law. The District Court declined to remand the case at Grable's behest after finding that the "claim does pose a significant question of federal law," and ruling that Grable's lack of a federal right of action to enforce its claim against Darue did not bar the exercise of federal jurisdiction. On the merits, the court granted summary judgment to Darue, holding that although § 6335 by its terms required personal service, substantial compliance with the statute was enough.

The Court of Appeals for the Sixth Circuit affirmed. On the jurisdictional question, the panel thought it sufficed that the title claim raised an issue of federal law that had to be resolved, and implicated a substantial federal interest (in construing federal tax law). The court went on to affirm the District Court's judgment on the merits. We granted certiorari on the jurisdictional question alone, to resolve a split within the Courts of Appeals on whether Merrell Dow Pharmaceuticals Inc. v. Thompson, 478 U.S. 804 (1986), always requires a federal cause of action as a condition for exercising federal-question jurisdiction. We now affirm.

II

Darue was entitled to remove the quiet title action if Grable could have brought it in federal district court originally, 28 U.S.C. § 1441(a), as a civil action "arising under the Constitution, laws, or treaties of the United States," § 1331. This provision for federal-question jurisdiction is invoked by and large by plaintiffs pleading a cause of action created by federal law .... There is, however, another longstanding, if less frequently encountered, variety of federal "arising under" jurisdiction, this Court having recognized for nearly 100 years that in certain cases federal question jurisdiction will lie over state-law claims that implicate significant federal issues. *E.g.*, Hopkins v. Walker, 244 U.S. 486, 490-491 (1917). The doctrine captures the commonsense notion that a federal court ought to be able to hear claims recognized under state law that nonetheless turn on substantial questions of federal law, and thus justify resort to the experience, solicitude, and hope of uniformity that a federal forum offers on federal issues.

The classic example is Smith v. Kansas City Title & Trust Co., 255 U.S. 180 (1921), a suit by a shareholder claiming that the defendant corporation could not lawfully buy certain bonds of the National Government because their issuance was unconstitutional. Although Missouri law provided the cause of action, the Court recognized federal-question jurisdiction because the principal issue in the case was the federal constitutionality of the bond issue. *Smith* thus held, in a somewhat generous statement of the scope of the doctrine, that a state-law claim could give rise to federal-question jurisdiction so long as it "appears from the [complaint] that the right to relief depends upon the construction or application of [federal law]."

The *Smith* statement has been subject to some trimming to fit earlier and later cases recognizing the vitality of the basic doctrine, but shying away from the expansive view that mere need to apply federal law in a state-law claim will suffice to open the "arising under" door. As early as 1912, this Court had confined federal-question jurisdiction over state-law claims to those that "really and substantially involv[e] a dispute or controversy respecting the validity, construction or effect of [federal] law." Shulthis v. McDougal, 225 U.S. 561, 569 (1912). . . . It has in fact become a constant refrain in such cases that federal jurisdiction demands not only a contested federal issue, but a substantial one, indicating a serious federal interest in claiming the advantages thought to be inherent in a federal forum.

But even when the state action discloses a contested and substantial federal question, the exercise of federal jurisdiction is subject to a possible veto. For the federal issue will ultimately qualify for a federal forum only if federal jurisdiction is consistent with congressional judgment about the sound division of labor between state and federal courts governing the application of § 1331. . . . Because arising-under jurisdiction to hear a state-law claim always raises the possibility of upsetting the state-federal line drawn (or at least assumed) by Congress, the presence of a disputed federal issue and the ostensible importance of a federal forum are never necessarily dispositive; there must always be an assessment of any disruptive portent in exercising federal jurisdiction. *See also Merrell Dow.*

These considerations have kept us from stating a "single, precise, all-embracing" test for jurisdiction over federal issues embedded in state-law claims between nondiverse parties. We have not kept them out simply because they appeared in state raiment, as Justice Holmes would have done, *see Smith, supra,* at 214 (dissenting opinion), but neither have we treated "federal issue" as a password opening federal courts to any state action embracing a point of federal law. Instead, the question is, does a state-law claim necessarily raise a stated federal issue, actually disputed and substantial, which a federal forum may entertain without disturbing any congressionally approved balance of federal and state judicial responsibilities.

III

A

This case warrants federal jurisdiction. Grable's state complaint must specify "the facts establishing the superiority of [its] claim," and Grable has premised its superior title claim on a failure by the IRS to give it adequate notice, as defined by federal law. Whether Grable was given notice within the meaning of the federal statute is thus an essential element of its quiet title claim, and the meaning of the federal statute is actually in dispute; it appears to be the only legal or factual issue contested in the case. The meaning of the federal tax provision is an important issue of federal law that sensibly belongs in a federal court. The Government has a strong interest in the "prompt and certain collection of delinquent taxes," and the ability of the IRS to satisfy its claims from the property of delinquents requires clear terms of notice to allow buyers like Darue to satisfy themselves that the Service has touched the bases necessary for good title. The Government thus has a direct interest in the availability of a federal forum to vindicate its own administrative action, and buyers (as well as tax delinquents) may find it valuable to come before judges used to federal tax matters. Finally, because it will be the rare state title case that raises a contested matter of federal law, federal jurisdiction to resolve genuine disagreement over federal tax title provisions will portend only a microscopic effect on the federal-state division of labor. . . .

B

Merrell Dow Pharmaceuticals Inc. v. Thompson, 478 U.S. 804 (1986), on which Grable rests its position, is not to the contrary. *Merrell Dow* considered a state tort claim resting in part on the allegation that the defendant drug company had violated a federal misbranding prohibition, and was thus presumptively negligent under Ohio law. The Court assumed that federal law would have to be applied to resolve the claim, but after closely examining the strength of the federal interest at stake and the implications of opening the federal forum, held federal jurisdiction unavailable. Congress had not provided a private federal cause of action for violation of the federal branding requirement, and the Court found "it would . . . flout, or at least undermine, congressional intent to conclude that federal courts might nevertheless exercise federal-question jurisdiction and provide remedies for violations of that federal statute solely because the violation . . . is said to be a . . . 'proximate cause' under state law."

Because federal law provides for no quiet title action that could be brought against Darue, Grable argues that there can be no federal jurisdiction here, stressing some broad language in *Merrell Dow* (including the passage just quoted) that on its face supports Grable's position. But an opinion is to be read as a whole, and *Merrell Dow* cannot be read whole as overturning decades of precedent, as it would have done by effectively adopting the Holmes dissent in *Smith,* and converting a federal cause of action from a sufficient condition for federal-question jurisdiction into a necessary one.

In the first place, *Merrell Dow* disclaimed the adoption of any bright-line rule, as when the Court reiterated that "in exploring the outer reaches of § 1331, determinations about federal jurisdiction require sensitive judgments about congressional intent, judicial power, and the federal system." The opinion included a lengthy footnote explaining that questions of jurisdiction over state-law claims require "careful judgments," about the "nature of the federal interest at stake." And as a final indication that it did not mean to make a federal right of action mandatory, it expressly approved the exercise of jurisdiction sustained in *Smith,* despite the want of any federal cause of action available to *Smith's* shareholder plaintiff. *Merrell Dow* then, did not toss out, but specifically retained the contextual enquiry that had been *Smith's* hallmark for over 60 years. At the end of *Merrell Dow,* Justice Holmes was still dissenting.

Accordingly, *Merrell Dow* should be read in its entirety as treating the absence of a federal private right of action as evidence relevant to, but not dispositive of, the "sensitive judgments about congressional intent" that § 1331 requires. The absence of any federal cause of action affected *Merrell Dow's* result two ways. The Court saw the fact as worth some consideration in the assessment of substantiality. But its primary importance emerged when the Court treated the combination of no federal cause of action and no preemption of state remedies for misbranding as an important clue to Congress's conception of the scope of jurisdiction to be exercised under

§ 1331. The Court saw the missing cause of action not as a missing federal door key, always required, but as a missing welcome mat, required in the circumstances, when exercising federal jurisdiction over a state misbranding action would have attracted a horde of original filings and removal cases raising other state claims with embedded federal issues. For if the federal labeling standard without a federal cause of action could get a state claim into federal court, so could any other federal standard without a federal cause of action. And that would have meant a tremendous number of cases.

... Expressing concern over the "increased volume of federal litigation," and noting the importance of adhering to "legislative intent," *Merrell Dow* thought it improbable that the Congress, having made no provision for a federal cause of action, would have meant to welcome any state-law tort case implicating federal law "solely because the violation of the federal statute is said to [create] a rebuttable presumption [of negligence] . . . under state law." In this situation, no welcome mat meant keep out. *Merrell Dow's* analysis thus fits within the framework of examining the importance of having a federal forum for the issue, and the consistency of such a forum with Congress's intended division of labor between state and federal courts.

As already indicated, however, a comparable analysis yields a different jurisdictional conclusion in this case. Although Congress also indicated ambivalence in this case by providing no private right of action to Grable, it is the rare state quiet title action that involves contested issues of federal law. Consequently, jurisdiction over actions like Grable's would not materially affect, or threaten to affect, the normal currents of litigation. Given the absence of threatening structural consequences and the clear interest the Government, its buyers, and its delinquents have in the availability of a federal forum, there is no good reason to shirk from federal jurisdiction over the dispositive and contested federal issue at the heart of the state-law title claim.

IV

The judgment of the Court of Appeals, upholding federal jurisdiction over Grable's quiet title action, is affirmed.

It is so ordered.

■ JUSTICE THOMAS, concurring.

The Court faithfully applies our precedents interpreting 28 U.S.C. § 1331 to authorize federal-court jurisdiction over some cases in which state law creates the cause of action but requires determination of an issue of federal law. In this case, no one has asked us to overrule those precedents and adopt the rule Justice Holmes set forth in American Well Works Co. v. Layne & Bowler Co., 241 U.S. 257 (1916), limiting § 1331 jurisdiction to cases in which federal law creates the cause of action pleaded on the face of the plaintiff's complaint. In an appropriate case, and perhaps with the benefit of better evidence as to the original meaning of § 1331's text, I would be willing to consider that course.

Jurisdictional rules should be clear. Whatever the virtues of the *Smith* standard, it is anything but clear. . . .

Whatever the vices of the *American Well Works* rule, it is clear. Moreover, it accounts for the "'vast majority'" of cases that come within § 1331 under our current case law — further indication that trying to sort out which cases fall within the smaller *Smith* category may not be worth the effort it entails. Accordingly, I would be willing in appropriate circumstances to reconsider our interpretation of § 1331.

* * * * * * *

EXXON MOBIL CORP. v. ALLAPATTAH SERVICES, INC.

545 U.S. 546 (2005)

■ JUSTICE KENNEDY delivered the opinion of the Court.

These consolidated cases* present the question whether a federal court in a diversity action may exercise supplemental jurisdiction over additional plaintiffs whose claims do not satisfy the minimum amount-in-controversy requirement, provided the claims are part of the same case or controversy as the claims of plaintiffs who do allege a sufficient amount in controversy. Our decision turns on the correct interpretation of 28 U.S.C. § 1367. The question has divided the Courts of Appeals, and we granted certiorari to resolve the conflict.

We hold that, where the other elements of jurisdiction are present and at least one named plaintiff in the action satisfies the amount-in-controversy requirement, § 1367 does authorize supplemental jurisdiction over the claims of other plaintiffs in the same Article III case or controversy, even if those claims are for less than the jurisdictional amount specified in the statute setting forth the requirements for diversity jurisdiction. We affirm the judgment of the Court of Appeals for the Eleventh Circuit in [*Allapattah*], and we reverse the judgment of the Court of Appeals for the First Circuit in [*Rosario Ortega*].

I

In 1991, about 10,000 Exxon dealers filed a class-action suit against the Exxon Corporation in the United States District Court for the Northern District of Florida. The dealers alleged an intentional and systematic scheme by Exxon under which they were overcharged for fuel purchased from Exxon. The plaintiffs invoked the District Court's § 1332(a) diversity jurisdiction. After a unanimous jury verdict in favor of the plaintiffs, the District Court certified the case for interlocutory review, asking whether it had properly exercised § 1367 supplemental jurisdiction over the claims of class members who did not meet the jurisdictional minimum amount in controversy.

The Court of Appeals for the Eleventh Circuit upheld the District Court's extension of supplemental jurisdiction to these class members. "[W]e find," the court held, "that § 1367 clearly and unambiguously provides

* *Exxon Mobil Corp. v. Allapattah Services, Inc.* was consolidated with *Rosario Ortega v. Star-Kist Foods, Inc.*, and this opinion decides both cases. — ED.

district courts with the authority in diversity class actions to exercise supplemental jurisdiction over the claims of class members who do not meet the minimum amount in controversy as long as the district court has original jurisdiction over the claims of at least one of the class representatives." This decision accords with the views of the Courts of Appeals for the Fourth, Sixth, and Seventh Circuits. The Courts of Appeals for the Fifth and Ninth Circuits, adopting a similar analysis of the statute, have held that in a diversity class action the unnamed class members need not meet the amount-in-controversy requirement, provided the named class members do. These decisions, however, are unclear on whether all the named plaintiffs must satisfy this requirement.

In the other case now before us the Court of Appeals for the First Circuit took a different position on the meaning of § 1367(a). In that case, a 9-year-old girl sued Star-Kist in a diversity action in the United States District Court for the District of Puerto Rico, seeking damages for unusually severe injuries she received when she sliced her finger on a tuna can. Her family joined in the suit, seeking damages for emotional distress and certain medical expenses. The District Court granted summary judgment to Star-Kist, finding that none of the plaintiffs met the minimum amount-in-controversy requirement. The Court of Appeals for the First Circuit, however, ruled that the injured girl, but not her family members, had made allegations of damages in the requisite amount.

The Court of Appeals then addressed whether, in light of the fact that one plaintiff met the requirements for original jurisdiction, supplemental jurisdiction over the remaining plaintiffs' claims was proper under § 1367. The court held that § 1367 authorizes supplemental jurisdiction only when the district court has original jurisdiction over the action, and that in a diversity case original jurisdiction is lacking if one plaintiff fails to satisfy the amount-in-controversy requirement. Although the Court of Appeals claimed to "express no view" on whether the result would be the same in a class action, its analysis is inconsistent with that of the Court of Appeals for the Eleventh Circuit. The Court of Appeals for the First Circuit's view of § 1367 is, however, shared by the Courts of Appeal for the Third, Eighth, and Tenth Circuits, and the latter two Courts of Appeals have expressly applied this rule to class actions.

II

A

The district courts of the United States, as we have said many times, are "courts of limited jurisdiction. They possess only that power authorized by Constitution and statute." In order to provide a federal forum for plaintiffs who seek to vindicate federal rights, Congress has conferred on the district courts original jurisdiction in federal-question cases — civil actions that arise under the Constitution, laws, or treaties of the United States. 28 U.S.C. § 1331. In order to provide a neutral forum for what have come to be known as diversity cases, Congress also has granted district courts original jurisdiction in civil actions between citizens of different States, between U.S. citizens and foreign citizens, or by foreign states against U.S. citizens. § 1332. To ensure that diversity jurisdiction does not flood the federal courts with minor disputes, § 1332(a) requires that the matter in controversy in a diversity case exceed a specified amount, currently $75,000.

Although the district courts may not exercise jurisdiction absent a statutory basis, it is well established — in certain classes of cases — that, once a court has original jurisdiction over some claims in the action, it may exercise supplemental jurisdiction over additional claims that are part of the same case or controversy. The leading modern case for this principle is Mine Workers v. Gibbs, 383 U.S. 715 (1966). In *Gibbs*, the plaintiff alleged the defendant's conduct violated both federal and state law. The District Court, *Gibbs* held, had original jurisdiction over the action based on the federal claims. *Gibbs* confirmed that the District Court had the additional power (though not the obligation) to exercise supplemental jurisdiction over related state claims that arose from the same Article III case or controversy.

As we later noted, the decision allowing jurisdiction over pendent state claims in *Gibbs* did not mention, let alone come to grips with, the text of the jurisdictional statutes and the bedrock principle that federal courts have no jurisdiction without statutory authorization. Finley v. United States, 490 U.S. 545, 548 (1989). In *Finley*, we nonetheless reaffirmed and rationalized *Gibbs* and its progeny by inferring from it the interpretive principle that, in cases involving supplemental jurisdiction over additional claims between parties properly in federal court, the jurisdictional statutes should be read broadly, on the assumption that in this context Congress intended to authorize courts to exercise their full Article III power to dispose of an "'entire action before the court [which] comprises but one constitutional "case."'"

We have not, however, applied *Gibbs*' expansive interpretive approach to other aspects of the jurisdictional statutes. For instance, we have consistently interpreted § 1332 as requiring complete diversity: In a case with multiple plaintiffs and multiple defendants, the presence in the action of a single plaintiff from the same State as a single defendant deprives the district court of original diversity jurisdiction over the entire action. Strawbridge v. Curtiss, 7 U.S. (3 Cranch) 267 (1806); Owen Equipment & Erection Co. v. Kroger, 437 U.S. 365, 375 (1978) . . . The Court . . . has adhered to the complete diversity rule in light of the purpose of the diversity requirement, which is to provide a federal forum for important disputes where state courts might favor, or be perceived as favoring, home-state litigants. The presence of parties from the same State on both sides of a case dispels this concern, eliminating a principal reason for conferring § 1332 jurisdiction over any of the claims in the action. The specific purpose of the complete diversity rule explains both why we have not adopted *Gibbs*' expansive interpretive approach to this aspect of the jurisdictional statute and why *Gibbs* does not undermine the complete diversity rule. In order for a federal court to invoke supplemental jurisdiction under *Gibbs*, it must first have original jurisdiction over at least one claim in the action. Incomplete diversity destroys original jurisdiction with respect to all claims, so there is nothing to which supplemental jurisdiction can adhere.

In contrast to the diversity requirement, most of the other statutory prerequisites for federal jurisdiction, including the federal-question and amount-in-controversy requirements, can be analyzed claim by claim. True, it does not follow by necessity from this that a district court has authority to exercise supplemental jurisdiction over all claims provided there is original jurisdiction over just one. Before the enactment of § 1367, the Court declined in contexts other than the pendent-claim instance to follow *Gibbs'* expansive approach to interpretation of the jurisdictional statutes. The Court took a more restrictive view of the proper interpretation of these statutes in so-called pendent-party cases involving supplemental jurisdiction over claims involving additional parties — plaintiffs or defendants — where the district courts would lack original jurisdiction over claims by each of the parties standing alone.

Thus, with respect to plaintiff-specific jurisdictional requirements, the Court held in Clark v. Paul Gray, Inc., 306 U.S. 583 (1939), that every plaintiff must separately satisfy the amount-in-controversy requirement. Though *Clark* was a federal-question case, at that time federal-question jurisdiction had an amount-in-controversy requirement analogous to the amount-in-controversy requirement for diversity cases. "Proper practice," *Clark* held, "requires that where each of several plaintiffs is bound to establish the jurisdictional amount with respect to his own claim, the suit should be dismissed as to those who fail to show that the requisite amount is involved." The Court reaffirmed this rule, in the context of a class action brought invoking § 1332(a) diversity jurisdiction, in Zahn v. International Paper Co., 414 U.S. 291 (1973). It follows "inescapably" from *Clark*, the Court held in *Zahn*, that "any plaintiff without the jurisdictional amount must be dismissed from the case, even though others allege jurisdictionally sufficient claims."

The Court took a similar approach with respect to supplemental jurisdiction over claims against additional defendants that fall outside the district courts' original jurisdiction. In Aldinger v. Howard, 427 U.S. 1 (1976), the plaintiff brought a 42 U.S.C. § 1983 action against county officials in district court . . . . The plaintiff further alleged the court had supplemental jurisdiction over her related state-law claims against the county, even though the county was not suable under § 1983 and so was not subject to § 1343(3)'s original jurisdiction. The Court held that supplemental jurisdiction could not be exercised because Congress . . . had declined (albeit implicitly) to extend federal jurisdiction over any party who could not be sued under the federal civil rights statutes. "Before it can be concluded that [supplemental] jurisdiction [over additional parties] exists," *Aldinger* held, "a federal court must satisfy itself not only that Art[icle] III permits it, but that Congress in the statutes conferring jurisdiction has not expressly or by implication negated its existence."

In Finley v. United States, 490 U.S. 545 (1989), we confronted a similar issue in a different statutory context. The plaintiff in *Finley* brought a

Federal Tort Claims Act negligence suit against the Federal Aviation Administration in District Court . . . . The plaintiff tried to add related claims against other defendants, invoking the District Court's supplemental jurisdiction over so-called pendent parties. We held that the District Court lacked a sufficient statutory basis for exercising supplemental jurisdiction over these claims. Relying primarily on *Zahn*, *Aldinger*, and *Kroger*, we held in *Finley* that "a grant of jurisdiction over claims involving particular parties does not itself confer jurisdiction over additional claims by or against different parties." While *Finley* did not "limit or impair" *Gibbs'* liberal approach to interpreting the jurisdictional statutes in the context of supplemental jurisdiction over additional claims involving the same parties, *Finley* nevertheless declined to extend that interpretive assumption to claims involving additional parties. *Finley* held that in the context of parties, in contrast to claims, "we will not assume that the full constitutional power has been congressionally authorized, and will not read jurisdictional statutes broadly."

As the jurisdictional statutes existed in 1989, then, here is how matters stood: First, the diversity requirement in § 1332(a) required complete diversity; absent complete diversity, the district court lacked original jurisdiction over all of the claims in the action. *Strawbridge*; *Kroger*. Second, if the district court had original jurisdiction over at least one claim, the jurisdictional statutes implicitly authorized supplemental jurisdiction over all other claims between the same parties arising out of the same Article III case or controversy. *Gibbs*. Third, even when the district court had original jurisdiction over one or more claims between particular parties, the jurisdictional statutes did not authorize supplemental jurisdiction over additional claims involving other parties. *Clark*; *Zahn*; *Finley*.

B

In *Finley* we emphasized that "[w]hatever we say regarding the scope of jurisdiction conferred by a particular statute can of course be changed by Congress." In 1990, Congress accepted the invitation. It passed the Judicial Improvements Act, which enacted § 1367, the provision which controls these cases. . . .

All parties to this litigation and all courts to consider the question agree that § 1367 overturned the result in *Finley*. There is no warrant, however, for assuming that § 1367 did no more than to overrule *Finley* and otherwise to codify the existing state of the law of supplemental jurisdiction. We must not give jurisdictional statutes a more expansive interpretation than their text warrants; but it is just as important not to adopt an artificial construction that is narrower than what the text provides. No sound canon of interpretation requires Congress to speak with extraordinary clarity in order to modify the rules of federal jurisdiction within appropriate constitutional bounds. Ordinary principles of statutory construction apply. In order to determine the scope of supplemental jurisdiction authorized by § 1367, then, we must examine the statute's text in light of context, structure, and related statutory provisions.

Section 1367(a) is a broad grant of supplemental jurisdiction over other claims within the same case or controversy, as long as the action is one in which the district courts would have original jurisdiction. The last sentence of § 1367(a) makes it clear that the grant of supplemental jurisdiction extends to claims involving joinder or intervention of additional parties. The single question before us, therefore, is whether a diversity case in which the claims of some plaintiffs satisfy the amount-in-controversy requirement, but the claims of other[ ] plaintiffs do not, presents a "civil action of which the district courts have original jurisdiction." If the answer is yes, § 1367(a) confers supplemental jurisdiction over all claims, including those that do not independently satisfy the amount-in-controversy requirement, if the claims are part of the same Article III case or controversy. If the answer is no, § 1367(a) is inapplicable and, in light of our holdings in *Clark* and *Zahn*, the district court has no statutory basis for exercising supplemental jurisdiction over the additional claims.

We now conclude the answer must be yes. When the well-pleaded complaint contains at least one claim that satisfies the amount-in-controversy requirement, and there are no other relevant jurisdictional defects, the district court, beyond all question, has original jurisdiction over that claim. The presence of other claims in the complaint, over which the district court may lack original jurisdiction, is of no moment. If the court has original jurisdiction over a single claim in the complaint, it has original jurisdiction over a "civil action" within the meaning of § 1367(a), even if the civil action over which it has jurisdiction comprises fewer claims than were included in the complaint. Once the court determines it has original jurisdiction over the civil action, it can turn to the question whether it has a constitutional and statutory basis for exercising supplemental jurisdiction over the other claims in the action.

Section 1367(a) commences with the direction that §§ 1367(b) and (c), or other relevant statutes, may provide specific exceptions, but otherwise § 1367(a) is a broad jurisdictional grant, with no distinction drawn between pendent-claim and pendent-party cases. In fact, the last sentence of § 1367(a) makes clear that the provision grants supplemental jurisdiction over claims involving joinder or intervention of additional parties. The terms of § 1367 do not acknowledge any distinction between pendent jurisdiction and the doctrine of so-called ancillary jurisdiction. Though the doctrines of pendent and ancillary jurisdiction developed separately as a historical matter, the Court has recognized that the doctrines are "two species of the same generic problem," *Kroger*. Nothing in § 1367 indicates a congressional intent to recognize, preserve, or create some meaningful, substantive distinction between the jurisdictional categories we have historically labeled pendent and ancillary.

If § 1367(a) were the sum total of the relevant statutory language, our holding would rest on that language alone. The statute, of course, instructs us to examine § 1367(b) to determine if any of its exceptions apply, so we proceed to that section. While § 1367(b) qualifies the broad rule of § 1367(a), it does not withdraw supplemental jurisdiction over the claims of the additional parties at issue here. The specific exceptions to § 1367(a) contained in § 1367(b), moreover, provide additional support for our conclusion that § 1367(a) confers supplemental jurisdiction over these claims. Section 1367(b), which applies only to diversity cases, withholds supplemental jurisdiction over the claims of plaintiffs proposed to be joined as indispensable parties under Federal Rule of Civil Procedure 19, or who seek to intervene pursuant to Rule 24. Nothing in the text of § 1367(b), however, withholds supplemental jurisdiction over the claims of plaintiffs permissively joined under Rule 20 (like the additional plaintiffs in [*Rosario Ortega*]) or certified as class-action members pursuant to Rule 23 (like the additional plaintiffs in [*Allapattah*]). The natural, indeed the necessary, inference is that § 1367 confers supplemental jurisdiction over claims by Rule 20 and Rule 23 plaintiffs. This inference, at least with respect to Rule 20 plaintiffs, is strengthened by the fact that § 1367(b) explicitly excludes supplemental jurisdiction over claims against defendants joined under Rule 20.

We cannot accept the view, urged by some of the parties, commentators, and Courts of Appeals, that a district court lacks original jurisdiction over a civil action unless the court has original jurisdiction over every claim in the complaint. As we understand this position, it requires assuming either that all claims in the complaint must stand or fall as a single, indivisible "civil action" as a matter of definitional necessity — what we will refer to as the "indivisibility theory" — or else that the inclusion of a claim or party falling outside the district court's original jurisdiction somehow contaminates every other claim in the complaint, depriving the court of original jurisdiction over any of these claims — what we will refer to as the "contamination theory."

The indivisibility theory is easily dismissed, as it is inconsistent with the whole notion of supplemental jurisdiction. If a district court must have original jurisdiction over every claim in the complaint in order to have "original jurisdiction" over a "civil action," then in *Gibbs* there was no civil action of which the district court could assume original jurisdiction under § 1331, and so no basis for exercising supplemental jurisdiction over any of the claims. The indivisibility theory is further belied by our practice — in both federal-question and diversity cases — of allowing federal courts to cure jurisdictional defects by dismissing the offending parties rather than dismissing the entire action. *Clark*, for example, makes clear that claims that are jurisdictionally defective as to amount in controversy do not destroy original jurisdiction over other claims. 306 U.S., at 590 (dismissing parties who failed to meet the amount-in-controversy requirement but retaining jurisdiction over the remaining party). If the presence of jurisdictionally problematic claims in the complaint meant the district court was without original jurisdiction over the single, indivisible civil action before it, then the district court would have to dismiss the whole action rather than particular parties. . . .

The contamination theory, as we have noted, can make some sense in the special context of the complete diversity requirement because the presence of nondiverse parties on both sides of a lawsuit eliminates the justification for providing a federal forum. The theory, however, makes little sense with respect to the amount-in-controversy requirement, which is meant to ensure that a dispute is sufficiently important to warrant federal-court attention. The presence of a single nondiverse party may eliminate the fear of bias with respect to all claims, but the presence of a claim that falls short of the minimum amount in controversy does nothing to reduce the importance of the claims that do meet this requirement. . .

We also reject the argument . . . that while the presence of additional claims over which the district court lacks jurisdiction does not mean the civil action is outside the purview of § 1367(a), the presence of additional parties does. The basis for this distinction is not altogether clear, and it is in considerable tension with statutory text. Section 1367(a) applies by its terms to any civil action of which the district courts have original jurisdiction, and the last sentence of § 1367(a) expressly contemplates that the court may have supplemental jurisdiction over additional parties. So it cannot be the case that the presence of those parties destroys the court's original jurisdiction, within the meaning of § 1367(a), over a civil action otherwise properly before it. Also, § 1367(b) expressly withholds supplemental jurisdiction in diversity cases over claims by plaintiffs joined as indispensable parties under Rule 19. If joinder of such parties were sufficient to deprive the district court of original jurisdiction over the civil action within the meaning of § 1367(a), this specific limitation on supplemental jurisdiction in § 1367(b) would be superfluous. The argument that the presence of additional parties removes the civil action from the scope of § 1367(a) also would mean that § 1367 left the *Finley* result undisturbed. *Finley*, after all, involved a Federal Tort Claims Act suit against a federal defendant and state-law claims against additional defendants not otherwise subject to federal jurisdiction. Yet all concede that one purpose of § 1367 was to change the result reached in *Finley*.

Finally, it is suggested that our interpretation of § 1367(a) creates an anomaly regarding the exceptions listed in § 1367(b): It is not immediately obvious why Congress would withhold supplemental jurisdiction over plaintiffs joined as parties "needed for just adjudication" under Rule 19 but would allow supplemental jurisdiction over plaintiffs permissively joined under Rule 20. The omission of Rule 20 plaintiffs from the list of exceptions in § 1367(b) may have been an "unintentional drafting gap." If that is the case, it is up to Congress rather than the courts to fix it. The omission may seem odd, but it is not absurd. . . .

And so we circle back to the original question. When the well-pleaded complaint in district court includes multiple claims, all part of the same case or controversy, and some, but not all, of the claims are within the court's original jurisdiction, does the court have before it "any civil action of which the district courts have original jurisdiction"? It does. Under § 1367, the court has original jurisdiction over the civil action comprising the claims for which there is no jurisdictional defect. No other reading of § 1367 is plausible in light of the text and structure of the jurisdictional statute.

Though the special nature and purpose of the diversity requirement mean that a single nondiverse party can contaminate every other claim in the lawsuit, the contamination does not occur with respect to jurisdictional defects that go only to the substantive importance of individual claims.

It follows from this conclusion that the threshold requirement of § 1367(a) is satisfied in cases, like those now before us, where some, but not all, of the plaintiffs in a diversity action allege a sufficient amount in controversy. We hold that § 1367 by its plain text overruled *Clark* and *Zahn* and authorized supplemental jurisdiction over all claims by diverse parties arising out of the same Article III case or controversy, subject only to enumerated exceptions not applicable in the cases now before us.

C

The proponents of the alternative view of § 1367 insist that the statute is at least ambiguous and that we should look to other interpretive tools, including the legislative history of § 1367, which supposedly demonstrate Congress did not intend § 1367 to overrule *Zahn*. We can reject this argument at the very outset simply because § 1367 is not ambiguous. For the reasons elaborated above, interpreting § 1367 to foreclose supplemental jurisdiction over plaintiffs in diversity cases who do not meet the minimum amount in controversy is inconsistent with the text, read in light of other statutory provisions and our established jurisprudence. Even if we were to stipulate, however, that the reading these proponents urge upon us is textually plausible, the legislative history cited to support it would not alter our view as to the best interpretation of § 1367.

Those who urge that the legislative history refutes our interpretation rely primarily on the House Judiciary Committee Report on the Judicial Improvements Act. This Report explained that § 1367 would "authorize jurisdiction in a case like *Finley*, as well as essentially restore the pre-*Finley* understandings of the authorization for and limits on other forms of supplemental jurisdiction."... The Report then remarked that § 1367(b) "is not intended to affect the jurisdictional requirements of [§ 1332] in diversity-only class actions, as those requirements were interpreted prior to *Finley*," citing, without further elaboration, *Zahn* and Supreme Tribe of Ben-Hur v. Cauble, 255 U.S. 356 (1921). . . .

As we have repeatedly held, the authoritative statement is the statutory text, not the legislative history or any other extrinsic material. Extrinsic materials have a role in statutory interpretation only to the extent they shed a reliable light on the enacting Legislature's understanding of otherwise ambiguous terms. Not all extrinsic materials are reliable sources of insight into legislative understandings, however, and legislative history in particular is vulnerable to two serious criticisms. First, legislative history is itself often murky, ambiguous, and contradictory. Judicial investigation of legislative history has a tendency to become, to borrow Judge Leventhal's memorable phrase, an exercise in "'looking over a crowd and picking out your friends.'" . . . Second, judicial reliance on legislative materials like committee reports, which are not themselves subject to the requirements of Article I, may give unrepresentative committee members — or, worse yet, unelected staffers and lobbyists — both the power and the incentive to attempt strategic manipulations of legislative history to secure results they were unable to achieve through the statutory text. We need not comment here on whether these problems are sufficiently prevalent to render legislative history inherently unreliable in all circumstances, a point on which Members of this Court have disagreed. It is clear, however, that in this instance both criticisms are right on the mark.

First of all, the legislative history of § 1367 is far murkier than selective quotation from the House Report would suggest. The text of § 1367 is based substantially on a draft proposal contained in a Federal Court[s] Study Committee working paper, which was drafted by a Subcommittee chaired by Judge Posner. While the Subcommittee explained, in language echoed by the House Report, that its proposal "basically restores the law as it existed prior to *Finley*," it observed in a footnote that its proposal would overrule *Zahn* and that this would be a good idea. Although the Federal Courts Study Committee did not expressly adopt the Subcommittee's specific reference to *Zahn*, it neither explicitly disagreed with the Subcommittee's conclusion that this was the best reading of the proposed text nor substantially modified the proposal to avoid this result. Therefore, even if the House Report could fairly be read to reflect an understanding that the text of § 1367 did not overrule *Zahn*, the Subcommittee Working Paper on which § 1367 was based reflected the opposite understanding. The House Report is no more authoritative than the Subcommittee Working Paper. The utility of either can extend no further than the light it sheds on how the enacting Legislature understood the statutory text. Trying to figure out how to square the Subcommittee Working Paper's understanding with the House Report's understanding, or which is more reflective of the understanding of the enacting legislators, is a hopeless task.

Second, the worst fears of critics who argue legislative history will be used to circumvent the Article I process were realized in this case. The telltale evidence is the statement, by three law professors who participated in drafting § 1367, that § 1367 "on its face" permits "supplemental jurisdiction over claims of class members that do not satisfy section 1332's jurisdictional amount requirement, which would overrule [*Zahn*]. [There is] a disclaimer of intent to accomplish this result in the legislative history . . . . It would have been better had the statute dealt explicitly with this problem, and the legislative history was an attempt to correct the oversight." Rowe, Burbank, & Mengler, *Compounding or Creating Confusion About Supplemental Jurisdiction? A Reply to Professor Freer*, 40 Emory L.J. 943, 960, n.90 (1991). The professors were frank to concede that if one refuses to consider the legislative history, one has no choice but to "conclude that section 1367 has wiped *Zahn* off the books." So there exists an acknowledgment, by parties who have detailed, specific knowledge of the statute and the drafting process, both that the plain text of § 1367 overruled *Zahn* and that language to the contrary in the House Report was a *post hoc* attempt to alter that result. One need not subscribe to the wholesale condemnation of legislative history to refuse to give any effect to such a deliberate effort to amend a statute through a committee report. . . .

The judgment of the Court of Appeals for the Eleventh Circuit is affirmed. The judgment of the Court of Appeals for the First Circuit is reversed, and the case is remanded for proceedings consistent with this opinion.

It is so ordered.

■ [The dissenting opinion of JUSTICE STEVENS, joined by JUSTICE BREYER, is omitted.]

■ JUSTICE GINSBURG, with whom JUSTICE STEVENS, JUSTICE O'CONNOR, and JUSTICE BREYER join, dissenting. . . .

The Court adopts a plausibly broad reading of § 1367, a measure that is hardly a model of the careful drafter's art. There is another plausible reading, however, one less disruptive of our jurisprudence regarding supplemental jurisdiction. If one reads § 1367(a) to instruct, as the statute's text suggests, that the district court must first have "original jurisdiction" over a "civil action" before supplemental jurisdiction can attach, then *Clark* and *Zahn* are preserved, and supplemental jurisdiction does not open the way for joinder of plaintiffs, or inclusion of class members, who do not independently meet the amount-in-controversy requirement. For the reasons that follow, I conclude that this narrower construction is the better reading of § 1367. . . .

II

A

Section 1367, by its terms, operates only in civil actions "of which the district courts have original jurisdiction." The "original jurisdiction" relevant here is diversity-of-citizenship jurisdiction, conferred by § 1332. The character of that jurisdiction is the essential backdrop for comprehension of § 1367. . . .

The statute today governing federal court exercise of diversity jurisdiction in the generality of cases, § 1332, like all its predecessors, incorporates both a diverse-citizenship requirement and an amount-in-controversy specification.[5] . . .

5. Endeavoring to preserve the "complete diversity" rule first stated in *Strawbridge v. Curtiss*, 7 U.S. (3 Cranch) 267 (1806), the Court's opinion drives a wedge between the two components of 28 U.S.C. § 1332, treating the diversity-of-citizenship requirement as essential, the amount-in-controversy requirement as more readily disposable. Section 1332 itself, however, does not rank order the two requirements. What "[o]rdinary principl[e] of statutory construction" or "sound canon of interpretation," allows the Court to slice up § 1332 this way? In partial explanation, the Court asserts that amount in controversy can be analyzed claim-by-claim, but the diversity requirement cannot. It is not altogether clear why that should be so. The cure for improper joinder of a nondiverse party is the same as the cure for improper joinder of a plaintiff who does not satisfy the

The rule that each plaintiff must independently satisfy the amount-in-controversy requirement, unless Congress expressly orders otherwise, was thus the solidly established reading of § 1332 when Congress enacted the Judicial Improvements Act of 1990, which added § 1367 to Title 28.

B

These cases present the question whether Congress abrogated the nonaggregation rule long tied to § 1332 when it enacted § 1367. In answering that question, "context [should provide] a crucial guide." The Court should assume, as it ordinarily does, that Congress legislated against a background of law already in place and the historical development of that law. Here, that background is the statutory grant of diversity jurisdiction, the amount-in-controversy condition that Congress, from the start, has tied to the grant, and the nonaggregation rule this Court has long applied to the determination of the "matter in controversy." . . .

The Court is unanimous in reading § 1367(a) to permit pendent-party jurisdiction in federal-question cases, and thus, to overrule *Finley*. . . .

The Court divides, however, on the impact of § 1367(a) on diversity cases controlled by § 1332. Under the majority's reading, § 1367(a) permits the joinder of related claims cut loose from the nonaggregation rule that has long attended actions under § 1332. Only the claims specified in § 1367(b) would be excluded from § 1367(a)'s expansion of § 1332's grant of diversity jurisdiction. And because § 1367(b) contains no exception for joinder of plaintiffs under Rule 20 or class actions under Rule 23, the Court concludes, *Clark* and *Zahn* have been overruled.

The Court's reading is surely plausible, especially if one detaches § 1367(a) from its context and attempts no reconciliation with prior interpretations of § 1332's amount-in-controversy requirement. But § 1367(a)'s text, as the First Circuit held, can be read another way, one that would involve no rejection of *Clark* and *Zahn*.

As explained by the First Circuit in *Ortega* . . . § 1367(a) addresses "civil action[s] of which the district courts have original jurisdiction," a formulation that, in diversity cases, is sensibly read to incorporate the rules on joinder and aggregation tightly tied to § 1332 at the time of § 1367's enactment. On this reading, a complaint must first meet that "original jurisdiction" measurement. If it does not, no supplemental jurisdiction is authorized. If it does, § 1367(a) authorizes "supplemental jurisdiction" over related claims. In other words, § 1367(a) would preserve undiminished, as part and parcel of § 1332 "original jurisdiction" determinations, both the "complete diversity" rule and the decisions restricting aggregation to arrive at the amount in controversy. . . . In contrast to the Court's construction of § 1367, which draws a sharp line between the diversity and amount-in-

jurisdictional amount. In both cases, original jurisdiction can be preserved by dismissing the nonqualifying party.

controversy components of § 1332, the interpretation presented here does not sever the two jurisdictional requirements.

The more restrained reading of § 1367 just outlined would yield affirmance of the First Circuit's judgment in *Ortega*, and reversal of the Eleventh Circuit's judgment in *Exxon*. It would not discard entirely, as the Court does, the judicially developed doctrines of pendent and ancillary jurisdiction as they existed when *Finley* was decided. Instead, it would recognize § 1367 essentially as a codification of those doctrines, placing them under a single heading, but largely retaining their substance, with overriding *Finley* the only basic change: Supplemental jurisdiction, once the district court has original jurisdiction, would now include "claims that involve the joinder or intervention of additional parties." . . .

What is the utility of § 1367(b) under my reading of § 1367(a)? Section 1367(a) allows parties other than the plaintiff to assert *reactive* claims once entertained under the heading ancillary jurisdiction. [Here the opinion lists claims, "including compulsory counterclaims and impleader claims, over which federal courts routinely exercised ancillary jurisdiction." — ED.] As earlier observed, § 1367(b) stops plaintiffs from circumventing § 1332's jurisdictional requirements by using another's claim as a hook to add a claim that the plaintiff could not have brought in the first instance. *Kroger* is the paradigm case. There, the Court held that ancillary jurisdiction did not extend to a plaintiff's claim against a nondiverse party who had been impleaded by the defendant under Rule 14. . . .

While §1367's enigmatic text defies flawless interpretation, the precedent-preservative reading, I am persuaded, better accords with the historical and legal context of Congress' enactment of the supplemental jurisdiction statute, and the established limits on pendent and ancillary jurisdiction. It does not attribute to Congress a jurisdictional enlargement broader than the one to which the legislators adverted, and it follows the sound counsel that "close questions of [statutory] construction should be resolved in favor of continuity and against change." Shapiro, *Continuity and Change in Statutory Interpretation*, 67 N.Y.U. L. REV. 921, 925 (1992).

For the reasons stated, I would hold that § 1367 does not overrule *Clark* and *Zahn*. I would therefore affirm the judgment of the Court of Appeals for the First Circuit and reverse the judgment of the Court of Appeals for the Eleventh Circuit.

FEDERAL RULES OF CIVIL PROCEDURE FOR THE UNITED STATES DISTRICT COURTS

WITH

SELECTED ADVISORY COMMITTEE NOTES

I. SCOPE OF RULES — ONE FORM OF ACTION

II. COMMENCEMENT OF ACTION; SERVICE OF PROCESS PLEADINGS, MOTIONS, AND ORDERS

III. PLEADINGS AND MOTIONS

XI. General Provisions

Appendix of Forms

I. SCOPE OF RULES — ONE FORM OF ACTION

Rule 1. Scope and Purpose of Rules

These rules govern the procedure in the United States district courts in all suits of a civil nature whether cognizable as cases at law or in equity or in admiralty, with the exceptions stated in Rule 81. They shall be construed and administered to secure the just, speedy, and inexpensive determination of every action.

ADVISORY COMMITTEE NOTES

1993 Amendments

The purpose of this revision, adding the words "and administered" to the second sentence, is to recognize the affirmative duty of the court to exercise the authority conferred by these rules to ensure that civil litigation is resolved not only fairly, but also without undue cost or delay. As officers of the court, attorneys share this responsibility with the judge to whom the case is assigned.

Rule 2. One Form of Action

There shall be one form of action to be known as "civil action".

II. COMMENCEMENT OF ACTION; SERVICE OF PROCESS, PLEADINGS, MOTIONS, AND ORDERS

Rule 3. Commencement of Action

A civil action is commenced by filing a complaint with the court.

Rule 4. Summons

(a) Form. The summons shall be signed by the clerk, bear the seal of the court, identify the court and the parties, be directed to the defendant, and state the name and address of the plaintiff's attorney or, if unrepresented, of the plaintiff. It shall also state the time within which the defendant must appear and defend, and notify the defendant that failure to do so will result in a judgment by default against the defendant for the relief demanded in the complaint. The court may allow a summons to be amended.

(b) Issuance. Upon or after filing the complaint, the plaintiff may present a summons to the clerk for signature and seal. If the summons is in proper form, the clerk shall sign, seal, and issue it to the plaintiff for service on the defendant. A summons, or a copy of the summons if addressed to multiple defendants, shall be issued for each defendant to be served.

(c) Service with Complaint; by Whom Made.

(1) A summons shall be served together with a copy of the complaint. The plaintiff is responsible for service of a summons and complaint within the time allowed under subdivision (m) and shall furnish the person effecting service with the necessary copies of the summons and complaint.

(2) Service may be effected by any person who is not a party and who is at least 18 years of age. At the request of the plaintiff, however, the court may direct that service be effected by a United States marshal, deputy United States marshal, or other person or officer specially appointed by the court for that purpose. Such an appointment must be made when the plaintiff is authorized to proceed in forma pauperis pursuant to 28 U.S.C. § 1915 or is authorized to proceed as a seaman under 28 U.S.C. § 1916.

(d) Waiver of Service; Duty to Save Costs of Service; Request to Waive.

(1) A defendant who waives service of a summons does not thereby waive any objection to the venue or to the jurisdiction of the court over the person of the defendant.

(2) An individual, corporation, or association that is subject to service under subdivision (e), (f), or (h) and that receives notice of an action in the manner provided in this paragraph has a duty to avoid unnecessary costs of serving the summons. To avoid costs, the plaintiff may notify such a defendant of the commencement of the action and request that the defendant waive service of a summons. The notice and request

(A) shall be in writing and shall be addressed directly to the defendant, if an individual, or else to an officer or managing or general agent (or other agent authorized by appointment or law to receive service of process) of a defendant subject to service under subdivision (h);

(B) shall be dispatched through first-class mail or other reliable means;

(C) shall be accompanied by a copy of the complaint and shall identify the court in which it has been filed;

(D) shall inform the defendant, by means of a text prescribed in an official form promulgated pursuant to Rule 84, of the consequences of compliance and of a failure to comply with the request;

(E) shall set forth the date on which the request is sent;

(F) shall allow the defendant a reasonable time to return the waiver, which shall be at least 30 days from the date on which the request is sent, or 60 days from that date if the defendant is addressed outside any judicial district of the United States; and

(G) shall provide the defendant with an extra copy of the notice and request, as well as a prepaid means of compliance in writing.

If a defendant located within the United States fails to comply with a request for waiver made by a plaintiff located within the United States, the court shall impose the costs subsequently incurred in effecting service on the defendant unless good cause for the failure be shown.

(3) A defendant that, before being served with process, timely returns a waiver so requested is not required to serve an answer to the complaint until 60 days after the date on which the request for waiver of service was sent, or 90 days after that date if the defendant was addressed outside any judicial district of the United States.

(4) When the plaintiff files a waiver of service with the court, the action shall proceed, except as provided in paragraph (3), as if a summons and complaint had been served at the time of filing the waiver, and no proof of service shall be required.

(5) The costs to be imposed on a defendant under paragraph (2) for failure to comply with a request to waive service of a summons shall include the costs subsequently incurred in effecting service under subdivision (e), (f), or (h), together with the costs, including a reasonable attorney's fee, of any motion required to collect the costs of service.

(e) Service Upon Individuals Within a Judicial District of the United States. Unless otherwise provided by federal law, service upon an individual from whom a waiver has not been obtained and filed, other than an infant or an incompetent person, may be effected in any judicial district of the United States:

(1) pursuant to the law of the state in which the district court is located, or in which service is effected, for the service of a summons upon the defendant in an action brought in the courts of general jurisdiction of the State; or

(2) by delivering a copy of the summons and of the complaint to the individual personally or by leaving copies thereof at the individual's dwelling house or usual place of abode with some person of suitable age and discretion then residing therein or by delivering a copy of the summons and of the complaint to an agent authorized by appointment or by law to receive service of process.

(f) Service Upon Individuals in a Foreign Country. Unless otherwise provided by federal law, service upon an individual from whom a waiver has not been obtained and filed, other than an infant or an incompetent person, may be effected in a place not within any judicial district of the United States:

(1) by any internationally agreed means reasonably calculated to give notice, such as those means authorized by the Hague Convention on the Service Abroad of Judicial and Extrajudicial Documents; or

(2) if there is no internationally agreed means of service or the applicable international agreement allows other means of service, provided that service is reasonably calculated to give notice:

(A) in the manner prescribed by the law of the foreign country for service in that country in an action in any of its courts of general jurisdiction; or

(B) as directed by the foreign authority in response to a letter rogatory or letter of request; or

(C) unless prohibited by the law of the foreign country, by

(i) delivery to the individual personally of a copy of the summons and the complaint; or

(ii) any form of mail requiring a signed receipt, to be addressed and dispatched by the clerk of the court to the party to be served; or

(3) by other means not prohibited by international agreement as may be directed by the court.

(g) Service Upon Infants and Incompetent Persons. Service upon an infant or an incompetent person in a judicial district of the United States shall be effected in the manner prescribed by the law of the state in which the service is made for the service of summons or other like process upon any such defendant in an action brought in the courts of general jurisdiction of that state. Service upon an infant or an incompetent person in a place not within any judicial district of the United States shall be effected in the manner prescribed by paragraph (2)(A) or (2)(B) of subdivision (f) or by such means as the court may direct.

(h) Service Upon Corporations and Associations. Unless otherwise provided by federal law, service upon a domestic or foreign corporation or upon a partnership or other unincorporated association that is subject to suit under a common name, and from which a waiver of service has not been obtained and filed, shall be effected:

(1) in a judicial district of the United States in the manner prescribed for individuals by subdivision (e)(1), or by delivering a copy of the summons and of the complaint to an officer, a managing or general agent, or to any other agent authorized by appointment or by law to receive service of process and, if the agent is one authorized by statute to receive service and the statute so requires, by also mailing a copy to the defendant, or

(2) in a place not within any judicial district of the United States in any manner prescribed for individuals by subdivision (f) except personal delivery as provided in paragraph (2)(C)(i) thereof.

(i) Serving the United States, Its Agencies, Corporations, Officers, or Employees.

(1) Service upon the United States shall be effected

(A) by delivering a copy of the summons and of the complaint to the United States attorney for the district in which the action is brought or to an assistant United States attorney or clerical employee designated by the United States attorney in a writing filed with the clerk of the court or by sending a copy of the summons and of the complaint by registered or certified mail addressed to the civil process clerk at the office of the United States attorney and

(B) by also sending a copy of the summons and of the complaint by registered or certified mail to the Attorney General of the United States at Washington, District of Columbia, and

(C) in any action attacking the validity of an order of an officer or agency of the United States not made a party, by also sending a copy of the summons and of the complaint by registered or certified mail to the officer or agency.

(2) (A) Service on an agency or corporation of the United States, or an officer or employee of the United States sued only in an official capacity, is effected by serving the United States in the manner prescribed by Rule 4(i)(1) and by also sending a copy of the summons and complaint by registered or certified mail to the officer, employee, agency, or corporation.

(B) Service on an officer or employee of the United States sued in an individual capacity for acts or omissions occurring in connection with the performance of duties on behalf of the United States — whether or not the officer or employee is sued also in an official capacity — is effected by serving the United States in the manner prescribed by Rule 4(i)(1) and by serving the officer or employee in the manner prescribed by Rule 4 (e), (f), or (g).

(3) The court shall allow a reasonable time to serve process under Rule 4(i) for the purpose of curing the failure to serve:

(A) all persons required to be served in an action governed by Rule 4(i)(2)(A), if the plaintiff has served either the United States attorney or the Attorney General of the United States, or

(B) the United States in an action governed by Rule 4(i)(2)(B), if the plaintiff has served an officer or employee of the United States sued in an individual capacity.

(j) Service Upon Foreign, State, or Local Governments.

(1) Service upon a foreign state or a political subdivision, agency, or instrumentality thereof shall be effected pursuant to 28 U.S.C. § 1608.

(2) Service upon a state, municipal corporation, or other governmental organization subject to suit shall be effected by delivering a copy of the summons and of the complaint to its chief executive officer or by serving the summons and complaint in the manner prescribed by the law of that state for the service of summons or other like process upon any such defendant.

(k) Territorial Limits of Effective Service.

(1) Service of a summons or filing a waiver of service is effective to establish jurisdiction over the person of a defendant

(A) who could be subjected to the jurisdiction of a court of general jurisdiction in the state in which the district court is located, or

(B) who is a party joined under Rule 14 or Rule 19 and is served at a place within a judicial district of the United States and not more than 100 miles from the place from which the summons issues, or

(C) who is subject to the federal interpleader jurisdiction under 28 U.S.C. § 1335, or

(D) when authorized by a statute of the United States.

(2) If the exercise of jurisdiction is consistent with the Constitution and laws of the United States, serving a summons or filing a waiver of service is also effective, with respect to claims arising under federal law, to establish personal jurisdiction over the person of any defendant who is not subject to the jurisdiction of the courts of general jurisdiction of any state.

(l) Proof of Service. If service is not waived, the person effecting service shall make proof thereof to the court. If service is made by a person other than a United States marshal or deputy United States marshal, the person shall make affidavit thereof. Proof of service in a place not within any judicial district of the United States shall, if effected under paragraph (1) of subdivision (f), be made pursuant to the applicable treaty or convention, and shall, if effected under paragraph (2) or (3) thereof, include a receipt signed by the addressee or other evidence of delivery to the addressee satisfactory to the court. Failure to make proof of service does not affect the validity of the service. The court may allow proof of service to be amended.

(m) Time Limit for Service. If service of the summons and complaint is not made upon a defendant within 120 days after the filing of the complaint, the court, upon motion or on its own initiative after notice to the plaintiff, shall dismiss the action without prejudice as to that defendant or direct that service be effected within a specified time; provided that if the plaintiff shows good cause for the failure, the court shall extend the time for service for an appropriate period. This subdivision does not apply to service in a foreign country pursuant to subdivision (f) or (j)(1).

(n) Seizure of Property; Service of Summons Not Feasible.

(1) If a statute of the United States so provides, the court may assert jurisdiction over property. Notice to claimants of the property shall then be sent in the manner provided by the statute or by service of a summons under this rule.

(2) Upon a showing that personal jurisdiction over a defendant cannot, in the district where the action is brought, be obtained with reasonable efforts by service of summons in any manner authorized by this rule, the court may assert jurisdiction over any of the defendant's assets found within the district by seizing the assets under the circumstances and in the manner provided by the law of the state in which the district court is located.

ADVISORY COMMITTEE NOTES

1993 Amendments [citations omitted without notation — Ed.]

. . .

Purposes of Revision. The general purpose of this revision is to facilitate the service of the summons and complaint. The revised rule explicitly authorizes a means for service of the summons and complaint on any defendant. While the methods of service so authorized always provide appropriate notice to persons against whom claims are made, effective service under this rule does not assure that personal jurisdiction has been established over the defendant served.

First, the revised rule authorizes the use of any means of service provided by the law not only of the forum state, but also of the state in which a defendant is served, unless the defendant is a minor or incompetent.

Second, the revised rule clarifies and enhances the cost-saving practice of securing the assent of the defendant to dispense with actual service of the summons and complaint. This practice was introduced to the rule in 1983 by an act of Congress authorizing "service-by-mail," a procedure that effects economic service with cooperation of the defendant. Defendants that magnify costs of service by requiring expensive service not necessary to achieve full notice of an action brought against them are required to bear the wasteful costs. This provision is made available in actions against defendants who cannot be served in the districts in which the actions are brought.

Third, the revision reduces the hazard of commencing an action against the United States or its officers, agencies, and corporations. A party failing to effect service on all the offices of the United States as required by the rule is assured adequate time to cure defects in service.

Fourth, the revision calls attention to the important effect of the Hague Convention and other treaties bearing on service of documents in foreign countries and favors the use of internationally agreed means of service. In some respects, these treaties have facilitated service in foreign countries but are not fully known to the bar.

Finally, the revised rule extends the reach of federal courts to impose jurisdiction over the person of all defendant[s] against whom federal law claims are made and who can be constitutionally subjected to the jurisdiction of the courts of the United States. The present territorial limits on the effectiveness of service to subject a defendant to the jurisdiction of the court over the defendant's person are retained for all actions in which there is a state in which personal jurisdiction can be asserted consistently with state law and the Fourteenth Amendment. A new provision enables district courts to exercise jurisdiction, if permissible under the Constitution and not precluded by statute, when a federal claim is made against a defendant not subject to the jurisdiction of any single state.

The revised rule is reorganized to make its provisions more accessible to those not familiar with all of them. Additional subdivisions in this rule allow for more captions; several overlaps among subdivisions are eliminated; and several disconnected provisions are removed, to be relocated in a new Rule 4.1.

The Caption of the Rule. Prior to this revision, Rule 4 was entitled "Process" and applied to the service of not only the summons but also other process as well, although these are not covered by the revised rule. Service of process in eminent domain proceedings is governed by Rule 71A. Service of a subpoena is governed by Rule 45, and service of papers such as orders, motions, notices, pleadings, and other documents is governed by Rule 5.

The revised rule is entitled "Summons" and applies only to that form of legal process. Unless service of the summons is waived, a summons must be served whenever a person is joined as a party against whom a claim is made. Those few provisions of the former rule which relate specifically to service of process other than a summons are relocated in Rule 4.1 in order to simplify the text of this rule.

Subdivision (a). Revised subdivision (a) contains most of the language of the former subdivision (b). The second sentence of the former subdivision (b) has been stricken, so that the federal court summons will be the same in all cases. Few states now employ, distinctive requirements of form for a summons and the applicability of such a requirement in federal court can only serve as a trap for an unwary party or attorney. A sentence is added to this subdivision authorizing an amendment of a summons. . . .

Subdivision (b). Revised subdivision (b) replaces the former subdivision (a). The revised text makes clear that the responsibility for filling in the summons falls on the plaintiff, not the clerk of the court. If there are multiple defendants, the plaintiff may secure issuance of a summons for each defendant, or may serve copies of a single original bearing the names of multiple defendants if the addressee of the summons is effectively identified.

Subdivision (c). . . .

The 1983 revision of Rule 4 relieved the marshals' offices of much of the burden of serving the summons. Subdivision (c) eliminates the requirement for service by the marshal's office in actions in which the party seeking service is the United States. The United States, like other civil litigants, is now permitted to designate any person who is 18 years of age and not a party to serve its summons.

The court remains obligated to appoint a marshal, a deputy, or some other person to effect service of a summons in two classes of cases specified by statute:

actions brought in forma pauperis or by a seaman. 28 U.S.C. §§ 1915, 1916. The court also retains discretion to appoint a process server on motion of a party. If a law enforcement presence appears to be necessary or advisable to keep the peace, the court should appoint a marshal or deputy or other official person to make the service. The Department of Justice may also call upon the Marshals Service to perform services in actions brought by the United States. 28 U.S.C. § 651.

Subdivision (d). This text is new, but is substantially derived from the former subdivisions (c)(2)(C) and (D), added to the rule by Congress in 1983. The aims of the provision are to eliminate the costs of service of a summons on many parties and to foster cooperation among adversaries and counsel. The rule operates to impose upon the defendant those costs that could have been avoided if the defendant had cooperated reasonably in the manner prescribed. This device is useful in dealing with defendants who are furtive, who reside in places not easily reached by process servers, or who are outside the United States and can be served only at substantial and unnecessary expense. Illustratively, there is no useful purpose achieved by requiring a plaintiff to comply with all the formalities of service in a foreign country, including costs of translation, when suing a defendant manufacturer, fluent in English, whose products are widely distributed in the United States. . . .

The former text described this process as service-by-mail. This language misled some plaintiffs into thinking that service could be effected by mail without the affirmative cooperation of the defendant. . . . It is more accurate to describe the communication sent to the defendant as a request for a waiver of formal service.

The request for waiver of service may be sent only to defendants subject to service under subdivision (e), (f), or (h). The United States is not expected to waive service for the reason that its mail receiving facilities are inadequate to assure that the notice is actually received by the correct person in the Department of Justice. The same principle is applied to agencies, corporations, and officers of the United States and to other governments and entities subject to service under subdivision (j). Moreover, there are policy reasons why governmental entities should not be confronted with the potential for bearing costs of service in cases in which they ultimately prevail. Infants or incompetent persons likewise are not called upon to waive service because, due to their presumed inability to understand the request and its consequences, they must generally be served through fiduciaries.

It was unclear whether the former rule authorized, mailing of a request for "acknowledgment of service" to defendants outside the forum state. See 1 R. Casad, Jurisdiction in Civil Actions (2d Ed.) 5-29, 30 (1991) and cases cited. But, as Professor Casad observed, there was no reason not to employ this device in an effort to obtain service outside the state, and there are many instances in which it was in fact so used, with respect both to defendants within the United States and to defendants in other countries.

The opportunity for waiver has distinct advantages to a foreign defendant. By waiving service, the defendant can reduce the costs that may ultimately be taxed against it if unsuccessful in the lawsuit, including the sometimes substantial expense of translation that may be wholly unnecessary for defendants fluent in English. Moreover, a foreign defendant that waives service is afforded substantially more time to defend against the action than if it had been formally served: under Rule 12, a defendant ordinarily has only 20 days after service in which to file its answer or raise objections by motion, but by signing a waiver it is allowed 90 days after the date the request for waiver was mailed in which to submit its defenses. Because of the additional time needed for mailing and the unreliability of some foreign mail services, a period of 60 days (rather than the 30 days required for domestic transmissions) is provided for a return of a waiver sent to a foreign country.

It is hoped that, since transmission of the notice and waiver forms is a private nonjudicial act, does not purport to effect service, and is not accompanied by any summons or directive from a court, use of the procedure will not offend foreign sovereignties, even those that have withheld their assent to formal service by mail or have objected to the "service-by-mail" provisions of the former rule. Unless the addressee consents, receipt of the request under the revised rule does not give rise to any obligation to answer the lawsuit, does not provide a basis for default judgment, and does not suspend the statute of limitations in those states where the period continues to run until service. Nor are there any adverse consequences to a foreign defendant, since the provisions for shifting the expense of service to a defendant that declines to waive service apply only if the plaintiff and defendant are both located in the United States.

With respect to a defendant located in a foreign country like the United Kingdom, which accepts documents in English, whose Central Authority acts promptly in effecting service, and whose policies discourage its residents from waiving formal service, there will be little reason for a plaintiff to send the notice and request under subdivision (d) rather than use convention methods. On the other hand, the procedure offers significant potential benefits to a plaintiff when suing a defendant that, though fluent in English, is located in a country where, as a condition to formal service under a convention, documents must be translated into another language or where formal service will be otherwise costly or time-consuming.

Paragraph (1) is explicit that a timely waiver of service of a summons does not prejudice the right of a defendant to object by means of a motion authorized by Rule 12(b)(2) to the absence of jurisdiction over the defendant's person, or to assert other defenses that may be available. The only issues eliminated are those involving the sufficiency of the summons or the sufficiency of the method by which it is served.

Paragraph (2) states what the present rule implies: the defendant has a duty to avoid costs associated with the service of a summons not needed to inform the defendant regarding the commencement of an action. The text of the rule also sets forth the requirements for a Notice and Request for Waiver sufficient to put the cost-shifting provision in place. These requirements are illustrated in Forms 1A and 1B, which replace the former Form 18-A.

Paragraph (2)(A) is explicit that a request for waiver of service by a corporate defendant must be addressed to a person qualified to receive service. The general mail rooms of large organizations cannot be required to identify the appropriate individual recipient for an institutional summons.

Paragraph (2)(B) permits the use of alternatives to the United States mails in sending the Notice and Request. While private messenger services or electronic communications may be more expensive than the mail, they may be equally reliable and on occasion more convenient to the parties. Especially with respect to transmissions to foreign countries, alternative means may be desirable, for in some countries facsimile transmission is the most efficient and economical means of communication. If electronic means such as facsimile transmission are employed, the sender should maintain a record of the transmission to assure proof of transmission if receipt is denied, but a party receiving such a transmission has a duty to cooperate and cannot avoid liability for the resulting cost of formal service if the transmission is prevented at the point of receipt.

A defendant failing to comply with a request for waiver shall be given an opportunity to show good cause for the failure, but sufficient cause should be rare. It is not a good cause for failure to waive service that the claim is unjust or that the court lacks jurisdiction. Sufficient cause not to shift the cost of service would exist, however, if the defendant did not receive the request or was insufficiently literate in English to understand it. It should be noted that the provisions for shifting the cost of service apply only if the plaintiff and the defendant are both located in the United States, and accordingly a foreign defendant need not show "good cause" for its failure to waive service.

Paragraph (3) extends the time for answer if, before being served with process, the defendant waives formal service. The extension is intended to serve as an inducement to waive service and to assure that a defendant will not gain any delay be declining to waive service and thereby causing the additional time needed to effect service. By waiving service, a defendant is not called upon to respond to the complaint until 60 days from the date the notice was sent to it — 90 days if the notice was sent to a foreign country — rather than within the 20 day period from date of service specified in Rule 12.

Paragraph (4) clarifies the effective date of service when service is waived; the provision is needed to resolve an issue arising when applicable law requires service of process to toll the statute of limitations. Cf. Walker v. Armco Steel Corp., 446 U.S. 740 (1980).

The provisions in former subdivision (c)(2)(C)(ii) of this rule may have been misleading to some parties. Some plaintiffs, not reading the rule carefully, supposed that receipt by the defendant of the mailed complaint had the effect both of establishing the jurisdiction of the court over the defendant's person and of tolling the statute of limitations in actions in which service of the summons is required to toll the limitations period. The revised rule is clear that, if the waiver is not returned and filed, the limitations period under such a law is not tolled and the action will not otherwise proceed until formal service of process is effected.

Some state limitations laws may toll an otherwise applicable statute at the time when the defendant receives notice of the action. Nevertheless, the device of requested waiver of service is not suitable if a limitations period which is about to expire is not tolled by filing the action. Unless there is ample time, the plaintiff should proceed directly to the formal methods for service identified in subdivisions (e), (f), or (h).

The procedure of requesting waiver of service should also not be used if the time for service under subdivision (m) will expire before the date on which the waiver must be returned. While a plaintiff has been allowed additional time for service in that situation, the court could refuse a request for additional time unless the defendant appears to have evaded service pursuant to subdivision (e) or (h). It may be noted that the presumptive time limit for service under subdivision (m) does not apply to service in a foreign country.

Paragraph (5) is a cost-shifting provision retained from the former rule. The costs that may be imposed on the defendant could include, for example, the cost of the time of a process server required to make contact with a defendant residing in a guarded apartment house or residential development. The paragraph is explicit that the costs of enforcing the cost-shifting provision are themselves recoverable from a defendant who fails to return the waiver. In the absence of such a provision, the purpose of the rule would be frustrated by the cost of its enforcement, which is likely to be high in relation to the small benefit secured by the plaintiff.

Some plaintiffs may send a notice and request for waiver and, without waiting for return of the waiver, also proceed with efforts to effect formal service on the defendant. To discourage this practice, the cost-shifting provisions in paragraphs (2) and (5) are limited to costs of effecting service incurred after the time expires for the defendant to return the waiver. Moreover, by returning the waiver within the time allowed and before being served with process, a defendant receives the benefit of the longer period for responding to the complaint afforded for waivers under paragraph (3).

Subdivision (e). This subdivision replaces former subdivisions (c)(2)(C)(i) and (d)(1). It provides a means for service of summons on individuals within a judicial district of the United States. Together with subdivision (f), it provides for service on persons anywhere, subject to constitutional and statutory constraints.

Service of the summons under this subdivision does not conclusively establish the jurisdiction of the court over the person of the defendant. A defendant may assert the territorial limits of the court's reach set forth in subdivision (k), including the constitutional limitations that may be imposed by the Due Process Clause of the Fifth Amendment.

Paragraph (1) authorizes service in any judicial district in conformity with state law. This paragraph sets forth the language of former subdivision (c)(2)(C)(i), which authorized the use of the law of the state in which the district court sits, but adds as an alternative the use of the law of the state in which the service is effected.

Paragraph (2) retains the text of the former subdivision (d)(1) and authorizes the use of the familiar methods of personal or abode service or service on an authorized agent in any judicial district. . . .

Subdivision (f). This subdivision provides for service on individuals who are in a foreign country, replacing the former subdivision (i) that was added to Rule 4 in 1963. Reflecting the pattern of Rule 4 in incorporating state law limitations on the exercise of jurisdiction over persons, the former subdivision (i) limited service outside the United States to cases in which extraterritorial service was authorized by state or federal law. The new rule eliminates the requirement of explicit authorization. On occasion, service in a foreign country was held to be improper for lack of statutory authority. This authority, however, was found to exist by implication. Given the substantial increase in the number of international transactions and events that are the subject of litigation in federal courts, it is appropriate to infer a general legislative authority to effect service on defendants in a foreign country.

A secondary effect of this provision for foreign service of a federal summons is to facilitate the use of federal long-arm law in actions brought to enforce the federal law against defendants who cannot be served under any state law but who can be constitutionally subjected to the jurisdiction of the federal court. Such a provision is set forth in paragraph (2) of subdivision (k) of this rule, applicable only to persons not subject to the territorial jurisdiction of any particular state.

Paragraph (1) gives effect to the Hague Convention on the Service Abroad of Judicial and Extrajudicial Documents, which entered into force for the United States on February 10, 1969. See 28 U.S.C.A., Fed. R. Civ. P. 4 (Supp. 1986). This Convention is an important means of dealing with problems of service in a foreign country. Use of the Convention procedures, when available, is mandatory if documents must be transmitted abroad to effect service. . . . Therefore, this paragraph provides that, when service is to be effected outside a judicial district of the United States, the methods of service appropriate under an applicable treaty shall be employed if available and if the treaty so requires.

The Hague Convention furnishes safeguards against the abridgment of rights of parties through inadequate notice. Article 15 provides for verification of actual notice or a demonstration that process was served by a method prescribed by the internal laws of the foreign state before a default judgment may be entered. Article 16 of the Convention also enables the judge to extend the time for appeal after judgment if the defendant shows a lack of adequate notice either to defend or to appeal the judgment, or has disclosed a prima facie case on the merits.

The Hague Convention does not specify a time within which a foreign country's Central Authority must effect service, but Article 15 does provide that alternate methods may be used if a Central Authority does not respond within six months. Generally, a Central Authority can be expected to respond much more quickly than that limit might permit, but there have been occasions when the signatory state was dilatory or refused to cooperate for substantive reasons. In such cases, resort may be had to the provision set forth in subdivision (f)(3). . . .

Paragraph (2) provides alternative methods for use when internationally agreed methods are not intended to be exclusive, or where there is no international agreement applicable. It contains most of the language formerly set forth in subdivision (i) of the rule. Service by methods that would violate foreign law is not generally authorized. Subparagraphs (A) and (B) prescribe the more appropriate methods for conforming to local practice or using a local authority. Subparagraph (C) prescribes other methods authorized by the former rule.

Paragraph (3) authorizes the court to approve other methods of service not prohibited by international agreements. The Hague Convention, for example, authorizes special forms of service in cases of urgency if convention methods will not permit service within the time required by the circumstances. Other circumstances that might justify the use of additional methods include the failure of the foreign country's Central Authority to effect service within the six-month period provided by the Convention, or the refusal of the Central Authority to serve a complaint seeking punitive damages or to enforce the antitrust laws of the United States. In such cases, the court may direct a special method of service not explicitly authorized by international agreement if not prohibited by the agreement. Inasmuch as our Constitution requires that reasonable notice be given, an earnest effort should be made to devise a method of communication that is consistent with due process and minimizes offense to foreign law. A court may in some instances specially authorize use of ordinary mail. Cf. Levin v. Ruby Trading Corp., 248 F. Supp. 537 (S.D.N.Y. 1965). . . .

Subdivision (i). This subdivision retains much of the text of former subdivisions (d)(4) and (d)(5). Paragraph (1) provides for service of a summons on the United States; it amends former subdivision (d)(4) to permit the United States attorney to be served by registered or certified mail. The rule does not authorize the use of the Notice and Request procedure of revised subdivision (d) when the United States is the defendant. To assure proper handling of mail in the United States attorney's office, the authorized mail service must be specifically addressed to the civil process clerk of the office of the United States attorney.

Paragraph (2) replaces former subdivision (d)(5). Paragraph (3) saves the plaintiff from the hazard of losing a substantive right because of failure to comply with the complex requirements of multiple service under this subdivision. That risk has proved to be more than nominal. This provision should be read in connection with the provisions of subdivision (c) of Rule 15 to preclude the loss of substantive rights against the United States or its agencies, corporations, or officers resulting from a plaintiff's failure to correctly identify and serve all the persons who should be named or served. . . .

Subdivision (k). This subdivision replaces the former subdivision (f), with no change in the title. Paragraph (1) retains the substance of the former rule in explicitly authorizing the exercise of personal jurisdiction over persons who can be reached under state long-arm law, the "100-mile bulge" provision added in 1963, or the federal interpleader act. Paragraph (1)(D) is new, but merely calls attention to federal legislation that may provide for nationwide or even world-wide service of process in cases arising under particular federal laws. Congress has provided for nationwide service of process and full exercise of territorial jurisdiction by all district courts with respect to specified federal actions.

Paragraph (2) is new. It authorizes the exercise of territorial jurisdiction over the person of any defendant against whom is made a claim arising under any federal law if that person is subject to personal jurisdiction in no state. This addition is a companion to the amendments made in revised subdivisions (e) and (f).

This paragraph corrects a gap in the enforcement of federal law. Under the former rule, a problem was presented when the defendant was a non-resident of the United States having contacts with the United States sufficient to justify the application of United States law and to satisfy federal standards of forum selection, but having insufficient contact with any single state to support jurisdiction under state long-arm legislation or meet the requirements of the Fourteenth Amendment limitation on state court territorial jurisdiction. In such cases, the defendant was shielded from the enforcement of federal law by the fortuity of a favorable limitation on the power of state courts, which was incorporated into the federal practice by the former rule. In this respect, the revision responds to the suggestion of the Supreme Court made in Omni Capital Int'l. v. Rudolf Wolff & Co., Ltd., 484 U.S. 97, 111 (1987).

There remain constitutional limitations on the exercise of territorial jurisdiction by federal courts over persons outside the United States. These restrictions arise from the Fifth Amendment rather than from the Fourteenth Amendment, which limits state-court reach and which was incorporated into federal practice by the reference to state law in the text of the former subdivision (e) that is deleted by this revision. The Fifth Amendment requires that any defendant have affiliating contacts with the United States sufficient to justify the exercise of personal jurisdiction over that party. There also may be a further Fifth Amendment constraint in that a plaintiff's forum selection might be so inconvenient to a defendant that it would be a denial of "fair play and substantial justice" required by the due process clause, even though the defendant had significant affiliating contacts with the United States. Compare World-Wide Volkswagen Corp. v. Woodson, 444 U.S. 286, 293-94 (1980); Insurance Corp. of Ireland v. Compagnie des Bauxites de Guinee, 456 U.S. 694, 702-03 (1982); Burger King Corp. v. Rudzewicz, 471 U.S. 462, 476-78 (1985); Asahi Metal Indus. v. Superior Court, 480 U.S. 102, 108-13 (1987).

This provision does not affect the operation of federal venue legislation. See generally 28 U.S.C. § 1391. Nor does it affect the operation of federal law providing for the change of venue. 28 U.S.C. §§ 1404, 1406. The availability of transfer for fairness and convenience under § 1404 should preclude most conflicts between the full exercise of territorial jurisdiction permitted by this rule and the Fifth Amendment requirement of "fair play and substantial justice."

The district court should be especially scrupulous to protect aliens who reside in a foreign country from forum selections so onerous that injustice could result. "[G]reat care and reserve should be exercised when extending our notions of personal jurisdiction into the international field." Asahi Metal Indus. v. Superior Court, 480 U.S. 102, 115 (1987), quoting United States v. First Nat'l City Bank, 379 U.S. 378, 404 (1965) (Harlan, J., dissenting).

This narrow extension of the federal reach applies only if a claim is made against the defendant under federal law. It does not establish personal jurisdiction if the only claims are those arising under state law or the law of another country, even though there might be diversity or alienage subject matter jurisdiction as to such claims. If, however, personal jurisdiction is established under this paragraph with respect to a federal claim, then 28 U.S.C. § 1367(a) provides supplemental jurisdiction over related claims against that defendant, subject to the court's discretion to decline exercise of that jurisdiction under 28 U.S.C. § 1367(c).

Subdivision (l). This subdivision assembles in one place all the provisions of the present rule bearing on proof of service. No material change in the rule is effected. . . .

Subdivision (m). This subdivision retains much of the language of the present subdivision (j).

The new subdivision explicitly provides that the court shall allow additional time if there is good cause for the plaintiff's failure to effect service in the prescribed 120 days, and authorizes the court to relieve a plaintiff of the consequences of an application of this subdivision even if there is no good cause shown. Such relief formerly was afforded in some cases, partly in reliance on Rule 6(b). Relief may be justified, for example, if the applicable statute of limitations would bar the refiled action, or if the defendant is evading service or conceals a defect in attempted service. A specific instance of good cause is set forth in paragraph (3) of this rule, which provides for extensions if necessary to correct oversights in compliance with the requirements of multiple service in actions against the United States or its officers, agencies, and corporations. The district court should also take care to protect pro se plaintiffs from consequences of confusion or delay attending the resolution of an in forma pauperis petition. . . .

Subdivision (n). This subdivision provides for in rem and quasi-in-rem jurisdiction. Paragraph (1) incorporates any requirements of 28 U.S.C. § 1655 or similar provisions bearing on seizures or liens.

Paragraph (2) provides for other uses of quasi-in-rem jurisdiction but limits its use to exigent circumstances. Provisional remedies may be employed as a means to secure jurisdiction over the property of a defendant whose person is not within reach of the court, but occasions for the use of this provision should be rare, as where the defendant is a fugitive or assets are in imminent danger of disappearing. Until 1963, it was not possible under Rule 4 to assert jurisdiction in a federal court over the property of a defendant not personally served. The 1963 amendment to subdivision (e) authorized the use of state law procedures authorizing seizures of assets as a basis for jurisdiction. Given the liberal availability of long-arm jurisdiction, the exercise of power quasi-in-rem has become almost an anachronism. Circumstances too spare to affiliate the defendant to the forum state sufficiently to support long-arm jurisdiction over the defendant's person are also inadequate to support seizure of the defendant's assets fortuitously found within the state. Shaffer v. Heitner, 433 U.S. 186 (1977).

Rule 4.1. Service of Other Process

(a) Generally. Process other than a summons as provided in Rule 4 or subpoena as provided in Rule 45 shall be served by a United States marshal, a deputy United States marshal, or a person specially appointed for that purpose, who shall make proof of service as provided in Rule 4(1). The process may be served anywhere within the territorial limits of the state in which the district court is located, and, when authorized by a statute of the United States, beyond the territorial limits of that state.

(b) Enforcement of Orders: Commitment for Civil Contempt. An order of civil commitment of a person held to be in contempt of a decree or injunction issued to enforce the laws of the United States may be served and enforced in any district. Other orders in civil contempt proceedings shall be served in the state in which the court issuing the order to be enforced is located or elsewhere within the United States if not more than 100 miles from the place at which the order to be enforced was issued.

Rule 5. Serving and Filing Pleadings and Other Papers

(a) Service: When required. Except as otherwise provided in these rules, every order required by its terms to be served, every pleading subsequent to the original complaint unless the court otherwise orders because of numerous defendants, every paper relating to discovery required to be served upon a party unless the court otherwise orders, every written motion other than one which may be heard ex parte, and every written notice, appearance, demand, offer of judgment, designation of record on appeal, and similar paper shall be served upon each of the parties. No service need be made on parties in default for failure to appear except that pleadings asserting new or additional claims for relief against them shall be served upon them in the manner provided for service of summons in Rule 4.

In an action begun by seizure of property, in which no person need be or is named as defendant, any service required to be made prior to the filing of an answer, claim, or appearance shall be made upon the person having custody or possession of the property at the time of its seizure.

(b) Making Service.

(1) Service under Rules 5(a) and 77(d) on a party represented by an attorney is made on the attorney unless the court orders service on the party.

(2) Service under Rule 5(a) is made by:

(A) Delivering a copy to the person served by:

(i) handing it to the person;

(ii) leaving it at the person's office with a clerk or other person in charge, or if no one is in charge leaving it in a conspicuous place in the office; or

(iii) if the person has no office or the office is closed, leaving it at the person's dwelling house or usual place of abode with someone of suitable age and discretion residing there.

(B) Mailing a copy to the last known address of the person served. Service by mail is complete on mailing.

(C) If the person served has no known address, leaving a copy with the clerk of the court.

(D) Delivering a copy by any other means, including electronic means, consented to in writing by the person served. Service by electronic means is complete on transmission; service by other consented means is complete when the person making service delivers the copy to the agency designated to make delivery. If authorized by local rule, a party may make service under this subparagraph (D) through the court's transmission facilities.

(3) Service by electronic means under Rule 5(b)(2)(D) is not effective if the party making service learns that the attempted service did not reach the person to be served.

(c) Same: Numerous Defendants. In any action in which there are unusually large numbers of defendants, the court, upon motion or of its own initiative, may order that service of the pleadings of the defendants and replies thereto need not be made as between the defendants and that any cross-claim, counterclaim, or matter constituting an avoidance or affirmative defense contained therein shall be deemed to be denied or avoided by all other parties and that the filing of any such pleading and service thereof upon the plaintiff constitutes due notice of it to the parties. A copy of every such order shall be served upon the parties in such manner and form as the court directs.

(d) Filing; Certificate of Service. All papers after the complaint required to be served upon a party, together with a certificate of service, must be filed with the court within a reasonable time after service, but disclosures under Rule 26(a)(1) or (2) and the following discovery requests and responses must not be filed until they are used in the proceeding or the court orders filing: (i) depositions, (ii) interrogatories, (iii) requests for documents or to permit entry upon land, and (iv) requests for admission.

(e) Filing with the Court Defined. The filing of papers with the court as required by these rules shall be made by filing them with the clerk of court, except that the judge may permit the papers to be filed with the judge, in which event the judge shall note thereon the filing date and forthwith transmit them to the office of the clerk. A court may by local rule permit papers to be filed, signed, or verified by electronic means that are consistent with technical standards, if any, that the Judicial Conference of the United States establishes. A local rule may require filing by electronic means only if reasonable exceptions are allowed. A paper filed by electronic means in compliance with a local rule constitutes a written paper for the purpose of applying these rules. The clerk shall not refuse to accept for filing any paper presented for that purpose solely because it is not presented in proper form as required by these rules or any local rules or practices.

ADVISORY COMMITTEE NOTES

2000 Amendment

Subdivision (d). Rule 5(d) is amended to provide that disclosures under Rule 26(a)(1) and (2), and discovery requests and responses under Rules 30, 31, 33, 34, and 36 must not be filed until they are used in the action. "Discovery requests" includes deposition notices and "discovery responses" includes objections. The rule supersedes and invalidates local rules that forbid, permit, or require filing of these materials before they are used in the action. The former Rule 26(a)(4) requirement that disclosures under Rule 26(a)(1) and (2) be filed has been removed. Disclosures under Rule 26(a)(3), however, must be promptly filed as provided in Rule 26(a)(3). Filings in connection with Rule 35 examinations, which involve a motion proceeding when the parties do not agree, are unaffected by these amendments.

Recognizing the costs imposed on parties and courts by required filing of discovery materials that are never used in an action, Rule 5(d) was amended in 1980 to authorize court orders that excuse filing. Since then, many districts have adopted local rules that excuse or forbid filing. In 1989 the Judicial Conference Local Rules Project concluded that these local rules were inconsistent with Rule 5(d), but urged the Advisory Committee to consider amending the rule. . . .

Although this amendment is based on widespread experience with local rules, and confirms the results directed by these local rules, it is designed to supersede and invalidate local rules. There is no apparent reason to have different filing rules in different districts. Even if districts vary in present capacities to store filed materials that are not used in an action, there is little reason to continue expending court resources for this purpose. These costs and burdens would likely change as parties make increased use of audio- and videotaped depositions. Equipment to facilitate review and reproduction of such discovery materials may prove costly to acquire, maintain, and operate.

The amended rule provides that discovery materials and disclosures under Rule 26(a)(1) and (a)(2) must not be filed until they are "used in the proceeding." This phrase is meant to refer to proceedings in court. This filing requirement is not triggered by "use" of discovery materials in other discovery activities, such as depositions. In connection with proceedings in court, however, the rule is to be interpreted broadly; any use of discovery materials in court in connection with a motion, a pretrial conference under Rule 16, or otherwise, should be interpreted as use in the proceeding.

Once discovery or disclosure materials are used in the proceeding, the filing requirements of Rule 5(d) should apply to them. But because the filing requirement applies only with regard to materials that are used, only those parts of voluminous materials that are actually used need be filed. Any party would be free to file other pertinent portions of materials that are so used. *See* Fed. R. Evid. 106; *cf.* Rule 32(a)(4). If the parties are unduly sparing in their submissions, the court may order further filings. By local rule, a court could provide appropriate direction regarding the filing of discovery materials, such as depositions, that are used in proceedings. . . .

2001 Amendments

. . .

Rule 5(b)(1) makes it clear that the provision for service on a party's attorney applies only to service made under Rules 5(a) and 77(d). Service under Rules 4, 4.1, 45(b), and 71A(d)(3) — as well as rules that invoke those rules — must be made as provided in those rules. . . .

Subparagraph (D) of Rule 5(b)(2) is new. It authorizes service by electronic means or any other means, but only if consent is obtained from the person served. The consent must be express, and cannot be implied from conduct. Early experience with electronic filing as authorized by Rule 5(d) is positive, supporting service by electronic means as well. Consent is required, however, because it is not yet possible to assume universal entry into the world of electronic communication. Subparagraph (D) also authorizes service by nonelectronic means. The Rule 5(b)(2)(B) provision making mail service complete on mailing is extended in subparagraph (D) to make service by electronic means complete on transmission; transmission is effected when the sender does the last act that must be performed by the sender. Service by other agencies is complete on delivery to the designated agency.

Finally, subparagraph (D) authorizes adoption of local rules providing for service through the court. Electronic case filing systems will come to include the capacity to make service by using the court's facilities to transmit all documents filed in the case. It may prove most efficient to establish an environment in which a party can file with the court, making use of the court's transmission facilities to serve the filed paper on all other parties. Transmission might be by such means as direct transmission of the paper, or by transmission of a notice of filing that includes an electronic link for direct access to the paper. Because service is under subparagraph (D), consent must be obtained from the persons served.

Consent to service under Rule 5(b)(2)(D) must be in writing, which can be provided by electronic means. Parties are encouraged to specify the scope and duration of the consent. The specification should include at least the persons to whom service should be made, the appropriate address or location for such service — such as the e-mail address or facsimile machine number, and the format to be used for attachments. A district court may establish a registry or other facility that allows advance consent to service by specified means for future actions.

Rule 6(e) is amended to allow additional time to respond when service is made under Rule 5(b)(2)(D). The additional time does not relieve a party who consents to service under Rule 5(b)(2)(D) of the responsibilities to monitor the facility designated for receiving service and to provide prompt notice of any address change.

Paragraph (3) addresses a question that may arise from a literal reading of the provision that service by electronic means is complete on transmission. Electronic communication is rapidly improving, but lawyers report continuing failures of transmission, particularly with respect to attachments. Ordinarily the risk of non-receipt falls on the person being served, who has consented to this form of service. But the risk should not extend to situations in which the person attempting service learns that the attempted service in fact did not reach the person to be served. Given actual knowledge that the attempt failed, service is not effected. The person attempting service must either try again or show circumstances that justify dispensing with service.

Paragraph (3) does not address the similar questions that may arise when a person attempting service learns that service by means other than electronic means in fact did not reach the person to be served. Case law provides few illustrations of circumstances in which a person attempting service actually knows that the attempt failed but seeks to act as if service had been made. This negative history suggests there is no need to address these problems in Rule 5(b)(3). This silence does not imply any view on these issues, nor on the circumstances that justify various forms of judicial action even though service has not been made.

2006 Amendment

Amended Rule 5(e) acknowledges that many courts have required electronic filing by means of a standing order, procedures manual, or local rule. These local practices reflect the advantages that courts and most litigants realize from electronic filing. Courts that mandate electronic filing recognize the need to make exceptions when requiring electronic filing imposes a hardship on a party. Under amended Rule 5(e), a local rule that requires electronic filing must include reasonable exceptions, but Rule 5(e) does not define the scope of those exceptions. Experience with the local rules that have been adopted and that will emerge will aid in drafting new local rules and will facilitate gradual convergence on uniform exceptions, whether in local rules or in an amended Rule 5(e).

Rule 5.1. Constitutional Challenge to a Statute — Notice, Certification, and Intervention

(a) Notice by a Party. A party that files a pleading, written motion, or other paper drawing into question the constitutionality of a federal or state statute must promptly:

(1) file a notice of constitutional question stating the question and identifying the paper that raises it, if:

(A) a federal statute is questioned and neither the United States nor any of its agencies, officers, or employees is a party in an official capacity, or

(B) a state statute is questioned and neither the state nor any of its agencies, officers, or employees is a party in an official capacity; and

(2) serve the notice and paper on the Attorney General of the United States if a federal statute is challenged — or on the state attorney general if a state statute is challenged — either by certified or registered mail or by sending it to an electronic address designated by the attorney general for this purpose.

(b) Certification by the Court. The court must, under 28 U.S.C. § 2403, certify to the Attorney General of the United States that there is a constitutional challenge to a federal statute, or certify to the state attorney general that there is a constitutional challenge to a state statute.

(c) Intervention; Final Decision on the Merits. Unless the court sets a later time, the attorney general may intervene within 60 days after the notice of constitutional question is filed or after the court certifies the challenge, whichever is earlier. Before the time to intervene expires, the court may reject the constitutional challenge, but may not enter a final judgment holding the statute unconstitutional.

(d) No Forfeiture. A party's failure to file and serve the notice, or the court's failure to certify, does not forfeit a constitutional claim or defense that is otherwise timely asserted.

Rule 6. Time

(a) Computation. In computing any period of time prescribed or allowed by these rules, by the local rules of any district court, by order of court, or by any applicable statute, the day of the act, event, or default from which the designated period of time begins to run shall not be included. The last day of the period so computed shall be included, unless it is a Saturday, a Sunday, or a legal holiday, or, when the act to be done is the filing of a paper in court, a day on which weather or other conditions have made the office of the clerk of the district court inaccessible, in which event the period runs until the end of the next day which is not one of the aforementioned days. When the period of time prescribed or allowed is less than 11 days, intermediate Saturdays, Sundays, and legal holidays shall be excluded in the computation. As used in this rule and in Rule 77(c), "legal holiday" includes New Year's Day, Birthday of Martin Luther King, Jr., Washington's Birthday, Memorial Day, Independence Day, Labor Day, Columbus Day, Veterans Day, Thanksgiving Day, Christmas Day, and any other day appointed as a holiday by the President or the Congress of the United States, or by the state in which the district court is held.

(b) Enlargement. When by these rules or by a notice given thereunder or by order of court an act is required or allowed to be done at or within a specified time, the court for cause shown may at any time in its discretion (1) with or without motion or notice order the period enlarged if request therefor is made before the expiration of the period originally prescribed or as extended by a previous order, or (2) upon motion made after the expiration of the specified period permit the act to be done where the failure to act was the result of excusable neglect; but it may not extend the time for taking any action under Rules 50(b) and (c)(2), 52(b), 59(b), (d) and (e), and 60(b), except to the extent and under the conditions stated in them.

(c) [Unaffected by Expiration of Term.] (Rescinded Feb. 28, 1966, effective July 1, 1966.)

(d) For Motions — Affidavits. A written motion, other than one which may be heard ex parte, and notice of the hearing thereof shall be served not later than 5 days before the time specified for the hearing, unless a different period is fixed by these rules or by order of the court. Such an order may for cause shown be made on ex parte application. When a motion is supported by affidavit, the affidavit shall be served with the motion; and, except as otherwise provided in Rule 59(c), opposing affidavits may be served not later than 1 day before the hearing, unless the court permits them to be served at some other time.

(e) Additional Time After Certain Kinds of Service. Whenever a party must or may act within a prescribed period after service and service is made under Rule 5(b)(2)(B), (C), or (D), 3 days are added after the prescribed period would otherwise expire under subdivision (a).

III. PLEADINGS AND MOTIONS

Rule 7. Pleadings Allowed; Form of Motions

(a) Pleadings. There shall be a complaint and an answer; a reply to a counterclaim denominated as such; an answer to a cross-claim, if the answer contains a cross-claim; a third-party complaint, if a person who was not an original party is summoned under the provisions of Rule 14; and a third-party answer, if a third-party complaint is served. No other pleading shall be allowed, except that the court may order a reply to an answer or a third-party answer.

(b) Motions and Other Papers.

(1) An application to the court for an order shall be by motion which, unless made during a hearing or trial, shall be made in writing, shall state with particularity the grounds therefor, and shall set forth the relief or order sought. The requirement of writing is fulfilled if the motion is stated in a written notice of the hearing of the motion.

(2) The rules applicable to captions and other matters of form of pleadings apply to all motions and other papers provided for by these rules.

(3) All motions shall be signed in accordance with Rule 11.

(c) Demurrers, Pleas, etc., Abolished. Demurrers, pleas, and exceptions for insufficiency of a pleading shall not be used.

Rule 7.1. Disclosure Statement

(a) Who Must File: Nongovernmental Corporate Party. A nongovernmental corporate party to an action or proceeding in a district court must file two copies of a statement that identifies any parent corporation and any publicly held corporation that owns 10% or more of its stock or states that there is no such corporation.

(b) Time for Filing; Supplemental Filing. A party must:

(1) file the Rule 7.1(a) statement with its first appearance, pleading, petition, motion, response, or other request addressed to the court, and

(2) promptly file a supplemental statement upon any change in the information that the statement requires.

Rule 8. General Rules of Pleading

(a) Claims for Relief. A pleading which sets forth a claim for relief, whether an original claim, counterclaim, cross-claim, or third-party claim, shall contain (1) a short and plain statement of the grounds upon which the court's jurisdiction depends, unless the court already has jurisdiction and the claim needs no new grounds of jurisdiction to support it, (2) a short and plain statement of the claim showing that the pleader is entitled to relief, and (3) a demand for judgment for the relief the pleader seeks. Relief in the alternative or of several different types may be demanded.

(b) Defenses; Form of Denials. A party shall state in short and plain terms the party's defenses to each claim asserted and shall admit or deny the averments upon which the adverse party relies. If a party is without knowledge or information sufficient to form a belief as to the truth of an averment, the party shall so state and this has the effect of a denial. Denials shall fairly meet the substance of the averments denied. When a pleader intends in good faith to deny only a part or a qualification of an averment, the pleader shall specify so much of it as is true and material and shall deny only the remainder. Unless the pleader intends in good faith to controvert all the averments of the preceding pleading, the pleader may make denials as specific denials of designated averments or paragraphs or may generally deny all the averments except such designated averments or paragraphs as the pleader expressly admits; but, when the pleader does so intend to controvert all its averments, including averments of the grounds upon which the court's jurisdiction depends, the pleader may do so by general denial subject to the obligations set forth in Rule 11.

(c) Affirmative Defenses. In pleading to a preceding pleading, a party shall set forth affirmatively accord and satisfaction, arbitration and award, assumption of risk, contributory negligence, discharge in bankruptcy, duress, estoppel, failure of consideration, fraud, illegality, injury by fellow servant, laches, license, payment, release, res judicata, statute of frauds, statute of limitations, waiver, and any other matter constituting an avoidance or affirmative defense. When a party has mistakenly designated a defense as a counterclaim or a counterclaim as a defense, the court on terms, if justice so requires, shall treat the pleading as if there had been a proper designation.

(d) Effect of Failure to Deny. Averments in a pleading to which a responsive pleading is required, other than those as to the amount of damage, are admitted when not denied in the responsive pleading. Averments in a pleading to which no responsive pleading is required or permitted shall be taken as denied or avoided.

(e) Pleading to be Concise and Direct; Consistency.

(1) Each averment of a pleading shall be simple, concise, and direct. No technical forms of pleading or motions are required.

(2) A party may set forth two or more statements of a claim or defense alternately or hypothetically, either in one count or defense or in separate counts or defenses. When two or more statements are made in the alternative and one of them if made independently would be sufficient, the pleading is not made insufficient by the insufficiency of one or more of the alternative statements. A party may also state as many separate claims or defenses as the party has regardless of consistency and whether based on legal, equitable, or maritime grounds. All statements shall be made subject to the obligations set forth in Rule 11.

(f) Construction of Pleadings. All pleadings shall be so construed as to do substantial justice.

ADVISORY COMMITTEE NOTES

1937 Adoption

Note to Subdivision (a). See [former] Equity Rules 25 (Bill of Complaint — Contents), and 30 (Answer — Contents — Counterclaim). Compare 2 Ind.Stat.Ann. (Burns, 1933) §§ 2-1004, 2-1015; 2 Ohio Gen.Code Ann. (Page, 1926) §§ 11305, 11314; Utah Rev.Stat.Ann. (1933) §§ 104-7-2, 104-9-1.

See Rule 19(c) for the requirement of a statement in a claim for relief of the names of persons who ought to be parties and the reason for their omission.

See Rule 23(b) [now Rule 23.1 — ED.] for particular requirements as to the complaint in a secondary action by shareholders.

Note to Subdivision (b). 1. This rule supersedes the methods of pleading prescribed in U.S.C., Title 19, § 508 (Persons making seizures pleading general issue and proving special matter); U.S.C. Title 35, [former] §§ 40d (Proving under general issue, upon notice, that a statement in application for an extended patent is not true), 69 [now 282] (Pleading and proof in actions for infringement) and similar statutes.

2. This rule is, in part, [former] Equity Rule 30 (Answer — Contents — Counterclaim), with the matter on denials largely from the Connecticut practice. See Conn. Practice Book (1934) §§ 107, 108, and 122; Conn.Gen.Stat. (1930) §§ 5508 to 5514. Compare the English practice, *English Rules Under the Judicature Act* (The Annual Practice, 1937) O. 19, r.r. 17-20.

Note to Subdivision (c). This follows substantially *English Rules Under the Judicature Act* (The Annual Practice, 1937) O. 19, r. 15 and N.Y.C.P.A. (1937) § 242, with "surprise" omitted in this rule.

Note to Subdivision (d). The first sentence is similar to former Equity Rule 30 (Answer — Contents — Counterclaim). For the second sentence see former Equity Rule 31 (Reply — When Required — When Cause at Issue). This is similar to *English Rules Under the Judicature Act* (The Annual Practice, 1937) O. 19, r.r. 13, 18; and to the practice of the States.

Note to Subdivision (e). This rule is an elaboration upon [former] Equity Rule 30 (Answer — Contents — Counterclaim), plus a statement of the actual practice under some codes. Compare also [former] Equity Rule 18 (Pleadings — Technical Forms Abrogated). See Clark, *Code Pleading* (1928), pp. 171-4, 432-5; Hankin, *Alternative and Hypothetical Pleading* (1924), 33 Yale L.J. 365.

Note to Subdivision (f). A provision of like import is of frequent occurrence in the codes. Smith-Hurd Ill.Stats. ch. 110, § 157(3); 2 Minn.Stat. (Mason, 1927) § 9266; N.Y.C.P.A. (1937) § 275; 2 N.D. Comp.Laws Ann. (1913) § 7458.

Rule 9. Pleading Special Matters

(a) Capacity. It is not necessary to aver the capacity of a party to sue or be sued or the authority of a party to sue or be sued in a representative capacity or the legal existence of an organized association of persons that is made a party, except to the extent required to show the jurisdiction of the court. When a party desires to raise an issue as to the legal existence of any party or the capacity of any party to sue or be sued or the authority of a party to sue or be sued in a representative capacity, the party desiring to raise the issue shall do so by specific negative averment, which shall include such supporting particulars as are peculiarly within the pleader's knowledge.

(b) Fraud, Mistake, Condition of the Mind. In all averments of fraud or mistake, the circumstances constituting fraud or mistake shall be stated with particularity. Malice, intent, knowledge, and other condition of mind of a person may be averred generally.

(c) Conditions Precedent. In pleading the performance or occurrence of conditions precedent, it is sufficient to aver generally that all conditions precedent have been performed or have occurred. A denial of performance or occurrence shall be made specifically and with particularity.

(d) Official Document or Act. In pleading an official document or official act it is sufficient to aver that the document was issued or the act done in compliance with law.

(e) Judgment. In pleading a judgment or decision of a domestic or foreign court, judicial or quasi-judicial tribunal, or of a board or officer, it is sufficient to aver the judgment or decision without setting forth matter showing jurisdiction to render it.

(f) Time and Place. For the purpose of testing the sufficiency of a pleading, averments of time and place are material and shall be considered like all other averments of material matter.

(g) Special Damage. When items of special damage are claimed, they shall be specifically stated.

(h) Admiralty and Maritime Claims. A pleading or count setting forth a claim for relief within the admiralty and maritime jurisdiction that is also within the jurisdiction of the district court on some other ground may contain a statement identifying the claim as an admiralty or maritime claim for the purposes of Rules 14(c), 38(e), 82, and the Supplemental Rules for Admiralty or Maritime Claims and Asset Forfeiture Actions. If the claim is cognizable only in admiralty, it is an admiralty or maritime claim for those purposes whether so identified or not. The amendment of a pleading to add or withdraw an identifying statement is governed by the principles of Rule 15. A case that includes an admiralty or maritime claim within this subdivision is an admiralty case within 28 U.S.C. § 1292(a)(3).

Rule 10. Form of Pleadings

(a) Caption; Names of Parties. Every pleading shall contain a caption setting forth the name of the court, the title of the action, the file number, and a designation as in Rule 7(a). In the complaint the title of the action shall include the names of all the parties, but in other pleadings it is sufficient to state the name of the first party on each side with an appropriate indication of other parties.

(b) Paragraphs; Separate Statements. All averments of claim or defense shall be made in numbered paragraphs, the contents of each of which shall be limited as far as practicable to a statement of a single set of circumstances; and a paragraph may be referred to by number in all succeeding pleadings. Each claim founded upon a separate transaction or occurrence and each defense other than denials shall be stated in a separate count or defense whenever a separation facilitates the clear presentation of the matters set forth.

(c) Adoption by Reference; Exhibits. Statements in a pleading may be adopted by reference in a different part of the same pleading or in another pleading or in any motion. A copy of any written instrument which is an exhibit to a pleading is a part thereof for all purposes.

Rule 11. Signing of Pleadings, Motions, and Other Papers; Representations to Court; Sanctions

(a) Signature. Every pleading, written motion, and other paper shall be signed by at least one attorney of record in the attorney's individual name, or, if the party is not represented by an attorney, shall be signed by the party. Each paper shall state the signer's address and telephone number, if any. Except when otherwise specifically provided by rule or statute, pleadings need not be verified or accompanied by affidavit. An unsigned paper shall be stricken unless omission of the signature is corrected promptly after being called to the attention of the attorney or party.

(b) Representations to Court. By presenting to the court (whether by signing, filing, submitting, or later advocating) a pleading, written motion, or other paper, an attorney or unrepresented party is certifying that to the best of the person's knowledge, information, and belief, formed after an inquiry reasonable under the circumstances, —

(1) it is not being presented for any improper purpose, such as to harass or to cause unnecessary delay or needless increase in the cost of litigation;

(2) the claims, defenses, and other legal contentions therein are warranted by existing law or by a nonfrivolous argument for the extension, modification, or reversal of existing law or the establishment of new law;

(3) the allegations and other factual contentions have evidentiary support or, if specifically so identified, are likely to have evidentiary support after a reasonable opportunity for further investigation or discovery; and

(4) the denials of factual contentions are warranted on the evidence or, if specifically so identified, are reasonably based on a lack of information or belief.

(c) Sanctions. If, after notice and a reasonable opportunity to respond, the court determines that subdivision (b) has been violated, the court may, subject to the conditions stated below, impose an appropriate sanction upon the attorneys, law firms, or parties that have violated subdivision (b) or are responsible for the violation.

(1) How Initiated.

(A) By Motion. A motion for sanctions under this rule shall be made separately from other motions or requests and shall describe the specific conduct alleged to violate subdivision (b). It shall be served as provided in Rule 5, but shall not be filed with or presented to the court unless, within 21 days after service of the motion (or such other period as the court may prescribe), the challenged paper, claim, defense, contention, allegation, or denial is not withdrawn or appropriately corrected. If warranted, the court may award to the party prevailing on the motion the reasonable expenses and attorney's fees incurred in presenting or opposing the motion. Absent exceptional circumstances, a law firm shall be held jointly responsible for violations committed by its partners, associates, and employees.

(B) On Court's Initiative. On its own initiative, the court may enter an order describing the specific conduct that appears to violate subdivision (b) and directing an attorney, law firm, or party to show cause why it has not violated subdivision (b) with respect thereto.

(2) Nature of Sanction; Limitations. A sanction imposed for violation of this rule shall be limited to what is sufficient to deter repetition of such conduct or comparable conduct by others similarly situated. Subject to the limitations in subparagraphs (A) and (B), the sanction may consist of, or include, directives of a nonmonetary nature, an order to pay a penalty into court, or, if imposed on motion and warranted for effective deterrence, an order directing payment to the movant of some or all of the reasonable attorneys' fees and other expenses incurred as a direct result of the violation.

(A) Monetary sanctions may not be awarded against a represented party for a violation of subdivision (b)(2).

(B) Monetary sanctions may not be awarded on the court's initiative unless the court issues its order to show cause before a voluntary dismissal or settlement of the claims made by or against the party which is, or whose attorneys are, to be sanctioned.

(3) Order. When imposing sanctions, the court shall describe the conduct determined to constitute a violation of this rule and explain the basis for the sanction imposed.

(d) Inapplicability to Discovery. Subdivisions (a) through (c) of this rule do not apply to disclosures and discovery requests, responses, objections, and motions that are subject to the provisions of Rules 26 through 37.

ADVISORY COMMITTEE NOTES

1983 Amendment [citations omitted without notation — ED.]

Since its original promulgation, Rule 11 has provided for the striking of pleadings and the imposition of disciplinary sanctions to check abuses in the signing of pleadings. Its provisions have always applied to motions and other papers by virtue of incorporation by reference in Rule 7(b)(2). The amendment and the addition of Rule 7(b)(3) expressly confirms this applicability.

Experience shows that in practice Rule 11 has not been effective in deterring abuses. There has been considerable confusion as to (1) the circumstances that should trigger striking a pleading or motion or taking disciplinary action, (2) the standard of conduct expected of attorneys who sign pleadings and motions, and (3) the range of available and appropriate sanctions. The new language is intended to reduce the reluctance of courts to impose sanctions, by emphasizing the responsibilities of the attorney and reenforcing those obligations by the imposition of sanctions.

The amended rule attempts to deal with the problem by building upon and expanding the equitable doctrine permitting the court to award expenses, including attorney's fees, to a litigant whose opponent acts in bad faith in instituting or conducting litigation. See, e.g., *Roadway Express, Inc. v. Piper*, 447 U.S. 752 (1980); *Hall v. Cole*, 412 U.S. 1, 5 (1973). Greater attention by the district courts to pleading and motion abuses and the imposition of sanctions when appropriate, should discourage dilatory or abusive tactics and help to streamline the litigation process by lessening frivolous claims or defenses.

The expanded nature of the lawyer's certification in the fifth sentence of amended Rule 11 recognizes that the litigation process may be abused for purposes other than delay.

The words "good ground to support" the pleading in the original rule were interpreted to have both factual and legal elements. They have been replaced by a standard of conduct that is more focused.

The new language stresses the need for some prefiling inquiry into both the facts and the law to satisfy the affirmative duty imposed by the rule. The standard is one of reasonableness under the circumstances. This standard is more stringent than the original good-faith formula and thus it is expected that a greater range of circumstances will trigger its violation.

The rule is not intended to chill an attorney's enthusiasm or creativity in pursuing factual or legal theories. The court is expected to avoid using the wisdom of hindsight and should test the signer's conduct by inquiring what was reasonable to believe at the time the pleading, motion, or other paper was submitted. Thus, what constitutes a reasonable inquiry may depend on such factors as how much time for investigation was available to the signer; whether he had to rely on a client for information as to the facts underlying the pleading, motion, or other paper; whether the pleading, motion, or other paper was based on a plausible view of the law; or whether he depended on forwarding counsel or another member of the bar.

The rule does not require a party or an attorney to disclose privileged communications or work product in order to show that the signing of the pleading, motion, or other paper is substantially justified. The provisions of Rule 26(c), including appropriate orders after *in camera* inspection by the court, remain available to protect a party claiming privilege or work product protection.

Amended Rule 11 continues to apply to anyone who signs a pleading, motion, or other paper. Although the standard is the same for unrepresented parties, who are obliged themselves to sign the pleadings, the court has sufficient discretion to take account of the special circumstances that often arise in *pro se* situations. See *Haines v. Kerner*, 404 U.S. 519 (1972).

The provision in the original rule for striking pleadings and motions as sham and false has been deleted. The passage has rarely been utilized, and decisions thereunder have tended to confuse the issue of attorney honesty with the merits of the action. Motions under this provision generally present issues better dealt with under Rules 8, 12, or 56.

The former reference to the inclusion of scandalous or indecent matter, which is itself strong indication that an improper purpose underlies the pleading, motion, or other paper, also has been deleted as unnecessary. Such matter may be stricken under Rule 12(f) as well as dealt with under the more general language of amended Rule 11.

The text of the amended rule seeks to dispel apprehensions that efforts to obtain enforcement will be fruitless by insuring that the rule will be applied when properly invoked. The word "sanctions" in the caption, for example, stresses a deterrent orientation in dealing with improper pleadings, motions or other papers. This corresponds to the approach in imposing sanctions for discovery abuses. See *National Hockey League v. Metropolitan Hockey Club*, 427 U.S. 639 (1976) (per curiam). And the words "shall impose" in the last sentence focus the court's attention on the need to impose sanctions for pleading and motion abuses. The court, however, retains the necessary flexibility to deal appropriately with violations of the rule. It has discretion to tailor sanctions to the particular facts of the case, with which it should be well acquainted.

The references in the former text to wilfulness as a prerequisite to disciplinary action has been deleted. However, in considering the nature and severity of the sanctions to be imposed, the court should take account of the state of the attorney's or party's actual or presumed knowledge when the pleading or other paper was signed. Thus, for example, when a party is not represented by counsel, the absence of legal advice is an appropriate factor to be considered.

Courts currently appear to believe they may impose sanctions on their own motion. Authority to do so has been made explicit in order to overcome the traditional reluctance of courts to intervene unless requested by one of the parties. The detection and punishment of a violation of the signing requirement, encouraged by the amended rule, is part of the court's responsibility for securing the system's effective operation.

If the duty imposed by the rule is violated, the court should have the discretion to impose sanctions on either the attorney, the party the signing attorney represents, or both, or on an unrepresented party who signed the pleading, and the new rule so provides. Although Rule 11 has been silent on the point, courts have claimed the power to impose sanctions on an attorney personally, either by imposing costs or employing the contempt technique. This power has been used infrequently. The amended rule should eliminate any doubt as to the propriety of assessing sanctions against the attorney.

Even though it is the attorney whose signature violates the rule, it may be appropriate under the circumstances of the case to impose a sanction on the client. This modification brings Rule 11 in line with practice under Rule 37, which allows sanctions for abuses during discovery to be imposed upon the party, the attorney, or both.

A party seeking sanctions should give notice to the court and the offending party promptly upon discovering a basis for doing so. The time when sanctions are to be imposed rests in the discretion of the trial judge. However, it is anticipated that in the case of pleadings the sanctions issue under Rule 11 normally will be determined at the end of the litigation, and in the case of motions at the time when the motion is decided or shortly thereafter. The procedure obviously must comport with due process requirements. The particular format to be followed should depend on the circumstances of the situation and the severity of the sanction under consideration. In many situations the judge's participation in the proceedings provides him with full knowledge of the relevant facts and little further inquiry will be necessary.

To assure that the efficiencies achieved through more effective operation of the pleading regimen will not be offset by the cost of satellite litigation over the imposition of sanctions, the court must to the extent possible limit the scope of sanction proceedings to the record. Thus, discovery should be conducted only by leave of the court, and then only in extraordinary circumstances.

Although the encompassing reference to "other papers" in new Rule 11 literally includes discovery papers, the certification requirement in that context is governed by proposed new Rule 26(g). Discovery motions, however, fall within the ambit of Rule 11.

1993 Amendments

Purpose of revision. This revision is intended to remedy problems that have arisen in the interpretation and application of the 1983 revision of the rule. For empirical examination of experience under the 1983 rule, see, *e.g.,* New York State Bar Committee on Federal Courts, *Sanctions and Attorneys' Fees* (1987); T. Willging, *The Rule 11 Sanctioning Process* (1989); American Judicature Society, *Report of the Third Circuit Task Force on Federal Rule of Civil Procedure 11* (S. Burbank ed., 1989); E. Wiggins, T. Willging, and D. Stienstra, *Report on Rule 11* (Federal Judicial Center 1991). . . .

The rule retains the principle that attorneys and pro se litigants have an obligation to the court to refrain from conduct that frustrates the aims of Rule 1. The revision broadens the scope of this obligation, but places greater constraints on the imposition of sanctions and should reduce the number of motions for sanctions presented to the court. New subdivision (d) removes from the ambit of this rule all discovery requests, responses, objections, and motions subject to the provisions of Rule 26 through 37.

Subdivision (a). Retained in this subdivision are the provisions requiring signatures on pleadings, written motions, and other papers. Unsigned papers are to be received by the Clerk, but then are to be stricken if the omission of the signature is not corrected promptly after being called to the attention of the attorney or pro se litigant. Correction can be made by signing the paper on file or by submitting a duplicate that contains the signature. A court may require by local rule that papers contain additional identifying information regarding the parties or attorneys, such as telephone numbers to facilitate facsimile transmissions, though, as for omission of a signature, the paper should not be rejected for failure to provide such information.

The sentence in the former rule relating to the effect of answers under oath is no longer needed and has been eliminated. The provision in the former rule that signing a paper constitutes a certificate that it has been read by the signer also has been eliminated as unnecessary. The obligations imposed under subdivision (b) obviously require that a pleading, written motion, or other paper be read before it is filed or submitted to the court.

Subdivisions (b) and (c). These subdivisions restate the provisions requiring attorneys and pro se litigants to conduct a reasonable inquiry into the law and facts before signing pleadings, written motions, and other documents, and prescribing sanctions for violation of these obligations. The revision in part expands the responsibilities of litigants to the court, while providing greater constraints and flexibility in dealing with infractions of the rule. The rule continues to require litigants to "stop-and-think" before initially making legal or factual contentions. It also, however, emphasizes the duty of candor by subjecting litigants to potential sanctions for insisting upon a position after it is no longer tenable and by generally providing protection against sanctions if they withdraw or correct contentions after a potential violation is called to their attention.

The rule applies only to assertions contained in papers filed with or submitted to the court. It does not cover matters arising for the first time during oral presentations to the court, when counsel may make statements that would not have been made if there had been more time for study and reflection. However, a litigant's obligations with respect to the contents of these papers are not measured solely as of the time they are filed with or submitted to the court, but include reaffirming to the court and advocating positions contained in those pleadings and motions after learning that they cease to have any merit. For example, an attorney who during a pretrial conference insists on a claim or defense should be viewed as "presenting to the court" that contention and would be subject to the obligations of subdivision (b) measured as of that time. Similarly, if after a notice of removal is filed, a party urges in federal court the allegations of a pleading filed in state court (whether as claims, defenses, or in disputes regarding removal or remand), it would be viewed as "presenting" — and hence certifying to the district court under Rule 11 — those allegations.

The certification with respect to allegations and other factual contentions is revised in recognition that sometimes a litigant may have good reason to believe that a fact is true or false but may need discovery, formal or informal, from opposing parties or third persons to gather and confirm the evidentiary basis for the allegation. Tolerance of factual contentions in initial pleadings by plaintiffs or defendants when specifically identified as made on information and belief does not relieve litigants from the obligation to conduct an appropriate investigation into the facts that is reasonable under the circumstances; it is not a license to join parties, make claims, or present defenses without any factual basis or justification. Moreover, if evidentiary support is not obtained after a reasonable opportunity for further investigation or discovery, the party has a duty under the rule not to persist with that contention. Subdivision (b) does not require a formal amendment to pleadings for which evidentiary support is not obtained, but rather calls upon a litigant not thereafter to advocate such claims or defenses.

The certification is that there is (or likely will be) "evidentiary support" for the allegation, not that the party will prevail with respect to its contention regarding the fact. That summary judgment is rendered against a party does not necessarily mean, for purposes of this certification, that it had no evidentiary support for its position. On the other hand, if a party has evidence with respect to a contention that would suffice to defeat a motion for summary judgment based thereon, it would have sufficient "evidentiary support" for purposes of Rule 11.

Denials of factual contentions involve somewhat different considerations. Often, of course, a denial is premised upon the existence of evidence contradicting the alleged fact. At other times a denial is permissible because, after an appropriate investigation, a party has no information concerning the matter or, indeed, has a reasonable basis for doubting the credibility of the only evidence relevant to the matter. A party should not deny an allegation it knows to be true; but it is not required, simply because it lacks contradictory evidence, to admit an allegation that it believes is not true.

The changes in subdivisions (b)(3) and (b)(4) will serve to equalize the burden of the rule upon plaintiffs and defendants, who under Rule 8(b) are in effect allowed to deny allegations by stating that from their initial investigation they lack sufficient information to form a belief as to the truth of the allegation. If, after further investigation or discovery, a denial is no longer warranted, the defendant should not continue to insist on that denial. While sometimes helpful, formal amendment of the pleadings to withdraw an allegation or denial is not required by subdivision (b).

Arguments for extensions, modifications, or reversals of existing law or for creation of new law do not violate subdivision (b)(2) provided they are "nonfrivolous." This establishes an objective standard, intended to eliminate any "empty-head pure-heart" justification for patently frivolous arguments. However, the extent to which a litigant has researched the issues and found some support for its theories even in minority opinions, in law review articles, or through consultation with other attorneys should certainly be taken into account in determining whether paragraph (2) has been violated. Although arguments for a change of law are not required to be specifically so identified, a contention that is so identified should be viewed with greater tolerance under the rule.

The court has available a variety of possible sanctions to impose for violations, such as striking the offending paper; issuing an admonition, reprimand, or censure; requiring participation in seminars or other educational programs; ordering a fine payable to the court; referring the matter to disciplinary authorities (or, in the case of government attorneys, to the Attorney General, Inspector General, or agency head), etc. *See Manual for Complex Litigation, Second*, § 42.3. The rule does not attempt to enumerate the factors a court should consider in deciding whether to impose a sanction or what sanctions would be appropriate in the circumstances; but, for emphasis, it does specifically note that a sanction may be nonmonetary as well as monetary. Whether the improper conduct was willful, or negligent; whether it was part of a pattern of activity, or an isolated event; whether it infected the entire pleading, or only one particular count or defense; whether the person has engaged in similar conduct in other litigation; whether it was intended to injure; what effect it had on the litigation process in time or expense; whether the responsible person is trained in the law; what amount, given the financial resources of the responsible person, is needed to deter that person from repetition in the same case; what amount is needed to deter similar activity by other litigants: all of these may in a particular case be proper considerations. The court has significant discretion in determining what sanctions, if any, should be imposed for a violation, subject to the principle that the sanctions should not be more severe than reasonably necessary to deter repetition of the conduct by the offending person or comparable conduct by similarly situated persons.

Since the purpose of Rule 11 sanctions is to deter rather than to compensate, the rule provides that, if a monetary sanction is imposed, it should ordinarily be paid into court as a penalty. However, under unusual circumstances, particularly for (b)(1) violations, deterrence may be ineffective unless the sanction not only requires the person violating the rule to make a monetary payment, but also directs that some or all of this payment be made to those injured by the violation. Accordingly, the rule authorizes the court, if requested in a motion and if so warranted, to award attorney's fees to another party. Any such award to another party, however, should not exceed the expenses and attorneys' fees for the services directly and unavoidably caused by the violation of the certification requirement. If, for example, a wholly unsupportable count were included in a multi-count complaint or counterclaim for the purpose of needlessly increasing the cost of litigation to an impecunious adversary, any award of expenses should be limited to those directly caused by inclusion of the improper count, and not those resulting from the filing of the complaint or answer itself. The award should not provide compensation for services that could have been avoided by an earlier disclosure of evidence or an earlier challenge to the groundless claims or defenses. Moreover, partial reimbursement of fees may constitute a sufficient deterrent with respect to violations by persons having modest financial resources. In cases brought under statutes providing for fees to be awarded to prevailing parties, the court should not employ cost-shifting under this rule in a manner that would be inconsistent with the standards that govern the statutory award of fees, such as stated in *Christiansburg Garment Co. v. EEOC*, 434 U.S. 412 (1978).

The sanction should be imposed on the persons — whether attorneys, law firms, or parties — who have violated the rule or who may be determined to be responsible for the violation. The person signing, filing, submitting, or advocating a document has a nondelegable responsibility to the court, and in most situations is the person to be sanctioned for a violation. Absent exceptional circumstances, a law firm is to be held also responsible when, as a result of a motion under subdivision (c)(1)(A), one of its partners, associates, or employees is determined to have violated the rule. Since such a motion may be filed only if the offending paper is not withdrawn or corrected within 21 days after service of the motion, it is appropriate that the law firm ordinarily be viewed as jointly responsible under established principles of agency. This provision is designed to remove the restrictions of the former rule. *Cf. Pavelic & LeFlore v. Marvel Entertainment Group*, 493 U.S. 120 (1989) (1983 version of Rule 11 does not permit sanctions against law firm of attorney signing groundless complaint).

The revision permits the court to consider whether other attorneys in the firm, co-counsel, other law firms, or the party itself should be held accountable for their part in causing a violation. When appropriate, the court can make an additional inquiry in order to determine whether the sanction should be imposed on such persons, firms, or parties either in addition to or, in unusual circumstances, instead of the person actually making the presentation to the court. For example, such an inquiry may be appropriate in cases involving governmental agencies or other institutional parties that frequently impose substantial restrictions on the discretion of individual attorneys employed by it.

Sanctions that involve monetary awards (such as a fine or an award of attorney's fees) may not be imposed on a represented party for causing a violation of subdivision (b)(2), involving frivolous contentions of law. Monetary responsibility for such violations is more properly placed solely on the party's attorneys. With this limitation, the rule should not be subject to attack under the Rules Enabling Act. See *Willy v. Coastal Corp.*, [503] U.S. [131] (1992); *Business Guides, Inc. v. Chromatic Communications Enter. Inc.*, [498] U.S. [533] (1991). This restriction does not limit the court's power to impose sanctions or remedial orders that may have collateral financial consequences upon a party, such as dismissal of a claim, preclusion of a defense, or preparation of amended pleadings.

Explicit provision is made for litigants to be provided notice of the alleged violation and an opportunity to respond before sanctions are imposed. Whether the matter should be decided solely on the basis of written submissions or should be scheduled for oral argument (or, indeed, for evidentiary presentation) will depend on the circumstances. If the court imposes a sanction, it must, unless waived, indicate its reasons in a written order or on the record; the court should not ordinarily have to explain its denial of a motion for sanctions. Whether a violation has occurred and what sanctions, if any, to impose for a violation are matters committed to the discretion of the trial court; accordingly, as under current law, the standard for appellate review of these decisions will be for abuse of discretion. *See Cooter & Gell v. Hartmarx Corp.*, 496 U.S. 384 (1990) . . . .

The revision leaves for resolution on a case-by-case basis, considering the particular circumstances involved, the question as to when a motion for violation of Rule 11 should be served and when, if filed, it should be decided. Ordinarily the motion should be served promptly after the inappropriate paper is filed, and, if delayed too long, may be viewed as untimely. In other circumstances, it should not be served until the other party has had a reasonable opportunity for discovery. Given the "safe harbor" provisions discussed below, a party cannot delay serving its Rule 11 motion until conclusion of the case (or judicial rejection of the offending contention).

Rule 11 motions should not be made or threatened for minor, inconsequential violations of the standards prescribed by subdivision (b). They should not be employed as a discovery device or to test the legal sufficiency or efficacy of allegations in the pleadings; other motions are available for those purposes. Nor should Rule 11 motions be prepared to emphasize the merits of a party's position, to exact an unjust settlement, to intimidate an adversary into withdrawing contentions that are fairly debatable, to increase the costs of litigation, to create a conflict of interest between attorney and client, or to seek disclosure of matters otherwise protected by the attorney-client privilege or the work-product doctrine. As under the prior rule, the court may defer its ruling (or its decision as to the identity of the persons to be sanctioned) until final resolution of the case in order to avoid immediate conflicts of interest and to reduce the disruption created if a disclosure of attorney-client communications is needed to determine whether a violation occurred or to identify the person responsible for the violation.

The rule provides that requests for sanctions must be made as a separate motion, *i.e.,* not simply included as an additional prayer for relief contained in another motion. The motion for sanctions is not, however, to be filed until at least 21 days (or such other period as the court may set) after being served. If, during this period, the alleged violation is corrected, as by withdrawing (whether formally or informally) some allegation or contention, the motion should not be filed with the court. These provisions are intended to provide a type of "safe harbor" against motions under Rule 11 in that a party will not be subject to sanctions on the basis of another party's motion unless, after receiving the motion, it refuses to withdraw that position or to acknowledge candidly that it does not currently have evidence to support a specified allegation. Under the former rule, parties were sometimes reluctant to abandon a questionable contention lest that be viewed as evidence of a violation of Rule 11; under the revision, the timely withdrawal of a contention will protect a party against a motion for sanctions.

To stress the seriousness of a motion for sanctions and to define precisely the conduct claimed to violate the rule, the revision provides that the "safe harbor" period begins to run only upon service of the motion. In most cases, however, counsel should be expected to give informal notice to the other party, whether in person or by a telephone call or letter, of a potential violation before proceeding to prepare and serve a Rule 11 motion.

As under former Rule 11, the filing of a motion for sanctions is itself subject to the requirements of the rule and can lead to sanctions. However, service of a cross motion under Rule 11 should rarely be needed since under the revision the court may award to the person who prevails on a motion under Rule 11 — whether the movant or the target of the motion — reasonable expenses, including attorney's fees, incurred in presenting or opposing the motion.

The power of the court to act on its own initiative is retained, but with the condition that this be done through a show cause order. This procedure provides the person with notice and an opportunity to respond. The revision provides that a monetary sanction imposed after a court-initiated show cause order be limited to a penalty payable to the court and that it be imposed only if the show cause order is issued before any voluntary dismissal or an agreement of the parties to settle the claims made by or against the litigant. Parties settling a case should not be subsequently faced with an unexpected order from the court leading to monetary sanctions that might have affected their willingness to settle or voluntarily dismiss a case. Since show cause orders will ordinarily be issued only in situations that are akin to a contempt of court, the rule does not provide a "safe harbor" to a litigant for withdrawing a claim, defense, etc., after a show cause order has been issued on the court's own initiative. Such corrective action, however, should be taken into account in deciding what — if any — sanction to impose if, after consideration of the litigant's response, the court concludes that a violation has occurred.

Subdivision (d). Rules 26(g) and 37 establish certification standards and sanctions that apply to discovery disclosures, requests, responses, objections, and motions. It is appropriate that Rules 26 through 37, which are specially designed for the discovery process, govern such documents and conduct rather than the more general provisions of Rule 11. Subdivision (d) has been added to accomplish this result.

Rule 11 is not the exclusive source for control of improper presentations of claims, defenses, or contentions. It does not supplant statutes permitting awards of attorney's fees to prevailing parties or alter the principles governing such awards. It does not inhibit the court in punishing for contempt, in exercising its inherent powers, or in imposing sanctions, awarding expenses, or directing remedial action authorized under other rules or under 28 U.S.C. § 1927. *See Chambers v. NASCO*, [501] U.S. [32] (1991). Chambers cautions, however, against reliance upon inherent powers if appropriate sanctions can be imposed under provisions such as Rule 11, and the procedures specified in Rule 11 — notice, opportunity to respond, and findings — should ordinarily be employed when imposing a sanction under the court's inherent powers. Finally, it should be noted that Rule 11 does not preclude a party from initiating an independent action for malicious prosecution or abuse of process.

Rule 12. Defenses and Objections — When and How Presented — By Pleading or Motion — Motion for Judgment on Pleadings

(a) When Presented.

(1) Unless a different time is prescribed in a statute of the United States, a defendant shall serve an answer

(A) within 20 days after being served with the summons and complaint, or

(B) if service of the summons has been timely waived on request under Rule 4(d), within 60 days after the date when the request for waiver was sent, or within 90 days after that date if the defendant was addressed outside any judicial district of the United States.

(2) A party served with a pleading stating a cross-claim against that party shall serve an answer thereto within 20 days after being served. The plaintiff shall serve a reply to a counterclaim in the answer within 20 days after service of the answer, or, if a reply is ordered by the court, within 20 days after service of the order, unless the order otherwise directs.

(3) **(A)** The United States, an agency of the United States, or an officer or employee of the United States sued in an official capacity, shall serve an answer to the complaint or cross-claim — or a reply to a counterclaim — within 60 days after the United States attorney is served with the pleading asserting the claim.

(B) An officer or employee of the United States sued in an individual capacity for acts or omissions occurring in connection with the performance of duties on behalf of the United States shall serve an answer to the complaint or cross-claim — or a reply to a counterclaim — within 60 days after service on the officer or employee, or service on the United States attorney, whichever is later.

(4) Unless a different time is fixed by court order, the service of a motion permitted under this rule alters these periods of time as follows:

(A) if the court denies the motion or postpones its disposition until the trial on the merits, the responsive pleading shall be served within 10 days after notice of the court's action; or

(B) if the court grants a motion for a more definite statement, the responsive pleading shall be served within 10 days after the service of the more definite statement.

(b) How Presented. Every defense, in law or fact, to a claim for relief in any pleading, whether a claim, counterclaim, cross-claim, or third-party claim, shall be asserted in the responsive pleading thereto if one is required, except that the following defenses may at the option of the pleader be made by motion: (1) lack of jurisdiction over the subject matter, (2) lack of jurisdiction over the person, (3) improper venue, (4) insufficiency of process, (5) insufficiency of service of process, (6) failure to state a claim upon which relief can be granted, (7) failure to join a party under Rule 19. A motion making any of these defenses shall be made before pleading if a further pleading is permitted. No defense or objection is waived by being joined with one or more other defenses or objections in a responsive pleading or motion. If a pleading sets forth a claim for relief to which the adverse party is not required to serve a responsive pleading, the adverse party may assert at the trial any defense in law or fact to that claim for relief. If, on a motion asserting the defense numbered (6) to dismiss for failure of the pleading to state a claim upon which relief can be granted, matters outside the pleading are presented to and not excluded by the court, the motion shall be treated as one for summary judgment and disposed of as provided in Rule 56, and all parties shall be given reasonable opportunity to present all material made pertinent to such a motion by Rule 56.

(c) Motion for Judgment on the Pleadings. After the pleadings are closed but within such time as not to delay the trial, any party may move for judgment on the pleadings. If, on a motion for judgment on the pleadings, matters outside the pleadings are presented to and not excluded by the court, the motion shall be treated as one for summary judgment and disposed of as provided in Rule 56, and all parties shall be given reasonable opportunity to present all material made pertinent to such a motion by Rule 56.

(d) Preliminary Hearings. The defenses specifically enumerated (1)-(7) in subdivision (b) of this rule, whether made in a pleading or by motion, and the motion for judgment mentioned in subdivision (c) of this rule shall be heard and determined before trial on application of any party, unless the court orders that the hearing and determination thereof be deferred until the trial.

(e) Motion for More Definite Statement. If a pleading to which a responsive pleading is permitted is so vague or ambiguous that a party cannot reasonably be required to frame a responsive pleading, the party may move for a more definite statement before interposing a responsive pleading. The motion shall point out the defects complained of and the details desired. If the motion is granted and the order of the court is not obeyed within 10 days after notice of the order or within such other time as the court may fix, the court may strike the pleading to which the motion was directed or make such order as it deems just.

(f) Motion to Strike. Upon motion made by a party before responding to a pleading or, if no responsive pleading is permitted by these rules, upon motion made by a party within 20 days after the service of the pleading upon the party or upon the court's own initiative at any time, the court may order stricken from any pleading any insufficient defense or any redundant, immaterial, impertinent, or scandalous matter.

(g) Consolidation of Defenses in Motion. A party who makes a motion under this rule may join with it any other motions herein provided for and then available to the party. If a party makes a motion under this rule but omits therefrom any defense or objection then available to the party which this rule permits to be raised by motion, the party shall not thereafter make a motion based on the defense or objection so omitted, except a motion as provided in subdivision (h)(2) hereof on any of the grounds there stated.

(h) Waiver or Preservation of Certain Defenses.

(1) A defense of lack of jurisdiction over the person, improper venue, insufficiency of process, or insufficiency of service of process is waived (A) if omitted from a motion in the circumstances described in subdivision (g), or (B) if it is neither made by motion under this rule nor included in a responsive pleading or an amendment thereof permitted by Rule 15(a) to be made as a matter of course.

(2) A defense of failure to state a claim upon which relief can be granted, a defense of failure to join a party indispensable under Rule 19, and an objection of failure to state a legal defense to a claim may be made in any pleading permitted or ordered under Rule 7(a), or by motion for judgment on the pleadings, or at the trial on the merits.

(3) Whenever it appears by suggestion of the parties or otherwise that the court lacks jurisdiction of the subject matter, the court shall dismiss the action.

ADVISORY COMMITTEE NOTES

1966 Amendment [citations omitted without notation — ED.]

. . .

Subdivision (g). Subdivision (g) has forbidden a defendant who makes a preanswer motion under this rule from making a further motion presenting any defense or objection which was available to him at the time he made the first motion and which he could have included, but did not in fact include therein. Thus if the defendant moves before answer to dismiss the complaint for failure to state a claim, he is barred from making a further motion presenting the defense of improper venue, if that defense was available to him when he made his original motion. Amended subdivision (g) is to the same effect. This required consolidation of defenses and objections in a Rule 12 motion is salutary in that it works against piecemeal consideration of a case. For exceptions to the requirement of consolidation, see the last clause of subdivision (g), referring to new subdivision (h)(2).

Subdivision (h). The question has arisen whether an omitted defense which cannot be made the basis of a second motion may nevertheless be pleaded in the answer. Subdivision (h) called for waiver of "... defenses and objections which he [defendant] does not present ... by motion ... or, if he has made no motion, in his answer ...." If the clause "if he has made no motion," was read literally, it seemed that the omitted defense was waived and could not be pleaded in the answer. On the other hand, the clause might be read as adding nothing of substance to the preceding words; in that event it appeared that a defense was not waived by reason of being omitted from the motion and might be set up in the answer. The decisions were divided.

Amended subdivision (h)(1)(A) eliminates the ambiguity and states that certain specified defenses which were available to a party when he made a preanswer motion, but which he omitted from the motion, are waived. The specified defenses are lack of jurisdiction over the person, improper venue, insufficiency of process, and insufficiency of service of process (see Rule 12(b)(2)-(5)). A party who by motion invites the court to pass upon a threshold defense should bring forward all the specified defenses he then has and thus allow the court to do a reasonably complete job. The waiver reinforces the policy of subdivision (g) forbidding successive motions.

By amended subdivision (h)(1)(B), the specified defenses, even if not waived by the operation of (A), are waived by the failure to raise them by a motion under Rule 12 or in the responsive pleading or any amendment thereof to which the party is entitled as a matter of course. The specified defenses are of such a character that they should not be delayed and brought up for the first time by means of an application to the court to amend the responsive pleading.

Since the language of the subdivisions is made clear, the party is put on fair notice of the effect of his actions and omissions and can guard himself against unintended waiver. It is to be noted that while the defenses specified in subdivision (h)(1) are subject to waiver as there provided, the more substantial defenses of failure to state a claim upon which relief can be granted, failure to join a party indispensable under Rule 19, and failure to state a legal defense to a claim (see Rule 12(b)(6), (7), (f)), as well as the defense of lack of jurisdiction over the subject matter (see Rule 12(b)(1)), are expressly preserved against waiver by amended subdivision (h)(2) and (3).

Rule 13. Counterclaim and Cross-Claim

(a) Compulsory Counterclaims. A pleading shall state as a counterclaim any claim which at the time of serving the pleading the pleader has against any opposing party, if it arises out of the transaction or occurrence that is the subject matter of the opposing party's claim and does not require for its adjudication the presence of third parties of whom the court cannot acquire jurisdiction. But the pleader need not state the claim if (1) at the time the action was commenced the claim was the subject of another pending action, or (2) the opposing party brought suit upon the claim by attachment or other process by which the court did not acquire jurisdiction to render a personal judgment on that claim, and the pleader is not stating any counterclaim under this Rule 13.

(b) Permissive Counterclaims. A pleading may state as a counterclaim any claim against an opposing party not arising out of the transaction or occurrence that is the subject matter of the opposing party's claim.

(c) Counterclaim Exceeding Opposing Claim. A counterclaim may or may not diminish or defeat the recovery sought by the opposing party. It may claim relief exceeding in amount or different in kind from that sought in the pleading of the opposing party.

(d) Counterclaim Against the United States. These rules shall not be construed to enlarge beyond the limits now fixed by law the right to assert counterclaims or to claim credits against the United States or an officer or agency thereof.

(e) Counterclaim Maturing or Acquired After Pleading. A claim which either matured or was acquired by the pleader after serving a pleading may, with the permission of the court, be presented as a counterclaim by supplemental pleading.

(f) Omitted Counterclaim. When a pleader fails to set up a counterclaim through oversight, inadvertence, or excusable neglect, or when justice requires, the pleader may by leave of court set up the counterclaim by amendment.

(g) Cross-Claim Against Co-Party. A pleading may state as a cross-claim any claim by one party against a co-party arising out of the transaction or occurrence that is the subject matter either of the original action or of a counterclaim therein or relating to any property that is the subject matter of the original action. Such cross-claim may include a claim that the party against whom it is asserted is or may be liable to the cross-claimant for all or part of a claim asserted in the action against the cross-claimant.

(h) Joinder of Additional Parties. Persons other than those made parties to the original action may be made parties to a counterclaim or cross-claim in accordance with the provisions of Rules 19 and 20.

(i) Separate Trials; Separate Judgments. If the court orders separate trials as provided in Rule 42(b), judgment on a counterclaim or cross-claim may be rendered in accordance with the terms of Rule 54(b) when the court has jurisdiction so to do, even if the claims of the opposing party have been dismissed or otherwise disposed of.

Rule 14. Third-Party Practice

(a) When Defendant May Bring in Third Party. At any time after commencement of the action a defending party, as a third-party plaintiff, may cause a summons and complaint to be served upon a person not a party to the action who is or may be liable to the third-party plaintiff for all or part of the plaintiff's claim against the third-party plaintiff. The third-party plaintiff need not obtain leave to make the service if the third-party plaintiff files the third-party complaint not later than 10 days after serving the original answer. Otherwise the third-party plaintiff must obtain leave on motion upon notice to all parties to the action. The person served with the summons and third-party complaint, hereinafter called the third-party defendant, shall make any defenses to the third-party plaintiff's claim as provided in Rule 12 and any counterclaims against the third-party plaintiff and cross-claims against other third-party defendants as provided in Rule 13. The third-party defendant may assert against the plaintiff any defenses which the third-party plaintiff has to the plaintiff's claim. The third-party defendant may also assert any claim against the plaintiff arising out of the transaction or occurrence that is the subject matter of the plaintiff's claim against the third-party plaintiff. The plaintiff may assert any claim against the third-party defendant arising out of the transaction or occurrence that is the subject matter of the plaintiff's claim against the third-party plaintiff, and the third-party defendant thereupon shall assert any defenses as provided in Rule 12 and any counterclaims and cross-claims as provided in Rule 13. Any party may move to strike the third-party claim, or for its severance or separate trial. A third-party defendant may proceed under this rule against any person not a party to the action who is or may be liable to the third-party defendant for all or part of the claim made in the action against the third-party defendant. The third-party complaint, if within the admiralty and maritime jurisdiction, may be in rem against a vessel, cargo, or other property subject to admiralty or maritime process in rem, in which case references in this rule to the summons include the warrant of arrest, and references to the third-party plaintiff or defendant include, where appropriate, a person who asserts a right under Supplemental Rule C(6)(a)(i) in the property arrested.

(b) When Plaintiff May Bring in Third Party. When a counterclaim is asserted against a plaintiff, the plaintiff may cause a third party to be brought in under circumstances which under this rule would entitle a defendant to do so.

(c) Admiralty and Maritime Claims. When a plaintiff asserts an admiralty or maritime claim within the meaning of Rule 9(h), the defendant or person who asserts a right under Supplemental Rule C(6)(a)(i), as a third-party plaintiff, may bring in a third-party defendant who may be wholly or partly liable, either to the plaintiff or to the third-party plaintiff, by way of remedy over, contribution, or otherwise on account of the same transaction, occurrence, or series of transactions or occurrences. In such a case the third-party plaintiff may also demand judgment against the third-party defendant in favor of the plaintiff, in which event the third-party defendant shall make any defenses to the claim of the plaintiff as well as to that of the third-party plaintiff in the manner provided in Rule 12 and the action shall proceed as if the plaintiff had commenced it against the third-party defendant as well as the third-party plaintiff.

Rule 15. Amended and Supplemental Pleadings

(a) Amendments. A party may amend the party's pleading once as a matter of course at any time before a responsive pleading is served or, if the pleading is one to which no responsive pleading is permitted and the action has not been placed upon the trial calendar, the party may so amend it at any time within 20 days after it is served. Otherwise a party may amend the party's pleading only by leave of court or by written consent of the adverse party; and leave shall be freely given when justice so requires. A party shall plead in response to an amended pleading within the time remaining for response to the original pleading or within 10 days after service of the amended pleading, whichever period may be the longer, unless the court otherwise orders.

notice + lack of prejudice

(b) Amendments to Conform to the Evidence. When issues not raised by the pleadings are tried by express or implied consent of the parties, they shall be treated in all respects as if they had been raised in the pleadings. Such amendment of the pleadings as may be necessary to cause them to conform to the evidence and to raise these issues may be made upon motion of any party at any time, even after judgment; but failure so to amend does not affect the result of the trial of these issues. If evidence is objected to at the trial on the ground that it is not within the issues made by the pleadings, the court may allow the pleadings to be amended and shall do so freely when the presentation of the merits of the action will be subserved thereby and the objecting party fails to satisfy the court that the admission of such evidence would prejudice the party in maintaining the party's action or defense upon the merits. The court may grant a continuance to enable the objecting party to meet such evidence.

(c) Relation Back of Amendments. An amendment of a pleading relates back to the date of the original pleading when

(1) relation back is permitted by the law that provides the statute of limitations applicable to the action, or

(2) the claim or defense asserted in the amended pleading arose out of the conduct, transaction, or occurrence set forth or attempted to be set forth in the original pleading, or

(3) the amendment changes the party or the naming of the party against whom a claim is asserted if the foregoing provision (2) is satisfied and, within the period provided by Rule 4(m) for service of the summons and complaint, the party to be brought in by amendment (A) has received such notice of the institution of the action that the party will not be prejudiced in maintaining a defense on the merits, and (B) knew or should have known that, but for a mistake concerning the identity of the proper party, the action would have been brought against the party.

The delivery or mailing of process to the United States Attorney, or United States Attorney's designee, or the Attorney General of the United States, or an agency or officer who would have been a proper defendant if named, satisfies the requirement of subparagraphs (A) and (B) of this paragraph (3) with respect to the United States or any agency or officer thereof to be brought into the action as a defendant.

(d) Supplemental Pleadings. Upon motion of a party the court may, upon reasonable notice and upon such terms as are just, permit the party to serve a supplemental pleading setting forth transactions or occurrences or events which have happened since the date of the pleading sought to be supplemented. Permission may be granted even though the original pleading is defective in its statement of a claim for relief or defense. If the court deems it advisable that the adverse party plead to the supplemental pleading, it shall so order, specifying the time therefor.

ADVISORY COMMITTEE NOTES

1991 Amendment [citations omitted without notation — ED.]

The rule has been revised to prevent parties against whom claims are made from taking unjust advantage of otherwise inconsequential pleading errors to sustain a limitations defense.

Paragraph (c)(1). This provision is new. It is intended to make it clear that the rule does not apply to preclude any relation back that may be permitted under the applicable limitations law. Generally, the applicable limitations law will be state law. If federal jurisdiction is based on the citizenship of the parties, the primary reference is the law of the state in which the district court sits. *Walker v. Armco Steel Corp.*, 446 U.S. 740 (1980). If federal jurisdiction is based on a federal question, the reference may be to the law of the state governing relations between the parties. *E.g.*, *Board of Regents v. Tomanio*, 446 U.S. 478 (1980). In some circumstances, the controlling limitations law may be federal law. *E.g.*, *West v. Conrail, Inc.*, [481 U.S. 35] (1987). Cf. *Burlington Northern R. Co. v. Woods*, 480 U.S. 1 (1987); *Stewart Organization v. Ricoh*, [487 U.S. 22] (1988). Whatever may be the controlling body of limitations law, if that law affords a more forgiving principle of relation back than the one provided in this rule, it should be available to save the claim. Accord, *Marshall v. Mulrenin,* 508 F.2d 39 (1st Cir. 1974). If *Schiavone v. Fortune*, [477 U.S. 21] (1986) implies the contrary, this paragraph is intended to make a material change in the rule.

Paragraph (c)(3). This paragraph has been revised to change the result in *Schiavone v. Fortune, supra,* with respect to the problem of a misnamed defendant. An intended defendant who is notified of an action within the period allowed by Rule 4(m) [present Rule 4(m) was proposed as part of these 1991 amendments but was withdrawn by the Supreme Court; Rule 4(m) was ultimately promulgated in 1993 — ED.] for service of a summons and complaint may not under the revised rule defeat the action on account of a defect in the pleading with respect to the defendant's name, provided that the requirements of clauses (A) and (B) have been met. If the notice requirement is met within the Rule 4(m) [see above — ED.]

period, a complaint may be amended at any time to correct a formal defect such as a misnomer or misidentification. On the basis of the text of the former rule, the Court reached a result in *Schiavone v. Fortune* that was inconsistent with the liberal pleading practices secured by Rule 8.

In allowing a name-correcting amendment within the time allowed by Rule 4([j]), this rule allows not only the 120 days specified in that rule, but also any additional time resulting from any extension ordered by the court pursuant to that rule, as may be granted, for example, if the defendant is a fugitive from service of the summons. . . .

Rule 16. Pretrial Conferences; Scheduling; Management

(a) Pretrial Conferences; Objectives. In any action, the court may in its discretion direct the attorneys for the parties and any unrepresented parties to appear before it for a conference or conferences before trial for such purposes as

(1) expediting the disposition of the action;

(2) establishing early and continuing control so that the case will not be protracted because of lack of management;

(3) discouraging wasteful pretrial activities;

(4) improving the quality of the trial through more thorough preparation, and;

(5) facilitating the settlement of the case.

(b) Scheduling and Planning. Except in categories of actions exempted by district court rule as inappropriate, the district judge, or a magistrate judge when authorized by district court rule, shall, after receiving the report from the parties under Rule 26(f) or after consulting with the attorneys for the parties and any unrepresented parties by a scheduling conference, telephone, mail, or other suitable means, enter a scheduling order that limits the time

(1) to join other parties and to amend the pleadings;

(2) to file motions; and

(3) to complete discovery.

The scheduling order may also include

(4) modifications of the times for disclosures under Rules 26(a) and 26(e)(1) and of the extent of discovery to be permitted;

(5) provisions for disclosure or discovery of electronically stored information;

(6) any agreements the parties reach for asserting claims of privilege or of protection as trial-preparation material after production;

(7) the date or dates for conferences before trial, a final pretrial conference, and trial; and

(8) any other matters appropriate in the circumstances of the case.

The order shall issue as soon as practicable but in any event within 90 days after the appearance of a defendant and within 120 days after the complaint has been served on a defendant. A schedule shall not be modified except upon a showing of good cause and by leave of the district judge or, when authorized by local rule, by a magistrate judge.

(c) Subjects for Consideration at Pretrial Conferences. At any conference under this rule consideration may be given, and the court may take appropriate action, with respect to

(1) the formulation and simplification of the issues, including the elimination of frivolous claims or defenses;

(2) the necessity or desirability of amendments to the pleadings;

(3) the possibility of obtaining admissions of fact and of documents which will avoid unnecessary proof, stipulations regarding the authenticity of documents, and advance rulings from the court on the admissibility of evidence;

(4) the avoidance of unnecessary proof and of cumulative evidence, and limitations or restrictions on the use of testimony under Rule 702 of the Federal Rules of Evidence;

(5) the appropriateness and timing of summary adjudication under Rule 56;

(6) the control and scheduling of discovery, including orders affecting disclosures and discovery pursuant to Rule 26 and Rules 29 through 37;

(7) the identification of witnesses and documents, the need and schedule for filing and exchanging pretrial briefs, and the date or dates for further conferences and for trial;

(8) the advisability of referring matters to a magistrate judge or master;

(9) settlement and the use of special procedures to assist in resolving the dispute when authorized by statute or local rule;

(10) the form and substance of the pretrial order;

(11) the disposition of pending motions;

(12) the need for adopting special procedures for managing potentially difficult or protracted actions that may involve complex issues, multiple parties, difficult legal questions, or unusual proof problems;

(13) an order for a separate trial pursuant to Rule 42(b) with respect to a claim, counterclaim, cross-claim, or third-party claim, or with respect to any particular issue in the case;

(14) an order directing a party or parties to present evidence early in the trial with respect to a manageable issue that could, on the evidence, be the basis for a judgment as a matter of law under Rule 50(a) or a judgment on partial findings under Rule 52(c);

(15) an order establishing a reasonable limit on the time allowed for presenting evidence; and

(16) such other matters as may facilitate the just, speedy, and inexpensive disposition of the action.

At least one of the attorneys for each party participating in any conference before trial shall have authority to enter into stipulations and to make admissions regarding all matters that the participants may reasonably anticipate may be discussed. If appropriate, the court may require that a party or its representative be present or reasonably available by telephone in order to consider possible settlement of the dispute.

(d) Final Pretrial Conference. Any final pretrial conference shall be held as close to the time of trial as reasonable under the circumstances. The participants at any such conference shall formulate a plan for trial, including a program for facilitating the admission of evidence. The conference shall be attended by at least one of the attorneys who will conduct the trial for each of the parties and by any unrepresented parties.

(e) Pretrial Orders. After any conference held pursuant to this rule, an order shall be entered reciting the action taken. This order shall control the subsequent course of the action unless modified by a subsequent order. The order following a final pretrial conference shall be modified only to prevent manifest injustice.

(f) Sanctions. If a party or party's attorney fails to obey a scheduling or pretrial order, or if no appearance is made on behalf of a party at a scheduling or pretrial conference, or if a party or party's attorney is substantially unprepared to participate in the conference, or if a party or party's attorney fails to participate in good faith, the judge, upon motion or the judge's own initiative, may make such orders with regard thereto as are just, and among others any of the orders provided in Rule 37(b)(2)(B), (C), (D). In lieu of or in addition to any other sanction, the judge shall require the party or the attorney representing the party or both to pay the reasonable expenses incurred because of any noncompliance with this rule, including attorney's fees, unless the judge finds that the noncompliance was substantially justified or that other circumstances make an award of expenses unjust.

ADVISORY COMMITTEE NOTES

1983 Amendment [citations omitted without notation — ED.]

Introduction

Rule 16 has not been amended since the Federal Rules were promulgated in 1938. In many respects, the rule has been a success. For example, there is evidence that pretrial conferences may improve the quality of justice rendered in the federal courts by sharpening the preparation and presentation of cases, tending to eliminate trial surprise, and improving, as well as facilitating, the settlement process. See 6 Wright & Miller, *Federal Practice and Procedure:* Civil § 1522 (1971). However, in other respects particularly with regard to case management, the rule has not always been as helpful as it might have been. Thus there has been a widespread feeling that amendment is necessary to encourage pretrial management that meets the needs of modern litigation. See *Report of the National Commission for the Review of Antitrust Laws and Procedures* (1979).

Major criticism of Rule 16 has centered on the fact that its application can result in over-regulation of some cases and under-regulation of others. In simple, run-of-the-mill cases, attorneys have found pretrial requirements burdensome. It is claimed that over-administration leads to a series of mini-trials that result in a waste of an attorney's time and needless expense to a client. Pollack, *Pretrial Procedures More Effectively Handled,* 65 F.R.D. 475 (1974). This is especially likely to be true when pretrial proceedings occur long before trial. At the other end of the spectrum, the discretionary character of Rule 16 and its orientation toward a single conference late in the pretrial process has led to under-administration of complex or protracted cases. Without judicial guidance beginning shortly after institution, these cases often become mired in discovery.

Four sources of criticism of pretrial have been identified. First, conferences often are seen as a mere exchange of legalistic contentions without any real analysis of the particular case. Second, the result frequently is nothing but a formal agreement on minutiae. Third, the conferences are seen as unnecessary and time-consuming in cases that will be settled before trial. Fourth, the meetings can be ceremonial and ritualistic, having little effect on the trial and being of minimal value, particularly when the attorneys attending the sessions are not the ones who will try the case or lack authority to enter into binding stipulations.

There also have been difficulties with the pretrial orders that issue following Rule 16 conferences. When an order is entered far in advance of trial, some issues may not be properly formulated. Counsel naturally are cautious and often try to preserve as many options as possible. If the judge who tries the case did not conduct the conference, he could find it difficult to determine exactly what was agreed to at the conference. But any insistence on a detailed order may be too burdensome, depending on the nature or posture of the case.

Given the significant changes in federal civil litigation since 1938 that are not reflected in Rule 16, it has been extensively rewritten and expanded to meet the challenges of modern litigation. Empirical studies reveal that when a trial judge intervenes personally at an early stage to assume judicial control over a case and to schedule dates for completion by the parties of the principal pretrial steps, the case is disposed of by settlement or trial more efficiently and with less cost and delay than when the parties are left to their own devices. Flanders, *Case Management and Court Management in United States District Courts* 17, Federal Judicial Center (1977). Thus, the rule mandates a pretrial scheduling order. However, although scheduling and pretrial conferences are encouraged in appropriate cases, they are not mandated.

Discussion

Subdivision (a); Pretrial Conferences; Objectives. The amended rule makes scheduling and case management an express goal of pretrial procedure. This is done in Rule 16(a) by shifting the emphasis away from a conference focused solely on the trial and toward a process of judicial management that embraces the entire pretrial phase, especially motions and discovery. In addition, the amendment explicitly recognizes some of the objectives of pretrial conferences and the powers that many courts already have assumed. Rule 16 thus will be a more accurate reflection of actual practice.

Subdivision (b); Scheduling and Planning. The most significant change in Rule 16 is the mandatory scheduling order described in Rule 16(b), which is based in part on Wisconsin Civil Procedure Rule 802.10. The idea of scheduling orders is not new. It has been used by many federal courts. See, *e.g.,* Southern District of Indiana, Local Rule 19.

Although a mandatory scheduling order encourages the court to become involved in case management early in the litigation, it represents a degree of judicial involvement that is not warranted in many cases. Thus, subdivision (b) permits each district court to promulgate a local rule under Rule 83 exempting certain categories of cases in which the burdens of scheduling orders exceed the administrative efficiencies that would be gained. See Eastern District of Virginia, Local Rule 12(1). Logical candidates for this treatment include social security disability matters, habeas corpus petitions, forfeitures, and reviews of certain administrative actions.

A scheduling conference may be requested either by the judge, a magistrate when authorized by district court rule, or a party within 120 days after the summons and complaint are filed. If a scheduling conference is not arranged within that time and the case is not exempted by local rule, a scheduling order must be issued under Rule 16(b), after some communication with the parties, which may be by telephone or mail rather than in person. The use of the term "judge" in subdivision (b) reflects the Advisory Committee's judgment that it is preferable that this task should be handled by a district judge rather than a magistrate, except when the magistrate is acting under 28 U.S.C. § 636(c). While personal supervision by the trial judge is preferred, the rule, in recognition of the impracticality or difficulty of complying with such a requirement in some districts, authorizes a district by local rule to delegate the duties to a magistrate. In order to formulate a practicable scheduling order, the judge, or a magistrate when authorized by district court rule, and attorneys are required to develop a timetable for the matters listed in Rule 16(b)(1)-(3). As indicated in Rule 16(b)(4)-(5), the order may also deal with a wide range of other matters. The rule is phrased permissively as to clauses (4) and (5), however, because scheduling these items at an early point may not be feasible or appropriate. Even though subdivision (b) relates only to scheduling, there is no reason why some of the procedural matters listed in Rule 16(c) cannot be addressed at the same time, at least when a scheduling conference is held.

Item (1) assures that at some point both the parties and the pleadings will be fixed, by setting a time within which joinder of parties shall be completed and the pleadings amended.

Item (2) requires setting time limits for interposing various motions that otherwise might be used as stalling techniques.

Item (3) deals with the problem of procrastination and delay by attorneys in a context in which scheduling is especially important-discovery. Scheduling the completion of discovery can serve some of the same functions as the conference described in Rule 26(f).

Item (4) refers to setting dates for conferences and for trial. Scheduling multiple pretrial conferences may well be desirable if the case is complex and the court believes that a more elaborate pretrial structure, such as that described in the *Manual for Complex Litigation,* should be employed. On the other hand, only one pretrial conference may be necessary in an uncomplicated case.

As long as the case is not exempted by local rule, the court must issue a written scheduling order even if no scheduling conference is called. The order, like pretrial orders under the former rule and those under new Rule 16(c), normally will "control the subsequent course of the action." See Rule 16(e). After consultation with the attorneys for the parties and any unrepresented parties-a formal motion is not necessary-the court may modify the schedule on a showing of good cause if it cannot reasonably be met despite the diligence of the party seeking the extension. Since the scheduling order is entered early in the litigation, this standard seems more appropriate than a "manifest injustice" or "substantial hardship" test. Otherwise, a fear that extensions will not be granted may encourage counsel to request the longest possible periods for completing pleading, joinder, and discovery. Moreover, changes in the court's calendar sometimes will oblige the judge or magistrate when authorized by district court rule to modify the scheduling order.

The district courts undoubtedly will develop several prototype scheduling orders for different types of cases. In addition, when no formal conference is held, the court may obtain scheduling information by telephone, mail, or otherwise. In many instances this will result in a scheduling order better suited to the individual case than a standard order, without taking the time that would be required by a formal conference.

Rule 16(b) assures that the judge will take some early control over the litigation, even when its character does not warrant holding a scheduling conference. Despite the fact that the process of preparing a scheduling order does not always bring the attorneys and judge together, the fixing of time limits serves

> to stimulate litigants to narrow the areas of inquiry and advocacy to those they believe are truly relevant and material. Time limits not only compress the amount of time for litigation, they should also reduce the amount of resources invested in litigation. Litigants are forced to establish discovery priorities and thus to do the most important work first.

Report of the National Commission for the Review of Antitrust Laws and Procedures 28 (1979).

Thus, except in exempted cases, the judge or a magistrate when authorized by district court rule will have taken some action in every case within 120 days after the complaint is filed that notifies the attorneys that the case will be moving toward trial. Subdivision (b) is reenforced by subdivision (f), which makes it clear that the sanctions for violating a scheduling order are the same as those for violating a pretrial order.

Subdivision (c); Subjects to be Discussed at Pretrial Conferences. This subdivision expands upon the list of things that may be discussed at a pretrial conference that appeared in original Rule 16. The intention is to encourage better planning and management of litigation. Increased judicial control during the pretrial process accelerates the processing and termination of cases. Flanders, *Case Management and Court Management in United States District Courts*, 39 Federal Judicial Center (1977). See also *Report of the National Commission for the Review of Antitrust Laws and Procedures* (1979).

The reference in Rule 16(c)(1) to "formulation" is intended to clarify and confirm the court's power to identify the litigable issues. It has been added in the hope of promoting efficiency and conserving judicial resources by identifying the real issues prior to trial, thereby saving time and expense for everyone. The notion is emphasized by expressly authorizing the elimination of frivolous claims or defenses at a pretrial conference. There is no reason to require that this await a formal motion for summary judgment. Nor is there any reason for the court to wait for the parties to initiate the process called for in Rule 16(c)(1).

The timing of any attempt at issue formulation is a matter of judicial discretion. In relatively simple cases it may not be necessary or may take the form of a stipulation between counsel or a request by the court that counsel work together to draft a proposed order.

Counsel bear a substantial responsibility for assisting the court in identifying the factual issues worthy of trial. If counsel fail to identify an issue for the court, the right to have the issue tried is waived. Although an order specifying the issues is intended to be binding, it may be amended at trial to avoid manifest injustice. See Rule 16(e). However, the rule's effectiveness depends on the court employing its discretion sparingly.

Clause (6) acknowledges the widespread availability and use of magistrates. The corresponding provision in the original rule referred only to masters and limited the function of the reference to the making of "findings to be used as evidence" in a case to be tried to a jury. The new text is not limited and broadens the potential use of a magistrate to that permitted by the Magistrate's Act.

Clause (7) explicitly recognizes that it has become commonplace to discuss settlement at pretrial conferences. Since it obviously eases crowded court dockets and results in savings to the litigants and the judicial system, settlement should be facilitated at as early a stage of the litigation as possible. Although it is not the purpose of Rule 16(b)(7) to impose settlement negotiations on unwilling litigants, it is believed that providing a neutral forum for discussing the subject might foster it. For instance, a judge to whom a case has been assigned may arrange, on his own motion or at a party's request, to have settlement conferences handled by another member of the court or by a magistrate. The rule does not make settlement conferences mandatory because they would be a waste of time in many cases. See Flanders, *Case Management and Court Management in the United States District Courts*, 39 Federal Judicial Center (1977). Requests for a conference from a party indicating a willingness to talk settlement normally should be honored, unless thought to be frivolous or dilatory.

A settlement conference is appropriate at any time. It may be held in conjunction with a pretrial or discovery conference, although various objectives of pretrial management, such as moving the case toward trial, may not always be compatible with settlement negotiations, and thus a separate settlement conference may be desirable.

In addition to settlement, Rule 16(c)(7) refers to exploring the use of procedures other than litigation to resolve the dispute. This includes urging the litigants to employ adjudicatory techniques outside the courthouse. See, for example, the experiment described in *Green, Marks & Olson, Settling Large Case Litigation: An Alternative Approach*, 11 Loyola of L.A. L. Rev. 493 (1978).

Rule 16(c)(10) authorizes the use of special pretrial procedures to expedite the adjudication of potentially difficult or protracted cases. Some district courts obviously have done so for many years. See Rubin, *The Managed Calendar: Some Pragmatic Suggestions About Achieving the Just, Speedy and Inexpensive Determination of Civil Cases in Federal Courts,* 4 Just. Sys. J. 135 (1976). Clause 10 provides an explicit authorization for such procedures and encourages their use. No particular techniques have been described; the Committee felt that flexibility and experience are the keys to efficient management of complex cases. Extensive guidance is offered in such documents as the *Manual for Complex Litigation.*

The rule simply identifies characteristics that make a case a strong candidate for special treatment. The four mentioned are illustrative, not exhaustive, and overlap to some degree. But experience has shown that one or more of them will be present in every protracted or difficult case and it seems desirable to set them out. See Kendig, *Procedures for Management of Non-Routine Cases,* 3 Hofstra L. Rev. 701 (1975).

The last sentence of subdivision (c) is new. See Wisconsin Civil Procedure Rule 802.11(2). It has been added to meet one of the criticisms of the present practice described earlier and insure proper preconference preparation so that the meeting is more than a ceremonial or ritualistic event. The reference to "authority" is not intended to insist upon the ability to settle the litigation. Nor should the rule be read to encourage the judge conducting the conference to compel attorneys to enter into stipulations or to make admissions that they consider to be unreasonable, that touch on matters that could not normally have been anticipated to arise at the conference, or on subjects of a dimension that normally require prior consultation with and approval from the client.

Subdivision (d); Final Pretrial Conference. This provision has been added to make it clear that the time between any final pretrial conference (which in a simple case may be the only pretrial conference) and trial should be as short as possible to be certain that the litigants make substantial progress with the case and avoid the inefficiency of having that preparation repeated when there is a delay between the last pretrial conference and trial. An optimum time of 10 days to two weeks has been suggested by one federal judge. Rubin, *The Managed Calendar: Some Pragmatic Suggestions About Achieving the Just, Speedy and Inexpensive Determination of Civil Cases in Federal Courts,* 4 Just. Sys. J. 135, 141 (1976). The Committee, however, concluded that it would be inappropriate to fix a precise time in the rule, given the numerous variables that could bear on the matter. Thus the timing has been left to the court's discretion.

At least one of the attorneys who will conduct the trial for each party must be present at the final pretrial conference. At this late date there should be no doubt as to which attorney or attorneys this will be. Since the agreements and stipulations made at this final conference will control the trial, the presence of lawyers who will be involved in it is especially useful to assist the judge in structuring the case, and to lead to a more effective trial.

Subdivision (e); Pretrial Orders. Rule 16(e) does not substantially change the portion of the original rule dealing with pretrial orders. The purpose of an order is to guide the course of the litigation and the language of the original rule making that clear has been retained. No compelling reason has been found for major revision, especially since this portion of the rule has been interpreted and clarified by over forty years of judicial decisions with comparatively little difficulty. See 6 Wright & Miller, *Federal Practice and Procedure*: Civil §§ 1521-30 (1971). Changes in language therefore have been kept to a minimum to avoid confusion.

Since the amended rule encourages more extensive pretrial management than did the original, two or more conferences may be held in many cases. The language of Rule 16(e) recognizes this possibility and the corresponding need to issue more than one pretrial order in a single case.

Once formulated, pretrial orders should not be changed lightly; but total inflexibility is undesirable. The exact words used to describe the standard for amending the pretrial order probably are less important than the meaning given them in practice. By not imposing any limitation on the ability to modify a pretrial order, the rule reflects the reality that in any process of continuous management, what is done at one conference may have to be altered at the next. In the case of the final pretrial order, however, a more stringent standard is called for and the words "to prevent manifest injustice," which appeared in the original rule, have been retained. They have the virtue of familiarity and adequately describe the restraint the trial judge should exercise.

Many local rules make the plaintiff's attorney responsible for drafting a proposed pretrial order, either before or after the conference. Others allow the court to appoint any of the attorneys to perform the task, and others leave it to the court. See Note, *Pretrial Conference: A Critical Examination of Local Rules Adopted by Federal District Courts,* 64 Va. L. Rev. 467 (1978). Rule 16 has never addressed this matter. Since there is no consensus about which method of drafting the order works best and there is no reason to believe that nationwide uniformity is needed, the rule has been left silent on the point. See *Handbook for Effective Pretrial Procedure,* 37 F.R.D. 225 (1964).

Subdivision (f); Sanctions. Original Rule 16 did not mention the sanctions that might be imposed for failing to comply with the rule. However, courts have not hesitated to enforce it by appropriate measures. See, e.g., *Link v. Wabash R.*

Co., 370 U.S. 628 (1962) (district court's dismissal under Rule 41(b) after plaintiff's attorney failed to appear at a pretrial conference upheld); Admiral Theatre Corp. v. Douglas Theatre, 585 F.2d 877 (8th Cir. 1978) (district court has discretion to exclude exhibits or refuse to permit the testimony of a witness not listed prior to trial in contravention of its pretrial order).

To reflect that existing practice, and to obviate dependence upon Rule 41(b) or the court's inherent power to regulate litigation, *cf. Societe Internationale Pour Participations Industrielles et Commerciales, S.A. v. Rogers*, 357 U.S. 197 (1958), Rule 16(f) expressly provides for imposing sanctions on disobedient or recalcitrant parties, their attorneys, or both in four types of situations. Rodes, Ripple & Mooney, *Sanctions Imposable for Violations of the Federal Rules of Civil Procedure* 65-67, 80-84, Federal Judicial Center (1981). Furthermore, explicit reference to sanctions reenforces the rule's intention to encourage forceful judicial management.

Rule 16(f) incorporates portions of Rule 37(b)(2), which prescribes sanctions for failing to make discovery. This should facilitate application of Rule 16(f), since courts and lawyers already are familiar with the Rule 37 standards. Among the sanctions authorized by the new subdivision are: preclusion order, striking a pleading, staying the proceeding, default judgment, contempt, and charging a party, his attorney, or both with the expenses, including attorney's fees, caused by noncompliance. The contempt sanction, however, is only available for a violation of a court order. The references in Rule 16(f) are not exhaustive.

As is true under Rule 37(b)(2), the imposition of sanctions may be sought by either the court or a party. In addition, the court has discretion to impose whichever sanction it feels is appropriate under the circumstances. Its action is reviewable under the abuse-of-discretion standard. See *National Hockey League v. Metropolitan Hockey Club, Inc.*, 427 U.S. 639 (1976).

1993 Amendments

Subdivision (b). One purpose of this amendment is to provide a more appropriate deadline for the initial scheduling order required by the rule. The former rule directed that the order be entered within 120 days from the filing of the complaint. This requirement has created problems because Rule 4(m) allows 120 days for service and ordinarily at least one defendant should be available to participate in the process of formulating the scheduling order. The revision provides that the order is to be entered within 90 days after the date a defendant first appears (whether by answer or by a motion under Rule 12) or, if earlier (as may occur in some actions against the United States or if service is waived under Rule 4), within 120 days after service of the complaint on a defendant. The longer time provided by the revision is not intended to encourage unnecessary delays in entering the scheduling order. Indeed, in most cases the order can and should be entered at a much earlier date. Rather, the additional time is intended to alleviate problems in multi-defendant cases and should ordinarily be adequate to enable participation by all defendants initially named in the action.

In many cases the scheduling order can and should be entered before this deadline. However, when setting a scheduling conference, the court should take into account the effect this setting will have in establishing deadlines for the parties to meet under revised Rule 26(f) and to exchange information under revised

Rule 26(a)(1). While the parties are expected to stipulate to additional time for making their disclosures when warranted by the circumstances, a scheduling conference held before defendants have had time to learn much about the case may result in diminishing the value of the Rule 26(f) meeting, the parties' proposed discovery plan, and indeed the conference itself.

New paragraph (4) has been added to highlight that it will frequently be desirable for the scheduling order to include provisions relating to the timing of disclosures under Rule 26(a). While the initial disclosures required by Rule 26(a)(1) will ordinarily have been made before entry of the scheduling order, the timing and sequence for disclosure of expert testimony and of the witnesses and exhibits to be used at trial should be tailored to the circumstances of the case and is a matter that should be considered at the initial scheduling conference. Similarly, the scheduling order might contain provisions modifying the extent of discovery (*e.g.*, number and length of depositions) otherwise permitted under these rules or by a local rule.

The report from the attorneys concerning their meeting and proposed discovery plan, as required by revised Rule 26(f), should be submitted to the court before the scheduling order is entered. Their proposals, particularly regarding matters on which they agree, should be of substantial value to the court in setting the timing and limitations on discovery and should reduce the time of the court needed to conduct a meaningful conference under Rule 16(b). As under the prior rule, while a scheduling order is mandated, a scheduling conference is not. However, in view of the benefits to be derived from the litigants and a judicial officer meeting in person, a Rule 16(b) conference should, to the extent practicable, be held in all cases that will involve discovery.

This subdivision, as well as subdivision (c)(8), also is revised to reflect the new title of United States Magistrate Judges pursuant to the Judicial Improvements Act of 1990.

Subdivision (c). The primary purposes of the changes in subdivision (c) are to call attention to the opportunities for structuring of trial under Rules 42, 50, and 52 and to eliminate questions that have occasionally been raised regarding the authority of the court to make appropriate orders designed either to facilitate settlement or to provide for an efficient and economical trial. The prefatory language of this subdivision is revised to clarify the court's power to enter appropriate orders at a conference notwithstanding the objection of a party. Of course settlement is dependent upon agreement by the parties and, indeed, a conference is most effective and productive when the parties participate in a spirit of cooperation and mindful of their responsibilities under Rule 1.

Paragraph (4) is revised to clarify that in advance of trial the court may address the need for, and possible limitations on, the use of expert testimony under Rule 702 of the Federal Rules of Evidence. Even when proposed expert testimony might be admissible under the standards of Rules 403 and 702 of the evidence rules, the court may preclude or limit such testimony if the cost to the litigants — which may include the cost to adversaries of securing testimony on the same subjects by other experts — would be unduly expensive given the needs of the case and the other evidence available at trial.

Paragraph (5) is added (and the remaining paragraphs renumbered) in recognition that use of Rule 56 to avoid or reduce the scope of trial is a topic that can, and often should, be considered at a pretrial conference. Renumbered paragraph (11) enables the court to rule on pending motions for summary adjudication that are ripe for decision at the time of the conference. Often, however, the potential use of Rule 56 is a matter that arises from discussions during a conference. The court may then call for motions to be filed.

Paragraph (6) is added to emphasize that a major objective of pretrial conferences should be to consider appropriate controls on the extent and timing of discovery. In many cases the court should also specify the times and sequence for disclosure of written reports from experts under revised Rule 26(a)(2)(B) and perhaps direct changes in the types of experts from whom written reports are required. Consideration should also be given to possible changes in the timing or form of the disclosure of trial witnesses and documents under Rule 26(a)(3).

Paragraph (9) is revised to describe more accurately the various procedures that, in addition to traditional settlement conferences, may be helpful in settling litigation. Even if a case cannot immediately be settled, the judge and attorneys can explore possible use of alternative procedures such as mini-trials, summary jury trials, mediation, neutral evaluation, and nonbinding arbitration that can lead to consensual resolution of the dispute without a full trial on the merits. The rule acknowledges the presence of statutes and local rules or plans that may authorize use of some of these procedures even when not agreed to by the parties. See 28 U.S.C. §§ 473(a)(6), 473(b)(4), 651-58; Section 104(b)(2), Pub. L. 101-650. The rule does not attempt to resolve questions as to the extent a court would be authorized to require such proceedings as an exercise of its inherent powers.

The amendment of paragraph (9) should be read in conjunction with the sentence added to the end of subdivision (c), authorizing the court to direct that, in appropriate cases, a responsible representative of the parties be present or available by telephone during a conference in order to discuss possible settlement of the case. The sentence refers to participation by a party or its representative. Whether this would be the individual party, an officer of a corporate party, a representative from an insurance carrier, or someone else would depend on the circumstances. Particularly in litigation in which governmental agencies or large amounts of money are involved, there may be no one with on-the-spot settlement authority, and the most that should be expected is access to a person who would have a major role in submitting a recommendation to the body or board with ultimate decision-making responsibility. The selection of the appropriate representative should ordinarily be left to the party and its counsel. Finally, it should be noted that the unwillingness of a party to be available, even by telephone, for a settlement conference may be a clear signal that the time and expense involved in pursuing settlement is likely to be unproductive and that personal participation by the parties should not be required.

The explicit authorization in the rule to require personal participation in the manner stated is not intended to limit the reasonable exercise of the court's inherent powers, *e.g., G. Heileman Brewing Co. v. Joseph Oat Corp.,* 871 F.2d 648 (7th Cir. 1989), or its power to require party participation under the Civil Justice Reform Act of 1990. See 28 U.S.C. § 473(b)(5) (civil justice expense and delay reduction plans adopted by district courts may include requirement that representatives "with authority to bind [parties] in settlement discussions" be available during settlement conferences).

New paragraphs (13) and (14) are added to call attention to the opportunities for structuring of trial under Rule 42 and under revised Rules 50 and 52.

Paragraph (15) is also new. It supplements the power of the court to limit the extent of evidence under Rules 403 and 611(a) of the Federal Rules of Evidence, which typically would be invoked as a result of developments during trial. Limits on the length of trial established at a conference in advance of trial can provide the parties with a better opportunity to determine priorities and exercise selectivity in presenting evidence than when limits are imposed during trial. Any such limits must be reasonable under the circumstances, and ordinarily the court should impose them only after receiving appropriate submissions from the parties outlining the nature of the testimony expected to be presented through various witnesses, and the expected duration of direct and cross-examination.

2006 Amendment

The amendment to Rule 16(b) is designed to alert the court to the possible need to address the handling of discovery of electronically stored information early in the litigation if such discovery is expected to occur. Rule 26(f) is amended to direct the parties to discuss discovery of electronically stored information if such discovery is contemplated in the action. Form 35 is amended to call for a report to the court about the results of this discussion. In many instances, the court's involvement early in the litigation will help avoid difficulties that might otherwise arise.

Rule 16(b) is also amended to include among the topics that may be addressed in the scheduling order any agreements that the parties reach to facilitate discovery by minimizing the risk of waiver of privilege or work-product protection. Rule 26(f) is amended to add to the discovery plan the parties' proposal for the court to enter a case-management or other order adopting such an agreement. The parties may agree to various arrangements. For example, they may agree to initial provision of requested materials without waiver of privilege or protection to enable the party seeking production to designate the materials desired or protection for actual production, with the privilege review of only those materials to follow. Alternatively, they may agree that if privileged or protected information is inadvertently produced, the producing party may by timely notice assert the privilege or protection and obtain return of the materials without waiver. Other arrangements are possible. In most circumstances, a party who receives information under such an arrangement cannot assert that production of the information waived a claim of privilege or of protection as trial-preparation material.

An order that includes the parties' agreement may be helpful in avoiding delay and excessive cost in discovery. *See Manual for Complex Litigation (4th)* § 11.446. Rule 16(b)(6) recognizes the propriety of including such agreements in the court's order. The rule does not provide the court with authority to enter such a case-management or other order without party agreement, or limit the court's authority to act on motion.

IV. PARTIES

Rule 17. Parties Plaintiff and Defendant; Capacity

(a) Real Party in Interest. Every action shall be prosecuted in the name of the real party in interest. An executor, administrator, guardian, bailee, trustee of an express trust, a party with whom or in whose name a contract has been made for the benefit of another, or a party authorized by statute may sue in that person's own name without joining the party for whose benefit the action is brought; and when a statute of the United States so provides, an action for the use or benefit of another shall be brought in the name of the United States. No action shall be dismissed on the ground that it is not prosecuted in the name of the real party in interest until a reasonable time has been allowed after objection for ratification of commencement of the action by, or joinder or substitution of, the real party in interest; and such ratification, joinder, or substitution shall have the same effect as if the action had been commenced in the name of the real party in interest.

(b) Capacity to Sue or be Sued. The capacity of an individual, other than one acting in a representative capacity, to sue or be sued shall be determined by the law of the individual's domicile. The capacity of a corporation to sue or be sued shall be determined by the law under which it was organized. In all other cases capacity to sue or be sued shall be determined by the law of the state in which the district court is held, except (1) that a partnership or other unincorporated association, which has no such capacity by the law of such state, may sue or be sued in its common name for the purpose of enforcing for or against it a substantive right existing under the Constitution or laws of the United States, and (2) that the capacity of a receiver appointed by a court of the United States to sue or be sued in a court of the United States is governed by Title 28, U.S.C., Sections 754 and 959(a).

(c) Infants or Incompetent Persons. Whenever an infant or incompetent person has a representative, such as a general guardian, committee, conservator, or other like fiduciary, the representative may sue or defend on behalf of the infant or incompetent person. An infant or incompetent person who does not have a duly appointed representative may sue by a next friend or by a guardian ad litem. The court shall appoint a guardian ad litem for an infant or incompetent person not otherwise represented in an action or shall make such other order as it deems proper for the protection of the infant or incompetent person.

Rule 18. Joinder of Claims and Remedies

(a) Joinder of Claims. A party asserting a claim to relief as an original claim, counterclaim, cross-claim, or third-party claim, may join, either as independent or as alternate claims, as many claims, legal, equitable, or maritime, as the party has against an opposing party.

(b) Joinder of Remedies; Fraudulent Conveyances. Whenever a claim is one heretofore cognizable only after another claim has been prosecuted to a conclusion, the two claims may be joined in a single action; but the court shall grant relief in that action only in accordance with the relative substantive rights of the parties. In particular, a plaintiff may state a claim for money and a claim to have set aside a conveyance fraudulent as to that plaintiff, without first having obtained a judgment establishing the claim for money.

Rule 19. Joinder of Persons Needed for Just Adjudication

(a) Persons to be Joined if Feasible. A person who is subject to service of process and whose joinder will not deprive the court of jurisdiction over the subject matter of the action shall be joined as a party in the action if (1) in the person's absence complete relief cannot be accorded among those already parties, or (2) the person claims an interest relating to the subject of the action and is so situated that the disposition of the action in the person's absence may (i) as a practical matter impair or impede the person's ability to protect that interest or (ii) leave any of the persons already parties subject to a substantial risk of incurring double, multiple, or otherwise inconsistent obligations by reason of the claimed interest. If the person has not been so joined, the court shall order that the person be made a party. If the person should join as a plaintiff but refuses to do so, the person may be made a defendant, or, in a proper case, an involuntary plaintiff. If the joined party objects to venue and joinder of that party would render the venue of the action improper, that party shall be dismissed from the action.

(b) Determination by Court Whenever Joinder not Feasible. If a person as described in subdivision (a)(1)-(2) hereof cannot be made a party, the court shall determine whether in equity and good conscience the action should proceed among the parties before it, or should be dismissed, the absent person being thus regarded as indispensable. The factors to be considered by the court include: first, to what extent a judgment rendered in the person's absence might be prejudicial to the person or those already parties; second, the extent to which, by protective provisions in the judgment, by the shaping of relief, or other measures, the prejudice can be lessened or avoided; third, whether a judgment rendered in the person's absence will be adequate; fourth, whether the plaintiff will have an adequate remedy if the action is dismissed for nonjoinder.

(c) Pleading Reasons for Nonjoinder. A pleading asserting a claim for relief shall state the names, if known to the pleader, of any persons as prescribed in subdivision (a)(1)-(2) hereof who are not joined, and the reasons why they are not joined.

(d) Exception of Class Actions. This rule is subject to the provisions of Rule 23.

Rule 20. Permissive Joinder of Parties

(a) Permissive Joinder. All persons may join in one action as plaintiffs if they assert any right to relief jointly, severally, or in the alternative in respect of or arising out of the same transaction, occurrence, or series of transactions or occurrences and if any question of law or fact common to all these persons will arise in the action. All persons (and any vessel, cargo or other property subject to admiralty process in rem) may be joined in one action as defendants if there is asserted against them jointly, severally, or in the alternative, any right to relief in respect of or arising out of the same transaction, occurrence, or series of transactions or occurrences and if any question of law or fact common to all defendants will arise in the action. A plaintiff or defendant need not be interested in obtaining or defending against all the relief demanded. Judgment may be given for one or more of the plaintiffs according to their respective rights to relief, and against one or more defendants according to their respective liabilities.

(b) Separate Trials. The court may make such orders as will prevent a party from being embarrassed, delayed, or put to expense by the inclusion of a party against whom the party asserts no claim and who asserts no claim against the party, and may order separate trials or make other orders to prevent delay or prejudice.

Rule 21. Misjoinder and Non-Joinder of Parties

Misjoinder of parties is not ground for dismissal of an action. Parties may be dropped or added by order of the court on motion of any party or of its own initiative at any stage of the action and on such terms as are just. Any claim against a party may be severed and proceeded with separately.

Rule 22. Interpleader

(1) Persons having claims against the plaintiff may be joined as defendants and required to interplead when their claims are such that the plaintiff is or may be exposed to double or multiple liability. It is not ground for objection to the joinder that the claims of the several claimants or the titles on which their claims depend do not have a common origin or are not identical but are adverse to and independent of one another, or that the plaintiff avers that the plaintiff is not liable in whole or in part to any or all of the claimants. A defendant exposed to similar liability may obtain such interpleader by way of cross-claim or counterclaim. The provisions of this rule supplement and do not in any way limit the joinder of parties permitted in Rule 20.

(2) The remedy herein provided is in addition to and in no way supersedes or limits the remedy provided by Title 28, U.S.C., §§ 1335, 1397, and 2361. Actions under those provisions shall be conducted in accordance with these rules.

Rule 23. Class Actions

(a) Prerequisites to a Class Action. One or more members of a class may sue or be sued as representative parties on behalf of all only if (1) the class is so numerous that joinder of all members is impracticable, (2) there are questions of law or fact common to the class, (3) the claims or defenses of the representative parties are typical of the claims or defenses of the class, and (4) the representative parties will fairly and adequately protect the interests of the class.

(b) Class Actions Maintainable. An action may be maintained as a class action if the prerequisites of subdivision (a) are satisfied, and in addition:

(1) the prosecution of separate actions by or against individual members of the class would create a risk of

(A) inconsistent or varying adjudications with respect to individual members of the class which would establish incompatible standards of conduct for the party opposing the class, or

(B) adjudications with respect to individual members of the class which would as a practical matter be dispositive of the interests of the other members not parties to the adjudications or substantially impair or impede their ability to protect their interests; or

(2) the party opposing the class has acted or refused to act on grounds generally applicable to the class, thereby making appropriate final injunctive relief or corresponding declaratory relief with respect to the class as a whole; or

(3) the court finds that the questions of law or fact common to the members of the class predominate over any questions affecting only individual members, and that a class action is superior to other available methods for the fair and efficient adjudication of the controversy. The matters pertinent to the findings include: (A) the interest of members of the class in individually controlling the prosecution or defense of separate actions; (B) the extent and nature of any litigation concerning the controversy already commenced by or against members of the class; (C) the desirability or undesirability of concentrating the litigation of the claims in the particular forum; (D) the difficulties likely to be encountered in the management of a class action.

(c) Determining by Order Whether to Certify a Class Action; Appointing Class Counsel; Notice and Membership in Class; Judgment; Multiple Classes and Subclasses.

(1) (A) When a person sues or is sued as a representative of a class, the court must — at an early practicable time — determine by order whether to certify the action as a class action.

(B) An order certifying a class action must define the class and the class claims, issues, or defenses, and must appoint class counsel under Rule 23(g).

(C) An order under Rule 23(c)(1) may be altered or amended before final judgment.

(2) (A) For any class certified under Rule 23(b)(1) or (2), the court may direct appropriate notice to the class.

(B) For any class certified under Rule 23(b)(3), the court must direct to class members the best notice practicable under the circumstances, including individual notice to all members who can be identified through reasonable effort. The notice must concisely and clearly state in plain, easily understood language:

- the nature of the action,
- the definition of the class certified,
- the class claims, issues, or defenses,
- that a class member may enter an appearance through counsel if the member so desires,

- that the court will exclude from the class any member who requests exclusion, stating when and how members may elect to be excluded, and
- the binding effect of a class judgment on class members under Rule 23(c)(3).

(3) The judgment in an action maintained as a class action under subdivision (b)(1) or (b)(2), whether or not favorable to the class, shall include and describe those whom the court finds to be members of the class. The judgment in an action maintained as a class action under subdivision (b)(3), whether or not favorable to the class, shall include and specify or describe those to whom the notice provided in subdivision (c)(2) was directed, and who have not requested exclusion, and whom the court finds to be members of the class.

(4) When appropriate (A) an action may be brought or maintained as a class action with respect to particular issues, or (B) a class may be divided into subclasses and each subclass treated as a class, and the provisions of this rule shall then be construed and applied accordingly.

(d) Orders in Conduct of Actions. In the conduct of actions to which this rule applies, the court may make appropriate orders: (1) determining the course of proceedings or prescribing measures to prevent undue repetition or complication in the presentation of evidence or argument; (2) requiring, for the protection of the members of the class or otherwise for the fair conduct of the action, that notice be given in such manner as the court may direct to some or all of the members of any step in the action, or of the proposed extent of the judgment, or of the opportunity of members to signify whether they consider the representation fair and adequate, to intervene and present claims or defenses, or otherwise to come into the action; (3) imposing conditions on the representative parties or on intervenors; (4) requiring that the pleadings be amended to eliminate therefrom allegations as to representation of absent persons, and that the action proceed accordingly; (5) dealing with similar procedural matters. The orders may be combined with an order under Rule 16, and may be altered or amended as may be desirable from time to time.

(e) Settlement, Voluntary Dismissal, or Compromise.

(1) (A) The court must approve any settlement, voluntary dismissal, or compromise of the claims, issues, or defenses of a certified class.

(B) The court must direct notice in a reasonable manner to all class members who would be bound by a proposed settlement, voluntary dismissal, or compromise.

settlement, voluntary dismissal, ass members only after a hearing ement, voluntary dismissal, or nd adequate.

val of a settlement, voluntary le 23(e)(1) must file a statement n connection with the proposed compromise.

ified as a class action under Rule rove a settlement unless it affords sion to individual class members equest exclusion but did not do so.

object to a proposed settlement, mise that requires court approval

ınder Rule 23(e)(4)(A) may be s approval.

ay in its discretion permit an appeal granting or denying class action ation is made to it within ten days s not stay proceedings in the district court of appeals so orders.

sel.

des otherwise, a court that certifies insel.

l to serve as class counsel must fairly interests of the class.

unsel, the court

unsel has done in identifying or potential claims in the action,

erience in handling class actions, other ation, and claims of the type asserted

- counsel's knowledge of the applicable law, and
- the resources counsel will commit to representing the class;

(ii) may consider any other matter pertinent to counsel's ability to fairly and adequately represent the interests of the class;

(iii) may direct potential class counsel to provide information on any subject pertinent to the appointment and to propose terms for attorney fees and nontaxable costs; and

(iv) may make further orders in connection with the appointment.

(2) Appointment Procedure.

(A) The court may designate interim counsel to act on behalf of the putative class before determining whether to certify the action as a class action.

(B) When there is one applicant for appointment as class counsel, the court may appoint that applicant only if the applicant is adequate under Rule 23(g)(1)(B) and (C). If more than one adequate applicant seeks appointment as class counsel, the court must appoint the applicant best able to represent the interests of the class.

(C) The order appointing class counsel may include provisions about the award of attorney fees or nontaxable costs under Rule 23(h).

(h) Attorney Fees Award. In an action certified as a class action, the court may award reasonable attorney fees and nontaxable costs authorized by law or by agreement of the parties as follows:

(1) Motion for Award of Attorney Fees. A claim for an award of attorney fees and nontaxable costs must be made by motion under Rule 54(d)(2), subject to the provisions of this subdivision, at a time set by the court. Notice of the motion must be served on all parties and, for motions by class counsel, directed to class members in a reasonable manner.

(2) Objections to Motion. A class member, or a party from whom payment is sought, may object to the motion.

(3) Hearing and Findings. The court may hold a hearing and must find the facts and state its conclusions of law on the motion under Rule 52(a).

(4) Reference to Special Master or Magistrate Judge. The court may refer issues related to the amount of the award to a special master or to a magistrate judge as provided in Rule 54(d)(2)(D).

ADVISORY COMMITTEE NOTES

1966 Amendment [citations omitted without notation — ED.]

. . .

The amended rule describes in more practical terms the occasions for maintaining class actions; provides that all class actions maintained to the end as such will result in judgments including those whom the court finds to be members of the class, whether or not the judgment is favorable to the class; and refers to the measures which can be taken to assure the fair conduct of these actions.

Subdivision (a) states the prerequisites for maintaining any class action in terms of the numerousness of the class making joinder of the members impracticable, the existence of questions common to the class, and the desired qualifications of the representative parties. These are necessary but not sufficient conditions for a class action. Subdivision (b) describes the additional elements which in varying situations justify the use of a class action.

Subdivision (b)(1). The difficulties which would be likely to arise if resort were had to separate actions by or against the individual members of the class here furnish the reasons for, and the principal key to, the propriety and value of utilizing the class-action device. The considerations stated under clauses (A) and (B) are comparable to certain of the elements which define the persons whose joinder in an action is desirable as stated in Rule 19(a), as amended.

Clause (A): One person may have rights against, or be under duties toward, numerous persons constituting a class, and be so positioned that conflicting or varying adjudications in lawsuits with individual members of the class might establish incompatible standards to govern his conduct. The class action device can be used effectively to obviate the actual or virtual dilemma which would thus confront the party opposing the class. The matter has been stated thus: "The felt necessity for a class action is greatest when the courts are called upon to order or sanction the alteration of the status quo in circumstances such that a large number of persons are in a position to call on a single person to alter the status quo, or to complain if it is altered, and the possibility exists that [the] actor might be called upon to act in inconsistent ways." To illustrate: Separate actions by individuals against a municipality to declare a bond issue invalid or condition or limit it, to prevent or limit the making of a particular appropriation or to compel or invalidate an assessment, might create a risk of inconsistent or varying determinations. In the same way, individual litigations of the rights and duties of riparian owners, or of landowners' rights and duties respecting a claimed nuisance, could create a possibility of incompatible adjudications. Actions by or against a class provide a ready and fair means of achieving unitary adjudication.

Clause (B): This clause takes in situations where the judgment in a nonclass action by or against an individual member of the class, while not technically concluding the other members, might do so as a practical matter. The vice of an individual action would lie in the fact that the other members of the class, thus practically concluded, would have had no representation in the lawsuit. In an action by policy holders against a fraternal benefit association attacking a financial reorganization of the society, it would hardly have been practical, if indeed it would have been possible, to confine the effects of a validation of the reorganization to the individual plaintiffs. Consequently a class action was called for with adequate representation of all members of the class. For much the same reason actions by shareholders to compel the declaration of a dividend[,] the proper recognition and handling of redemption or pre-emption rights, or the like (or actions by the corporation for corresponding declarations of rights), should ordinarily be conducted as class actions, although the matter has been much obscured by the insistence that each shareholder has an individual claim. The same reasoning applies to an action which charges a breach of trust by an indenture trustee or other fiduciary similarly affecting the members of a large class of security holders or other beneficiaries, and which requires an accounting or like measures to restore the subject of the trust.

In various situations an adjudication as to one or more members of the class will necessarily or probably have an adverse practical effect on the interests of other members who should therefore be represented in the lawsuit. This is plainly the case when claims are made by numerous persons against a fund insufficient to satisfy all claims. A class action by or against representative members to settle the validity of the claims as a whole, or in groups, followed by separate proof of the amount of each valid claim and proportionate distribution of the fund, meets the problem. The same reasoning applies to an action by a creditor to set aside a fraudulent conveyance by the debtor and to appropriate the property to his claim, when the debtor's assets are insufficient to pay all creditors' claims. Similar problems, however, can arise in the absence of a fund either present or potential. A negative or mandatory injunction secured by one of a numerous class may disable the opposing party from performing claimed duties toward the other members of the class or materially affect his ability to do so. An adjudication as to movie "clearances and runs" nominally affecting only one exhibitor would often have practical effects on all the exhibitors in the same territorial area. Assuming a sufficiently numerous class of exhibitors, a class action would be advisable. (Here representation of subclasses of exhibitors could become necessary; see subdivision (c)(3)(B).)

Subdivision (b)(2). This subdivision is intended to reach situations where a party has taken action or refused to take action with respect to a class, and final relief of an injunctive nature or of a corresponding declaratory nature, settling the legality of the behavior with respect to the class as a whole, is appropriate. Declaratory relief "corresponds" to injunctive relief when as a practical matter it affords injunctive relief or serves as a basis for later injunctive relief. The subdivision does not extend to cases in which the appropriate final relief relates exclusively or predominantly to money damages. Action or inaction is directed to a class within the meaning of this subdivision even if it has taken effect or is threatened only as to one or a few members of the class, provided it is based on grounds which have general application to the class.

Illustrative are various actions in the civil-rights field where a party is charged with discriminating unlawfully against a class, usually one whose members are incapable of specific enumeration. Subdivision (b)(2) is not limited to civil-rights cases. Thus an action looking to specific or declaratory relief could be brought by a numerous class of purchasers, say retailers of a given description, against a seller alleged to have undertaken to sell to that class at prices higher than those set for other purchasers, say retailers of another description, when the applicable law forbids such a pricing differential. So also a patentee of a machine, charged with selling or licensing the machine on condition that purchasers or licensees also purchase or obtain licenses to use an ancillary unpatented machine, could be sued on a class basis by a numerous group of purchasers or licensees, or by a numerous group of competing sellers or licensors of the unpatented machine, to test the legality of the "tying" condition.

Subdivision (b)(3). In the situations to which this subdivision relates, class-action treatment is not as clearly called for as in those described above, but it may nevertheless be convenient and desirable depending upon the particular facts. Subdivision (b)(3) encompasses those cases in which a class action would achieve economies of time, effort, and expense, and promote uniformity of decision as to persons similarly situated, without sacrificing procedural fairness or bringing about other undesirable results.

The court is required to find, as a condition of holding that a class action may be maintained under this subdivision, that the questions common to the class predominate over the questions affecting individual members. It is only where this predominance exists that economies can be achieved by means of the class-action device. In this view, a fraud perpetrated on numerous persons by the use of similar misrepresentations may be an appealing situation for a class action, and it may remain so despite the need, if liability is found, for separate determination of the damages suffered by individuals within the class. On the other hand, although having some common core, a fraud case may be unsuited for treatment as a class action if there was material variation in the representations made or in the kinds or degrees of reliance by the persons to whom they were addressed. A "mass accident" resulting in injuries to numerous persons is ordinarily not appropriate for a class action because of the likelihood that significant questions, not only of damages but of liability and defenses of liability, would be present, affecting the individuals in different ways. In these circumstances an action conducted nominally as a class action would degenerate in practice into multiple lawsuits separately tried. Private damage claims by numerous individuals arising out of concerted antitrust violations may or may not involve predominating common questions.

That common questions predominate is not itself sufficient to justify a class action under subdivision (b)(3), for another method of handling the litigious situation may be available which has greater practical advantages. Thus one or more actions agreed to by the parties as test or model actions may be preferable to a class action; or it may prove feasible and preferable to consolidate actions. Even when a number of separate actions are proceeding simultaneously, experience shows that the burdens on the parties and the courts can sometimes be reduced by arrangements for avoiding repetitious discovery or the like. Currently the Coordinating Committee on Multiple Litigation in the United States District Courts (a subcommittee of the Committee on Trial Practice and Technique of the Judicial Conference of the United States) is charged with developing methods for expediting such massive litigation. To reinforce the point that the court with the aid of the parties ought to assess the relative advantages of alternative procedures for handling the total controversy, subdivision (b)(3) requires, as a further condition of maintaining the class action, that the court shall find that that procedure is "superior" to the others in the particular circumstances.

Factors (A)-(D) are listed, non-exhaustively, as pertinent to the findings. The court is to consider the interests of individual members of the class in controlling their own litigations and carrying them on as they see fit.

In this connection the court should inform itself of any litigation actually pending by or against the individuals. The interests of individuals in conducting separate lawsuits may be so strong as to call for denial of a class action. On the other hand, these interests may be theoretic rather than practical; the class may have a high degree of cohesion and prosecution of the action through representatives would be quite unobjectionable, or the amounts at stake for individuals may be so small that separate suits would be impracticable. The burden that separate suits would impose on the party opposing the class, or upon the court calendars, may also fairly be considered. (See the discussion, under subdivision (c)(2) below, of the right of members to be excluded from the class upon their request.)

Also pertinent is the question of the desirability of concentrating the trial of the claims in the particular forum by means of a class action, in contrast to allowing the claims to be litigated separately in forums to which they would ordinarily be brought. Finally, the court should consider the problems of management which are likely to arise in the conduct of a class action.

Subdivision (c)(1). In order to give clear definition to the action, this provision requires the court to determine, as early in the proceedings as may be practicable, whether an action brought as a class action is to be so maintained. The determination depends in each case on satisfaction of the terms of subdivision (a) and the relevant provisions of subdivision (b).

An order embodying a determination can be conditional; the court may rule, for example, that a class action may be maintained only if the representation is improved through intervention of additional parties of a stated type. A determination once made can be altered or amended before the decision on the merits if, upon fuller development of the facts, the original determination appears unsound. A negative determination means that the action should be stripped of its character as a class action. See subdivision (d)(4). Although an action thus becomes a nonclass action, the court may still be receptive to interventions before the decision on the merits so that the litigation may cover as many interests as can be conveniently handled; the questions whether the intervenors in the nonclass action shall be permitted to claim "ancillary" jurisdiction or the benefit of the date of the commencement of the action for purposes of the statute of limitations are to be decided by reference to the laws governing jurisdiction and limitations as they apply in particular contexts.

Whether the court should require notice to be given to members of the class of its intention to make a determination, or of the order embodying it, is left to the court's discretion under subdivision (d)(2).

Subdivision (c)(2) makes special provision for class actions maintained under subdivision (b)(3). As noted in the discussion of the latter subdivision, the interests of the individuals in pursing their own litigations may be so strong here as to warrant denial of a class action altogether. Even when a class action is maintained under subdivision (b)(3), this individual interest is respected. Thus the court is required to direct notice to the members of the class of the right of each member to be excluded from the class upon his request. A member who does not request exclusion may, if he wishes, enter an appearance in the action through his counsel; whether or not he does so, the judgment in the action will embrace him.

The notice[,] setting forth the alternatives open to the members of the class, is to be the best practicable under the circumstances, and shall include individual notice to the members who can be identified through reasonable effort. (For further discussion of this notice, see the statement under subdivision (d)(2) below.)

Subdivision (c)(3). The judgment in a class action maintained as such to the end will embrace the class, that is, in a class action under subdivision (b)(1) or (b)(2), those found by the court to be class members; in a class action under subdivision (b)(3), those to whom the notice prescribed by subdivision (c)(2) was directed, excepting those who requested exclusion or who are ultimately found by the court not to be members of the class. The judgment has this scope whether it is favorable or unfavorable to the class. In a (b)(1) or (b)(2) action the judgment "describes" the members of the class, but need not specify the individual members; in a (b)(3) action the judgment "specifies" the individual members who have been identified and described the others.

Compare subdivision (c)(4) as to actions conducted as class actions only with respect to particular issues. Where the class-action character of the lawsuit is based solely on the existence of a "limited fund," the judgment, while extending to all claims of class members against the fund, has ordinarily left unaffected the personal claims of nonappearing members against the debtor.

Hitherto, in a few actions conducted as "spurious" class actions and thus nominally designed to extend only to parties and others intervening before the determination of liability, courts have held or intimated that class members might be permitted to intervene after a decision on the merits favorable to their interests, in order to secure the benefits of the decision for themselves, although they would presumably be unaffected by an unfavorable decision. See, as to the propriety of this so-called "one-way" intervention in "spurious" actions, the conflicting views expressed in [several lower-court cases]. Under proposed subdivision (c)(3), one-way intervention is excluded; the action will have been early determined to be a class or nonclass action, and in the former case the judgment, whether or not favorable, will include the class, as above stated.

Although thus declaring that the judgment in a class action includes the class, as defined, subdivision (c)(3) does not disturb the recognized principle that the court conducting the action cannot predetermine the *res judicata* effect of the judgment; this can be tested only in a subsequent action. The court, however, in framing the judgment in any suit brought as a class action, must decide what its extent or coverage shall be, and if the matter is carefully considered, questions of *res judicata* are less likely to be raised at a later time and if raised will be more satisfactorily answered.

Subdivision (c)(4). This provision recognizes that an action may be maintained as a class action as to particular issues only. For example, in a fraud or similar case the action may retain its "class" character only through the adjudication of liability to the class; the members of the class may thereafter be required to come in individually and prove the amounts of their respective claims.

Two or more classes may be represented in a single action. Where a class is found to include subclasses divergent in interest, the class may be divided correspondingly, and each subclass treated as a class.

Subdivision (d) is concerned with the fair and efficient conduct of the action and lists some types of orders which may be appropriate.

The court should consider how the proceedings are to be arranged in sequence, and what measures should be taken to simplify the proof and argument. See subdivision (d)(1). The orders resulting from this consideration, like the others referred to in subdivision (d), may be combined with a pretrial order under Rule 16, and are subject to modification as the case proceeds.

Subdivision (d)(2) sets out a non-exhaustive list of possible occasions for orders requiring notice to the class. Such notice is not a novel conception. For example, in "limited fund" cases, members of the class have been notified to present individual claims after the basic class decision. Notice has gone to members of a class so that they might express any opposition to the representation, and notice may encourage interventions to improve the representation of the class. Notice has been used to poll members on a proposed modification of a consent decree.

Subdivision (d)(2) does not require notice at any stage, but rather calls attention to its availability and invokes the court's discretion. In the degree that there is cohesiveness or unity in the class and the representation is effective, the need for notice to the class will tend toward a minimum. These indicators suggest that notice under subdivision (d)(2) may be particularly useful and advisable in certain class actions maintained under subdivision (b)(3), for example, to permit members of the class to object to the representation. Indeed, under subdivision (c)(2), notice must be ordered, and is not merely discretionary, to give the members in a subdivision (b)(3) class action an opportunity to secure exclusion from the class. This mandatory notice pursuant to subdivision (c)(2), together with any discretionary notice which the court may find it advisable to give under subdivision (d)(2), is designed to fulfill requirements of due process to which the class action procedure is of course subject.

Notice to members of the class, whenever employed under amended Rule 23, should be accommodated to the particular purpose but need not comply with the formalities for service of process. The fact that notice is given at one stage of the action does not mean that it must be given at subsequent stages. Notice is available fundamentally "for the protection of the members of the class or otherwise for the fair conduct of the action" and should not be used merely as a device for the undesirable solicitation of claims.

In appropriate cases the court should notify interested government agencies of the pendency of the action or of particular steps therein.

Subdivision (d)(3) reflects the possibility of conditioning the maintenance of a class action, e.g., on the strengthening of the representation, see subdivision (c)(1) above; and recognizes that the imposition of conditions on intervenors may be required for the proper and efficient conduct of the action. . . .

Subdivision (e) requires approval of the court, after notice, for the dismissal or compromise of any class action.

1998 Amendments

Subdivision (f). This permissive interlocutory appeal provision is adopted under the power conferred by 28 U.S.C. § 1292(e). Appeal from an order granting or denying class certification is permitted in the sole discretion of the court of appeals. No other type of Rule 23 order is covered by this provision. The court of appeals is given unfettered discretion whether to permit the appeal, akin to the discretion exercised by the Supreme Court in acting on a petition for certiorari. This discretion suggests an analogy to the provision in 28 U.S.C. § 1292(b) for permissive appeal on certification by a district court. Subdivision (f), however, departs from the § 1291(b) model in two significant ways. It does not require that the district court certify the certification ruling for appeal, although the district court often can assist the parties and court of appeals by offering advice on the desirability of appeal. And it does not include the potentially limiting requirements of § 1292(b) that the district court order "involve[] a controlling question of law as to which there is substantial ground for difference of opinion and that an immediate appeal from the order may materially advance the ultimate termination of the litigation.["]

The courts of appeals will develop standards for granting review that reflect the changing areas of uncertainty in class litigation. The Federal Judicial Center study supports the view that many suits with class-action allegations present familiar and almost routine issues that are no more worthy of immediate appeal than many other interlocutory rulings. Yet several concerns justify expansion of present opportunities to appeal. An order denying certification may confront the plaintiff with a situation in which the only sure path to appellate review is by proceeding to final judgment on the merits of an individual claim that, standing alone, is far smaller than the costs of litigation. An order granting certification, on the other hand, may force a defendant to settle rather than incur the costs of defending a class action and run the risk of potentially ruinous liability. These concerns can be met at low cost by establishing in the court of appeals a discretionary power to grant interlocutory review in cases that show appeal-worthy certification issues.

Permission to appeal may be granted or denied on the basis of any consideration that the court of appeals finds persuasive. Permission is most likely to be granted when the certification decision turns on a novel or unsettled question of law, or when, as a practical matter, the decision on certification is likely dispositive of the litigation.

The district court, having worked through the certification decision, often will be able to provide cogent advice on the factors that bear on the decision whether to permit appeal. This advice can be particularly valuable if the certification decision is tentative. Even as to a firm certification decision, a statement of reasons bearing on the probably benefits and costs of immediate appeal can help focus the court of appeals decision, and may persuade the disappointed party that an attempt to appeal would be fruitless.

The 10-day period for seeking permission to appeal is designed to reduce the risk that attempted appeals will disrupt continuing proceedings. It is expected that the courts of appeals will act quickly in making the preliminary determination whether to permit appeal. Permission to appeal does not stay trial court proceedings. A stay should be sought first from the trial court. If the trial court refuses a stay, its action and any explanation of its views should weigh heavily with the court of appeals. . . .

2003 Amendments [citations omitted without notation — ED.]

Subdivision (c). Subdivision (c) is amended in several respects. The requirement that the court determine whether to certify a class "as soon as practicable after commencement of an action" is replaced by requiring determination "at an early practicable time." The notice provisions are substantially revised.

Paragraph (1). Subdivision (c)(1)(A) is changed to require that the determination whether to certify a class be made "at an early practicable time." The "as soon as practicable" exaction neither reflect s prevailing practice nor captures the many valid reasons that may justify deferring the initial certification decision.

Time may be needed to gather information necessary to make the certification decision. Although an evaluation of the probable outcome on the merits is not properly part of the certification decision, discovery in aid of the certification decision often includes information required to identify the nature of the issues that actually will be presented at trial. In this sense it is appropriate to conduct controlled discovery into the "merits," limited to those aspects relevant to making the certification decision on an informed basis. Active judicial supervision may be required to achieve the most effective balance that expedites an informed certification determination without forcing an artificial and ultimately wasteful division between "certification discovery" and "merits discovery." A critical need is to determine how the case will be tried. An increasing number of courts require a party requesting class certification to present a "trial plan" that describes the issues likely to be presented at trial and tests whether they are susceptible of class-wide proof.

Other considerations may affect the timing of the certification decision. The party opposing the class may prefer to win dismissal or summary judgment as to the individual plaintiffs without certification and without binding the class that might have been certified. Time may be needed to explore designation of class counsel under Rule 23(g), recognizing that in many cases the need to progress toward the certification determination may require designation of interim counsel under Rule 23(g)(2)(A).

Although many circumstances may justify deferring the certification decision, active management may be necessary to ensure that the certification decision is not unjustifiably delayed.

Subdivision (c)(1)(C) reflects two amendments. The provision that a class certification "may be conditional" is deleted. A court that is not satisfied that the requirements of Rule 23 have been met should refuse certification until they have been met. The provision that permits alteration or amendment of an order granting or denying class certification is amended to set the cut-off point at final judgment rather than "the decision on the merits." This change avoids the possible ambiguity in referring to "the decision on the merits." Following a determination of liability, for example, proceedings to define the remedy may demonstrate the need to amend the class definition or subdivide the class. In this setting the final judgment concept is pragmatic. It is not the same as the concept used for appeal purposes, but it should be flexible, particularly in protracted litigation.

The authority to amend an order under Rule 23(c)(1) before final judgment does not restore the practice of "one-way intervention" that was rejected by the 1966 revision of Rule 23. A determination of liability after certification, however, may show a need to amend the class definition. Decertification may be warranted after further proceedings.

If the definition of a class certified under Rule 23(b)(3) is altered to include members who have not been afforded notice and an opportunity to request exclusion, notice — including an opportunity to request exclusion — must be directed to the new class members under Rule 23(c)(2)(B).

Paragraph (2). The first change made in Rule 23(c)(2) is to call attention to the court's authority — already established in part by Rule 23(d)(2) — to direct notice of certification to a Rule 23(b)(1) or (b)(2) class. The present rule expressly requires notice only in actions certified under Rule 23(b)(3). Members of classes certified under Rules 23(b)(1) or (b)(2) have interests that may deserve protection by notice.

The authority to direct notice to class members in a (b)(1) or (b)(2) class action should be exercised with care. For several reasons, there may be less need for notice than in a (b)(3) class action. There is no right to request exclusion from a (b)(1) or (b)(2) class. The characteristics of the class may reduce the need for formal notice. The cost of providing notice, moreover, could easily cripple actions that do not seek damages. The court may decide not to direct notice after balancing the risk that notice costs may deter the pursuit of class relief against the benefits of notice.

When the court does direct certification notice in a (b)(1) or (b)(2) class action, the discretion and flexibility established by subdivision (c)(2)(A) extend to the method of giving notice. Notice facilitates the opportunity to participate. Notice calculated to reach a significant number of class members often will protect the interests of all. Informal methods may prove effective. A simple posting in a place visited by many class members, directing attention to a source of more detailed information, may suffice. The court should consider the costs of notice in relation to the probable reach of inexpensive methods.

If a Rule 23(b)(3) class is certified in conjunction with a (b)(2) class, the (c)(2)(B) notice requirements must be satisfied as to the (b)(3) class.

The direction that class-certification notice be couched in plain, easily understood language is a reminder of the need to work unremittingly at the difficult task of communicating with class members. It is difficult to provide information about most class actions that is both accurate and easily understood by class members who are not themselves lawyers. Factual uncertainty, legal complexity, and the complication of class-action procedure raise the barriers high. The Federal Judicial Center has created illustrative clear-notice forms that provide a helpful starting point for actions similar to those described in the forms.

Subdivision (e). Subdivision (e) is amended to strengthen the process of reviewing proposed class-action settlements. Settlement may be a desirable means of resolving a class action. But court review and approval are essential to assure adequate representation of class members who have not participated in shaping the settlement.

Paragraph (1). Subdivision (e)(1)(A) expressly recognizes the power of a class representative to settle class claims, issues, or defenses.

Rule 23(e)(1)(A) resolves the ambiguity in former Rule 23(e)'s reference to dismissal or compromise of "a class action." That language could be — and at times was — read to require court approval of settlements with putative class representatives that resolved only individual claims. The new rule requires approval only if the claims, issues, or defenses of a certified class are resolved by a settlement, voluntary dismissal, or compromise.

Subdivision (e)(1)(B) carries forward the notice requirement of present Rule 23(e) when the settlement binds the class through claim or issue preclusion; notice is not required when the settlement binds only the individual class representatives. Notice of a settlement binding on the class is required either when the settlement follows class certification or when the decisions on certification and settlement proceed simultaneously.

Reasonable settlement notice may require individual notice in the manner required by Rule 23(c)(2)(B) for certification notice to a Rule 23(b)(3) class. Individual notice is appropriate, for example, if class members are required to take action — such as filing claims — to participate in the judgment, or if the court orders a settlement opt-out opportunity under Rule 23(e)(3).

Subdivision (e)(1)(C) confirms and mandates the already common practice of holding hearings as part of the process of approving settlement, voluntary dismissal, or compromise that would bind members of a class.

Subdivision (e)(1)(C) states the standard for approving a proposed settlement that would bind class members. The settlement must be fair, reasonable, and adequate. A helpful review of many factors that may deserve consideration is provided by *In re: Prudential Ins. Co. America Sales Practice Litigation Agent Actions,* 148 F.3d 283, 316-324 (3d Cir. 1998). Further guidance can be found in the Manual for Complex Litigation.

The court must make findings that support the conclusion that the settlement is fair, reasonable, and adequate. The findings must be set out in sufficient detail to explain to class members and the appellate court the factors that bear on applying the standard.

Settlement review also may provide an occasion to review the cogency of the initial class definition. The terms of the settlement themselves, or objections, may reveal divergent interests of class members and demonstrate the need to redefine the class or to designate subclasses. Redefinition of a class certified under Rule 23(b)(3) may require notice to new class members under Rule 23(c)(2)(B). See Rule 23(c)(1)(C).

Paragraph (2). Subdivision (e)(2) requires parties seeking approval of a settlement, voluntary dismissal, or compromise under Rule 23(e)(1) to file a statement identifying any agreement made in connection with the settlement. This provision does not change the basic requirement that the parties disclose all terms of the settlement or compromise that the court must approve under Rule

23(e)(1). It aims instead at related undertakings that, although seemingly separate, may have influenced the terms of the settlement by trading away possible advantages for the class in return for advantages for others. Doubts should be resolved in favor of identification.

Further inquiry into the agreements identified by the parties should not become the occasion for discovery by the parties or objectors. The court may direct the parties to provide to the court or other parties a summary or copy of the full terms of any agreement identified by the parties. The court also may direct the parties to provide a summary or copy of any agreement not identified by the parties that the court considers relevant to its review of a proposed settlement. In exercising discretion under this rule, the court may act in steps, calling first for a summary of any agreement that may have affected the settlement and then for a complete version if the summary does not provide an adequate basis for review. A direction to disclose a summary or copy of an agreement may raise concerns of confidentiality. Some agreements may include information that merits protection against general disclosure. And the court must provide an opportunity to claim work-product or other protections.

Paragraph (3). Subdivision (e)(3) authorizes the court to refuse to approve a settlement unless the settlement affords class members a new opportunity to request exclusion from a class certified under Rule 23(b)(3) after settlement terms are known. An agreement by the parties themselves to permit class members to elect exclusion at this point by the settlement agreement may be one factor supporting approval of the settlement. Often there is an opportunity to opt out at this point because the class is certified and settlement is reached in circumstances that lead to simultaneous notice of certification and notice of settlement. In these cases, the basic opportunity to elect exclusion applies without further complication. In some cases, particularly if settlement appears imminent at the time of certification, it may be possible to achieve equivalent protection by deferring notice and the opportunity to elect exclusion until actual settlement terms are known. This approach avoids the cost and potential confusion of providing two notices and makes the single notice more meaningful. But notice should not be delayed unduly after certification in the hope of settlement.

Rule 23(e)(3) authorizes the court to refuse to approve a settlement unless the settlement affords a new opportunity to elect exclusion in a case that settles after a certification decision if the earlier opportunity to elect exclusion provided with the certification notice has expired by the time of the settlement notice. A decision to remain in the class is likely to be more carefully considered and is better informed when settlement terms are known.

The opportunity to request exclusion from a proposed settlement is limited to members of a (b)(3) class. Exclusion may be requested only by individual class members; no class member may purport to opt out other class members by way of another class action.

The decision whether to approve a settlement that does not allow a new opportunity to elect exclusion is confided to the court's discretion. The court may make this decision before directing notice to the class under Rule 23(e)(1)(B) or after the Rule 23(e)(1)(C) hearing. Many factors may influence the court's decision. Among these are changes in the information available to class members since expiration of the first opportunity to request exclusion, and the nature of the individual class members' claims.

The terms set for permitting a new opportunity to elect exclusion from the proposed settlement of a Rule 23(b)(3) class action may address concerns of potential misuse. The court might direct, for example, that class members who elect exclusion are bound by rulings on the merits made before the settlement was proposed for approval. Still other terms or conditions may be appropriate.

Paragraph (4). Subdivision (e)(4) confirms t he right of class members to object to a proposed settlement, voluntary dismissal, or compromise. The right is defined in relation to a disposition that, because it would bind the class, requires court approval under subdivision (e)(1)(C).

Subdivision (e)(4)(B) requires court approval for withdrawal of objections made under subdivision (e)(4)(A). Review follows automatically if the objections are withdrawn on terms that lead to modification of the settlement with the class. Review also is required if the objector formally withdraws the objections. If the objector simply abandons pursuit of the objection, the court may inquire into the circumstances.

Approval under paragraph (4)(B) may be given or denied with little need for further inquiry if the objection and the disposition go only to a protest that the individual treatment afforded the objector under the proposed settlement is unfair because of factors that distinguish the objector from other class members. Different considerations may apply if the objector has protested that the proposed settlement is not fair, reasonable, or adequate on grounds that apply generally to a class or subclass. Such objections, which purport to represent class-wide interests, may augment the opportunity for obstruction or delay. If such objections are surrendered on terms that do not affect the class settlement or the objector's participation in the class settlement, the court often can approve withdrawal of the objections without elaborate inquiry.

Once an objector appeals, control of the proceeding lies in the court of appeals. The court of appeals may undertake review and approval of a settlement with the objector, perhaps as part of appeal settlement procedures, or may remand to the district court to take advantage of the district court's familiarity with the action and settlement.

Subdivision (g). Subdivision (g) is new. It responds to the reality that the selection and activity of class counsel are often critically important to the successful handling of a class action. Until now, courts have scrutinized proposed class counsel as well as the class representative under Rule 23(a)(4). This experience has recognized the importance of judicial evaluation of the proposed lawyer for the class, and this new subdivision builds on that experience rather than introducing an entirely new element into the class certification process. Rule 23(a)(4) will continue to call for scrutiny of the proposed class representative, while this subdivision will guide the court in assessing proposed class counsel as part of the certification decision. This subdivision recognizes the importance of class counsel, states the obligation to represent the interests of the class, and provides a framework for selection of class counsel. The procedure and standards for appointment vary depending on whether there are multiple applicants to be class counsel. The new subdivision also provides a method by which the court may make directions from the outset about the potential fee award to class counsel in the event the action is successful.

Paragraph (1) sets out the basic requirement that class counsel be appointed if a class is certified and articulates the obligation of class counsel to represent the interests of the class, as opposed to the potentially conflicting interests of individual class members. It also sets out the factors the court should consider in assessing proposed class counsel.

Paragraph (1)(A) requires that the court appoint class counsel to represent the class. Class counsel must be appointed for all classes, including each subclass that the court certifies to represent divergent interests.

Paragraph (1)(A) does not apply if "a statute provides otherwise." This recognizes that provisions of the Private Securities Litigation Reform Act of 1995, Pub. L. No. 104-67, 109 Stat. 737 (1995) (codified in various sections of 15 U.S.C.), contain directives that bear on selection of a lead plaintiff and the retention of counsel. This subdivision does not purport to supersede or to affect the interpretation of those provisions, or any similar provisions of other legislation.

Paragraph 1(B) recognizes t hat t he primary responsibility of class counsel, resulting from appointment as class counsel, is to represent the best interests of the class. The rule thus establishes the obligation of class counsel, an obligation that may be different from the customary obligations of counsel to individual clients. Appointment as class counsel means that the primary obligation of counsel is to the class rather than to any individual members of it. The class representatives do not have an unfettered right to "fire" class counsel. In the same vein, the class representatives cannot command class counsel to accept or reject a settlement proposal. To the contrary, class counsel must determine whether seeking the court's approval of a settlement would be in the best interests of the class as a whole.

Paragraph (1)(C) articulates the basic responsibility of the court to appoint class counsel who will provide the adequate representation called for by paragraph (1)(B). It identifies criteria that must be considered and invites the court to consider any other pertinent matters. Although couched in terms of the court's duty, the listing also informs counsel seeking appointment about the topics that should be addressed in an application for appointment or in the motion for class certification.

The court may direct potential class counsel to provide additional information about the topics mentioned in paragraph (1)(C) or about any other relevant topic. For example, the court may direct applicants to inform the court concerning any agreements about a prospective award of attorney fees or nontaxable costs, as such agreements may sometimes be significant in the selection of class counsel. The court might also direct that potential class counsel indicate how parallel litigation might be coordinated or consolidated with the action before the court.

The court may also direct counsel to propose terms for a potential award of attorney fees and nontaxable costs. Attorney fee awards are an important feature of class action practice, and attention to this subject from the outset may often be a productive technique. Paragraph (2)(C) therefore authorizes the court to provide directions about attorney fees and costs when appointing class counsel. Because there will be numerous class actions in which this information is not likely to be useful, the court need not consider it in all class actions.

Some information relevant to class counsel appointment may involve matters that include adversary preparation in a way that should be shielded from disclosure to other parties. An appropriate protective order may be necessary to preserve confidentiality.

In evaluating prospective class counsel, the court should weigh all pertinent factors. No single factor should necessarily be determinative in a given case. For example, the resources counsel will commit to the case must be appropriate to its needs, but the court should be careful not to limit consideration to lawyers with the greatest resources.

If, after review of all applicants, the court concludes that none would be satisfactory class counsel, it may deny class certification, reject all applications, recommend that an application be modified, invite new applications, or make any other appropriate order regarding selection and appointment of class counsel.

Paragraph (2). This paragraph sets out the procedure that should be followed in appointing class counsel. Although it affords substantial flexibility, it provides the framework for appointment of class counsel in all class actions. For counsel who filed the action, the materials submitted in support of the motion for class certification may suffice to justify appointment so long as the information described in paragraph (g)(1)(C) is included. If there are other applicants, they ordinarily would file a formal application detailing their suitability for the position.

In a plaintiff class action the court usually would appoint as class counsel only an attorney or attorneys who have sought appointment. Different considerations may apply in defendant class actions.

The rule states that the court should appoint "class counsel." In many instances, the applicant will be an individual attorney. In other cases, however, an entire firm, or perhaps numerous attorneys who are not otherwise affiliated but are collaborating on the action will apply. No rule of thumb exists to determine when such arrangements are appropriate; the court should be alert to the need for adequate staffing of the case, but also to the risk of overstaffing or an ungainly counsel structure.

Paragraph (2)(A) authorizes the court to designate interim counsel during the pre-certification period if necessary to protect the interests of the putative class. Rule 23(c)(1)(B) directs that the order certifying the class include appointment of class counsel. Before class certification, however, it will usually be important for an attorney to take action to prepare for the certification decision. The amendment to Rule 23(c)(1) recognizes that some discovery is often necessary for that determination. It also may be important to make or respond to motions before certification. Settlement may be discussed before certification. Ordinarily, such work is handled by the lawyer who filed the action. In some cases, however, there may be rivalry or uncertainty that makes formal designation of interim counsel appropriate. Rule 23(g)(2)(A) authorizes the court to designate interim counsel to act on behalf of the putative class before the certification decision is made. Failure to make the formal designation does not prevent the attorney who filed the action from proceeding in it. Whether or not formally designated interim counsel, an attorney who acts on behalf of the class before certification must act in the best interests of the class as a whole. For example, an attorney who negotiates a pre-certification settlement must seek a settlement that is fair, reasonable, and adequate for the class.

Rule 23(c)(1) provides that the court should decide whether to certify the class "at an early practicable time," and directs that class counsel should be appointed in the order certifying the class. In some cases, it may be appropriate for the court to allow a reasonable period after commencement of the action for filing applications to serve as class counsel. The primary ground for deferring appointment would be that there is reason to anticipate competing applications to serve as class counsel. Examples might include instances in which more than one class action has been filed, or in which other attorneys have filed individual actions on behalf of putative class members. The purpose of facilitating competing applications in such a case is to afford the best possible representation for the class. Another possible reason for deferring appointment would be that the initial applicant was found inadequate, but it seems appropriate to permit additional applications rather than deny class certification.

Paragraph (2)(B) states the basic standard the court should use in deciding whether to certify the class and appoint class counsel in the single applicant situation — that the applicant be able to provide the representation called for by paragraph (1)(B) in light of the factors identified in paragraph (1)(C).

If there are multiple adequate applicants, paragraph (2)(B) directs the court to select the class counsel best able to represent the interests of the class. This decision should also be made using the factors outlined in paragraph (1)(C), but in the multiple applicant situation the court is to go beyond scrutinizing the adequacy of counsel and make a comparison of the strengths of the various applicants. As with the decision whether to appoint the sole applicant for the position, no single factor should be dispositive in selecting class counsel in cases in which there are multiple applicants. The fact that a given attorney filed the instant action, for example, might not weigh heavily in the decision if that lawyer had not done significant work identifying or investigating claims. Depending on the nature of the case, one important consideration might be the applicant's existing attorney-client relationship with the proposed class representative.

Paragraph (2)(C) builds on the appointment process by authorizing the court to include provisions regarding attorney fees in the order appointing class counsel. Courts may find it desirable to adopt guidelines for fees or nontaxable costs, or to direct class counsel to report to the court at regular intervals on the efforts undertaken in the action, to facilitate the court's later determination of a reasonable attorney fee.

Subdivision (h). Subdivision (h) is new. Fee awards are a powerful influence on the way attorneys initiate, develop, and conclude class actions. Class action attorney fee awards have heretofore been handled, along with all other attorney fee awards, under Rule 54(d)(2), but that rule is not addressed to the particular concerns of class actions. This subdivision is designed to work in tandem with new subdivision (g) on appointment of class counsel, which may afford an opportunity for the court to provide an early framework for an eventual fee award, or for monitoring the work of class counsel during the pendency of the action.

Subdivision (h) applies to "an action certified as a class action." This includes cases in which there is a simultaneous proposal for class certification and settlement even though technically the class may not be certified unless the court approves the settlement pursuant to review under Rule 23(e). When a settlement is proposed for Rule 23(e) approval, either after certification or with a request for certification, notice to class members about class counsel's fee motion would ordinarily accompany the notice to the class about the settlement proposal itself.

This subdivision does not undertake to create new grounds for an award of attorney fees or nontaxable costs. Instead, it applies when such awards are authorized by law or by agreement of the parties. Against that background, it provides a format for all awards of attorney fees and nontaxable costs in connection with a class action, not only the award to class counsel. In some situations, there may be a basis for making an award to other counsel whose work produced a beneficial result for the class, such as attorneys who acted for the class before certification but were not appointed class counsel, or attorneys who represented objectors to a proposed settlement under Rule 23(e) or to the fee motion of class counsel. Other situations in which fee awards are authorized by law or by agreement of the parties may exist.

This subdivision authorizes an award of "reasonable" attorney fees and nontaxable costs. This is the customary term for measurement of fee awards in cases in which counsel may obtain an award of fees under the "common fund" theory that applies in many class actions, and is used in many fee-shifting statutes. Depending on the circumstances, courts have approached the determination of what is reasonable in different ways. In particular, there is some variation among courts about whether in "common fund" cases the court should use the lodestar or a percentage method of determining what fee is reasonable. The rule does not attempt to resolve the question whether the lodestar or percentage approach should be viewed as preferable.

Active judicial involvement in measuring fee awards is singularly important to the proper operation of the class-action process. Continued reliance on caselaw development of fee-award measures does not diminish the court's responsibility. In a class action, the district court must ensure that the amount and mode of payment of attorney fees are fair and proper whether the fees come from a common fund or are otherwise paid. Even in the absence of objections, the court bears this responsibility.

Courts discharging this responsibility have looked to a variety of factors. One fundamental focus is the result actually achieved for class members, a basic consideration in any case in which fees are sought on the basis of a benefit achieved for class members. The Private Securities Litigation Reform Act of 1995 explicitly makes this factor a cap for a fee award in actions to which it applies. See 15 U.S.C. §§ 77z-1(a)(6); 78u-4(a)(6) (fee award should not exceed a "reasonable percentage of the amount of any damages and prejudgment interest actually paid to the class"). For a percentage approach to fee measurement, results achieved is the basic starting point.

In many instances, the court may need to proceed with care in assessing the value conferred on class members. Settlement regimes that provide for future payments, for example, may not result in significant actual payments to class members. In this connection, the court may need to scrutinize the manner and operation of any applicable claims procedure. In some cases, it may be appropriate to defer some portion of the fee award until actual payouts to class members are known. Settlements involving nonmonetary provisions for class members also deserve careful scrutiny to ensure that these provisions have actual value to the class. On occasion the court's Rule 23(e) review will provide a solid basis for this sort of evaluation, but in any event it is also important to assessing the fee award for the class.

At the same time, it is important to recognize that in some class actions the monetary relief obtained is not the sole determinant of an appropriate attorney fees award.

Any directions or orders made by the court in connection with appointing class counsel under Rule 23(g) should weigh heavily in making a fee award under this subdivision.

Courts have also given weight to agreements among the parties regarding the fee motion, and to agreements between class counsel and others about the fees claimed by the motion. Rule 54(d)(2)(B) provides: "If directed by the court, the motion shall also disclose the terms of any agreement with respect to fees to be paid for the services for which claim is made." The agreement by a settling party not to oppose a fee application up to a certain amount, for example, is worthy of consideration, but the court remains responsible to determine a reasonable fee. "Side agreements" regarding fees provide at least perspective pertinent to an appropriate fee award.

In addition, courts may take account of the fees charged by class counsel or other attorneys for representing individual claimants or objectors in the case. In determining a fee for class counsel, the court's objective is to ensure an overall fee that is fair for counsel and equitable within the class. In some circumstances individual fee agreements between class counsel and class members might have provisions inconsistent with those goals, and the court might determine that adjustments in the class fee award were necessary as a result.

Finally, it is important to scrutinize separately the application for an award covering nontaxable costs. If costs were addressed in the order appointing class counsel, those directives should be a presumptive starting point in determining what is an appropriate award.

Paragraph (1). Any claim for an award of attorney fees must be sought by motion under Rule 54(d)(2), which invokes the provisions for timing of appeal in Rule 58 and Appellate Rule 4. Owing to the distinctive features of class action fee motions, however, the provisions of this subdivision control disposition of fee motions in class actions, while Rule 54(d)(2) applies to matters not addressed in this subdivision.

The court should direct when the fee motion must be filed. For motions by class counsel in cases subject to court review of a proposed settlement under Rule 23(e), it would be important to require the filing of at least the initial motion in time for inclusion of information about the motion in the notice to the class about the proposed settlement that is required by Rule 23(e). In cases litigated to judgment, the court might also order class counsel's motion to be filed promptly so that notice to the class under this subdivision (h) can be given.

Besides service of the motion on all parties, notice of class counsel's motion for attorney fees must be "directed to the class in a reasonable manner." Because members of the class have an interest in the arrangements for payment of class counsel whether that payment comes from the class fund or is made directly by another party, notice is required in all instances. In cases in which settlement approval is contemplated under Rule 23(e), notice of class counsel's fee motion should be combined with notice of the proposed settlement, and the provision regarding notice to the class is parallel to the requirements for notice under Rule 23(e). In adjudicated class actions, the court may calibrate the notice to avoid undue expense.

Paragraph (2). A class member and any party from whom payment is sought may object to the fee motion. Other parties — for example, nonsettling defendants — may not object because they lack a sufficient interest in the amount the court awards. The rule does not specify a time limit for making an objection. In setting the date objections are due, the court should provide sufficient time after the full fee motion is on file to enable potential objectors to examine the motion.

The court may allow an objector discovery relevant to the objections. In determining whether to allow discovery, the court should weigh the need for the information against the cost and delay that would attend discovery. See Rule 26(b)(2). One factor in determining whether to authorize discovery is the completeness of the material submitted in support of the fee motion, which depends in part on the fee measurement standard applicable to the case. If the motion provides thorough information, the burden should be on the objector to justify discovery to obtain further information.

Paragraph (3). Whether or not there are formal objections, the court must determine whether a fee award is justified and, if so, set a reasonable fee. The rule does not require a formal hearing in all cases. The form and extent of a hearing depend on the circumstances of the case. The rule does require findings and conclusions under Rule 52(a).

Paragraph (4). By incorporating Rule 54(d)(2), this provision gives the court broad authority to obtain assistance in determining the appropriate amount to award. In deciding whether to direct submission of such questions to a special master or magistrate judge, the court should give appropriate consideration to the cost and delay that such a process might entail.

Rule 23.1. Derivative Actions by Shareholders

In a derivative action brought by one or more shareholders or members to enforce a right of a corporation or of an unincorporated association, the corporation or association having failed to enforce a right which may properly be asserted by it, the complaint shall be verified and shall allege (1) that the plaintiff was a shareholder or member at the time of the transaction of which the plaintiff complains or that the plaintiff's share or membership thereafter devolved on the plaintiff by operation of law, and (2) that the action is not a collusive one to confer jurisdiction on a court of the United States which it would not otherwise have. The complaint shall also allege with particularity the efforts, if any, made by the plaintiff to obtain the action the plaintiff desires from the directors or comparable authority and, if necessary, from the shareholders or members, and the reasons for the plaintiff's failure to obtain the action or for not making the effort. The derivative action may not be maintained if it appears that the plaintiff does not fairly and adequately represent the interests of the shareholders or members similarly situated in enforcing the right of the corporation or association. The action shall not be dismissed or compromised without the approval of the court, and notice of the proposed dismissal or compromise shall be given to shareholders or members in such manner as the court directs.

Rule 23.2. Actions Relating to Unincorporated Associations

An action brought by or against the members of an unincorporated association as a class by naming certain members as representative parties may be maintained only if it appears that the representative parties will fairly and adequately protect the interests of the association and its members. In the conduct of the action the court may make appropriate orders corresponding with those described in Rule 23(d), and the procedure for dismissal or compromise of the action shall correspond with that provided in Rule 23(e).

Rule 24. Intervention

(a) Intervention of Right. Upon timely application anyone shall be permitted to intervene in an action: (1) when a statute of the United States confers an unconditional right to intervene; or (2) when the applicant claims an interest relating to the property or transaction which is the subject of the action and the applicant is so situated that the disposition of the action may as a practical matter impair or impede the applicant's ability to protect that interest, unless the applicant's interest is adequately represented by existing parties.

(b) Permissive Intervention. Upon timely application anyone may be permitted to intervene in an action: (1) when a statute of the United States confers a conditional right to intervene; or (2) when an applicant's claim or defense and the main action have a question of law or fact in common. When a party to an action relies for ground of claim or defense upon any statute or executive order administered by a federal or state governmental officer or agency or upon any regulation, order, requirement, or agreement issued or made pursuant to the statute or executive order, the officer or agency upon timely application may be permitted to intervene in the action. In exercising its discretion the court shall consider whether the intervention will unduly delay or prejudice the adjudication of the rights of the original parties.

(c) Procedure. A person desiring to intervene shall serve a motion to intervene upon the parties as provided in Rule 5. The motion shall state the grounds therefor and shall be accompanied by a pleading setting forth the claim or defense for which intervention is sought. The same procedure shall be followed when a statute of the United States gives a right to intervene.

ADVISORY COMMITTEE NOTES

1966 Amendment [citations omitted without notation — Ed.]

. . .

The amendment provides that an applicant is entitled to intervene in an action when his position is comparable to that of a person under Rule 19(a)(2)(i), as amended, unless his interest is already adequately represented in the action by existing parties. The Rule 19(a)(2)(i) criterion imports practical considerations, and the deletion of the "bound" language similarly frees the rule from undue preoccupation with strict considerations of res judicata.

The representation whose adequacy comes into question under the amended rule is not confined to formal representation like that provided by a trustee for his beneficiary or a representative party in a class action for a member of the class. A party to an action may provide practical representation to the absentee seeking intervention although no such formal relationship exists between them, and the adequacy of this practical representation will then have to be weighed.

An intervention of right under the amended rule may be subject to appropriate conditions or restrictions responsive among other things to the requirements of efficient conduct of the proceedings.

Rule 25. Substitution of Parties

(a) Death.

(1) If a party dies and the claim is not thereby extinguished, the court may order substitution of the proper parties. The motion for substitution may be made by any party or by the successors or representatives of the deceased party and, together with the notice of hearing, shall be served on the parties as provided in Rule 5 and upon persons not parties in the manner provided in Rule 4 for the service of a summons, and may be served in any judicial district. Unless the motion for substitution is made not later than 90 days after the death is suggested upon the record by service of a statement of the fact of the death as provided herein for the service of the motion, the action shall be dismissed as to the deceased party.

(2) In the event of the death of one or more of the plaintiffs or of one or more of the defendants in an action in which the right sought to be enforced survives only to the surviving plaintiffs or only against the surviving defendants, the action does not abate. The death shall be suggested upon the record and the action shall proceed in favor of or against the surviving parties.

(b) Incompetency. If a party becomes incompetent, the court upon motion served as provided in subdivision (a) of this rule may allow the action to be continued by or against the party's representative.

(c) Transfer of Interest. In case of any transfer of interest, the action may be continued by or against the original party, unless the court upon motion directs the person to whom the interest is transferred to be substituted in the action or joined with the original party. Service of the motion shall be made as provided in subdivision (a) of this rule.

(d) Public Officers; Death or Separation from Office.

(1) When a public officer is a party to an action in his official capacity and during its pendency dies, resigns, or otherwise ceases to hold office, the action does not abate and the officer's successor is automatically substituted as a party. Proceedings following the substitution shall be in the name of the substituted party, but any misnomer not affecting the substantial rights of the parties shall be disregarded. An order of substitution may be entered at any time, but the omission to enter such an order shall not affect the substitution.

(2) A public officer who sues or is sued in an official capacity may be described as a party by the officer's official title rather than by name; but the court may require the officer's name to be added.

V. DEPOSITIONS AND DISCOVERY

Rule 26. General Provisions Governing Discovery; Duty of Disclosure

(a) Required Disclosures; Methods to Discover Additional Matter.

(1) Initial Disclosures. Except in categories of proceedings specified in Rule 26(a)(1)(E), or to the extent otherwise stipulated or directed by order, a party must, without awaiting a discovery request, provide to other parties:

(A) the name and, if known, the address and telephone number of each individual likely to have discoverable information that the disclosing party may use to support its claims or defenses, unless solely for impeachment, identifying the subjects of the information;

(B) a copy of, or a description by category and location of, all documents, electronically stored information, and tangible things that are in the possession, custody, or control of the party and that the disclosing party may use to support its claims or defenses, unless solely for impeachment;

(C) a computation of any category of damages claimed by the disclosing party, making available for inspection and copying as under Rule 34 the documents or other evidentiary material, not privileged or protected from disclosure, on which such computation is based, including materials bearing on the nature and extent of injuries suffered; and

(D) for inspection and copying as under Rule 34 any insurance agreement under which any person carrying on an insurance business may be liable to satisfy part or all of a judgment which may be entered in the action or to indemnify or reimburse for payments made to satisfy the judgment.

(E) The following categories of proceedings are exempt from initial disclosure under Rule 26(a)(1):

(i) an action for review on an administrative record;

(ii) a forfeiture action in rem arising from a federal statute;

(iii) a petition for habeas corpus or other proceeding to challenge a criminal conviction or sentence;

(iv) an action brought without counsel by a person in custody of the United States, a state, or a state subdivision;

(v) an action to enforce or quash an administrative summons or subpoena;

(vi) an action by the United States to recover benefit payments;

(vii) an action by the United States to collect on a student loan guaranteed by the United States;

(viii) a proceeding ancillary to proceedings in other courts; and

(ix) an action to enforce an arbitration award.

These disclosures must be made at or within 14 days after the Rule 26(f) conference unless a different time is set by stipulation or court order, or unless a party objects during the conference that initial disclosures are not appropriate in the circumstances of the action and states the objection in the Rule 26(f) discovery plan. In ruling on the objection, the court must determine what disclosures — if any — are to be made, and set the time for disclosure. Any party first served or otherwise joined after the Rule 26(f) conference must make these disclosures within 30 days after being served or joined unless a different time is set by stipulation or court order. A party must make its initial disclosures based on the information then reasonably available to it and is not excused from making its disclosures because it has not fully completed its investigation of the case or because it challenges the sufficiency of another party's disclosures or because another party has not made its disclosures.

(2) Disclosure of Expert Testimony.

(A) In addition to the disclosures required by paragraph (1), a party shall disclose to other parties the identity of any person who may be used at trial to present evidence under Rules 702, 703, or 705 of the Federal Rules of Evidence.

(B) Except as otherwise stipulated or directed by the court, this disclosure shall, with respect to a witness who is retained or specially employed to provide expert testimony in the case or whose duties as an employee of the party regularly involve giving expert testimony, be accompanied by a written report prepared and signed by the witness. The report shall contain a complete statement of all opinions to be expressed and the basis and reasons therefor; the data or other information considered by the witness in forming the opinions; any exhibits to be used as a summary of or support for the opinions; the qualifications of the witness, including a list of all publications authored by the witness within the preceding ten years; the compensation to be paid for the study and testimony; and a listing of any other cases in which the witness has testified as an expert at trial or by deposition within the preceding four years.

(C) These disclosures shall be made at the times and in the sequence directed by the court. In the absence of other directions from the court or stipulation by the parties, the disclosures shall be made at least 90 days before the trial date or the date the case is to be ready for trial or, if the evidence is intended solely to contradict or rebut evidence on the same subject matter identified by another party under paragraph (2)(B), within 30 days after the disclosure made by the other party. The parties shall supplement these disclosures when required under subdivision (e)(1).

(3) Pretrial Disclosures. In addition to the disclosures required by Rule 26(a)(1) and (2), a party must provide to other parties and promptly file with the court the following information regarding the evidence that it may present at trial other than solely for impeachment:

(A) the name and, if not previously provided, the address and telephone number of each witness, separately identifying those whom the party expects to present and those whom the party may call if the need arises;

(B) the designation of those witnesses whose testimony is expected to be presented by means of a deposition and, if not taken stenographically, a transcript of the pertinent portions of the deposition testimony; and

(C) an appropriate identification of each document or other exhibit, including summaries of other evidence, separately identifying those which the party expects to offer and those which the party may offer if the need arises.

Unless otherwise directed by the court, these disclosures must be made at least 30 days before trial. Within 14 days thereafter, unless a different time is specified by the court, a party may serve and promptly file a list disclosing (i) any objections to the use under Rule 32(a) of a deposition designated by another party under Rule 26(a)(3)(B), and (ii) any objection, together with the grounds therefor, that may be made to the admissibility of materials identified under Rule 26(a)(3)(C). Objections not so disclosed, other than objections under Rules 402 and 403 of the Federal Rules of Evidence, are waived unless excused by the court for good cause.

(4) Form of Disclosures. Unless the court orders otherwise, all disclosures under Rules 26(a)(1) through (3) must be made in writing, signed, and served.

(5) Methods to Discover Additional Matter. Parties may obtain discovery by one or more of the following methods: depositions upon oral examination or written questions; written interrogatories; production of documents or things or permission to enter upon land or other property under Rule 34 or 45(a)(1)(C), for inspection and other purposes; physical and mental examinations; and requests for admission.

(b) Discovery Scope and Limits. Unless otherwise limited by order of the court in accordance with these rules, the scope of discovery is as follows:

(1) In General. Parties may obtain discovery regarding any matter, not privileged, that is relevant to the claim or defense of any party, including the existence, description, nature, custody, condition, and location of any books, documents, or other tangible things and the identity and location of persons having knowledge of any discoverable matter. For good cause, the court may order discovery of any matter relevant to the subject matter involved in the action. Relevant information need not be admissible at the trial if the discovery appears reasonably calculated to lead to the discovery of admissible evidence. All discovery is subject to the limitations imposed by Rule 26(b)(2)(i), (ii), and (iii).

(2) Limitations.

(A) By order, the court may alter the limits in these rules on the number of depositions and interrogatories or the length of depositions under Rule 30. By order or local rule, the court may also limit the number of requests under Rule 36.

(B) A party need not provide discovery of electronically stored information from sources that the party identifies as not reasonably accessible because of undue burden or cost. On motion to compel discovery or for a protective order, the party from whom discovery is sought must show that the information is not reasonably accessible because of undue burden or cost. If that showing is made, the court may nonetheless order discovery from such sources if the requesting party shows good cause, considering the limitations of Rule 26(b)(2)(C). The court may specify conditions for the discovery.

(C) The frequency or extent of use of the discovery methods otherwise permitted under these rules and by any local rule shall be limited by the court if it determines that: (i) the discovery sought is unreasonably cumulative or duplicative, or is obtainable from some other source that is more convenient, less burdensome, or less expensive; (ii) the party seeking discovery has had ample opportunity by discovery in the action to obtain the information sought; or (iii) the burden or expense of the proposed discovery outweighs its likely benefit, taking into account the needs of the case, the amount in controversy, the parties' resources, the importance of the issues at stake in the litigation, and the importance of the proposed discovery in resolving the issues. The court may act upon its own initiative after reasonable notice or pursuant to a motion under Rule 26(c).

(3) Trial Preparation: Materials. Subject to the provisions of subdivision (b)(4) of this rule, a party may obtain discovery of documents and tangible things otherwise discoverable under subdivision (b)(1) of this rule and prepared in anticipation of litigation or for trial by or for another party or by or for that other party's representative (including the other party's attorney, consultant, surety, indemnitor, insurer, or agent) only upon a showing that the party seeking discovery has substantial need of the materials in the preparation of the party's case and that the party is unable without undue hardship to obtain the substantial equivalent of the materials by other means. In ordering discovery of such materials when the required showing has been made, the court shall protect against disclosure of the mental impressions, conclusions, opinions, or legal theories of an attorney or other representative of a party concerning the litigation.

A party may obtain without the required showing a statement concerning the action or its subject matter previously made by that party. Upon request, a person not a party may obtain without the required showing a statement concerning the action or its subject matter previously made by that person. If the request is refused, the person may move for a court order. The provisions of Rule 37(a)(4) apply to the award of expenses incurred in relation to the motion. For purposes of this paragraph, a statement previously made is (A) a written statement signed or otherwise adopted or approved by the person making it, or (B) a stenographic, mechanical, electrical, or other recording, or a transcription thereof, which is a substantially verbatim recital of an oral statement by the person making it and contemporaneously recorded.

(4) Trial Preparation: Experts.

(A) A party may depose any person who has been identified as an expert whose opinions may be presented at trial. If a report from the expert is required under subdivision (a)(2)(B), the deposition shall not be conducted until after the report is provided.

(B) A party may, through interrogatories or by deposition, discover facts known or opinions held by an expert who has been retained or specially employed by another party in anticipation of litigation or preparation for trial and who is not expected to be called as a witness at trial, only as provided in Rule 35(b) or upon a showing of exceptional circumstances under which it is impracticable for the party seeking discovery to obtain facts or opinions on the same subject by other means.

(C) Unless manifest injustice would result, (i) the court shall require that the party seeking discovery pay the expert a reasonable fee for time spent in responding to discovery under this subdivision; and (ii) with respect to discovery obtained under subdivision (b)(4)(B) of this rule the court shall require the party seeking discovery to pay the other party a fair portion of the fees and expenses reasonably incurred by the latter party in obtaining facts and opinions from the expert.

(5) Claims of Privilege or Protection of Trial-Preparation Materials.

(A) Information Withheld. When a party withholds information otherwise discoverable under these rules by claiming that it is privileged or subject to protection as trial-preparation material, the party shall make the claim expressly and shall describe the nature of the documents, communications, or things not produced or disclosed in a manner that, without revealing information itself privileged or protected, will enable other parties to assess the applicability of the privilege or protection.

(B) Information Produced. If information is produced in discovery that is subject to a claim of privilege or of protection as trial-preparation material, the party making the claim may notify any party that received the information of the claim and the basis for it. After being notified, a party must promptly return, sequester, or destroy the specified information and any copies it has and may not use or disclose the information until the claim is resolved. A receiving party may promptly present the information to the court under seal for a determination of the claim. If the receiving party disclosed the information before being notified, it must take reasonable steps to retrieve it. The producing party must preserve the information until the claim is resolved.

(c) Protective Orders. Upon motion by a party or by the person from whom discovery is sought, accompanied by a certification that the movant has in good faith conferred or attempted to confer with other affected parties in an effort to resolve the dispute without court action, and for good cause shown, the court in which the action is pending or alternatively, on matters relating to a deposition, the court in the district where the deposition is to be taken may make any order which justice requires to protect a party or person from annoyance, embarrassment, oppression, or undue burden or expense, including one or more of the following:

(1) that the disclosure or discovery not be had;

(2) that the disclosure or discovery may be had only on specified terms and conditions, including a designation of the time or place;

(3) that the discovery may be had only by a method of discovery other than that selected by the party seeking discovery;

(4) that certain matters not be inquired into, or that the scope of the disclosure or discovery be limited to certain matters;

(5) that discovery be conducted with no one present except persons designated by the court;

(6) that a deposition, after being sealed, be opened only by order of the court;

(7) that a trade secret or other confidential research, development, or commercial information not be revealed or be revealed only in a designated way; and

(8) that the parties simultaneously file specified documents or information enclosed in sealed envelopes to be opened as directed by the court.

If the motion for a protective order is denied in whole or in part, the court may, on such terms and conditions as are just, order that any party or other person provide or permit discovery. The provisions of Rule 37(a)(4) apply to the award of expenses incurred in relation to the motion.

(d) Timing and Sequence of Discovery. Except in categories of proceedings exempted from initial disclosure under Rule 26(a)(1)(E), or when authorized under these rules or by order or agreement of the parties, a party may not seek discovery from any source before the parties have conferred as required by Rule 26(f). Unless the court upon motion, for the convenience of parties and witnesses and in the interests of justice, orders otherwise, methods of discovery may be used in any sequence, and the fact that a party is conducting discovery, whether by deposition or otherwise, does not operate to delay any other party's discovery.

(e) Supplementation of Disclosures and Responses. A party who has made a disclosure under subdivision (a) or responded to a request for discovery with a disclosure or response is under a duty to supplement or correct the disclosure or response to include information thereafter acquired if ordered by the court or in the following circumstances:

(1) A party is under a duty to supplement at appropriate intervals its disclosures under subdivision (a) if the party learns that in some material respect the information disclosed is incomplete or incorrect and if the additional or corrective information has not otherwise been made known to the other parties during the discovery process or in writing. With respect to testimony of an expert from whom a report is required under subdivision (a)(2)(B) the duty extends both to information contained in the report and to information provided through a deposition of the expert, and any additions or other changes to this information shall be disclosed by the time the party's disclosures under Rule 26(a)(3) are due.

(2) A party is under a duty seasonably to amend a prior response to an interrogatory, request for production, or request for admission if the party learns that the response is in some material respect incomplete or incorrect and if the additional or corrective information has not otherwise been made known to the other parties during the discovery process or in writing.

(f) Conference of Parties; Planning for Discovery. Except in categories of proceedings exempted from initial disclosure under Rule 26(a)(1)(E) or when otherwise ordered, the parties must, as soon as practicable and in any event at least 21 days before a scheduling conference is held or a scheduling order is due under Rule 16(b), confer to consider the nature and basis of their claims and defenses and the possibilities for a prompt settlement or resolution of the case, to make or arrange for the disclosures required by Rule 26(a)(1), to discuss any issues relating to preserving discoverable information, and to develop a proposed discovery plan that indicates the parties' views and proposals concerning:

(1) what changes should be made in the timing, form, or requirement for disclosures under Rule 26(a), including a statement as to when disclosures under Rule 26(a)(1) were made or will be made;

(2) the subjects on which discovery may be needed, when discovery should be completed, and whether discovery should be conducted in phases or be limited to or focused upon particular issues;

(3) any issues relating to disclosure or discovery of electronically stored information, including the form or forms in which it should be produced;

(4) any issues relating to claims of privilege or of protection as trial-preparation material, including — if the parties agree on a procedure to assert such claims after production — whether to ask the court to include their agreement in an order;

(5) what changes should be made in the limitations on discovery imposed under these rules or by local rule, and what other limitations should be imposed; and

(6) any other orders that should be entered by the court under Rule 26(c) or under Rule 16(b) and (c).

The attorneys of record and all unrepresented parties that have appeared in the case are jointly responsible for arranging the conference, for attempting in good faith to agree on the proposed discovery plan, and for submitting to the court within 14 days after the conference a written report outlining the plan. A court may order that the parties or attorneys attend the conference in person. If necessary to comply with its expedited schedule for Rule 16(b) conferences, a court may by local rule (i) require that the conference between the parties occur fewer than 21 days before the scheduling conference is held or a scheduling order is due under Rule 16(b), and (ii) require that the written report outlining the discovery plan be filed fewer than 14 days after the conference between the parties, or excuse the parties from submitting a written report and permit them to report orally on their discovery plan at the Rule 16(b) conference.

(g) Signing of Disclosures, Discovery Requests, Responses, and Objections.

(1) Every disclosure made pursuant to subdivision (a)(1) or subdivision (a)(3) shall be signed by at least one attorney of record in the attorney's individual name, whose address shall be stated. An unrepresented party shall sign the disclosure and state the party's address. The signature of the attorney or party constitutes a certification that to the best of the signer's knowledge, information, and belief, formed after a reasonable inquiry, the disclosure is complete and correct as of the time it is made.

(2) Every discovery request, response, or objection made by a party represented by an attorney shall be signed by at least one attorney of record in the attorney's individual name, whose address shall be stated. An unrepresented party shall sign the request, response, or objection and state the party's address. The signature of the attorney or party constitutes a certification that to the best of the signer's knowledge, information, and belief, formed after a reasonable inquiry, the request, response, or objection is:

(A) consistent with these rules and warranted by existing law or a good faith argument for the extension, modification, or reversal of existing law;

(B) not interposed for any improper purpose, such as to harass or to cause unnecessary delay or needless increase in the cost of litigation; and

(C) not unreasonable or unduly burdensome or expensive, given the needs of the case, the discovery already had in the case, the amount in controversy, and the importance of the issues at stake in the litigation.

If a request, response, or objection is not signed, it shall be stricken unless it is signed promptly after the omission is called to the attention of the party making the request, response, or objection, and a party shall not be obligated to take any action with respect to it until it is signed.

(3) If without substantial justification a certification is made in violation of the rule, the court, upon motion or upon its own initiative, shall impose upon the person who made the certification, the party on whose behalf the disclosure, request, response, or objection is made, or both, an appropriate sanction, which may include an order to pay the amount of the reasonable expenses incurred because of the violation, including a reasonable attorney's fee.

ADVISORY COMMITTEE NOTES

1970 Amendment [citations omitted without notation — Ed.]

. . .

Subdivision (b)(3) — Trial Preparation: Materials. Some of the most controversial and vexing problems to emerge from the discovery rules have arisen out of requests for the production of documents or things prepared in anticipation of litigation or for trial. The existing rules make no explicit provision for such materials. . . .

The rules are amended by eliminating the general requirement of "good cause" from Rule 34 but retaining a requirement of a special showing for trial preparation materials in this subdivision. The required showing is expressed, not in terms of "good cause" whose generality has tended to encourage confusion and controversy, but in terms of the elements of the special showing to be made: substantial need of the materials in the preparation of the case and inability without undue hardship to obtain the substantial equivalent of the materials by other means.

These changes conform to the holdings of the cases, when viewed in light of their facts. Apart from trial preparation, the fact that the materials sought are documentary does not in and of itself require a special showing beyond relevance and absence of privilege. The protective provisions are of course available, and if the party from whom production is sought raises a special issue of privacy (as with respect to income tax returns or grand jury minutes) or points to evidence primarily impeaching, or can show serious burden or expense, the court will exercise its traditional power to decide whether to issue a protective order. On the other hand, the requirement of a special showing for discovery of trial preparation materials reflects the view that each side's informal evaluation of its case should be protected, that each side should be encouraged to prepare independently, and that one side should not automatically have the benefit of the detailed preparatory work of the other side. . . .

Materials assembled in the ordinary course of business, or pursuant to public requirements unrelated to litigation, or for other nonlitigation purposes are not under the qualified immunity provided by this subdivision. No change is made in the existing doctrine, noted in the *Hickman* case, that one party may discover relevant facts known or available to the other party, even though such facts are contained in a document which is not itself discoverable.

Treatment of Lawyers; Special Protection of Mental Impressions, Conclusions, Opinions, and Legal Theories Concerning the Litigation. — The courts are divided as to whether the work-product doctrine extends to the preparatory work only of lawyers. The *Hickman* case left this issue open since the statements in that case were taken by a lawyer. . . .

Subdivision (b)(3) reflects the trend of the cases by requiring a special showing, not merely as to materials prepared by an attorney, but also as to materials prepared in anticipation of litigation or preparation for trial by or for a party or any representative acting on his behalf. The subdivision then goes on to protect against disclosure the mental impressions, conclusions, opinions, or legal theories concerning the litigation of an attorney or other representative of a party. The *Hickman* opinion drew special attention to the need for protecting an attorney against discovery of memoranda prepared from recollection of oral interviews. The courts have steadfastly safeguarded against disclosure of lawyers' mental impressions and legal theories, as well as mental impressions and subjective evaluations of investigators and claim-agents. In enforcing this provision of the subdivision, the courts will sometimes find it necessary to order disclosure of a document but with portions deleted.

Rules 33 and 36 have been revised in order to permit discovery calling for opinions, contentions, and admissions relating not only to fact but also to the application of law to fact. Under those rules, a party and his attorney or other representative may be required to disclose, to some extent, mental impressions, opinions, or conclusions. But documents or parts of documents containing these matters are protected against discovery by this subdivision. Even though a party may ultimately have to disclose in response to interrogatories or requests to admit, he is entitled to keep confidential documents containing such matters prepared for internal use. . . .

1983 Amendment [citations omitted without notation — ED.]

Excessive discovery and evasion or resistance to reasonable discovery requests pose significant problems. Recent studies have made some attempt to determine the sources and extent of the difficulties. See Brazil, *Civil Discovery: Lawyers' Views of its Effectiveness, Principal Problems and Abuses,* American Bar Foundation (1980); Connolly, Holleman & Kuhlman, *Judicial Controls and the Civil Litigative Process: Discovery,* Federal Judicial Center (1978); Ellington, *A Study of Sanctions for Discovery Abuse,* Department of Justice (1979); Schroeder & Frank, *The Proposed Changes in the Discovery Rules,* 1978 Ariz. St. L.J. 475.

The purpose of discovery is to provide a mechanism for making relevant information available to the litigants. "Mutual knowledge of all the relevant facts gathered by both parties is essential to proper litigation." *Hickman v. Taylor,* 329 U.S. 495, 507 (1947). Thus the spirit of the rules is violated when advocates attempt to use discovery tools as tactical weapons rather than to expose the facts and illuminate the issues by overuse of discovery or unnecessary use of defensive weapons or evasive responses. All of this results in excessively costly and time-consuming activities that are disproportionate to the nature of the case, the amount involved, or the issues or values at stake.

Given our adversary tradition and the current discovery rules, it is not surprising that there are many opportunities, if not incentives, for attorneys to engage in discovery that, although authorized by the broad, permissive terms of the rules, nevertheless results in delay. As a result, it has been said that the rules have "not infrequently [been] exploited to the disadvantage of justice." *Herbert v. Lando,* 441 U.S. 153, 179 (1979) (Powell, J., concurring). These practices impose costs on an already overburdened system and impede the fundamental goal of the "just, speedy, and inexpensive determination of every action." Fed. R. Civ. P. 1.

Subdivision (a); Discovery Methods. The deletion of the last sentence of Rule 26(a)(1), which provided that unless the court ordered otherwise under Rule 26(c) "the frequency of use" of the various discovery methods was not to be limited, is an attempt to address the problem of duplicative, redundant, and excessive discovery and to reduce it. The amendment, in conjunction with the changes in Rule 26(b)(1), is designed to encourage district judges to identify instances of needless discovery and to limit the use of the various discovery devices accordingly. The question may be raised by one of the parties, typically on a motion for a protective order, or by the court on its own initiative. It is entirely appropriate to consider a limitation on the frequency of use of discovery at a discovery conference under Rule 26(f) or at any other pretrial conference authorized by these rules. In considering the discovery needs of a particular case, the court should consider the factors described in Rule 26(b)(1).

Subdivision (b); Discovery Scope and Limits. Rule 26(b)(1) has been amended to add a sentence to deal with the problem of over-discovery. The objective is to guard against redundant or disproportionate discovery by giving the court authority to reduce the amount of discovery that may be directed to matters that are otherwise proper subjects of inquiry. The new sentence is intended to encourage judges to be more aggressive in identifying and discouraging discovery overuse. The grounds mentioned in the amended rule for limiting discovery reflect the existing practice of many courts in issuing protective orders under Rule 26(c).

The first element of the standard, Rule 26(b)(1)(i), is designed to minimize redundancy in discovery and encourage attorneys to be sensitive to the comparative costs of different methods of securing information. Subdivision (b)(1)(ii) also seeks to reduce repetitiveness and to oblige lawyers to think through their discovery activities in advance so that full utilization is made of each deposition, document request, or set of interrogatories. The elements of Rule 26(b)(1)(iii) address the problem of discovery that is disproportionate to the individual lawsuit as measured by such matters as its nature and complexity, the importance of the issues at stake in a case seeking damages, the limitations on a financially weak litigant to withstand extensive opposition to a discovery program or to respond to discovery requests, and the significance of the substantive issues, as measured in philosophic, social, or institutional terms. Thus the rule recognizes that many cases in public policy spheres, such as employment practices, free speech, and other matters, may have importance far beyond the monetary amount involved. The court must apply the standards in an even-handed manner that will prevent use of discovery to wage a war of attrition or as a device to coerce a party, whether financially weak or affluent.

The rule contemplates greater judicial involvement in the discovery process and thus acknowledges the reality that it cannot always operate on a self-regulating basis. In an appropriate case the court could restrict the number of depositions, interrogatories, or the scope of a production request. But the court must be careful not to deprive a party of discovery that is reasonably necessary to afford a fair opportunity to develop and prepare the case.

The court may act on motion, or its own initiative. It is entirely appropriate to resort to the amended rule in conjunction with a discovery conference under Rule 26(f) or one of the other pretrial conferences authorized by the rules.

Subdivision (g); Signing of Discovery Requests, Responses, and Objections. Rule 26(g) imposes an affirmative duty to engage in pretrial discovery in a responsible manner that is consistent with the spirit and purposes of Rules 26 through 37. In addition, Rule 26(g) is designed to curb discovery abuse by explicitly encouraging the imposition of sanctions. The subdivision provides a deterrent to both excessive discovery and evasion by imposing a certification requirement that obliges each attorney to stop and think about the legitimacy of a discovery request, a response thereto, or an objection. The term "response" includes answers to interrogatories and to requests to admit as well as responses to production requests.

If primary responsibility for conducting discovery is to continue to rest with the litigants, they must be obliged to act responsibly and avoid abuse. With this in mind, Rule 26(g), which parallels the amendments to Rule 11, requires an attorney or unrepresented party to sign each discovery request, response, or objection. Motions relating to discovery are governed by Rule 11. However, since a discovery request, response, or objection usually deals with more specific subject matter than motions or papers, the elements that must be certified in connection with the former are spelled out more completely. The signature is a certification of the elements set forth in Rule 26(g).

Although the certification duty requires the lawyer to pause and consider the reasonableness of his request, response, or objection, it is not meant to discourage or restrict necessary and legitimate discovery. The rule simply requires that the attorney make a reasonable inquiry into the factual basis of his response, request, or objection.

The duty to make a "reasonable inquiry" is satisfied if the investigation undertaken by the attorney and the conclusions drawn therefrom are reasonable under the circumstances. It is an objective standard similar to the one imposed by Rule 11. See the Advisory Committee Note to Rule 11. In making the inquiry, the attorney may rely on assertions by the client and on communications with other counsel in the case as long as that reliance is appropriate under the circumstances. Ultimately, what is reasonable is a matter for the court to decide on the totality of the circumstances.

Rule 26(g) does not require the signing attorney to certify the truthfulness of the client's factual responses to a discovery request. Rather, the signature certifies that the lawyer has made a reasonable effort to assure that the client has provided all the information and documents available to him that are responsive to the discovery demand. Thus, the lawyer's certification under Rule 26(g) should be distinguished from other signature requirements in the rules, such as those in Rules 30(e) and 33.

Nor does the rule require a party or an attorney to disclose privileged communications or work product in order to show that a discovery request, response, or objection is substantially justified. The provisions of Rule 26(c), including appropriate orders after *in camera* inspection by the court, remain available to protect a party claiming privilege or work product protection.

The signing requirement means that every discovery request, response, or objection should be grounded on a theory that is reasonable under the precedents or a good faith belief as to what should be the law. This standard is heavily dependent on the circumstances of each case. The certification speaks as of the time it is made. The duty to supplement discovery responses continues to be governed by Rule 26(e). . . .

1993 Amendments

Subdivision (a). Through the addition of paragraphs (1)-(4), this subdivision imposes on parties a duty to disclose, without awaiting formal discovery requests, certain basic information that is needed in most cases to prepare for trial or make an informed decision about settlement. The rule requires all parties (1) early in the case to exchange information regarding potential witnesses, documentary evidence, damages, and insurance, (2) at an appropriate time during the discovery period to identify expert witnesses and provide a detailed written statement of the testimony that may be offered at trial through specially retained experts, and (3) as the trial date approaches to identify the particular evidence that may be offered at trial. The enumeration in Rule 26(a) of items to be disclosed does not prevent a court from requiring by order or local rule that the parties disclose additional information without a discovery request. Nor are parties precluded from using traditional discovery methods to obtain further information regarding these matters, as for example asking an expert during a deposition about testimony given in other litigation beyond the four-year period specified in Rule 26(a)(2)(B).

A major purpose of the revision is to accelerate the exchange of basic information about the case and to eliminate the paper work involved in requesting such information, and the rule should be applied in a manner to achieve those objectives. . . .

The rule is based upon the experience of district courts that have required disclosure of some of this information through local rules, court-approved standard interrogatories, and standing orders. Most have required pretrial disclosure of the kind of information described in Rule 26(a)(3). Many have required written reports from experts containing information like that specified in Rule 26(a)(2)(B). While far more limited, the experience of the few state and federal courts that have required pre-discovery exchange of core information such as is contemplated in Rule 26(a)(1) indicates that savings in time and expense can be achieved, particularly if the litigants meet and discuss the issues in the case as a predicate for this exchange and if a judge supports the process, as by using the results to guide further proceedings in the case. Courts in Canada and the United Kingdom have for many years required disclosure of certain information without awaiting a request from an adversary.

Paragraph (1). As the functional equivalent of court-ordered interrogatories, this paragraph requires early disclosure, without need for any request, of four types of information that have been customarily secured early in litigation through formal discovery. The introductory clause permits the court, by local rule, to exempt all or particular types of cases from these disclosure requirement[s] or to modify the nature of the information to be disclosed. . . . The disclosure obligations specified in paragraph (1) will not be appropriate for all cases, and it is expected that changes in these obligations will be made by the court or parties when the circumstances warrant. . . .

Subdivision (e). This subdivision is revised to provide that the requirement for supplementation applies to all disclosures required by subdivisions (a)(1)-(3). Like the former rule, the duty, while imposed on a "party," applies whether the corrective information is learned by the client or by the attorney. Supplementations need not be made as each new item of information is learned but should be made at appropriate intervals during the discovery period, and with special promptness as the trial date approaches. It may be useful for the scheduling order to specify the time or times when supplementations should be made.

The revision also clarifies that the obligation to supplement responses to formal discovery requests applies to interrogatories, requests for production, and requests for admissions, but not ordinarily to deposition testimony. However, with respect to experts from whom a written report is required under subdivision (a)(2)(B), changes in the opinions expressed by the expert whether in the report or at a subsequent deposition are subject to a duty of supplemental disclosure under subdivision (e)(1).

The obligation to supplement disclosures and discovery responses applies whenever a party learns that its prior disclosures or responses are in some material respect incomplete or incorrect. There is, however, no obligation to provide supplemental or corrective information that has been otherwise made known to the parties in writing or during the discovery process, as when a witness not previously disclosed is identified during the taking of a deposition or when an expert during a deposition corrects information contained in an earlier report.

Subdivision (f). This subdivision was added in 1980 to provide a party threatened with abusive discovery with a special means for obtaining judicial intervention other than through discrete motions under Rules 26(c) and 37(a). . . .

The desirability of some judicial control of discovery can hardly be doubted. Rule 16, as revised, requires that the court set a time for completion of discovery and authorizes various other orders affecting the scope, timing, and extent of discovery and disclosures. Before entering such orders, the court should consider the views of the parties, preferably by means of a conference, but at the least through written submissions. Moreover, it is desirable that the parties' proposals regarding discovery be developed through a process where they meet in person, informally explore the nature and basis of the issues, and discuss how discovery can be conducted most efficiently and economically.

. . . [F]ormer subdivision (f) envisioned the development of proposed discovery plans as an optional procedure to be used in relatively few cases. The revised rule directs that in all cases not exempted by local rule or special order the litigants must meet in person and plan for discovery. Following this meeting, the parties submit to the court their proposals for a discovery plan and can begin formal discovery. Their report will assist the court in seeing that the timing and scope of disclosures under revised Rule 26(a) and the limitations on the extent of discovery under these rules and local rules are tailored to the circumstances of the particular case. . . .

Subdivision (g). Paragraph (1) is added to require signatures on disclosures, a requirement that parallels the provisions of paragraph (2) with respect to discovery requests, responses, and objections. The provisions of paragraph (3) have been modified to be consistent with Rules 37(a)(4) and 37(c)(1); in combination, these rules establish sanctions for violation of the rules regarding disclosures and discovery matters. Amended Rule 11 no longer applies to such violations.

2000 Amendment [citations omitted without notation — ED.]

Purposes of amendments. The Rule 26(a)(1) initial disclosure provisions are amended to establish a nationally uniform practice. The scope of the disclosure obligation is narrowed to cover only information that the disclosing party may use to support its position. In addition, the rule exempts specified categories of proceedings from initial disclosure, and permits a party who contends that disclosure is not appropriate in the circumstances of the case to present its objections to the court, which must then determine whether disclosure should be made. Related changes are made in Rules 26(d) and (f).

The initial disclosure requirements added by the 1993 amendments permitted local rules directing that disclosure would not be required or altering its operation. The inclusion of the "opt out" provision reflected the strong opposition to initial disclosure felt in some districts, and permitted experimentation with differing disclosure rules in those districts that were favorable to disclosure. The local option also recognized that — partly in response to the first publication in 1991 of a proposed disclosure rule — many districts had adopted a variety of disclosure programs under the aegis of the Civil Justice Reform Act. It was hoped that developing experience under a variety of disclosure systems would support eventual refinement of a uniform national disclosure practice. In addition, there was hope that local experience could identify categories of actions in which disclosure is not useful.

A striking array of local regimes in fact emerged for disclosure and related features introduced in 1993. . . .

The Committee has discerned widespread support for national uniformity. . . .

These amendments restore national uniformity to disclosure practice. . . .

Subdivision (a)(1). The amendments remove the authority to alter or opt out of the national disclosure requirements by local rule, invalidating not only formal local rules but also informal "standing" orders of an individual judge or court that purport to create exemptions from — or limit or expand — the disclosure provided under the national rule. *See* Rule 83. Case-specific orders remain proper, however, and are expressly required if a party objects that initial disclosure is not appropriate in the circumstances of the action. Specified categories of proceedings are excluded from initial disclosure under subdivision (a)(1)(E). In addition, the parties can stipulate to forgo disclosure, as was true before. But even in a case excluded by subdivision (a)(1)(E) or in which the parties stipulate to bypass disclosure, the court can order exchange of similar information in managing the action under Rule 16.

The initial disclosure obligation of subdivisions (a)(1)(A) and (B) has been narrowed to identification of witnesses and documents that the disclosing party may use to support its claims or defenses. "Use" includes any use at a pretrial conference, to support a motion, or at trial. The disclosure obligation is also triggered by intended use in discovery, apart from use to respond to a discovery request; use of a document to question a witness during a deposition is a common example. The disclosure obligation attaches both to witnesses and documents a party intends to use and also to witnesses and to documents the party intends to use if — in the language of Rule 26(a)(3) — "the need arises."

A party is no longer obligated to disclose witnesses or documents, whether favorable or unfavorable, that it does not intend to use. The obligation to disclose information the party may use connects directly to the exclusion sanction of Rule 37(c)(1). Because the disclosure obligation is limited to material that the party may use, it is no longer tied to particularized allegations in the pleadings. Subdivision (e)(1), which is unchanged, requires supplementation if information later acquired would have been subject to the disclosure requirement. As case preparation continues, a party must supplement its disclosures when it determines that it may use a witness or document that it did not previously intend to use.

The disclosure obligation applies to "claims and defenses," and therefore requires a party to disclose information it may use to support its denial or rebuttal of the allegations, claim, or defense of another party. It thereby bolsters the requirements of Rule 11(b)(4), which authorizes denials "warranted on the evidence," and disclosure should include the identity of any witness or document that the disclosing party may use to support such denials.

Subdivision (a)(3) presently excuses pretrial disclosure of information solely for impeachment. Impeachment information is similarly excluded from the initial disclosure requirement.

Subdivisions (a)(1)(C) and (D) are not changed. Should a case be exempted from initial disclosure by Rule 26(a)(1)(E) or by agreement or order, the insurance information described by subparagraph (D) should be subject to discovery, as it would have been under the principles of former Rule 26(b)(2), which was added in 1970 and deleted in 1993 as redundant in light of the new initial disclosure obligation.

New subdivision (a)(1)(E) excludes eight specified categories of proceedings from initial disclosure. The objective of this listing is to identify cases in which there is likely to be little or no discovery, or in which initial disclosure appears unlikely to contribute to the effective development of the case. The list was developed after a review of the categories excluded by local rules in various districts from the operation of Rule 16(b) and the conference requirements of subdivision (f). Subdivision (a)(1)(E) refers to categories of "proceedings" rather than categories of "actions" because some might not properly be labeled " actions." Case designations made by the parties or the clerk's office at the time of filing do not control application of the exemptions. The descriptions in the rule are generic and are intended to be administered by the parties — and, when needed, the courts — with the flexibility needed to adapt to gradual evolution in the types of proceedings that fall within these general categories. The exclusion of an action for review on an administrative record, for example, is intended to reach a proceeding that is framed as an " appeal" based solely on an administrative record. The exclusion should not apply to a proceeding in a form that commonly permits admission of new evidence to supplement the record. . . .

Subdivision (a)(1)(E) is likely to exempt a substantial proportion of the cases in most districts from the initial disclosure requirement. Based on 1996 and 1997 case filing statistics, Federal Judicial Center staff estimate that, nationwide, these categories total approximately one-third of all civil filings.

The categories of proceedings listed in subdivision (a)(1)(E) are also exempted from the subdivision (f) conference requirement and from the subdivision (d) moratorium on discovery. Although there is no restriction on commencement of discovery in these cases, it is not expected that this opportunity will often lead to abuse since there is likely to be little or no discovery in most such cases. Should a defendant need more time to respond to discovery requests filed at the beginning of an exempted action, it can seek relief by motion under Rule 26(c) if the plaintiff is unwilling to defer the due date by agreement.

Subdivision (a)(1)(E)'s enumeration of exempt categories is exclusive. Although a case-specific order can alter or excuse initial disclosure, local rules or "standing" orders that purport to create general exemptions are invalid. *See* Rule 83.

The time for initial disclosure is extended to 14 days after the subdivision (f) conference unless the court orders otherwise. This change is integrated with corresponding changes requiring that the subdivision (f) conference be held 21 days before the Rule 16(b) scheduling conference or scheduling order, and that the report on the subdivision (f) conference be submitted to the court 14 days after the meeting. These changes provide a more orderly opportunity for the parties to review the disclosures, and for the court to consider the report. In many instances, the subdivision (f) conference and the effective preparation of the case would benefit from disclosure before the conference, and earlier disclosure is encouraged.

The presumptive disclosure date does not apply if a party objects to initial disclosure during the subdivision (f) conference and states its objection in the subdivision (f) discovery plan. The right to object to initial disclosure is not intended to afford parties an opportunity to "opt out" of disclosure unilaterally. It does provide an opportunity for an objecting party to present to the court its position that disclosure would be "inappropriate in the circumstances of the action." Making the objection permits the objecting party to present the question to the judge before any party is required to make disclosure. The court must then rule on the objection and determine what disclosures — if any — should be made. Ordinarily, this determination would be included in the Rule 16(b) scheduling order, but the court could handle the matter in a different fashion. Even when circumstances warrant suspending some disclosure obligations, others — such as the damages and insurance information called for by subdivisions (a)(1)(C) and (D) — may continue to be appropriate.

The presumptive disclosure date is also inapplicable to a party who is "first served or otherwise joined" after the subdivision (f) conference. This phrase refers to the date of service of a claim on a party in a defensive posture (such as a defendant or third-party defendant), and the date of joinder of a party added as a claimant or an intervenor. Absent court order or stipulation, a new party has 30 days in which to make its initial disclosures. But it is expected that later-added parties will ordinarily be treated the same as the original parties when the original parties have stipulated to forgo initial disclosure, or the court has ordered disclosure in a modified form.

Subdivision (a)(3). The amendment to Rule 5(d) forbids filing disclosures under subdivisions (a)(1) and (a)(2) until they are used in the proceeding, and this change is reflected in an amendment to subdivision (a)(4). Disclosures under subdivision (a)(3), however, may be important to the court in connection with the final pretrial conference or otherwise in preparing for trial. The requirement that objections to certain matters be filed points up the court's need to be provided with these materials. Accordingly, the requirement that subdivision (a)(3) materials be filed has been moved from subdivision (a)(4) to subdivision (a)(3), and it has also been made clear that they — and any objections — should be filed "promptly."

Subdivision (a)(4). The filing requirement has been removed from this subdivision. Rule 5(d) has been amended to provide that disclosures under subdivisions (a)(1) and (a)(2) must not be filed until used in the proceeding. Subdivision (a)(3) has been amended to require that the disclosures it directs, and objections to them, be filed promptly. Subdivision (a)(4) continues to require that all disclosures under subdivisions (a)(1), (a)(2), and (a)(3) be in writing, signed, and served. . . .

Subdivision (b)(1). In 1978, the Committee published for comment a proposed amendment, suggested by the Section of Litigation of the American Bar Association, to refine the scope of discovery by deleting the "subject matter" language. This proposal was withdrawn, and the Committee has since then made other changes in the discovery rules to address concerns about overbroad discovery. Concerns about costs and delay of discovery have persisted nonetheless, and other bar groups have repeatedly renewed similar proposals for amendment to this subdivision to delete the "subject matter" language. Nearly one-third of the lawyers surveyed in 1997 by the Federal Judicial Center endorsed narrowing the scope of discovery as a means of reducing litigation expense without interfering with fair case resolutions. The Committee has heard that in some instances, particularly cases involving large quantities of discovery, parties seek to justify discovery requests that sweep far beyond the claims and defenses of the parties on the ground that they nevertheless have a bearing on the "subject matter" involved in the action.

The amendments proposed for subdivision (b)(1) include one element of these earlier proposals but also differ from these proposals in significant ways. The similarity is that the amendments describe the scope of party- controlled discovery in terms of matter relevant to the claim or defense of any party. The court, however, retains authority to order discovery of any matter relevant to the subject matter involved in the action for good cause. The amendment is designed to involve the court more actively in regulating the breadth of sweeping or contentious discovery. The Committee has been informed repeatedly by lawyers that involvement of the court in managing discovery is an important method of controlling problems of inappropriately broad discovery. Increasing the availability of judicial officers to resolve discovery disputes and increasing court management of discovery were both strongly endorsed by the attorneys surveyed by the Federal Judicial Center. Under the amended provisions, if there is an objection that discovery goes beyond material relevant to the parties' claims or defenses, the court would become involved to determine whether the discovery is relevant to the claims or defenses and, if not, whether good cause exists for authorizing it so long as it is relevant to the subject matter of the action. The good-cause standard warranting broader discovery is meant to be flexible.

The Committee intends that the parties and the court focus on the actual claims and defenses involved in the action. The dividing line between information relevant to the claims and defenses and that relevant only to the subject matter of the action cannot be defined with precision. A variety of types of information not directly pertinent to the incident in suit could be relevant to the claims or defenses raised in a given action. For example, other incidents of the same type, or involving the same product, could be properly discoverable under the revised standard. Information about organizational arrangements or filing systems of a party could be discoverable if likely to yield or lead to the discovery of admissible information. Similarly, information that could be used to impeach a likely witness, although not otherwise relevant to the claims or defenses, might be properly discoverable. In each instance, the determination whether such information is discoverable because it is relevant to the claims or defenses depends on the circumstances of the pending action.

The rule change signals to the court that it has the authority to confine discovery to the claims and defenses asserted in the pleadings, and signals to the parties that they have no entitlement to discovery to develop new claims or defenses that are not already identified in the pleadings. In general, it is hoped that reasonable lawyers can cooperate to manage discovery without the need for judicial intervention. When judicial intervention is invoked, the actual scope of discovery should be determined according to the reasonable needs of the action. The court may permit broader discovery in a particular case depending on the circumstances of the case, the nature of the claims and defenses, and the scope of the discovery requested.

The amendments also modify the provision regarding discovery of information not admissible in evidence. As added in 1946, this sentence was designed to make clear that otherwise relevant material could not be withheld because it was hearsay or otherwise inadmissible. The Committee was concerned that the "reasonably calculated to lead to the discovery of admissible evidence" standard set forth in this sentence might swallow any other limitation on the scope of discovery. Accordingly, this sentence has been amended to clarify that information must be relevant to be discoverable, even though inadmissible, and that discovery of such material is permitted if reasonably calculated to lead to the discovery of admissible evidence. As used here, "relevant" means within the scope of discovery as defined in this subdivision, and it would include information relevant to the subject matter involved in the action if the court has ordered discovery to that limit based on a showing of good cause.

Finally, a sentence has been added calling attention to the limitations of subdivision (b)(2)(i), (ii), and (iii). These limitations apply to discovery that is otherwise within the scope of subdivision (b)(1). The Committee has been told repeatedly that courts have not implemented these limitations with the vigor that was contemplated. This otherwise redundant cross-reference has been added to emphasize the need for active judicial use of subdivision (b)(2) to control excessive discovery. *Cf. Crawford-El v. Britton*, [523 U.S. 574, 598-99] (1998) (quoting Rule 26(b)(2)(iii) and stating that "Rule 26 vests the trial judge with broad discretion to tailor discovery narrowly").

Subdivision (b)(2). Rules 30, 31, and 33 establish presumptive national limits on the numbers of depositions and interrogatories. New Rule 30(d)(2) establishes a presumptive limit on the length of depositions. Subdivision (b)(2) is amended to remove the previous permission for local rules that establish different presumptive limits on these discovery activities. There is no reason to believe that unique circumstances justify varying these nationally-applicable presumptive limits in certain districts. The limits can be modified by court order or agreement in an individual action, but "standing" orders imposing different presumptive limits are not authorized. Because there is no national rule limiting the number of Rule 36 requests for admissions, the rule continues to authorize local rules that impose numerical limits on them. This change is not intended to interfere with differentiated case management in districts that use this technique by case-specific order as part of their Rule 16 process.

Subdivision (d). The amendments remove the prior authority to exempt cases by local rule from the moratorium on discovery before the subdivision (f) conference, but the categories of proceedings exempted from initial disclosure under subdivision (a)(1)(E) are excluded from subdivision (d). The parties may agree to disregard the moratorium where it applies, and the court may so order in a case, but "standing" orders altering the moratorium are not authorized.

Subdivision (f). As in subdivision (d), the amendments remove the prior authority to exempt cases by local rule from the conference requirement. The Committee has been informed that the addition of the conference was one of the most successful changes made in the 1993 amendments, and it therefore has determined to apply the conference requirement nationwide. The categories of proceedings exempted from initial disclosure under subdivision (a)(1)(E) are exempted from the conference requirement for the reasons that warrant exclusion from initial disclosure. The court may order that the conference need not occur in a case where otherwise required, or that it occur in a case otherwise exempted by subdivision (a)(1)(E). "Standing" orders altering the conference requirement for categories of cases are not authorized.

The rule is amended to require only a "conference" of the parties, rather than a "meeting." There are important benefits to face-to-face discussion of the topics to be covered in the conference, and those benefits may be lost if other means of conferring were routinely used when face-to- face meetings would not impose burdens. Nevertheless, geographic conditions in some districts may exact costs far out of proportion to these benefits. The amendment allows the court by case-specific order to require a face-to- face meeting, but "standing" orders so requiring are not authorized.

As noted concerning the amendments to subdivision (a)(1), the time for the conference has been changed to at least 21 days before the Rule 16 scheduling conference, and the time for the report is changed to no more than 14 days after the Rule 26(f) conference. This should ensure that the court will have the report well in advance of the scheduling conference or the entry of the scheduling order.

Since Rule 16 was amended in 1983 to mandate some case management activities in all courts, it has included deadlines for Completing these tasks to ensure that all courts do so within a reasonable time. Rule 26(f) was fit into this scheme when it was adopted in 1993. It was never intended, however, that the national requirements that certain activities be completed by a certain time should delay case management in districts that move much faster than the national rules direct, and the rule is therefore amended to permit such a court to adopt a local rule that shortens the period specified for the completion of these tasks. . . .

2006 Amendment

Subdivision (a). Rule 26(a)(1)(B) is amended to parallel Rule 34(a) by recognizing that a party must disclose electronically stored information as well as documents that it may use to support its claims or defenses. The term "electronically stored information" has the same broad meaning in Rule 26(a)(1) as in Rule 34(a). This amendment is consistent with the 1993 addition of Rule 26(a)(1)(B). The term "data compilations" is deleted as unnecessary because it is a subset of both documents and electronically stored information.

Subdivision (b)(2). The amendment to Rule 26(b)(2) is designed to address issues raised by difficulties in locating, retrieving, and providing discovery of some electronically stored information. Electronic storage systems often make it easier to locate and retrieve information. These advantages are properly taken into account in determining the reasonable scope of discovery in a particular case. But some sources of electronically stored information can be accessed only with substantial burden and cost. In a particular case, these burdens and costs may make the information on such sources not reasonably accessible.

It is not possible to define in a rule the different types of technological features that may affect the burdens and costs of accessing electronically stored information. Information systems are designed to provide ready access to information used in regular ongoing activities. They also may be designed so as to provide ready access to information that is not regularly used. But a system may retain information on sources that are accessible only by incurring substantial burdens or costs. Subparagraph (B) is added to regulate discovery from such sources.

Under this rule, a responding party should produce electronically stored information that is relevant, not privileged, and reasonably accessible, subject to the (b)(2)(C) limitations that apply to all discovery. The responding party must also identify, by category or type, the sources containing potentially responsive information that it is neither searching nor producing. The identification should, to the extent possible, provide enough detail to enable the requesting party to evaluate the burdens and costs of providing the discovery and the likelihood of finding responsive information on the identified sources.

A party's identification of sources of electronically stored information as not reasonably accessible does not relieve the party of its common-law or statutory duties to preserve evidence. Whether a responding party is required to preserve unsearched sources of potentially responsive information that it believes are not reasonably accessible depends on the circumstances of each case. It is often useful for the parties to discuss this issue early in discovery.

The volume of — and the ability to search — much electronically stored information means that in many cases the responding party will be able to produce information from reasonably accessible sources that will fully satisfy the parties' discovery needs. In many circumstances the requesting party should obtain and evaluate the information from such sources before insisting that the responding party search and produce information contained on sources that are not reasonably accessible. If the requesting party continues to seek discovery of information from sources identified as not reasonably accessible, the parties should discuss the burdens and costs of accessing and retrieving the information, the needs that may establish good cause for requiring all or part of the requested discovery even if the information sought is not reasonably accessible, and conditions on obtaining and producing the information that may be appropriate.

If the parties cannot agree whether, or on what terms, sources identified as not reasonably accessible should be searched and discoverable information produced, the issue may be raised either by a motion to compel discovery or by a motion for a protective order. The parties must confer before bringing either motion. If the parties do not resolve the issue and the court must decide, the responding party must show that the identified sources of information are not reasonably accessible because of undue burden or cost. The requesting party may need discovery to test this assertion. Such discovery might take the form of requiring the responding party to conduct a sampling of information contained on the sources identified as not reasonably accessible; allowing some form of inspection of such sources; or taking depositions of witnesses knowledgeable about the responding party's information systems.

Once it is shown that a source of electronically stored information is not reasonably accessible, the requesting party may still obtain discovery by showing good cause, considering the limitations of Rule 26(b)(2)(C) that balance the costs and potential benefits of discovery. The decision whether to require a responding party to search for and produce information that is not reasonably accessible depends not only on the burdens and costs of doing so, but also on whether those burdens and costs can be justified in the circumstances of the case. Appropriate considerations may include: (1) the specificity of the discovery request; (2) the quantity of information available from other and more easily accessed sources; (3) the failure to produce relevant information that seems likely to have existed but is no longer available on more easily accessed sources; (4) the likelihood of finding relevant, responsive information that cannot be obtained from other, more easily accessed sources; (5) predictions as to the importance and usefulness of the further information; (6) the importance of the issues at stake in the litigation; and (7) the parties' resources.

The responding party has the burden as to one aspect of the inquiry — whether the identified sources are not reasonably accessible in light of the burdens and costs required to search for, retrieve, and produce whatever responsive information may be found. The requesting party has the burden of showing that its need for the discovery outweighs the burdens and costs of locating, retrieving, and producing the information. In some cases, the court will be able to determine whether the identified sources are not reasonably accessible and whether the requesting party has shown good cause for some or all of the discovery, consistent with the limitations of Rule 26(b)(2)(C), through a single proceeding or presentation. The good-cause determination, however, may be complicated because the court and parties may know little about what information the sources identified as not reasonably accessible might contain, whether it is relevant, or how valuable it may be to the litigation. In such cases, the parties may need some focused discovery, which may include sampling of the sources, to learn more about what burdens and costs are involved in accessing the information, what the information consists of, and how valuable it is for the litigation in light of information that can be obtained by exhausting other opportunities for discovery.

The good-cause inquiry and consideration of the Rule 26(b)(2)(C) limitations are coupled with the authority to set conditions for discovery. The conditions may take the form of limits on the amount, type, or sources of information required to be accessed and produced. The conditions may also include payment by the requesting party of part or all of the reasonable costs of obtaining information from sources that are not reasonably accessible. A requesting party's willingness to share or bear the access costs may be weighed by the court in determining whether there is good cause. But the producing party's burdens in reviewing the information for relevance and privilege may weigh against permitting the requested discovery.

The limitations of Rule 26(b)(2)(C) continue to apply to all discovery of electronically stored information, including that stored on reasonably accessible electronic sources.

Subdivision (b)(5). The Committee has repeatedly been advised that the risk of privilege waiver, and the work necessary to avoid it, add to the costs and delay of discovery. When the review is of electronically stored information, the risk of waiver, and the time and effort required to avoid it, can increase substantially because of the volume of electronically stored information and the difficulty in ensuring that all information to be produced has in fact been reviewed. Rule 26(b)(5)(A) provides a procedure for a party that has withheld information on the basis of privilege or protection as trial-preparation material to make the claim so that the requesting party can decide whether to contest the claim and the court can resolve the dispute. Rule 26(b)(5)(B) is added to provide a procedure for a party to assert a claim of privilege or trial-preparation material protection after information is produced in discovery in the action and, if the claim is contested, permit any party that received the information to present the matter to the court for resolution.

Rule 26(b)(5)(B) does not address whether the privilege or protection that is asserted after production was waived by the production. The courts have developed principles to determine whether, and under what circumstances, waiver results from inadvertent production of privileged or protected information. Rule 26(b)(5)(B) provides a procedure for presenting and addressing these issues. Rule 26(b)(5)(B) works in tandem with Rule 26(f), which is amended to direct the parties to discuss privilege issues in preparing their discovery plan, and which, with amended Rule 16(b), allows the parties to ask the court to include in an order any agreements the parties reach regarding issues of privilege or trial-preparation material protection. Agreements reached under Rule 26(f)(4) and orders including such agreements entered under Rule 16(b)(6) may be considered when a court determines whether a waiver has occurred. Such agreements and orders ordinarily control if they adopt procedures different from those in Rule 26(b)(5)(B).

A party asserting a claim of privilege or protection after production must give notice to the receiving party. That notice should be in writing unless the circumstances preclude it. Such circumstances could include the assertion of the claim during a deposition. The notice should be as specific as possible in identifying the information and stating the basis for the claim. Because the receiving party must decide whether to challenge the claim and may sequester the information and submit it to the court for a ruling on whether the claimed privilege or protection applies and whether it has been waived, the notice should be sufficiently detailed so as to enable the receiving party and the court to understand the basis for the claim and to determine whether waiver has occurred. Courts will continue to examine whether a claim of privilege or protection was made at a reasonable time when delay is part of the waiver determination under the governing law.

After receiving notice, each party that received the information must promptly return, sequester, or destroy the information and any copies it has. The option of sequestering or destroying the information is included in part because the receiving party may have incorporated the information in protected trial-preparation materials. No receiving party may use or disclose the information pending resolution of the privilege claim. The receiving party may present to the court the questions whether the information is privileged or protected as trial-preparation material, and whether the privilege or protection has been waived. If it does so, it must provide the court with the grounds for the privilege or protection specified in the producing party's notice, and serve all parties. In presenting the question, the party may use the content of the information only to the extent permitted by the applicable law of privilege, protection for trial-preparation material, and professional responsibility.

If a party disclosed the information to nonparties before receiving notice of a claim of privilege or protection as trial-preparation material, it must take reasonable steps to retrieve the information and to return it, sequester it until the claim is resolved, or destroy it.

Whether the information is returned or not, the producing party must preserve the information pending the court's ruling on whether the claim of privilege or of protection is properly asserted and whether it was waived. As with claims made under Rule 26(b)(5)(A), there may be no ruling if the other parties do not contest the claim.

Subdivision (f). Rule 26(f) is amended to direct the parties to discuss discovery of electronically stored information during their discovery-planning conference. The rule focuses on "issues relating to disclosure or discovery of electronically stored information"; the discussion is not required in cases not involving electronic discovery, and the amendment imposes no additional requirements in those cases. When the parties do anticipate disclosure or discovery of electronically stored information, discussion at the outset may avoid later difficulties or ease their resolution.

When a case involves discovery of electronically stored information, the issues to be addressed during the Rule 26(f) conference depend on the nature and extent of the contemplated discovery and of the parties' information systems. It may be important for the parties to discuss those systems, and accordingly important for counsel to become familiar with those systems before the conference. With that information, the parties can develop a discovery plan that takes into account the capabilities of their computer systems. In appropriate cases identification of, and early discovery from, individuals with special knowledge of a party's computer systems may be helpful.

The particular issues regarding electronically stored information that deserve attention during the discovery planning stage depend on the specifics of the given case. *See Manual for Complex Litigation (4th)* § 40.25(2) (listing topics for discussion in a proposed order regarding meet-and-confer sessions). For example, the parties may specify the topics for such discovery and the time period for which discovery will be sought. They may identify the various sources of such information within a party's control that should be searched for electronically stored information. They may discuss whether the information is reasonably accessible to the party that has it, including the burden or cost of retrieving and reviewing the information. *See* Rule 26(b)(2)(B). Rule 26(f)(3) explicitly directs the parties to discuss the form or forms in which electronically stored information might be produced. The parties may be able to reach agreement on the forms of production, making discovery more efficient. Rule 34(b) is amended to permit a requesting party to specify the form or forms in which it wants electronically stored information produced. If the requesting party does not specify a form, Rule 34(b) directs the responding party to state the forms it intends to use in the production. Early discussion of the forms of production may facilitate the application of Rule 34(b) by allowing the parties to determine what forms of production will meet both parties' needs. Early identification of disputes over the forms of production may help avoid the expense and delay of searches or productions using inappropriate forms.

Rule 26(f) is also amended to direct the parties to discuss any issues regarding preservation of discoverable information during their conference as they develop a discovery plan. This provision applies to all sorts of discoverable information, but can be particularly important with regard to electronically stored information. The volume and dynamic nature of electronically stored information may complicate preservation obligations. The ordinary operation of computers involves both the automatic creation and the automatic deletion or overwriting of certain information. Failure to address preservation issues early in the litigation increases uncertainty and raises a risk of disputes.

The parties' discussion should pay particular attention to the balance between the competing needs to preserve relevant evidence and to continue routine operations critical to ongoing activities. Complete or broad cessation of a party's routine computer operations could paralyze the party's activities. *Cf. Manual for Complex Litigation (4th)* § 11.422 ("A blanket preservation order may be prohibitively expensive and unduly burdensome for parties dependent on computer systems for their day-to-day operations.") The parties should take account of these considerations in their discussions, with the goal of agreeing on reasonable preservation steps.

The requirement that the parties discuss preservation does not imply that courts should routinely enter preservation orders. A preservation order entered over objections should be narrowly tailored. Ex parte preservation orders should issue only in exceptional circumstances.

Rule 26(f) is also amended to provide that the parties should discuss any issues relating to assertions of privilege or of protection as trial-preparation materials, including whether the parties can facilitate discovery by agreeing on procedures for asserting claims of privilege or protection after production and whether to ask the court to enter an order that includes any agreement the parties reach. The Committee has repeatedly been advised about the discovery difficulties that can result from efforts to guard against waiver of privilege and work-product protection. Frequently parties find it necessary to spend large amounts of time reviewing materials requested through discovery to avoid waiving privilege. These efforts are necessary because materials subject to a claim of privilege or protection are often difficult to identify. A failure to withhold even one such item may result in an argument that there has been a waiver of privilege as to all other privileged materials on that subject matter. Efforts to avoid the risk of waiver can impose substantial costs on the party producing the material and the time required for the privilege review can substantially delay access for the party seeking discovery.

These problems often become more acute when discovery of electronically stored information is sought. The volume of such data, and the informality that attends use of e-mail and some other types of electronically stored information, may make privilege determinations more difficult, and privilege review correspondingly more expensive and time consuming. Other aspects of electronically stored information pose particular difficulties for privilege review. For example, production may be sought of information automatically included in electronic files but not apparent to the creator or to readers. Computer programs may retain draft language, editorial comments, and other deleted matter (sometimes referred to as "embedded data" or "embedded edits") in an electronic file but not make them apparent to the reader. Information describing the history, tracking, or management of an electronic file (sometimes called "metadata") is usually not apparent to the reader viewing a hard copy or a screen image. Whether this information should be produced may be among the topics discussed in the Rule 26(f) conference. If it is, it may need to be reviewed to ensure that no privileged information is included, further complicating the task of privilege review.

Parties may attempt to minimize these costs and delays by agreeing to protocols that minimize the risk of waiver. They may agree that the responding party will provide certain requested materials for initial examination without waiving any privilege or protection — sometimes known as a "quick peek." The requesting party then designates the documents it wishes to have actually produced. This designation is the Rule 34 request. The responding party then responds in the usual course, screening only those documents actually requested for formal production and asserting privilege claims as provided in Rule 26(b)(5)(A). On other occasions, parties enter agreements — sometimes called "clawback agreements"— that production without intent to waive privilege or protection should not be a waiver so long as the responding party identifies the documents mistakenly produced, and that the documents should be returned under those circumstances. Other voluntary arrangements may be appropriate depending on the circumstances of each litigation. In most circumstances, a party who receives information under such an arrangement cannot assert that production of the information waived a claim of privilege or of protection as trial-preparation material.

Although these agreements may not be appropriate for all cases, in certain cases they can facilitate prompt and economical discovery by reducing delay before the discovering party obtains access to documents, and by reducing the cost and burden of review by the producing party. A case-management or other order including such agreements may further facilitate the discovery process. Form 35 is amended to include a report to the court about any agreement regarding protections against inadvertent forfeiture or waiver of privilege or protection that the parties have reached, and Rule 16(b) is amended to recognize that the court may include such an agreement in a case-management or other order. If the parties agree to entry of such an order, their proposal should be included in the report to the court.

Rule 26(b)(5)(B) is added to establish a parallel procedure to assert privilege or protection as trial-preparation material after production, leaving the question of waiver to later determination by the court.

Rule 27. Depositions Before Action or Pending Appeal

(a) Before Action.

(1) Petition. A person who desires to perpetuate testimony regarding any matter that may be cognizable in any court of the United States may file a verified petition in the United States district court in the district of the residence of any expected adverse party. The petition shall be entitled in the name of the petitioner and shall show: 1, that the petitioner expects to be a party to an action cognizable in a court of the United States but is presently unable to bring it or cause it to be brought, 2, the subject matter of the expected action and the petitioner's interest therein, 3, the facts which the petitioner desires to establish by the proposed testimony and the reasons for desiring to perpetuate it, 4, the names or a description of the persons the petitioner expects will be adverse parties and their addresses so far as known, and 5, the names and addresses of the persons to be examined and the substance of the testimony which the petitioner expects to elicit from each, and shall ask for an order authorizing the petitioner to take the depositions of the persons to be examined named in the petition, for the purpose of perpetuating their testimony.

(2) Notice and Service. At least 20 days before the hearing date, the petitioner must serve each expected adverse party with a copy of the petition and a notice stating the time and place of the hearing. The notice may be served either inside or outside the district or state in the manner provided in Rule 4. If that service cannot be made with due diligence on an expected adverse party, the court may order service by publication or otherwise. The court must appoint an attorney to represent persons not served in the manner provided by Rule 4 and to cross-examine the deponent if an unserved person is not otherwise represented. Rule 17(c) applies if any expected adverse party is a minor or is incompetent.

(3) Order and Examination. If the court is satisfied that the perpetuation of the testimony may prevent a failure or delay of justice, it shall make an order designating or describing the persons whose depositions may be taken and specifying the subject matter of the examination and whether the depositions shall be taken upon oral examination or written interrogatories. The depositions may then be taken in accordance with these rules; and the court may make orders of the character provided for by Rules 34 and 35. For the purpose of applying these rules to depositions for perpetuating testimony, each reference therein to the court in which the action is pending shall be deemed to refer to the court in which the petition for such deposition was filed.

(4) Use of Deposition. If a deposition to perpetuate testimony is taken under these rules or if, although not so taken, it would be admissible in evidence in the courts of the state in which it is taken, it may be used in any action involving the same subject matter subsequently brought in a United States district court, in accordance with the provisions of Rule 32(a).

(b) Pending Appeal. If an appeal has been taken from a judgment of a district court or before the taking of an appeal if the time therefor has not expired, the district court in which the judgment was rendered may allow the taking of the depositions of witnesses to perpetuate their testimony for use in the event of further proceedings in the district court. In such case the party who desires to perpetuate the testimony may make a motion in the district court for leave to take the depositions, upon the same notice and service thereof as if the action was pending in the district court. The motion shall show (1) the names and addresses of persons to be examined and the substance of the testimony which the party expects to elicit from each; (2) the reasons for perpetuating their testimony. If the court finds that the perpetuation of the testimony is proper to avoid a failure or delay of justice, it may make an order allowing the depositions to be taken and may make orders of the character provided for by Rules 34 and 35, and thereupon the depositions may be taken and used in the same manner and under the same conditions as are prescribed in these rules for depositions taken in actions pending in the district court.

(c) Perpetuation by Action. This rule does not limit the power of a court to entertain an action to perpetuate testimony.

Rule 28. Persons Before Whom Depositions may be Taken

(a) Within the United States. Within the United States or within a territory or insular possession subject to the jurisdiction of the United States, depositions shall be taken before an officer authorized to administer oaths by the laws of the United States or of the place where the examination is held, or before a person appointed by the court in which the action is pending. A person so appointed has power to administer oaths and take testimony. The term officer as used in Rules 30, 31 and 32 includes a person appointed by the court or designated by the parties under Rule 29.

(b) In Foreign Countries. Depositions may be taken in a foreign country (1) pursuant to any applicable treaty or convention, or (2) pursuant to a letter of request (whether or not captioned a letter rogatory), or (3) on notice before a person authorized to administer oaths in the place where the examination is held, either by the law thereof or by the law of the United States, or (4) before a person commissioned by the court, and a person so commissioned shall have the power by virtue of the commission to administer any necessary oath and take testimony. A commission or a letter of request shall be issued on application and notice and on terms that are just and appropriate. It is not requisite to the issuance of a commission or a letter of request that the taking of the deposition in any other manner is impracticable or inconvenient; and both a commission and a letter of request may be issued in proper cases. A notice or commission may designate the person before whom the deposition is to be taken either by name or descriptive title. A letter of request may be addressed "To the Appropriate Authority in [here name the country]." When a letter of request or any other device is used pursuant to any applicable treaty or convention, it shall be captioned in the form prescribed by that treaty or convention. Evidence obtained in response to a letter of request need not be excluded merely because it is not a verbatim transcript, because the testimony was not taken under oath, or because of any similar departure from the requirements for depositions taken within the United States under these rules.

(c) Disqualification for Interest. No deposition shall be taken before a person who is a relative or employee or attorney or counsel of any of the parties, or is a relative or employee of such attorney or counsel, or is financially interested in the action.

Rule 29. Stipulations Regarding Discovery Procedure

Unless otherwise directed by the court, the parties may by written stipulation (1) provide that depositions may be taken before any person, at any time or place, upon any notice, and in any manner and when so taken may be used like other depositions, and (2) modify other procedures governing or limitations placed upon discovery, except that stipulations extending the time provided in Rules 33, 34, and 36 for responses to discovery may, if they would interfere with any time set for completion of discovery, for hearing of a motion, or for trial, be made only with the approval of the court.

Rule 30. Depositions Upon Oral Examination

(a) When Depositions May Be Taken; When Leave Required.

(1) A party may take the testimony of any person, including a party, by deposition upon oral examination without leave of court except as provided in paragraph (2). The attendance of witnesses may be compelled by subpoena as provided in Rule 45.

(2) A party must obtain leave of court, which shall be granted to the extent consistent with the principles stated in Rule 26(b)(2), if the person to be examined is confined in prison or if, without the written stipulation of the parties,

(A) a proposed deposition would result in more than ten depositions being taken under this rule or Rule 31 by the plaintiffs, or by the defendants, or by third-party defendants;

(B) the person to be examined already has been deposed in the case; or

(C) a party seeks to take a deposition before the time specified in Rule 26(d) unless the notice contains a certification, with supporting facts, that the person to be examined is expected to leave the United States and be unavailable for examination in this country unless deposed before that time.

(b) Notice of Examination: General Requirements; Method of Recording; Production of Documents and Things; Deposition of Organization; Deposition by Telephone.

(1) A party desiring to take the deposition of any person upon oral examination shall give reasonable notice in writing to every other party to the action. The notice shall state the time and place for taking the deposition and the name and address of each person to be examined, if known, and, if the name is not known, a general description sufficient to identify the person or the particular class or group to which the person belongs. If a subpoena duces tecum is to be served on the person to be examined, the designation of the materials to be produced as set forth in the subpoena shall be attached to, or included in, the notice.

(2) The party taking the deposition shall state in the notice the method by which the testimony shall be recorded. Unless the court orders otherwise, it may be recorded by sound, sound-and-visual, or stenographic means, and the party taking the deposition shall bear the cost of the recording. Any party may arrange for a transcription to be made from the recording of a deposition taken by nonstenographic means.

(3) With prior notice to the deponent and other parties, any party may designate another method to record the deponent's testimony in addition to the method specified by the person taking the deposition. The additional record or transcript shall be made at that party's expense unless the court otherwise orders.

(4) Unless otherwise agreed by the parties, a deposition shall be conducted before an officer appointed or designated under Rule 28 and shall begin with a statement on the record by the officer that includes (A) the officer's name and business address; (B) the date, time, and place of the deposition; (C) the name of the deponent; (D) the administration of the oath or affirmation to the deponent; and (E) an identification of all persons present. If the deposition is recorded other than stenographically, the officer shall repeat items (A) through (C) at the beginning of each unit of recorded tape or other recording medium. The appearance or demeanor of deponents or attorneys shall not be distorted through camera or sound-recording techniques. At the end of the deposition, the officer shall state on the record that the deposition is complete and shall set forth any stipulations made by counsel concerning the custody of the transcript or recording and the exhibits, or concerning other pertinent matters.

(5) The notice to a party deponent may be accompanied by a request made in compliance with Rule 34 for the production of documents and tangible things at the taking of the deposition. The procedure of Rule 34 shall apply to the request.

(6) A party may in the party's notice and in a subpoena name as the deponent a public or private corporation or a partnership or association or governmental agency and describe with reasonable particularity the matters on which examination is requested. In that event, the organization so named shall designate one or more officers, directors, or managing agents, or other persons who consent to testify on its behalf, and may set forth, for each person designated, the matters on which the person will testify. A subpoena shall advise a non-party organization of its duty to make such a designation. The persons so designated shall testify as to matters known or reasonably available to the organization. This subdivision (b)(6) does not preclude taking a deposition by any other procedure authorized in these rules.

(7) The parties may stipulate in writing or the court may upon motion order that a deposition be taken by telephone or other remote electronic means. For the purposes of this rule and Rules 28(a), 37(a)(1), and 37(b)(1), a deposition taken by such means is taken in the district and at the place where the deponent is to answer questions.

(c) Examination and Cross-Examination; Record of Examination; Oath; Objections. Examination and cross-examination of witnesses may proceed as permitted at the trial under the provisions of the Federal Rules of Evidence except Rules 103 and 615. The officer before whom the deposition is to be taken shall put the witness on oath or affirmation and shall personally, or by someone acting under the officer's direction and in the officer's presence, record the testimony of the witness. The testimony shall be taken stenographically or recorded by any other method authorized by subdivision (b)(2) of this rule. All objections made at the time of the examination to the qualifications of the officer taking the deposition, to the manner of taking it, to the evidence presented, to the conduct of any party, or to any other aspect of the proceedings shall be noted by the officer upon the record of the deposition; but the examination shall proceed, with the testimony being taken subject to the objections. In lieu of participating in the oral examination, parties may serve written questions in a sealed envelope on the party taking the deposition and the party taking the deposition shall transmit them to the officer, who shall propound them to the witness and record the answers verbatim.

(d) Schedule and Duration; Motion to Terminate or Limit Examination.

(1) Any objection during a deposition must be stated concisely and in a non-argumentative and non-suggestive manner. A person may instruct a deponent not to answer only when necessary to preserve a privilege, to enforce a limitation directed by the court, or to present a motion under Rule 30(d)(4).

(2) Unless otherwise authorized by the court or stipulated by the parties, a deposition is limited to one day of seven hours. The court must allow additional time consistent with Rule 26(b)(2) if needed for a fair examination of the deponent or if the deponent or another person, or other circumstance, impedes or delays the examination.

(3) If the court finds that any impediment, delay, or other conduct has frustrated the fair examination of the deponent, it may impose upon the persons responsible an appropriate sanction, including the reasonable costs and attorney's fees incurred by any parties as a result thereof.

(4) At any time during a deposition, on motion of a party or of the deponent and upon a showing that the examination is being conducted in bad faith or in such manner as unreasonably to annoy, embarrass, or oppress the deponent or party, the court in which the action is pending or the court in the district where the deposition is being taken may order the officer conducting the examination to cease forthwith from taking the deposition, or may limit the scope and manner of the taking of the deposition as provided in Rule 26(c). If the order made terminates the examination, it may be resumed thereafter only upon the order of the court in which the action is pending. Upon demand of the objecting party or deponent, the taking of the deposition must be suspended for the time necessary to make a motion for an order. The provisions of Rule 37(a)(4) apply to the award of expenses incurred in relation to the motion.

(e) Review by Witness; Changes; Signing. If requested by the deponent or a party before completion of the deposition, the deponent shall have 30 days after being notified by the officer that the transcript or recording is available in which to review the transcript or recording and, if there are changes in form or substance, to sign a statement reciting such changes and the reasons given by the deponent for making them. The officer shall indicate in the certificate prescribed by subdivision (f)(1) whether any review was requested and, if so, shall append any changes made by the deponent during the period allowed.

(f) Certification and Delivery by Officer; Exhibits; Copies.

(1) The officer must certify that the witness was duly sworn by the officer and that the deposition is a true record of the testimony given by the witness. This certificate must be in writing and accompany the record of the deposition. Unless otherwise ordered by the court, the officer must securely seal the deposition in an envelope or package indorsed with the title of the action and marked "Deposition of [here insert name of witness]" and must promptly send it to the attorney who arranged for the transcript or recording, who must store it under conditions that will protect it against loss, destruction, tampering, or deterioration. Documents and things produced for inspection during the examination of the witness must, upon the request of a party, be marked for identification and annexed to the deposition and may be inspected and copied by any party, except that if the person producing the materials desires to retain them the person may (A) offer copies to be marked for identification and annexed to the deposition and to serve thereafter as originals if the person affords to all parties fair opportunity to verify the copies by comparison with the originals, or (B) offer the originals to be marked for identification, after giving to each party an opportunity to inspect and copy them, in which event the materials may then be used in the same manner as if annexed to the deposition. Any party may move for an order that the original be annexed to and returned with the deposition to the court, pending final disposition of the case.

(2) Unless otherwise ordered by the court or agreed by the parties, the officer shall retain stenographic notes of any deposition taken stenographically or a copy of the recording of any deposition taken by another method. Upon payment of reasonable charges therefor, the officer shall furnish a copy of the transcript or other recording of the deposition to any party or to the deponent.

(3) The party taking the deposition shall give prompt notice of its filing to all other parties.

(g) Failure to Attend or to Serve Subpoena; Expenses.

(1) If the party giving the notice of the taking of a deposition fails to attend and proceed therewith and another party attends in person or by attorney pursuant to the notice, the court may order the party giving the notice to pay to such other party the reasonable expenses incurred by that party and that party's attorney in attending, including reasonable attorney's fees.

(2) If the party giving the notice of the taking of a deposition of a witness fails to serve a subpoena upon the witness and the witness because of such failure does not attend, and if another party attends in person or by attorney because that party expects the deposition of that witness to be taken, the court may order the party giving the notice to pay to such other party the reasonable expenses incurred by that party and that party's attorney in attending, including reasonable attorney's fees.

ADVISORY COMMITTEE NOTES

1993 Amendments

Subdivision (a). . . .

Paragraph (2)(A) is new. It provides a limit on the number of depositions the parties may take, absent leave of court or stipulation with the other parties. One aim of this revision is to assure judicial review under the standards stated in Rule 26(b)(2) before any side will be allowed to take more than ten depositions in a case without agreement of the other parties. A second objective is to emphasize that counsel have a professional obligation to develop a mutual cost-effective plan for discovery in the case. Leave to take additional depositions should be granted when consistent with the principles of Rule 26(b)(2), and in some cases the ten-per-side limit should be reduced in accordance with those same principles. Consideration should ordinarily be given at the planning meeting of the parties under Rule 26(f) and at the time of a scheduling conference under Rule 16(b) as to enlargements or reductions in the number of depositions, eliminating the need for special motions.

A deposition under Rule 30(b)(6) should, for purposes of this limit, be treated as a single deposition even though more than one person may be designated to testify.

In multi-party cases, the parties on any side are expected to confer and agree as to which depositions are most needed, given the presumptive limit on the number of depositions they can take without leave of court. If these disputes cannot be amicably resolved, the court can be requested to resolve the dispute or permit additional depositions.

Paragraph (2)(B) is new. It requires leave of court if any witness is to be deposed in the action more than once. This requirement does not apply when a deposition is temporarily recessed for convenience of counsel or the deponent or to enable additional materials to be gathered before resuming the deposition. If significant travel costs would be incurred to resume the deposition, the parties should consider the feasibility of conducting the balance of the examination by telephonic means.

Paragraph (2)(C) revises the second sentence of the former subdivision (a) as to when depositions may be taken. Consistent with the changes made in Rule 26(d), providing that formal discovery ordinarily not commence until after the litigants have met and conferred as directed in revised Rule 26(f), the rule requires leave of court or agreement of the parties if a deposition is to be taken before that time (except when a witness is about to leave the country).

Subdivision (b). The primary change in subdivision (b) is that parties will be authorized to record deposition testimony by nonstenographic means without first having to obtain permission of the court or agreement from other counsel. . . .

New paragraph (2) confers on the party taking the deposition the choice of the method of recording, without the need to obtain prior court approval for one taken other than stenographically. A party choosing to record a deposition only by videotape or audiotape should understand that a transcript will be required by Rule 26(a)(3)(B) and Rule 32(c) if the deposition is later to be offered as evidence at trial or on a dispositive motion under Rule 56. Objections to the nonstenographic recording of a deposition, when warranted by the circumstances, can be presented to the court under Rule 26(c).

Paragraph (3) provides that other parties may arrange, at their own expense, for the recording of a deposition by a means (stenographic, visual, or sound) in addition to the method designated by the person noticing the deposition. The former provisions of this paragraph, relating to the court's power to change the date of a deposition, have been eliminated as redundant in view of Rule 26(c)(2). . . .

Paragraph (7) is revised to authorize the taking of a deposition not only by telephone but also by other remote electronic means, such as satellite television, when agreed to by the parties or authorized by the court.

Subdivision (c). Minor changes are made in this subdivision to reflect those made in subdivision (b) and to complement the new provisions of subdivision (d)(1), aimed at reducing the number of interruptions during depositions.

In addition, the revision addresses a recurring problem as to whether other potential deponents can attend a deposition. Courts have disagreed . . . . The revision provides that other witnesses are not automatically excluded from a deposition simply by the request of a party. Exclusion, however, can be ordered under Rule 26(c)(5) when appropriate; and, if exclusion is ordered, consideration should be given as to whether the excluded witnesses likewise should be precluded from reading, or being otherwise informed about, the testimony given in the earlier depositions. The revision addresses only the matter of attendance by potential deponents, and does not attempt to resolve issues concerning attendance by others, such as members of the public or press.

Subdivision (d). The first sentence of new paragraph (1) provides that any objections during a deposition must be made concisely and in a non-argumentative and non-suggestive manner. Depositions frequently have been unduly prolonged, if not unfairly frustrated, by lengthy objections and colloquy, often suggesting how the deponent should respond. While objections may, under the revised rule, be made during a deposition, they ordinarily should be limited to those that under Rule 32(d)(3) might be waived if not made at that time, *i.e.,* objections on grounds that might be immediately obviated, removed, or cured, such as to the form of a question or the responsiveness of an answer. Under Rule 32(b), other objections can, even without the so-called "usual stipulation" preserving objections, be raised for the first time at trial and therefore should be kept to a minimum during a deposition.

Directions to a deponent not to answer a question can be even more disruptive than objections. The second sentence of new paragraph (1) prohibits such directions except in the three circumstances indicated: to claim a privilege or protection against disclosure (*e.g.*, as work product), to enforce a court directive limiting the scope or length of permissible discovery, or to suspend a deposition to enable presentation of a motion under paragraph (3).

Paragraph (2) is added to this subdivision to dispel any doubts regarding the power of the court by order or local rule to establish limits on the length of depositions. The rule also explicitly authorizes the court to impose the cost resulting from obstructive tactics that unreasonably prolong a deposition on the person engaged in such obstruction. This sanction may be imposed on a non-party witness as well as a party or attorney, but is otherwise congruent with Rule 26(g).

It is anticipated that limits on the length of depositions prescribed by local rules would be presumptive only, subject to modification by the court or by agreement of the parties. Such modifications typically should be discussed by the parties in their meeting under Rule 26(f) and included in the scheduling order required by Rule 16(b). Additional time, moreover, should be allowed under the revised rule when justified under the principles stated in Rule 26(b)(2). To reduce the number of special motions, local rules should ordinarily permit — and indeed encourage — the parties to agree to additional time, as when, during the taking of a deposition, it becomes clear that some additional examination is needed.

Paragraph (3) authorizes appropriate sanctions not only when a deposition is unreasonably prolonged, but also when an attorney engages in other practices that improperly frustrate the fair examination of the deponent, such as making improper objections or giving directions not to answer prohibited by paragraph (1). In general, counsel should not engage in any conduct during a deposition that would not be allowed in the presence of a judicial officer. The making of an excessive number of unnecessary objections may itself constitute sanctionable conduct, as may the refusal of an attorney to agree with other counsel on a fair apportionment of the time allowed for examination of a deponent or a refusal to agree to a reasonable request for some additional time to complete a deposition, when that is permitted by the local rule or order. . . .

2000 Amendment

Subdivision (d). Paragraph (1) has been amended to clarify the terms regarding behavior during depositions. The references to objections " to evidence" and limitations "on evidence" have been removed to avoid disputes about what is "evidence" and whether an objection is to, or a limitation is on, discovery instead. It is intended that the rule apply to any objection to a question or other issue arising during a deposition, and to any limitation imposed by the court in connection with a deposition, which might relate to duration or other matters.

The current rule places limitations on instructions that a witness not answer only when the instruction is made by a "party." Similar limitations should apply with regard to anyone who might purport to instruct a witness not to answer a question. Accordingly, the rule is amended to apply the limitation to instructions by any person. The amendment is not intended to confer new authority on nonparties to instruct witnesses to refuse to answer deposition questions. The amendment makes it clear that, whatever the legitimacy of giving such instructions, the nonparty is subject to the same limitations as parties.

Paragraph (2) imposes a presumptive durational limitation of one day of seven hours for any deposition. The Committee has been informed that overlong depositions can result in undue costs and delays in some circumstances. This limitation contemplates that there will be reasonable breaks during the day for lunch and other reasons, and that the only time to be counted is the time occupied by the actual deposition. For purposes of this durational limit, the deposition of each person designated under Rule 30(b)(6) should be considered a separate deposition. The presumptive duration may be extended, or otherwise altered, by agreement. Absent agreement, a court order is needed. The party seeking a court order to extend the examination, or otherwise alter the limitations, is expected to show good cause to justify such an order.

Parties considering extending the time for a deposition — and courts asked to order an extension — might consider a variety of factors. For example, if the witness needs an interpreter, that may prolong the examination. If the examination will cover events occurring over a long period of time, that may justify allowing additional time. In cases in which the witness will be questioned about numerous or lengthy documents, it is often desirable for the interrogating party to send copies of the documents to the witness sufficiently in advance of the deposition so that the witness can become familiar with them. Should the witness nevertheless not read the documents in advance, thereby prolonging the deposition, a court could consider that a reason for extending the time limit. If the examination reveals that documents have been requested but not produced, that may justify further examination once production has occurred. In multi-party cases, the need for each party to examine the witness may warrant additional time, although duplicative questioning should be avoided and parties with similar interests should strive to designate one lawyer to question about areas of common interest. Similarly, should the lawyer for the witness want to examine the witness, that may require additional time. Finally, with regard to expert witnesses, there may more often be a need for additional time — even after the submission of the report required by Rule 26(a)(2) — for full exploration of the theories upon which the witness relies.

It is expected that in most instances the parties and the witness will make reasonable accommodations to avoid the need for resort to the court. The limitation is phrased in terms of a single day on the assumption that ordinarily a single day would be preferable to a deposition extending over multiple days; if alternative arrangements would better suit the parties, they may agree to them. It is also assumed that there will be reasonable breaks during the day. Preoccupation with timing is to be avoided.

The rule directs the court to allow additional time where consistent with Rule 26(b)(2) if needed for a fair examination of the deponent. In addition, if the deponent or another person impedes or delays the examination, the court must authorize extra time. The amendment makes clear that additional time should also be allowed where the examination is impeded by an "other circumstance," which might include a power outage, a health emergency, or other event.

In keeping with the amendment to Rule 26(b)(2), the provision added in 1993 granting authority to adopt a local rule limiting the time permitted for depositions has been removed. The court may enter a case-specific order directing shorter depositions for all depositions in a case or with regard to a specific witness. The court may also order that a deposition be taken for limited periods on several days.

Paragraph (3) includes sanctions provisions formerly included in paragraph (2). It authorizes the court to impose an appropriate sanction on any person responsible for an impediment that frustrated the fair examination of the deponent. This could include the deponent, any party, or any other person involved in the deposition. If the impediment or delay results from an "other circumstance" under paragraph (2), ordinarily no sanction would be appropriate. . . .

Subdivision (f)(1)[.] This subdivision is amended because Rule 5(d) has been amended to direct that discovery materials, including depositions, ordinarily should not be filed. . . . Rule 5(d) provides that, once the deposition is used in the proceeding, the attorney must file it with the court. . . .

Rule 31. Depositions Upon Written Questions

(a) Serving Questions; Notice.

(1) A party may take the testimony of any person, including a party, by deposition upon written questions without leave of court except as provided in paragraph (2). The attendance of witnesses may be compelled by the use of subpoena as provided in Rule 45.

(2) A party must obtain leave of court, which shall be granted to the extent consistent with the principles stated in Rule 26(b)(2), if the person to be examined is confined in prison or if, without the written stipulation of the parties.

(A) a proposed deposition would result in more than ten depositions being taken under this rule or Rule 30 by the plaintiffs, or by the defendants, or by third-party defendants;

(B) the person to be examined has already been deposed in the case; or

(C) a party seeks to take a deposition before the time specified in Rule 26(d).

(3) A party desiring to take a deposition upon written questions shall serve them upon every other party with a notice stating (1) the name and address of the person who is to answer them, if known, and if the name is not known, a general description sufficient to identify the person or the particular class or group to which the person belongs, and (2) the name or descriptive title and address of the officer before whom the deposition is to be taken. A deposition upon written questions may be taken of a public or private corporation or a partnership or association or governmental agency in accordance with the provisions of Rule 30(b)(6).

(4) Within 14 days after the notice and written questions are served, a party may serve cross questions upon all other parties. Within 7 days after being served with cross questions, a party may serve redirect questions upon all other parties. Within 7 days after being served with redirect questions, a party may serve recross questions upon all other parties. The court may for cause shown enlarge or shorten the time.

(b) Officer to Take Responses and Prepare Record. A copy of the notice and copies of all questions served shall be delivered by the party taking the deposition to the officer designated in the notice, who shall proceed promptly, in the manner provided by Rule 30(c), (e), and (f), to take the testimony of the witness in response to the questions and to prepare, certify, and file or mail the deposition, attaching thereto the copy of the notice and the questions received by the officer.

(c) Notice of Filing. When the deposition is filed the party taking it shall promptly give notice thereof to all other parties.

Rule 32. Use of Depositions in Court Proceedings

(a) Use of Depositions. At the trial or upon the hearing of a motion or an interlocutory proceeding, any part or all of a deposition, so far as admissible under the rules of evidence applied as though the witness were then present and testifying, may be used against any party who was present or represented at the taking of the deposition or who had reasonable notice thereof, in accordance with any of the following provisions:

(1) Any deposition may be used by any party for the purpose of contradicting or impeaching the testimony of deponent as a witness, or for any other purpose permitted by the Federal Rules of Evidence.

(2) The deposition of a party or of anyone who at the time of taking the deposition was an officer, director, or managing agent, or a person designated under Rule 30(b)(6) or 31(a) to testify on behalf of a public or private corporation, partnership or association or governmental agency which is a party may be used by an adverse party for any purpose.

(3) The deposition of a witness, whether or not a party, may be used by any party for any purpose if the court finds:

(A) that the witness is dead; or

(B) that the witness is at a greater distance than 100 miles from the place of trial or hearing, or is out of the United States, unless it appears that the absence of the witness was procured by the party offering the deposition; or

(C) that the witness is unable to attend or testify because of age, illness, infirmity, or imprisonment; or

(D) that the party offering the deposition has been unable to procure the attendance of the witness by subpoena; or

(E) upon application and notice, that such exceptional circumstances exist as to make it desirable, in the interest of justice and with due regard to the importance of presenting the testimony of witnesses orally in open court, to allow the deposition to be used.

A deposition taken without leave of court pursuant to a notice under Rule 30(a)(2)(C) shall not be used against a party who demonstrates that, when served with the notice, it was unable through the exercise of diligence to obtain counsel to represent it at the taking of the deposition; nor shall a deposition be used against a party who, having received less than 11 days notice of a deposition, has promptly upon receiving such notice filed a motion for a protective order under Rule

26(c)(2) requesting that the deposition not be held or be held at a different time or place and such motion is pending at the time the deposition is held.

(4) If only part of a deposition is offered in evidence by a party, an adverse party may require the offeror to introduce any other part which ought in fairness to be considered with the part introduced, and any party may introduce any other parts.

Substitution of parties pursuant to Rule 25 does not affect the right to use depositions previously taken; and, when an action has been brought in any court of the United States or of any State and another action involving the same subject matter is afterward brought between the same parties or their representatives or successors in interest, all depositions lawfully taken and duly filed in the former action may be used in the latter as if originally taken therefor. A deposition previously taken may also be used as permitted by the Federal Rules of Evidence.

(b) Objections to Admissibility. Subject to the provisions of Rule 28(b) and subdivision (d)(3) of this rule, objection may be made at the trial or hearing to receiving in evidence any deposition or part thereof for any reason which would require the exclusion of the evidence if the witness were then present and testifying.

(c) Form of Presentation. Except as otherwise directed by the court, a party offering deposition testimony pursuant to this rule may offer it in stenographic or nonstenographic form, but, if in nonstenographic form, the party shall also provide the court with a transcript of the portions so offered. On request of any party in a case tried before a jury, deposition testimony offered other than for impeachment purposes shall be presented in nonstenographic form, if available, unless the court for good cause orders otherwise.

(d) Effect of Errors and Irregularities in Depositions.

(1) As to Notice. All errors and irregularities in the notice for taking a deposition are waived unless written objection is promptly served upon the party giving the notice.

(2) As to Disqualification of Officer. Objection to taking a deposition because of disqualification of the officer before whom it is to be taken is waived unless made before the taking of the deposition begins or as soon thereafter as the disqualification becomes known or could be discovered with reasonable diligence.

(3) As to Taking of Deposition.

(A) Objections to the competency of a witness or to the competency, relevancy, or materiality of testimony are not waived by failure to make them before or during the taking of the deposition, unless the ground of the objection is one which might have been obviated or removed if presented at that time.

(B) Errors and irregularities occurring at the oral examination in the manner of taking the deposition, in the form of the questions or answers, in the oath or affirmation, or in the conduct of parties, and errors of any kind which might be obviated, removed, or cured if promptly presented, are waived unless seasonable objection thereto is made at the taking of the deposition.

(C) Objections to the form of written questions submitted under Rule 31 are waived unless served in writing upon the party propounding them within the time allowed for serving the succeeding cross or other questions and within 5 days after service of the last questions authorized.

(4) As to Completion and Return of Deposition. Errors and irregularities in the manner in which the testimony is transcribed or the deposition is prepared, signed, certified, sealed, indorsed, transmitted, filed, or otherwise dealt with by the officer under Rules 30 and 31 are waived unless a motion to suppress the deposition or some part thereof is made with reasonable promptness after such defect is, or with due diligence might have been, ascertained.

Rule 33. Interrogatories to Parties

(a) Availability. Without leave of court or written stipulation, any party may serve upon any other party written interrogatories, not exceeding 25 in number including all discrete subparts, to be answered by the party served or, if the party served is a public or private corporation or a partnership or association or governmental agency, by any officer or agent, who shall furnish such information as is available to the party. Leave to serve additional interrogatories shall be granted to the extent consistent with the principles of Rule 26(b)(2). Without leave of court or written stipulation, interrogatories may not be served before the time specified in Rule 26(d).

(b) Answers and Objections.

(1) Each interrogatory shall be answered separately and fully in writing under oath, unless it is objected to, in which event the objecting party shall state the reasons for objection and shall answer to the extent the interrogatory is not objectionable.

(2) The answers are to be signed by the person making them, and the objections signed by the attorney making them.

(3) The party upon whom the interrogatories have been served shall serve a copy of the answers, and objections if any, within 30 days after the service of the interrogatories. A shorter or longer time may be directed by the court or, in the absence of such an order, agreed to in writing by the parties subject to Rule 29.

(4) All grounds for an objection to an interrogatory shall be stated with specificity. Any ground not stated in a timely objection is waived unless the party's failure to object is excused by the court for good cause shown.

(5) The party submitting the interrogatories may move for an order under Rule 37(a) with respect to any objection to or other failure to answer an interrogatory.

(c) Scope; Use at Trial. Interrogatories may relate to any matters which can be inquired into under Rule 26(b)(1), and the answers may be used to the extent permitted by the rules of evidence.

An interrogatory otherwise proper is not necessarily objectionable merely because an answer to the interrogatory involves an opinion or contention that relates to fact or the application of law to fact, but the court may order that such an interrogatory need not be answered until after designated discovery has been completed or until a pre-trial conference or other later time.

(d) Option to Produce Business Records. Where the answer to an interrogatory may be derived or ascertained from the business records, including electronically stored information, of the party upon whom the interrogatory has been served or from an examination, audit or inspection of such business records, including a compilation, abstract or summary thereof, and the burden of deriving or ascertaining the answer is substantially the same for the party serving the interrogatory as for the party served, it is a sufficient answer to such interrogatory to specify the records from which the answer may be derived or ascertained and to afford to the party serving the interrogatory reasonable opportunity to examine, audit or inspect such records and to make copies, compilations, abstracts or summaries. A specification shall be in sufficient detail to permit the interrogating party to locate and to identify, as readily as can the party served, the records from which the answer may be ascertained.

ADVISORY COMMITTEE NOTES

1980 Amendment

Subdivision (c). The Committee is advised that parties upon whom interrogatories are served have occasionally responded by directing the interrogating party to a mass of business records or by offering to make all of their records available, justifying the response by the option provided by this subdivision. Such practices are an abuse of the option. A party who is permitted by the terms of this subdivision to offer records for inspection in lieu of answering an interrogatory should offer them in a manner than permits the same direct and economical access that is available to the party. If the information sought exists in the form of compilations, abstracts or summaries then available to the responding party, those should be made available to the interrogating party. The final sentence is added to make it clear that a responding party has the duty to specify, by category and location, the records from which answers to interrogatories can be derived.

1993 Amendments

Purpose of Revision. The purpose of this revision is to reduce the frequency and increase the efficiency of interrogatory practice. The revision is based on experience with local rules. For ease of reference, subdivision (a) is divided into two subdivisions and the remaining subdivisions renumbered.

Subdivision (a). Revision of this subdivision limits interrogatory practice. Because Rule 26(a)(1)-(3) requires disclosure of much of the information previously obtained by this form of discovery, there should be less occasion to use it. Experience in over half of the district courts has confirmed that limitations on the number of interrogatories are useful and manageable. Moreover, because the device can be costly and may be used as a means of harassment, it is desirable to subject its use to the control of the court consistent with the principles stated in Rule 26(b)(2), particularly in multi-party cases where it has not been unusual for the same interrogatory to be propounded to a party by more than one of its adversaries.

Each party is allowed to serve 25 interrogatories upon any other party, but must secure leave of court (or a stipulation from the opposing party) to serve a larger number. Parties cannot evade this presumptive limitation through the device of joining as "subparts" questions that seek information about discrete separate subjects. However, a question asking about communications of a particular type should be treated as a single interrogatory even though it requests that the time, place, persons present, and contents be stated separately for each such communication.

As with the number of depositions authorized by Rule 30, leave to serve additional interrogatories is to be allowed when consistent with Rule 26(b)(2). The aim is not to prevent needed discovery, but to provide judicial scrutiny before parties make potentially excessive use of this discovery device. In many cases it will be appropriate for the court to permit a larger number of interrogatories in the scheduling order entered under Rule 16(b).

Unless leave of court is obtained, interrogatories may not be served prior to the meeting of the parties under Rule 26(f).

When a case with outstanding interrogatories exceeding the number permitted by this rule is removed to federal court, the interrogating party must seek leave allowing the additional interrogatories, specify which twenty-five are to be answered, or resubmit interrogatories that comply with the rule. Moreover, under Rule 26(d), the time for response would be measured from the date of the parties' meeting under Rule 26(f). See Rule 81(c), providing that these rules govern procedures after removal.

Subdivision (b). A separate subdivision is made of the former second paragraph of subdivision (a). Language is added to paragraph (1) of this subdivision to emphasize the duty of the responding party to provide full answers to the extent not objectionable. If, for example, an interrogatory seeking information about numerous facilities or products is deemed objectionable, but an interrogatory seeking information about a lesser number of facilities or products would not have been objectionable, the interrogatory should be answered with respect to the latter even though an objection is raised as to the balance of the facilities or products. Similarly, the fact that additional time may be needed to respond to some questions (or to some aspects of questions) should not justify a delay in responding to those questions (or other aspects of questions) that can be answered within the prescribed time.

Paragraph (4) is added to make clear that objections must be specifically justified, and that unstated or untimely grounds for objection ordinarily are waived. Note also the provisions of revised Rule 26(b)(5), which require a responding party to indicate when it is withholding information under a claim of privilege or as trial preparation materials.

These provisions should be read in light of Rule 26(g), authorizing the court to impose sanctions on a party and attorney making an unfounded objection to an interrogatory. . . .

2006 Amendment

Rule 33(d) is amended to parallel Rule 34(a) by recognizing the importance of electronically stored information. The term "electronically stored information" has the same broad meaning in Rule 33(d) as in Rule 34(a). Much business information is stored only in electronic form; the Rule 33(d) option should be available with respect to such records as well.

Special difficulties may arise in using electronically stored information, either due to its form or because it is dependent on a particular computer system. Rule 33(d) allows a responding party to substitute access to documents or electronically stored information for an answer only if the burden of deriving the answer will be substantially the same for either party. Rule 33(d) states that a party electing to respond to an interrogatory by providing electronically stored information must ensure that the interrogating party can locate and identify it "as readily as can the party served," and that the responding party must give the interrogating party a "reasonable opportunity to examine, audit, or inspect" the information. Depending on the circumstances, satisfying these provisions with regard to electronically stored information may require the responding party to provide some combination of technical support, information on application software, or other assistance. The key question is whether such support enables the interrogating party to derive or ascertain the answer from the electronically stored information as readily as the responding party. A party that wishes to invoke Rule 33(d) by specifying electronically stored information may be required to provide direct access to its electronic information system, but only if that is necessary to afford the requesting party an adequate opportunity to derive or ascertain the answer to the interrogatory. In that situation, the responding party's need to protect sensitive interests of confidentiality or privacy may mean that it must derive or ascertain and provide the answer itself rather than invoke Rule 33(d).

Rule 34. Production of Documents, Electronically Stored Information, and Things and Entry Upon Land for Inspection and Other Purposes

(a)Scope. Any party may serve on any other party a request (1) to produce and permit the party making the request, or someone acting on the requestor's behalf, to inspect, copy, test, or sample any designated documents or electronically stored information — including writings, drawings, graphs, charts, photographs, sound recordings, images and other data or data compilations stored in any medium from which information can be obtained — translated, if necessary, by the respondent into reasonably usable form, or to inspect, copy, test, or sample any designated tangible things which constitute or contain matters within the scope of Rule 26(b) and which are in the possession, custody or control of the party upon whom the request is served; or (2) to permit entry upon designated land or other property in the possession or control of the party upon whom the request is served for the purpose of inspection and measuring, surveying, photographing, testing, or sampling the property or any designated object or operation thereon, within the scope of Rule 26(b).

(b) Procedure. The request shall set forth, either by individual item or by category, the items to be inspected, and describe each with reasonable particularity. The request shall specify a reasonable time, place, and manner of making the inspection and performing the related acts. The request may specify the form or forms in which electronically stored information is to be produced. Without leave of court or written stipulation, a request may not be served before the time specified in Rule 26(d).

The party upon whom the request is served shall serve a written response within 30 days after the service of the request. A shorter or longer time may be directed by the court or, in the absence of such an order, agreed to in writing by the parties, subject to Rule 29. The response shall state, with respect to each item or category, that inspection and related activities will be permitted as requested, unless the request is objected to, including an objection to the requested form or forms for producing electronically stored information, stating the reasons for the objection. If objection is made to part of an item or category, the part shall be specified and inspection permitted of the remaining parts. If objection is made to the requested form or forms for producing electronically stored information — or if no form was specified in the request — the responding party must state the form or forms it intends to use. The party submitting the request may move for an order under Rule 37(a) with respect to any objection to or other failure to respond to the request or any part thereof, or any failure to permit inspection as requested.

Unless the parties otherwise agree, or the court otherwise orders:

(i) a party who produces documents for inspection shall produce them as they are kept in the usual course of business or shall organize and label them to correspond with the categories in the request;

(ii) if a request does not specify the form or forms for producing electronically stored information, a responding party must produce the information in a form or forms in which it is ordinarily maintained or in a form or forms that are reasonably usable; and

(iii) a party need not produce the same electronically stored information in more than one form.

(c) Persons Not Parties. A person not a party to the action may be compelled to produce documents and things or to submit to an inspection as provided in Rule 45.

ADVISORY COMMITTEE NOTES

2006 Amendment

Subdivision (a). As originally adopted, Rule 34 focused on discovery of "documents" and "things." In 1970, Rule 34(a) was amended to include discovery of data compilations, anticipating that the use of computerized information would increase. Since then, the growth in electronically stored information and in the variety of systems for creating and storing such information has been dramatic. Lawyers and judges interpreted the term "documents" to include electronically stored information because it was obviously improper to allow a party to evade discovery obligations on the basis that the label had not kept pace with changes in information technology. But it has become increasingly difficult to say that all forms of electronically stored information, many dynamic in nature, fit within the traditional concept of a "document." . . . Rule 34(a) is amended to confirm that discovery of electronically stored information stands on equal footing with discovery of paper documents. . . . At the same time, a Rule 34 request for production of "documents" should be understood to encompass, and the response should include, electronically stored information unless discovery in the action has clearly distinguished between electronically stored information and "documents."

Discoverable information often exists in both paper and electronic form, and the same or similar information might exist in both. The items listed in Rule 34(a) show different ways in which information may be recorded or stored. Images, for example, might be hard-copy documents or electronically stored information. The wide variety of computer systems currently in use, and the rapidity of technological change, counsel against a limiting or precise definition of electronically stored information. Rule 34(a)(1) is expansive and includes any type of information that is stored electronically. A common example often sought in discovery is electronic communications, such as e-mail. The rule covers — either as documents or as electronically stored information — information "stored in any medium," to encompass future developments in computer technology. Rule 34(a)(1) is intended to be broad enough to cover all current types of computer-based information, and flexible enough to encompass future changes and developments.

References elsewhere in the rules to "electronically stored information" should be understood to invoke this expansive approach. A companion change is made to Rule 33(d), making it explicit that parties choosing to respond to an interrogatory by permitting access to responsive records may do so by providing access to electronically stored information. More generally, the term used in Rule 34(a)(1) appears in a number of other amendments, such as those to Rules 26(a)(1), 26(b)(2), 26(b)(5)(B), 26(f), 34(b), 37(f), and 45. In each of these rules, electronically stored information has the same broad meaning it has under Rule 34(a)(1). References to "documents" appear in discovery rules that are not amended, including Rules 30(f), 36(a), and 37(c)(2). These references should be interpreted to include electronically stored information as circumstances warrant.

The term "electronically stored information" is broad, but whether material that falls within this term should be produced, and in what form, are separate questions that must be addressed under Rules 26(b), 26(c), and 34(b). . . .

Rule 34(a)(1) is also amended to make clear that parties may request an opportunity to test or sample materials sought under the rule in addition to inspecting and copying them. That opportunity may be important for both electronically stored information and hard-copy materials. The current rule is not clear that such testing or sampling is authorized; the amendment expressly permits it. As with any other form of discovery, issues of burden and intrusiveness raised by requests to test or sample can be addressed under Rules 26(b)(2) and 26(c). Inspection or testing of certain types of electronically stored information or of a responding party's electronic information system may raise issues of confidentiality or privacy. The addition of testing and sampling to Rule 34(a) with regard to documents and electronically stored information is not meant to create a routine right of direct access to a party's electronic information system, although such access might be justified in some circumstances. Courts should guard against undue intrusiveness resulting from inspecting or testing such systems. . . .

Subdivision (b). . . .

The amendment to Rule 34(b) permits the requesting party to designate the form or forms in which it wants electronically stored information produced. The form of production is more important to the exchange of electronically stored information than of hard-copy materials, although a party might specify hard copy as the requested form. Specification of the desired form or forms may facilitate the orderly, efficient, and cost-effective discovery of electronically stored information. The rule recognizes that different forms of production may be appropriate for different types of electronically stored information. Using current technology, for example, a party might be called upon to produce word processing documents, e-mail messages, electronic spreadsheets, different image or sound files, and material from databases. Requiring that such diverse types of electronically stored information all be produced in the same form could prove impossible, and even if possible could increase the cost and burdens of producing and using the information. The rule therefore provides that the requesting party may ask for different forms of production for different types of electronically stored information.

The rule does not require that the requesting party choose a form or forms of production. The requesting party may not have a preference. In some cases, the requesting party may not know what form the producing party uses to maintain its electronically stored information, although Rule 26(f)(3) is amended to call for discussion of the form of production in the parties' prediscovery conference. . . .

If the requesting party is not satisfied with the form stated by the responding party, or if the responding party has objected to the form specified by the requesting party, the parties must meet and confer under Rule 37(a)(2)(B) in an effort to resolve the matter before the requesting party can file a motion to compel. If they cannot agree and the court resolves the dispute, the court is not limited to the forms initially chosen by the requesting party, stated by the responding party, or specified in this rule for situations in which there is no court order or party agreement.

If the form of production is not specified by party agreement or court order, the responding party must produce electronically stored information either in a form or forms in which it is ordinarily maintained or in a form or forms that are reasonably usable. Rule 34(a) requires that, if necessary, a responding party "translate" information it produces into a "reasonably usable" form. Under some circumstances, the responding party may need to provide some reasonable amount of technical support, information on application software, or other reasonable assistance to enable the requesting party to use the information. The rule does not require a party to produce electronically stored information in the form it which it is ordinarily maintained, as long as it is produced in a reasonably usable form. But the option to produce in a reasonably usable form does not mean that a responding party is free to convert electronically stored information from the form in which it is ordinarily maintained to a different form that makes it more difficult or burdensome for the requesting party to use the information efficiently in the litigation. If the responding party ordinarily maintains the information it is producing in a way that makes it searchable by electronic means, the information should not be produced in a form that removes or significantly degrades this feature.

Some electronically stored information may be ordinarily maintained in a form that is not reasonably usable by any party. One example is "legacy" data that can be used only by superseded systems. The questions whether a producing party should be required to convert such information to a more usable form, or should be required to produce it at all, should be addressed under Rule 26(b)(2)(B).

Whether or not the requesting party specified the form of production, Rule 34(b) provides that the same electronically stored information ordinarily need be produced in only one form.

Rule 35. Physical and Mental Examinations of Persons

(a) Order for Examination. When the mental or physical condition (including the blood group) of a party or of a person in the custody or under the legal control of a party, is in controversy, the court in which the action is pending may order the party to submit to a physical or mental examination by a suitably licensed or certified examiner or to produce for examination the person in the party's custody or legal control. The order may be made only on motion for good cause shown and upon notice to the person to be examined and to all parties and shall specify the time, place, manner, conditions, and scope of the examination and the person or persons by whom it is to be made.

(b) Report of Examiner.

(1) If requested by the party against whom an order is made under Rule 35(a) or the person examined, the party causing the examination to be made shall deliver to the requesting party a copy of the detailed written report of the examiner setting out the examiner's findings, including results of all tests made, diagnoses and conclusions, together with like reports of all earlier examinations of the same condition. After delivery the party causing the examination shall be entitled upon request to receive from the party against whom the order is made a like report of any examination, previously or thereafter made, of the same condition, unless, in the case of a report of examination of a person not a party, the party shows that the party is unable to obtain it. The court on motion may make an order against a party requiring delivery of a report on such terms as are just, and if an examiner fails or refuses to make a report the court may exclude the examiner's testimony if offered at trial.

(2) By requesting and obtaining a report of the examination so ordered or by taking the deposition of the examiner, the party examined waives any privilege the party may have in that action or any other involving the same controversy, regarding the testimony of every other person who has examined or may thereafter examine the party in respect of the same mental or physical condition.

(3) This subdivision applies to examinations made by agreement of the parties, unless the agreement expressly provides otherwise. This subdivision does not preclude discovery of a report of an examiner or the taking of a deposition of the examiner in accordance with the provisions of any other rule.

Rule 36. Requests for Admission

(a) Request for Admission. A party may serve upon any other party a written request for the admission, for purposes of the pending action only, of the truth of any matters within the scope of Rule 26(b)(1) set forth in the request that relate to statements or opinions of fact or of the application of law to fact, including the genuineness of any documents described in the request. Copies of documents shall be served with the request unless they have been or are otherwise furnished or made available for inspection and copying. Without leave of court or written stipulation, requests for admission may not be served before the time specified in Rule 26(d).

Each matter of which an admission is requested shall be separately set forth. The matter is admitted unless, within 30 days after service of the request, or within such shorter or longer time as the court may allow or as the parties may agree to in writing, subject to Rule 29, the party to whom the request is directed serves upon the party requesting the admission a written answer or objection addressed to the matter, signed by the party or by the party's attorney. If objection is made, the reasons therefor shall be stated. The answer shall specifically deny the matter or set forth in detail the reasons why the answering party cannot truthfully admit or deny the matter. A denial shall fairly meet the substance of the requested admission, and when good faith requires that a party qualify an answer or deny only a part of the matter of which an admission is requested, the party shall specify so much of it as is true and qualify or deny the remainder. An answering party may not give lack of information or knowledge as a reason for failure to admit or deny unless the party states that the party has made reasonable inquiry and that the information known or readily obtainable by the party is insufficient to enable the party to admit or deny. A party who considers that a matter of which an admission has been requested presents a genuine issue for trial may not, on that ground alone, object to the request; the party may, subject to the provisions of Rule 37(c), deny the matter or set forth reasons why the party cannot admit or deny it.

The party who has requested the admissions may move to determine the sufficiency of the answers or objections. Unless the court determines that an objection is justified, it shall order that an answer be served. If the court determines that an answer does not comply with the requirements of this rule, it may order either that the matter is admitted or that an amended answer be served. The court may, in lieu of these orders, determine that final disposition of the request be made at a pre-trial conference or at a designated time prior to trial. The provisions of Rule 37(a)(4) apply to the award of expenses incurred in relation to the motion.

(b) Effect of Admission. Any matter admitted under this rule is conclusively established unless the court on motion permits withdrawal or amendment of the admission. Subject to the provision of Rule 16 governing amendment of a pre-trial order, the court may permit withdrawal or amendment when the presentation of the merits of the action will be subserved thereby and the party who obtained the admission fails to satisfy the court that withdrawal or amendment will prejudice that party in maintaining the action or defense on the merits. Any admission made by a party under this rule is for the purpose of the pending action only and is not an admission for any other purpose nor may it be used against the party in any other proceeding.

Rule 37. Failure to Make Disclosure or Cooperate in Discovery; Sanctions

(a) Motion For Order Compelling Disclosure or Discovery. A party, upon reasonable notice to other parties and all persons affected thereby, may apply for an order compelling disclosure or discovery as follows:

(1) Appropriate Court. An application for an order to a party shall be made to the court in which the action is pending. An application for an order to a person who is not a party shall be made to the court in the district where the discovery is being, or is to be, taken.

(2) Motion.

(A) If a party fails to make a disclosure required by Rule 26(a), any other party may move to compel disclosure and for appropriate sanctions. The motion must include a certification that the movant has in good faith conferred or attempted to confer with the party not making the disclosure in an effort to secure the disclosure without court action.

(B) If a deponent fails to answer a question propounded or submitted under Rules 30 or 31, or a corporation or other entity fails to make a designation under Rule 30(b)(6) or 31(a), or a party fails to answer an interrogatory submitted under Rule 33, or if a party, in response to a request for inspection submitted under Rule 34, fails to respond that inspection will be permitted as requested or fails to permit inspection as requested, the discovering party may move for an order compelling an answer, or a designation, or an order compelling inspection in accordance with the request. The motion must include a certification that the movant has in good faith conferred or attempted to confer with the person or party failing to make the discovery in an effort to secure the information or material without court action. When taking a deposition on oral examination, the proponent of the question may complete or adjourn the examination before applying for an order.

(3) Evasive or Incomplete Disclosure, Answer, or Response. For purposes of this subdivision an evasive or incomplete disclosure, answer, or response is to be treated as a failure to disclose, answer, or respond.

(4) Expenses and Sanctions.

(A) If the motion is granted or if the disclosure or requested discovery is provided after the motion was filed, the court shall, after affording an opportunity to be heard, require the party or deponent whose conduct necessitated the motion or the party or attorney advising such conduct or both of them to pay to the moving party the reasonable expenses incurred in making the motion, including attorney's fees, unless the court finds that the motion was filed without the movant's first making a good faith effort to obtain the disclosure or discovery without court action, or that the opposing party's nondisclosure, response, or objection was substantially justified, or that other circumstances make an award of expenses unjust.

(B) If the motion is denied, the court may enter any protective order authorized under Rule 26(c) and shall, after affording an opportunity to be heard, require the moving party or the attorney filing the motion or both of them to pay to the party or deponent who opposed the motion the reasonable expenses incurred in opposing the motion, including attorney's fees, unless the court finds that the making of the motion was substantially justified or that other circumstances make an award of expenses unjust.

(C) If the motion is granted in part and denied in part, the court may enter any protective order authorized under Rule 26(c) and may, after affording an opportunity to be heard, apportion the reasonable expenses incurred in relation to the motion among the parties and persons in a just manner.

(b) Failure to Comply With Order.

(1) Sanctions by Court in District Where Deposition is Taken. If a deponent fails to be sworn or to answer a question after being directed to do so by the court in the district in which the deposition is being taken, the failure may be considered a contempt of that court.

(2) Sanctions by Court in Which Action is Pending. If a party or an officer, director, or managing agent of a party or a person designated under Rule 30(b)(6) or 31(a) to testify on behalf of a party fails to obey an order to provide or permit discovery, including an order made under subdivision (a) of this rule or Rule 35, or if a party fails to obey an order entered under Rule 26(f), the court in which the action is pending may make such orders in regard to the failure as are just, and among others the following:

(A) An order that the matters regarding which the order was made or any other designated facts shall be taken to be established for the purposes of the action in accordance with the claim of the party obtaining the order;

(B) An order refusing to allow the disobedient party to support or oppose designated claims or defenses, or prohibiting that party from introducing designated matters in evidence;

(C) An order striking out pleadings or parts thereof, or staying further proceedings until the order is obeyed, or dismissing the action or proceeding or any part thereof, or rendering a judgment by default against the disobedient party;

(D) In lieu of any of the foregoing orders or in addition thereto, an order treating as a contempt of court the failure to obey any orders except an order to submit to a physical or mental examination;

(E) Where a party has failed to comply with an order under Rule 35(a) requiring that party to produce another for examination, such orders as are listed in paragraphs (A), (B), and (C) of this subdivision, unless the party failing to comply shows that that party is unable to produce such person for examination.

In lieu of any of the foregoing orders or in addition thereto, the court shall require the party failing to obey the order or the attorney advising that party or both to pay the reasonable expenses, including attorney's fees, caused by the failure, unless the court finds that the failure was substantially justified or that other circumstances make an award of expenses unjust.

(c) Failure to Disclose; False or Misleading Disclosure; Refusal to Admit.

(1) A party that without substantial justification fails to disclose information required by Rule 26(a) or 26(e)(1), or to amend a prior response to discovery as required by Rule 26(e)(2), is not, unless such failure is harmless, permitted to use as evidence at a trial, at a hearing, or on a motion any witness or information not so disclosed. In addition to or in lieu of this sanction, the court, on motion and after affording an opportunity to be heard, may impose other appropriate sanctions. In addition to requiring payment of reasonable expenses, including attorney's fees, caused by the failure, these sanctions may include any of the actions authorized under Rule 37(b)(2)(A), (B), and

(C) and may include informing the jury of the failure to make the disclosure.

(2) If a party fails to admit the genuineness of any document or the truth of any matter as requested under Rule 36, and if the party requesting the admissions thereafter proves the genuineness of the document or the truth of the matter, the requesting party may apply to the court for an order requiring the other party to pay the reasonable expenses incurred in making that proof, including reasonable attorney's fees. The court shall make the order unless it finds that (A) the request was held objectionable pursuant to Rule 36(a), or (B) the admission sought was of no substantial importance, or (C) the party failing to admit had reasonable ground to believe that the party might prevail on the matter, or (D) there was other good reason for the failure to admit.

(d) Failure of Party to Attend at Own Deposition or Serve Answers to Interrogatories or Respond to Request for Inspection. If a party or an officer, director, or managing agent of a party or a person designated under Rule 30(b)(6) or 31(a) to testify on behalf of a party fails (1) to appear before the officer who is to take the deposition, after being served with a proper notice, or (2) to serve answers or objections to interrogatories submitted under Rule 33, after proper service of the interrogatories, or (3) to serve a written response to a request for inspection submitted under Rule 34, after proper service of the request, the court in which the action is pending on motion may make such orders in regard to the failure as are just, and among others it may take any action authorized under subparagraphs (A), (B), and (C) of subdivision (b)(2) of this rule. Any motion specifying a failure under clause (2) or (3) of this subdivision shall include a certification that the movant has in good faith conferred or attempted to confer with the party ailing to answer or respond in an effort to obtain such answer or response without court action. In lieu of any order or in addition thereto, the court shall require the party failing to act or the attorney advising that party or both to pay the reasonable expenses, including attorney's fees, caused by the failure unless the court finds that the failure was substantially justified or that other circumstances make an award of expenses unjust.

The failure to act described in this subdivision may not be excused on the ground that the discovery sought is objectionable unless the party failing to act has a pending motion for a protective order as provided by Rule 26(c).

(e) [Subpoena of Person in Foreign Country.] (Abrogated Apr. 29, 1990, effective Aug. 1, 1980.)

(f) Electronically Stored Information. Absent exceptional circumstances, a court may not impose sanctions under these rules on a party for failing to provide electronically stored information lost as a result of the routine, good-faith operation of an electronic information system.

(g) Failure to Participate in the Framing of a Discovery Plan. If a party or a party's attorney fails to participate in good faith in the development and submission of a proposed discovery plan as required by Rule 26(f), the court may, after opportunity for hearing, require such party or attorney to pay to any other party the reasonable expenses, including attorney's fees, caused by the failure.

ADVISORY COMMITTEE NOTES

2006 Amendment

Subdivision (f). Subdivision (f) is new. It focuses on a distinctive feature of computer operations, the routine alteration and deletion of information that attends ordinary use. Many steps essential to computer operation may alter or destroy information, for reasons that have nothing to do with how that information might relate to litigation. As a result, the ordinary operation of computer systems creates a risk that a party may lose potentially discoverable information without culpable conduct on its part. Under Rule 37(f), absent exceptional circumstances, sanctions cannot be imposed for loss of electronically stored information resulting from the routine, good-faith operation of an electronic information system.

Rule 37(f) applies only to information lost due to the "routine operation of an electronic information system" — the ways in which such systems are generally designed, programmed, and implemented to meet the party's technical and business needs. The "routine operation" of computer systems includes the alteration and overwriting of information, often without the operator's specific direction or awareness, a feature with no direct counterpart in hard-copy documents. Such features are essential to the operation of electronic information systems.

Rule 37(f) applies to information lost due to the routine operation of an information system only if the operation was in good faith. Good faith in the routine operation of an information system may involve a party's intervention to modify or suspend certain features of that routine operation to prevent the loss of information, if that information is subject to a preservation obligation. A preservation obligation may arise from many sources, including common law, statutes, regulations, or a court order in the case. The good faith requirement of Rule 37(f) means that a party is not permitted to exploit the routine operation of an information system to thwart discovery obligations by allowing that operation to continue in order to destroy specific stored information that it is required to preserve. When a party is under a duty to preserve information because of pending or reasonably anticipated litigation, intervention in the routine operation of an information system is one aspect of what is often called a "litigation hold." Among the factors that bear on a party's good faith in the routine operation of an information system are the steps the party took to comply with a court order in the case or party agreement requiring preservation of specific electronically stored information.

Whether good faith would call for steps to prevent the loss of information on sources that the party believes are not reasonably accessible under Rule 26(b)(2) depends on the circumstances of each case. One factor is whether the party reasonably believes that the information on such sources is likely to be discoverable and not available from reasonably accessible sources.

The protection provided by Rule 37(f) applies only to sanctions "under these rules." It does not affect other sources of authority to impose sanctions or rules of professional responsibility.

This rule restricts the imposition of "sanctions." It does not prevent a court from making the kinds of adjustments frequently used in managing discovery if a party is unable to provide relevant responsive information. For example, a court could order the responding party to produce an additional witness for deposition, respond to additional interrogatories, or make similar attempts to provide substitutes or alternatives for some or all of the lost information.

VI. TRIALS

Rule 38. Jury Trial of Right

(a) Right Preserved. The right of trial by jury as declared by the Seventh Amendment to the Constitution or as given by a statute of the United States shall be preserved to the parties inviolate.

(b) Demand. Any party may demand a trial by jury of any issue triable of right by a jury by (1) serving upon the other parties a demand therefor in writing at any time after the commencement of the action and not later than 10 days after the service of the last pleading directed to such issue, and (2) filing the demand as required by Rule 5(d). Such demand may be indorsed upon a pleading of the party. Answer

(c) Same: Specification of Issues. In the demand a party may specify the issues which the party wishes so tried; otherwise the party shall be deemed to have demanded trial by jury for all the issues so triable. If the party has demanded trial by jury for only some of the issues, any other party within 10 days after service of the demand or such lesser time as the court may order, may serve a demand for trial by jury of any other or all of the issues of fact in the action.

(d) Waiver. The failure of a party to serve and file a demand as required by this rule constitutes a waiver by the party of trial by jury. A demand for trial by jury made as herein provided may not be withdrawn without the consent of the parties.

(e) Admiralty and Maritime Claims. These rules shall not be construed to create a right to trial by jury of the issues in an admiralty or maritime claim within the meaning of Rule 9(h).

Rule 39. Trial by Jury or by the Court

(a) By Jury. When trial by jury has been demanded as provided in Rule 38, the action shall be designated upon the docket as a jury action. The trial of all issues so demanded shall be by jury, unless (1) the parties or their attorneys of record, by written stipulation filed with the court or by an oral stipulation made in open court and entered in the record, consent to trial by the court sitting without a jury or (2) the court upon motion or of its own initiative finds that a right of trial by jury of some or all of those issues does not exist under the Constitution or statutes of the United States.

(b) By the Court. Issues not demanded for trial by jury as provided in Rule 38 shall be tried by the court; but, notwithstanding the failure of a party to demand a jury in an action in which such a demand might have been made of right, the court in its discretion upon motion may order a trial by a jury of any or all issues.

(c) Advisory Jury and Trial by Consent. In all actions not triable of right by a jury the court upon motion or of its own initiative may try any issue with an advisory jury or, except in actions against the United States when a statute of the United States provides for trial without a jury, the court, with the consent of both parties, may order a trial with a jury whose verdict has the same effect as if trial by jury had been a matter of right.

Rule 40. Assignment of Cases for Trial

The district courts shall provide by rule for the placing of actions upon the trial calendar (1) without request of the parties or (2) upon request of a party and notice to the other parties or (3) in such other manner as the courts deem expedient. Precedence shall be given to actions entitled thereto by any statute of the United States.

Rule 41. Dismissal of Actions

(a) Voluntary Dismissal: Effect Thereof.

(1) By Plaintiff; by Stipulation. Subject to the provisions of Rule 23(e), of Rule 66, and of any statute of the United States, an action may be dismissed by the plaintiff without order of court (i) by filing a notice of dismissal at any time before service by the adverse party of an answer or of a motion for summary judgment, whichever first occurs, or (ii) by filing a stipulation of dismissal signed by all parties who have appeared in the action. Unless otherwise stated in the notice of dismissal or stipulation, the dismissal is without prejudice, except that a notice of dismissal operates as an adjudication upon the merits when filed by a plaintiff who has once dismissed in any court of the United States or of any state an action based on or including the same claim.

(2) By Order of Court. Except as provided in paragraph (1) of this subdivision of this rule, an action shall not be dismissed at the plaintiff's instance save upon order of the court and upon such terms and conditions as the court deems proper. If a counterclaim has been pleaded by a defendant prior to the service upon the defendant of the plaintiff's motion to dismiss, the action shall not be dismissed against the defendant's objection unless the counterclaim can remain pending for independent adjudication by the court. Unless otherwise specified in the order, a dismissal under this paragraph is without prejudice.

(b) Involuntary Dismissal: Effect Thereof. For failure of the plaintiff to prosecute or to comply with these rules or any order of court, a defendant may move for dismissal of an action or of any claim against the defendant. Unless the court in its order for dismissal otherwise specifies, a dismissal under this subdivision and any dismissal not provided for in this rule, other than a dismissal for lack of jurisdiction, for improper venue, or for failure to join a party under Rule 19, operates as an adjudication upon the merits.

(c) Dismissal of Counterclaim, Cross-Claim, or Third-Party Claim. The provisions of this rule apply to the dismissal of any counterclaim, cross-claim, or third-party claim. A voluntary dismissal by the claimant alone pursuant to paragraph (1) of subdivision (a) of this rule shall be made before a responsive pleading is served or, if there is none, before the introduction of evidence at the trial or hearing.

(d) Costs of Previously-Dismissed Action. If a plaintiff who has once dismissed an action in any court commences an action based upon or including the same claim against the same defendant, the court may make such order for the payment of costs of the action previously dismissed as it may deem proper and may stay the proceedings in the action until the plaintiff has complied with the order.

Rule 42. Consolidation; Separate Trials

(a) Consolidation. When actions involving a common question of law or fact are pending before the court, it may order a joint hearing or trial of any or all the matters in issue in the actions; it may order all the actions consolidated; and it may make such orders concerning proceedings therein as may tend to avoid unnecessary costs or delay.

(b) Separate Trials. The court, in furtherance of convenience or to avoid prejudice, or when separate trials will be conducive to expedition and economy, may order a separate trial of any claim, cross-claim, counterclaim, or third-party claim, or of any separate issue or of any number of claims, cross-claims, counterclaims, third-party claims, or issues, always preserving inviolate the right of trial by jury as declared by the Seventh Amendment to the Constitution or as given by a statute of the United States.

Rule 43. Taking of Testimony

(a) Form. In every trial, the testimony of witnesses shall be taken in open court, unless a federal law, these rules, the Federal Rules of Evidence, or other rules adopted by the Supreme Court provide otherwise. The court may, for good cause shown in compelling circumstances and upon appropriate safeguards, permit presentation of testimony in open court by contemporaneous transmission from a different location.

(b) [Scope of Examination and Cross-Examination.] (Abrogated Nov. 20, 1972, and Dec. 18, 1972, effective July 1, 1975.)

(c) [Record of Excluded Evidence.] (Abrogated Nov. 20, 1982, and Dec. 18, 1972, eff. July 1, 1975.)

(d) Affirmation in Lieu of Oath. Whenever under these rules an oath is required to be taken, a solemn affirmation may be accepted in lieu thereof.

(e) Evidence on Motions. When a motion is based on facts not appearing of record the court may hear the matter on affidavits presented by the respective parties, but the court may direct that the matter be heard wholly or partly on oral testimony or deposition.

(f) Interpreters. The court may appoint an interpreter of its own selection and may fix the interpreter's reasonable compensation. The compensation shall be paid out of funds provided by law or by one or more of the parties as the court may direct, and may be taxed ultimately as costs, in the discretion of the court.

Rule 44. Proof of Official Record

(a) Authentication.

(1) Domestic. An official record kept within the United States, or any state, district, or commonwealth, or within a territory subject to the administrative or judicial jurisdiction of the United States, or an entry therein, when admissible for any purpose, may be evidenced by an official publication thereof or by a copy attested by the officer having the legal custody of the record, or by the officer's deputy, and accompanied by a certificate that such officer has the custody. The certificate may be made by a judge of a court of record of the district or political subdivision in which the record is kept, authenticated by the seal of the court, or may be made by any public officer having a seal of office and having official duties in the district or political subdivision in which the record is kept, authenticated by the seal of the officer's office.

(2) Foreign. A foreign official record, or an entry therein, when admissible for any purpose, may be evidenced by an official publication thereof; or a copy thereof, attested by a person authorized to make the attestation, and accompanied by a final certification as to the genuineness of the signature and official position (i) of the attesting person, or (ii) of any foreign official whose certificate of genuineness of signature and official position relates to the attestation or is in a chain of certificates of genuineness of signature and official position relating to the attestation. A final certification may be made by a secretary of embassy or legation, consul general, vice consul, or consular agent of the United States, or a diplomatic or consular official of the foreign country assigned or accredited to the United States. If reasonable opportunity has been given to all parties to investigate the authenticity and accuracy of the documents, the court may, for good cause shown, (i) admit an attested copy without final certification or (ii) permit the foreign official record to be evidenced by an attested summary with or without a final certification. The final certification is unnecessary if the record and the attestation are certified as provided in a treaty or convention to which the United States and the foreign country in which the official record is located are parties.

(b) Lack of Record. A written statement that after diligent search no record or entry of a specified tenor is found to exist in the records designated by the statement, authenticated as provided in subdivision (a)(1) of this rule in the case of a domestic record, or complying with the requirements of subdivision (a)(2) of this rule for a summary in the case of a foreign record, is admissible as evidence that the records contain no such record or entry.

(c) Other Proof. This rule does not prevent the proof of official records or of entry or lack of entry therein by any other method authorized by law.

Rule 44.1. Determination of Foreign Law

A party who intends to raise an issue concerning the law of a foreign country shall give notice by pleadings or other reasonable written notice. The court, in determining foreign law, may consider any relevant material or source, including testimony, whether or not submitted by a party or admissible under the Federal Rules of Evidence. The court's determination shall be treated as a ruling on a question of law.

Rule 45. Subpoena

(a) Form; Issuance.

(1) Every subpoena shall

(A) state the name of the court from which it is issued; and

(B) state the title of the action, the name of the court in which it is pending, and its civil action number; and

(C) command each person to whom it is directed to attend and give testimony or to produce and permit inspection, copying, testing, or sampling of designated books, documents, electronically stored information, or tangible things in the possession, custody or control of that person, or to permit inspection of premises, at a time and place therein specified; and

(D) set forth the text of subdivisions (c) and (d) of this rule.

A command to produce evidence or to permit inspection, copying, testing, or sampling may be joined with a command to appear at trial or hearing or at deposition, or may be issued separately. A subpoena may specify the form or forms in which electronically stored information is to be produced.

(2) A subpoena must issue as follows:

(A) for attendance at a trial or hearing, from the court for the district where the trial or hearing is to be held;

(B) for attendance at a deposition, from the court for the district where the deposition is to be taken, stating the method for recording the testimony; and

(C) for production, inspection, copying, testing, or sampling, if separate from a subpoena commanding a person's attendance, from the court for the district where the production or inspection is to be made.

(3) The clerk shall issue a subpoena, signed but otherwise in blank, to a party requesting it, who shall complete it before service. An attorney as officer of the court may also issue and sign a subpoena on behalf of

(A) a court in which the attorney is authorized to practice; or

(B) a court for a district in which a deposition or production is compelled by the subpoena, if the deposition or production pertains to an action pending in a court in which the attorney is authorized to practice.

(b) Service.

(1) A subpoena may be served by any person who is not a party and is not less than 18 years of age. Service of a subpoena upon a person named therein shall be made by delivering a copy thereof to such person and, if the person's attendance is commanded, by tendering to that person the fees for one day's attendance and the mileage allowed by law. When the subpoena is issued on behalf of the United States or an officer or agency thereof, fees and mileage need not be tendered. Prior notice of any commanded production of documents and things or inspection of premises before trial shall be served on each party in the manner prescribed by Rule 5(b).

(2) Subject to the provisions of clause (ii) of subparagraph (c)(3)(A) of this rule, a subpoena may be served at any place within the district of the court by which it is issued, or at any place without the district that is within 100 miles of the place of the deposition, hearing, trial, production, inspection, copying, testing, or sampling specified in the subpoena or at any place within the state where a state statute or rule of court permits service of a subpoena issued by a state court of general jurisdiction sitting in the place of the deposition, hearing, trial, production, inspection, copying, testing, or sampling specified in the subpoena. When a statute of the United States provides therefor, the court upon proper application and cause shown may authorize the service of a subpoena at any other place. A subpoena directed to a witness in a foreign country who is a national or resident of the United States shall issue under the circumstances and in the manner and be served as provided in Title 28, U.S.C. § 1783.

(3) Proof of service when necessary shall be made by filing with the clerk of the court by which the subpoena is issued a statement of the date and manner of service and of the names of the persons served, certified by the person who made the service.

(c) Protection of Persons Subject to Subpoenas.

(1) A party or an attorney responsible for the issuance and service of a subpoena shall take reasonable steps to avoid imposing undue burden or expense on a person subject to that subpoena. The court on behalf of which the subpoena was issued shall enforce this duty and impose upon the party or attorney in breach of this duty an appropriate sanction, which may include, but is not limited to, lost earnings and a reasonable attorney's fee.

(2) (A) A person commanded to produce and permit inspection, copying, testing, or sampling of designated electronically stored information, books, papers, documents or tangible things, or inspection of premises need not appear in person at the place of production or inspection unless commanded to appear for deposition, hearing or trial.

(B) Subject to paragraph (d)(2) of this rule, a person commanded to produce and permit inspection, copying, testing, or sampling may, within 14 days after service of the subpoena or before the time specified for compliance if such time is less than 14 days after service, serve upon the party or attorney designated in the subpoena written objection to producing any or all of the designated materials or inspection of the premises — or to producing electronically stored information in the form or forms requested. If objection is made, the party serving the subpoena shall not be entitled to inspect, copy, test, or sample the materials or inspect the premises except pursuant to an order of the court by which the subpoena was issued. If objection has been made, the party serving the subpoena may, upon notice to the person commanded to produce, move at any time for an order to compel the production, inspection, copying, testing, or sampling. Such an order to compel shall protect any person who is not a party or an officer of a party from significant expense resulting from the inspection, copying, testing, or sampling commanded.

(3) (A) On timely motion, the court by which a subpoena was issued shall quash or modify the subpoena if it

(i) fails to allow reasonable time for compliance;

(ii) requires a person who is not a party or an officer of a party to travel to a place more than 100 miles from the place where that person resides, is employed or regularly transacts business in person, except that, subject to the provisions of clause (c)(3)(B)(iii) of this rule, such a person may in order to attend trial be commanded to travel from any such place within the state in which the trial is held;

(iii) requires disclosure of privileged or other protected matter and no exception or waiver applies; or

(iv) subjects a person to undue burden.

(B) If a subpoena

(i) requires disclosure of a trade secret or other confidential research, development, or commercial information, or

(ii) requires disclosure of an unretained expert's opinion or information not describing specific events or occurrences in dispute and resulting from the expert's study made not at the request of any party, or

(iii) requires a person who is not a party or an officer of a party to incur substantial expense to travel more than 100 miles to attend trial,

the court may, to protect a person subject to or affected by the subpoena, quash or modify the subpoena or, if the party in whose behalf the subpoena is issued shows a substantial need for the testimony or material that cannot be otherwise met without undue hardship and assures that the person to whom the subpoena is addressed will be reasonably compensated, the court may order appearance or production only upon specified conditions.

(d) Duties in Responding to Subpoena.

(1) (A) A person responding to a subpoena to produce documents shall produce them as they are kept in the usual course of business or shall organize and label them to correspond with the categories in the demand.

(B) If a subpoena does not specify the form or forms for producing electronically stored information, a person responding to a subpoena must produce the information in a form or forms in which the person ordinarily maintains it or in a form or forms that are reasonably usable.

(C) A person responding to a subpoena need not produce the same electronically stored information in more than one form.

(D) A person responding to a subpoena need not provide discovery of electronically stored information from sources that the person identifies as not reasonably accessible because of undue burden or cost. On motion to compel discovery or to quash, the person from whom discovery is sought must show that the information sought is not reasonably accessible because of undue burden or cost. If that showing is made, the court may nonetheless order discovery from such sources if the requesting party shows good cause, considering the limitations of Rule 26(b)(2)(C). The court may specify conditions for the discovery.

(2) (A) When information subject to a subpoena is withheld on a claim that it is privileged or subject to protection as trial-preparation materials, the claim shall be made expressly and shall be supported by a description of the nature of the documents, communications, or things not produced that is sufficient to enable the demanding party to contest the claim.

(B) If information is produced in response to a subpoena that is subject to a claim of privilege or of protection as trial-preparation material, the person making the claim may notify any party that received the information of the claim and the basis for it. After being notified, a party must promptly return, sequester, or destroy the specified information and any copies it has and may not use or disclose the information until the claim is resolved. A receiving party may promptly present the information to the court under seal for a determination of the claim. If the receiving party disclosed the information before being notified, it must take reasonable steps to retrieve it. The person who produced the information must preserve the information until the claim is resolved.

(e) Contempt. Failure of any person without adequate excuse to obey a subpoena served upon that person may be deemed a contempt of the court from which the subpoena issued. An adequate cause for failure to obey exists when a subpoena purports to require a nonparty to attend or produce at a place not within the limits provided by clause (ii) of subparagraph (c)(3)(A).

ADVISORY COMMITTEE NOTES

1991 Amendment [citations omitted without notation — ED.]

Purposes of Revision. The purposes of this revision are (1) to clarify and enlarge the protections afforded persons who are required to assist the court by giving information or evidence; (2) to facilitate access outside the deposition procedure provided by Rule 30 to documents and other information in the possession of persons who are not parties; (3) to facilitate service of subpoenas for depositions or productions of evidence at places distant from the district in which an action is proceeding; (4) to enable the court to compel a witness found within the state in which the court sits to attend trial; (5) to clarify the organization of the text of the rule.

Subdivision (a). This subdivision is amended in seven significant respects.

First, Paragraph (a)(3) modifies the requirement that a subpoena be issued by the clerk of court. Provision is made for the issuance of subpoenas by attorneys as officers of the court. This revision perhaps culminates an evolution. Subpoenas were long issued by specific order of the court. As this became a burden to the court, general orders were made authorizing clerks to issue subpoenas on request. Since 1948, they have been issued in blank by the clerk of any federal court to any lawyer, the clerk serving as stationer to the bar. In allowing counsel to issue the subpoena, the rule is merely a recognition of present reality.

Although the subpoena is in a sense the command of the attorney who completes the form, defiance of a subpoena is nevertheless an act in defiance of a court order and exposes the defiant witness to contempt sanctions. In *ICC v. Brimson,* 154 U.S. 447 (1894), the Court upheld a statute directing federal courts to issue subpoenas to compel testimony before the ICC. In *CAB v. Hermann,* 353 U.S. 322 (1957), the Court approved as established practice the issuance of administrative subpoenas as a matter of absolute agency right. And in *NLRB v. Warren Co.,* 350 U.S. 107 (1955), the Court held that the lower court had no discretion to withhold sanctions against a contemnor who violated such subpoenas. The 1948 revision of Rule 45 put the attorney in a position similar to that of the administrative agency, as a public officer entitled to use the court's contempt power to investigate facts in dispute. Two courts of appeals have touched on the issue and have described lawyer-issued subpoenas as mandates of the court. *Waste Conversion, Inc. v. Rollins Environmental Services (NJ), Inc.,* 893 F.2d 605 (3d Cir., 1990); *Fisher v. Marubent Cotton Corp.,* 526 F.2d 1338, 1340 (8th cir., 1975). Cf. *Young v. United States ex rel Vuitton et Fils S.A.,* 481 U.S. 787, 821 (1987) (Scalia, J., concurring). This revision makes the rule explicit that the attorney acts as an officer of the court in issuing and signing subpoenas.

Necessarily accompanying the evolution of this power of the lawyer as officer of the court is the development of increased responsibility and liability for the misuse of this power. The latter development is reflected in the provisions of subdivision (c) of this rule, and also in the requirement imposed by paragraph (3) of this subdivision that the attorney issuing a subpoena must sign it.

Second, Paragraph (a)(3) authorizes attorneys in distant districts to serve as officers authorized to issue commands in the name of the court. Any attorney permitted to represent a client in a federal court, even one admitted pro haec vice, has the same authority as a clerk to issue a subpoena from any federal court for the district in which the subpoena is served and enforced. In authorizing attorneys to issue subpoenas from distant courts, the amended rule effectively authorizes service of a subpoena anywhere in the United States by an attorney representing any party. This change is intended to ease the administrative burdens of inter-district law practice. The former rule resulted in delay and expense caused by the need to secure forms from clerks' offices some distance from the place at which the action proceeds. This change does not enlarge the burden on the witness.

Pursuant to Paragraph (a)(2), a subpoena for a deposition must still issue from the court in which the deposition or production would be compelled. Accordingly, a motion to quash such a subpoena if it overbears the limits of the subpoena power must, as under the previous rule, be presented to the court for the district in which the deposition would occur. Likewise, the court in whose name the subpoena is issued is responsible for its enforcement.

Third, in order to relieve attorneys of the need to secure an appropriate seal to affix to a subpoena issued as an officer of a distant court, the requirement that a subpoena be under seal is abolished by the provisions of Paragraph (a)(1).

Fourth, Paragraph (a)(1) authorizes the issuance of a subpoena to compel a non-party to produce evidence independent of any deposition. This revision spares the necessity of a deposition of the custodian of evidentiary material required to be produced. A party seeking additional production from a person subject to such a subpoena may serve an additional subpoena requiring additional production at the same time and place.

Fifth, Paragraph (a)(2) makes clear that the person subject to the subpoena is required to produce materials in that person's control whether or not the materials are located within the district or within the territory within which the subpoena can be served. The non-party witness is subject to the same scope of discovery under this rule as that person would be as a party to whom a request is addressed pursuant to Rule 34.

Sixth, Paragraph (a)(1) requires that the subpoena include a statement of the rights and duties of witnesses by setting forth in full the text of the new subdivisions (c) and (d).

Seventh, the revised rule authorizes the issuance of a subpoena to compel the inspection of premises in the possession of a non-party. Rule 34 has authorized such inspections of premises in the possession of a party as discovery compelled under Rule 37, but prior practice required an independent proceeding to secure such relief ancillary to the federal proceeding when the premises were not in the possession of a party. Practice in some states has long authorized such use of a subpoena for this purpose without apparent adverse consequence.

Subdivision (b). Paragraph (b)(1) retains the text of the former subdivision (c) with minor changes.

The reference to the United States marshal and deputy marshal is deleted because of the infrequency of the use of these officers for this purpose. Inasmuch as these officers meet the age requirement, they may still be used if available.

A provision requiring service of prior notice pursuant to Rule 5 of compulsory pretrial production or inspection has been added to paragraph (b)(1). The purpose of such notice is to afford other parties an opportunity to object to the production or inspection, or to serve a demand for additional documents or things. Such additional notice is not needed with respect to a deposition because of the requirement of notice imposed by Rule 30 or 31. But when production or inspection is sought independently of a deposition, other parties may need notice in order to monitor the discovery and in order to pursue access to any information that may or should be produced.

Paragraph (b)(2) retains language formerly set forth in subdivision (e) and extends its application to subpoenas for depositions or production.

Paragraph (b)(3) retains language formerly set forth in paragraph (d)(1) and extends its applications to subpoenas for trial or hearing or production.

Subdivision (c). This provision is new and states the rights of witnesses. It is not intended to diminish rights conferred by Rules 26-37 or any other authority.

Paragraph (c)(1) gives specific application to the principle stated in Rule 26(g) and specifies liability for earnings lost by a non-party witness as a result of a misuse of the subpoena. No change in existing law is thereby effected. Abuse of a subpoena is an actionable tort, and the duty of the attorney to the non-party is also embodied in Model Rule of Professional Conduct 4.4. The liability of the attorney is correlative to the expanded power of the attorney to issue subpoenas. The liability may include the cost of fees to collect attorneys' fees owed as a result of a breach of this duty.

Paragraph (c)(2) retains language from the former subdivision (b) and paragraph (d)(1). The 10-day period for response to a subpoena is extended to 14 days to avoid the complex calculations associated with short time periods under Rule 6 and to allow a bit more time for such objections to be made.

A non-party required to produce documents or materials is protected against significant expense resulting from involuntary assistance to the court. This provision applies, for example, to a non-party required to provide a list of class members. The court is not required to fix the costs in advance of production, although this will often be the most satisfactory accommodation to protect the party seeking discovery from excessive costs. In some instances, it may be preferable to leave uncertain costs to be determined after the materials have been produced, provided that the risk of uncertainty is fully disclosed to the discovering party.

Paragraph (c)(3) explicitly authorizes the quashing of a subpoena as a means of protecting a witness from misuse of the subpoena power. It replaces and enlarges on the former subdivision (b) of this rule and tracks the provisions of Rule 26(c). While largely repetitious, this rule is addressed to the witness who may read it on the subpoena, where it is required to be printed by the revised paragraph (a)(1) of this rule.

Subparagraph (c)(3)(A) identifies those circumstances in which a subpoena must be quashed or modified. It restates the former provisions with respect to the limits of mandatory travel that are set forth in the former paragraphs (d)(2) and (e)(1), with one important change. Under the revised rule, a federal court can compel a witness to come from any place in the state to attend trial, whether or not the local state law so provides. This extension is subject to the qualification provided in the next paragraph, which authorizes the court to condition enforcement of a subpoena compelling a non-party witness to bear substantial expense to attend trial. The traveling non-party witness may be entitled to reasonable compensation for the time and effort entailed.

Clause (c)(3)(A)(iv) requires the court to protect all persons from undue burden imposed by the use of the subpoena power. Illustratively, it might be unduly burdensome to compel an adversary to attend trial as a witness if the adversary is known to have no personal knowledge of matters in dispute, especially so if the adversary would be required to incur substantial travel burdens.

Subparagraph (c)(3)(B) identifies circumstances in which a subpoena should be quashed unless the party serving the subpoena shows a substantial need and the court can devise an appropriate accommodation to protect the interests of the witness. An additional circumstance in which such action is required is a request for costly production of documents; that situation is expressly governed by subparagraph (b)(2)(B) [probably should read "(c)(2)(B)" — Ed.].

Clause (c)(3)(B)(i) authorizes the court to quash, modify, or condition a subpoena to protect the person subject to or affected by the subpoena from unnecessary or unduly harmful disclosures of confidential information. It corresponds to Rule 26(c)(7).

Clause (c)(3)(B)(ii) provides appropriate protection for the intellectual property of the non-party witness; it does not apply to the expert retained by a party, whose information is subject to the provisions of Rule 26(b)(4). A growing problem has been the use of subpoenas to compel the giving of evidence and information by unretained experts. Experts are not exempt from the duty to give evidence, even if they cannot be compelled to prepare themselves to give effective testimony, but compulsion to give evidence may threaten the intellectual property of experts denied the opportunity to bargain for the value of their services. Arguably the compulsion to testify can be regarded as a "taking" of intellectual property. The rule establishes the right of such persons to withhold their expertise, at least unless the party seeking it makes the kind of showing required for a conditional denial of a motion to quash as provided in the final sentence of subparagraph (c)(3)(B); that requirement is the same as that necessary to secure work product under Rule 26(b)(3) and gives assurance of reasonable compensation. The Rule thus approves the accommodation of competing interests exemplified in *United States v. Columbia Broadcasting Systems Inc.,* 666 F.2d 364 (9th Cir, 1982).

As stated in *Kaufman v. Edelstein,* 539 F.2d 811, 822 (2d Cir, 1976), the district court's discretion in these matters should be informed by "the degree to which the expert is being called because of his knowledge of facts relevant to the case rather than in order to give opinion testimony; the difference between testifying to a previously formed or expressed opinion and forming a new one; the possibility that, for other reasons, the witness is a unique expert; the extent to which the calling party is able to show the unlikelihood that any comparable witness will willingly testify; and the degree to which the witness is able to show that he has been oppressed by having continually to testify . . . ."

Clause (c)(3)(B)(iii) protects non-party witnesses who may be burdened to perform the duty to travel in order to provide testimony at trial. The provision requires the court to condition a subpoena requiring travel of more than 100 miles on reasonable compensation.

Subdivision (d). This provision is new. Paragraph (d)(1) extends to non-parties the duty imposed on parties by the last paragraph of Rule 34(b), which was added in 1980.

Paragraph (d)(2) is new . . . . Its purpose is to provide a party whose discovery is constrained by a claim of privilege or work product protection with information sufficient to evaluate such a claim and to resist if it seems unjustified. The person claiming a privilege or protection cannot decide the limits of that party's own entitlement.

A party receiving a discovery request who asserts a privilege or protection but fails to disclose that claim is at risk of waiving the privilege or protection. A person claiming a privilege or protection who fails to provide adequate information about the privilege or protection claim to the party seeking the information is subject to an order to show cause why the person should not be held in contempt under subdivision (e). Motions for such orders and responses to motions are subject to the sanctions provisions of Rules 7 and 11.

A person served a subpoena that is too broad may be faced with a burdensome task to provide full information regarding all that person's claims to privilege or work product protection. Such a person is entitled to protection that may be secured through an objection made pursuant to paragraph (c)(2).

Subdivision (e). This provision retains most of the language of the former subdivision (f).

"Adequate cause" for a failure to obey a subpoena remains undefined. In at least some circumstances, a non-party might be guilty of contempt for refusing to obey a subpoena even though the subpoena manifestly overreaches the appropriate limits of the subpoena power. *E.g., Walker v. City of Birmingham,* 388 U.S. 307 (1967). But, because the command of the subpoena is not in fact one uttered by a judicial officer, contempt should be very sparingly applied when the non-party witness has been overborne by a party or attorney. The language added to subdivision (f) is intended to assure that result where a non-party has been commanded, on the signature of an attorney, to travel greater distances than can be compelled pursuant to this rule.

2006 Amendment

Rule 45 is amended to conform the provisions for subpoenas to changes in other discovery rules, largely related to discovery of electronically stored information. Rule 34 is amended to provide in greater detail for the production of electronically stored information. Rule 45(a)(1)(C) is amended to recognize that electronically stored information, as defined in Rule 34(a), can also be sought by subpoena. Like Rule 34(b), Rule 45(a)(1) is amended to provide that the subpoena can designate a form or forms for production of electronic data. Rule 45(c)(2) is amended, like Rule 34(b), to authorize the person served with a subpoena to object to the requested form or forms. In addition, as under Rule 34(b), Rule 45(d)(1)(B) is amended to provide that if the subpoena does not specify the form or forms for electronically stored information, the person served with the subpoena must produce electronically stored information in a form or forms in which it is usually maintained or in a form or forms that are reasonably usable. Rule 45(d)(1)(C) is added to provide that the person producing electronically stored information should not have to produce the same information in more than one form unless so ordered by the court for good cause.

As with discovery of electronically stored information from parties, complying with a subpoena for such information may impose burdens on the responding person. Rule 45(c) provides protection against undue impositions on nonparties. For example, Rule 45(c)(1) directs that a party serving a subpoena "shall take reasonable steps to avoid imposing undue burden or expense on a person subject to the subpoena," and Rule 45(c)(2)(B) permits the person served with the subpoena to object to it and directs that an order requiring compliance "shall protect a person who is neither a party nor a party's officer from significant expense resulting from" compliance. Rule 45(d)(1)(D) is added to provide that the responding person need not provide discovery of electronically stored information from sources the party identifies as not reasonably accessible, unless the court orders such discovery for good cause, considering the limitations of Rule 26(b)(2)(C), on terms that protect a nonparty against significant expense. A parallel provision is added to Rule 26(b)(2).

Rule 45(a)(1)(B) is also amended, as is Rule 34(a), to provide that a subpoena is available to permit testing and sampling as well as inspection and copying. As in Rule 34, this change recognizes that on occasion the opportunity to perform testing or sampling may be important, both for documents and for electronically stored information. Because testing or sampling may present particular issues of burden or intrusion for the person served with the subpoena, however, the protective provisions of Rule 45(c) should be enforced with vigilance when such demands are made. Inspection or testing of certain types of electronically stored information or of a person's electronic information system may raise issues of confidentiality or privacy. The addition of sampling and testing to Rule 45(a) with regard to documents and electronically stored information is not meant to create a routine right of direct access to a person's electronic information system, although such access might be justified in some circumstances. Courts should guard against undue intrusiveness resulting from inspecting or testing such systems.

Rule 45(d)(2) is amended, as is Rule 26(b)(5), to add a procedure for assertion of privilege or of protection as trial-preparation materials after production. The receiving party may submit the information to the court for resolution of the privilege claim, as under Rule 26(b)(5)(B). . . .

Rule 46. Exceptions Unnecessary

Formal exceptions to rulings or orders of the court are unnecessary; but for all purposes for which an exception has heretofore been necessary it is sufficient that a party, at the time the ruling or order of the court is made or sought, makes known to the court the action which the party desires the court to take or the party's objection to the action of the court and the grounds therefor; and, if a party has no opportunity to object to a ruling or order at the time it is made, the absence of an objection does not thereafter prejudice the party.

Rule 47. Selection of Jurors

(a) Examination of Jurors. The court may permit the parties or their attorneys to conduct the examination of prospective jurors or may itself conduct the examination. In the latter event, the court shall permit the parties or their attorneys to supplement the examination by such further inquiry as it deems proper or shall itself submit to the prospective jurors such additional questions of the parties or their attorneys as it deems proper.

(b) Peremptory Challenges. The court shall allow the number of peremptory challenges provided by 28 U.S.C. § 1870.

(c) Excuse. The court may for good cause excuse a juror from service during trial or deliberation.

Rule 48. Number of Jurors — Participation in Verdict

The court shall seat a jury of not fewer than six and not more than twelve members and all jurors shall participate in the verdict unless excused from service by the court pursuant to Rule 47(c). Unless the parties otherwise stipulate, (1) the verdict shall be unanimous and (2) no verdict shall be taken from a jury reduced in size to fewer than six members.

ADVISORY COMMITTEE NOTES

1991 Amendment

. . .

It appears that the minimum size of a jury consistent with the Seventh Amendment is six. *Cf. Ballew v. Georgia*, 435 U.S. 223 (1978) (holding that a conviction based on a jury of less than six is a denial of due process of law). If the parties agree to trial before a smaller jury, a verdict can be taken, but the parties should not other than in exceptional circumstances be encouraged to waive the right to a jury of six, not only because of the constitutional stature of the right, but also because smaller juries are more erratic and less effective in serving to distribute responsibility for the exercise of judicial power.

Because the institution of the alternate juror has been abolished by the proposed revision of Rule 47, it will ordinarily be prudent and necessary, in order to provide for sickness or disability among jurors, to seat more than six jurors. The use of jurors in excess of six increases the representativeness of the jury and harms no interest of a party. *Ray v. Parkside Surgery Center*, 13 F.R. Serv. 585 (6th Cir, 1989).

If the court takes the precaution of seating a jury larger than six, an illness occurring during the deliberation period will not result in a mistrial, as it did formerly, because all seated jurors will participate in the verdict and a sufficient number will remain to render a unanimous verdict of six or more.

In exceptional circumstances, as where a jury suffers depletions during trial and deliberation that are greater than can reasonably be expected, the parties may agree to be bound by a verdict rendered by fewer than six jurors. The court should not, however, rely upon the availability of such an agreement, for the use of juries smaller than six is problematic for reasons fully explained in *Ballew v. Georgia*, supra.

Rule 49. Special Verdicts and Interrogatories

(a) Special Verdicts. The court may require a jury to return only a special verdict in the form of a special written finding upon each issue of fact. In that event the court may submit to the jury written questions susceptible of categorical or other brief answer or may submit written forms of the several special findings which might properly be made under the pleadings and evidence; or it may use such other method of submitting the issues and requiring the written findings thereon as it deems most appropriate. The court shall give to the jury such explanation and instruction concerning the matter thus submitted as may be necessary to enable the jury to make its findings upon each issue. If in so doing the court omits any issue of fact raised by the pleadings or by the evidence, each party waives the right to a trial by jury of the issue so omitted unless before the jury retires the party demands its submission to the jury. As to an issue omitted without such demand the court may make a finding; or, if it fails to do so, it shall be deemed to have made a finding in accord with the judgment on the special verdict.

(b) General Verdict Accompanied by Answer to Interrogatories. The court may submit to the jury, together with appropriate forms for a general verdict, written interrogatories upon one or more issues of fact the decision of which is necessary to a verdict. The court shall give such explanation or instruction as may be necessary to enable the jury both to make answers to the interrogatories and to render a general verdict, and the court shall direct the jury both to make written answers and to render a general verdict. When the general verdict and the answers are harmonious, the appropriate judgment upon the verdict and answers shall be entered pursuant to Rule 58. When the answers are consistent with each other but one or more is inconsistent with the general verdict, judgment may be entered pursuant to Rule 58 in accordance with the answers, notwithstanding the general verdict, or the court may return the jury for further consideration of its answers and verdict or may order a new trial. When the answers are inconsistent with each other and one or more is likewise inconsistent with the general verdict, judgment shall not be entered, but the court shall return the jury for further consideration of its answers and verdict or shall order a new trial.

Rule 50. Judgment as a Matter of Law in Jury Trials; Alternative Motion for New Trial; Conditional Rulings

(a) Judgment as a Matter of Law.

(1)**In General.** If a party has been fully heard on an issue during a jury trial and the court finds that a reasonable jury would not have a legally sufficient evidentiary basis to find for the party on that issue, the court may:

(A) resolve the issue against the party; and

(B) grant a motion for judgment as a matter of law against the party on a claim or defense that, under the controlling law, can be maintained or defeated only with a favorable finding on that issue.

(2) Motion. A motion for judgment as a matter of law may be made at any time before the case is submitted to the jury. The motion must specify the judgment sought and the law and facts that entitle the movant to the judgment.

(b) Renewing the Motion After Trial; Alternative Motion for a New Trial. If the court does not grant a motion for judgment as a matter of law made under subdivision (a), the court is considered to have submitted the action to the jury subject to the court's later deciding the legal questions raised by the motion. The movant may renew its request for judgment as a matter of law by filing a motion no later than 10 days after the entry of judgment or — if the motion addresses a jury issue not decided by a verdict — no later than 10 days after the jury was discharged. The movant may alternatively request a new trial or join a motion for a new trial under Rule 59. In ruling on a renewed motion, the court may:

(1) if a verdict was returned:

(A) allow the judgment to stand,

(B) order a new trial, or

(C) direct entry of judgment as a matter of law; or

(2) if no verdict was returned:

(A) order a new trial, or

(B) direct entry of judgment as a matter of law.

(c) Granting Renewed Motion for Judgment as a Matter of Law; Conditional Rulings; New Trial Motion.

(1) If the renewed motion for judgment as a matter of law is granted, the court shall also rule on the motion for a new trial, if any, by determining whether it should be granted if the judgment is thereafter vacated or reversed, and shall specify the grounds for granting or denying the motion for the new trial. If the motion for a new trial is thus conditionally granted, the order thereon does not affect the finality of the judgment. In case the motion for a new trial has been conditionally granted and the judgment is reversed on appeal, the new trial shall proceed unless the appellate court has otherwise ordered. In case the motion for a new trial has been conditionally denied, the appellee on appeal may assert error in that denial; and if the judgment is reversed on appeal, subsequent proceedings shall be in accordance with the order of the appellate court.

(2) Any motion for a new trial under Rule 59 by a party against whom judgment as a matter of law is rendered shall be filed no later than 10 days after entry of the judgment.

(d) Same: Denial of Motion for Judgment as a Matter of Law. If the motion for judgment as a matter of law is denied, the party who prevailed on that motion may, as appellee, assert grounds entitling the party to a new trial in the event the appellate court concludes that the trial court erred in denying the motion for judgment. If the appellate court reverses the judgment, nothing in this rule precludes it from determining that the appellee is entitled to a new trial, or from directing the trial court to determine whether a new trial shall be granted.

ADVISORY COMMITTEE NOTES

1963 Amendment [citations omitted without notation — ED.]

Subdivision (a). The practice, after the court has granted a motion for a directed verdict, of requiring the jury to express assent to a verdict they did not reach by their own deliberations serves no useful purpose and may give offense to the members of the jury. The final sentence of the subdivision, added by amendment, provides that the court's order granting a motion for a directed verdict is effective in itself, and that no action need be taken by the foreman or other members of the jury. No change is intended in the standard to be applied in deciding the motion. To assure this interpretation, and in the interest of simplicity, the traditional term, "directed verdict," is retained.

Subdivision (b). A motion for judgment notwithstanding the verdict will not lie unless it was preceded by a motion for a directed verdict made at the close of all the evidence.

The amendment of the second sentence of this subdivision sets the time limit for making the motion for judgment n.o.v. at 10 days after the entry of judgment, rather than 10 days after the reception of the verdict. Thus the time provision is made consistent with that contained in Rule 59(b) (time for motion for new trial) and Rule 52(b) (time for motion to amend findings by the court).

Subdivision (c) deals with the situation where a party joins a motion for a new trial with his motion for judgment n.o.v., or prays for a new trial in the alternative, and the motion for judgment n.o.v. is granted. The procedure to be followed in making rulings on the motion for the new trial, and the consequences of the rulings thereon, were partly set out in *Montgomery Ward & Co. v. Duncan,* 311 U.S. 243, 253 (1940), and have been further elaborated in later cases. See *Cone v. West Virginia Pulp & Paper Co.,* 330 U.S. 212 (1947); *Globe Liquor Co., Inc. v. San Roman,* 332 U.S. 571 (1948); *Fountain v. Filson,* 336 U.S. 681 (1949); *Johnson v. New York, N.H. & H.R.R. Co.*, 344 U.S. 48 (1952). However, courts as well as counsel have often misunderstood the procedure, and it will be helpful to summarize the proper practice in the text of the rule. The amendments do not alter the effects of a jury verdict or the scope of appellate review.

In the situation mentioned, subdivision (c)(1) requires that the court make a "conditional" ruling on the new-trial motion, i.e., a ruling which goes on the assumption that the motion for judgment n.o.v. was erroneously granted and will be reversed or vacated; and the court is required to state its grounds for the conditional ruling. Subdivision (c)(1) then spells out the consequences of a reversal of the judgment in the light of the conditional ruling on the new-trial motion.

If the motion for new trial has been conditionally granted, and the judgment is reversed, "the new trial shall proceed unless the appellate court has otherwise ordered." The party against whom the judgment n.o.v. was entered below may, as appellant, besides seeking to overthrow that judgment, also attack the conditional grant of the new trial. And the appellate court, if it reverses the judgment n.o.v., may in an appropriate case also reverse the conditional grant of the new trial and direct that judgment be entered on the verdict.

If the motion for a new trial has been conditionally denied, and the judgment is reversed, "subsequent proceedings shall be in accordance with the order of the appellate court." The party in whose favor judgment n.o.v. was entered below may, as appellee, besides seeking to uphold that judgment, also urge on the appellate court that the trial court committed error in conditionally denying the new trial. The appellee may assert this error in his brief, without taking a cross-appeal. If the appellate court concludes that the judgment cannot stand, but accepts the appellee's contention that there was error in the conditional denial of the new trial, it may order a new trial in lieu of directing the entry of judgment upon the verdict.

Subdivision (c)(2), which also deals with the situation where the trial court has granted the motion for judgment n.o.v., states that the verdict-winner may apply to the trial court for a new trial pursuant to Rule 59 after the judgment n.o.v. has been entered against him. In arguing to the trial court in opposition to the motion for judgment n.o.v., the verdict-winner may, and often will, contend that he is entitled, at the least, to a new trial, and the court has a range of discretion to grant a new trial or (where plaintiff won the verdict) to order a dismissal of the action without prejudice instead of granting judgment n.o.v. See *Cone v. West Virginia Pulp & Paper Co.,* supra, 330 U.S. at 217, 218. Subdivision (c)(2) is a reminder that the verdict-winner is entitled, even after entry of judgment n.o.v. against him, to move for a new trial in the usual course. If in these circumstances the motion is granted, the judgment is superseded.

In some unusual circumstances, however, the grant of the new-trial motion may be only conditional, and the judgment will not be superseded. See the situation in *Tribble v. Bruin,* 279 F.2d 424 (4th Cir. 1960) (upon a verdict for plaintiff, defendant moves for and obtains judgment n.o.v.; plaintiff moves for a new trial on the ground of inadequate damages; trial court might properly have granted plaintiff's motion, conditional upon reversal of the judgment n.o.v.).

Even if the verdict-winner makes no motion for a new trial, he is entitled upon his appeal from the judgment n.o.v. not only to urge that that judgment should be reversed and judgment entered upon the verdict, but that errors were committed during the trial which at the least entitle him to a new trial.

Subdivision (d) deals with the situation where judgment has been entered on the jury verdict, the motion for judgment n.o.v. and any motion for a new trial having been denied by the trial court. The verdict-winner, as appellee, besides seeking to uphold the judgment may urge upon the appellate court that in case the trial court is found to have erred in entering judgment on the verdict, there are grounds for granting him a new trial instead of directing the entry of judgment for his opponent. In appropriate cases the appellate court is not precluded from itself directing that a new trial be had. See *Weade v. Dichmann, Wright & Pugh, Inc.,* 337 U.S. 801 (1949). Nor is it precluded in proper cases from remanding the case for a determination by the trial court as to whether a new trial should be granted. The latter course is advisable where the grounds urged are suitable for the exercise of trial court discretion.

Subdivision (d) does not attempt a regulation of all aspects of the procedure where the motion for judgment n.o.v. and any accompanying motion for a new trial are denied, since the problems have not been fully canvassed in the decisions and the procedure is in some respects still in a formative stage. It is, however, designed to give guidance on certain important features of the practice.

1991 Amendment [citations omitted without notation — ED.]

Subdivision (a). The revision of this subdivision aims to facilitate the exercise by the court of its responsibility to assure the fidelity of its judgment to the controlling law, a responsibility imposed by the Due Process Clause of the Fifth Amendment. *Cf. Galloway v. United States,* 319 U.S. 372 (1943).

The revision abandons the familiar terminology of *direction of verdict* for several reasons. The term is misleading as a description of the relationship between judge and jury. It is also freighted with anachronisms some of which are the subject of the text of former subdivision (a) of this rule that is deleted in this revision. Thus, it should not be necessary to state in the text of this rule that a motion made pursuant to it is not a waiver of the right to jury trial, and only the antiquities of directed verdict practice suggest that it might have been. The term "judgment as a matter of law" is an almost equally familiar term and appears in the text of Rule 56; its use in Rule 50 calls attention to the relationship between the two rules. Finally, the change enables the rule to refer to preverdict and post-verdict motions with a terminology that does not conceal the common identity of two motions made at different times in the proceeding.

If a motion is denominated a motion for directed verdict or for judgment notwithstanding the verdict, the party's error is merely formal. Such a motion should be treated as a motion for judgment as a matter of law in accordance with this rule.

Paragraph (a)(1) articulates the standard for the granting of a motion for judgment as a matter of law. It effects no change in the existing standard. That existing standard was not expressed in the former rule, but was articulated in long-standing case law. *See generally* Cooper, *Directions for Directed Verdicts: A Compass for Federal Courts,* 55 MINN. L. REV. 903 (1971). The expressed standard makes clear that action taken under the rule is a performance of the court's duty to assure enforcement of the controlling law and is not an intrusion on any responsibility for factual determinations conferred on the jury by the Seventh Amendment or any other provision of federal law. Because this standard is also used as a reference point for entry of summary judgment under 56(a), it serves to link the two related provisions.

The revision authorizes the court to perform its duty to enter judgment as a matter of law at any time during the trial, as soon as it is apparent that either party is unable to carry a burden of proof that is essential to that party's case. Thus, the second sentence of paragraph (a)(1) authorizes the court to consider a motion for judgment as a matter of law as soon as a party has completed a presentation on a fact essential to that party's case. Such early action is appropriate when economy and expedition will be served. In no event, however, should the court enter judgment against a party who has not been apprised of the materiality of the dispositive fact and been afforded an opportunity to present any available evidence bearing on that fact. In order further to facilitate the exercise of the authority provided by this rule, Rule 16 is also revised to encourage the court to schedule an order of trial that proceeds first with a presentation on an issue that is likely to be dispositive, if such an issue is identified in the course of pretrial. Such scheduling can be appropriate where the court is uncertain whether favorable action should be taken under Rule 56. Thus, the revision affords the court the alternative of denying a motion for summary judgment while scheduling a separate trial of the issue under Rule 42(b) or scheduling the trial to begin with a presentation on that essential fact which the opposing party seems unlikely to be able to maintain.

Paragraph (a)(2) retains the requirement that a motion for judgment be made prior to the close of the trial, subject to renewal after a jury verdict has been rendered. The purpose of this requirement is to assure the responding party an opportunity to cure any deficiency in that party's proof that may have been overlooked until called to the party's attention by a late motion for judgment. Cf. *Farley Transp. Co. v. Santa Fe Trail Transp. Co.,* 786 F.2d 1342 (9th Cir, 1986) ("If the moving party is then permitted to make a later attack on the evidence through a motion for judgment notwithstanding the verdict or an appeal, the opposing party may be prejudiced by having lost the opportunity to present additional evidence before the case was submitted to the jury"); *Benson v. Allphin,* 786 F.2d 268 (7th Cir, 1986) ("the motion for directed verdict at the close of all the evidence provides the nonmovant an opportunity to do what he can to remedy the deficiencies in his case . . .) At one time, this requirement was held to be of constitutional stature, being compelled by the Seventh Amendment. Cf. *Slocum v. New York Insurance Co.,* 228 U.S. 364 (1913). But cf. *Baltimore & Carolina Line v. Redman,* 295 U.S. 654 (1935).

The second sentence of paragraph (a)(2) does impose a requirement that the moving party articulate the basis on which a judgment as a matter of law might be rendered. The articulation is necessary to achieve the purpose of the requirement that the motion be made before the case is submitted to the jury, so that the responding party may seek to correct any overlooked deficiencies in the proof. The revision thus alters the result in cases in which courts have used various techniques to avoid the requirement that a motion for a directed verdict be made as a predicate to a motion for judgment notwithstanding the verdict. . . . The information required with the motion may be supplied by explicit reference to materials and argument previously supplied to the court.

This subdivision deals only with the entry of judgment and not with the resolution of particular factual issues as a matter of law. The court may, as before, properly refuse to instruct a jury to decide an issue if a reasonable jury could on the evidence presented decide that issue in only one way.

Subdivision (b). This provision retains the concept of the former rule that the post-verdict motion is a renewal of an earlier motion made at the close of the evidence. One purpose of this concept was to avoid any question arising under the Seventh Amendment. *Montgomery Ward & Co. v. Duncan,* 311 U.S. 243 (1940).

It remains useful as a means of defining the appropriate issue posed by the post-verdict motion. A post-trial motion for judgment can be granted only on grounds advanced in the pre-verdict motion.

Often it appears to the court or to the moving party that a motion for judgment as a matter of law made at the close of the evidence should be reserved for a post-verdict decision. This is so because a jury verdict for the moving party moots the issue and because a preverdict ruling gambles that a reversal may result in a new trial that might have been avoided. For these reasons, the court may often wisely decline to rule on a motion for judgment as a matter of law made at the close of the evidence, and it is not inappropriate for the moving party to suggest such a postponement of the ruling until after the verdict has been rendered.

In ruling on such a motion, the court should disregard any jury determination for which there is no legally sufficient evidentiary basis enabling a reasonable jury to make it. The court may then decide such issues as a matter of law and enter judgment if all other material issues have been decided by the jury on the basis of legally sufficient evidence, or by the court as a matter of law.

The revised rule is intended for use in this manner with Rule 49. Thus, the court may combine facts established as a matter of law either before trial under Rule 56 or at trial on the basis of the evidence presented with other facts determined by the jury under instructions provided under Rule 49 to support a proper judgment under this rule.

This provision also retains the former requirement that a post-trial motion under the rule must be made within 10 days after entry of a contrary judgment. The renewed motion must be served and filed as provided by Rule 5. A purpose of this requirement is to meet the requirements of F.R. App. P. 4(a)(4). . . .

1995 Amendments

The only change, other than stylistic, intended by this revision is to prescribe a uniform explicit time for filing of post-judgment motions under this rule — no later than 10 days after entry of the judgment. Previously, there was an inconsistency in the wording of Rules 50, 52, and 59 with respect to whether certain post-judgment motions had to be filed, or merely served, during that period. This inconsistency caused special problems when motions for a new trial were joined with other post-judgment motions. These motions affect the finality of the judgment, a matter often of importance to third persons as well as the parties and the court. The Committee believes that each of these rules should be revised to require filing before end of the 10-day period. Filing is an event that can be determined with certainty from court records. The phrase "no later than" is used — rather than "within" — to include post-judgment motions that sometimes are filed before actual entry of the judgment by the clerk. It should be noted that under Rule 6(a) Saturdays, Sundays, and legal holidays are excluded in measuring the 10-day period, and that under Rule 5 the motions when filed are to contain a certificate of service on other parties.

2006 Amendment

. . .

Rule 50(b) is amended to permit renewal of any Rule 50(a) motion for judgment as a matter of law, deleting the requirement that a motion be made at the close of all the evidence. Because the Rule 50(b) motion is only a renewal of the preverdict motion, it can be granted only on grounds advanced in the preverdict motion. The earlier motion informs the opposing party of the challenge to the sufficiency of the evidence and affords a clear opportunity to provide additional evidence that may be available. The earlier motion also alerts the court to the opportunity to simplify the trial by resolving some issues, or even all issues, without submission to the jury. This fulfillment of the functional needs that underlie present Rule 50(b) also satisfies the Seventh Amendment. Automatic reservation of the legal questions raised by the motion conforms to the decision in *Baltimore & Carolina Line v. Redman*, 297 U.S. 654 (1935).

This change responds to many decisions that have begun to move away from requiring a motion for judgment as a matter of law at the literal close of all the evidence. Although the requirement has been clearly established for several decades, lawyers continue to overlook it. The courts are slowly working away from the formal requirement. The amendment establishes the functional approach that courts have been unable to reach under the present rule and makes practice more consistent and predictable.

Many judges expressly invite motions at the close of all the evidence. The amendment is not intended to discourage this useful practice.

Finally, an explicit time limit is added for making a posttrial motion when the trial ends without a verdict or with a verdict that does not dispose of all issues suitable for resolution by verdict. The motion must be made no later than 10 days after the jury was discharged.

Rule 51. Instructions to Jury; Objections; Preserving a Claim of Error

(a) Requests.

(1) A party may, at the close of the evidence or at an earlier reasonable time that the court directs, file and furnish to every other party written requests that the court instruct the jury on the law as set forth in the requests.

(2) After the close of the evidence, a party may:

(A) file requests for instructions on issues that could not reasonably have been anticipated at an earlier time for requests set under Rule 51(a)(1), and

(B) with the court's permission file untimely requests for instructions on any issue.

(b) Instructions. The court:

(1) must inform the parties of its proposed instructions and proposed action on the requests before instructing the jury and before final jury arguments;

(2) must give the parties an opportunity to object on the record and out of the jury's hearing to the proposed instructions and actions on requests before the instructions and arguments are delivered; and

(3) may instruct the jury at any time after trial begins and before the jury is discharged.

(c) Objections.

(1) A party who objects to an instruction or the failure to give an instruction must do so on the record, stating distinctly the matter objected to and the grounds of the objection.

(2) An objection is timely if:

(A) a party that has been informed of an instruction or action on a request before the jury is instructed and before final jury arguments, as provided by Rule 51(b)(1), objects at the opportunity for objection required by Rule 51(b)(2); or

(B) a party that has not been informed of an instruction or action on a request before the time for objection provided under Rule 51(b)(2) objects promptly after learning that the instruction or request will be, or has been, given or refused.

(d) Assigning Error; Plain Error.

(1) A party may assign as error:

(A) an error in an instruction actually given if that party made a proper objection under Rule 51(c), or

(B) a failure to give an instruction if that party made a proper request under Rule 51(a), and — unless the court made a definitive ruling on the record rejecting the request — also made a proper objection under Rule 51(c).

(2) A court may consider a plain error in the instructions affecting substantial rights that has not been preserved as required by Rule 51(d)(1)(A) or (B).

ADVISORY COMMITTEE NOTES

2003 Amendments

Rule 51 is revised to capture many of the interpretations that have emerged in practice. The revisions in text will make uniform the conclusions reached by a majority of decisions on each point. Additions also are made to cover some practices that cannot now be anchored in the text of Rule 51.

Scope. Rule 51 governs instructions to the trial jury on the law that governs the verdict. A variety of other instructions cannot practicably be brought within Rule 51. Among these instructions are preliminary instructions to a venire, and cautionary or limiting instructions delivered in immediate response to events at trial.

Requests. Subdivision (a) governs requests. Apart from the plain error doctrine recognized in subdivision (d)(2), a court is not obliged to instruct the jury on issues raised by the evidence unless a party requests an instruction. The revised rule recognizes the court's authority to direct that requests be submitted before trial.

The close-of-the-evidence deadline may come before trial is completed on all potential issues. Trial may be formally bifurcated or may be sequenced in some less formal manner. The close of the evidence is measured by the occurrence of two events: completion of all intended evidence on an identified phase of the trial and impending submission to the jury with instructions.

The risk in directing a pretrial request deadline is that trial evidence may raise new issues or reshape issues the parties thought they had understood. Courts need not insist on pretrial requests in all cases. Even if the request time is set before trial or early in the trial, subdivision (a)(2)(A) permits requests after the close of the evidence to address issues that could not reasonably have been anticipated at the earlier time for requests set by the court.

Subdivision (a)(2)(B) expressly recognizes the court's discretion to act on an untimely request. The most important consideration in exercising the discretion confirmed by subdivision (a)(2)(B) is the importance of the issue to the case — the closer the issue lies to the "plain error" that would be recognized under subdivision (d)(2), the better the reason to give an instruction. The cogency of the reason for failing to make a timely request also should be considered. To be considered under subdivision (a)(2)(B) a request should be made before final instructions and before final jury arguments. What is a "final" instruction and argument depends on the sequence of submitting the case to the jury. If separate portions of the case are submitted to the jury in sequence, the final arguments and final instructions are those made on submitting to the jury the portion of the case addressed by the arguments and instructions.

Instructions. Subdivision (b)(1) requires the court to inform the parties, before instructing the jury and before final jury arguments related to the instruction, of the proposed instructions as well as the proposed action on instruction requests. The time limit is addressed to final jury arguments to reflect the practice that allows interim argument s during trial in complex cases; it may not be feasible to develop final instructions before such interim arguments. It is enough that counsel know of the intended instructions before making final arguments addressed to the issue. If the trial is sequenced or bifurcated, the final arguments addressed to an issue may occur before the close of the entire trial.

Subdivision (b)(2) complements subdivision (b)(1) by carrying forward the opportunity to object established by present Rule 51. It makes explicit the opportunity to object on the record, ensuring a clear memorial of the objection.

Subdivision (b)(3) reflects common practice by authorizing instructions at any time after trial begins and before the jury is discharged.

Objections. Subdivision (c) states the right to object to an instruction or the failure to give an instruction. It carries forward the formula of present Rule 51 requiring that the objection state distinctly the matter objected to and the grounds of the objection, and makes explicit the requirement that the objection be made on the record. The provisions on the time to object make clear that it is timely to object promptly after learning of an instruction or action on a request when the court has not provided advance information as required by subdivision (b)(1). The need to repeat a request by way of objection is continued by new subdivision (d)(1)(B) except where the court made a definitive ruling on the record.

Preserving a claim of error and plain error. Many cases hold that a proper request for a jury instruction is not alone enough to preserve the right to appeal failure to give the instruction. The request must be renewed by objection. This doctrine is appropriate when the court may not have sufficiently focused on the request, or may believe that the request has been granted in substance although in different words. But this doctrine may also prove a trap for the unwary who fail to add an objection after the court has made it clear that the request has been considered and rejected on the merits. Subdivision (d)(1)(B) establishes authority to review the failure to grant a timely request, despite a failure to add an objection, when the court has made a definitive ruling on the record rejecting the request.

Many circuits have recognized that an error not preserved under Rule 51 may be reviewed in exceptional circumstances. The language adopted to capture these decisions in subdivision (d)(2) is borrowed from Criminal Rule 52. Although the language is the same, the context of civil litigation often differs from the context of criminal prosecution; actual application of the plain-error standard takes account of the differences. The Supreme Court has summarized application of Criminal Rule 52 as involving four elements: (1) there must be an error; (2) the error must be plain; (3) the error must affect substantial rights; and (4) the error must seriously affect the fairness, integrity, or public reputation of judicial proceedings. Johnson v. U.S., 520 U.S. 461, 466-467, 469-470 (1997). (The Johnson case quoted the fourth element from its decision in a civil action, U.S. v. Atkinson, 297 U.S. 157, 160 (1936): "In exceptional circumstances, especially in criminal cases, appellate courts, in the public interest, may, of their own motion, notice errors to which no exception has been taken, if the errors are obvious, or if they otherwise substantially affect the fairness, integrity, or public reputation of judicial proceedings.")

The court's duty to give correct jury instructions in a civil action is shaped by at least four factors.

The factor most directly implied by a "plain" error rule is the obviousness of the mistake. The importance of the error is a second major factor. The costs of correcting an error reflect a third factor that is affected by a variety of circumstances. In a case that seems close to the fundamental error line, account also may be taken of the impact a verdict may have on nonparties.

Rule 52. Findings by the Court; Judgment on Partial Findings

(a) Effect. In all actions tried upon the facts without a jury or with an advisory jury, the court shall find the facts specially and state separately its conclusions of law thereon, and judgment shall be entered pursuant to

Rule 58; and in granting or refusing interlocutory injunctions the court shall similarly set forth the findings of fact and conclusions of law which constitute the grounds of its action. Requests for findings are not necessary for purposes of review. Findings of fact, whether based on oral or documentary evidence, shall not be set aside unless clearly erroneous, and due regard shall be given to the opportunity of the trial court to judge of the credibility of the witnesses. The findings of a master, to the extent that the court adopts them, shall be considered as the findings of the court. It will be sufficient if the findings of fact and conclusions of law are stated orally and recorded in open court following the close of the evidence or appear in an opinion or memorandum of decision filed by the court. Findings of fact and conclusions of law are unnecessary on decisions of motions under Rule 12 or 56 or any other motion except as provided in subdivision (c) of this rule.

(b) Amendment. On a party's motion filed no later than 10 days after entry of judgment, the court may amend its findings — or make additional findings — and may amend the judgment accordingly. The motion may accompany a motion for a new trial under Rule 59. When findings of fact are made in actions tried without a jury, the sufficiency of the evidence supporting the findings may be later questioned whether or not in the district court the party raising the question objected to the findings, moved to amend them, or moved for partial findings.

(c) Judgment on Partial Findings. If during a trial without a jury a party has been fully heard on an issue and the court finds against the party on that issue, the court may enter judgment as a matter of law against that party with respect to a claim or defense that cannot under the controlling law be maintained or defeated without a favorable finding on that issue, or the court may decline to render any judgment until the close of all the evidence. Such a judgment shall be supported by findings of fact and conclusions of law as required by subdivision (a) of this rule.

Rule 53. Masters

(a) Appointment.

(1) Unless a statute provides otherwise, a court may appoint a master only to:

(A) perform duties consented to by the parties;

(B) hold trial proceedings and make or recommend findings of fact on issues to be decided by the court without a jury if appointment is warranted by

(i) some exceptional condition, or

(ii) the need to perform an accounting or resolve a difficult computation of damages; or

(C) address pretrial and post-trial matters that cannot be addressed effectively and timely by an available district judge or magistrate judge of the district.

(2) A master must not have a relationship to the parties, counsel, action, or court that would require disqualification of a judge under 28 U.S.C. § 455 unless the parties consent with the court's approval to appointment of a particular person after disclosure of any potential grounds for disqualification.

(3) In appointing a master, the court must consider the fairness of imposing the likely expenses on the parties and must protect against unreasonable expense or delay.

(b) Order Appointing Master.

(1) Notice. The court must give the parties notice and an opportunity to be heard before appointing a master. A party may suggest candidates for appointment.

(2) Contents. The order appointing a master must direct the master to proceed with all reasonable diligence and must state:

(A) the master's duties, including any investigation or enforcement duties, and any limits on the master's authority under Rule 53(c);

(B) the circumstances — if any — in which the master may communicate ex parte with the court or a party;

(C) the nature of the materials to be preserved and filed as the record of the master's activities;

(D) the time limits, method of filing the record, other procedures, and standards for reviewing the master's orders, findings, and recommendations; and

(E) the basis, terms, and procedure for fixing the master's compensation under Rule 53(h).

(3) Entry of Order. The court may enter the order appointing a master only after the master has filed an affidavit disclosing whether there is any ground for disqualification under 28 U.S.C. § 455 and, if a ground for disqualification is disclosed, after the parties have consented with the court's approval to waive the disqualification.

(4) Amendment. The order appointing a master may be amended at any time after notice to the parties, and an opportunity to be heard.

(c) Master's Authority. Unless the appointing order expressly directs otherwise, a master has authority to regulate all proceedings and take all appropriate measures to perform fairly and efficiently the assigned duties. The master may by order impose upon a party any noncontempt sanction provided by Rule 37 or 45, and may recommend a contempt sanction against a party and sanctions against a nonparty.

(d) Evidentiary Hearings. Unless the appointing order expressly directs otherwise, a master conducting an evidentiary hearing may exercise the power of the appointing court to compel, take, and record evidence.

(e) Master's Orders. A master who makes an order must file the order and promptly serve a copy on each party. The clerk must enter the order on the docket.

(f) Master's Reports. A master must report to the court as required by the order of appointment. The master must file the report and promptly serve a copy of the report on each party unless the court directs otherwise.

(g) Action on Master's Order, Report, or Recommendations.

(1) Action. In acting on a master's order, report, or recommendations, the court must afford an opportunity to be heard and may receive evidence, and may: adopt or affirm; modify; wholly or partly reject or reverse; or resubmit to the master with instructions.

(2) Time To Object or Move. A party may file objections to — or a motion to adopt or modify — the master's order, report, or recommendations no later than 20 days from the time the master's order, report, or recommendations are served, unless the court sets a different time.

(3) Fact Findings. The court must decide de novo all objections to findings of fact made or recommended by a master unless the parties stipulate with the court's consent that:

(A) the master's findings will be reviewed for clear error, or

(B) the findings of a master appointed under Rule 53(a)(1)(A) or (C) will be final.

(4) Legal Conclusions. The court must decide de novo all objections to conclusions of law made or recommended by a master.

(5) Procedural Matters. Unless the order of appointment establishes a different standard of review, the court may set aside a master's ruling on a procedural matter only for an abuse of discretion.

(h) Compensation.

(1) Fixing Compensation. The court must fix the master's compensation before or after judgment on the basis and terms stated in the order of appointment, but the court may set a new basis and terms after notice and an opportunity to be heard.

(2) Payment. The compensation fixed under Rule 53(h)(1) must be paid either:

(A) by a party or parties; or

(B) from a fund or subject matter of the action within the court's control.

(3) Allocation. The court must allocate payment of the master's compensation among the parties after considering the nature and amount of the controversy, the means of the parties, and the extent to which any party is more responsible than other parties for the reference to a master. An interim allocation may be amended to reflect a decision on the merits.

(i) Appointment of Magistrate Judge. A magistrate judge is subject to this rule only when the order referring a matter to the magistrate judge expressly provides that the reference is made under this rule.

VII. JUDGMENT

Rule 54. Judgments; Costs

(a) Definition; Form. "Judgment" as used in these rules includes a decree and any order from which an appeal lies. A judgment shall not contain a recital of pleadings, the report of a master, or the record of prior proceedings.

(b) Judgment Upon Multiple Claims or Involving Multiple Parties. When more than one claim for relief is presented in an action, whether as a claim, counterclaim, cross-claim, or third-party claim, or when multiple parties are involved, the court may direct the entry of a final judgment as to one or more but fewer than all of the claims or parties only upon an express determination that there is no just reason for delay and upon an express direction for the entry of judgment. In the absence of such determination and direction, any order or other form of decision, however designated, which adjudicates fewer than all the claims or the rights and liabilities of fewer than all the parties shall not terminate the action as to any of the claims or parties, and the order or other form of decision is subject to revision at any time before the entry of judgment adjudicating all the claims and the rights and liabilities of all the parties.

(c) Demand for Judgment. A judgment by default shall not be different in kind from or exceed in amount that prayed for in the demand for judgment. Except as to a party against whom a judgment is entered by default, every final judgment shall grant the relief to which the party in whose favor it is rendered is entitled, even if the party has not demanded such relief in the party's pleadings.

(d) Costs; Attorneys' Fees.

(1) Costs Other than Attorneys' Fees. Except when express provision therefor is made either in a statute of the United States or in these rules, costs other than attorneys' fees shall be allowed as of course to the prevailing party unless the court otherwise directs; but costs against the United States, its officers, and agencies shall be imposed only to the extent permitted by law. Such costs may be taxed by the clerk on one day's notice. On motion served within 5 days thereafter, the action of the clerk may be reviewed by the court.

(2) Attorneys' Fees.

(A) Claims for attorneys' fees and related nontaxable expenses shall be made by motion unless the substantive law governing the action provides for the recovery of such fees as an element of damages to be proved at trial.

(B) Unless otherwise provided by statute or order of the court, the motion must be filed no later than 14 days after entry of judgment; must specify the judgment and the statute, rule, or other grounds entitling the moving party to the award; and must state the amount or provide a fair estimate of the amount sought. If directed by the court, the motion shall also disclose the terms of any agreement with respect to fees to be paid for the services for which claim is made.

(C) On request of a party or class member, the court shall afford an opportunity for adversary submissions with respect to the motion in accordance with Rule 43(e) or Rule 78. The court may determine issues of liability for fees before receiving submissions bearing on issues of evaluation of services for which liability is imposed by the court. The court shall find the facts and state its conclusions of law as provided in Rule 52(a).

(D) By local rule the court may establish special procedures by which issues relating to such fees may be resolved without extensive evidentiary hearings. In addition, the court may refer issues relating to the value of services to a special master under

Rule 53 without regard to the provisions of Rule 53(a)(1) and may refer a motion for attorneys' fees to a magistrate judge under Rule 72(b) as if it were a dispositive pretrial matter.

(E) The provisions of subparagraphs (A) through (D) do not apply to claims for fees and expenses as sanctions for violations of these rules or under 28 U.S.C. § 1927.

Rule 55. Default

(a) Entry. When a party against whom a judgment for affirmative relief is sought has failed to plead or otherwise defend as provided by these rules and that fact is made to appear by affidavit or otherwise, the clerk shall enter the party's default.

(b) Judgment. Judgment by default may be entered as follows:

(1) By the Clerk. When the plaintiff's claim against a defendant is for a sum certain or for a sum which can by computation be made certain, the clerk upon request of the plaintiff and upon affidavit of the amount due shall enter judgment for that amount and costs against the defendant, if the defendant has been defaulted for failure to appear and is not an infant or incompetent person.

(2) By the Court. In all other cases the party entitled to a judgment by default shall apply to the court therefor; but no judgment by default shall be entered against an infant or incompetent person unless represented in the action by a general guardian, committee, conservator, or other such representative who has appeared therein. If the party against whom judgment by default is sought has appeared in the action, the party (or, if appearing by representative, the party's representative) shall be served with written notice of the application for judgment at least 3 days prior to the hearing on such application. If, in order to enable the court to enter judgment or to carry it into effect, it is necessary to take an account or to determine the amount of damages or to establish the truth of any averment by evidence or to make an investigation of any other matter, the court may conduct such hearings or order such references as it deems necessary and proper and shall accord a right of trial by jury to the parties when and as required by any statute of the United States.

(c) Setting Aside Default. For good cause shown the court may set aside an entry of default and, if a judgment by default has been entered, may likewise set it aside in accordance with Rule 60(b).

(d) Plaintiffs, Counterclaimants, Cross-Claimants. The provisions of this rule apply whether the party entitled to the judgment by default is a plaintiff, a third-party plaintiff, or a party who has pleaded a cross-claim or counterclaim. In all cases a judgment by default is subject to the limitations of Rule 54(c).

(e) Judgment Against the United States. No judgment by default shall be entered against the United States or an officer or agency thereof unless the claimant establishes a claim or right to relief by evidence satisfactory to the court.

Rule 56. Summary Judgment

(a) For Claimant. A party seeking to recover upon a claim, counterclaim, or cross-claim or to obtain a declaratory judgment may, at any time after the expiration of 20 days from the commencement of the action or after service of a motion for summary judgment by the adverse party, move with or without supporting affidavits for a summary judgment in the party's favor upon all or any part thereof.

(b) For Defending Party. A party against whom a claim, counterclaim, or cross-claim is asserted or a declaratory judgment is sought may, at any time, move with or without supporting affidavits for a summary judgment in the party's favor as to all or any part thereof.

(c) Motion and Proceedings Thereon. The motion shall be served at least 10 days before the time fixed for the hearing. The adverse party prior to the day of hearing may serve opposing affidavits. The judgment sought shall be rendered forthwith if the pleadings, depositions, answers to interrogatories, and admissions on file, together with the affidavits, if any, show that there is no genuine issue as to any material fact and that the moving party is entitled to a judgment as a matter of law. A summary judgment, interlocutory in character, may be rendered on the issue of liability alone although there is a genuine issue as to the amount of damages.

(d) Case Not Fully Adjudicated on Motion. If on motion under this rule judgment is not rendered upon the whole case or for all the relief asked and a trial is necessary, the court at the hearing of the motion, by examining the pleadings and the evidence before it and by interrogating counsel, shall if practicable ascertain what material facts exist without substantial controversy and what material facts are actually and in good faith controverted. It shall thereupon make an order specifying the facts that appear without substantial controversy, including the extent to which the amount of damages or other relief is not in controversy, and directing such further proceedings in the action as are just. Upon the trial of the action the facts so specified shall be deemed established, and the trial shall be conducted accordingly.

(e) Form of Affidavits; Further Testimony; Defense Required. Supporting and opposing affidavits shall be made on personal knowledge, shall set forth such facts as would be admissible in evidence, and shall show affirmatively that the affiant is competent to testify to the matters stated therein. Sworn or certified copies of all papers or parts thereof referred to in an affidavit shall be attached thereto or served therewith. The court may permit affidavits to be supplemented or opposed by depositions, answers to interrogatories, or further affidavits. When a motion for summary judgment is made and supported as provided in this rule, an adverse party may not rest upon the mere allegations or denials of the adverse party's pleading, but the adverse party's response, by affidavits or as otherwise provided in this rule, must set forth specific facts showing that there is a genuine issue for trial. If the adverse party does not so respond, summary judgment, if appropriate, shall be entered against the adverse party.

(f) When Affidavits are Unavailable. Should it appear from the affidavits of a party opposing the motion that the party cannot for reasons stated present by affidavit facts essential to justify the party's opposition, the court may refuse the application for judgment or may order a continuance to permit affidavits to be obtained or depositions to be taken or discovery to be had or may make such other order as is just.

(g) Affidavits Made in Bad Faith. Should it appear to the satisfaction of the court at any time that any of the affidavits presented pursuant to this rule are presented in bad faith or solely for the purpose of delay, the court shall forthwith order the party employing them to pay to the other party the amount of the reasonable expenses which the filing of the affidavits caused the other party to incur, including reasonable attorney's fees, and any offending party or attorney may be adjudged guilty of contempt.

ADVISORY COMMITTEE NOTES

1963 Amendment [citations omitted without notation — Ed.]

. . .

Subdivision (e). . . .

The last two sentences are added to overcome a line of cases, chiefly in the Third Circuit, which has impaired the utility of the summary judgment device. A typical case is as follows: A party supports his motion for summary judgment by affidavits or other evidentiary matter sufficient to show that there is no genuine issue as to a material fact. The adverse party, in opposing the motion, does not produce any evidentiary matter, or produces some but not enough to establish that there is a genuine issue for trial. Instead, the adverse party rests on averments of his pleadings which on their face present an issue. In this situation Third

Circuit cases have taken the view that summary judgment must be denied, at least if the averments are "well-pleaded," and not suppositious, conclusory, or ultimate.

The very mission of the summary judgment procedure is to pierce the pleadings and to assess the proof in order to see whether there is a genuine need for trial. The Third Circuit doctrine, which permits the pleadings themselves to stand in the way of granting an otherwise justified summary judgment, is incompatible with the basic purpose of the rule.

It is hoped that the amendment will contribute to the more effective utilization of the salutary device of summary judgment.

The amendment is not intended to derogate from the solemnity of the pleadings. Rather it recognizes that, despite the best efforts of counsel to make his pleadings accurate, they may be overwhelmingly contradicted by the proof available to his adversary.

Nor is the amendment designed to affect the ordinary standards applicable to the summary judgment motion. So, for example: Where an issue as to a material fact cannot be resolved without observation of the demeanor of witnesses in order to evaluate their credibility, summary judgment is not appropriate. Where the evidentiary matter in support of the motion does not establish the absence of a genuine issue, summary judgment must be denied even if no opposing evidentiary matter is presented. And summary judgment may be inappropriate where the party opposing it shows under subdivision (f) that he cannot at the time present facts essential to justify his opposition.

Rule 57. Declaratory Judgments

The procedure for obtaining a declaratory judgment pursuant to Title 28, U.S.C., § 2201, shall be in accordance with these rules, and the right to trial by jury may be demanded under the circumstances and in the manner provided in Rules 38 and 39. The existence of another adequate remedy does not preclude a judgment for declaratory relief in cases where it is appropriate. The court may order a speedy hearing of an action for a declaratory judgment and may advance it on the calendar.

Rule 58. Entry of Judgment

(a) Separate Document.

(1) Every judgment and amended judgment must be set forth on a separate document, but a separate document is not required for an order disposing of a motion:

(A) for judgment under Rule 50(b);

(B) to amend or make additional findings of fact under Rule 52(b);

(C) for attorney fees under Rule 54;

(D) for a new trial, or to alter or amend the judgment, under Rule 59; or

(E) for relief under Rule 60.

(2) Subject to Rule 54(b):

(A) unless the court orders otherwise, the clerk must, without awaiting the court's direction, promptly prepare, sign, and enter the judgment when:

(i) the jury returns a general verdict,

(ii) the court awards only costs or a sum certain, or

(iii) the court denies all relief;

(B) the court must promptly approve the form of the judgment, which the clerk must promptly enter, when:

(i) the jury returns a special verdict or a general verdict accompanied by interrogatories, or

(ii) the court grants other relief not described in Rule 58(a)(2).

(b) Time of Entry. Judgment is entered for purposes of these rules:

(1) if Rule 58(a)(1) does not require a separate document, when it is entered in the civil docket under Rule 79(a), and

(2) if Rule 58(a)(1) requires a separate document, when it is entered in the civil docket under Rule 79(a) and when the earlier of these events occurs:

(A) when it is set forth on a separate document, or

(B) when 150 days have run from entry in the civil docket under Rule 79(a).

(c) Cost or Fee Awards.

(1) Entry of judgment may not be delayed, nor the time for appeal extended, in order to tax costs or award fees, except as provided in Rule 58(c)(2).

(2) When a timely motion for attorney fees is made under Rule 54(d)(2), the court may act before a notice of appeal has been filed and has become effective to order that the motion have the same effect under Federal Rule of Appellate Procedure 4(a)(4) as a timely motion under Rule 59.

(d) Request for Entry. A party may request that judgment be set forth on a separate document as required by Rule 58(a)(1).

Rule 59. New Trials; Amendment of Judgments

(a) Grounds. A new trial may be granted to all or any of the parties and on all or part of the issues (1) in an action in which there has been a trial by jury, for any of the reasons for which new trials have heretofore been granted in actions at law in the courts of the United States; and (2) in an action tried without a jury, for any of the reasons for which rehearings have heretofore been granted in suits in equity in the courts of the United States. On a motion for a new trial in an action tried without a jury, the court may open the judgment if one has been entered, take additional testimony, amend findings of fact and conclusions of law or make new findings and conclusions, and direct the entry of a new judgment.

(b) Time for Motion. Any motion for a new trial shall be filed no later than 10 days after entry of the judgment.

(c) Time for Serving Affidavits. When a motion for new trial is based on affidavits, they shall be filed with the motion. The opposing party has 10 days after service to file opposing affidavits, but that period may be extended for up to 20 days, either by the court for good cause or by the parties' written stipulation. The court may permit reply affidavits.

(d) On Court's Initiative; Notice; Specifying Grounds. No later than 10 days after entry of judgment the court, on its own, may order a new trial for any reason that would justify granting one on a party's motion. After giving the parties notice and an opportunity to be heard, the court may grant a timely motion for a new trial for a reason not stated in the motion. When granting a new trial on its own initiative or for a reason not stated in a motion, the court shall specify the grounds in its order.

(e) Motion to Alter or Amend Judgment. Any motion to alter or amend a judgment shall be filed no later than 10 days after entry of the judgment.

Rule 60. Relief From Judgment or Order

(a) Clerical Mistakes. Clerical mistakes in judgments, orders or other parts of the record and errors therein arising from oversight or omission may be corrected by the court at any time of its own initiative or on the motion of any party and after such notice, if any, as the court orders. During the pendency of an appeal, such mistakes may be so corrected before the appeal is docketed in the appellate court, and thereafter while the appeal is pending may be so corrected with leave of the appellate court.

(b) Mistakes; Inadvertence; Excusable Neglect; Newly Discovered Evidence; Fraud, Etc. On motion and upon such terms as are just, the court may relieve a party or a party's legal representative from a final judgment, order, or proceeding for the following reasons: (1) mistake, inadvertence, surprise, or excusable neglect; (2) newly discovered evidence which by due diligence could not have been discovered in time to move for a new trial under Rule 59(b); (3) fraud (whether heretofore denominated intrinsic or extrinsic), misrepresentation, or other misconduct of an adverse party; (4) the judgment is void; (5) the judgment has been satisfied, released, or discharged, or a prior judgment upon which it is based has been reversed or otherwise vacated, or it is no longer equitable that the judgment should have prospective application; or (6) any other reason justifying relief from the operation of the judgment. The motion shall be made within a reasonable time, and for reasons (1), (2), and (3) not more than one year after the judgment, order, or proceeding was entered or taken. A motion under this subdivision (b) does not affect the finality of a judgment or suspend its operation. This rule does not limit the power of a court to entertain an independent action to relieve a party from a judgment, order, or proceeding, or to grant relief to a defendant not actually personally notified as provided in Title 28, U.S.C., § 1655, or to set aside a judgment for fraud upon the court. Writs of coram nobis, coram vobis, audita querela, and bills of review and bills in the nature of a bill of review, are abolished, and the procedure for obtaining any relief from a judgment shall be by motion as prescribed in these rules or by an independent action.

Rule 61. Harmless Error

No error in either the admission or the exclusion of evidence and no error or defect in any ruling or order or in anything done or omitted by the court or by any of the parties is ground for granting a new trial or for setting aside a verdict or for vacating, modifying, or otherwise disturbing a judgment or order, unless refusal to take such action appears to the court inconsistent with substantial justice. The court at every stage of the proceeding must disregard any error or defect in the proceeding which does not affect the substantial rights of the parties.

Rule 62. Stay of Proceedings to Enforce a Judgment

(a) Automatic Stay; Exceptions — Injunctions, Receiverships, and Patent Accountings. Except as stated herein, no execution shall issue upon a judgment nor shall proceedings be taken for its enforcement until the expiration of 10 days after its entry. Unless otherwise ordered by the court, an interlocutory or final judgment in an action for an injunction or in a receivership action, or a judgment or order directing an accounting in an action for infringement of letters patent, shall not be stayed during the period after its entry and until an appeal is taken or during the pendency of an appeal. The provisions of subdivision (c) of this rule govern the suspending, modifying, restoring, or granting of an injunction during the pendency of an appeal.

(b) Stay on Motion for New Trial or for Judgment. In its discretion and on such conditions for the security of the adverse party as are proper, the court may stay the execution of or any proceedings to enforce a judgment pending the disposition of a motion for a new trial or to alter or amend a judgment made pursuant to Rule 59, or of a motion for relief from a judgment or order made pursuant to Rule 60, or of a motion for judgment in accordance with a motion for a directed verdict made pursuant to Rule 50, or of a motion for amendment to the findings or for additional findings made pursuant to Rule 52(b).

(c) Injunction Pending Appeal. When an appeal is taken from an interlocutory or final judgment granting, dissolving, or denying an injunction, the court in its discretion may suspend, modify, restore, or grant an injunction during the pendency of the appeal upon such terms as to bond or otherwise as it considers proper for the security of the rights of the adverse party. If the judgment appealed from is rendered by a district court of three judges specially constituted pursuant to a statute of the United States, no such order shall be made except (1) by such court sitting in open court or (2) by the assent of all the judges of such court evidenced by their signatures to the order.

(d) Stay Upon Appeal. When an appeal is taken the appellant by giving a supersedeas bond may obtain a stay subject to the exceptions contained in subdivision (a) of this rule. The bond may be given at or after the time of filing the notice of appeal or of procuring the order allowing the appeal, as the case may be. The stay is effective when the supersedeas bond is approved by the court.

(e) Stay in Favor of the United States or Agency Thereof. When an appeal is taken by the United States or an officer or agency thereof or by direction of any department of the Government of the United States and the operation or enforcement of the judgment is stayed, no bond, obligation, or other security shall be required from the appellant.

(f) Stay According to State Law. In any state in which a judgment is a lien upon the property of the judgment debtor and in which the judgment debtor is entitled to a stay of execution, a judgment debtor is entitled, in the district court held therein, to such stay as would be accorded the judgment debtor had the action been maintained in the courts of that state.

(g) Power of Appellate Court Not Limited. The provisions in this rule do not limit any power of an appellate court or of a judge or justice thereof to stay proceedings during the pendency of an appeal or to suspend, modify, restore, or grant an injunction during the pendency of an appeal or to make any order appropriate to preserve the status quo or the effectiveness of the judgment subsequently to be entered.

(h) Stay of Judgment as to Multiple Claims or Multiple Parties. When a court has ordered a final judgment under the conditions stated in Rule 54(b), the court may stay enforcement of that judgment until the entering of a subsequent judgment or judgments and may prescribe such conditions as are necessary to secure the benefit thereof to the party in whose favor the judgment is entered.

Rule 63. Inability of a Judge to Proceed

If a trial or hearing has been commenced and the judge is unable to proceed, any other judge may proceed with it upon certifying familiarity with the record and determining that the proceedings in the case may be completed without prejudice to the parties. In a hearing or trial without a jury, the successor judge shall at the request of a party recall any witness whose testimony is material and disputed and who is available to testify again without undue burden. The successor judge may also recall any other witness.

VIII. PROVISIONAL AND FINAL REMEDIES

Rule 64. Seizure of Person or Property

At the commencement of and during the course of an action, all remedies providing for seizure of person or property for the purpose of securing satisfaction of the judgment ultimately to be entered in the action are available under the circumstances and in the manner provided by the law of the state in which the district court is held, existing at the time the remedy is sought, subject to the following qualifications: (1) any existing statute of the United States governs to the extent to which it is applicable; (2) the action in which any of the foregoing remedies is used shall be commenced and prosecuted or, if removed from a state court, shall be prosecuted after removal, pursuant to these rules. The remedies thus available include arrest, attachment, garnishment, replevin, sequestration, and other corresponding or equivalent remedies, however designated and regardless of whether by state procedure the remedy is ancillary to an action or must be obtained by an independent action.

Rule 65. Injunctions

(a) Preliminary Injunction.

(1) Notice. No preliminary injunction shall be issued without notice to the adverse party.

(2) Consolidation of Hearing With Trial on Merits. Before or after the commencement of the hearing of an application for a preliminary injunction, the court may order the trial of the action on the merits to be advanced and consolidated with the hearing of the application. Even when this consolidation is not ordered, any evidence received upon an application for a preliminary injunction which would be admissible upon the trial on the merits becomes part of the record on the trial and need not be repeated upon the trial. This subdivision (a)(2) shall be so construed and applied as to save to the parties any rights they may have to trial by jury.

(b) Temporary Restraining Order; Notice; Hearing; Duration. A temporary restraining order may be granted without written or oral notice to the adverse party or that party's attorney only if (1) it clearly appears from specific facts shown by affidavit or by the verified complaint that immediate and irreparable injury, loss, or damage will result to the applicant before the adverse party or that party's attorney can be heard in opposition, and (2) the applicant's attorney certifies to the court in writing the efforts, if any, which have been made to give the notice and the reasons supporting the claim that notice should not be required. Every temporary restraining order granted without notice shall be indorsed with the date and hour of issuance; shall be filed forthwith in the clerk's office and entered of record; shall define the injury and state why it is irreparable and why the order was granted without notice; and shall expire by its terms within such time after entry, not to exceed 10 days, as the court fixes, unless within the time so fixed the order, for good cause shown, is extended for a like period or unless the party against whom the order is directed consents that it may be extended for a longer period. The reasons for the extension shall be entered of record. In case a temporary restraining order is granted without notice, the motion for a preliminary injunction shall be set down for hearing at the earliest possible time and takes precedence of all matters except older matters of the same character; and when the motion comes on for hearing the party who obtained the temporary restraining order shall proceed with the application for a preliminary injunction and, if the party does not do so, the court shall dissolve the temporary restraining order. On 2 days' notice to the party who obtained the temporary restraining order without notice or on such shorter notice to that party as the court may prescribe, the adverse party may appear and move its dissolution or modification and in that event the court shall proceed to hear and determine such motion as expeditiously as the ends of justice require.

(c) Security. No restraining order or preliminary injunction shall issue except upon the giving of security by the applicant, in such sum as the court deems proper, for the payment of such costs and damages as may be incurred or suffered by any party who is found to have been wrongfully enjoined or restrained. No such security shall be required of the United States or of an officer or agency thereof.

The provisions of Rule 65.1 apply to a surety upon a bond or undertaking under this rule.

(d) Form and Scope of Injunction or Restraining Order. Every order granting an injunction and every restraining order shall set forth the reasons for its issuance; shall be specific in terms; shall describe in reasonable detail, and not by reference to the complaint or other document, the act or acts sought to be restrained; and is binding only upon the parties to the action, their officers, agents, servants, employees, and attorneys, and upon those persons in active concert or participation with them who receive actual notice of the order by personal service or otherwise.

(e) Employer and Employee; Interpleader; Constitutional Cases. These rules do not modify any statute of the United States relating to temporary restraining orders and preliminary injunctions in actions affecting employer and employee; or the provisions of Title 28, U.S.C., § 2361, relating to preliminary injunctions in actions of interpleader or in the nature of interpleader; or Title 28, U.S.C., § 2284, relating to actions required by Act of Congress to be heard and determined by a district court of three judges.

(f) Copyright Impoundment. This rule applies to copyright impoundment proceedings.

Rule 65.1. Security: Proceedings Against Sureties

Whenever these rules, including the Supplemental Rules for Admiralty or Maritime Claims and Asset Forfeiture Actions, require or permit the giving of security by a party, and security is given in the form of a bond or stipulation or other undertaking with one or more sureties, each surety submits to the jurisdiction of the court and irrevocably appoints the clerk of the court as the surety's agent upon whom any papers affecting the surety's liability on the bond or undertaking may be served. The surety's liability may be enforced on motion without the necessity of an independent action. The motion and such notice of the motion as the court prescribes may be served on the clerk of the court, who shall forthwith mail copies to the sureties if their addresses are known.

Rule 66. Receivers Appointed by Federal Courts

An action wherein a receiver has been appointed shall not be dismissed except by order of the court. The practice in the administration of estates by receivers or by other similar officers appointed by the court shall be in accordance with the practice heretofore followed in the courts of the United States or as provided in rules promulgated by the district courts. In all other respects the action in which the appointment of a receiver is sought or which is brought by or against a receiver is governed by these rules.

Rule 67. Deposit in Court

In an action in which any part of the relief sought is a judgment for a sum of money or the disposition of a sum of money or the disposition of any other thing capable of delivery, a party, upon notice to every other party, and by leave of court, may deposit with the court all or any part of such sum or thing, whether or not that party claims all or any part of the sum or thing. The party making the deposit shall serve the order permitting deposit on the clerk of the court. Money paid into court under this rule shall be deposited and withdrawn in accordance with the provisions of Title 28, U.S.C., §§ 2041, and 2042; the Act of June 26, 1934, c. 756, § 23, as amended (48 Stat. 1236, 58 Stat. 845), U.S.C., Title 31, § 725v; or any like statute. The fund shall be deposited in an interest-bearing account or invested in an interest-bearing instrument approved by the court.

Rule 68. Offer of Judgment

At any time more than 10 days before the trial begins, a party defending against a claim may serve upon the adverse party an offer to allow judgment to be taken against the defending party for the money or property or to the effect specified in the offer, with costs then accrued. If within 10 days after the service of the offer the adverse party serves written notice that the offer is accepted, either party may then file the offer and notice of acceptance together with proof of service thereof and thereupon the clerk shall enter judgment. An offer not accepted shall be deemed withdrawn and evidence thereof is not admissible except in a proceeding to determine costs. If the judgment finally obtained by the offeree is not more favorable than the offer, the offeree must pay the costs incurred after the making of the offer. The fact that an offer is made but not accepted does not preclude a subsequent offer. When the liability of one party to another has been determined by verdict or order or judgment, but the amount or extent of the liability remains to be determined by further proceedings, the party adjudged liable may make an offer of judgment, which shall have the same effect as an offer made before trial if it is served within a reasonable time not less than 10 days prior to the commencement of hearings to determine the amount or extent of liability.

Rule 69. Execution

(a) In General. Process to enforce a judgment for the payment of money shall be a writ of execution, unless the court directs otherwise. The procedure on execution, in proceedings supplementary to and in aid of a judgment, and in proceedings on and in aid of execution shall be in accordance with the practice and procedure of the state in which the district court is held, existing at the time the remedy is sought, except that any statute of the United States governs to the extent that it is applicable. In aid of the judgment or execution, the judgment creditor or a successor in interest when that interest appears of record, may obtain discovery from any person, including the judgment debtor, in the manner provided in these rules or in the manner provided by the practice of the state in which the district court is held.

(b) Against Certain Public Officers. When a judgment has been entered against a collector or other officer of revenue under the circumstances stated in Title 28, U.S.C., § 2006, or against an officer of Congress in an action mentioned in the Act of March 3, 1875, ch. 130, § 8 (18 Stat. 401), U.S.C., Title 2, § 118, and when the court has given the certificate of probable cause for the officer's act as provided in those statutes, execution shall not issue against the officer or the officer's property but the final judgment shall be satisfied as provided in such statutes.

Rule 70. Judgment for Specific Acts; Vesting Title

If a judgment directs a party to execute a conveyance of land or to deliver deeds or other documents or to perform any other specific act and the party fails to comply within the time specified, the court may direct the act to be done at the cost of the disobedient party by some other person appointed by the court and the act when so done has like effect as if done by the party. On application of the party entitled to performance, the clerk shall issue a writ of attachment or sequestration against the property of the disobedient party to compel obedience to the judgment. The court may also in proper cases adjudge the party in contempt. If real or personal property is within the district, the court in lieu of directing a conveyance thereof may enter a judgment divesting the title of any party and vesting it in others and such judgment has the effect of a conveyance executed in due form of law. When any order or judgment is for the delivery of possession, the party in whose favor it is entered is entitled to a writ of execution or assistance upon application to the clerk.

Rule 71. Process in Behalf of and Against Persons not Parties

When an order is made in favor of a person who is not a party to the action, that person may enforce obedience to the order by the same process as if a party; and, when obedience to an order may be lawfully enforced against a person who is not a party, that person is liable to the same process for enforcing obedience to the order as if a party.

IX. SPECIAL PROCEEDINGS

Rule 71A. Condemnation of Property

(a) Applicability of Other Rules. The Rules of Civil Procedure for the United States District Courts govern the procedure for the condemnation of real and personal property under the power of eminent domain, except as otherwise provided in this rule.

(b) Joinder of Properties. The plaintiff may join in the same action one or more separate pieces of property, whether in the same or different ownership and whether or not sought for the same use.

(c) Complaint.

(1) Caption. The complaint shall contain a caption as provided in Rule 10(a), except that the plaintiff shall name as defendants the property, designated generally by kind, quantity, and location, and at least one of the owners of some part of or interest in the property.

(2) Contents. The complaint shall contain a short and plain statement of the authority for the taking, the use for which the property is to be taken, a description of the property sufficient for its identification, the interests to be acquired, and as to each separate piece of property a designation of the defendants who have been joined as owners thereof or of some interest therein. Upon the commencement of the action, the plaintiff need join as defendants only the persons having or claiming an interest in the property whose names are then known, but prior to any hearing involving the compensation to be paid for a piece of property, the plaintiff shall add as defendants all persons having or claiming an interest in that property whose names can be ascertained by a reasonably diligent search of the records, considering the character and value of the property involved and the interests to be acquired, and also those whose names have otherwise been learned. All others may be made defendants under the designation "Unknown Owners." Process shall be served as provided in subdivision (d) of this rule upon all defendants, whether named as defendants at the time of the commencement of the action or subsequently added, and a defendant may answer as provided in subdivision (e) of this rule. The court meanwhile may order such distribution of a deposit as the facts warrant.

(3) Filing. In addition to filing the complaint with the court, the plaintiff shall furnish to the clerk at least one copy thereof for the use of the defendants and additional copies at the request of the clerk or of a defendant.

(d) Process.

(1) Notice; Delivery. Upon the filing of the complaint the plaintiff shall forthwith deliver to the clerk joint or several notices directed to the defendants named or designated in the complaint. Additional notices directed to defendants subsequently added shall be so delivered. The delivery of the notice and its service have the same effect as the delivery and service of the summons under Rule 4.

(2) Same; Form. Each notice shall state the court, the title of the action, the name of the defendant to whom it is directed, that the action is to condemn property, a description of the defendant's property sufficient for its identification, the interest to be taken, the authority for the taking, the uses for which the property is to be taken, that the defendant may serve upon the plaintiff's attorney an answer within 20 days after service of the notice, and that the failure so to serve an answer constitutes a consent to the taking and to the authority of the court to proceed to hear the action and to fix the compensation. The notice shall conclude with the name of the plaintiff's attorney and an address within the district in which action is brought where the attorney may be served. The notice need contain a description of no other property than that to be taken from the defendants to whom it is directed.

(3) Service of Notice.

(A) Personal Service. Personal service of the notice (but without copies of the complaint) shall be made in accordance with

Rule 4 upon a defendant whose residence is known and who resides within the United States or a territory subject to the administrative or judicial jurisdiction of the United States.

(B) Service by Publication. Upon the filing of a certificate of the plaintiff's attorney stating that the attorney believes a defendant cannot be personally served, because after diligent inquiry within the state in which the complaint is filed the defendant's place of residence cannot be ascertained by the plaintiff or, if ascertained, that it is beyond the territorial limits of personal service as provided in this rule, service of the notice shall be made on this defendant by publication in a newspaper published in the county where the property is located, or if there is no such newspaper, then in a newspaper having a general circulation where the property is located, once a week for not less than three successive weeks. Prior to the last publication, a copy of the notice shall also be mailed to a defendant who cannot be personally served as provided in this rule but whose place of residence is then known. Unknown owners may be served by publication in like manner by a notice addressed to "Unknown Owners."

Service by publication is complete upon the date of the last publication. Proof of publication and mailing shall be made by certificate of the plaintiff's attorney, to which shall be attached a printed copy of the published notice with the name and dates of the newspaper marked thereon.

(4) Return; Amendment. Proof of service of the notice shall be made and amendment of the notice or proof of its service allowed in the manner provided for the return and amendment of the summons under Rule 4.

(e) Appearance or Answer. If a defendant has no objection or defense to the taking of the defendant's property, the defendant may serve a notice of appearance designating the property in which the defendant claims to be interested. Thereafter, the defendant shall receive notice of all proceedings affecting it. If a defendant has any objection or defense to the taking of the property, the defendant shall serve an answer within 20 days after the service of notice upon the defendant. The answer shall identify the property in which the defendant claims to have an interest, state the nature and extent of the interest claimed, and state all the defendant's objections and defenses to the taking of the property. A defendant waives all defenses and objections not so presented, but at the trial of the issue of just compensation, whether or not the defendant has previously appeared or answered, the defendant may present evidence as to the amount of the compensation to be paid for the property, and the defendant may share in the distribution of the award. No other pleading or motion asserting any additional defense or objection shall be allowed.

(f) Amendment of Pleadings. Without leave of court, the plaintiff may amend the complaint at any time before the trial of the issue of compensation and as many times as desired, but no amendment shall be made which will result in a dismissal forbidden by subdivision (i) of this rule. The plaintiff need not serve a copy of an amendment, but shall serve notice of the filing, as provided in Rule 5(b), upon any party affected thereby who has appeared and, in the manner provided in subdivision (d) of this rule, upon any party affected thereby who has not appeared. The plaintiff shall furnish to the clerk of the court for the use of the defendants at least one copy of each amendment and shall furnish additional copies on the request of the clerk or of a defendant. Within the time allowed by subdivision (e) of this rule a defendant may serve an answer to the amended pleading, in the form and manner and with the same effect as there provided.

(g) Substitution of Parties. If a defendant dies or becomes incompetent or transfers an interest after the defendant's joinder, the court may order substitution of the proper party upon motion and notice of hearing. If the motion and notice of hearing are to be served upon a person not already a party, service shall be made as provided in subdivision (d)(3) of this rule.

(h) Trial. If the action involves the exercise of the power of eminent domain under the law of the United States, any tribunal specially constituted by an Act of Congress governing the case for the trial of the issue of just compensation shall be the tribunal for the determination of that issue; but if there is no such specially constituted tribunal any party may have a trial by jury of the issue of just compensation by filing a demand therefor within the time allowed for answer or within such further time as the court may fix, unless the court in its discretion orders that, because of the character, location, or quantity of the property to be condemned, or for other reasons in the interest of justice, the issue of compensation shall be determined by a commission of three persons appointed by it.

In the event that a commission is appointed the court may direct that not more than two additional persons serve as alternate commissioners to hear the case and replace commissioners who, prior to the time when a decision is filed, are found by the court to be unable or disqualified to perform their duties. An alternate who does not replace a regular commissioner shall be discharged after the commission renders its final decision. Before appointing the members of the commission and alternates the court shall advise the parties of the identity and qualifications of each prospective commissioner and alternate and may permit the parties to examine each such designee. The parties shall not be permitted or required by the court to suggest nominees. Each party shall have the right to object for valid cause to the appointment of any person as a commissioner or alternate. If a commission is appointed it shall have the authority of a master provided in Rule 53(c) and proceedings before it shall be governed by the provisions of Rule 53(d). Its action and report shall be determined by a majority and its findings and report shall have the effect, and be dealt with by the court in accordance with the practice, prescribed in Rule 53(e), (f), and (g). Trial of all issues shall otherwise be by the court.

(i) Dismissal of Action.

(1) As of Right. If no hearing has begun to determine the compensation to be paid for a piece of property and the plaintiff has not acquired the title or a lesser interest in or taken possession, the plaintiff may dismiss the action as to that property, without an order of the court, by filing a notice of dismissal setting forth a brief description of the property as to which the action is dismissed.

(2) By Stipulation. Before the entry of any judgment vesting the plaintiff with title or a lesser interest in or possession of property, the action may be dismissed in whole or in part, without an order of the court, as to any property by filing a stipulation of dismissal by the plaintiff and the defendant affected thereby; and, if the parties so stipulate, the court may vacate any judgment that has been entered.

(3) By Order of the Court. At any time before compensation for a piece of property has been determined and paid and after motion and hearing, the court may dismiss the action as to that property, except that it shall not dismiss the action as to any part of the property of which the plaintiff has taken possession or in which the plaintiff has taken title or a lesser interest, but shall award just compensation for the possession, title or lesser interest so taken. The court at any time may drop a defendant unnecessarily or improperly joined.

(4) Effect. Except as otherwise provided in the notice, or stipulation of dismissal, or order of the court, any dismissal is without prejudice.

(j) Deposit and its Distribution. The plaintiff shall deposit with the court any money required by law as a condition to the exercise of the power of eminent domain; and, although not so required, may make a deposit when permitted by statute. In such cases the court and attorneys shall expedite the proceedings for the distribution of the money so deposited and for the ascertainment and payment of just compensation. If the compensation finally awarded to any defendant exceeds the amount which has been paid to that defendant on distribution of the deposit, the court shall enter judgment against the plaintiff and in favor of that defendant for the deficiency. If the compensation finally awarded to any defendant is less than the amount which has been paid to that defendant, the court shall enter judgment against that defendant and in favor of the plaintiff for the overpayment.

(k) Condemnation Under a State's Power of Eminent Domain. The practice as herein prescribed governs in actions involving the exercise of the power of eminent domain under the law of a state, provided that if the state law makes provision for trial of any issue by jury, or for trial of the issue of compensation by jury or commission or both, that provision shall be followed.

(l) Costs. Costs are not subject to Rule 54(d).

Rule 72. Magistrate Judges; Pretrial Orders

(a) Nondispositive Matters. A magistrate judge to whom a pretrial matter not dispositive of a claim or defense of a party is referred to hear and determine shall promptly conduct such proceedings as are required and when appropriate enter into the record a written order setting forth the disposition of the matter. Within 10 days after being served with a copy of the magistrate judge's order, a party may serve and file objections to the order; a party may not thereafter assign as error a defect in the magistrate judge's order to which objection was not timely made. The district judge to whom the case is assigned shall consider such objections and shall modify or set aside any portion of the magistrate judge's order found to be clearly erroneous or contrary to law.

(b) Dispositive Motions and Prisoner Petitions. A magistrate judge assigned without consent of the parties to hear a pretrial matter dispositive of a claim or defense of a party or a prisoner petition challenging the conditions of confinement shall promptly conduct such proceedings as are required. A record shall be made of all evidentiary proceedings before the magistrate judge, and a record may be made of such other proceedings as the magistrate judge deems necessary. The magistrate judge shall enter into the record a recommendation for disposition of the matter, including proposed findings of fact when appropriate. The clerk shall forthwith mail copies to all parties.

A party objecting to the recommended disposition of the matter shall promptly arrange for the transcription of the record, or portions of it as all parties may agree upon or the magistrate judge deems sufficient, unless the district judge otherwise directs. Within 10 days after being served with a copy of the recommended disposition, a party may serve and file specific, written objections to the proposed findings and recommendations.

A party may respond to another party's objections within 10 days after being served with a copy thereof. The district judge to whom the case is assigned shall make a de novo determination upon the record, or after additional evidence, of any portion of the magistrate judge's disposition to which specific written objection has been made in accordance with this rule. The district judge may accept, reject, or modify the recommended decision, receive further evidence, or recommit the matter to the magistrate judge with instructions.

Rule 73. Magistrate Judges; Trial by Consent and Appeal Options

(a) Powers; Procedure. When specially designated to exercise such jurisdiction by local rule or order of the district court and when all parties consent thereto, a magistrate judge may exercise the authority provided by Title 28, U.S.C. § 636(c) and may conduct any or all proceedings, including a jury or nonjury trial, in a civil case. A record of the proceedings shall be made in accordance with the requirements of Title 28, U.S.C. § 636(c)(5).

(b) Consent. When a magistrate judge has been designated to exercise civil trial jurisdiction, the clerk shall give written notice to the parties of their opportunity to consent to the exercise by a magistrate judge of civil jurisdiction over the case, as authorized by Title 28, U.S.C. § 636(c). If, within the period specified by local rule, the parties agree to a magistrate judge's exercise of such authority, they shall execute and file a joint form of consent or separate forms of consent setting forth such election.

A district judge, magistrate judge, or other court official may again advise the parties of the availability of the magistrate judge, but, in so doing, shall also advise the parties that they are free to withhold consent without adverse substantive consequences. A district judge or magistrate judge shall not be informed of a party's response to the clerk's notification, unless all parties have consented to the referral of the matter to a magistrate judge.

The district judge, for good cause shown on the judge's own initiative, or under extraordinary circumstances shown by a party, may vacate a reference of a civil matter to a magistrate judge under this subdivision.

(c) Appeal. In accordance with Title 28, U.S.C. § 636(c)(3), appeal from a judgment entered upon direction of a magistrate judge in proceedings under this rule will lie to the court of appeals as it would from a judgment of the district court.

(d) [Optional Appeal Route.] (Abrogated April 11, 1997, effective Dec. 1, 1997.)

Rule 74. [Method of Appeal From Magistrate Judge to District Judge Under Title 28, U.S.C. § 636(c)(4) and Rule 73(d)]

(Abrogated Apr. 11, 1997, effective Dec. 1, 1997.)

Rule 75. [Proceedings on Appeal From Magistrate Judge to District Judge Under Rule 73(d)]

(Abrogated Apr. 11, 1997, effective Dec. 1, 1997.)

Rule 76. [Judgment of the District Judge on the Appeal Under Rule 73(d) and Costs]

(Abrogated Apr. 11, 1997, effective Dec. 1, 1997.)

X. DISTRICT COURTS AND CLERKS

Rule 77. District Courts and Clerks

(a) District Courts Always Open. The district courts shall be deemed always open for the purpose of filing any pleading or other proper paper, of issuing and returning mesne and final process, and of making and directing all interlocutory motions, orders, and rules.

(b) Trials and Hearings; Orders in Chambers. All trials upon the merits shall be conducted in open court and so far as convenient in a regular court room. All other acts or proceedings may be done or conducted by a judge in chambers, without the attendance of the clerk or other court officials and at any place either within or without the district; but no hearing, other than one ex parte, shall be conducted outside the district without the consent of all parties affected thereby.

(c) Clerk's Office and Orders by Clerk. The clerk's office with the clerk or a deputy in attendance shall be open during business hours on all days except Saturdays, Sundays, and legal holidays, but a district court may provide by local rule or order that its clerk's office shall be open for specified hours on Saturdays or particular legal holidays other than New Year's Day, Birthday of Martin Luther King, Jr., Washington's Birthday, Memorial Day, Independence Day, Labor Day, Columbus Day, Veterans Day, Thanksgiving Day, and Christmas Day. All motions and applications in the clerk's office for issuing mesne process, for issuing final process to enforce and execute judgments, for entering defaults or judgments by default, and for other proceedings which do not require allowance or order of the court are grantable of course by the clerk; but the clerk's action may be suspended or altered or rescinded by the court upon cause shown.

(d) Notice of Orders or Judgments. Immediately upon the entry of an order or judgment the clerk shall serve a notice of the entry in the manner provided for in Rule 5(b) upon each party who is not in default for failure to appear, and shall make a note in the docket of the service. Any party may in addition serve a notice of such entry in the manner provided in Rule 5(b) for the service of papers. Lack of notice of the entry by the clerk does not affect the time to appeal or relieve or authorize the court to relieve a party for failure to appeal within the time allowed, except as permitted in Rule 4(a) of the Federal Rules of Appellate Procedure.

Rule 78. Motion Day

Unless local conditions make it impracticable, each district court shall establish regular times and places, at intervals sufficiently frequent for the prompt dispatch of business, at which motions requiring notice and hearing may be heard and disposed of; but the judge at any time or place and on such notice, if any, as the judge considers reasonable may make orders for the advancement, conduct, and hearing of actions.

To expedite its business, the court may make provision by rule or order for the submission and determination of motions without oral hearing upon brief written statements of reasons in support and opposition.

Rule 79. Books and Records Kept by the Clerk and Entries Therein

(a) Civil Docket. The clerk shall keep a book known as "civil docket" of such form and style as may be prescribed by the Director of the Administrative Office of the United States Courts with the approval of the Judicial Conference of the United States, and shall enter therein each civil action to which these rules are made applicable. Actions shall be assigned consecutive file numbers. The file number of each action shall be noted on the folio of the docket whereon the first entry of the action is made. All papers filed with the clerk, all process issued and returns made thereon, all appearances, orders, verdicts, and judgments shall be entered chronologically in the civil docket on the folio assigned to the action and shall be marked with its file number. These entries shall be brief but shall show the nature of each paper filed or writ issued and the substance of each order or judgment of the court and of the returns showing execution of process. The entry of an order or judgment shall show the date the entry is made. When in an action trial by jury has been properly demanded or ordered the clerk shall enter the word "jury" on the folio assigned to that action.

(b) Civil Judgments and Orders. The clerk shall keep, in such form and manner as the Director of the Administrative Office of the United States Courts with the approval of the Judicial Conference of the United States may prescribe, a correct copy of every final judgment or appealable order, or order affecting title to or lien upon real or personal property, and any other order which the court may direct to be kept.

(c) Indices; Calendars. Suitable indices of the civil docket and of every civil judgment and order referred to in subdivision (b) of this rule shall be kept by the clerk under the direction of the court. There shall be prepared under the direction of the court calendars of all actions ready for trial, which shall distinguish "jury actions" from "court actions."

(d) Other Books and Records of the Clerk. The clerk shall also keep such other books and records as may be required from time to time by the Director of the Administrative Office of the United States Courts with the approval of the Judicial Conference of the United States.

Rule 80. Stenographer; Stenographic Report or Transcript as Evidence

(a) [Stenographer.] (Abrogated Dec. 27, 1946, effective Mar. 19, 1948.)

(b) [Official Stenographer.] (Abrogated Dec. 27, 1946, effective Mar. 19, 1948.)

(c) Stenographic Report or Transcript as Evidence. Whenever the testimony of a witness at a trial or hearing which was stenographically reported is admissible in evidence at a later trial, it may be proved by the transcript thereof duly certified by the person who reported the testimony.

XI. GENERAL PROVISIONS

Rule 81. Applicability in General

(a) To What Proceedings Applicable.

(1) These rules do not apply to prize proceedings in admiralty governed by Title 10, U.S.C., §§ 7651-7681. They do apply to proceedings in bankruptcy to the extent provided by the Federal Rules of Bankruptcy Procedure.

(2) These rules are applicable to proceedings for admission to citizenship, habeas corpus, and quo warranto, to the extent that the practice in such proceedings is not set forth in statutes of the United States, the Rules Governing Section 2254 Cases, or the Rules Governing Section 2255 Proceedings, and has heretofore conformed to the practice in civil actions.

(3) In proceedings under Title 9, U.S.C., relating to arbitration, or under the Act of May 20, 1926, ch. 347, § 9 (44 Stat. 585), U.S.C., Title 45, § 159, relating to boards of arbitration of railway labor disputes, these rules apply only to the extent that matters of procedure are not provided for in those statutes. These rules apply to proceedings to compel the giving of testimony or production of documents in accordance with a subpoena issued by an officer or agency of the United States under any statute of the United States except as otherwise provided by statute or by rules of the district court or by order of the court in the proceedings.

(4) These rules do not alter the method prescribed by the Act of February 18, 1922, ch. 57, § 2 (42 Stat. 388), U.S.C., Title 7, § 292; or by the Act of June 10, 1930, ch. 436, § 7 (46 Stat. 534), as amended, U.S.C., Title 7, § 499g(c), for instituting proceedings in the United States district courts to review orders of the Secretary of Agriculture; or prescribed by the Act of June 25, 1934, ch. 742, § 2 (48 Stat. 1214), U.S.C., Title 15, § 522, for instituting proceedings to review orders of the Secretary of the Interior; or prescribed by the Act of February 22, 1935, ch. 18, § 5 (49 Stat. 31), U.S.C., Title 15, § 715d(c), as extended, for instituting proceedings to review orders of petroleum control boards; but the conduct of such proceedings in the district courts shall be made to conform to these rules so far as applicable.

(5) These rules do not alter the practice in the United States district courts prescribed in the Act of July 5, 1935, ch. 372, §§ 9 and 10 (49 Stat. 453), as amended, U.S.C., Title 29, §§ 159 and 160, for beginning and conducting proceedings to enforce orders of the National Labor Relations Board; and in respects not covered by those statutes, the practice in the district courts shall conform to these rules so far as applicable.

(6) These rules apply to proceedings for enforcement or review of compensation orders under the Longshoremen's and Harbor Workers' Compensation Act, Act of March 4, 1927, c. 509, §§ 18, 21 (44 Stat. 1434, 1436), as amended, U.S.C., Title 33, §§ 918, 921, except to the extent that matters of procedure are provided for in that Act. The provisions for service by publication and for answer in proceedings to cancel certificates of citizenship under the Act of June 27, 1952, c. 477,

Title III, c. 2, § 340 (66 Stat. 260), U.S.C., Title 8, § 1451, remain in effect.

(7) (Abrogated Apr. 30, 1951, effective Aug. 1, 1951.)

(b) Scire Facias and Mandamus. The writs of scire facias and mandamus are abolished. Relief heretofore available by mandamus or scire facias may be obtained by appropriate action or by appropriate motion under the practice prescribed in these rules.

(c) Removed Actions. These rules apply to civil actions removed to the United States district courts from the state courts and govern procedure after removal. Repleading is not necessary unless the court so orders. In a removed action in which the defendant has not answered, the defendant shall answer or present the other defenses or objections available under these rules within 20 days after the receipt through service or otherwise of a copy of the initial pleading setting forth the claim for relief upon which the action or proceeding is based, or within 20 days after the service of summons upon such initial pleading, then filed, or within 5 days after the filing of the petition for removal, whichever period is longest. If at the time of removal all necessary pleadings have been served, a party entitled to trial by jury under Rule 38 shall be accorded it, if the party's demand therefor is served within 10 days after the petition for removal is filed if the party is the petitioner, or if not the petitioner within 10 days after service on the party of the notice of filing the petition. A party who, prior to removal, has made an express demand for trial by jury in accordance with state law, need not make a demand after removal. If state law applicable in the court from which the case is removed does not require the parties to make express demands in order to claim trial by jury, they need not make demands after removal unless the court directs that they do so within a specified time if they desire to claim trial by jury. The court may make this direction on its own motion and shall do so as a matter of course at the request of any party. The failure of a party to make demand as directed constitutes a waiver by that party of trial by jury.

(d) [District of Columbia; Courts and Judges.] (Abrogated Dec. 29, 1948, effective Oct. 20, 1949.)

(e) Law Applicable. Whenever in these rules the law of the state in which the district court is held is made applicable, the law applied in the District of Columbia governs proceedings in the United States District Court for the District of Columbia. When the word "state" is used, it includes, if appropriate, the District of Columbia. When the term "statute of the United States" is used, it includes, so far as concerns proceedings in the United States District Court for the District of Columbia, any Act of Congress locally applicable to and in force in the District of Columbia.

When the law of a state is referred to, the word "law" includes the statutes of that state and the state judicial decisions construing them.

(f) References to Officer of the United States. Under any rule in which reference is made to an officer or agency of the United States, the term "officer" includes a district director of internal revenue, a former district director or collector of internal revenue, or the personal representative of a deceased district director or collector of internal revenue.

Rule 82. Jurisdiction and Venue Unaffected

These rules shall not be construed to extend or limit the jurisdiction of the United States district courts or the venue of actions therein. An admiralty or maritime claim within the meaning of Rule 9(h) shall not be treated as a civil action for the purposes of Title 28, U.S.C., §§ 1391-1392.

Rule 83. Rules by District Courts; Judge's Directives

(a) Local Rules.

(1) Each district court, acting by a majority of its district judges, may, after giving appropriate public notice and an opportunity for comment, make and amend rules governing its practice. A local rule shall be consistent with — but not duplicative of — Acts of Congress and rules adopted under 28 U.S.C. §§ 2072 and 2075, and shall conform to any uniform numbering system prescribed by the Judicial Conference of the United States. A local rule takes effect on the date specified by the district court and remains in effect unless amended by the court or abrogated by the judicial council of the circuit. Copies of rules and amendments shall, upon their promulgation, be furnished to the judicial council and the Administrative Office of the United States Courts and be made available to the public.

(2) A local rule imposing a requirement of form shall not be enforced in a manner that causes a party to lose rights because of a nonwillful failure to comply with the requirement.

(b) Procedures When There is No Controlling Law. A judge may regulate practice in any manner consistent with federal law, rules adopted under 28 U.S.C. §§ 2072 and 2075, and local rules of the district. No sanction or other disadvantage may be imposed for noncompliance with any requirement not in federal law, federal rules, or the local district rules unless the alleged violator has been furnished in the particular case with actual notice of the requirement.

Rule 84. Forms

The forms contained in the Appendix of Forms are sufficient under the rules and are intended to indicate the simplicity and brevity of statement which the rules contemplate.

Rule 85. Title

These rules may be known and cited as the Federal Rules of Civil Procedure.

Rule 86. Effective Date

(a) These rules will take effect on the day which is 3 months subsequent to the adjournment of the second regular session of the 75th Congress, but if that day is prior to September 1, 1938, then these rules will take effect on September 1, 1938. They govern all proceedings in actions brought after they take effect and also all further proceedings in actions then pending, except to the extent that in the opinion of the court their application in a particular action pending when the rules take effect would not be feasible or would work injustice, in which event the former procedure applies.

(b) Effective Date of Amendments. The amendments adopted by the Supreme Court on December 27, 1946, and transmitted to the Attorney General on January 2, 1947, shall take effect on the day which is three months subsequent to the adjournment of the first regular session of the 80th Congress, but, if that day is prior to September 1, 1947, then these amendments shall take effect on September 1, 1947. They govern all proceedings in actions brought after they take effect and also all further proceedings in actions then pending, except to the extent that in the opinion of the court their application in a particular action pending when the amendments take effect would not be feasible or would work injustice, in which event the former procedure applies.

(c) Effective Date of Amendments. The amendments adopted by the Supreme Court on December 29, 1948, and transmitted to the Attorney General on December 31, 1948, shall take effect on the day following the adjournment of the first regular session of the 81st Congress.

(d) Effective Date of Amendments. The amendments adopted by the Supreme Court on April 17, 1961, and transmitted to the Congress on April 18, 1961, shall take effect on July 19, 1961. They govern all proceedings in actions brought after they take effect and also all further proceedings in actions then pending, except to the extent that in the opinion of the court their application in a particular action pending when the amendments take effect would not be feasible or would work injustice, in which event the former procedure applies.

(e) Effective Date of Amendments. The amendments adopted by the Supreme Court on January 21, 1963, and transmitted to the Congress on January 21, 1963, shall take effect on July 1, 1963. They govern all proceedings in actions brought after they take effect and also all further proceedings in actions then pending, except to the extent that in the opinion of the court their application in a particular action pending when the amendments take effect would not be feasible or would work injustice, in which event the former procedure applies.

APPENDIX OF FORMS

(See Rule 84)

INTRODUCTORY STATEMENT

1. The following forms are intended for illustration only. They are limited in number. No attempt is made to furnish a manual of forms. Each form assumes the action to be brought in the Southern District of New York. If the district in which an action is brought has divisions, the division should be indicated in the caption.

2. Except where otherwise indicated each pleading, motion, and other paper should have a caption similar to that of the summons, with the designation of the particular paper substituted for the word "Summons." In the caption of the summons and in the caption of the complaint all parties must be named but in other pleadings and papers, it is sufficient to state the name of the first party on either side, with an appropriate indication of other parties. See Rules 4(b), 7(b)(2), and 10(a).

3. In Form 3 and the forms following, the words, "Allegation of jurisdiction," are used to indicate the appropriate allegation in Form 2.

4. Each pleading, motion, and other paper is to be signed in his individual name by at least one attorney of record (Rule 11). The attorney's name is to be followed by his address as indicated in Form 3. In forms following Form 3 the signature and address are not indicated.

5. If a party is not represented by an attorney, the signature and address of the party are required in place of those of the attorney.

Form 1. Summons

United States District Court for the
Southern District of New York

Civil Action, File Number ________

A. B., Plaintiff)
v.) *Summons*
C. D., Defendant)

To the above-named Defendant:

You are hereby summoned and required to serve upon ______, plaintiff's attorney, whose address is ______, an answer to the complaint which is herewith served upon you, within 20[1] days after service of this summons upon you, exclusive of the day of service. If you fail to do so, judgment by default will be taken against you for the relief demanded in the complaint.

______________________,
Clerk of Court.

[Seal of the U.S. District Court]

Dated ________

(This summons is issued pursuant to Rule 4 of the Federal Rules of Civil Procedure)

Form 1A. Notice of Lawsuit and Request for Waiver of Service of Summons

TO: (A)

[as (B) of (C)]

A lawsuit has been commenced against you (or the entity on whose behalf you are addressed). A copy of the complaint is attached to this notice. It has been filed in the United States District Court for the (D) and has been assigned docket number (E).

This is not a formal summons or notification from the court, but rather my request that you sign and return the enclosed waiver of service in order to save the cost of serving you with a judicial summons and an additional copy of the complaint. The cost of service will be avoided if I receive a signed copy of the waiver within (F) days after the date designated below as the date on which this Notice and Request is sent. I enclose a stamped

1. If the United States or an officer or agency there of is a defendant, the time to be inserted as to it is 60 days.

and addressed envelope (or other means of cost-free return) for your use. An extra copy of the waiver is also attached for your records.

If you comply with this request and return the signed waiver, it will be filed with the court and no summons will be served on you. The action will then proceed as if you had been served on the date the waiver is filed, except that you will not be obligated to answer the complaint before 60 days from the date designated below as the date on which this notice is sent (or before 90 days from that date if your address is not in any judicial district of the United States).

If you do not return the signed waiver within the time indicated, I will take appropriate steps to effect formal service in a manner authorized by the Federal Rules of Civil Procedure and will then, to the extent authorized by those Rules, ask the court to require you (or the party on whose behalf you are addressed) to pay the full costs of such service. In that connection, please read the statement concerning the duty of parties to waive the service of the summons, which is set forth on the reverse side (or at the foot) of the waiver form.

I affirm that this request is being sent to you on behalf of the plaintiff, this ___ day of ______, ______.

Signature of Plaintiff's Attorney or Unrepresented Plaintiff

Notes:

A — Name of individual defendant (or name of officer or agent of corporate defendant)

B — Title, or other relationship of individual to corporate defendant

C — Name of corporate defendants, if any

D — District

E — Docket number of action

F — Addresses must be given at least 30 days (60 days if located in foreign country) in which to return waiver.

Form 1B. Waiver of Service of Summons

TO: (name of plaintiff's attorney or unrepresented plaintiff)

I acknowledge receipt of your request that I waive service of a summons in the action of (caption of action), which is case number (docket number) in the United States District Court for the (district). I have also received a copy of the complaint in the action, two copies of this instrument, and a means by which I can return the signed waiver to you without cost to me.

I agree to save the cost of service of a summons and an additional copy of the complaint in this lawsuit by not requiring that I (or the entity on whose behalf I am acting) be served with judicial process in the manner provided by Rule 4.

I (or the entity on whose behalf I am acting) will retain all defenses or objections to the lawsuit or to the jurisdiction or venue of the court except for objections based on a defect in the summons or in the service of the summons.

I understand that a judgment may be entered against me (or the party on whose behalf I am acting) if an answer or motion under Rule 12 is not served upon you within 60 days after (date request was sent), or within 90 days after that date if the request was sent outside the United States.

____________________ ________________________________

Date Signature

Printed/typed name: ____

[as ______________________________]

[of ______________________________]

To be printed on reverse side of the waiver form or set forth at the foot of the form:

Duty to Avoid Unnecessary Costs of Service of Summons

Rule 4 of the Federal Rules of Civil Procedure requires certain parties to cooperate in saving unnecessary costs of service of the summons and complaint. A defendant located in the United States who, after being notified of an action and asked by a plaintiff located in the United States to waive service of a summons, fails to do so will be required to bear the cost of such service unless good cause be shown for its failure to sign and return the waiver.

It is not good cause for a failure to waive service that a party believes that the complaint is unfounded, or that the action has been brought in an improper place or in a court that lacks jurisdiction over the subject matter of the action or over its person or property. A party who waives service of the summons retains all defenses and objections (except any relating to the summons or the service of the summons), and may later object to the jurisdiction of the court or to the place where the action has been brought.

A defendant who waives service must within the time specified on the waiver form serve on the plaintiff's attorney (or unrepresented plaintiff) a response to the complaint and must also file a signed copy of the response with the court. If the answer or motion is not served within this time, a default judgment may be taken against that defendant. By waiving service, a defendant is allowed more time to answer than if the summons had been actually served when the request for waiver of service was received.

Form 2. Allegation of Jurisdiction

(a) Jurisdiction founded on diversity of citizenship and amount.

Plaintiff is a [citizen of the State of Connecticut][1] [corporation incorporated under the laws of the State of Connecticut having its principal place of business in the State of Connecticut] and defendant is a corporation incorporated under the laws of the State of New York having its principal place of business in a State other than the State of Connecticut. The matter in controversy exceeds, exclusive of interest and costs, the sum specified by 28 U.S.C. § 1332.

(b) Jurisdiction founded on the existence of a Federal question.

The action arises under [the Constitution of the United States, Article ___, Section ___]; [the ___ Amendment to the Constitution of the United States, Section ___]; [the Act of ___, ___ Stat. ___; U.S.C., Title ___, § ___]; [the Treaty of the United States (here describe the treaty)][2] as hereinafter more fully appears.

(c) Jurisdiction founded on the existence of a question arising under particular statutes.

The action arises under the Act of ___, ___ Stat. ___; U.S.C., Title ___, § ___, as hereinafter more fully appears.

(d) Jurisdiction founded on the admiralty or maritime character of the claim.

This is a case of admiralty and maritime jurisdiction, as hereinafter more fully appears. [If the pleader wishes to invoke the distinctively maritime procedures referred to in Rule 9(h), add the following or its substantial equivalent: This is an admiralty or maritime claim within the meaning of Rule 9(h).]

NOTES

1. Diversity of citizenship. U.S.C., Title 28, § 1332 (Diversity of citizenship; amount in controversy; costs), as amended by PL 85-554, 72 Stat. 415, July 25, 1958, states in subsection (c) that "For the purposes of this section and section 1441 of this title [removable actions], a corporation shall be deemed a

1. Form for natural person.

2. Use the appropriate phrase or phrases. The general allegation of the existence of a Federal question is ineffective unless the matters constituting the claim for relief as set forth in the complaint raise a Federal question.

citizen of any State by which it has been incorporated and of the State where it has its principal place of business." Thus if the defendant corporation in Form 2(a) had its principal place of business in Connecticut, diversity of citizenship would not exist. An allegation regarding the principal place of business of each corporate party must be made in addition to an allegation regarding its place of incorporation.

2. **Jurisdictional amount.** U.S.C., Title 28, § 1331 (Federal question; amount in controversy; costs) and § 1332 (Diversity of citizenship; amount in controversy; costs), as amended by PL 85-554, 72 Stat. 415, July 25, 1958, require that the amount in controversy, exclusive of interest and costs, be in excess of $10,000 [Ed. — This amount has been raised by subsequent legislation to the present $75,000.]. The allegation as to the amount in controversy may be omitted in any case where by law no jurisdictional amount is required. See, for example, U.S.C., Title 28, § 1338 (Patents, copyrights, trade-marks, and unfair competition), § 1343 (Civil rights and elective franchise).

3. **Pleading venue.** Since improper venue is a matter of defense, it is not necessary for plaintiff to include allegations showing the venue to be proper. See 1 *Moore's Federal Practice,* par. 0.140[1-4] (2d ed. 1959).

Form 3. Complaint on a Promissory Note

1. Allegation of jurisdiction.

2. Defendant on or about June 1, 1935, executed and delivered to plaintiff a promissory note [in the following words and figures: (here set out the note verbatim)]; [a copy of which is hereto annexed as Exhibit A]; [whereby defendant promised to pay to plaintiff or order on June 1, 1936 the sum of _____ dollars with interest thereon at the rate of six percent. per annum].

3. Defendant owes to plaintiff the amount of said note and interest.

Wherefore plaintiff demands judgment against defendant for the sum of _____ dollars, interest, and costs.

Signed: ______________________

Attorney for Plaintiff.

Address: ______________________

Notes

1. The pleader may use the material in one of the three sets of brackets. His choice will depend upon whether he desires to plead the document verbatim, or by exhibit, or according to its legal effect.

2. Under the rules free joinder of claims is permitted. See rules 8(e) and 18. Consequently the claims set forth in each and all of the following forms may be joined with this complaint or with each other. Ordinarily each claim should be stated in a separate division of the complaint, and the divisions should be

designated as counts successively numbered. In particular the rules permit alternative and inconsistent pleading. See Form 10.

Form 4. Complaint on an Account

1. Allegation of jurisdiction.

2. Defendant owes plaintiff _____ dollars according to the account hereto annexed as Exhibit A.

Wherefore (etc. as in Form 3).

Form 5. Complaint for Goods Sold and Delivered

1. Allegation of jurisdiction.

2. Defendant owes plaintiff _____ dollars for goods sold and delivered by plaintiff to defendant between June 1, 1936 and December 1, 1936.

Wherefore (etc. as in Form 3).

NOTE

This form may be used where the action is for an agreed price or for the reasonable value of the goods.

Form 6. Complaint for Money Lent

1. Allegation of jurisdiction.

2. Defendant owes plaintiff _____ dollars for money lent by plaintiff to defendant on June 1, 1936.

Wherefore (etc. as in Form 3).

Form 7. Complaint for Money Paid by Mistake

1. Allegation of jurisdiction.

2. Defendant owes plaintiff _____ dollars for money paid by plaintiff to defendant by mistake on June 1, 1936, under the following circumstances: [here state the circumstances with particularity — see Rule 9(b)].

Wherefore (etc. as in Form 3).

Form 8. Complaint for Money Had and Received

1. Allegation of jurisdiction.

2. Defendant owes plaintiff _____ dollars for money had and received from one G. H. on June 1, 1936, to be paid by defendant to plaintiff.

Wherefore (etc. as in Form 3).

Form 9. Complaint for Negligence

1. Allegation of jurisdiction.

2. On June 1, 1936, in a public highway called Boylston Street in Boston, Massachusetts, defendant negligently drove a motor vehicle against plaintiff who was then crossing said highway.

3. As a result plaintiff was thrown down and had his leg broken and was otherwise injured, was prevented from transacting his business, suffered great pain of body and mind, and incurred expenses for medical attention and hospitalization in the sum of one thousand dollars.

Wherefore plaintiff demands judgment against defendant in the sum of _____ dollars and costs.

NOTE

Since contributory negligence is an affirmative defense, the complaint need contain no allegation of due care of plaintiff.

Form 10. Complaint for Negligence Where Plaintiff is Unable to Determine Definitely Whether the Person Responsible is C. D. or E. F. or Whether Both are Responsible and Where his Evidence may Justify a Finding of Wilfulness or of Recklessness or of Negligence

A. B., Plaintiff)
v.) *Complaint*
C. D. and E. F., Defendants)

1. Allegation of jurisdiction.

2. On June 1, 1936, in a public highway called Boylston Street in Boston, Massachusetts, defendant C. D. or defendant E. F., or both defendants C. D. and E. F. wilfully or recklessly or negligently drove or caused to be driven a motor vehicle against plaintiff who was then crossing said highway.

3. As a result plaintiff was thrown down and had his leg broken and was otherwise injured, was prevented from transacting his business, suffered great pain of body and mind, and incurred expenses for medical attention and hospitalization in the sum of one thousand dollars.

Wherefore plaintiff demands judgment against C. D. or against E. F. or against both in the sum of _____ dollars and costs.

Form 11. Complaint for Conversion

1. Allegation of jurisdiction.

2. On or about December 1, 1936, defendant converted to his own use ten bonds of the _____ Company (here insert brief identification as by number and issue) of the value of _____ dollars, the property of plaintiff.

Wherefore plaintiff demands judgment against defendant in the sum of _____ dollars, interest, and costs.

Form 12. Complaint for Specific Performance of Contract to Convey Land

1. Allegation of jurisdiction.

2. On or about December 1, 1936, plaintiff and defendant entered into an agreement in writing a copy of which is hereto annexed as Exhibit A.

3. In accord with the provisions of said agreement plaintiff tendered to defendant the purchase price and requested a conveyance of the land, but defendant refused to accept the tender and refused to make the conveyance.

4. Plaintiff now offers to pay the purchase price.

Wherefore plaintiff demands (1) that defendant be required specifically to perform said agreement, (2) damages in the sum of one thousand dollars, and (3) that if specific performance is not granted plaintiff have judgment against defendant in the sum of _____ dollars.

NOTE

Here, as in Form 3, plaintiff may set forth the contract verbatim in the complaint or plead it, as indicated, by exhibit, or plead it according to its legal effect. Furthermore, plaintiff may seek legal or equitable relief or both even though this was impossible under the system in operation before these rules.

Form 13. Complaint on Claim for Debt and to Set Aside Fraudulent Conveyance Under Rule 18(b)

A. B., Plaintiff)
v.) *Complaint*
C. D. and E. F., Defendants)

1. Allegation of jurisdiction.

2. Defendant C. D. on or about _____ executed and delivered to plaintiff a promissory note [in the following words and figures: (here set out the note verbatim)]; [a copy of which is hereto annexed as Exhibit A]; [whereby defendant C. D. promised to pay to plaintiff or order on _____ the sum of five thousand dollars with interest thereon at the rate of _____ percent. per annum].

3. Defendant C. D. owes to plaintiff the amount of said note and interest.

4. Defendant C. D. on or about _____ conveyed all his property, real and personal [or specify and describe] to defendant E. F. for the purpose of defrauding plaintiff and hindering and delaying the collection of the indebtedness evidenced by the note above referred to.

Wherefore plaintiff demands:

(1) That plaintiff have judgment against defendant C. D. for _____ dollars and interest; (2) that the aforesaid conveyance to defendant E. F. be declared void and the judgment herein be declared a lien on said property; (3) that plaintiff have judgment against the defendants for costs.

Form 14. Complaint for Negligence Under Federal Employer's Liability Act

1. Allegation of jurisdiction.

2. During all the times herein mentioned defendant owned and operated in interstate commerce a railroad which passed through a tunnel located at _____ and known as Tunnel No. ___.

3. On or about June 1, 1936, defendant was repairing and enlarging the tunnel in order to protect interstate trains and passengers and freight from injury and in order to make the tunnel more conveniently usable for interstate commerce.

4. In the course of thus repairing and enlarging the tunnel on said day defendant employed plaintiff as one of its workmen, and negligently put plaintiff to work in a portion of the tunnel which defendant had left unprotected and unsupported.

5. By reason of defendant's negligence in thus putting plaintiff to work in that portion of the tunnel, plaintiff was, while so working pursuant to defendant's orders, struck and crushed by a rock, which fell from the unsupported portion of the tunnel, and was (here describe plaintiff's injuries).

6. Prior to these injuries, plaintiff was a strong, able-bodied man, capable of earning and actually earning _____ dollars per day. By these injuries he has been made incapable of any gainful activity, has suffered great physical and mental pain, and has incurred expense in the amount of _____ dollars for medicine, medical attendance, and hospitalization.

Wherefore plaintiff demands judgment against defendant in the sum of _____ dollars and costs.

Form 15. Complaint for Damages Under Merchant Marine Act

1. Allegation of jurisdiction. [If the pleader wishes to invoke the distinctively maritime procedures referred to in Rule 9(h), add the following or its substantial equivalent: This is an admiralty or maritime claim within the meaning of Rule 9(h).]

2. During all the times herein mentioned defendant was the owner of the steamship _____ and used it in the transportation of freight for hire by water in interstate and foreign commerce.

3. During the first part of (month and year) at _____ plaintiff entered the employ of defendant as an able seaman on said steamship under seamen's articles of customary form for a voyage from _____ ports to the Orient and return at a wage of _____ dollars per month and found, which is equal to a wage of _____ dollars per month as a shore worker.

4. On June 1, 1936, said steamship was about ___ days out of the port of _____ and was being navigated by the master and crew on the return voyage to _____ ports. (Here describe weather conditions and the condition of the ship and state as in an ordinary complaint for personal injuries the negligent conduct of defendant.)

5. By reason of defendant's negligence in thus (brief statement of defendant's negligent conduct) and the unseaworthiness of said steamship, plaintiff was (here describe plaintiff's injuries).

6. Prior to these injuries, plaintiff was a strong, able-bodied man, capable of earning and actually earning _____ dollars per day. By these injuries he has been made incapable of any gainful activity; has suffered great physical and mental pain, and has incurred expense in the amount of _____ dollars for medicine, medical attendance, and hospitalization.

Wherefore plaintiff demands judgment against defendant in the sum of _____ dollars and costs.

Form 16. Complaint for Infringement of Patent

1. Allegation of jurisdiction.

2. On May 16, 1934, United States Letters Patent No. ___ were duly and legally issued to plaintiff for an invention in an electric motor; and since that date plaintiff has been and still is the owner of those Letters Patent.

3. Defendant has for a long time past been and still is infringing those Letters Patent by making, selling, and using electric motors embodying the patented invention, and will continue to do so unless enjoined by this court.

4. Plaintiff has placed the required statutory notice on all electric motors manufactured and sold by him under said Letters Patent, and has given written notice to defendant of his said infringement.

Wherefore plaintiff demands a preliminary and final injunction against continued infringement, an accounting for damages, and an assessment of interest and costs against defendant.

Form 17. Complaint for Infringement of Copyright and Unfair Competition

1. Allegation of jurisdiction.

2. Prior to March, 1936, plaintiff, who then was and ever since has been a citizen of the United States, created and wrote an original book, entitled _____.

3. This book contains a large amount of material wholly original with plaintiff and is copyrightable subject matter under the laws of the United States.

4. Between March 2, 1936, and March 10, 1936, plaintiff complied in all respects with the Act of (give citation) and all other laws governing copyright, and secured the exclusive rights and privileges in and to the copyright of said book, and received from the Register of Copyrights a certificate of registration, dated and identified as follows: "March 10, 1936, Class ___, No. ___."

5. Since March 10, 1936, said book has been published by plaintiff and all copies of it made by plaintiff or under his authority or license have been printed, bound, and published in strict conformity with the provisions of the Act of _____ and all other laws governing copyright.

6. Since March 10, 1936, plaintiff has been and still is the sole proprietor of all rights, title, and interest in and to the copyright in said book.

7. After March 10, 1936, defendant infringed said copyright by publishing and placing upon the market a book entitled _____, which was copied largely from plaintiff's copyrighted book, entitled _____.

8. A copy of plaintiff's copyrighted book is hereto attached as "Exhibit 1"; and a copy of defendant's infringing book is hereto attached as "Exhibit 2."

9. Plaintiff has notified defendant that defendant has infringed the copyright of plaintiff, and defendant has continued to infringe the copyright.

10. After March 10, 1936, and continuously since about _____, defendant has been publishing, selling and otherwise marketing the book entitled _____, and has thereby been engaging in unfair trade practices and unfair competition against plaintiff to plaintiff's irreparable damage.

Wherefore plaintiff demands:

(1) That defendant, his agents, and servants be enjoined during the pendency of this action and permanently from infringing said copyright of said plaintiff in any manner, and from publishing, selling, marketing or otherwise disposing of any copies of the book entitled _____.

(2) That defendant be required to pay to plaintiff such damages as plaintiff has sustained in consequence of defendant's infringement of said copyright and said unfair trade practices and unfair competition and to account for

(a) all gains, profits and advantages derived by defendant by said trade practices and unfair competition and

(b) all gains, profits, and advantages derived by defendant by his infringement of plaintiff's copyright or such damages as to the court shall appear proper within the provisions of the copyright statutes, but not less than two hundred and fifty dollars.

(3) That defendant be required to deliver up to be impounded during the pendency of this action all copies of said book entitled _____ in his possession or under his control and to deliver up for destruction all infringing copies and all plates, molds, and other matter for making such infringing copies.

(4) That defendant pay to plaintiff the costs of this action and reasonable attorney's fees to be allowed to the plaintiff by the court.

(5) That plaintiff have such other and further relief as is just.

Form 18. Complaint for Interpleader and Declaratory Relief

1. Allegation of jurisdiction.

2. On or about June 1, 1935, plaintiff issued to G. H. a policy of life insurance whereby plaintiff promised to pay to K. L. as beneficiary the sum of _____ dollars upon the death of G. H. The policy required the payment by G. H. of a stipulated premium on June 1, 1936, and annually thereafter as a condition precedent to its continuance in force.

3. No part of the premium due June 1, 1936, was ever paid and the policy ceased to have any force or effect on July 1, 1936.

4. Thereafter, on September 1, 1936, G. H. and K. L. died as the result of a collision between a locomotive and the automobile in which G. H. and K. L. were riding.

5. Defendant C. D. is the duly appointed and acting executor of the will of G. H.; defendant E. F. is the duly appointed and acting executor of the will of K. L.; defendant X. Y. claims to have been duly designated as beneficiary of said policy in place of K. L.

6. Each of defendants, C. D., E. F., and X. Y. is claiming that the above-mentioned policy was in full force and effect at the time of the death of G. H.; each of them is claiming to be the only person entitled to receive payment of the amount of the policy and has made demand for payment thereof.

7. By reason of these conflicting claims of the defendants, plaintiff is in great doubt as to which defendant is entitled to be paid the amount of the policy, if it was in force at the death of G. H.

Wherefore plaintiff demands that the court adjudge:

(1) That none of the defendants is entitled to recover from plaintiff the amount of said policy or any part thereof.

(2) That each of the defendants be restrained from instituting any action against plaintiff for the recovery of the amount of said policy or any part thereof.

(3) That, if the court shall determine that said policy was in force at the death of G. H., the defendants be required to interplead and settle between themselves their rights to the money due under said policy, and that plaintiff be discharged from all liability in the premises except to the person whom the court shall adjudge entitled to the amount of said policy.

(4) That plaintiff recover its costs.

Form 18-A. [Notice and Acknowledgment for Service by Mail]

(Abrogated Apr. 22, 1993, effective Dec. 1, 1993.)

Form 19. Motion to Dismiss, Presenting Defenses of Failure to State a Claim, of Lack of Service of Process, of Improper Venue, and of Lack of Jurisdiction Under Rule 12(b)

The defendant moves the court as follows:

1. To dismiss the action because the complaint fails to state a claim against defendant upon which relief can be granted.

2. To dismiss the action or in lieu thereof to quash the return of service of summons on the grounds (a) that the defendant is a corporation organized under the laws of Delaware and was not and is not subject to service of process within the Southern District of New York, and (b) that the defendant has not been properly served with process in this action, all of which more clearly appears in the affidavits of M. N. and X. Y. hereto annexed as Exhibit A and Exhibit B respectively.

3. To dismiss the action on the ground that it is in the wrong district because (a) the jurisdiction of this court is invoked solely on the ground that the action arises under the Constitution and laws of the United States and (b) the defendant is a corporation incorporated under the laws of the State of Delaware and is not licensed to do or doing business in the Southern District of New York, all of which more clearly appears in the affidavits of K. L. and V. W. hereto annexed as Exhibits C and D, respectively.

4. To dismiss the action on the ground that the court lacks jurisdiction because the amount actually in controversy is less than ten thousand dollars exclusive of interest and costs.

Signed: ____________________
Attorney for Defendant.

Address: ____________________

Notice of Motion

To: ____________________
Attorney for Plaintiff.

____

Please take notice, that the undersigned will bring the above motion on for hearing before this Court at Room ___, United States Court House, Foley Square, City of New York, on the ___ day of _____, 20___, at 10 o'clock in the forenoon of that day or as soon thereafter as counsel can be heard.

Signed: ____________________
Attorney for Defendant.

Address: ____________________

NOTES

1. The above motion and notice of motion may be combined and denominated Notice of Motion. See Rule 7(b).

2. As to paragraph 3, see U.S.C., Title 28, § 1391 (Venue generally), subsections (b) and (c).

3. As to paragraph 4, see U.S.C., Title 28, § 1331 (Federal question; amount in controversy; costs), as amended by P.L. 85-554, 72 Stat. 415, July 25, 1958, requiring that the amount in controversy, exclusive of interest and costs, be in excess of $10,000.

Form 20. Answer Presenting Defenses Under Rule 12(b)

First Defense

The complaint fails to state a claim against defendant upon which relief can be granted.

Second Defense

If defendant is indebted to plaintiffs for the goods mentioned in the complaint, he is indebted to them jointly with G. H. G. H. is alive; is a citizen of the State of New York and a resident of this district, is subject to the jurisdiction of this court, as to both service of process and venue; can be made a party without depriving this court of jurisdiction of the present parties, and has not been made a party.

Third Defense

Defendant admits the allegation contained in paragraphs 1 and 4 of the complaint; alleges that he is without knowledge or information sufficient to form a belief as to the truth of the allegations contained in paragraph 2 of the complaint; and denies each and every other allegation contained in the complaint.

Fourth Defense

The right of action set forth in the complaint did not accrue within six years next before the commencement of this action.

Counterclaim

(Here set forth any claim as a counterclaim in the manner in which a claim is pleaded in a complaint. No statement of the grounds on which the court's jurisdiction depends need be made unless the counterclaim requires independent grounds of jurisdiction.)

Cross-Claim Against Defendant M. N.

(Here set forth the claim constituting a cross-claim against defendant M. N. in the manner in which a claim is pleaded in a complaint. The statement of grounds upon which the court's jurisdiction depends need not be made unless the cross-claim requires independent grounds of jurisdiction.)

NOTE

The above form contains examples of certain defenses provided for in Rule 12(b). The first defense challenges the legal sufficiency of the complaint. It is a substitute for a general demurrer or a motion to dismiss.

The second defense embodies the old plea in abatement; the decision thereon, however, may well provide under Rules 19 and 21 for the citing in of the party rather than an abatement of the action.

The third defense is an answer on the merits.

The fourth defense is one of the affirmative defenses provided for in Rule 8(c).

The answer also includes a counterclaim and a cross-claim.

Form 21. Answer to Complaint Set Forth in Form 8, With Counterclaim for Interpleader

Defense

Defendant admits the allegations stated in paragraph 1 of the complaint; and denies the allegations stated in paragraph 2 to the extent set forth in the counterclaim herein.

Counterclaim for Interpleader

1. Defendant received the sum of _____ dollars as a deposit from E. F.

2. Plaintiff has demanded the payment of such deposit to him by virtue of an assignment of it which he claims to have received from E. F.

3. E. F. has notified the defendant that he claims such deposit, that the purported assignment is not valid, and that he holds the defendant responsible for the deposit.

Wherefore defendant demands:

(1) That the court order E. F. to be made a party defendant to respond to the complaint and to this counterclaim.[1]

(2) That the court order the plaintiff and E. F. to interplead their respective claims.

(3) That the court adjudge whether the plaintiff or E. F. is entitled to the sum of money.

1. Rule 13(h) provides for the court ordering parties to a counterclaim, but who are not parties to the original action, to be brought in as defendants.

(4) That the court discharge defendant from all liability in the premises except to the person it shall adjudge entitled to the sum of money.

(5) That the court award to the defendant its costs and attorney's fees.

Form 22. [Motion to Bring in Third-Party Defendant]

(Eliminated effective Jul. 1, 1963.)

Form 22-A. Summons and Complaint Against Third-Party Defendant

United States District Court for the
Southern District of New York

Civil Action, File Number ___

A. B., Plaintiff)	
v.)	
C. D., Defendant and)	
Third-Party Plaintiff)	*Summons*
v.)	
E. F., Third-Party Defendant)	

To the above-named Third-Party Defendant:

You are hereby summoned and required to serve upon _____, plaintiff's attorney whose address is ________, and upon _____, who is attorney for C. D., defendant and third-party plaintiff, and whose address is ________, an answer to the third-party complaint which is herewith served upon you within 20 days after the service of this summons upon you exclusive of the day of service. If you fail to do so, judgment by default will be taken against you for the relief demanded in the third-party complaint. There is also served upon you herewith a copy of the complaint of the plaintiff which you may but are not required to answer.

____________________________________,
Clerk of Court.

[Seal of the U.S. District Court]

Dated _________

United States District Court for the
Southern District of New York

Civil Action, File Number ___

A. B., Plaintiff)
v.)
C. D., Defendant and)
Third-Party Plaintiff) *Third-Party Complaint*
v.)
E. F., Third-Party Defendant)

1. Plaintiff A. B. has filed against defendant C. D. a complaint, a copy of which is hereto attached as "Exhibit A."

2. (Here state the grounds upon which C. D. is entitled to recover from E. F., all or part of what A. B. may recover from C. D. The statement should be framed as in an original complaint.)

Wherefore C. D. demands judgment against third-party defendant E. F. for all sums[1] that may be adjudged against defendant C. D. in favor of plaintiff A. B.

Signed: ______________________
Attorney for C. D., Third-Party Plaintiff.

Address: ______________________

Form 22-B. Motion to Bring in Third-Party Defendant

Defendant moves for leave, as third-party plaintiff, to cause to be served upon E. F. a summons and third-party complaint, copies of which are hereto attached as Exhibit X.

Signed: ______________________
Attorney for Defendant C. D.

Address: ______________________

Notice of Motion

(Contents the same as in Form 19. The notice should be addressed to all parties to the action.)

Exhibit X

(Contents the same as in Form 22-A.)

1. Make appropriate change where C. D. is entitled to only partial recovery-over against E. F.

Form 23. Motion to Intervene as a Defendant Under Rule 24

(Based upon the complaint, Form 16)

United States District Court for the
Southern District of New York

Civil Action, File Number ___

A. B., plaintiff	)	
v.	)	*Motion to intervene*
	)	*as a defendant*
C. D., defendant	)	
E. F., applicant	)	
for intervention	)	

E. F. moves for leave to intervene as a defendant in this action, in order to assert the defenses set forth in his proposed answer, of which a copy is hereto attached, on the ground that he is the manufacturer and vendor to the defendant, as well as to others, of the articles alleged in the complaint to be an infringement of plaintiff's patent, and as such has a defense to plaintiff's claim presenting both questions of law and of fact which are common to the main action.[1]

Signed: ______________________
Attorney for E. F., Applicant For Intervention.

Address: ______________________

Notice of Motion

(Contents the same as in Form 19)

United States District Court for the
Southern District of New York

Civil Action, File Number ___

A. B., plaintiff	)	
v.	)	*Intervener's Answer*
C. D., defendant	)	
E. F., intervener	)	

First Defense

Intervener admits the allegations stated in paragraphs 1 and 4 of the complaint; denies the allegations in paragraph 3, and denies the allegations in paragraph 2 in so far as they assert the legality of the issuance of the Letters Patent to plaintiff.

1. For other grounds of intervention, either of right or in the discretion of the court, see Rule 24(a) and (b).

Second Defense

Plaintiff is not the first inventor of the articles covered by the Letters Patent specified in his complaint, since articles substantially identical in character were previously patented in Letters Patent granted to intervener on January 5, 1920.

Signed: ______________________

Attorney for E. F., Intervener.

Address: ______________________

Form 24. Request for Production of Documents, etc., Under Rule 34

Plaintiff A. B. requests defendant C. D. to respond within ______ days to the following requests:

(1) That defendant produce and permit plaintiff to inspect and to copy each of the following documents:

(Here list the documents either individually or by category and describe each of them.)

(Here state the time, place, and manner of making the inspection and performance of any related acts.)

(2) That defendant produce and permit plaintiff to inspect and to copy, test, or sample each of the following objects:

(Here list the objects either individually or by category and describe each of them.)

(Here state the time, place, and manner of making the inspection and performance of any related acts.)

(3) That defendant permit plaintiff to enter (here describe property to be entered) and to inspect and to photograph, test or sample (here describe the portion of the real property and the objects to be inspected).

(Here state the time, place, and manner of making the inspection and performance of any related acts.)

Signed: ______________________

Attorney for Plaintiff.

Address: ______________________

Form 25. Request for Admission Under Rule 36

Plaintiff A. B. requests defendant C. D. within ___ days after service of this request to make the following admissions for the purpose of this action only and subject to all pertinent objections to admissibility which may be interposed at the trial:

1. That each of the following documents, exhibited with this request, is genuine.

(Here list the documents and describe each document.)

2. That each of the following statements is true.

(Here list the statements.)

Signed: ______________________
Attorney for Plaintiff.

Address: ______________________

Form 26. Allegation of Reason for Omitting Party

When it is necessary, under Rule 19(c), for the pleader to set forth in his pleading the names of persons who ought to be made parties, but who are not so made, there should be an allegation such as the one set out below:

John Doe named in this complaint is not made a party to this action [because he is not subject to the jurisdiction of this court]; [because he cannot be made a party to this action without depriving this court of jurisdiction].

Form 27. [Notice of Appeal to Court of Appeals Under Rule 73(b)]

(Abrogated Dec. 4, 1967, effective Jul. 1, 1968.)

Form 28. Notice: Condemnation

United States District Court for the
Southern District of New York

Civil Action, File Number ___

United States of America, Plaintiff)
v.)
1,000 Acres of Land in [here insert a) *Notice*
general location as "City of _____" or)
"County of _____"], John Doe et al.)
and Unknown Owners, Defendants)

To (here insert the names of the defendants to whom the notice is directed):

You are hereby notified that a complaint in condemnation has heretofore been filed in the office of the clerk of the United States District Court for the Southern District of New York, in the United States Court House in New York City, New York, for the taking (here state the interest to be acquired, as "an estate in fee simple") for use (here state briefly the use, "as a site for a post-office building") of the following described property in which you have or claim an interest.

(Here insert brief description of the property in which the defendants, to whom the notice is directed, have or claim an interest.)

The authority for the taking is (here state briefly, as "the Act of _____, _____ Stat. _____, U.S.C., Title _____, § ____".)[1]

You are further notified that if you desire to present any objection or defense to the taking of your property you are required to serve your answer on the plaintiff's attorney at the address herein designated within twenty days after ____________________.[2]

Your answer shall identify the property in which you claim to have an interest, state the nature and extent of the interest you claim, and state all of your objections and defenses to the taking of your property. All defenses and objections not so presented are waived. And in case of your failure so to answer the complaint, judgment of condemnation of that part of the above-described property in which you have or claim an interest will be rendered.

But without answering, you may serve on the plaintiff's attorney a notice of appearance designating the property in which you claim to be interested. Thereafter you will receive notice of all proceedings affecting it. At the trial of the issue of just compensation, whether or not you have previously appeared or answered, you may present evidence as to the amount of the compensation to be paid for your property, and you may share in the distribution of the award.

____

United States Attorney.

Address: ______________________________

(Here state an address within the district where the United States Attorney may be served as "United States Court House, New York, N.Y.".)

Dated __________

1. And where appropriate add a citation to any applicable Executive Order.

2. Here insert the words "personal service of this notice upon you," if personal service is to be made pursuant to subdivision (d)(3)(i) of this rule [Rule 71A]; or, insert the date of the last publication of notice, if service by publication is to be made pursuant to subdivision (d)(3)(ii) of this rule.

Form 29. Complaint: Condemnation

United States District Court for the
Southern District of New York

Civil Action, File Number ___

United States of America, Plaintiff)
v.)
1,000 Acres of Land in [here insert a) *Complaint*
general location as "City of _____" or)
"County of _____"], John Doe et al.)
and Unknown Owners, Defendants)

1. This is an action of a civil nature brought by the United States of America for the taking of property under the power of eminent domain and for the ascertainment and award of just compensation to the owners and parties in interest.[1]

2. The authority for the taking is (here state briefly, as "the Act of _____, _____ Stat. _____, U.S.C., Title _____, § ___").[2]

3. The use for which the property is to be taken is (here state briefly the use, "as a site for a post-office building").

4. The interest to be acquired in the property is (here state the interest as "an estate in fee simple").

5. The property so to be taken is (here set forth a description of the property sufficient for its identification) or (described in Exhibit A hereto attached and made a part hereof).

6. The persons known to the plaintiff to have or claim an interest in the property[3] are:

(Here set forth the names of such persons and the interests claimed.)[4]

1. If the plaintiff is not the United States, but is, for example, a corporation invoking the power of eminent domain delegated to it by the state, then this paragraph 1 of the complaint should be appropriately modified and should be preceded by a paragraph appropriately alleging federal jurisdiction for the action, such as diversity. See Form 2.

2. And where appropriate add a citation to any applicable Executive Order.

3. At the commencement of the action the plaintiff need name as defendants only the persons having or claiming an interest in the property whose names are then known, but prior to any hearing involving the compensation to be paid for a particular piece of property the plaintiff must add as defendants all persons having or claiming an interest in that property whose names can be ascertained by an appropriate search of the records and also those whose names have otherwise been learned. See Rule 71A(c)(2).

4. The plaintiff should designate, as to each separate piece of property, the defendants who have been joined as owners thereof or of some interest therein. See Rule 71A(c)(2).

7. In addition to the persons named, there are or may be others who have or may claim some interest in the property to be taken, whose names are unknown to the plaintiff and on diligent inquiry have not been ascertained. They are made parties to the action under the designation "Unknown Owners."

Wherefore the plaintiff demands judgment that the property be condemned and that just compensation for the taking be ascertained and awarded and for such other relief as may be lawful and proper.

____

United States Attorney.

Address: ______________________________

(Here state an address within the district where the United States Attorney may be served as "United States Court House, New York, N.Y.".)

Form 30. Suggestion of Death Upon the Record Under Rule 25(a)(1)

A. B. [describe as a party, or as executor, administrator, or other representative or successor of C. D., the deceased party] suggests upon the record, pursuant to Rule 25(a)(1), the death of C. D. [describe as party] during the pendency of this action.

Form 31. Judgment on Jury Verdict

United States District Court for the
Southern District of New York

Civil Action, File Number ___

A. B., Plaintiff)
v.) *Judgment*
C. D., Defendant)

This action came on for trial before the Court and a jury, Honorable John Marshall, District Judge, presiding, and the issues having been duly tried and the jury having duly rendered its verdict,

It is Ordered and Adjudged

[that the plaintiff A. B. recover of the defendant C. D. the sum of _____, with interest thereon at the rate of _____ percent as provided by law, and his costs of action.]

[that the plaintiff take nothing, that the action be dismissed on the merits, and that the defendant C. D. recover of the plaintiff A. B. his costs of action.]

Dated at New York, New York, this ___ day of _____, 20__.

______________________________,
Clerk of Court.

NOTE

1. This Form is illustrative of the judgment to be entered upon the general verdict of a jury. It deals with the cases where there is a general jury verdict awarding the plaintiff money damages or finding for the defendant, but is adaptable to other situations of jury verdicts.

2. The clerk, unless the court otherwise orders, is required forthwith to prepare, sign, and enter the judgment upon a general jury verdict without awaiting any direction by the court. The form of the judgment upon a special verdict or a general verdict accompanied by answers to interrogatories shall be promptly approved by the court, and the clerk shall thereupon enter it. See Rule 58, as amended.

3. The Rules contemplate a simple judgment promptly entered. See Rule 54(a). Every judgment shall be set forth on a separate document. See Rule 58, as amended.

4. Attorneys are not to submit forms of judgment unless directed in exceptional cases to do so by the court. See Rule 58, as amended.

Form 32. Judgment on Decision by the Court

United States District Court for th
Southern District of New York

Civil Action, File Number ___

A. B., Plaintiff)
v.) *Judgment*
C. D., Defendant)

This action came on for [trial] [hearing] before the Court, Honorable John Marshall, District Judge, presiding, and the issues having been duly [tried] [heard] and a decision having been duly rendered,

It is Ordered and Adjudged

[that the plaintiff A. B. recover of the defendant C. D. the sum of _____, with interest thereon at the rate of _____ percent as provided by law, and his costs of action.]

[that the plaintiff take nothing, that the action be dismissed on the merits, and that the defendant C. D. recover of the plaintiff A. B. his costs of action.]

Dated at New York, New York, this ___ day of _____, 20__.

_________________________,

Clerk of Court.

NOTES

1. This Form is illustrative of the judgment to be entered upon a decision of the court. It deals with the cases of decisions by the court awarding a party only money damages or costs, but is adaptable to other decisions by the court.

2. The clerk, unless the court otherwise orders, is required forthwith, without awaiting any direction by the court, to prepare, sign, and enter the judgment upon a decision by the court that a party shall recover only a sum certain or costs or that all relief shall be denied. The form of the judgment upon a decision by the court granting other relief shall be promptly approved by the court, and the clerk shall thereupon enter it. See Rule 58, as amended.

3. See also paragraphs 3-4 of the Explanatory Note to Form 31.

Form 33. Notice of Availability of Magistrate Judge to Exercise Jurisdiction

In accordance with the provisions of Title 28, U.S.C. § 636(c), you are hereby notified that a United States magistrate judge of this district court is available to exercise the court's jurisdiction and to conduct any or all proceedings in this case including a jury or nonjury trial, and entry of a final judgment. Exercise of this jurisdiction by a magistrate judge is, however, permitted only if all parties voluntarily consent.

You may, without adverse substantive consequences, withhold your consent, but this will prevent the court's jurisdiction from being exercised by a magistrate judge. If any party withholds consent, the identity of the parties consenting or withholding consent will not be communicated to any magistrate judge or to the district judge to whom the case has been assigned.

An appeal from a judgment entered by a magistrate judge may be taken directly to the United States court of appeals for this judicial circuit in the same manner as an appeal from any other judgment of a district court.

Copies of the Form for the "Consent to Jurisdiction by a United States Magistrate Judge" are available from the clerk of the court.

Form 34. Consent to Exercise of Jurisdiction by a United States Magistrate Judge

UNITED STATES DISTRICT COURT
_____ DISTRICT OF _____

	)	
Plaintiff,	)	
	)	
vs.	)	Docket No. _________
	)	
Defendant.	)	

CONSENT TO JURISDICTION BY
A UNITED STATES MAGISTRATE JUDGE

In accordance with the provisions of Title 28, U.S.C. § 636(c), the undersigned party or parties to the above-captioned civil matter hereby voluntarily consent to have a United States magistrate judge conduct any and all further proceedings in the case, including trial, and order the entry of a final judgment.

____________________ ______________________________

Date Signature

Note: Return this form to the Clerk of the Court if you consent to jurisdiction by a magistrate judge. Do not send a copy of this form to any district judge or magistrate judge.

Form 34A. Order of Reference

UNITED STATES DISTRICT COURT
_____ DISTRICT OF _____

	)	
Plaintiff,	)	
	)	
vs.	)	Docket No. _________
	)	
Defendant.	)	

ORDER OF REFERENCE

IT IS HEREBY ORDERED that the above-captioned matter be referred to United States Magistrate Judge for all further proceedings and entry of judgment in accordance with Title 28, U.S.C. § 636(c) and the consent of the parties.

____

U.S. District Judge

Form 35. Report of Parties' Planning Meeting

[Caption and Names of Parties]

1. Pursuant to Fed. R. Civ. P. 26(f), a meeting was held on (date) at (place) and was attended by:

(name) for plaintiff(s)

(name) for defendant(s) (party name)

(name) for defendant(s) (party name)

2. Pre-Discovery Disclosures. The parties [have exchanged] [will exchange by (date)] the information required by [Fed. R. Civ. P. 26(a)(1)] [local rule ___].

3. Discovery Plan. The parties jointly propose to the court the following discovery plan: [Use separate paragraphs or subparagraphs as necessary if parties disagree.]

Discovery will be needed on the following subjects: (brief description of subjects on which discovery will be needed)

Disclosure or discovery of electronically stored information should be handled as follows: (brief description of parties' proposals)

The parties have agreed to an order regarding claims of privilege or of protection as trial-preparation material asserted after production, as follows: (brief description of provisions of proposed order).

All discovery commenced in time to be completed by ___(date)___. [Discovery on ___ (issue for early discovery) to be completed by ___(date)___.]

Maximum of ___ interrogatories by each party to any other party. [Responses due ___ days after service.]

Maximum of ___ requests for admission by each party to any other party. [Responses due ___ days after service.]

Maximum of ___ depositions by plaintiff(s) and ___ by defendant(s).

Each deposition [other than of ______] limited to maximum of ___ hours unless extended by agreement of parties.

Reports from retained experts under Rule 26(a)(2) due:

from plaintiff(s) by ___(date)___

from defendant(s) by ___(date)___

Supplementations under Rule 26(e) due ___ time(s) or interval(s))___.

4. Other Items. [Use separate paragraphs or subparagraphs as necessary if parties disagree.]

The parties [request] [do not request] a conference with the court before entry of the scheduling order.

The parties request a pretrial conference in ___(month and year)___.

Plaintiff(s) should be allowed until ___(date)___ to join additional parties and until ___(date)___ to amend the pleadings.

Defendant(s) should be allowed until ___(date)___ to join additional parties and until ___(date)___ to amend the pleadings.

All potentially dispositive motions should be filed by ___(date)___.

Settlement [is likely] [is unlikely] [cannot be evaluated prior to ___(date)___] [may be enhanced by use of the following alternative dispute resolution procedure: [______].

Final lists of witnesses and exhibits under Rule 26(a)(3) should be due

from plaintiff(s) by ___(date)___

from defendant(s) by ___(date)___

Parties should have ___ days after service of final lists of witnesses and exhibits to list objections under Rule 26(a)(3).

The case should be ready for trial by ___(date)___ [and at this time is expected to take approximately ___(length of time)___].

[Other matters.]

Date: ______

SUPPLEMENTAL RULES FOR ADMIRALTY OR MARITIME CLAIMS AND ASSET FORFEITURE ACTIONS

[Omitted.]

FEDERAL RULES OF APPELLATE PROCEDURE: SELECTED SECTIONS

TITLE I. APPLICABILITY OF RULES

Rule 1. Scope of Rules; Title

(a) Scope of Rules.

(1) These rules govern procedure in the United States courts of appeals.

(2) When these rules provide for filing a motion or other document in the district court, the procedure must comply with the practice of the district court. . . .

(c) Title. These rules are to be known as the Federal Rules of Appellate Procedure.

TITLE II. APPEAL FROM A JUDGMENT OR ORDER OF A DISTRICT COURT

Rule 3. Appeal as of Right — How Taken

(a) Filing the Notice of Appeal.

(1) An appeal permitted by law as of right from a district court to a court of appeals may be taken only by filing a notice of appeal with the district clerk within the time allowed by Rule 4. . . .

(3) An appeal from a judgment by a magistrate judge in a civil case is taken in the same way as an appeal from any other district court judgment.

(4) An appeal by permission under 28 U.S.C. § 1292(b) . . . may be taken only in the manner prescribed by Rule[ ] 5 . . . .

(c) Contents of the Notice of Appeal.

(1) The notice of appeal must:

(A) specify the party or parties taking the appeal by naming each one in the caption or body of the notice, but an attorney representing more than one party may describe those parties with such terms as "all plaintiffs," "the defendants," "the plaintiffs A, B, et al.," or "all defendants except X";

(B) designate the judgment, order, or part thereof being appealed; and

(C) name the court to which the appeal is taken. . . .

(3) In a class action, whether or not the class has been certified, the notice of appeal is sufficient if it names one person qualified to bring the appeal as representative of the class.

(4) An appeal must not be dismissed for informality of form or title of the notice of appeal, or for failure to name a party whose intent to appeal is otherwise clear from the notice. . . .

(d) Serving the Notice of Appeal.

(1) The district clerk must serve notice of the filing of a notice of appeal by mailing a copy to each party's counsel of record — excluding the appellant's — or, if a party is proceeding pro se, to the party's last known address. . . . The clerk must promptly send a copy of the notice of appeal and of the docket entries — and any later docket entries — to the clerk of the court of appeals named in the notice. The district clerk must note, on each copy, the date when the notice of appeal was filed.

(e) Payment of Fees. Upon filing a notice of appeal, the appellant must pay the district clerk all required fees. The district clerk receives the appellate docket fee on behalf of the court of appeals.

Rule 4. Appeal as of Right — When Taken

(a) Appeal in a Civil Case.

(1) Time for Filing a Notice of Appeal.

(A) In a civil case, except as provided in Rules 4(a)(1)(B), 4(a)(4), and 4(c), the notice of appeal required by Rule 3 must be filed with the district clerk within 30 days after the judgment or order appealed from is entered.

(B) When the United States or its officer or agency is a party, the notice of appeal may be filed by any party within 60 days after the judgment or order appealed from is entered. . . .

(2) Filing Before Entry of Judgment. A notice of appeal filed after the court announces a decision or order--but before the entry of the judgment or order — is treated as filed on the date of and after the entry.

(3) Multiple Appeals. If one party timely files a notice of appeal, any other party may file a notice of appeal within 14 days after the date when the first notice was filed, or within the time otherwise prescribed by this Rule 4(a), whichever period ends later.

(4) Effect of a Motion on a Notice of Appeal.

(A) If a party timely files in the district court any of the following motions under the Federal Rules of Civil Procedure, the time to file an appeal runs for all parties from the entry of the order disposing of the last such remaining motion:

(i) for judgment under Rule 50(b);

(ii) to amend or make additional factual findings under Rule 52(b), whether or not granting the motion would alter the judgment;

(iii) for attorney's fees under Rule 54 if the district court extends the time to appeal under Rule 58;

(iv) to alter or amend the judgment under Rule 59;

(v) for a new trial under Rule 59; or

(vi) for relief under Rule 60 if the motion is filed no later than 10 days after the judgment is entered.

(B) (i) If a party files a notice of appeal after the court announces or enters a judgment — but before it disposes of any motion listed in Rule 4(a)(4)(A) — the notice becomes effective to appeal a judgment or order, in whole or in part, when the order disposing of the last such remaining motion is entered.

(ii) A party intending to challenge an order disposing of any motion listed in Rule 4(a)(4)(A), or a judgment altered or amended upon such a motion, must file a notice of appeal, or an amended notice of appeal — in compliance with Rule 3(c) — within the time prescribed by this Rule measured from the entry of the order disposing of the last such remaining motion.

. . .

(5) Motion for Extension of Time.

(A) The district court may extend the time to file a notice of appeal if:

(i) a party so moves no later than 30 days after the time prescribed by this Rule 4(a) expires; and

(ii) regardless of whether its motion is filed before or during the 30 days after the time prescribed by this Rule 4(a) expires, that party shows excusable neglect or good cause.

(B) A motion filed before the expiration of the time prescribed in Rule 4(a)(1) or (3) may be ex parte unless the court requires otherwise. If the motion is filed after the expiration of the prescribed time, notice must be given to the other parties in accordance with local rules.

(C) No extension under this Rule 4(a)(5) may exceed 30 days after the prescribed time or 10 days after the date when the order granting the motion is entered, whichever is later.

(6) Reopening the Time to File an Appeal. The district court may reopen the time to file an appeal for a period of 14 days after the date when its order to reopen is entered, but only if all the following conditions are satisfied:

(A) the court finds that the moving party did not receive notice under Federal Rule of Civil Procedure 77(d) of the entry of the judgment or order sought to be appealed within 21 days after entry;

(B) the motion is filed within 180 days after the judgment or order is entered or within 7 days after the moving party receives or observes written notice of the entry from any source, whichever is earlier; and

(C) the court finds that no party would be prejudiced.

(7) Entry Defined.

(A) A judgment or order is entered for purposes of this Rule 4(a):

(i) if Federal Rule of Civil Procedure 58(a)(1) does not require a separate document, when the judgment or order is entered in the civil docket under Federal Rule of Civil Procedure 79(a); or

(ii) if Federal Rule of Civil Procedure 58(a)(1) requires a separate document, when the judgment or order is entered in the civil docket under Federal Rule of Civil Procedure 79(a) and when the earlier of these events occurs:

- the judgment or order is set forth on a separate document, or
- 150 days have run from entry of the judgment or order in the civil docket under Federal Rule of Civil Procedure 79(a).

(B) A failure to set forth a judgment or order on a separate document when required by Federal Rule of Civil Procedure 58(a)(1) does not affect the validity of an appeal from that judgment or order. . . .

(d) Mistaken Filing in the Court of Appeals. If a notice of appeal in either a civil or a criminal case is mistakenly filed in the court of appeals, the clerk of that court must note on the notice the date when it was received and send it to the district clerk. The notice is then considered filed in the district court on the date so noted.

Rule 5. Appeal by Permission

(a) Petition for Permission to Appeal.

(1) To request permission to appeal when an appeal is within the court of appeals' discretion, a party must file a petition for permission to appeal. The petition must be filed with the circuit clerk with proof of service on all other parties to the district-court action.

(2) The petition must be filed within the time specified by the statute or rule authorizing the appeal or, if no such time is specified, within the time provided by Rule 4(a) for filing a notice of appeal.

(3) If a party cannot petition for appeal unless the district court first enters an order granting permission to do so or stating that the necessary conditions are met, the district court may amend its order, either on its own or in response to a party's motion, to include the required permission or statement. In that event, the time to petition runs from entry of the amended order.

(b) Contents of the Petition; Answer or Cross-Petition; Oral Argument.

(1) The petition must include the following:

(A) the facts necessary to understand the question presented;

(B) the question itself;

(C) the relief sought;

(D) the reasons why the appeal should be allowed and is authorized by a statute or rule; and

(E) an attached copy of:

(i) the order, decree, or judgment complained of and any related opinion or memorandum, and

(ii) any order stating the district court's permission to appeal or finding that the necessary conditions are met.

(2) A party may file an answer in opposition or a cross-petition within 7 days after the petition is served. . . .

TITLE VII. GENERAL PROVISIONS

Rule 35. En Banc Determination

(a) When Hearing or Rehearing En Banc May Be Ordered. A majority of the circuit judges who are in regular active service and who are not disqualified may order that an appeal or other proceeding be heard or reheard by the court of appeals en banc. An en banc hearing or rehearing is not favored and ordinarily will not be ordered unless:

(1) en banc consideration is necessary to secure or maintain uniformity of the court's decisions; or

(2) the proceeding involves a question of exceptional importance.

. . .

(c) Time for Petition for Hearing or Rehearing En Banc. A petition that an appeal be heard initially en banc must be filed by the date when the appellee's brief is due. A petition for a rehearing en banc must be filed within the time prescribed by Rule 40 for filing a petition for rehearing. . . .

(e) Response. No response may be filed to a petition for an en banc consideration unless the court orders a response. . . .

Rule 38. Frivolous Appeal — Damages and Costs

If a court of appeals determines that an appeal is frivolous, it may, after a separately filed motion or notice from the court and reasonable opportunity to respond, award just damages and single or double costs to the appellee.

Rule 40. Petition for Panel Rehearing

(a) Time to File; Contents; Answer; Action by the Court if Granted.

(1) Time. Unless the time is shortened or extended by order or local rule, a petition for panel rehearing may be filed within 14 days after entry of judgment. But in a civil case, if the United States or its officer or agency is a party, the time within which any party may seek rehearing is 45 days after entry of judgment, unless an order shortens or extends the time.

(2) Contents. The petition must state with particularity each point of law or fact that the petitioner believes the court has overlooked or misapprehended and must argue in support of the petition. Oral argument is not permitted.

(3) Answer. Unless the court requests, no answer to a petition for panel rehearing is permitted. But ordinarily rehearing will not be granted in the absence of such a request.

(4) Action by the Court. If a petition for panel rehearing is granted, the court may do any of the following:

(A) make a final disposition of the case without reargument;

(B) restore the case to the calendar for reargument or resubmission; or

(C) issue any other appropriate order. . . .

RULES OF THE SUPREME COURT OF THE UNITED STATES: SELECTED SECTIONS

PART I. THE COURT

Rule 3. Term

The Court holds a continuous annual Term commencing on the first Monday in October and ending on the day before the first Monday in October of the following year. See 28 U.S.C. § 2. At the end of each Term, all cases pending on the docket are continued to the next Term.

Rule 4. Sessions and Quorum

1. Open sessions of the Court are held beginning at 10 a.m. on the first Monday in October of each year, and thereafter as announced by the Court. Unless it orders otherwise, the Court sits to hear arguments from 10 a.m. until noon and from 1 p.m. until 3 p.m.

2. Six Members of the Court constitute a quorum. See 28 U.S.C. § 1. In the absence of a quorum on any day appointed for holding a session of the Court, the Justices attending — or if no Justice is present, the Clerk or a Deputy Clerk — may announce that the Court will not meet until there is a quorum.

3. When appropriate, the Court will direct the Clerk or the Marshal to announce recesses.

PART III. JURISDICTION ON WRIT OF CERTIORARI

Rule 10. Considerations Governing Review on Certiorari

Review on a writ of certiorari is not a matter of right, but of judicial discretion. A petition for a writ of certiorari will be granted only for compelling reasons. The following, although neither controlling nor fully measuring the Court's discretion, indicate the character of the reasons the Court considers:

(a) a United States court of appeals has entered a decision in conflict with the decision of another United States court of appeals on the same important matter; has decided an important federal question in a way that conflicts with a decision by a state court of last resort; or has so far departed from the accepted and usual course of judicial proceedings, or sanctioned such a departure by a lower court, as to call for an exercise of this Court's supervisory power;

(b) a state court of last resort has decided an important federal question in a way that conflicts with the decision of another state court of last resort or of a United States court of appeals;

(c) a state court or a United States court of appeals has decided an important question of federal law that has not been, but should be, settled by this Court, or has decided an important federal question in a way that conflicts with relevant decisions of this Court.

A petition for a writ of certiorari is rarely granted when the asserted error consists of erroneous factual findings or the misapplication of a properly stated rule of law.

Rule 11. Certiorari to a United States Court of Appeals Before Judgment

A petition for a writ of certiorari to review a case pending in a United States court of appeals, before judgment is entered in that court, will be granted only upon a showing that the case is of such imperative public importance as to justify deviation from normal appellate practice and to require immediate determination in this Court. See 28 U.S.C. § 2101(e).

Rule 13. Review on Certiorari: Time for Petitioning

1. Unless otherwise provided by law, a petition for a writ of certiorari to review a judgment in any case, civil or criminal, entered by a state court of last resort or a United States court of appeals (including the United States Court of Appeals for the Armed Forces) is timely when it is filed with the Clerk of this Court within 90 days after entry of the judgment. A petition for a writ of certiorari seeking review of a judgment of a lower state court that is subject to discretionary review by the state court of last resort is timely when it is filed with the Clerk within 90 days after entry of the order denying discretionary review.

2. The Clerk will not file any petition for a writ of certiorari that is jurisdictionally out of time. See, *e.g.*, 28 U.S.C. § 2101(c).

3. The time to file a petition for a writ of certiorari runs from the date of entry of the judgment or order sought to be reviewed, and not from the issuance date of the mandate (or its equivalent under local practice). But if a petition for rehearing is timely filed in the lower court by any party, or if the lower court appropriately entertains an untimely petition for rehearing or *sua sponte* considers rehearing, the time to file the petition for a writ of certiorari for all parties (whether or not they requested rehearing or joined in the petition for rehearing) runs from the date of the denial of the petition for rehearing or, if the petition for rehearing is granted, the subsequent entry of judgment.

4. A cross-petition for a writ of certiorari is timely when it is filed with the Clerk as provided in paragraphs 1, 3, and 5 of this Rule, or in Rule 12.5. However, a conditional cross-petition (which except for Rule 12.5 would be untimely) will not be granted unless another party's timely petition for a writ of certiorari is granted.

5. For good cause, a Justice may extend the time to file a petition for a writ of certiorari for a period not exceeding 60 days. An application to extend the time to file shall set out the basis for jurisdiction in this Court, identify the judgment sought to be reviewed, include a copy of the opinion and any order respecting rehearing, and set out specific reasons why an extension of time is justified. The application must be filed with the Clerk at least 10 days before the date the petition is due, except in extraordinary circumstances. For the time and manner of presenting the application, see Rules 21, 22, 30, and 33.2. An application to extend the time to file a petition for a writ of certiorari is not favored.

Rule 16. Disposition of a Petition for a Writ of Certiorari

1. After considering the documents [filed regarding a petition for certiorari], the Court will enter an appropriate order. The order may be a summary disposition on the merits.

2. Whenever the Court grants a petition for a writ of certiorari, the Clerk will prepare, sign, and enter an order to that effect and will notify forthwith counsel of record and the court whose judgment is to be reviewed. The case then will be scheduled for briefing and oral argument. If the record has not previously been filed in this Court, the Clerk will request the clerk of the court having possession of the record to certify and transmit it. A formal writ will not issue unless specially directed.

3. Whenever the Court denies a petition for a writ of certiorari, the Clerk will prepare, sign, and enter an order to that effect and will notify forthwith counsel of record and the court whose judgment was sought to be reviewed. The order of denial will not be suspended pending disposition of a petition for rehearing except by order of the Court or a Justice.

Rule 18. Appeal from a United States District Court

1. When a direct appeal from a decision of a United States district court is authorized by law, the appeal is commenced by filing a notice of appeal with the clerk of the district court within the time provided by law after entry of the judgment sought to be reviewed. The time to file may not be extended. The notice of appeal shall specify the parties taking the appeal, designate the judgment, or part thereof, appealed from and the date of its entry, and specify the statute or statutes under which the appeal is taken. . . .

Rule 19. Procedure on a Certified Question

1. A United States court of appeals may certify to this Court a question or proposition of law on which it seeks instruction for the proper decision of a case. The certificate shall contain a statement of the nature of the case and the facts on which the question or proposition of law arises. Only questions or propositions of law may be certified, and they shall be stated separately and with precision. The certificate shall be prepared as required by Rule 33.2 and shall be signed by the clerk of the court of appeals.

2. When a question is certified by a United States court of appeals, this Court, on its own motion or that of a party, may consider and decide the entire matter in controversy. See 28 U.S.C. § 1254(2). . . .

PART IV. OTHER JURISDICTION

Rule 20. Procedure on a Petition for an Extraordinary Writ

1. Issuance by the Court of an extraordinary writ authorized by 28 U.S.C. § 1651(a) is not a matter of right, but of discretion sparingly exercised. To justify the granting of any such writ, the petition must show that the writ will be in aid of the Court's appellate jurisdiction, that exceptional circumstances warrant the exercise of the Court's discretionary powers, and that adequate relief cannot be obtained in any other form or from any other court. . . .

UNITED STATES CODE: SELECTED SECTIONS

TITLE 28. JUDICIARY AND JUDICIAL PROCEDURE

PART I — ORGANIZATION OF COURTS

CHAPTER 1 — SUPREME COURT

§ 1. Number of justices; quorum

The Supreme Court of the United States shall consist of a Chief Justice of the United States and eight associate justices, any six of whom shall constitute a quorum.

CHAPTER 3 — COURTS OF APPEALS

§ 41. Number and composition of circuits

The thirteen judicial circuits of the United States are constituted as follows:

Circuits	*Composition*
District of Columbia	District of Columbia.
First	Maine, Massachusetts, New Hampshire, Puerto Rico, Rhode Island.
Second	Connecticut, New York, Vermont.
Third	Delaware, New Jersey, Pennsylvania, Virgin Islands.
Fourth	Maryland, North Carolina, South Carolina, Virginia, West Virginia.
Fifth	District of the Canal Zone, Louisiana, Mississippi, Texas.
Sixth	Kentucky, Michigan, Ohio, Tennessee.
Seventh	Illinois, Indiana, Wisconsin.
Eighth	Arkansas, Iowa, Minnesota, Missouri, Nebraska, North Dakota, South Dakota.

Ninth	Alaska, Arizona, California, Idaho, Montana, Nevada, Oregon, Washington, Guam, Hawaii.
Tenth	Colorado, Kansas, New Mexico, Oklahoma, Utah, Wyoming.
Eleventh	Alabama, Florida, Georgia.
Federal	All Federal judicial districts.

§ 43. Creation and composition of courts

(a) There shall be in each circuit a court of appeals, which shall be a court of record, known as the United States Court of Appeals for the circuit.

(b) Each court of appeals shall consist of the circuit judges of the circuit in regular active service. The circuit justice and justices or judges designated or assigned shall be competent to sit as judges of the court.

§ 46. Assignment of judges; panels; hearings; quorum

(a) Circuit judges shall sit on the court and its panels in such order and at such times as the court directs.

(b) In each circuit the court may authorize the hearing and determination of cases and controversies by separate panels, each consisting of three judges, at least a majority of whom shall be judges of that court, unless such judges cannot sit because recused or disqualified, or unless the chief judge of that court certifies that there is an emergency including, but not limited to, the unavailability of a judge of the court because of illness. . . .

(c) Cases and controversies shall be heard and determined by a court or panel of not more than three judges . . . unless a hearing or rehearing before the court in banc is ordered by a majority of the circuit judges of the circuit who are in regular active service. A court in banc shall consist of all circuit judges in regular active service [with limited exceptions].

CHAPTER 5 — DISTRICT COURTS

§ 132. Creation and composition of district courts

(a) There shall be in each judicial district a district court which shall be a court of record known as the United States District Court for the district.

(b) Each district court shall consist of the district judge or judges for the district in regular active service. Justices or judges designated or assigned shall be competent to sit as judges of the court.

(c) Except as otherwise provided by law, or rule or order of court, the judicial power of a district court with respect to any action, suit or proceeding may be exercised by a single judge, who may preside alone and hold a regular or special session of court at the same time other sessions are held by other judges.

§ 144. Bias or prejudice of judge

Whenever a party to any proceeding in a district court makes and files a timely and sufficient affidavit that the judge before whom the matter is pending has a personal bias or prejudice either against him or in favor of any adverse party, such judge shall proceed no further therein, but another judge shall be assigned to hear such proceeding.

The affidavit shall state the facts and the reasons for the belief that bias or prejudice exists, and shall be filed not less than ten days before the beginning of the term at which the proceeding is to be heard, or good cause shall be shown for failure to file it within such time. A party may file only one such affidavit in any case. It shall be accompanied by a certificate of counsel of record stating that it is made in good faith.

CHAPTER 13 — ASSIGNMENT OF JUDGES TO OTHER COURTS

§ 291. Circuit judges

(a) The Chief Justice of the United States may, in the public interest, designate and assign temporarily any circuit judge to act as circuit judge in another circuit upon request by the chief judge or circuit justice of such circuit.

(b) The chief judge of a circuit or the circuit justice may, in the public interest, designate and assign temporarily any circuit judge within the circuit, including a judge designated and assigned to temporary duty therein, to hold a district court in any district within the circuit.

§ 292. District judges

(a) The chief judge of a circuit may designate and assign one or more district judges within the circuit to sit upon the court of appeals or a division thereof whenever the business of that court so requires. Such designations or assignments shall be in conformity with the rules or orders of the court of appeals of the circuit.

(b) The chief judge of a circuit may, in the public interest, designate and assign temporarily any district judge of the circuit to hold a district court in any district within the circuit. . . .

(d) The Chief Justice of the United States may designate and assign temporarily a district judge of one circuit for service in another circuit, either in a district court or court of appeals, upon presentation of a certificate of necessity by the chief judge or circuit justice of the circuit wherein the need arises. . . .

Chapter 21 — General Provisions Applicable to Courts and Judges

§ 451. Definitions

As used in this title:

The term "court of the United States" includes the Supreme Court of the United States, courts of appeals, district courts constituted by chapter 5 of this title, including the Court of International Trade and any court created by Act of Congress the judges of which are entitled to hold office during good behavior.

The terms "district court" and "district court of the United States" mean the courts constituted by chapter 5 of this title.

The term "judge of the United States" includes judges of the courts of appeals, district courts, Court of International Trade and any court created by Act of Congress, the judges of which are entitled to hold office during good behavior.

The term "justice of the United States" includes the Chief Justice of the United States and the associate justices of the Supreme Court.

The term "district" and "judicial district" mean the districts enumerated in Chapter 5 of this title.

The term "department" means one of the executive departments enumerated in section 1 of Title 5, unless the context shows that such term was intended to describe the executive, legislative, or judicial branches of the government.

The term "agency" includes any department, independent establishment, commission, administration, authority, board or bureau of the United States or any corporation in which the United States has a proprietary interest, unless the context shows that such term was intended to be used in a more limited sense.

§ 452. Courts always open; powers unrestricted by expiration of sessions

All courts of the United States shall be deemed always open for the purpose of filing proper papers, issuing and returning process, and making motions and orders.

The continued existence or expiration of a session of a court in no way affects the power of the court to do any act or take any proceeding.

§ 453. Oaths of justices and judges

Each justice or judge of the United States shall take the following oath or affirmation before performing the duties of his office: "I, ______ ______, do solemnly swear (or affirm) that I will administer justice without respect to persons, and do equal right to the poor and to the rich, and that I will faithfully and impartially discharge and perform all the duties incumbent upon me as ______ under the Constitution and laws of the United States. So help me God."

§ 454. Practice of law by justices and judges

Any justice or judge appointed under the authority of the United States who engages in the practice of law is guilty of a high misdemeanor.

§ 455. Disqualification of justice, judge, or magistrate judge

(a) Any justice, judge, or magistrate judge of the United States shall disqualify himself in any proceeding in which his impartiality might reasonably be questioned.

(b) He shall also disqualify himself in the following circumstances:

(1) Where he has a personal bias or prejudice concerning a party, or personal knowledge of disputed evidentiary facts concerning the proceeding;

(2) Where in private practice he served as lawyer in the matter in controversy, or a lawyer with whom he previously practiced law served during such association as a lawyer concerning the matter, or the judge or such lawyer has been a material witness concerning it;

(3) Where he has served in governmental employment and in such capacity participated as counsel, adviser or material witness concerning the proceeding or expressed an opinion concerning the merits of the particular case in controversy;

(4) He knows that he, individually or as a fiduciary, or his spouse or minor child residing in his household, has a financial interest in the subject matter in controversy or in a party to the proceeding, or any other interest that could be substantially affected by the outcome of the proceeding;

(5) He or his spouse, or a person within the third degree of relationship to either of them, or the spouse of such a person:

(i) Is a party to the proceeding, or an officer, director, or trustee of a party;

(ii) Is acting as a lawyer in the proceeding;

(iii) Is known by the judge to have an interest that could be substantially affected by the outcome of the proceeding;

(iv) Is to the judge's knowledge likely to be a material witness in the proceeding.

(c) A judge should inform himself about his personal and fiduciary financial interests, and make a reasonable effort to inform himself about the personal financial interests of his spouse and minor children residing in his household.

(d) For the purposes of this section the following words or phrases shall have the meaning indicated:

(1) "proceeding" includes pretrial, trial, appellate review, or other stages of litigation;

(2) the degree of relationship is calculated according to the civil law system;

(3) "fiduciary" includes such relationships as executor, administrator, trustee, and guardian;

(4) "financial interest" means ownership of a legal or equitable interest, however small, or a relationship as director, adviser, or other active participant in the affairs of a party, except that:

(i) Ownership in a mutual or common investment fund that holds securities is not a "financial interest" in such securities unless the judge participates in the management of the fund;

(ii) An office in an educational, religious, charitable, fraternal, or civic organization is not a "financial interest" in securities held by the organization;

(iii) The proprietary interest of a policyholder in a mutual insurance company, of a depositor in a mutual savings association, or a similar proprietary interest, is a "financial interest" in the organization only if the outcome of the proceeding could substantially affect the value of the interest;

(iv) Ownership of government securities is a "financial interest" in the issuer only if the outcome of the proceeding could substantially affect the value of the securities.

(e) No justice, judge, or magistrate judge shall accept from the parties to the proceeding a waiver of any ground for disqualification enumerated in subsection (b). Where the ground for disqualification arises only under subsection (a), waiver may be accepted provided it is preceded by a full disclosure on the record of the basis for disqualification.

(f) Notwithstanding the preceding provisions of this section, if any justice, judge, magistrate judge, or bankruptcy judge to whom a matter has been assigned would be disqualified, after substantial judicial time has been devoted to the matter, because of the appearance or discovery, after the matter was assigned to him or her, that he or she individually or as a fiduciary, or his or her spouse or minor child residing in his or her household, has a financial interest in a party (other than an interest that could be substantially affected by the outcome), disqualification is not required if the justice, judge, magistrate judge, bankruptcy judge, spouse or minor child, as the case may be, divests himself or herself of the interest that provides the grounds for the disqualification.

PART III — COURT OFFICERS AND EMPLOYEES

CHAPTER 43 — UNITED STATES MAGISTRATE JUDGES

§ 631. Appointment and tenure

(a) The judges of each United States district court and the district courts of the Virgin Islands, Guam, and the Northern Mariana Islands shall appoint United States magistrate judges in such numbers and to serve at such locations within the judicial districts as the Judicial Conference may determine under this chapter. In the case of a magistrate judge appointed by the district court of the Virgin Islands, Guam, or the Northern Mariana Islands, this chapter shall apply as though the court appointing such a magistrate judge were a United States district court. Where there is more than one judge of a district court, the appointment, whether an original appointment or a reappointment, shall be by the concurrence of a majority of all the judges of such district court, and when there is no such concurrence, then by the chief judge. Where the conference deems it desirable, a magistrate judge may be designated to serve in one or more districts adjoining the district for which he is appointed. Such a designation shall be made by the concurrence of a majority of the judges of each of the district courts involved and shall specify the duties to be performed by the magistrate judge in the adjoining district or districts. . . .

(e) The appointment of any individual as a full-time magistrate judge shall be for a term of eight years, and the appointment of any individuals as a part-time magistrate judge shall be for a term of four years . . .

§ 636. Jurisdiction, powers, and temporary assignment

. . .

(b) (1) Notwithstanding any provision of law to the contrary —

(A) a judge may designate a magistrate judge to hear and determine any pretrial matter pending before the court, except a motion for injunctive relief, for judgment on the pleadings, for summary judgment, to dismiss or quash an indictment or information made by the defendant, to suppress evidence in a criminal case, to dismiss or to permit maintenance of a class action, to dismiss for failure to state a claim upon which relief can be granted, and to involuntarily dismiss an action. A judge of the court may reconsider any pretrial matter under this subparagraph (A) where it has been shown that the magistrate judge's order is clearly erroneous or contrary to law.

(B) a judge may also designate a magistrate judge to conduct hearings, including evidentiary hearings, and to submit to a judge of the court proposed findings of fact and recommendations for the disposition, by a judge of the court, of any motion excepted in subparagraph (A), of applications for posttrial relief made by individuals convicted of criminal offenses and of prisoner petitions challenging conditions of confinement.

(C) the magistrate judge shall file his proposed findings and recommendations under subparagraph (B) with the court and a copy shall forthwith be mailed to all parties.

Within ten days after being served with a copy, any party may serve and file written objections to such proposed findings and recommendations as provided by rules of court. A judge of the court shall make a de novo determination of those portions of the report or specified proposed findings or recommendations to which objection is made. A judge of the court may accept, reject, or modify, in whole or in part, the findings or recommendations made by the magistrate judge. The judge may also receive further evidence or recommit the matter to the magistrate judge with instructions. . . .

(3) A magistrate judge may be assigned such additional duties as are not inconsistent with the Constitution and laws of the United States. . . .

(c) Notwithstanding any provision of law to the contrary —

(1) Upon the consent of the parties, a full-time United States magistrate judge or a part-time United States magistrate judge who serves as a full-time judicial officer may conduct any or all proceedings in a jury or nonjury civil matter and order the entry of judgment in the case, when specially designated to exercise such jurisdiction by the district court or courts he serves. . . .

(2) If a magistrate judge is designated to exercise civil jurisdiction under paragraph (1) of this subsection, the clerk of court shall, at the time the action is filed, notify the parties of the availability of a magistrate judge to exercise such jurisdiction. The decision of the parties shall be communicated to the clerk of court. Thereafter, either the district court judge or the magistrate judge may again advise the parties of the availability of the magistrate judge, but in so doing, shall also advise the parties that they are free to withhold consent without adverse substantive consequences. Rules of court for the reference of civil matters to magistrate judges shall include procedures to protect the voluntariness of the parties' consent.

(3) Upon entry of judgment in any case referred under paragraph (1) of this subsection, an aggrieved party may appeal directly to the appropriate United States court of appeals from the judgment of the magistrate judge in the same manner as an appeal from any other judgment of a district court. The consent of the parties allows a magistrate judge designated to exercise civil jurisdiction under paragraph (1) of this subsection to direct the entry of a judgment of the district court in accordance with the Federal Rules of Civil Procedure. Nothing in this paragraph shall be construed as a limitation of any party's right to seek review by the Supreme Court of the United States.

(4) The court may, for good cause shown on its own motion, or under extraordinary circumstances shown by any party, vacate a reference of a civil matter to a magistrate judge under this subsection. . . .

(d) The practice and procedure for the trial of cases before officers serving under this chapter shall conform to rules promulgated by the Supreme Court pursuant to section 2072 of this title. . . .

CHAPTER 44 — ALTERNATIVE DISPUTE RESOLUTION

§ 651. Authorization of alternative dispute resolution

(a) **Definition.** — For purposes of this chapter, an alternative dispute resolution process includes any process or procedure, other than an adjudication by a presiding judge, in which a neutral third party participates to assist in the resolution of issues in controversy, through processes such as early neutral evaluation, mediation, minitrial, and arbitration as provided in sections 654 through 658.

(b) **Authority.** — Each United States district court shall authorize, by local rule adopted under section 2071(a), the use of alternative dispute resolution processes in all civil actions, including adversary proceedings in bankruptcy, in accordance with this chapter, except that the use of arbitration may be authorized only as provided in section 654. Each United States district court shall devise and implement its own alternative dispute resolution program, by local rule adopted under section 2071(a), to encourage and promote the use of alternative dispute resolution in its district.

(c) **Existing alternative dispute resolution programs.** — In those courts where an alternative dispute resolution program is in place on the date of the enactment of the Alternative Dispute Resolution Act of 1998, the court shall examine the effectiveness of that program and adopt such improvements to the program as are consistent with the provisions and purposes of this chapter. . . .

§ 652. Jurisdiction

(a) **Consideration of alternative dispute resolution in appropriate cases.** — Notwithstanding any provision of law to the contrary and except as provided in subsections (b) and (c), each district court shall, by local rule adopted under section 2071(a), require that litigants in all civil cases consider the use of an alternative dispute resolution process at an appropriate stage in the litigation. Each district court shall provide litigants in all civil cases with at least one alternative dispute resolution process, including, but not limited to, mediation, early neutral evaluation, minitrial, and arbitration as authorized in sections 654 through 658. Any district court that elects to require the use of alternative dispute resolution in certain cases may do so only with respect to mediation, early neutral evaluation, and, if the parties consent, arbitration.

(b) **Actions exempted from consideration of alternative dispute resolution.** — Each district court may exempt from the requirements of this section specific cases or categories of cases in which use of alternative dispute resolution would not be appropriate. In defining these exemptions, each district court shall consult with members of the bar, including the United States Attorney for that district. . . .

(d) **Confidentiality provisions.** — Until such time as rules are adopted under chapter 131 of this title providing for the confidentiality of alternative dispute resolution processes under this chapter, each district court shall, by local rule adopted under section 2071(a), provide for the confidentiality of the alternative dispute resolution processes and to prohibit disclosure of confidential dispute resolution communications.

§ 654. Arbitration

(a) **Referral of actions to arbitration.** — Notwithstanding any provision of law to the contrary and except as provided in subsections (a), (b), and (c) of section 652 and subsection (d) of this section, a district court may allow the referral to arbitration of any civil action (including any adversary proceeding in bankruptcy) pending before it when the parties consent, except that referral to arbitration may not be made where —

(1) the action is based on an alleged violation of a right secured by the Constitution of the United States;

(2) jurisdiction is based in whole or in part on section 1343 of this title; or

(3) the relief sought consists of money damages in an amount greater than $150,000.

(b) **Safeguards in consent cases.** — Until such time as rules are adopted under chapter 131 of this title relating to procedures described in this subsection, the district court shall, by local rule adopted under section 2071(a), establish procedures to ensure that any civil action in which arbitration by consent is allowed under subsection (a) —

(1) consent to arbitration is freely and knowingly obtained; and

(2) no party or attorney is prejudiced for refusing to participate in arbitration.

§ 657. Arbitration award and judgment

(a) **Filing and effect of arbitration award.** — An arbitration award made by an arbitrator under this chapter, along with proof of service of such award on the other party by the prevailing party or by the plaintiff, shall be filed promptly after the arbitration hearing is concluded with the clerk of the district court that referred the case to arbitration. Such award shall be entered as the judgment of the court after the time has expired for requesting a trial de novo. The judgment so entered shall be subject to the same provisions of law and shall have the same force and effect as a judgment of the court in a civil action, except that the judgment shall not be subject to review in any other court by appeal or otherwise.

(b) **Sealing of arbitration award.** — The district court shall provide, by local rule adopted under section 2071(a), that the contents of any arbitration award made under this chapter shall not be made known to any judge who might be assigned to the case until the district court has entered final judgment in the action or the action has otherwise terminated.

(c) **Trial de novo of arbitration awards.** —

(1) **Time for filing demand.** — Within 30 days after the filing of an arbitration award with a district court under subsection (a), any party may file a written demand for a trial de novo in the district court.

(2) **Action restored to court docket.** — Upon a demand for a trial de novo, the action shall be restored to the docket of the court and treated for all purposes as if it had not been referred to arbitration.

(3) **Exclusion of evidence of arbitration.** — The court shall not admit at the trial de novo any evidence that there has been an arbitration proceeding, the nature or amount of any award, or any other matter concerning the conduct of the arbitration proceeding, unless —

(A) the evidence would otherwise be admissible in the court under the Federal Rules of Evidence; or

(B) the parties have otherwise stipulated.

PART IV — JURISDICTION AND VENUE

CHAPTER 81 — SUPREME COURT

§ 1251. Original jurisdiction

(a) The Supreme Court shall have original and exclusive jurisdiction of all controversies between two or more States.

(b) The Supreme Court shall have original but not exclusive jurisdiction of:

(1) All actions or proceedings to which ambassadors, other public ministers, consuls, or vice consuls of foreign states are parties;

(2) All controversies between the United States and a State;

(3) All actions or proceedings by a State against the citizens of another State or against aliens.

§ 1253. Direct appeals from decisions of three-judge courts

Except as otherwise provided by law, any party may appeal to the Supreme Court from an order granting or denying, after notice and hearing, an interlocutory or permanent injunction in any civil action, suit or proceeding required by any Act of Congress to be heard and determined by a district court of three judges.

§ 1254. Courts of appeals; certiorari; certified questions

Cases in the courts of appeals may be reviewed by the Supreme Court by the following methods:

(1) By writ of certiorari granted upon the petition of any party to any civil or criminal case, before or after rendition of judgment or decree;

(2) By certification at any time by a court of appeals of any question of law in any civil or criminal case as to which instructions are desired, and upon such certification the Supreme Court may give binding instructions or require the entire record to be sent up for decision of the entire matter in controversy.

§ 1257. State courts; certiorari

(a) Final judgments or decrees rendered by the highest court of a State in which a decision could be had, may be reviewed by the Supreme Court by writ of certiorari where the validity of a treaty or statute of the United States is drawn in question or where the validity of a statute of any State is drawn in question on the ground of its being repugnant to the Constitution, treaties, or laws of the United States, or where any title, right, privilege, or immunity is specially set up or claimed under the Constitution or the treaties or statutes of, or any commission held or authority exercised under, the United States.

(b) For the purposes of this section, the term "highest court of a State" includes the District of Columbia Court of Appeals.

§ 1258. Supreme Court of Puerto Rico; certiorari

Final judgments or decrees rendered by the Supreme Court of the Commonwealth of Puerto Rico may be reviewed by the Supreme Court by writ of certiorari where the validity of a treaty or statute of the United States is drawn in question or where the validity of a statute of the Commonwealth of Puerto Rico is drawn in question on the ground of its being repugnant to the Constitution, treaties, or laws of the United States, or where any title, right, privilege, or immunity is specially set up or claimed under the Constitution or the treaties or statutes of, or any commission held or authority exercised under, the United States.

§ 1259. Court of Appeals for the Armed Forces; certiorari

Decisions of the United States Court of Appeals for the Armed Forces may be reviewed by the Supreme Court by writ of certiorari in the following cases:

(1) Cases reviewed by the Court of Appeals for the Armed Forces under section 867(a)(1) of title 10.

(2) Cases certified to the Court of Appeals for the Armed Forces by the Judge Advocate General under section 867(a)(2) of title 10.

(3) Cases in which the Court of Appeals for the Armed Forces granted a petition for review under section 867(a)(3) of title 10.

(4) Cases, other than those described in paragraphs (1), (2), and (3) of this subsection, in which the Court of Appeals for the Armed Forces granted relief.

CHAPTER 83 — COURTS OF APPEALS

§ 1291. Final decisions of district courts

The courts of appeals (other than the United States Court of Appeals for the Federal Circuit) shall have jurisdiction of appeals from all final decisions of the district courts of the United States, the United States District Court for the District of the Canal Zone, the District Court of Guam, and the District Court of the Virgin Islands, except where a direct review may be had in the Supreme Court. The jurisdiction of the United States Court of Appeals for the Federal Circuit shall be limited to the jurisdiction described in sections 1292(c) and (d) and 1295 of this title.

§ 1292. Interlocutory decisions

(a) Except as provided in subsections (c) and (d) of this section, the courts of appeals shall have jurisdiction of appeals from:

(1) Interlocutory orders of the district courts of the United States, the United States District Court for the District of the Canal Zone, the District Court of Guam, and the District Court of the Virgin Islands, or of the judges thereof, granting, continuing, modifying, refusing or dissolving injunctions, or refusing to dissolve or modify injunctions, except where a direct review may be had in the Supreme Court;

(2) Interlocutory orders appointing receivers, or refusing orders to wind up receiverships or to take steps to accomplish the purposes thereof, such as directing sales or other disposals of property;

(3) Interlocutory decrees of such district courts or the judges thereof determining the rights and liabilities of the parties to admiralty cases in which appeals from final decrees are allowed.

(b) When a district judge, in making in a civil action an order not otherwise appealable under this section, shall be of the opinion that such order involves a controlling question of law as to which there is substantial ground for difference of opinion and that an immediate appeal from the order may materially advance the ultimate termination of the litigation, he shall so state in writing in such order. The Court of Appeals which would have jurisdiction of an appeal of such action may thereupon, in its discretion, permit an appeal to be taken from such order, if application is made to it within ten days after the entry of the order: *Provided, however,* That application for an appeal hereunder shall not stay proceedings in the district court unless the district judge or the Court of Appeals or a judge thereof shall so order. . . .

(c) The United States Court of Appeals for the Federal Circuit shall have exclusive jurisdiction —

(1) of an appeal from an interlocutory order or decree described in subsection (a) or (b) of this section in any case over which the court would have jurisdiction of an appeal under section 1295 of this title; and

(2) of an appeal from a judgment in a civil action for patent infringement which would otherwise be appealable to the United States Court of Appeals for the Federal Circuit and is final except for an accounting.

(d) [Omitted.]

(e) The Supreme Court may prescribe rules, in accordance with section 2072 of this title, to provide for an appeal of an interlocutory decision to the courts of appeals that is not otherwise provided for under subsection (a), (b), (c), or (d).

§ 1294. Circuits in which decisions reviewable

Except as provided in sections 1292(c), 1292(d), and 1295 of this title, appeals from reviewable decisions of the district and territorial courts shall be taken to the courts of appeals as follows:

(1) From a district court of the United States to the court of appeals for the circuit embracing the district;

(2) From the United States District Court for the District of the Canal Zone, to the Court of Appeals for the Fifth Circuit;

(3) From the District Court of the Virgin Islands, to the Court of Appeals for the Third Circuit;

(4) From the District Court of Guam, to the Court of Appeals for the Ninth Circuit.

§ 1295. Jurisdiction of the United States Court of Appeals for the Federal Circuit

(a) The United States Court of Appeals for the Federal Circuit shall have exclusive jurisdiction [of appeals from final decisions of the district courts in cases "based, in whole or in part, on section 1338 of this title, except that a case involving a claim arising under any Act of Congress relating to copyrights, exclusive rights in mask works, or trademarks and no other claims under section 1338(a) shall be governed by sections 1291, 1292, and 1294 of this title"; of appeals in government-contract disputes; and of appeals in various other matters.]

CHAPTER 85 — DISTRICT COURTS; JURISDICTION

§ 1331. Federal question

The district courts shall have original jurisdiction of all civil actions arising under the Constitution, laws, or treaties of the United States.

§ 1332. Diversity of citizenship; amount in controversy; costs

(a) The district courts shall have original jurisdiction of all civil actions where the matter in controversy exceeds the sum or value of $75,000, exclusive of interest and costs, and is between —

(1) citizens of different States;

(2) citizens of a State and citizens or subjects of a foreign state;

(3) citizens of different States and in which citizens or subjects of a foreign state are additional parties; and

(4) a foreign state, defined in section 1603(a) of this title [part of the Foreign Sovereign Immunities Act, not included in this supplement — ED.], as plaintiff and citizens of a State or of different States.

For the purposes of this section, section 1335, and section 1441, an alien admitted to the United States for permanent residence shall be deemed a citizen of the State in which such alien is domiciled.

(b) Except when express provision therefor is otherwise made in a statute of the United States, where the plaintiff who files the case originally in the Federal courts is finally adjudged to be entitled to recover less than the sum or value of $75,000, computed without regard to any setoff or counterclaim to which the defendant may be adjudged to be entitled, and exclusive of interest and costs, the district court may deny costs to the plaintiff and, in addition, may impose costs on the plaintiff.

(c) For the purposes of this section and section 1441 of this title —

(1) a corporation shall be deemed to be a citizen of any State by which it has been incorporated and of the State where it has its principal place of business, except that in any direct action against the insurer of a policy or contract of liability insurance, whether incorporated or unincorporated, to which action the insured is not joined as a party-defendant, such insurer shall be deemed a citizen of the State of which the insured is a citizen, as well as of any State by which the insurer has been incorporated and of the State where it has its principal place of business; and

(2) the legal representative of the estate of a decedent shall be deemed to be a citizen only of the same State as the decedent, and the legal representative of an infant or incompetent shall be deemed to be a citizen only of the same State as the infant or incompetent.

(d) (1) In this subsection —

(A) the term "class" means all of the class members in a class action;

(B) the term "class action" means any civil action filed under rule 23 of the Federal Rules of Civil Procedure or similar State statute or rule of judicial procedure authorizing an action to be brought by 1 or more representative persons as a class action;

(C) the term "class certification order" means an order issued by a court approving the treatment of some or all aspects of a civil action as a class action; and

(D) the term "class members" means the persons (named or unnamed) who fall within the definition of the proposed or certified class in a class action.

(2) The district courts shall have original jurisdiction of any civil action in which the matter in controversy exceeds the sum or value of $5,000,000, exclusive of interest and costs, and is a class action in which —

(A) any member of a class of plaintiffs is a citizen of a State different from any defendant;

(B) any member of a class of plaintiffs is a foreign state or a citizen or subject of a foreign state and any defendant is a citizen of a State; or

(C) any member of a class of plaintiffs is a citizen of a State and any defendant is a foreign state or a citizen or subject of a foreign state.

(3) A district court may, in the interests of justice and looking at the totality of the circumstances, decline to exercise jurisdiction under paragraph (2) over a class action in which greater than one-third but less than two-thirds of the members of all proposed plaintiff classes in the aggregate and the primary defendants are citizens of the State in which the action was originally filed based on consideration of —

(A) whether the claims asserted involve matters of national or interstate interest;

(B) whether the claims asserted will be governed by laws of the State in which the action was originally filed or by the laws of other States;

(C) whether the class action has been pleaded in a manner that seeks to avoid Federal jurisdiction;

(D) whether the action was brought in a forum with a distinct nexus with the class members, the alleged harm, or the defendants;

(E) whether the number of citizens of the State in which the action was originally filed in all proposed plaintiff classes in the aggregate is substantially larger than the number of citizens from any other State, and the citizenship of the other members of the proposed class is dispersed among a substantial number of States; and

(F) whether, during the 3-year period preceding the filing of that class action, 1 or more other class actions asserting the same or similar claims on behalf of the same or other persons have been filed.

(4) A district court shall decline to exercise jurisdiction under paragraph (2) —

(A) (i) over a class action in which —

(I) greater than two-thirds of the members of all proposed plaintiff classes in the aggregate are citizens of the State in which the action was originally filed;

(II) at least 1 defendant is a defendant —

(aa) from whom significant relief is sought by members of the plaintiff class;

(bb) whose alleged conduct forms a significant basis for the claims asserted by the proposed plaintiff class; and

(cc) who is a citizen of the State in which the action was originally filed; and

(III) principal injuries resulting from the alleged conduct or any related conduct of each defendant were incurred in the State in which the action was originally filed; and

(ii) during the 3-year period preceding the filing of that class action, no other class action has been filed asserting the same or similar factual allegations against any of the defendants on behalf of the same or other persons; or

(B) two-thirds or more of the members of all proposed plaintiff classes in the aggregate, and the primary defendants, are citizens of the State in which the action was originally filed.

(5) Paragraphs (2) through (4) shall not apply to any class action in which —

(A) the primary defendants are States, State officials, or other governmental entities against whom the district court may be foreclosed from ordering relief; or

(B) the number of members of all proposed plaintiff classes in the aggregate is less than 100.

(6) In any class action, the claims of the individual class members shall be aggregated to determine whether the matter in controversy exceeds the sum or value of $5,000,000, exclusive of interest and costs.

(7) Citizenship of the members of the proposed plaintiff classes shall be determined for purposes of paragraphs (2) through (6) as of the date of filing of the complaint or amended complaint, or, if the case stated by the initial pleading is not subject to Federal jurisdiction, as of the date of service by plaintiffs of an amended pleading, motion, or other paper, indicating the existence of Federal jurisdiction.

(8) This subsection shall apply to any class action before or after the entry of a class certification order by the court with respect to that action.

(9) Paragraph (2) shall not apply to any class action that solely involves a claim —

(A) concerning a covered security as defined under 16(f)(3) of the Securities Act of 1933 (15 U.S.C. 78p(f)(3)) and section

28(f)(5)(E) of the Securities Exchange Act of 1934 (15 U.S.C. 78bb(f)(5)(E));

(B) that relates to the internal affairs or governance of a corporation or other form of business enterprise and that arises under or by virtue of the laws of the State in which such corporation or business enterprise is incorporated or organized; or

(C) that relates to the rights, duties (including fiduciary duties), and obligations relating to or created by or pursuant to any security (as defined under section 2(a)(1) of the Securities Act of 1933 (15 U.S.C. 77b(a)(1)) and the regulations issued thereunder).

(10) For purposes of this subsection and section 1453, an unincorporated association shall be deemed to be a citizen of the State where it has its principal place of business and the State under whose laws it is organized.

(11)(A) For purposes of this subsection and section 1453, a mass action shall be deemed to be a class action removable under paragraphs (2) through (10) if it otherwise meets the provisions of those paragraphs.

(B) (i) As used in subparagraph (A), the term "mass action" means any civil action (except a civil action within the scope of section 1711(2)) in which monetary relief claims of 100 or more persons are proposed to be tried jointly on the ground that the plaintiffs' claims involve common questions of law or fact, except that jurisdiction shall exist only over those plaintiffs whose claims in a mass action satisfy the jurisdictional amount requirements under subsection (a).

(ii) As used in subparagraph (A), the term "mass action" shall not include any civil action in which —

(I) all of the claims in the action arise from an event or occurrence in the State in which the action was filed, and that allegedly resulted in injuries in that State or in States contiguous to that State;

(II) the claims are joined upon motion of a defendant;

(III) all of the claims in the action are asserted on behalf of the general public (and not on behalf of individual claimants or members of a purported class) pursuant to a State statute specifically authorizing such action; or

(IV) the claims have been consolidated or coordinated solely for pretrial proceedings.

(C) (i) Any action(s) removed to Federal court pursuant to this subsection shall not thereafter be transferred to any other court pursuant to section 1407, or the rules promulgated thereunder, unless a majority of the plaintiffs in the action request transfer pursuant to section 1407.

(ii) This subparagraph will not apply —

(I) to cases certified pursuant to rule 23 of the Federal Rules of Civil Procedure; or

(II) if plaintiffs propose that the action proceed as a class action pursuant to rule 23 of the Federal Rules of Civil Procedure.

(D) The limitations periods on any claims asserted in a mass action that is removed to Federal court pursuant to this subsection shall be deemed tolled during the period that the action is pending in Federal court.

(e) The word "States", as used in this section, includes the Territories, the District of Columbia, and the Commonwealth of Puerto Rico.

§ 1333. Admiralty, maritime and prize cases

The district courts shall have original jurisdiction, exclusive of the courts of the States, of:

(1) Any civil case of admiralty or maritime jurisdiction, saving to suitors in all cases all other remedies to which they are otherwise entitled.

(2) Any prize brought into the United States and all proceedings for the condemnation of property taken as prize.

§ 1335. Interpleader

(a) The district courts shall have original jurisdiction of any civil action of interpleader or in the nature of interpleader filed by any person, firm, or corporation, association, or society having in his or its custody or possession money or property of the value of $500 or more, or having issued a note, bond, certificate, policy of insurance, or other instrument of value or amount of $500 or more, or providing for the delivery or payment or the loan of money or property of such amount or value, or being under any obligation written or unwritten to the amount of $500 or more, if

(1) Two or more adverse claimants, of diverse citizenship as defined in subsection (a) or (d) of section 1332 of this title, are claiming or may claim to be entitled to such money or property, or to any one or more of the benefits arising by virtue of any note, bond, certificate, policy or other instrument, or arising by virtue of any such obligation; and if (2)

the plaintiff has deposited such money or property or has paid the amount of or the loan or other value of such instrument or the amount due under such obligation into the registry of the court, there to abide the judgment of the court, or has given bond payable to the clerk of the court in such amount and with such surety as the court or judge may deem proper, conditioned upon the compliance by the plaintiff with the future order or judgment of the court with respect to the subject matter of the controversy.

(b) Such an action may be entertained although the titles or claims of the conflicting claimants do not have a common origin, or are not identical, but are adverse to and independent of one another.

§ 1337. Commerce and antitrust regulations; amount in controversy, costs

(a) The district courts shall have original jurisdiction of any civil action or proceeding arising under any Act of Congress regulating commerce or protecting trade and commerce against restraints and monopolies: *Provided, however*, That the district courts shall have original jurisdiction of an action brought under section 11706 or 14706 of title 49, only if the matter in controversy for each receipt or bill of lading exceeds $10,000, exclusive of interest and costs.

(b) Except when express provision therefor is otherwise made in a statute of the United States, where a plaintiff who files the case under section 11706 or 14706 of title 49, originally in the Federal courts is finally adjudged to be entitled to recover less than the sum or value of $10,000, computed without regard to any setoff or counterclaim to which the defendant may be adjudged to be entitled, and exclusive of any interest and costs, the district court may deny costs to the plaintiff and, in addition, may impose costs on the plaintiff. . . .

§ 1338. Patents, plant variety protection, copyrights, mask works, designs, trademarks, and unfair competition

(a) The district courts shall have original jurisdiction of any civil action arising under any Act of Congress relating to patents, plant variety protection, copyrights and trademarks. Such jurisdiction shall be exclusive of the courts of the states in patent, plant variety protection and copyright cases.

(b) The district courts shall have original jurisdiction of any civil action asserting a claim of unfair competition when joined with a substantial and related claim under the copyright, patent, plant variety protection or trademark laws. . . .

§ 1341. Taxes by States

The district courts shall not enjoin, suspend or restrain the assessment, levy or collection of any tax under State law where a plain, speedy and efficient remedy may be had in the courts of such State.

§ 1343. Civil rights and elective franchise

(a) The district courts shall have original jurisdiction of any civil action authorized by law to be commenced by any person:

(1) To recover damages for injury to his person or property, or because of the deprivation of any right or privilege of a citizen of the United States, by any act done in furtherance of any conspiracy mentioned in section 1985 of Title 42;

(2) To recover damages from any person who fails to prevent or to aid in preventing any wrongs mentioned in section 1985 of Title 42 which he had knowledge were about to occur and power to prevent;

(3) To redress the deprivation, under color of any State law, statute, ordinance, regulation, custom or usage, of any right, privilege or immunity secured by the Constitution of the United States or by any Act of Congress providing for equal rights of citizens or of all persons within the jurisdiction of the United States;

(4) To recover damages or to secure equitable or other relief under any Act of Congress providing for the protection of civil rights, including the right to vote.

(b) For purposes of this section —

(1) the District of Columbia shall be considered to be a State; and

(2) any Act of Congress applicable exclusively to the District of Columbia shall be considered to be a statute of the District of Columbia.

§ 1345. United States as plaintiff

Except as otherwise provided by Act of Congress, the district courts shall have original jurisdiction of all civil actions, suits or proceedings commenced by the United States, or by any agency or officer thereof expressly authorized to sue by Act of Congress.

§ 1346. United States as defendant

(a) The district courts shall have original jurisdiction, concurrent with the United States Court of Federal Claims, of:

(1) Any civil action against the United States for the recovery of any internal-revenue tax alleged to have been erroneously or illegally

assessed or collected, or any penalty claimed to have been collected without authority or any sum alleged to have been excessive or in any manner wrongfully collected under the internal-revenue laws;

(2) Any other civil action or claim against the United States, not exceeding $10,000 in amount, founded either upon the Constitution, or any Act of Congress, or any regulation of an executive department, or upon any express or implied contract with the United States, or for liquidated or unliquidated damages in cases not sounding in tort [subject to certain exceptions].

(b) (1) Subject to the provisions of chapter 171 of this title, the district courts, together with the United States District Court for the District of the Canal Zone and the District Court of the Virgin Islands, shall have exclusive jurisdiction of civil actions on claims against the United States, for money damages, accruing on and after January 1, 1945, for injury or loss of property, or personal injury or death caused by the negligent or wrongful act or omission of any employee of the Government while acting within the scope of his office or employment, under circumstances where the United States, if a private person, would be liable to the claimant in accordance with the law of the place where the act or omission occurred. . . .

§ 1358. Eminent domain

The district courts shall have original jurisdiction of all proceedings to condemn real estate for the use of the United States or its departments or agencies.

§ 1359. Parties collusively joined or made

A district court shall not have jurisdiction of a civil action in which any party, by assignment or otherwise, has been improperly or collusively made or joined to invoke the jurisdiction of such court.

§ 1361. Action to compel an officer of the United States to perform his duty

The district courts shall have original jurisdiction of any action in the nature of mandamus to compel an officer or employee of the United States or any agency thereof to perform a duty owed to the plaintiff.

§ 1367. Supplemental jurisdiction

(a) Except as provided in subsections (b) and (c) or as expressly provided otherwise by Federal statute, in any civil action of which the district courts have original jurisdiction, the district courts shall have supplemental jurisdiction over all other claims that are so related to claims

expect that they would normally be tried together?

common nucleus of operative facts
Gibbs

in the action within such original jurisdiction that they form part of the same case or controversy under Article III of the United States Constitution. Such supplemental jurisdiction shall include claims that involve the joinder or intervention of additional parties.

(b) In any civil action of which the district courts have original jurisdiction founded solely on section 1332 of this title, the district courts shall not have supplemental jurisdiction under subsection (a) over claims by plaintiffs against persons made parties under Rule 14, 19, 20, or 24 of the Federal Rules of Civil Procedure, or over claims by persons proposed to be joined as plaintiffs under Rule 19 of such rules, or seeking to intervene as plaintiffs under Rule 24 of such rules, when exercising supplemental jurisdiction over such claims would be inconsistent with the jurisdictional requirements of section 1332.

(c) The district courts may decline to exercise supplemental jurisdiction over a claim under subsection (a) if—

(1) the claim raises a novel or complex issue of State law,

(2) the claim substantially predominates over the claim or claims over which the district court has original jurisdiction,

(3) the district court has dismissed all claims over which it has original jurisdiction, or

(4) in exceptional circumstances, there are other compelling reasons for declining jurisdiction.

(d) The period of limitations for any claim asserted under subsection (a), and for any other claim in the same action that is voluntarily dismissed at the same time as or after the dismissal of the claim under subsection (a), shall be tolled while the claim is pending and for a period of 30 days after it is dismissed unless State law provides for a longer tolling period.

(e) As used in this section, the term "State" includes the District of Columbia, the Commonwealth of Puerto Rico, and any territory or possession of the United States.

§ 1369. Multiparty, multiforum jurisdiction

(a) **In general.** — The district courts shall have original jurisdiction of any civil action involving minimal diversity between adverse parties that arises from a single accident, where at least 75 natural persons have died in the accident at a discrete location, if—

(1) a defendant resides in a State and a substantial part of the accident took place in another State or other location, regardless of whether that defendant is also a resident of the State where a substantial part of the accident took place;

(2) any two defendants reside in different States, regardless of whether such defendants are also residents of the same State or States; or

(3) substantial parts of the accident took place in different States.

(b) **Limitation of jurisdiction of district courts.** — The district court shall abstain from hearing any civil action described in subsection (a) in which —

(1) the substantial majority of all plaintiffs are citizens of a single State of which the primary defendants are also citizens; and

(2) the claims asserted will be governed primarily by the laws of that State.

(c) **Special rules and definitions.** — For purposes of this section —

(1) minimal diversity exists between adverse parties if any party is a citizen of a State and any adverse party is a citizen of another State, a citizen or subject of a foreign state, or a foreign state as defined in section 1603(a) of this title [part of the Foreign Sovereign Immunities Act, not included in this supplement — ED.];

(2) a corporation is deemed to be a citizen of any State, and a citizen or subject of any foreign state, in which it is incorporated or has its principal place of business, and is deemed to be a resident of any State in which it is incorporated or licensed to do business or is doing business;

(3) the term "injury" means —

(A) physical harm to a natural person; and

(B) physical damage to or destruction of tangible property, but only if physical harm described in subparagraph (A) exists;

(4) the term "accident" means a sudden accident, or a natural event culminating in an accident, that results in death incurred at a discrete location by at least 75 natural persons; and

(5) the term "State" includes the District of Columbia, the Commonwealth of Puerto Rico, and any territory or possession of the United States.

(d) **Intervening parties.** — In any action in a district court which is or could have been brought, in whole or in part, under this section, any person with a claim arising from the accident described in subsection (a) shall be permitted to intervene as a party plaintiff in the action, even if that person could not have brought an action in a district court as an original matter.

(e) **Notification of judicial panel on multidistrict litigation.** — A district court in which an action under this section is pending shall promptly notify the judicial panel on multidistrict litigation of the pendency of the action.

CHAPTER 87 — DISTRICT COURTS; VENUE

§ 1391. Venue generally

(a) A civil action wherein jurisdiction is founded only on diversity of citizenship may, except as otherwise provided by law, be brought only in (1) a judicial district where any defendant resides, if all defendants reside in the same State, (2) a judicial district in which a substantial part of the events or omissions giving rise to the claim occurred, or a substantial part of property that is the subject of the action is situated, or (3) a judicial district in which any defendant is subject to personal jurisdiction at the time the action is commenced, if there is no district in which the action may otherwise be brought.

(b) A civil action wherein jurisdiction is not founded solely on diversity of citizenship may, except as otherwise provided by law, be brought only in (1) a judicial district where any defendant resides, if all defendants reside in the same State, (2) a judicial district in which a substantial part of the events or omissions giving rise to the claim occurred, or a substantial part of property that is the subject of the action is situated, or (3) a judicial district in which any defendant may be found, if there is no district in which the action may otherwise be brought.

(c) For purposes of venue under this chapter, a defendant that is a corporation shall be deemed to reside in any judicial district in which it is subject to personal jurisdiction at the time the action is commenced. In a State which has more than one judicial district and in which a defendant that is a corporation is subject to personal jurisdiction at the time an action is commenced, such corporation shall be deemed to reside in any district in that State within which its contacts would be sufficient to subject it to personal jurisdiction if that district were a separate State, and, if there is no such district, the corporation shall be deemed to reside in the district within which it has the most significant contacts.

(d) An alien may be sued in any district.

(e) A civil action in which a defendant is an officer or employee of the United States or any agency thereof acting in his official capacity or under color of legal authority, or an agency of the United States, or the United States, may, except as otherwise provided by law, be brought in any judicial district in which (1) a defendant in the action resides, (2) a substantial part of the events or omissions giving rise to the claim occurred, or a substantial part of property that is the subject of the action is situated, or (3) the plaintiff resides if no real property is involved in the action. Additional persons may be joined as parties to any such action in accordance with the Federal Rules of Civil Procedure and with such other venue requirements as would be applicable if the United States or one of its officers, employees, or agencies were not a party.

The summons and complaint in such an action shall be served as provided by the Federal Rules of Civil Procedure except that the delivery of the summons and complaint to the officer or agency as required by the rules may be made by certified mail beyond the territorial limits of the district in which the action is brought. . . .

(g) A civil action in which jurisdiction of the district court is based upon section 1369 of this title may be brought in any district in which any defendant resides or in which a substantial part of the accident giving rise to the action took place.

§ 1392. Defendants or property in different districts in same State

Any civil action, of a local nature, involving property located in different districts in the same State, may be brought in any of such districts.

§ 1397. Interpleader

Any civil action of interpleader or in the nature of interpleader under section 1335 of this title may be brought in the judicial district in which one or more of the claimants reside.

§ 1400. Patents and copyrights, mask works, and designs

(a) Civil actions, suits, or proceedings arising under any Act of Congress relating to copyrights or exclusive rights in mask works or designs may be instituted in the district in which the defendant or his agent resides or may be found.

(b) Any civil action for patent infringement may be brought in the judicial district where the defendant resides, or where the defendant has committed acts of infringement and has a regular and established place of business.

§ 1404. Change of venue

(a) For the convenience of parties and witnesses, in the interest of justice, a district court may transfer any civil action to any other district or division where it might have been brought.

(b) Upon motion, consent or stipulation of all parties, any action, suit or proceeding of a civil nature or any motion or hearing thereof, may be transferred, in the discretion of the court, from the division in which pending to any other division in the same district. Transfer of proceedings in rem brought by or on behalf of the United States may be transferred under this section without the consent of the United States where all other parties request transfer.

(c) A district court may order any civil action to be tried at any place within the division in which it is pending. . . .

§ 1406. Cure or waiver of defects

(a) The district court of a district in which is filed a case laying venue in the wrong division or district shall dismiss, or if it be in the interest of justice, transfer such case to any district or division in which it could have been brought.

(b) Nothing in this chapter shall impair the jurisdiction of a district court of any matter involving a party who does not interpose timely and sufficient objection to the venue. . . .

§ 1407. Multidistrict litigation

(a) When civil actions involving one or more common questions of fact are pending in different districts, such actions may be transferred to any district for coordinated or consolidated pretrial proceedings. Such transfers shall be made by the judicial panel on multidistrict litigation authorized by this section upon its determination that transfers for such proceedings will be for the convenience of parties and witnesses and will promote the just and efficient conduct of such actions. Each action so transferred shall be remanded by the panel at or before the conclusion of such pretrial proceedings to the district from which it was transferred unless it shall have been previously terminated: *Provided, however*, That the panel may separate any claim, cross-claim, counter-claim, or third-party claim and remand any of such claims before the remainder of the action is remanded.

(b) Such coordinated or consolidated pretrial proceedings shall be conducted by a judge or judges to whom such actions are assigned by the judicial panel on multidistrict litigation. For this purpose, upon request of the panel, a circuit judge or a district judge may be designated and assigned temporarily for service in the transferee district by the Chief Justice of the United States or the chief judge of the circuit, as may be required, in accordance with the provisions of chapter 13 of this title. With the consent of the transferee district court, such actions may be assigned by the panel to a judge or judges of such district. The judge or judges to whom such actions are assigned, the members of the judicial panel on multidistrict litigation, and other circuit and district judges designated when needed by the panel may exercise the powers of a district judge in any district for the purpose of conducting pretrial depositions in such coordinated or consolidated pretrial proceedings.

(c) Proceedings for the transfer of an action under this section may be initiated by —

(i) the judicial panel on multidistrict litigation upon its own initiative, or

(ii) motion filed with the panel by a party in any action in which transfer for coordinated or consolidated pretrial proceedings under this section may be appropriate. A copy of such motion shall be filed in the district court in which the moving party's action is pending.

The panel shall give notice to the parties in all actions in which transfers for coordinated or consolidated pretrial proceedings are contemplated, and such notice shall specify the time and place of any hearing to determine whether such transfer shall be made. Orders of the panel to set a hearing and other orders of the panel issued prior to the order either directing or denying transfer shall be filed in the office of the clerk of the district court in which a transfer hearing is to be or has been held. The panel's order of transfer shall be based upon a record of such hearing at which material evidence may be offered by any party to an action pending in any district that would be affected by the proceedings under this section, and shall be supported by findings of fact and conclusions of law based upon such record. Orders of transfer and such other orders as the panel may make thereafter shall be filed in the office of the clerk of the district court of the transferee district and shall be effective when thus filed. The clerk of the transferee district court shall forthwith transmit a certified copy of the panel's order to transfer to the clerk of the district court from which the action is being transferred. An order denying transfer shall be filed in each district wherein there is a case pending in which the motion for transfer has been made.

(d) The judicial panel on multidistrict litigation shall consist of seven circuit and district judges designated from time to time by the Chief Justice of the United States, no two of whom shall be from the same circuit. The concurrence of four members shall be necessary to any action by the panel.

(e) No proceedings for review of any order of the panel may be permitted except by extraordinary writ pursuant to the provisions of title 28, section 1651, United States Code. Petitions for an extraordinary writ to review an order of the panel to set a transfer hearing and other orders of the panel issued prior to the order either directing or denying transfer shall be filed only in the court of appeals having jurisdiction over the district in which a hearing is to be or has been held. Petitions for an extraordinary writ to review an order to transfer or orders subsequent to transfer shall be filed only in the court of appeals having jurisdiction over the transferee district. There shall be no appeal or review of an order of the panel denying a motion to transfer for consolidated or coordinated proceedings.

(f) The panel may prescribe rules for the conduct of its business not inconsistent with Acts of Congress and the Federal Rules of Civil Procedure.

(g) Nothing in this section shall apply to any action in which the United States is a complainant arising under the antitrust laws. . . .

CHAPTER 89 — DISTRICT COURTS; REMOVAL OF CASES FROM STATE COURTS

§ 1441. Actions removable generally

(a) Except as otherwise expressly provided by Act of Congress, any civil action brought in a State court of which the district courts of the United States have original jurisdiction, may be removed by the defendant or the defendants, to the district court of the United States for the district and division embracing the place where such action is pending. For purposes of removal under this chapter, the citizenship of defendants sued under fictitious names shall be disregarded.

(b) Any civil action of which the district courts have original jurisdiction founded on a claim or right arising under the Constitution, treaties or laws of the United States shall be removable without regard to the citizenship or residence of the parties. Any other such action shall be removable only if none of the parties in interest properly joined and served as defendants is a citizen of the State in which such action is brought.

(c) Whenever a separate and independent claim or cause of action within the jurisdiction conferred by section 1331 of this title is joined with one or more otherwise non-removable claims or causes of action, the entire case may be removed and the district court may determine all issues therein, or, in its discretion, may remand all matters in which State law predominates. . . .

(e) (1) Notwithstanding the provisions of subsection (b) of this section, a defendant in a civil action in a State court may remove the action to the district court of the United States for the district and division embracing the place where the action is pending if—

(A) the action could have been brought in a United States district court under section 1369 of this title; or

(B) the defendant is a party to an action which is or could have been brought, in whole or in part, under section 1369 in a United States district court and arises from the same accident as the action in State court, even if the action to be removed could not have been brought in a district court as an original matter.

The removal of an action under this subsection shall be made in accordance with section 1446 of this title, except that a notice of removal may also be filed before trial of the action in State court within 30 days after the date on which the defendant first becomes a party to an action under section 1369 in a United States district court that arises from the same accident as the action in State court, or at a later time with leave of the district court.

(2) Whenever an action is removed under this subsection and the district court to which it is removed or transferred under section 1407(j) has made a liability determination requiring further proceedings as to damages, the district court shall remand the action to the State court from which it had been removed for the determination of damages, unless the court finds that, for the convenience of parties and witnesses and in the interest of justice, the action should be retained for the determination of damages.

(3) Any remand under paragraph (2) shall not be effective until 60 days after the district court has issued an order determining liability and has certified its intention to remand the removed action for the determination of damages. An appeal with respect to the liability determination of the district court may be taken during that 60-day period to the court of appeals with appellate jurisdiction over the district court. In the event a party files such an appeal, the remand shall not be effective until the appeal has been finally disposed of. Once the remand has become effective, the liability determination shall not be subject to further review by appeal or otherwise.

(4) Any decision under this subsection concerning remand for the determination of damages shall not be reviewable by appeal or otherwise.

(5) An action removed under this subsection shall be deemed to be an action under section 1369 and an action in which jurisdiction is

based on section 1369 of this title for purposes of this section and sections 1407, 1697, and 1785 of this title.

(6) Nothing in this subsection shall restrict the authority of the district court to transfer or dismiss an action on the ground of inconvenient forum.

(f) The court to which a civil action is removed under this section is not precluded from hearing and determining any claim in such civil action because the State court from which such civil action is removed did not have jurisdiction over that claim.

§ 1442. Federal officers or agencies sued or prosecuted

(a) A civil action or criminal prosecution commenced in a State court against any of the following may be removed by them to the district court of the United States for the district and division embracing the place wherein it is pending:

(1) The United States or any agency thereof or any officer (or any person acting under that officer) of the United States or of any agency thereof, sued in an official or individual capacity for any act under color of such office or on account of any right, title or authority claimed under any Act of Congress for the apprehension or punishment of criminals or the collection of the revenue.

(2) A property holder whose title is derived from any such officer, where such action or prosecution affects the validity of any law of the United States.

(3) Any officer of the courts of the United States, for any act under color of office or in the performance of his duties;

(4) Any officer of either House of Congress, for any act in the discharge of his official duty under an order of such House.

(b) A personal action commenced in any State court by an alien against any citizen of a State who is, or at the time the alleged action accrued was, a civil officer of the United States and is a nonresident of such State, wherein jurisdiction is obtained by the State court by personal service of process, may be removed by the defendant to the district court of the United States for the district and division in which the defendant was served with process.

§ 1442a. Members of armed forces sued or prosecuted

A civil or criminal prosecution in a court of a State of the United States against a member of the armed forces of the United States on account of an act done under color of his office or status, or in respect to which he claims any right, title, or authority under a law of the United States respecting the armed forces thereof, or under the law of war, may at any time before the trial or final hearing thereof be removed for trial into the district court of the United States for the district where it is pending in the manner prescribed by law, and it shall thereupon be entered on the docket of the district court, which shall proceed as if the cause had been originally commenced therein and shall have full power to hear and determine the cause.

§ 1443. Civil rights cases

Any of the following civil actions or criminal prosecutions, commenced in a State court may be removed by the defendant to the district court of the United States for the district and division embracing the place wherein it is pending:

(1) Against any person who is denied or cannot enforce in the courts of such State a right under any law providing for the equal civil rights of citizens of the United States, or of all persons within the jurisdiction thereof;

(2) For any act under color of authority derived from any law providing for equal rights, or for refusing to do any act on the ground that it would be inconsistent with such law.

§ 1445. Nonremovable actions

(a) A civil action in any State court against a railroad or its receivers or trustees, arising under sections 1-4 and 5-10 of the Act of April 22, 1908 (45 U.S.C. 51-54, 55-60), may not be removed to any district court of the United States.

(b) A civil action in any State court against a carrier or its receivers or trustees to recover damages for delay, loss, or injury of shipments, arising under section 11706 or 14706 of title 49, may not be removed to any district court of the United States unless the matter in controversy exceeds $10,000, exclusive of interest and costs.

(c) A civil action in any State court arising under the workmen's compensation laws of such State may not be removed to any district court of the United States.

(d) A civil action in any State court arising under section 40302 of the Violence Against Women Act of 1994 may not be removed to any district court of the United States.

§ 1446. Procedure for removal

(a) A defendant or defendants desiring to remove any civil action or criminal prosecution from a State court shall file in the district court of the

United States for the district and division within which such action is pending a notice of removal signed pursuant to Rule 11 of the Federal Rules of Civil Procedure and containing a short and plain statement of the grounds for removal, together with a copy of all process, pleadings, and orders served upon such defendant or defendants in such action.

(b) The notice of removal of a civil action or proceeding shall be filed within thirty days after the receipt by the defendant, through service or otherwise, of a copy of the initial pleading setting forth the claim for relief upon which such action or proceeding is based, or within thirty days after the service of summons upon the defendant if such initial pleading has then been filed in court and is not required to be served on the defendant, whichever period is shorter.

If the case stated by the initial pleading is not removable, a notice of removal may be filed within thirty days after receipt by the defendant, through service or otherwise, of a copy of an amended pleading, motion, order or other paper from which it may first be ascertained that the case is one which is or has become removable, except that a case may not be removed on the basis of jurisdiction conferred by section 1332 of this title more than 1 year after commencement of the action. . . .

(d) Promptly after the filing of such notice of removal of a civil action the defendant or defendants shall give written notice thereof to all adverse parties and shall file a copy of the notice with the clerk of such State court, which shall effect the removal and the State court shall proceed no further unless and until the case is remanded. . . .

§ 1447. Procedure after removal generally

(a) In any case removed from a State court, the district court may issue all necessary orders and process to bring before it all proper parties whether served by process issued by the State court or otherwise.

(b) It may require the removing party to file with its clerk copies of all records and proceedings in such State court or may cause the same to be brought before it by writ of certiorari issued to such State court.

(c) A motion to remand the case on the basis of any defect other than lack of subject matter jurisdiction must be made within 30 days after the filing of the notice of removal under section 1446(a). If at any time before final judgment it appears that the district court lacks subject matter jurisdiction, the case shall be remanded. An order remanding the case may require payment of just costs and any actual expenses, including attorney fees, incurred as a result of the removal. A certified copy of the order of remand shall be mailed by the clerk to the clerk of the State court. The State court may thereupon proceed with such case.

(d) An order remanding a case to the State court from which it was removed is not reviewable on appeal or otherwise, except that an order remanding a case to the State court from which it was removed pursuant to section 1443 of this title shall be reviewable by appeal or otherwise.

(e) If after removal the plaintiff seeks to join additional defendants whose joinder would destroy subject matter jurisdiction, the court may deny joinder, or permit joinder and remand the action to the State court.

§ 1448. Process after removal

In all cases removed from any State court to any district court of the United States in which any one or more of the defendants has not been served with process or in which the service has not been perfected prior to removal, or in which process served proves to be defective, such process or service may be completed or new process issued in the same manner as in cases originally filed in such district court.

This section shall not deprive any defendant upon whom process is served after removal of his right to move to remand the case.

§ 1453. Removal of class actions

(a) **Definitions.** — In this section, the terms “class”, “class action”, “class certification order”, and “class member” shall have the meanings given such terms under section 1332(d)(1).

(b) **In general.** — A class action may be removed to a district court of the United States in accordance with section 1446 (except that the 1-year limitation under section 1446(b) shall not apply), without regard to whether any defendant is a citizen of the State in which the action is brought, except that such action may be removed by any defendant without the consent of all defendants.

(c) **Review of remand orders.** —

(1) **In general.** — Section 1447 shall apply to any removal of a case under this section, except that notwithstanding section 1447(d), a court of appeals may accept an appeal from an order of a district court granting or denying a motion to remand a class action to the State court from which it was removed if application is made to the court of appeals not less than 7 days after entry of the order.

(2) **Time period for judgment.** — If the court of appeals accepts an appeal under paragraph (1), the court shall complete all action on such appeal, including rendering judgment, not later than 60 days after the date on which such appeal was filed, unless an extension is granted under paragraph (3).

(3) **Extension of time period.** — The court of appeals may grant an extension of the 60-day period described in paragraph (2) if —

(A) all parties to the proceeding agree to such extension, for any period of time; or

(B) such extension is for good cause shown and in the interests of justice, for a period not to exceed 10 days.

(4) **Denial of appeal.** — If a final judgment on the appeal under paragraph (1) is not issued before the end of the period described in paragraph (2), including any extension under paragraph (3), the appeal shall be denied.

(d) **Exception.** — This section shall not apply to any class action that solely involves —

(1) a claim concerning a covered security as defined under section 16(f)(3) of the Securities Act of 1933 (15 U.S.C. 78p(f)(3)) and section 28(f)(5)(E) of the Securities Exchange Act of 1934 (15 U.S.C. 78bb(f)(5)(E));

(2) a claim that relates to the internal affairs or governance of a corporation or other form of business enterprise and arises under or by virtue of the laws of the State in which such corporation or business enterprise is incorporated or organized; or

(3) a claim that relates to the rights, duties (including fiduciary duties), and obligations relating to or created by or pursuant to any security (as defined under section 2(a)(1) of the Securities Act of 1933 (15 U.S.C. 77b(a)(1)) and the regulations issued thereunder).

CHAPTER 99 — GENERAL PROVISIONS

§ 1631. Transfer to cure want of jurisdiction

Whenever a civil action is filed in a court as defined in section 610 of this title or an appeal, including a petition for review of administrative action, is noticed for or filed with such a court and that court finds that there is a want of jurisdiction, the court shall, if it is in the interest of justice, transfer such action or appeal to any other such court in which the action or appeal could have been brought at the time it was filed or noticed, and the action or appeal shall proceed as if it had been filed in or noticed for the court to which it is transferred on the date upon which it was actually filed in or noticed for the court from which it is transferred.

PART V — PROCEDURE

CHAPTER 111 — GENERAL PROVISIONS

§ 1651. Writs

(a) The Supreme Court and all courts established by Act of Congress may issue all writs necessary or appropriate in aid of their respective jurisdictions and agreeable to the usages and principles of law. . . .

§ 1652. State laws as rules of decision

The laws of the several states, except where the Constitution or treaties of the United States or Acts of Congress otherwise require or provide, shall be regarded as rules of decision in civil actions in the courts of the United States, in cases where they apply.

§ 1653. Amendment of pleadings to show jurisdiction

Defective allegations of jurisdiction may be amended, upon terms, in the trial or appellate courts.

§ 1655. Lien enforcement; absent defendants

In an action in a district court to enforce any lien upon or claim to, or to remove any incumbrance or lien or cloud upon the title to, real or personal property within the district, where any defendant cannot be served within the State, or does not voluntarily appear, the court may order the absent defendant to appear or plead by a day certain.

Such order shall be served on the absent defendant personally if practicable, wherever found, and also upon the person or persons in possession or charge of such property, if any. Where personal service is not practicable, the order shall be published as the court may direct, not less than once a week for six consecutive weeks.

If an absent defendant does not appear or plead within the time allowed, the court may proceed as if the absent defendant had been served with process within the State, but any adjudication shall, as regards the absent defendant without appearance, affect only the property which is the subject of the action. When a part of the property is within another district, but within the same state, such action may be brought in either district.

Any defendant not so personally notified may, at any time within one year after final judgment, enter his appearance, and thereupon the court shall set aside the judgment and permit such defendant to plead on payment of such costs as the court deems just.

CHAPTER 113 — PROCESS

§ 1696. Service in foreign and international litigation

(a) The district court of the district in which a person resides or is found may order service upon him of any document issued in connection with a proceeding in a foreign or international tribunal. The order may be made pursuant to a letter rogatory issued, or request made, by a foreign or international tribunal or upon application of any interested person and shall direct the manner of service. Service pursuant to this subsection does not, of itself, require the recognition or enforcement in the United States of a judgment, decree, or order rendered by a foreign or international tribunal.

(b) This section does not preclude service of such a document without an order of court.

§ 1697. Service in multiparty, multiforum actions

When the jurisdiction of the district court is based in whole or in part upon section 1369 of this title, process, other than subpoenas, may be served at any place within the United States, or anywhere outside the United States if otherwise permitted by law.

CHAPTER 114 — CLASS ACTIONS

§ 1711. Definitions

In this chapter:

(1) **Class.** — The term "class" means all of the class members in a class action.

(2) **Class action.** — The term "class action" means any civil action filed in a district court of the United States under rule 23 of the Federal Rules of Civil Procedure or any civil action that is removed to a district court of the United States that was originally filed under a State statute or rule of judicial procedure authorizing an action to be brought by 1 or more representatives as a class action.

(3) **Class counsel.** — The term "class counsel" means the persons who serve as the attorneys for the class members in a proposed or certified class action.

(4) **Class members.** — The term "class members" means the persons (named or unnamed) who fall within the definition of the proposed or certified class in a class action.

(5) **Plaintiff class action.** — The term "plaintiff class action" means a class action in which class members are plaintiffs.

(6) **Proposed settlement.** — The term "proposed settlement" means an agreement regarding a class action that is subject to court approval and that, if approved, would be binding on some or all class members.

§ 1712. Coupon settlements

(a) **Contingent fees in coupon settlements.** — If a proposed settlement in a class action provides for a recovery of coupons to a class member, the portion of any attorney's fee award to class counsel that is attributable to the award of the coupons shall be based on the value to class members of the coupons that are redeemed.

(b) **Other attorney's fee awards in coupon settlements.** —

(1) **In general.** — If a proposed settlement in a class action provides for a recovery of coupons to class members, and a portion of the recovery of the coupons is not used to determine the attorney's fee to be paid to class counsel, any attorney's fee award shall be based upon the amount of time class counsel reasonably expended working on the action.

(2) **Court approval.** — Any attorney's fee under this subsection shall be subject to approval by the court and shall include an appropriate attorney's fee, if any, for obtaining equitable relief, including an injunction, if applicable. Nothing in this subsection shall be construed to prohibit application of a lodestar with a multiplier method of determining attorney's fees.

(c) **Attorney's fee awards calculated on a mixed basis in coupon settlements.** — If a proposed settlement in a class action provides for an award of coupons to class members and also provides for equitable relief, including injunctive relief —

(1) that portion of the attorney's fee to be paid to class counsel that is based upon a portion of the recovery of the coupons shall be calculated in accordance with subsection (a); and

(2) that portion of the attorney's fee to be paid to class counsel that is not based upon a portion of the recovery of the coupons shall be calculated in accordance with subsection (b).

(d) **Settlement valuation expertise.** — In a class action involving the awarding of coupons, the court may, in its discretion upon the motion of a party, receive expert testimony from a witness qualified to provide information on the actual value to the class members of the coupons that are redeemed.

(e) **Judicial scrutiny of coupon settlements.** — In a proposed settlement under which class members would be awarded coupons, the court may approve the proposed settlement only after a hearing to determine whether, and making a written finding that, the settlement is fair, reasonable, and adequate for class members. The court, in its discretion, may also require that a proposed settlement agreement provide for the distribution of a portion of the value of unclaimed coupons to 1 or more charitable or governmental organizations, as agreed to by the parties. The distribution and redemption of any proceeds under this subsection shall not be used to calculate attorneys' fees under this section.

§ 1713. Protection against loss by class members

The court may approve a proposed settlement under which any class member is obligated to pay sums to class counsel that would result in a net loss to the class member only if the court makes a written finding that nonmonetary benefits to the class member substantially outweigh the monetary loss.

§ 1714. Protection against discrimination based on geographic location

The court may not approve a proposed settlement that provides for the payment of greater sums to some class members than to others solely on the basis that the class members to whom the greater sums are to be paid are located in closer geographic proximity to the court.

§ 1715. Notifications to appropriate Federal and State officials

(a) **Definitions.** —

(1) **Appropriate Federal official.** — In this section, the term "appropriate Federal official" means —

(A) the Attorney General of the United States; or

(B) in any case in which the defendant is a Federal depository institution, a State depository institution, a depository institution holding company, a foreign bank, or a nondepository institution subsidiary of the foregoing (as such terms are defined in section 3 of the Federal Deposit Insurance Act (12 U.S.C. 1813)), the person who has the primary Federal regulatory or supervisory responsibility with respect to the defendant, if some or all of the matters alleged in the class action are subject to regulation or supervision by that person.

(2) **Appropriate State official.** — In this section, the term "appropriate State official" means the person in the State who has the

primary regulatory or supervisory responsibility with respect to the defendant, or who licenses or otherwise authorizes the defendant to conduct business in the State, if some or all of the matters alleged in the class action are subject to regulation by that person. If there is no primary regulator, supervisor, or licensing authority, or the matters alleged in the class action are not subject to regulation or supervision by that person, then the appropriate State official shall be the State attorney general.

(b) **In general.** — Not later than 10 days after a proposed settlement of a class action is filed in court, each defendant that is participating in the proposed settlement shall serve upon the appropriate State official of each State in which a class member resides and the appropriate Federal official, a notice of the proposed settlement consisting of —

(1) a copy of the complaint and any materials filed with the complaint and any amended complaints (except such materials shall not be required to be served if such materials are made electronically available through the Internet and such service includes notice of how to electronically access such material);

(2) notice of any scheduled judicial hearing in the class action;

(3) any proposed or final notification to class members of —

(A) (i) the members' rights to request exclusion from the class action; or

(ii) if no right to request exclusion exists, a statement that no such right exists; and

(B) a proposed settlement of a class action;

(4) any proposed or final class action settlement;

(5) any settlement or other agreement contemporaneously made between class counsel and counsel for the defendants;

(6) any final judgment or notice of dismissal;

(7) (A) if feasible, the names of class members who reside in each State and the estimated proportionate share of the claims of such members to the entire settlement to that State's appropriate State official; or

(B) if the provision of information under subparagraph (A) is not feasible, a reasonable estimate of the number of class members residing in each State and the estimated proportionate share of the claims of such members to the entire settlement; and

(8) any written judicial opinion relating to the materials described under subparagraphs (3) through (6).

(c) **Depository institutions notification.** —

(1) **Federal and other depository institutions.** — In any case in which the defendant is a Federal depository institution, a depository institution holding company, a foreign bank, or a non-depository institution subsidiary of the foregoing, the notice requirements of this section are satisfied by serving the notice required under subsection (b) upon the person who has the primary Federal regulatory or supervisory responsibility with respect to the defendant, if some or all of the matters alleged in the class action are subject to regulation or supervision by that person.

(2) **State depository institutions.** — In any case in which the defendant is a State depository institution (as that term is defined in section 3 of the Federal Deposit Insurance Act (12 U.S.C. 1813)), the notice requirements of this section are satisfied by serving the notice required under subsection (b) upon the State bank supervisor (as that term is defined in section 3 of the Federal Deposit Insurance Act (12 U.S.C. 1813)) of the State in which the defendant is incorporated or chartered, if some or all of the matters alleged in the class action are subject to regulation or supervision by that person, and upon the appropriate Federal official.

(d) **Final approval.** — An order giving final approval of a proposed settlement may not be issued earlier than 90 days after the later of the dates on which the appropriate Federal official and the appropriate State official are served with the notice required under subsection (b).

(e) **Noncompliance if notice not provided.** —

(1) **In general.** — A class member may refuse to comply with and may choose not to be bound by a settlement agreement or consent decree in a class action if the class member demonstrates that the notice required under subsection (b) has not been provided.

(2) **Limitation.** — A class member may not refuse to comply with or to be bound by a settlement agreement or consent decree under paragraph (1) if the notice required under subsection (b) was directed to the appropriate Federal official and to either the State attorney general or the person that has primary regulatory, supervisory, or licensing authority over the defendant.

(3) **Application of rights.** — The rights created by this subsection shall apply only to class members or any person acting on a class member's behalf, and shall not be construed to limit any other rights affecting a class member's participation in the settlement.

(f) **Rule of construction.** — Nothing in this section shall be construed to expand the authority of, or impose any obligations, duties, or responsibilities upon, Federal or State officials.

CHAPTER 115 — EVIDENCE; DOCUMENTARY

§ 1738. State and Territorial statutes and judicial proceedings; full faith and credit

The Acts of the legislature of any State, Territory, or Possession of the United States, or copies thereof, shall be authenticated by affixing the seal of such State, Territory or Possession thereto.

The records and judicial proceedings of any court of any such State, Territory or Possession, or copies thereof, shall be proved or admitted in other courts within the United States and its Territories and Possessions by the attestation of the clerk and seal of the court annexed, if a seal exists, together with a certificate of a judge of the court that the said attestation is in proper form.

Such Acts, records and judicial proceedings or copies thereof, so authenticated, shall have the same full faith and credit in every court within the United States and its Territories and Possessions as they have by law or usage in the courts of such State, Territory or Possession from which they are taken.

CHAPTER 117 — EVIDENCE; DEPOSITIONS

§ 1781. Transmittal of letter rogatory or request

(a) The Department of State has power, directly, or through suitable channels —

(1) to receive a letter rogatory issued, or request made, by a foreign or international tribunal, to transmit it to the tribunal, officer, or agency in the United States to whom it is addressed, and to receive and return it after execution; and

(2) to receive a letter rogatory issued, or request made, by a tribunal in the United States, to transmit it to the foreign or international tribunal, officer, or agency to whom it is addressed, and to receive and return it after execution.

(b) This section does not preclude —

(1) the transmittal of a letter rogatory or request directly from a foreign or international tribunal to the tribunal, officer, or agency in

the United States to whom it is addressed and its return in the same manner; or

(2) the transmittal of a letter rogatory or request directly from a tribunal in the United States to the foreign or international tribunal, officer, or agency to whom it is addressed and its return in the same manner.

§ 1782. Assistance to foreign and international tribunals and to litigants before such tribunals

(a) The district court of the district in which a person resides or is found may order him to give his testimony or statement or to produce a document or other thing for use in a proceeding in a foreign or international tribunal, including criminal investigations conducted before formal accusation. The order may be made pursuant to a letter rogatory issued, or request made, by a foreign or international tribunal or upon the application of any interested person and may direct that the testimony or statement be given, or the document or other thing be produced, before a person appointed by the court. By virtue of his appointment, the person appointed has power to administer any necessary oath and take the testimony or statement. The order may prescribe the practice and procedure, which may be in whole or part the practice and procedure of the foreign country or the international tribunal, for taking the testimony or statement or producing the document or other thing. To the extent that the order does not prescribe otherwise, the testimony or statement shall be taken, and the document or other thing produced, in accordance with the Federal Rules of Civil Procedure.

A person may not be compelled to give his testimony or statement or to produce a document or other thing in violation of any legally applicable privilege.

(b) This chapter does not preclude a person within the United States from voluntarily giving his testimony or statement, or producing a document or other thing, for use in a proceeding in a foreign or international tribunal before any person and in any manner acceptable to him.

§ 1783. Subpoena of person in foreign country

(a) A court of the United States may order the issuance of a subpoena requiring the appearance as a witness before it, or before a person or body designated by it, of a national or resident of the United States who is in a foreign country, or requiring the production of a specified document or other thing by him, if the court finds that particular testimony or the production of the document or other thing by him is necessary in the interest of justice, and, in other than a criminal action or proceeding, if the court finds, in addition, that it is not possible to obtain his testimony in admissible form without his personal appearance or to obtain the production of the document or other thing in any other manner.

(b) The subpoena shall designate the time and place for the appearance or for the production of the document or other thing. Service of the subpoena and any order to show cause, rule, judgment, or decree authorized by this section or by section 1784 of this title shall be effected in accordance with the provisions of the Federal Rules of Civil Procedure relating to service of process on a person in a foreign country. The person serving the subpoena shall tender to the person to whom the subpoena is addressed his estimated necessary travel and attendance expenses, the amount of which shall be determined by the court and stated in the order directing the issuance of the subpoena.

§ 1785. Subpoenas in multiparty, multiforum actions

When the jurisdiction of the district court is based in whole or in part upon section 1369 of this title, a subpoena for attendance at a hearing or trial may, if authorized by the court upon motion for good cause shown, and upon such terms and conditions as the court may impose, be served at any place within the United States, or anywhere outside the United States if otherwise permitted by law.

CHAPTER 121 — JURIES; TRIAL BY JURY

§ 1861. Declaration of policy

It is the policy of the United States that all litigants in Federal courts entitled to trial by jury shall have the right to grand and petit juries selected at random from a fair cross section of the community in the district or division wherein the court convenes. It is further the policy of the United States that all citizens shall have the opportunity to be considered for service on grand and petit juries in the district courts of the United States, and shall have an obligation to serve as jurors when summoned for that purpose.

§ 1862. Discrimination prohibited

No citizen shall be excluded from service as a grand or petit juror in the district courts of the United States or in the Court of International Trade on account of race, color, religion, sex, national origin, or economic status.

§ 1863. Plan for random jury selection

(a) Each United States district court shall devise and place into operation a written plan for random selection of grand and petit jurors that shall be designed to achieve the objectives of sections 1861 and 1862 of this title, and that shall otherwise comply with the provisions of this title. The plan shall be placed into operation after approval by a reviewing panel consisting of the members of the judicial council of the circuit and either the chief judge of the district whose plan is being reviewed or such other active district judge of that district as the chief judge of the district may designate. The panel shall examine the plan to ascertain that it complies with the provisions of this title. If the reviewing panel finds that the plan does not comply, the panel shall state the particulars in which the plan fails to comply and direct the district court to present within a reasonable time an alternative plan remedying the defect or defects. Separate plans may be adopted for each division or combination of divisions within a judicial district. The district court may modify a plan at any time and it shall modify the plan when so directed by the reviewing panel. The district court shall promptly notify the panel, the Administrative Office of the United States Courts, and the Attorney General of the United States, of the initial adoption and future modifications of the plan by filing copies therewith. Modifications of the plan made at the instance of the district court shall become effective after approval by the panel. Each district court shall submit a report on the jury selection process within its jurisdiction to the Administrative Office of the United States Courts in such form and at such times as the Judicial Conference of the United States may specify. The Judicial Conference of the United States may, from time to time, adopt rules and regulations governing the provisions and the operation of the plans formulated under this title. . . .

§ 1865. Qualifications for jury service

(a) The chief judge of the district court, or such other district court judge as the plan may provide, on his initiative or upon recommendation of the clerk or jury commission, or the clerk under supervision of the court if the court's jury selection plan so authorizes, shall determine solely on the basis of information provided on the juror qualification form and other competent evidence whether a person is unqualified for, or exempt, or to be excused from jury service. The clerk shall enter such determination in the space provided on the juror qualification form and in any alphabetical list of names drawn from the master jury wheel. If a person did not appear in response to a summons, such fact shall be noted on said list.

(b) In making such determination the chief judge of the district court, or such other district court judge as the plan may provide, or the clerk if the court's jury selection plan so provides, shall deem any person qualified to serve on grand and petit juries in the district court unless he —

(1) is not a citizen of the United States eighteen years old who has resided for a period of one year within the judicial district;

(2) is unable to read, write, and understand the English language with a degree of proficiency sufficient to fill out satisfactorily the juror qualification form;

(3) is unable to speak the English language;

(4) is incapable, by reason of mental or physical infirmity, to render satisfactory jury service; or

(5) has a charge pending against him for the commission of, or has been convicted in a State or Federal court of record of, a crime punishable by imprisonment for more than one year and his civil rights have not been restored.

§ 1867. Challenging compliance with selection procedures

. . .

(c) In civil cases, before the voir dire examination begins, or within seven days after the party discovered or could have discovered, by the exercise of diligence, the grounds therefor, whichever is earlier, any party may move to stay the proceedings on the ground of substantial failure to comply with the provisions of this title in selecting the petit jury.

(d) Upon motion filed under subsection . . . (c) of this section, containing a sworn statement of facts which, if true, would constitute a substantial failure to comply with the provisions of this title, the moving party shall be entitled to present in support of such motion the testimony of the jury commission or clerk, if available, any relevant records and papers not public or otherwise available used by the jury commissioner or clerk, and any other relevant evidence. . . . If the court determines that there has been a substantial failure to comply with the provisions of this title in selecting the petit jury, the court shall stay the proceedings pending the selection of a petit jury in conformity with this title.

(e) The procedures prescribed by this section shall be the exclusive means by which . . . a party in a civil case may challenge any jury on the ground that such jury was not selected in conformity with the provisions of this title. Nothing in this section shall preclude any person or the United States from pursuing any other remedy, civil or criminal, which may be available for the vindication or enforcement of any law prohibiting discrimination on account of race, color, religion, sex, national origin or economic status in the selection of persons for service on grand or petit juries.

§ 1870. Challenges

In civil cases, each party shall be entitled to three peremptory challenges. Several defendants or several plaintiffs may be considered as a single party for the purposes of making challenges, or the court may allow additional peremptory challenges and permit them to be exercised separately or jointly.

All challenges for cause or favor, whether to the array or panel or to individual jurors, shall be determined by the court.

CHAPTER 123 — FEES AND COSTS

§ 1920. Taxation of costs

A judge or clerk of any court of the United States may tax as costs the following:

(1) Fees of the clerk and marshal;

(2) Fees of the court reporter for all or any part of the stenographic transcript necessarily obtained for use in the case;

(3) Fees and disbursements for printing and witnesses;

(4) Fees for exemplification and copies of papers necessarily obtained for use in the case;

(5) Docket fees under section 1923 of this title;

(6) Compensation of court appointed experts, compensation of interpreters, and salaries, fees, expenses, and costs of special interpretation services under section 1828 of this title.

A bill of costs shall be filed in the case and, upon allowance, included in the judgment or decree.

§ 1927. Counsel's liability for excessive costs

Any attorney or other person admitted to conduct cases in any court of the United States or any Territory thereof who so multiplies the proceedings in any case unreasonably and vexatiously may be required by the court to satisfy personally the excess costs, expenses, and attorneys' fees reasonably incurred because of such conduct.

CHAPTER 125 — PENDING ACTIONS AND JUDGMENTS

§ 1963. Registration of judgments for enforcement in other districts

A judgment in an action for the recovery of money or property entered in any court of appeals, district court, bankruptcy court, or in the Court of International Trade may be registered by filing a certified copy of the judgment in any other district or, with respect to the Court of International Trade, in any judicial district, when the judgment has become final by appeal or expiration of the time for appeal or when ordered by the court that entered the judgment for good cause shown. Such a judgment entered in favor of the United States may be so registered any time after judgment is entered. A judgment so registered shall have the same effect as a judgment of the district court of the district where registered and may be enforced in like manner.

A certified copy of the satisfaction of any judgment in whole or in part may be registered in like manner in any district in which the judgment is a lien.

The procedure prescribed under this section is in addition to other procedures provided by law for the enforcement of judgments.

PART VI — PARTICULAR PROCEEDINGS

CHAPTER 131 — RULES OF COURTS

§ 2071. Rule-making power generally

(a) The Supreme Court and all courts established by Act of Congress may from time to time prescribe rules for the conduct of their business. Such rules shall be consistent with Acts of Congress and rules of practice and procedure prescribed under section 2072 of this title.

(b) Any rule prescribed by a court, other than the Supreme Court, under subsection (a) shall be prescribed only after giving appropriate public notice and an opportunity for comment. Such rule shall take effect upon the date specified by the prescribing court and shall have such effect on pending proceedings as the prescribing court may order.

(c) (1) A rule of a district court prescribed under subsection (a) shall remain in effect unless modified or abrogated by the judicial council of the relevant circuit.

(2) Any other rule prescribed by a court other than the Supreme Court under subsection (a) shall remain in effect unless modified or abrogated by the Judicial Conference.

(d) Copies of rules prescribed under subsection (a) by a district court shall be furnished to the judicial council, and copies of all rules prescribed by a court other than the Supreme Court under subsection (a) shall be furnished to the Director of the Administrative Office of the United States Courts and made available to the public.

(e) If the prescribing court determines that there is an immediate need for a rule, such court may proceed under this section without public notice and opportunity for comment, but such court shall promptly thereafter afford such notice and opportunity for comment.

(f) No rule may be prescribed by a district court other than under this section.

§ 2072. Rules of procedure and evidence; power to prescribe

(a) The Supreme Court shall have the power to prescribe general rules of practice and procedure and rules of evidence for cases in the United States district courts (including proceedings before magistrate judges thereof) and courts of appeals.

(b) Such rules shall not abridge, enlarge or modify any substantive right. All laws in conflict with such rules shall be of no further force or effect after such rules have taken effect.

(c) Such rules may define when a ruling of a district court is final for the purposes of appeal under section 1291 of this title.

§ 2073. Rules of procedure and evidence; method of prescribing

(a) (1) The Judicial Conference shall prescribe and publish the procedures for the consideration of proposed rules under this section.

(2) The Judicial Conference may authorize the appointment of committees to assist the Conference by recommending rules to be prescribed under sections 2072 . . . of this title. Each such committee shall consist of members of the bench and the professional bar, and trial and appellate judges.

(b) The Judicial Conference shall authorize the appointment of a standing committee on rules of practice, procedure, and evidence under subsection (a) of this section. Such standing committee shall review each recommendation of any other committees so appointed and recommend to the Judicial Conference rules of practice, procedure, and evidence and such changes in rules proposed by a committee appointed under subsection (a)(2) of this section as may be necessary to maintain consistency and otherwise promote the interest of justice.

(c) (1) Each meeting for the transaction of business under this chapter by any committee appointed under this section shall be open to the public, except when the committee so meeting, in open session and with a majority present, determines that it is in the public interest that all or part of the remainder of the meeting on that day shall be closed to the public, and states the reason for so closing the meeting. Minutes of each meeting for the transaction of business under this chapter shall be maintained by the committee and made available to the public, except that any portion of such minutes, relating to a closed meeting and made available to the public, may contain such deletions as may be necessary to avoid frustrating the purposes of closing the meeting.

(2) Any meeting for the transaction of business under this chapter, by a committee appointed under this section, shall be preceded by sufficient notice to enable all interested persons to attend.

(d) In making a recommendation under this section or under section 2072 . . ., the body making that recommendation shall provide a proposed rule, an explanatory note on the rule, and a written report explaining the body's action, including any minority or other separate views.

(e) Failure to comply with this section does not invalidate a rule prescribed under section 2072 . . . of this title.

§ 2074. Rules of procedure and evidence; submission to Congress; effective date

(a) The Supreme Court shall transmit to the Congress not later than May 1 of the year in which a rule prescribed under section 2072 is to become effective a copy of the proposed rule. Such rule shall take effect no earlier than December 1 of the year in which such rule is so transmitted unless otherwise provided by law. The Supreme Court may fix the extent such rule shall apply to proceedings then pending, except that the Supreme Court shall not require the application of such rule to further proceedings then pending to the extent that, in the opinion of the court in which such proceedings are pending, the application of such rule in such proceedings would not be feasible or would work injustice, in which event the former rule applies.

(b) Any such rule creating, abolishing, or modifying an evidentiary privilege shall have no force or effect unless approved by Act of Congress.

CHAPTER 133 — REVIEW — MISCELLANEOUS PROVISIONS

§ 2111. Harmless error

On the hearing of any appeal or writ of certiorari in any case, the court shall give judgment after an examination of the record without regard to errors or defects which do not affect the substantial rights of the parties.

PART VI — PARTICULAR PROCEEDINGS

CHAPTER 151 — DECLARATORY JUDGMENTS

§ 2201. Creation of remedy

(a) In a case of actual controversy within its jurisdiction, except with respect to Federal taxes other than actions brought under section 7428 of the Internal Revenue Code of 1986, a proceeding under section 505 or 1146 of title 11, or in any civil action involving an antidumping or countervailing duty proceeding regarding a class or kind of merchandise of a free trade area country (as defined in section 516A(f)(10) of the Tariff Act of 1930), as determined by the administering authority, any court of the United States, upon the filing of an appropriate pleading, may declare the rights and other legal relations of any interested party seeking such declaration, whether or not further relief is or could be sought. Any such declaration shall have the force and effect of a final judgment or decree and shall be reviewable as such. . . .

§ 2202. Further relief

Further necessary or proper relief based on a declaratory judgment or decree may be granted, after reasonable notice and hearing, against any adverse party whose rights have been determined by such judgment.

CHAPTER 155 — INJUNCTIONS; THREE-JUDGE COURTS

§ 2283. Stay of State court proceedings

A court of the United States may not grant an injunction to stay proceedings in a State court except as expressly authorized by Act of Congress, or where necessary in aid of its jurisdiction, or to protect or effectuate its judgments.

CHAPTER 159 — INTERPLEADER

§ 2361. Process and procedure

In any civil action of interpleader or in the nature of interpleader under section 1335 of this title, a district court may issue its process for all claimants and enter its order restraining them from instituting or prosecuting any proceeding in any State or United States court affecting the property, instrument or obligation involved in the interpleader action until further order of the court. Such process and order shall be returnable at such time as the court or judge thereof directs, and shall be addressed to and served by the United States marshals for the respective districts where the claimants reside or may be found.

Such district court shall hear and determine the case, and may discharge the plaintiff from further liability, make the injunction permanent, and make all appropriate orders to enforce its judgment.

* * * * * * *

TITLE 29. LABOR

CHAPTER 14 — AGE DISCRIMINATION IN EMPLOYMENT

§ 623. Prohibition of age discrimination

(a) **Employer practices**

It shall be unlawful for an employer —

(1) to fail or refuse to hire or to discharge any individual or otherwise discriminate against any individual with respect to his compensation, terms, conditions, or privileges of employment, because of such individual's age;

(2) to limit, segregate, or classify his employees in any way which would deprive or tend to deprive any individual of employment opportunities or otherwise adversely affect his status as an employee, because of such individual's age; or

(3) to reduce the wage rate of any employee in order to comply with this chapter. . . .

* * * * * * *

TITLE 42. THE PUBLIC HEALTH AND WELFARE

CHAPTER 21 — CIVIL RIGHTS

§ 1983. Civil action for deprivation of rights

Every person who, under color of any statute, ordinance, regulation, custom, or usage, of any State or Territory or the District of Columbia, subjects, or causes to be subjected, any citizen of the United States or other person within the jurisdiction thereof to the deprivation of any rights, privileges, or immunities secured by the Constitution and laws, shall be liable to the party injured in an action at law, suit in equity, or other proper proceeding for redress, except that in any action brought against a judicial officer for an act or omission taken in such officer's judicial capacity, injunctive relief shall not be granted unless a declaratory decree was violated or declaratory relief was unavailable. For the purposes of this section, any Act of Congress applicable exclusively to the District of Columbia shall be considered to be a statute of the District of Columbia.

§ 1988. Proceedings in vindication of civil rights

(a) **Applicability of statutory and common law**

The jurisdiction in civil and criminal matters conferred on the district courts by the provisions of titles 13, 24, and 70 of the Revised Statutes for the protection of all persons in the United States in their civil rights, and for their vindication, shall be exercised and enforced in conformity with the laws of the United States, so far as such laws are suitable to carry the same into effect; but in all cases where they are not adapted to the object, or are deficient in the provisions necessary to furnish suitable remedies and punish offenses against law, the common law, as modified and changed by the constitution and statutes of the State wherein the court having jurisdiction of such civil or criminal cause is held, so far as the same is not inconsistent with the Constitution and laws of the United States, shall be extended to and govern the said courts in the trial and disposition of the cause, and, if it is of a criminal nature, in the infliction of punishment on the party found guilty.

(b) **Attorney's fees**

In any action or proceeding to enforce a provision of [section 1983 or various other listed civil rights statutes], the court, in its discretion, may allow the prevailing party, other than the United States, a reasonable attorney's fee as part of the costs, except that in any action brought against a judicial officer for an act or omission taken in such officer's judicial capacity such officer shall not be held liable for any costs, including attorney's fees, unless such action was clearly in excess of such officer's jurisdiction.

(c) **Expert fees**

In awarding an attorney's fee under subsection (b) of this section in any action or proceeding to enforce a provision of section 1981 or 1981a of this title, the court, in its discretion, may include expert fees as part of the attorney's fee.

§ 2000e-2. Unlawful employment practices

(a) **Employer practices**

It shall be an unlawful employment practice for an employer —

(1) to fail or refuse to hire or to discharge any individual, or otherwise to discriminate against any individual with respect to his compensation, terms, conditions, or privileges of employment, because of such individual's race, color, religion, sex, or national origin; or

(2) to limit, segregate, or classify his employees or applicants for employment in any way which would deprive or tend to deprive any individual of employment opportunities or otherwise adversely affect his status as an employee, because of such individual's race, color, religion, sex, or national origin. . . .

THE UNITED STATES CONSTITUTION

PREAMBLE

WE THE PEOPLE of the United States, in Order to form a more perfect Union, establish Justice, insure domestic Tranquility, provide for the common defence, promote the general Welfare, and secure the Blessings of Liberty to ourselves and our Posterity, do ordain and establish this CONSTITUTION for the United States of America.

ARTICLE I.

SECTION 1. All legislative Powers herein granted shall be vested in a Congress of the United States, which shall consist of a Senate and House of Representatives.

SECTION 2. The House of Representatives shall be composed of Members chosen every second Year by the People of the several States, and the Electors in each State shall have the Qualifications requisite for Electors of the most numerous Branch of the State Legislature.

No Person shall be a Representative who shall not have attained to the Age of twenty five Years, and been seven Years a Citizen of the United States, and who shall not, when elected, be an Inhabitant of that State in which he shall be chosen.

Representatives and direct Taxes shall be apportioned among the several States which may be included within this Union, according to their respective Numbers, which shall be determined by adding to the whole Number of free Persons, including those bound to Service for a Term of Years, and excluding Indians not taxed, three fifths of all other Persons. The actual Enumeration shall be made within three Years after the first Meeting of the Congress of the United States, and within every subsequent Term of ten Years, in such Manner as they shall by Law direct. The Number of Representatives shall not exceed one for every thirty Thousand, but each State shall have at Least one Representative; and until such enumeration shall be made, the State of New Hampshire shall be entitled to chuse three, Massachusetts eight, Rhode Island and Providence Plantations one, Connecticut five, New York six, New Jersey four, Pennsylvania eight, Delaware one, Maryland six, Virginia ten, North Carolina five, South Carolina five, and Georgia three.

When vacancies happen in the Representation from any State, the Executive Authority thereof shall issue Writs of Election to fill such Vacancies.

The House of Representatives shall chuse their Speaker and other Officers; and shall have the sole Power of Impeachment.

SECTION 3. The Senate of the United States shall be composed of two Senators from each State, chosen by the Legislature thereof, for six Years; and each Senator shall have one Vote.

Immediately after they shall be assembled in Consequence of the first Election, they shall be divided as equally as may be into three Classes. The Seats of the Senators of the first Class shall be vacated at the Expiration of the second Year, of the second Class at the Expiration of the fourth Year, and of the third Class at the Expiration of the sixth Year, so that one third may be chosen every second Year; and if Vacancies happen by Resignation, or otherwise, during the Recess of the Legislature of any State, the Executive thereof may make temporary Appointments until the next Meeting of the Legislature, which shall then fill such Vacancies.

No Person shall be a Senator who shall not have attained to the Age of thirty Years, and been nine Years a Citizen of the United States, and who shall not, when elected, be an Inhabitant of that State for which he shall be chosen.

The Vice President of the United States shall be President of the Senate, but shall have no Vote, unless they be equally divided.

The Senate shall chuse their other Officers, and also a President pro tempore, in the Absence of the Vice President, or when he shall exercise the Office of President of the United States.

The Senate shall have the sole Power to try all Impeachments. When sitting for that Purpose, they shall be on Oath or Affirmation. When the President of the United States is tried, the Chief Justice shall preside: And no Person shall be convicted without the Concurrence of two thirds of the Members present.

Judgment in Cases of Impeachment shall not extend further than to removal from Office, and disqualification to hold and enjoy any Office of honor, Trust or Profit under the United States: but the Party convicted shall nevertheless be liable and subject to Indictment, Trial, Judgment and Punishment, according to Law.

SECTION 4. The Times, Places and Manner of holding Elections for Senators and Representatives, shall be prescribed in each State by the Legislature thereof; but the Congress may at any time by Law make or alter such Regulations, except as to the Places of chusing Senators.

The Congress shall assemble at least once in every Year, and such Meeting shall be on the first Monday in December, unless they shall by Law appoint a different Day.

SECTION 5. Each House shall be the Judge of the Elections, Returns and Qualifications of its own Members, and a Majority of each shall constitute a Quorum to do Business; but a smaller Number may adjourn from day to day, and may be authorized to compel the Attendance of absent Members, in such Manner, and under such Penalties as each House may provide.

Each House may determine the Rules of its Proceedings, punish its Members for disorderly Behaviour, and, with the Concurrence of two thirds, expel a Member.

Each House shall keep a Journal of its Proceedings, and from time to time publish the same, excepting such Parts as may in their Judgment require Secrecy; and the Yeas and Nays of the Members of either House on any question shall, at the Desire of one fifth of those Present, be entered on the Journal.

Neither House, during the Session of Congress, shall, without the Consent of the other, adjourn for more than three days, nor to any other Place than that in which the two Houses shall be sitting.

SECTION 6. The Senators and Representatives shall receive a Compensation for their Services, to be ascertained by Law, and paid out of the Treasury of the United States. They shall in all Cases, except Treason, Felony and Breach of the Peace, be privileged from Arrest during their Attendance at the Session of their respective Houses, and in going to and returning from the same; and for any Speech or Debate in either House, they shall not be questioned in any other Place.

No Senator or Representative shall, during the Time for which he was elected, be appointed to any civil Office under the Authority of the United States, which shall have been created, or the Emoluments whereof shall have been encreased during such time; and no Person holding any Office under the United States, shall be a Member of either House during his Continuance in Office.

SECTION 7. All Bills for raising Revenue shall originate in the House of Representatives; but the Senate may propose or concur with Amendments as on other Bills.

Every Bill which shall have passed the House of Representatives and the Senate, shall, before it become a Law, be presented to the President of the United States; If he approve he shall sign it, but if not he shall return it, with his Objections to that House in which it shall have originated, who shall enter the Objections at large on their Journal, and proceed to reconsider it. If after such Reconsideration two thirds of that House shall agree to pass the Bill, it shall be sent, together with the Objections, to the other House, by which it shall likewise be reconsidered, and if approved by two thirds of that House, it shall become a Law. But in all such Cases the Votes of both Houses shall be determined by Yeas and Nays, and the

Names of the Persons voting for and against the Bill shall be entered on the Journal of each House respectively. If any Bill shall not be returned by the President within ten Days (Sundays excepted) after it shall have been presented to him, the Same shall be a Law, in like Manner as if he had signed it, unless the Congress by their Adjournment prevent its Return, in which Case it shall not be a Law.

Every Order, Resolution, or Vote to which the Concurrence of the Senate and House of Representatives may be necessary (except on a question of Adjournment) shall be presented to the President of the United States; and before the Same shall take Effect, shall be approved by him, or being disapproved by him, shall be repassed by two thirds of the Senate and House of Representatives, according to the Rules and Limitations prescribed in the Case of a Bill.

SECTION 8. The Congress shall have Power To lay and collect Taxes, Duties, Imposts and Excises, to pay the Debts and provide for the common Defence and general Welfare of the United States; but all Duties, Imposts and Excises shall be uniform throughout the United States;

To borrow Money on the credit of the United States;

To regulate Commerce with foreign Nations, and among the several States, and with the Indian Tribes;

To establish an uniform Rule of Naturalization, and uniform Laws on the subject of Bankruptcies throughout the United States;

To coin Money, regulate the Value thereof, and of foreign Coin, and fix the Standard of Weights and Measures;

To provide for the Punishment of counterfeiting the Securities and current Coin of the United States;

To establish Post Offices and post Roads;

To promote the Progress of Science and useful Arts, by securing for limited Times to Authors and Inventors the exclusive Right to their respective Writings and Discoveries;

To constitute Tribunals inferior to the supreme Court;

To define and punish Piracies and Felonies committed on the high Seas, and Offences against the Law of Nations;

To declare War, grant Letters of Marque and Reprisal, and make Rules concerning Captures on Land and Water;

To raise and support Armies, but no Appropriation of Money to that Use shall be for a longer Term than two Years;

To provide and maintain a Navy;

To make Rules for the Government and Regulation of the land and naval Forces;

To provide for calling forth the Militia to execute the Laws of the Union, suppress Insurrections and repel Invasions;

To provide for organizing, arming, and disciplining, the Militia, and for governing such Part of them as may be employed in the Service of the United States, reserving to the States respectively, the Appointment of the Officers, and the Authority of training the Militia according to the discipline prescribed by Congress;

To exercise exclusive Legislation in all Cases whatsoever, over such District (not exceeding ten Miles square) as may, by Cession of particular States, and the Acceptance of Congress, become the Seat of the Government of the United States, and to exercise like Authority over all Places purchased by the Consent of the Legislature of the State in which the Same shall be, for the Erection of Forts, Magazines, Arsenals, dock-Yards, and other needful Buildings; — And

To make all Laws which shall be necessary and proper for carrying into Execution the foregoing Powers, and all other Powers vested by this Constitution in the Government of the United States, or in any Department or Officer thereof.

SECTION 9. The Migration or Importation of such Persons as any of the States now existing shall think proper to admit, shall not be prohibited by the Congress prior to the Year one thousand eight hundred and eight, but a Tax or duty may be imposed on such Importation, not exceeding ten dollars for each Person.

The Privilege of the Writ of Habeas Corpus shall not be suspended, unless when in Cases of Rebellion or Invasion the public Safety may require it.

No Bill of Attainder or ex post facto Law shall be passed.

No Capitation, or other direct, Tax shall be laid, unless in Proportion to the Census or Enumeration herein before directed to be taken.

No Tax or Duty shall be laid on Articles exported from any State.

No Preference shall be given by any Regulation of Commerce or Revenue to the Ports of one State over those of another: nor shall Vessels bound to, or from, one State, be obliged to enter, clear, or pay Duties in another.

No Money shall be drawn from the Treasury, but in Consequence of Appropriations made by Law; and a regular Statement and Account of the Receipts and Expenditures of all public Money shall be published from time to time.

No Title of Nobility shall be granted by the United States: And no Person holding any Office of Profit or Trust under them, shall, without the Consent of the Congress, accept of any present, Emolument, Office, or Title, of any kind whatever, from any King, Prince, or foreign State.

SECTION 10. No State shall enter into any Treaty, Alliance, or Confederation; grant Letters of Marque and Reprisal; coin Money; emit Bills of Credit; make any Thing but gold and silver Coin a Tender in Payment of Debts; pass any Bill of Attainder, ex post facto Law, or Law impairing the Obligation of Contracts, or grant any Title of Nobility.

No State shall, without the Consent of the Congress, lay any Imposts or Duties on Imports or Exports, except what may be absolutely necessary for executing it's inspection Laws: and the net Produce of all Duties and Imposts, laid by any State on Imports or Exports, shall be for the Use of the Treasury of the United States; and all such Laws shall be subject to the Revision and Controul of the Congress.

No State shall, without the Consent of Congress, lay any Duty of Tonnage, keep Troops, or Ships of War in time of Peace, enter into any Agreement or Compact with another State, or with a foreign Power, or engage in War, unless actually invaded, or in such imminent Danger as will not admit of delay.

ARTICLE II.

SECTION 1. The executive Power shall be vested in a President of the United States of America. He shall hold his Office during the Term of four Years, and, together with the Vice President, chosen for the same Term, be elected, as follows

Each State shall appoint, in such Manner as the Legislature thereof may direct, a Number of Electors, equal to the whole Number of Senators and Representatives to which the State may be entitled in the Congress: but no Senator or Representative, or Person holding an Office of Trust or Profit under the United States, shall be appointed an Elector.

The Electors shall meet in their respective States, and vote by Ballot for two Persons, of whom one at least shall not be an Inhabitant of the same State with themselves. And they shall make a List of all the Persons voted for, and of the Number of Votes for each; which List they shall sign and certify, and transmit sealed to the Seat of the Government of the United States, directed to the President of the Senate. The President of the Senate shall, in the Presence of the Senate and House of Representatives, open all the Certificates, and the Votes shall then be counted. The Person having the greatest Number of Votes shall be the President, if such Number be a Majority of the whole Number of Electors appointed; and if there be more than one who have such Majority, and have an equal Number of Votes, then the House of Representatives shall immediately chuse by Ballot one of them for President; and if no Person have a Majority, then from the five highest on the List the said House shall in like Manner chuse the President. But in chusing the President, the Votes shall be taken by States, the Representation from each State having one Vote; a quorum for this Purpose shall consist of a Member or Members from two thirds of the States, and a Majority of all the States shall be necessary to a Choice. In every Case, after the Choice of the President, the Person having the greatest Number of Votes of the Electors shall be the Vice President. But if there should remain two or more who have equal Votes, the Senate shall chuse from them by Ballot the Vice President.

The Congress may determine the Time of chusing the Electors, and the Day on which they shall give their Votes; which Day shall be the same throughout the United States.

No Person except a natural born Citizen, or a Citizen of the United States, at the time of the Adoption of this Constitution, shall be eligible to the Office of President; neither shall any Person be eligible to that Office who shall not have attained to the Age of thirty five Years, and been fourteen Years a Resident within the United States.

In Case of the Removal of the President from Office, or of his Death, Resignation, or Inability to discharge the Powers and Duties of the said Office, the Same shall devolve on the Vice President, and the Congress may by Law provide for the Case of Removal, Death, Resignation or Inability, both of the President and Vice President, declaring what Officer shall then act as President, and such Officer shall act accordingly, until the Disability be removed, or a President shall be elected.

The President shall, at stated Times, receive for his Services, a Compensation, which shall neither be encreased nor diminished during the Period for which he shall have been elected, and he shall not receive within that Period any other Emolument from the United States, or any of them.

Before he enter on the Execution of his Office, he shall take the following Oath or Affirmation: — "I do solemnly swear (or affirm) that I will faithfully execute the Office of President of the United States, and will to the best of my Ability, preserve, protect and defend the Constitution of the United States."

SECTION 2. The President shall be Commander in Chief of the Army and Navy of the United States, and of the Militia of the several States, when called into the actual Service of the United States; he may require the Opinion, in writing, of the principal Officer in each of the executive Departments, upon any Subject relating to the Duties of their respective

Offices, and he shall have Power to grant Reprieves and Pardons for Offences against the United States, except in Cases of Impeachment.

He shall have Power, by and with the Advice and Consent of the Senate, to make Treaties, provided two thirds of the Senators present concur; and he shall nominate, and by and with the Advice and Consent of the Senate, shall appoint Ambassadors, other public Ministers and Consuls, Judges of the supreme Court, and all other Officers of the United States, whose Appointments are not herein otherwise provided for, and which shall be established by Law: but the Congress may by Law vest the Appointment of such inferior Officers, as they think proper, in the President alone, in the Courts of Law, or in the Heads of Departments.

The President shall have Power to fill up all Vacancies that may happen during the Recess of the Senate, by granting Commissions which shall expire at the End of their next Session.

SECTION 3. He shall from time to time give to the Congress Information of the State of the Union, and recommend to their Consideration such Measures as he shall judge necessary and expedient; he may, on extraordinary Occasions, convene both Houses, or either of them, and in Case of Disagreement between them, with Respect to the Time of Adjournment, he may adjourn them to such Time as he shall think proper; he shall receive Ambassadors and other public Ministers; he shall take Care that the Laws be faithfully executed, and shall Commission all the Officers of the United States.

SECTION 4. The President, Vice President and all civil Officers of the United States, shall be removed from Office on Impeachment for, and Conviction of, Treason, Bribery, or other high Crimes and Misdemeanors.

ARTICLE III.

SECTION 1. The judicial Power of the United States, shall be vested in one supreme Court, and in such inferior Courts as the Congress may from time to time ordain and establish. The Judges, both of the supreme and inferior Courts, shall hold their Offices during good Behaviour, and shall, at stated Times, receive for their Services, a Compensation, which shall not be diminished during their Continuance in Office.

SECTION 2. The judicial Power shall extend to all Cases, in Law and Equity, arising under this Constitution, the Laws of the United States, and Treaties made, or which shall be made, under their Authority; — to all Cases affecting Ambassadors, other public Ministers and Consuls; — to all Cases of admiralty and maritime Jurisdiction; — to Controversies to which the United States shall be a Party; — to Controversies between two or more States; — between a State and Citizens of another State; — between

Citizens of different States; — between Citizens of the same State claiming Lands under Grants of different States, and between a State, or the Citizens thereof, and foreign States, Citizens or Subjects.

In all Cases affecting Ambassadors, other public Ministers and Consuls, and those in which a State shall be Party, the supreme Court shall have original Jurisdiction. In all the other Cases before mentioned, the supreme Court shall have appellate Jurisdiction, both as to Law and Fact, with such Exceptions, and under such Regulations as the Congress shall make.

The Trial of all Crimes, except in Cases of Impeachment, shall be by Jury; and such Trial shall be held in the State where the said Crimes shall have been committed; but when not committed within any State, the Trial shall be at such Place or Places as the Congress may by Law have directed.

SECTION 3. Treason against the United States, shall consist only in levying War against them, or in adhering to their Enemies, giving them Aid and Comfort. No Person shall be convicted of Treason unless on the Testimony of two Witnesses to the same overt Act, or on Confession in open Court.

The Congress shall have Power to declare the Punishment of Treason, but no Attainder of Treason shall work Corruption of Blood, or Forfeiture except during the Life of the Person attainted.

ARTICLE IV.

SECTION 1. Full Faith and Credit shall be given in each State to the public Acts, Records, and judicial Proceedings of every other State. And the Congress may by general Laws prescribe the Manner in which such Acts, Records and Proceedings shall be proved, and the Effect thereof.

SECTION 2. The Citizens of each State shall be entitled to all Privileges and Immunities of Citizens in the several States.

A Person charged in any State with Treason, Felony, or other Crime, who shall flee from Justice, and be found in another State, shall on Demand of the executive Authority of the State from which he fled, be delivered up, to be removed to the State having Jurisdiction of the Crime.

No Person held to Service or Labour in one State, under the Laws thereof, escaping into another, shall, in Consequence of any Law or Regulation therein, be discharged from such Service or Labour, but shall be delivered up on Claim of the Party to whom such Service or Labour may be due.

SECTION 3. New States may be admitted by the Congress into this Union; but no new State shall be formed or erected within the Jurisdiction of any other State; nor any State be formed by the Junction of two or more States, or Parts of States, without the Consent of the Legislatures of the States concerned as well as of the Congress.

The Congress shall have Power to dispose of and make all needful Rules and Regulations respecting the Territory or other Property belonging to the United States; and nothing in this Constitution shall be so construed as to Prejudice any Claims of the United States, or of any particular State.

SECTION 4. The United States shall guarantee to every State in this Union a Republican Form of Government, and shall protect each of them against Invasion; and on Application of the Legislature, or of the Executive (when the Legislature cannot be convened) against domestic Violence.

ARTICLE V.

The Congress, whenever two thirds of both Houses shall deem it necessary, shall propose Amendments to this Constitution, or, on the Application of the Legislatures of two thirds of the several States, shall call a Convention for proposing Amendments, which, in either Case, shall be valid to all Intents and Purposes, as Part of this Constitution, when ratified by the Legislatures of three fourths of the several States, or by Conventions in three fourths thereof, as the one or the other Mode of Ratification may be proposed by the Congress; Provided that no Amendment which may be made prior to the Year One thousand eight hundred and eight shall in any Manner affect the first and fourth Clauses in the Ninth Section of the first Article; and that no State, without its Consent, shall be deprived of its equal Suffrage in the Senate.

ARTICLE VI.

All Debts contracted and Engagements entered into, before the Adoption of this Constitution, shall be as valid against the United States under this Constitution, as under the Confederation.

This Constitution, and the Laws of the United States which shall be made in Pursuance thereof; and all Treaties made, or which shall be made, under the Authority of the United States, shall be the supreme Law of the Land; and the Judges in every State shall be bound thereby, any Thing in the Constitution or Laws of any State to the Contrary notwithstanding.

The Senators and Representatives before mentioned, and the Members of the several State Legislatures, and all executive and judicial Officers, both of the United States and of the several States, shall be bound by Oath or Affirmation, to support this Constitution; but no religious Test shall ever be required as a Qualification to any Office or public Trust under the United States.

ARTICLE VII.

The Ratification of the Conventions of nine States, shall be sufficient for the Establishment of this Constitution between the States so ratifying the Same.

Done in Convention by the Unanimous Consent of the States present the Seventeenth Day of September in the Year of Our Lord one thousand seven hundred and Eighty seven and of the Independence of the United States of America the Twelfth. IN WITNESS whereof We have hereunto subscribed our Names.

GO. WASHINGTON — *Presidt.*
and deputy from Virginia

[Signatories omitted.]

* * * * *

ARTICLES IN ADDITION TO, AND AMENDMENT OF, THE CONSTITUTION OF THE UNITED STATES OF AMERICA, PROPOSED BY CONGRESS, AND RATIFIED BY THE LEGISLATURES OF THE SEVERAL STATES, PURSUANT TO THE FIFTH ARTICLE OF THE ORIGINAL CONSTITUTION

AMENDMENT I [1791]

Congress shall make no law respecting an establishment of religion, or prohibiting the free exercise thereof; or abridging the freedom of speech, or of the press; or the right of the people peaceably to assemble, and to petition the Government for a redress of grievances.

AMENDMENT II [1791]

A well regulated Militia, being necessary to the security of a free State, the right of the people to keep and bear Arms, shall not be infringed.

AMENDMENT III [1791]

No Soldier shall, in time of peace be quartered in any house, without the consent of the Owner, nor in time of war, but in a manner to be prescribed by law.

AMENDMENT IV [1791]

The right of the people to be secure in their persons, houses, papers, and effects, against unreasonable searches and seizures, shall not be violated, and no Warrants shall issue, but upon probable cause, supported by Oath or affirmation, and particularly describing the place to be searched, and the persons or things to be seized.

AMENDMENT V [1791]

No person shall be held to answer for a capital, or otherwise infamous crime, unless on a presentment or indictment of a Grand Jury, except in cases arising in the land or naval forces, or in the Militia, when in actual service in time of War or public danger; nor shall any person be subject for the same offence to be twice put in jeopardy of life or limb; nor shall be compelled in any criminal case to be a witness against himself, nor be deprived of life, liberty, or property, without due process of law; nor shall private property be taken for public use, without just compensation.

AMENDMENT VI [1791]

In all criminal prosecutions, the accused shall enjoy the right to a speedy and public trial, by an impartial jury of the State and district wherein the crime shall have been committed, which district shall have been previously ascertained by law, and to be informed of the nature and cause of the accusation; to be confronted with the witnesses against him; to have compulsory process for obtaining witnesses in his favor, and to have the Assistance of Counsel for his defence.

AMENDMENT VII [1791]

In Suits at common law, where the value in controversy shall exceed twenty dollars, the right of trial by jury shall be preserved, and no fact tried by a jury, shall be otherwise re-examined in any Court of the United States, than according to the rules of the common law.

AMENDMENT VIII [1791]

Excessive bail shall not be required, nor excessive fines imposed, nor cruel and unusual punishments inflicted.

AMENDMENT IX [1791]

The enumeration in the Constitution, of certain rights, shall not be construed to deny or disparage others retained by the people.

AMENDMENT X [1791]

The powers not delegated to the United States by the Constitution, nor prohibited by it to the States, are reserved to the States respectively, or to the people.

AMENDMENT XI [1798]

The Judicial power of the United States shall not be construed to extend to any suit in law or equity, commenced or prosecuted against one of the United States by Citizens of another State, or by Citizens or Subjects of any Foreign State.

AMENDMENT XII [1804]

The Electors shall meet in their respective states, and vote by ballot for President and Vice-President, one of whom, at least, shall not be an inhabitant of the same state with themselves; they shall name in their ballots the person voted for as President, and in distinct ballots the person voted for as Vice-President, and they shall make distinct lists of all persons voted for as President, and of all persons voted for as Vice-President, and of the number of votes for each, which lists they shall sign and certify, and transmit sealed to the seat of the government of the United States, directed to the President of the Senate; — The President of the Senate shall, in the presence of the Senate and House of Representatives, open all the certificates and the votes shall then be counted; — The person having the greatest number of votes for President, shall be the President, if such number be a majority of the whole number of Electors appointed; and if no person have such majority, then from the persons having the highest numbers not exceeding three on the list of those voted for as President, the House of Representatives shall choose immediately, by ballot, the President. But in choosing the President, the votes shall be taken by states, the representation from each state having one vote; a quorum for this purpose shall consist of a member or members from two-thirds of the states, and a majority of all the states shall be necessary to a choice. And if the House of Representatives shall not choose a President whenever the right of choice shall devolve upon them, before the fourth day of March next following, then the Vice-President shall act as President, as in the case of the death or other constitutional disability of the President. — The person having the greatest number of votes as Vice-President, shall be the Vice-President, if such number be a majority of the whole number of Electors appointed, and if no person have a majority, then from the two highest numbers on the list, the Senate shall choose the Vice-President; a quorum for the purpose shall consist of two-thirds of the whole number of Senators, and a majority of the whole number shall be necessary to a choice. But no person constitutionally ineligible to the office of President shall be eligible to that of Vice-President of the United States.

AMENDMENT XIII [1865]

SECTION 1. Neither slavery nor involuntary servitude, except as a punishment for crime whereof the party shall have been duly convicted, shall exist within the United States, or any place subject to their jurisdiction.

SECTION 2. Congress shall have power to enforce this article by appropriate legislation.

AMENDMENT XIV [1868]

SECTION 1. All persons born or naturalized in the United States, and subject to the jurisdiction thereof, are citizens of the United States and of the State wherein they reside. No State shall make or enforce any law which shall abridge the privileges or immunities of citizens of the United States; nor shall any State deprive any person of life, liberty, or property, without due process of law; nor deny to any person within its jurisdiction the equal protection of the laws.

SECTION 2. Representatives shall be apportioned among the several States according to their respective numbers, counting the whole number of persons in each State, excluding Indians not taxed. But when the right to vote at any election for the choice of electors for President and Vice President of the United States, Representatives in Congress, the Executive and Judicial officers of a State, or the members of the Legislature thereof, is denied to any of the male inhabitants of such State, being twenty-one years of age, and citizens of the United States, or in any way abridged, except for participation in rebellion, or other crime, the basis of representation therein shall be reduced in the proportion which the number of such male citizens shall bear to the whole number of male citizens twenty-one years of age in such State.

SECTION 3. No person shall be a Senator or Representative in Congress, or elector of President and Vice President, or hold any office, civil or military, under the United States, or under any State, who, having previously taken an oath, as a member of Congress, or as an officer of the United States, or as a member of any State legislature, or as an executive or judicial officer of any State, to support the Constitution of the United States, shall have engaged in insurrection or rebellion against the same, or given aid or comfort to the enemies thereof. But Congress may by a vote of two-thirds of each House, remove such disability.

SECTION 4. The validity of the public debt of the United States, authorized by law, including debts incurred for payment of pensions and bounties for services in suppressing insurrection or rebellion, shall not be questioned. But neither the United States nor any State shall assume or pay any debt or obligation incurred in aid of insurrection or rebellion against the United States, or any claim for the loss or emancipation of any slave; but all such debts, obligations and claims shall be held illegal and void.

SECTION 5. The Congress shall have power to enforce, by appropriate legislation, the provisions of this article.

AMENDMENT XV [1870]

SECTION 1. The right of citizens of the United States to vote shall not be denied or abridged by the United States or by any State on account of race, color, or previous condition of servitude.

SECTION 2. The Congress shall have power to enforce this article by appropriate legislation.

AMENDMENT XVI [1913]

The Congress shall have power to lay and collect taxes on incomes, from whatever source derived, without apportionment among the several States, and without regard to any census or enumeration.

AMENDMENT XVII [1913]

The Senate of the United States shall be composed of two Senators from each State, elected by the people thereof, for six years; and each Senator shall have one vote. The electors in each State shall have the qualifications requisite for electors of the most numerous branch of the State legislatures.

When vacancies happen in the representation of any State in the Senate, the executive authority of such State shall issue writs of election to fill such vacancies: *Provided*, That the legislature of any State may empower the executive thereof to make temporary appointments until the people fill the vacancies by election as the legislature may direct.

This Article shall not be so construed as to affect the election or term of any Senator chosen before it becomes valid as part of the Constitution.

AMENDMENT XVIII [1919]

SECTION 1. After one year from the ratification of this article the manufacture, sale, or transportation of intoxicating liquors within, the importation thereof into, or the exportation thereof from the United States and all territory subject to the jurisdiction thereof for beverage purposes is hereby prohibited.

SECTION 2. The Congress and the several States shall have concurrent power to enforce this article by appropriate legislation.

SECTION 3. This article shall be inoperative unless it shall have been ratified as an amendment to the Constitution by the legislatures of the several States, as provided in the Constitution, within seven years from the date of the submission hereof to the States by the Congress.

AMENDMENT XIX [1920]

The right of citizens of the United States to vote shall not be denied or abridged by the United States or by any State on account of sex.

Congress shall have power to enforce this article by appropriate legislation.

AMENDMENT XX [1933]

SECTION 1. The terms of the President and Vice President shall end at noon on the 20th day of January, and the terms of Senators and Representatives at noon on the 3d day of January, of the years in which such terms would have ended if this article had not been ratified; and the terms of their successors shall then begin.

SECTION 2. The Congress shall assemble at least once in every year, and such meeting shall begin at noon on the 3d day of January, unless they shall by law appoint a different day.

SECTION 3. If, at the time fixed for the beginning of the term of the President, the President elect shall have died, the Vice President elect shall become President. If a President shall not have been chosen before the time fixed for the beginning of his term, or if the President elect shall have failed to qualify, then the Vice President elect shall act as President until a President shall have qualified; and the Congress may by law provide for the case wherein neither a President elect nor a Vice President elect shall have qualified, declaring who shall then act as President, or the manner in which one who is to act shall be selected, and such person shall act accordingly until a President or Vice President shall have qualified.

SECTION 4. The Congress may by law provide for the case of the death of any of the persons from whom the House of Representatives may choose a President whenever the right of choice shall have devolved upon them, and for the case of the death of any of the persons from whom the Senate may choose a Vice President whenever the right of choice shall have devolved upon them.

SECTION 5. Sections 1 and 2 shall take effect on the 15th day of October following the ratification of this article.

SECTION 6. This article shall be inoperative unless it shall have been ratified as an amendment to the Constitution by the legislatures of three-fourths of the several States within seven years from the date of its submission.

AMENDMENT XXI [1933]

SECTION 1. The eighteenth article of amendment to the Constitution of the United States is hereby repealed.

SECTION 2. The transportation or importation into any State, Territory, or possession of the United States for delivery or use therein of intoxicating liquors, in violation of the laws thereof, is hereby prohibited.

SECTION 3. This article shall be inoperative unless it shall have been ratified as an amendment to the Constitution by conventions in the several States, as provided in the Constitution, within seven years from the date of the submission hereof to the States by the Congress.

AMENDMENT XXII [1951]

SECTION 1. No person shall be elected to the office of the President more than twice, and no person who has held the office of President, or acted as President, for more than two years of a term to which some other person was elected President shall be elected to the office of the President more than once. But this article shall not apply to any person holding the office of President when this article was proposed by the Congress, and shall not prevent any person who may be holding the office of President, or acting as President, during the term within which this article becomes operative from holding the office of President or acting as President during the remainder of such term.

SECTION 2. This article shall be inoperative unless it shall have been ratified as an amendment to the Constitution by the legislatures of three-fourths of the several states within seven years from the date of its submission to the states by the Congress.

AMENDMENT XXIII [1961]

SECTION 1. The District constituting the seat of government of the United States shall appoint in such manner as the Congress may direct: A number of electors of President and Vice President equal to the whole number of Senators and Representatives in Congress to which the District would be entitled if it were a state, but in no event more than the least populous state; they shall be in addition to those appointed by the states, but they shall be considered, for the purposes of the election of President and Vice President, to be electors appointed by a state; and they shall meet in the District and perform such duties as provided by the twelfth article of amendment.

SECTION 2. The Congress shall have power to enforce this article by appropriate legislation.

AMENDMENT XXIV [1964]

SECTION 1. The right of citizens of the United States to vote in any primary or other election for President or Vice President, for electors for President or Vice President, or for Senator or Representative in Congress, shall not be denied or abridged by the United States or any state by reason of failure to pay any poll tax or other tax.

SECTION 2. The Congress shall have power to enforce this article by appropriate legislation.

AMENDMENT XXV [1967]

SECTION 1. In case of the removal of the President from office or of his death or resignation, the Vice President shall become President.

SECTION 2. Whenever there is a vacancy in the office of the Vice President, the President shall nominate a Vice President who shall take office upon confirmation by a majority vote of both Houses of Congress.

SECTION 3. Whenever the President transmits to the President pro tempore of the Senate and the Speaker of the House of Representatives his written declaration that he is unable to discharge the powers and duties of his office, and until he transmits to them a written declaration to the contrary, such powers and duties shall be discharged by the Vice President as Acting President.

SECTION 4. Whenever the Vice President and a majority of either the principal officers of the executive departments or of such other body as Congress may by law provide, transmit to the President pro tempore of the Senate and the Speaker of the House of Representatives their written declaration that the President is unable to discharge the powers and duties of his office, the Vice President shall immediately assume the powers and duties of the office as Acting President.

Thereafter, when the President transmits to the President pro tempore of the Senate and the Speaker of the House of Representatives his written declaration that no inability exists, he shall resume the powers and duties of his office unless the Vice President and a majority of either the principal officers of the executive department or of such other body as Congress may by law provide, transmit within four days to the President pro tempore of the Senate and the Speaker of the House of Representatives their written declaration that the President is unable to discharge the powers and duties of his office. Thereupon Congress shall decide the issue, assembling within forty-eight hours for that purpose if not in session. If the Congress, within twenty-one days after receipt of the latter written declaration, or, if Congress is not in session, within twenty-one days after Congress is required to assemble, determines by two-thirds vote of both Houses that the President is unable to discharge the powers and duties of his office, the Vice President shall continue to discharge the same as Acting President; otherwise, the President shall resume the powers and duties of his office.

AMENDMENT XXVI [1971]

SECTION 1. The right of citizens of the United States, who are 18 years of age or older, to vote, shall not be denied or abridged by the United States or any state on account of age.

SECTION 2. The Congress shall have the power to enforce this article by appropriate legislation.

AMENDMENT XXVII [1992][*]

No law varying the compensation for the services of the Senators and Representatives shall take effect until an election of Representatives shall have intervened.

[*] This amendment was proposed by Congress in 1789 as one of the original amendments constituting the Bill of Rights. The last of the requisite three-quarters of state legislatures ratified the amendment in 1992. — ED.

PENDING AMENDMENTS TO THE FEDERAL RULES OF CIVIL PROCEDURE*

TITLE I. SCOPE OF RULES; FORM OF ACTION

Rule 1. Scope and Purpose

These rules govern the procedure in all civil actions and proceedings in the United States district courts, except as stated in Rule 81. They should be construed and administered to secure the just, speedy, and inexpensive determination of every action and proceeding.

Rule 2. One Form of Action

There is one form of action — the civil action.

TITLE II. COMMENCING AN ACTION; SERVICE OF PROCESS, PLEADINGS, MOTIONS, AND ORDERS

Rule 3. Commencing an Action

A civil action is commenced by filing a complaint with the court.

Rule 4. Summons

(a) Contents; Amendments.

(1) Contents. A summons must:

(A) name the court and the parties;

(B) be directed to the defendant;

(C) state the name and address of the plaintiff's attorney or — if unrepresented — of the plaintiff;

(D) state the time within which the defendant must appear and defend;

* On April 30, 2007, the Supreme Court adopted these amendments to the Federal Rules of Civil Procedure and, pursuant to 28 U.S.C. § 2074(a), transmitted them to Congress. The amendments will become effective on December 1, 2007 unless Congress enacts legislation disapproving, delaying, or modifying them. A few new provisions have been added, but the basic point of these amendments is to make the Rules easier to comprehend. The Rules were re-written stem to stern, and many subsections were redesignated. Hence, even though some of the Rules remain unchanged, we reproduce the pending amendments in their entirety. — ED.

(E) notify the defendant that a failure to appear and defend will result in a default judgment against the defendant for the relief demanded in the complaint;

(F) be signed by the clerk; and

(G) bear the court's seal.

(2) ***Amendments.*** The court may permit a summons to be amended.

(b) Issuance. On or after filing the complaint, the plaintiff may present a summons to the clerk for signature and seal. If the summons is properly completed, the clerk must sign, seal, and issue it to the plaintiff for service on the defendant. A summons — or a copy of a summons that is addressed to multiple defendants — must be issued for each defendant to be served.

(c) Service.

(1) ***In General.*** A summons must be served with a copy of the complaint. The plaintiff is responsible for having the summons and complaint served within the time allowed by Rule 4(m) and must furnish the necessary copies to the person who makes service.

(2) ***By Whom.*** Any person who is at least 18 years old and not a party may serve a summons and complaint.

(3) ***By a Marshal or Someone Specially Appointed.*** At the plaintiff's request, the court may order that service be made by a United States marshal or deputy marshal or by a person specially appointed by the court. The court must so order if the plaintiff is authorized to proceed in forma pauperis under 28 U.S.C. §1915 or as a seaman under 28 U.S.C. § 1916.

(d) Waiving Service.

(1) ***Requesting a Waiver.*** An individual, corporation, or association that is subject to service under Rule 4(e), (f), or (h) has a duty to avoid unnecessary expenses of serving the summons. The plaintiff may notify such a defendant that an action has been commenced and request that the defendant waive service of a summons. The notice and request must:

(A) be in writing and be addressed:

(i) to the individual defendant; or

(ii) for a defendant subject to service under Rule 4(h), to an officer, a managing or general agent, or any other agent authorized by appointment or by law to receive service of process;

(B) name the court where the complaint was filed;

(C) be accompanied by a copy of the complaint, two copies of a waiver form, and a prepaid means for returning the form;

(D) inform the defendant, using text prescribed in Form 5, of the consequences of waiving and not waiving service;

(E) state the date when the request is sent;

(F) give the defendant a reasonable time of at least 30 days after the request was sent — or at least 60 days if sent to the defendant outside any judicial district of the United States — to return the waiver; and

(G) be sent by first-class mail or other reliable means.

(2) ***Failure to Waive.*** If a defendant located within the United States fails, without good cause, to sign and return a waiver requested by a plaintiff located within the United States, the court must impose on the defendant:

(A) the expenses later incurred in making service; and

(B) the reasonable expenses, including attorney's fees, of any motion required to collect those service expenses.

(3) ***Time to Answer After a Waiver.*** A defendant who, before being served with process, timely returns a waiver need not serve an answer to the complaint until 60 days after the request was sent — or until 90 days after it was sent to the defendant outside any judicial district of the United States.

(4) ***Results of Filing a Waiver.*** When the plaintiff files a waiver, proof of service is not required and these rules apply as if a summons and complaint had been served at the time of filing the waiver.

(5) ***Jurisdiction and Venue Not Waived.*** Waiving service of a summons does not waive any objection to personal jurisdiction or to venue.

(e) Serving an Individual Within a Judicial District of the United States. Unless federal law provides otherwise, an individual — other than a minor, an incompetent person, or a person whose waiver has been filed — may be served in a judicial district of the United States by:

(1) following state law for serving a summons in an action brought in courts of general jurisdiction in the state where the district court is located or where service is made; or

(2) doing any of the following:

(A) delivering a copy of the summons and of the complaint to the individual personally;

(B) leaving a copy of each at the individual's dwelling or usual place of abode with someone of suitable age and discretion who resides there; or

(C) delivering a copy of each to an agent authorized by appointment or by law to receive service of process.

(f) Serving an Individual in a Foreign Country. Unless federal law provides otherwise, an individual — other than a minor, an incompetent person, or a person whose waiver has been filed — may be served at a place not within any judicial district of the United States:

(1) by any internationally agreed means of service that is reasonably calculated to give notice, such as those authorized by the Hague Convention on the Service Abroad of Judicial and Extrajudicial Documents;

(2) if there is no internationally agreed means, or if an international agreement allows but does not specify other means, by a method that is reasonably calculated to give notice:

(A) as prescribed by the foreign country's law for service in that country in an action in its courts of general jurisdiction;

(B) as the foreign authority directs in response to a letter rogatory or letter of request; or

(C) unless prohibited by the foreign country's law, by:

(i) delivering a copy of the summons and of the complaint to the individual personally; or

(ii) using any form of mail that the clerk addresses and sends to the individual and that requires a signed receipt; or

(3) by other means not prohibited by international agreement, as the court orders.

(g) Serving a Minor or an Incompetent Person. A minor or an incompetent person in a judicial district of the United States must be served by following state law for serving a summons or like process on such a defendant in an action brought in the courts of general jurisdiction of the state where service is made. A minor or an incompetent person who is not within any judicial district of the United States must be served in the manner prescribed by Rule 4(f)(2)(A), (f)(2)(B), or (f)(3).

(h) Serving a Corporation, Partnership, or Association. Unless federal law provides otherwise or the defendant's waiver has been filed, a domestic or foreign corporation, or a partnership or other unincorporated association that is subject to suit under a common name, must be served:

(1) in a judicial district of the United States:

(A) in the manner prescribed by Rule 4(e)(1) for serving an individual; or

(B) by delivering a copy of the summons and of the complaint to an officer, a managing or general agent, or any other agent authorized by appointment or by law to receive service of process and — if the agent is one authorized by statute and the statute so requires — by also mailing a copy of each to the defendant; or

(2) at a place not within any judicial district of the United States, in any manner prescribed by Rule 4(f) for serving an individual, except personal delivery under (f)(2)(C)(i).

(i) Serving the United States and Its Agencies, Corporations, Officers, or Employees.

(1) ***United States.*** To serve the United States, a party must:

(A) **(i)** deliver a copy of the summons and of the complaint to the United States attorney for the district where the action is brought — or to an assistant United States attorney or clerical employee whom the United States attorney designates in a writing filed with the court clerk — or

(ii) send a copy of each by registered or certified mail to the civil-process clerk at the United States attorney's office;

(B) send a copy of each by registered or certified mail to the Attorney General of the United States at Washington, D.C.; and

(C) if the action challenges an order of a nonparty agency or officer of the United States, send a copy of each by registered or certified mail to the agency or officer.

(2) ***Agency; Corporation; Officer or Employee Sued in an Official Capacity.*** To serve a United States agency or corporation, or a United States officer or employee sued only in an official capacity, a party must serve the United States and also send a copy of the summons and of the complaint by registered or certified mail to the agency, corporation, officer, or employee.

(3) ***Officer or Employee Sued Individually.*** To serve a United States officer or employee sued in an individual capacity for an act or omission occurring in connection with duties performed on the United States' behalf (whether or not the officer or employee is also sued in an official capacity), a party must serve the United States and also serve the officer or employee under Rule 4(e), (f), or (g).

(4) ***Extending Time.*** The court must allow a party a reasonable time to cure its failure to:

(A) serve a person required to be served under Rule 4(i)(2), if the party has served either the United States attorney or the Attorney General of the United States; or

(B) serve the United States under Rule 4(i)(3), if the party has served the United States officer or employee.

(j) Serving a Foreign, State, or Local Government.

(1) ***Foreign State.*** A foreign state or its political subdivision, agency, or instrumentality must be served in accordance with 28 U.S.C. § 1608.

(2) ***State or Local Government.*** A state, a municipal corporation, or any other state-created governmental organization that is subject to suit must be served by:

(A) delivering a copy of the summons and of the complaint to its chief executive officer; or

(B) serving a copy of each in the manner prescribed by that state's law for serving a summons or like process on such a defendant.

(k) Territorial Limits of Effective Service.

(1) ***In General.*** Serving a summons or filing a waiver of service establishes personal jurisdiction over a defendant:

(A) who is subject to the jurisdiction of a court of general jurisdiction in the state where the district court is located;

(B) who is a party joined under Rule 14 or 19 and is served within a judicial district of the United States and not more than 100 miles from where the summons was issued;

(C) when authorized by a federal statute.

(2) ***Federal Claim Outside State-Court Jurisdiction.*** For a claim that arises under federal law, serving a summons or filing a waiver of service establishes personal jurisdiction over a defendant if:

(A) the defendant is not subject to jurisdiction in any state's courts of general jurisdiction; and

(B) exercising jurisdiction is consistent with the United States Constitution and laws.

(l) Proving Service.

(1) ***Affidavit Required.*** Unless service is waived, proof of service must be made to the court. Except for service by a United States marshal or deputy marshal, proof must be by the server's affidavit.

(2) ***Service Outside the United States.*** Service not within any judicial district of the United States must be proved as follows:

(A) if made under Rule 4(f)(1), as provided in the applicable treaty or convention; or

(B) if made under Rule 4(f)(2) or (f)(3), by a receipt signed by the addressee, or by other evidence satisfying the court that the summons and complaint were delivered to the addressee.

(3) ***Validity of Service; Amending Proof.*** Failure to prove service does not affect the validity of service. The court may permit proof of service to be amended.

(m) Time Limit for Service. If a defendant is not served within 120 days after the complaint is filed, the court — on motion or on its own after notice to the plaintiff — must dismiss the action without prejudice against that defendant or order that service be made within a specified time. But if the plaintiff shows good cause for the failure, the court must extend the time for service for an appropriate period. This subdivision (m) does not apply to service in a foreign country under Rule 4(f) or 4(j)(1).

(n) Asserting Jurisdiction over Property or Assets.

(1) ***Federal Law.*** The court may assert jurisdiction over property if authorized by a federal statute. Notice to claimants of the property must be given as provided in the statute or by serving a summons under this rule.

(2) ***State Law.*** On a showing that personal jurisdiction over a defendant cannot be obtained in the district where the action is brought by reasonable efforts to serve a summons under this rule, the court may assert jurisdiction over the defendant's assets found in the district. Jurisdiction is acquired by seizing the assets under the circumstances and in the manner provided by state law in that district.

Rule 4.1. Serving Other Process

(a) In General. Process — other than a summons under Rule 4 or a subpoena under Rule 45 — must be served by a United States marshal or deputy marshal or by a person specially appointed for that purpose. It may be served anywhere within the territorial limits of the state where the district court is located and, if authorized by a federal statute, beyond those limits. Proof of service must be made under Rule 4(l).

(b) Enforcing Orders: Committing for Civil Contempt. An order committing a person for civil contempt of a decree or injunction issued to enforce federal law may be served and enforced in any district. Any other order in a civil-contempt proceeding may be served only in the state where the issuing court is located or elsewhere in the United States within 100 miles from where the order was issued.

Rule 5. Serving and Filing Pleadings and Other Papers

(a) Service: When Required.

(1) ***In General.*** Unless these rules provide otherwise, each of the following papers must be served on every party:

(A) an order stating that service is required;

(B) a pleading filed after the original complaint, unless the court orders otherwise under Rule 5(c) because there are numerous defendants;

(C) a discovery paper required to be served on a party, unless the court orders otherwise;

(D) a written motion, except one that may be heard ex parte; and

(E) a written notice, appearance, demand, or offer of judgment, or any similar paper.

(2) ***If a Party Fails to Appear.*** No service is required on a party who is in default for failing to appear. But a pleading that asserts a new claim for relief against such a party must be served on that party under Rule 4.

(3) ***Seizing Property.*** If an action is begun by seizing property and no person is or need be named as a defendant, any service required before the filing of an appearance, answer, or claim must be made on the person who had custody or possession of the property when it was seized.

(b) Service: How Made.

(1) ***Serving an Attorney.*** If a party is represented by an attorney, service under this rule must be made on the attorney unless the court orders service on the party.

(2) ***Service in General.*** A paper is served under this rule by:

(A) handing it to the person;

(B) leaving it:

(i) at the person's office with a clerk or other person in charge or, if no one is in charge, in a conspicuous place in the office; or

(ii) if the person has no office or the office is closed, at the person's dwelling or usual place of abode with someone of suitable age and discretion who resides there;

(C) mailing it to the person's last known address — in which event service is complete upon mailing;

(D) leaving it with the court clerk if the person has no known address;

(E) sending it by electronic means if the person consented in writing — in which event service is complete upon transmission, but is not effective if the serving party learns that it did not reach the person to be served; or

(F) delivering it by any other means that the person consented to in writing — in which event service is complete when the person making service delivers it to the agency designated to make delivery.

(3) ***Using Court Facilities.*** If a local rule so authorizes, a party may use the court's transmission facilities to make service under Rule 5(b)(2)(E).

(c) Serving Numerous Defendants.

(1) ***In General.*** If an action involves an unusually large number of defendants, the court may, on motion or on its own, order that:

(A) defendants' pleadings and replies to them need not be served on other defendants;

(B) any crossclaim, counterclaim, avoidance, or affirmative defense in those pleadings and replies to them will be treated as denied or avoided by all other parties; and

(C) filing any such pleading and serving it on the plaintiff constitutes notice of the pleading to all parties.

(2) ***Notifying Parties.*** A copy of every such order must be served on the parties as the court directs.

(d) Filing.

(1) ***Required Filings; Certificate of Service.*** Any paper after the complaint that is required to be served — together with a certificate of service — must be filed within a reasonable time after service. But disclosures under Rule 26(a)(1) or (2) and the following discovery requests and responses must not be filed until they are used in the proceeding or the court orders filing: depositions, interrogatories, requests for documents or tangible things or to permit entry onto land, and requests for admission.

(2) ***How Filing Is Made — In General.*** A paper is filed by delivering it:

(A) to the clerk; or

(B) to a judge who agrees to accept it for filing, and who must then note the filing date on the paper and promptly send it to the clerk.

(3) ***Electronic Filing, Signing, or Verification.*** A court may, by local rule, allow papers to be filed, signed, or verified by electronic means that are consistent with any technical standards established by the Judicial Conference of the United States. A local rule may require electronic filing only if reasonable exceptions are allowed. A paper filed electronically in compliance with a local rule is a written paper for purposes of these rules.

(4) ***Acceptance by the Clerk.*** The clerk must not refuse to file a paper solely because it is not in the form prescribed by these rules or by a local rule or practice.

Rule 5.1. Constitutional Challenge to a Statute — Notice, Certification, and Intervention

(a) Notice by a Party. A party that files a pleading, written motion, or other paper drawing into question the constitutionality of a federal or state statute must promptly:

(1) file a notice of constitutional question stating the question and identifying the paper that raises it, if:

(A) a federal statute is questioned and the parties do not include the United States, one of its agencies, or one of its officers or employees in an official capacity; or

(B) a state statute is questioned and the parties do not include the state, one of its agencies, or one of its officers or employees in an official capacity; and

(2) serve the notice and paper on the Attorney General of the United States if a federal statute is questioned — or on the state attorney general if a state statute is questioned — either by certified or registered mail or by sending it to an electronic address designated by the attorney general for this purpose.

(b) Certification by the Court. The court must, under 28 U.S.C. § 2403, certify to the appropriate attorney general that a statute has been questioned.

(c) Intervention; Final Decision on the Merits. Unless the court sets a later time, the attorney general may intervene within 60 days after the notice is filed or after the court certifies the challenge, whichever is earlier. Before the time to intervene expires, the court may reject the constitutional challenge, but may not enter a final judgment holding the statute unconstitutional.

(d) No Forfeiture. A party's failure to file and serve the notice, or the court's failure to certify, does not forfeit a constitutional claim or defense that is otherwise timely asserted.

Rule 5.2. Privacy Protection For Filings Made with the Court

(a) Redacted Filings. Unless the court orders otherwise, in an electronic or paper filing with the court that contains an individual's social-security number, taxpayer-identification number, or birth date, the name of an individual known to be a minor, or a financial-account number, a party or nonparty making the filing may include only:

(1) the last four digits of the social-security number and taxpayer-identification number;

(2) the year of the individual's birth;

(3) the minor's initials; and

(4) the last four digits of the financial-account number.

(b) Exemptions from the Redaction Requirement. The redaction requirement does not apply to the following:

(1) a financial-account number that identifies the property allegedly subject to forfeiture in a forfeiture proceeding;

(2) the record of an administrative or agency proceeding;

(3) the official record of a state-court proceeding;

(4) the record of a court or tribunal, if that record was not subject to the redaction requirement when originally filed;

(5) a filing covered by Rule 5.2(c) or (d); and

(6) a pro se filing in an action brought under 28 U.S.C. §§ 2241, 2254, or 2255.

(c) Limitations on Remote Access to Electronic Files; Social-Security Appeals and Immigration Cases. Unless the court orders otherwise, in an action for benefits under the Social Security Act, and in an action or proceeding relating to an order of removal, to relief from removal, or to immigration benefits or detention, access to an electronic file is authorized as follows:

(1) the parties and their attorneys may have remote electronic access to any part of the case file, including the administrative record;

(2) any other person may have electronic access to the full record at the courthouse, but may have remote electronic access only to:

(A) the docket maintained by the court; and

(B) an opinion, order, judgment, or other disposition of the court, but not any other part of the case file or the administrative record.

(d) Filings Made Under Seal. The court may order that a filing be made under seal without redaction. The court may later unseal the filing or order the person who made the filing to file a redacted version for the public record.

(e) Protective Orders. For good cause, the court may by order in a case:

(1) require redaction of additional information; or

(2) limit or prohibit a nonparty's remote electronic access to a document filed with the court.

(f) Option for Additional Unredacted Filing Under Seal. A person making a redacted filing may also file an unredacted copy under seal. The court must retain the unredacted copy as part of the record.

(g) Option for Filing a Reference List. A filing that contains redacted information may be filed together with a reference list that identifies each item of redacted information and specifies an appropriate identifier that uniquely corresponds to each item listed. The list must be filed under seal and may be amended as of right. Any reference in the case to a listed identifier will be construed to refer to the corresponding item of information.

(h) Waiver of Protection of Identifiers. A person waives the protection of Rule 5.2(a) as to the person's own information by filing it without redaction and not under seal.

Rule 6. Computing and Extending Time; Time for Motion Papers

(a) Computing Time. The following rules apply in computing any time period specified in these rules or in any local rule, court order, or statute:

(1) ***Day of the Event Excluded.*** Exclude the day of the act, event, or default that begins the period.

(2) ***Exclusions from Brief Periods.*** Exclude intermediate Saturdays, Sundays, and legal holidays when the period is less than 11 days.

(3) ***Last Day.*** Include the last day of the period unless it is a Saturday, Sunday, legal holiday, or — if the act to be done is filing a paper in court — a day on which weather or other conditions make the clerk's office inaccessible. When the last day is excluded, the period runs until the end of the next day that is not a Saturday, Sunday, legal holiday, or day when the clerk's office is inaccessible.

(4) ***"Legal Holiday" Defined.*** As used in these rules, "legal holiday" means:

(A) the day set aside by statute for observing New Year's Day, Martin Luther King Jr.'s Birthday, Washington's Birthday, Memorial Day, Independence Day, Labor Day, Columbus Day, Veterans' Day, Thanksgiving Day, or Christmas Day; and

(B) any other day declared a holiday by the President, Congress, or the state where the district court is located.

(b) Extending Time.

(1) ***In General.*** When an act may or must be done within a specified time, the court may, for good cause, extend the time:

(A) with or without motion or notice if the court acts, or if a request is made, before the original time or its extension expires; or

(B) on motion made after the time has expired if the party failed to act because of excusable neglect.

(2) ***Exceptions.*** A court must not extend the time to act under Rules 50(b) and (d), 52(b), 59(b), (d), and (e), and 60(b), except as those rules allow.

(c) Motions, Notices of Hearing, and Affidavits.

(1) ***In General.*** A written motion and notice of the hearing must be served at least 5 days before the time specified for the hearing, with the following exceptions:

(A) when the motion may be heard ex parte;

(B) when these rules set a different time; or

(C) when a court order — which a party may, for good cause, apply for ex parte — sets a different time.

(2) ***Supporting Affidavit.*** Any affidavit supporting a motion must be served with the motion. Except as Rule 59(c) provides otherwise, any opposing affidavit must be served at least 1 day before the hearing, unless the court permits service at another time.

(d) Additional Time After Certain Kinds of Service. When a party may or must act within a specified time after service and service is made under Rule 5(b)(2)(C), (D), (E), or (F), 3 days are added after the period would otherwise expire under Rule 6(a).

TITLE III. PLEADINGS AND MOTIONS

Rule 7. Pleadings Allowed; Form of Motions and Other Papers

(a) Pleadings. Only these pleadings are allowed:

(1) a complaint;

(2) an answer to a complaint;

(3) an answer to a counterclaim designated as a counterclaim;

(4) an answer to a crossclaim;

(5) a third-party complaint;

(6) an answer to a third-party complaint; and

(7) if the court orders one, a reply to an answer.

(b) Motions and Other Papers.

(1) ***In General.*** A request for a court order must be made by motion. The motion must:

(A) be in writing unless made during a hearing or trial;

(B) state with particularity the grounds for seeking the order; and

(C) state the relief sought.

(2) ***Form.*** The rules governing captions and other matters of form in pleadings apply to motions and other papers.

Rule 7.1. Disclosure Statement

(a) Who Must File; Contents. A nongovernmental corporate party must file two copies of a disclosure statement that:

(1) identifies any parent corporation and any publicly held corporation owning 10% or more of its stock; or

(2) states that there is no such corporation.

(b) Time to File; Supplemental Filing. A party must:

(1) file the disclosure statement with its first appearance, pleading, petition, motion, response, or other request addressed to the court; and

(2) promptly file a supplemental statement if any required information changes.

Rule 8. General Rules of Pleading

(a) Claim for Relief. A pleading that states a claim for relief must contain:

(1) a short and plain statement of the grounds for the court's jurisdiction, unless the court already has jurisdiction and the claim needs no new jurisdictional support;

(2) a short and plain statement of the claim showing that the pleader is entitled to relief; and

(3) a demand for the relief sought, which may include relief in the alternative or different types of relief.

(b) Defenses; Admissions and Denials.

(1) ***In General.*** In responding to a pleading, a party must:

(A) state in short and plain terms its defenses to each claim asserted against it; and

(B) admit or deny the allegations asserted against it by an opposing party.

(2) ***Denials — Responding to the Substance.*** A denial must fairly respond to the substance of the allegation.

(3) ***General and Specific Denials.*** A party that intends in good faith to deny all the allegations of a pleading — including the jurisdictional grounds — may do so by a general denial. A party that does not intend to deny all the allegations must either specifically deny designated allegations or generally deny all except those specifically admitted.

(4) ***Denying Part of an Allegation.*** A party that intends in good faith to deny only part of an allegation must admit the part that is true and deny the rest.

(5) ***Lacking Knowledge or Information.*** A party that lacks knowledge or information sufficient to form a belief about the truth of an allegation must so state, and the statement has the effect of a denial.

(6) ***Effect of Failing to Deny.*** An allegation — other than one relating to the amount of damages — is admitted if a responsive pleading is required and the allegation is not denied. If a responsive pleading is not required, an allegation is considered denied or avoided.

(c) Affirmative Defenses.

(1) ***In General.*** In responding to a pleading, a party must affirmatively state any avoidance or affirmative defense, including:

- accord and satisfaction;
- arbitration and award;
- assumption of risk;
- contributory negligence;
- discharge in bankruptcy;
- duress;
- estoppel;
- failure of consideration;
- fraud;
- illegality;
- injury by fellow servant;
- laches;
- license;
- payment;
- release;
- res judicata;
- statute of frauds;
- statute of limitations; and
- waiver.

(2) ***Mistaken Designation.*** If a party mistakenly designates a defense as a counterclaim, or a counterclaim as a defense, the court must, if justice requires, treat the pleading as though it were correctly designated, and may impose terms for doing so.

(d) Pleading to Be Concise and Direct; Alternative Statements; Inconsistency.

(1) ***In General.*** Each allegation must be simple, concise, and direct. No technical form is required.

(2) ***Alternative Statements of a Claim or Defense.*** A party may set out two or more statements of a claim or defense alternatively or hypothetically, either in a single count or defense or in separate ones. If a party makes alternative statements, the pleading is sufficient if any one of them is sufficient.

(3) ***Inconsistent Claims or Defenses.*** A party may state as many separate claims or defenses as it has, regardless of consistency.

(e) Construing Pleadings. Pleadings must be construed so as to do justice.

Rule 9. Pleading Special Matters

(a) Capacity or Authority to Sue; Legal Existence.

(1) ***In General.*** Except when required to show that the court has jurisdiction, a pleading need not allege:

(A) a party's capacity to sue or be sued;

(B) a party's authority to sue or be sued in a representative capacity; or

(C) the legal existence of an organized association of persons that is made a party.

(2) ***Raising Those Issues.*** To raise any of those issues, a party must do so by a specific denial, which must state any supporting facts that are peculiarly within the party's knowledge.

(b) Fraud or Mistake; Conditions of Mind. In alleging fraud or mistake, a party must state with particularity the circumstances constituting fraud or mistake. Malice, intent, knowledge, and other conditions of a person's mind may be alleged generally.

(c) Conditions Precedent. In pleading conditions precedent, it suffices to allege generally that all conditions precedent have occurred or been performed. But when denying that a condition precedent has occurred or been performed, a party must do so with particularity.

(d) Official Document or Act. In pleading an official document or official act, it suffices to allege that the document was legally issued or the act legally done.

(e) Judgment. In pleading a judgment or decision of a domestic or foreign court, a judicial or quasi-judicial tribunal, or a board or officer, it suffices to plead the judgment or decision without showing jurisdiction to render it.

(f) Time and Place. An allegation of time or place is material when testing the sufficiency of a pleading.

(g) Special Damages. If an item of special damage is claimed, it must be specifically stated.

(h) Admiralty or Maritime Claim.

(1) ***How Designated.*** If a claim for relief is within the admiralty or maritime jurisdiction and also within the court's subject-matter jurisdiction on some other ground, the pleading may designate the claim as an admiralty or maritime claim for purposes of Rules 14(c), 38(e), and 82 and the Supplemental Rules for Admiralty or Maritime Claims and Asset Forfeiture Actions. A claim cognizable only in the admiralty or maritime jurisdiction is an admiralty or maritime claim for those purposes, whether or not so designated.

(2) ***Designation for Appeal.*** A case that includes an admiralty or maritime claim within this subdivision (h) is an admiralty case within 28 U.S.C. § 1292(a)(3).

Rule 10. Form of Pleadings

(a) Caption; Names of Parties. Every pleading must have a caption with the court's name, a title, a file number, and a Rule 7(a) designation. The title of the complaint must name all the parties; the title of other pleadings, after naming the first party on each side, may refer generally to other parties.

(b) Paragraphs; Separate Statements. A party must state its claims or defenses in numbered paragraphs, each limited as far as practicable to a single set of circumstances. A later pleading may refer by number to a paragraph in an earlier pleading. If doing so would promote clarity, each claim founded on a separate transaction or occurrence — and each defense other than a denial — must be stated in a separate count or defense.

(c) Adoption by Reference; Exhibits. A statement in a pleading may be adopted by reference elsewhere in the same pleading or in any other pleading or motion. A copy of a written instrument that is an exhibit to a pleading is a part of the pleading for all purposes.

Rule 11. Signing Pleadings, Motions, and Other Papers; Representations to the Court; Sanctions

(a) Signature. Every pleading, written motion, and other paper must be signed by at least one attorney of record in the attorney's name — or by a party personally if the party is unrepresented. The paper must state the signer's address, e-mail address, and telephone number. Unless a rule or statute specifically states otherwise, a pleading need not be verified or accompanied by an affidavit. The court must strike an unsigned paper unless the omission is promptly corrected after being called to the attorney's or party's attention.

(b) Representations to the Court. By presenting to the court a pleading, written motion, or other paper — whether by signing, filing, submitting, or later advocating it — an attorney or unrepresented party certifies that to the best of the person's knowledge, information, and belief, formed after an inquiry reasonable under the circumstances:

(1) it is not being presented for any improper purpose, such as to harass, cause unnecessary delay, or needlessly increase the cost of litigation;

(2) the claims, defenses, and other legal contentions are warranted by existing law or by a nonfrivolous argument for extending, modifying, or reversing existing law or for establishing new law;

(3) the factual contentions have evidentiary support or, if specifically so identified, will likely have evidentiary support after a reasonable opportunity for further investigation or discovery; and

(4) the denials of factual contentions are warranted on the evidence or, if specifically so identified, are reasonably based on belief or a lack of information.

(c) Sanctions.

(1) ***In General.*** If, after notice and a reasonable opportunity to respond, the court determines that Rule 11(b) has been violated, the court may impose an appropriate sanction on any attorney, law firm, or party that violated the rule or is responsible for the violation. Absent exceptional circumstances, a law firm must be held jointly responsible for a violation committed by its partner, associate, or employee.

(2) ***Motion for Sanctions.*** A motion for sanctions must be made separately from any other motion and must describe the specific conduct that allegedly violates Rule 11(b). The motion must be served under Rule 5, but it must not be filed or be presented to the court if the challenged paper, claim, defense, contention, or denial is withdrawn or appropriately corrected within 21 days after service or within another time the court sets. If warranted, the court may award to the prevailing party the reasonable expenses, including attorney's fees, incurred for the motion.

(3) ***On the Court's Initiative.*** On its own, the court may order an attorney, law firm, or party to show cause why conduct specifically described in the order has not violated Rule 11(b).

(4) ***Nature of a Sanction.*** A sanction imposed under this rule must be limited to what suffices to deter repetition of the conduct or comparable conduct by others similarly situated. The sanction may include nonmonetary directives; an order to pay a penalty into court; or, if imposed on motion and warranted for effective deterrence, an order directing payment to the movant of part or all of the reasonable attorney's fees and other expenses directly resulting from the violation.

(5) ***Limitations on Monetary Sanctions.*** The court must not impose a monetary sanction:

(A) against a represented party for violating Rule 11(b)(2); or

(B) on its own, unless it issued the show-cause order under Rule 11(c)(3) before voluntary dismissal or settlement of the claims made by or against the party that is, or whose attorneys are, to be sanctioned.

(6) ***Requirements for an Order.*** An order imposing a sanction must describe the sanctioned conduct and explain the basis for the sanction.

(d) Inapplicability to Discovery. This rule does not apply to disclosures and discovery requests, responses, objections, and motions under Rules 26 through 37.

Rule 12. Defenses and Objections: When and How Presented; Motion for Judgment on the Pleadings; Consolidating Motions; Waiving Defenses; Pretrial Hearing

(a) Time to Serve a Responsive Pleading.

(1) ***In General.*** Unless another time is specified by this rule or a federal statute, the time for serving a responsive pleading is as follows:

(A) A defendant must serve an answer:

(i) within 20 days after being served with the summons and complaint; or

(ii) if it has timely waived service under Rule 4(d), within 60 days after the request for a waiver was sent, or within 90 days after it was sent to the defendant outside any judicial district of the United States.

(B) A party must serve an answer to a counterclaim or crossclaim within 20 days after being served with the pleading that states the counterclaim or crossclaim.

(C) A party must serve a reply to an answer within 20 days after being served with an order to reply, unless the order specifies a different time.

(2) ***United States and Its Agencies, Officers, or Employees Sued in an Official Capacity.*** The United States, a United States agency, or a United States officer or employee sued only in an official capacity must serve an answer to a complaint, counterclaim, or crossclaim within 60 days after service on the United States attorney.

(3) ***United States Officers or Employees Sued in an Individual Capacity.*** A United States officer or employee sued in an individual capacity for an act or omission occurring in connection with duties performed on the United States' behalf must serve an answer to a complaint, counterclaim, or crossclaim within 60 days after service on the officer or employee or service on the United States attorney, whichever is later.

(4) ***Effect of a Motion.*** Unless the court sets a different time, serving a motion under this rule alters these periods as follows:

(A) if the court denies the motion or postpones its disposition until trial, the responsive pleading must be served within 10 days after notice of the court's action; or

(B) if the court grants a motion for a more definite statement, the responsive pleading must be served within 10 days after the more definite statement is served.

(b) How to Present Defenses. Every defense to a claim for relief in any pleading must be asserted in the responsive pleading if one is required. But a party may assert the following defenses by motion:

(1) lack of subject-matter jurisdiction;

(2) lack of personal jurisdiction;

(3) improper venue;

(4) insufficient process;

(5) insufficient service of process;

(6) failure to state a claim upon which relief can be granted; and

(7) failure to join a party under Rule 19.

A motion asserting any of these defenses must be made before pleading if a responsive pleading is allowed. If a pleading sets out a claim for relief that does not require a responsive pleading, an opposing party may assert at trial any defense to that claim. No defense or objection is waived by joining it with one or more other defenses or objections in a responsive pleading or in a motion.

(c) Motion for Judgment on the Pleadings. After the pleadings are closed — but early enough not to delay trial — a party may move for judgment on the pleadings.

(d) Result of Presenting Matters Outside the Pleadings. If, on a motion under Rule 12(b)(6) or 12(c), matters outside the pleadings are presented to and not excluded by the court, the motion must be treated as one for summary judgment under Rule 56. All parties must be given a reasonable opportunity to present all the material that is pertinent to the motion.

(e) Motion for a More Definite Statement. A party may move for a more definite statement of a pleading to which a responsive pleading is allowed but which is so vague or ambiguous that the party cannot reasonably prepare a response. The motion must be made before filing a responsive pleading and must point out the defects complained of and the details desired. If the court orders a more definite statement and the order is not obeyed within 10 days after notice of the order or within the time the court sets, the court may strike the pleading or issue any other appropriate order.

(f) Motion to Strike. The court may strike from a pleading an insufficient defense or any redundant, immaterial, impertinent, or scandalous matter. The court may act:

(1) on its own; or

(2) on motion made by a party either before responding to the pleading or, if a response is not allowed, within 20 days after being served with the pleading.

(g) Joining Motions.

(1) ***Right to Join.*** A motion under this rule may be joined with any other motion allowed by this rule.

(2) ***Limitation on Further Motions.*** Except as provided in Rule 12(h)(2) or (3), a party that makes a motion under this rule must not make another motion under this rule raising a defense or objection that was available to the party but omitted from its earlier motion.

(h) Waiving and Preserving Certain Defenses.

(1) ***When Some Are Waived.*** A party waives any defense listed in Rule 12(b)(2)-(5) by:

(A) omitting it from a motion in the circumstances described in Rule 12(g)(2); or

(B) failing to either:

(i) make it by motion under this rule; or

(ii) include it in a responsive pleading or in an amendment allowed by Rule 15(a)(1) as a matter of course.

(2) ***When to Raise Others.*** Failure to state a claim upon which relief can be granted, to join a person required by Rule 19(b), or to state a legal defense to a claim may be raised:

(A) in any pleading allowed or ordered under Rule 7(a);

(B) by a motion under Rule 12(c); or

(C) at trial.

(3) ***Lack of Subject-Matter Jurisdiction.*** If the court determines at any time that it lacks subject-matter jurisdiction, the court must dismiss the action.

(i) Hearing Before Trial. If a party so moves, any defense listed in Rule 12(b)(1)-(7) — whether made in a pleading or by motion — and a motion under Rule 12(c) must be heard and decided before trial unless the court orders a deferral until trial.

Rule 13. Counterclaim and Crossclaim

(a) Compulsory Counterclaim.

(1) ***In General.*** A pleading must state as a counterclaim any claim that — at the time of its service — the pleader has against an opposing party if the claim:

(A) arises out of the transaction or occurrence that is the subject matter of the opposing party's claim; and

(B) does not require adding another party over whom the court cannot acquire jurisdiction.

(2) ***Exceptions.*** The pleader need not state the claim if:

(A) when the action was commenced, the claim was the subject of another pending action; or

(B) the opposing party sued on its claim by attachment or other process that did not establish personal jurisdiction over the pleader on that claim, and the pleader does not assert any counterclaim under this rule.

(b) Permissive Counterclaim. A pleading may state as a counterclaim against an opposing party any claim that is not compulsory.

(c) Relief Sought in a Counterclaim. A counterclaim need not diminish or defeat the recovery sought by the opposing party. It may request relief that exceeds in amount or differs in kind from the relief sought by the opposing party.

(d) Counterclaim Against the United States. These rules do not expand the right to assert a counterclaim — or to claim a credit — against the United States or a United States officer or agency.

(e) Counterclaim Maturing or Acquired After Pleading. The court may permit a party to file a supplemental pleading asserting a counterclaim that matured or was acquired by the party after serving an earlier pleading.

(f) Omitted Counterclaim. The court may permit a party to amend a pleading to add a counterclaim if it was omitted through oversight, inadvertence, or excusable neglect or if justice so requires.

(g) Crossclaim Against a Coparty. A pleading may state as a crossclaim any claim by one party against a coparty if the claim arises out of the transaction or occurrence that is the subject matter of the original action or of a counterclaim, or if the claim relates to any property that is the subject matter of the original action. The crossclaim may include a claim that the coparty is or may be liable to the crossclaimant for all or part of a claim asserted in the action against the crossclaimant.

(h) Joining Additional Parties. Rules 19 and 20 govern the addition of a person as a party to a counterclaim or crossclaim.

(i) Separate Trials; Separate Judgments. If the court orders separate trials under Rule 42(b), it may enter judgment on a counterclaim or crossclaim under Rule 54(b) when it has jurisdiction to do so, even if the opposing party's claims have been dismissed or otherwise resolved.

Rule 14. Third-Party Practice

(a) When a Defending Party May Bring in a Third Party.

(1) ***Timing of the Summons and Complaint.*** A defending party may, as third-party plaintiff, serve a summons and complaint on a nonparty who is or may be liable to it for all or part of the claim against it. But the third-party plaintiff must, by motion, obtain the court's leave if it files the third-party complaint more than 10 days after serving its original answer.

(2) ***Third-Party Defendant's Claims and Defenses.*** The person served with the summons and third-party complaint — the "third-party defendant":

(A) must assert any defense against the third-party plaintiff's claim under Rule 12;

(B) must assert any counterclaim against the third-party plaintiff under Rule 13(a), and may assert any counterclaim against the third-party plaintiff under Rule 13(b) or any crossclaim against another third-party defendant under Rule 13(g);

(C) may assert against the plaintiff any defense that the third-party plaintiff has to the plaintiff's claim; and

(D) may also assert against the plaintiff any claim arising out of the transaction or occurrence that is the subject matter of the plaintiff's claim against the third-party plaintiff.

(3) ***Plaintiff's Claims Against a Third-Party Defendant.*** The plaintiff may assert against the third-party defendant any claim arising out of the transaction or occurrence that is the subject matter of the plaintiff's claim against the third-party plaintiff. The third-party defendant must then assert any defense under Rule 12 and any counterclaim under Rule 13(a), and may assert any counterclaim under Rule 13(b) or any crossclaim under Rule 13(g).

(4) ***Motion to Strike, Sever, or Try Separately.*** Any party may move to strike the third-party claim, to sever it, or to try it separately.

(5) ***Third-Party Defendant's Claim Against a Nonparty.*** A third-party defendant may proceed under this rule against a nonparty who is or may be liable to the third-party defendant for all or part of any claim against it.

(6) ***Third-Party Complaint In Rem.*** If it is within the admiralty or maritime jurisdiction, a third-party complaint may be in rem. In that event, a reference in this rule to the "summons" includes the warrant of arrest, and a reference to the defendant or third-party plaintiff includes, when appropriate, a person who asserts a right under Supplemental Rule C(6)(a)(i) in the property arrested.

(b) When a Plaintiff May Bring in a Third Party. When a claim is asserted against a plaintiff, the plaintiff may bring in a third party if this rule would allow a defendant to do so.

(c) Admiralty or Maritime Claim.

(1) ***Scope of Impleader.*** If a plaintiff asserts an admiralty or maritime claim under Rule 9(h), the defendant or a person who asserts a right under Supplemental Rule C(6)(a)(i) may, as a third-party plaintiff, bring in a third-party defendant who may be wholly or partly liable — either to the plaintiff or to the third-party plaintiff — for remedy over, contribution, or otherwise on account of the same transaction, occurrence, or series of transactions or occurrences.

(2) ***Defending Against a Demand for Judgment for the Plaintiff.*** The third-party plaintiff may demand judgment in the plaintiff's favor against the third-party defendant. In that event, the third-party defendant must defend under Rule 12 against the plaintiff's claim as well as the third-party plaintiff's claim; and the action proceeds as if the plaintiff had sued both the third-party defendant and the third-party plaintiff.

Rule 15. Amended and Supplemental Pleadings

(a) Amendments Before Trial.

(1) ***Amending as a Matter of Course.*** A party may amend its pleading once as a matter of course:

(A) before being served with a responsive pleading; or

(B) within 20 days after serving the pleading if a responsive pleading is not allowed and the action is not yet on the trial calendar.

(2) ***Other Amendments.*** In all other cases, a party may amend its pleading only with the opposing party's written consent or the court's leave. The court should freely give leave when justice so requires.

(3) ***Time to Respond.*** Unless the court orders otherwise, any required response to an amended pleading must be made within the time remaining to respond to the original pleading or within 10 days after service of the amended pleading, whichever is later.

(b) Amendments During and After Trial.

(1) ***Based on an Objection at Trial.*** If, at trial, a party objects that evidence is not within the issues raised in the pleadings, the court may permit the pleadings to be amended. The court should freely permit an amendment when doing so will aid in presenting the merits and the objecting party fails to satisfy the court that the evidence would prejudice that party's action or defense on the merits. The court may grant a continuance to enable the objecting party to meet the evidence.

(2) ***For Issues Tried by Consent.*** When an issue not raised by the pleadings is tried by the parties' express or implied consent, it must be treated in all respects as if raised in the pleadings. A party may move — at any time, even after judgment — to amend the pleadings to conform them to the evidence and to raise an unpleaded issue. But failure to amend does not affect the result of the trial of that issue.

(c) Relation Back of Amendments.

(1) *When an Amendment Relates Back.* An amendment to a pleading relates back to the date of the original pleading when:

(A) the law that provides the applicable statute of limitations allows relation back;

(B) the amendment asserts a claim or defense that arose out of the conduct, transaction, or occurrence set out — or attempted to be set out — in the original pleading; or

(C) the amendment changes the party or the naming of the party against whom a claim is asserted, if Rule 15(c)(1)(B) is satisfied and if, within the period provided by Rule 4(m) for serving the summons and complaint, the party to be brought in by amendment:

(i) received such notice of the action that it will not be prejudiced in defending on the merits; and

(ii) knew or should have known that the action would have been brought against it, but for a mistake concerning the proper party's identity.

(2) *Notice to the United States.* When the United States or a United States officer or agency is added as a defendant by amendment, the notice requirements of Rule 15(c)(1)(C)(i) and (ii) are satisfied if, during the stated period, process was delivered or mailed to the United States attorney or the United States attorney's designee, to the Attorney General of the United States, or to the officer or agency.

(d) Supplemental Pleadings. On motion and reasonable notice, the court may, on just terms, permit a party to serve a supplemental pleading setting out any transaction, occurrence, or event that happened after the date of the pleading to be supplemented. The court may permit supplementation even though the original pleading is defective in stating a claim or defense. The court may order that the opposing party plead to the supplemental pleading within a specified time.

Rule 16. Pretrial Conferences; Scheduling; Management

(a) Purposes of a Pretrial Conference. In any action, the court may order the attorneys and any unrepresented parties to appear for one or more pretrial conferences for such purposes as:

(1) expediting disposition of the action;

(2) establishing early and continuing control so that the case will not be protracted because of lack of management;

(3) discouraging wasteful pretrial activities;

(4) improving the quality of the trial through more thorough preparation; and

(5) facilitating settlement.

(b) Scheduling.

(1) ***Scheduling Order.*** Except in categories of actions exempted by local rule, the district judge — or a magistrate judge when authorized by local rule — must issue a scheduling order:

(A) after receiving the parties' report under Rule 26(f); or

(B) after consulting with the parties' attorneys and any unrepresented parties at a scheduling conference or by telephone, mail, or other means.

(2) ***Time to Issue.*** The judge must issue the scheduling order as soon as practicable, but in any event within the earlier of 120 days after any defendant has been served with the complaint or 90 days after any defendant has appeared.

(3) ***Contents of the Order.***

(A) ***Required Contents.*** The scheduling order must limit the time to join other parties, amend the pleadings, complete discovery, and file motions.

(B) ***Permitted Contents.*** The scheduling order may:

(i) modify the timing of disclosures under Rules 26(a) and 26(e)(1);

(ii) modify the extent of discovery;

(iii) provide for disclosure or discovery of electronically stored information;

(iv) include any agreements the parties reach for asserting claims of privilege or of protection as trial-preparation material after information is produced;

(v) set dates for pretrial conferences and for trial; and

(vi) include other appropriate matters.

(4) ***Modifying a Schedule.*** A schedule may be modified only for good cause and with the judge's consent.

(c) Attendance and Matters for Consideration at a Pretrial Conference.

(1) ***Attendance.*** A represented party must authorize at least one of its attorneys to make stipulations and admissions about all matters that can reasonably be anticipated for discussion at a pretrial conference. If appropriate, the court may require that a party or its representative be present or reasonably available by other means to consider possible settlement.

(2) ***Matters for Consideration.*** At any pretrial conference, the court may consider and take appropriate action on the following matters:

(A) formulating and simplifying the issues, and eliminating frivolous claims or defenses;

(B) amending the pleadings if necessary or desirable;

(C) obtaining admissions and stipulations about facts and documents to avoid unnecessary proof, and ruling in advance on the admissibility of evidence;

(D) avoiding unnecessary proof and cumulative evidence, and limiting the use of testimony under Federal Rule of Evidence 702;

(E) determining the appropriateness and timing of summary adjudication under Rule 56;

(F) controlling and scheduling discovery, including orders affecting disclosures and discovery under Rule 26 and Rules 29 through 37;

(G) identifying witnesses and documents, scheduling the filing and exchange of any pretrial briefs, and setting dates for further conferences and for trial;

(H) referring matters to a magistrate judge or a master;

(I) settling the case and using special procedures to assist in resolving the dispute when authorized by statute or local rule;

(J) determining the form and content of the pretrial order;

(K) disposing of pending motions;

(L) adopting special procedures for managing potentially difficult or protracted actions that may involve complex issues, multiple parties, difficult legal questions, or unusual proof problems;

(M) ordering a separate trial under Rule 42(b) of a claim, counterclaim, crossclaim, third-party claim, or particular issue;

(N) ordering the presentation of evidence early in the trial on a manageable issue that might, on the evidence, be the basis for a judgment as a matter of law under Rule 50(a) or a judgment on partial findings under Rule 52(c);

(O) establishing a reasonable limit on the time allowed to present evidence; and

(P) facilitating in other ways the just, speedy, and inexpensive disposition of the action.

(d) Pretrial Orders. After any conference under this rule, the court should issue an order reciting the action taken. This order controls the course of the action unless the court modifies it.

(e) Final Pretrial Conference and Orders. The court may hold a final pretrial conference to formulate a trial plan, including a plan to facilitate the admission of evidence. The conference must be held as close to the start of trial as is reasonable, and must be attended by at least one attorney who will conduct the trial for each party and by any unrepresented party. The court may modify the order issued after a final pretrial conference only to prevent manifest injustice.

(f) Sanctions.

(1) *In General.* On motion or on its own, the court may issue any just orders, including those authorized by Rule 37(b)(2)(A)(ii)-(vii), if a party or its attorney:

(A) fails to appear at a scheduling or other pretrial conference;

(B) is substantially unprepared to participate — or does not participate in good faith — in the conference; or

(C) fails to obey a scheduling or other pretrial order.

(2) *Imposing Fees and Costs.* Instead of or in addition to any other sanction, the court must order the party, its attorney, or both to pay the reasonable expenses — including attorney's fees — incurred because of any noncompliance with this rule, unless the noncompliance was substantially justified or other circumstances make an award of expenses unjust.

TITLE IV. PARTIES

Rule 17. Plaintiff and Defendant; Capacity; Public Officers

(a) Real Party in Interest.

(1) *Designation in General.* An action must be prosecuted in the name of the real party in interest. The following may sue in their own names without joining the person for whose benefit the action is brought:

(A) an executor;

(B) an administrator;

(C) a guardian;

(D) a bailee;

(E) a trustee of an express trust;

(F) a party with whom or in whose name a contract has been made for another's benefit; and

(G) a party authorized by statute.

(2) ***Action in the Name of the United States for Another's Use or Benefit.*** When a federal statute so provides, an action for another's use or benefit must be brought in the name of the United States.

(3) ***Joinder of the Real Party in Interest.*** The court may not dismiss an action for failure to prosecute in the name of the real party in interest until, after an objection, a reasonable time has been allowed for the real party in interest to ratify, join, or be substituted into the action. After ratification, joinder, or substitution, the action proceeds as if it had been originally commenced by the real party in interest.

(b) Capacity to Sue or Be Sued. Capacity to sue or be sued is determined as follows:

(1) for an individual who is not acting in a representative capacity, by the law of the individual's domicile;

(2) for a corporation, by the law under which it was organized; and

(3) for all other parties, by the law of the state where the court is located, except that:

(A) a partnership or other unincorporated association with no such capacity under that state's law may sue or be sued in its common name to enforce a substantive right existing under the United States Constitution or laws; and

(B) 28 U.S.C. §§ 754 and 959(a) govern the capacity of a receiver appointed by a United States court to sue or be sued in a United States court.

(c) Minor or Incompetent Person.

(1) ***With a Representative.*** The following representatives may sue or defend on behalf of a minor or an incompetent person:

(A) a general guardian;

(B) a committee;

(C) a conservator; or

(D) a like fiduciary.

(2) ***Without a Representative.*** A minor or an incompetent person who does not have a duly appointed representative may sue by a next friend or by a guardian ad litem. The court must appoint a guardian ad litem — or issue another appropriate order — to protect a minor or incompetent person who is unrepresented in an action.

(d) Public Officer's Title and Name. A public officer who sues or is sued in an official capacity may be designated by official title rather than by name, but the court may order that the officer's name be added.

Rule 18. Joinder of Claims

(a) In General. A party asserting a claim, counterclaim, crossclaim, or third-party claim may join, as independent or alternative claims, as many claims as it has against an opposing party.

(b) Joinder of Contingent Claims. A party may join two claims even though one of them is contingent on the disposition of the other; but the court may grant relief only in accordance with the parties' relative substantive rights. In particular, a plaintiff may state a claim for money and a claim to set aside a conveyance that is fraudulent as to that plaintiff, without first obtaining a judgment for the money.

Rule 19. Required Joinder of Parties

(a) Persons Required to Be Joined if Feasible.

(1) *Required Party.* A person who is subject to service of process and whose joinder will not deprive the court of subject-matter jurisdiction must be joined as a party if:

(A) in that person's absence, the court cannot accord complete relief among existing parties; or

(B) that person claims an interest relating to the subject of the action and is so situated that disposing of the action in the person's absence may:

(i) as a practical matter impair or impede the person's ability to protect the interest; or

(ii) leave an existing party subject to a substantial risk of incurring double, multiple, or otherwise inconsistent obligations because of the interest.

(2) *Joinder by Court Order.* If a person has not been joined as required, the court must order that the person be made a party. A person who refuses to join as a plaintiff may be made either a defendant or, in a proper case, an involuntary plaintiff.

(3) ***Venue.*** If a joined party objects to venue and the joinder would make venue improper, the court must dismiss that party.

(b) When Joinder Is Not Feasible. If a person who is required to be joined if feasible cannot be joined, the court must determine whether, in equity and good conscience, the action should proceed among the existing parties or should be dismissed. The factors for the court to consider include:

(1) the extent to which a judgment rendered in the person's absence might prejudice that person or the existing parties;

(2) the extent to which any prejudice could be lessened or avoided by:

(A) protective provisions in the judgment;

(B) shaping the relief; or

(C) other measures;

(3) whether a judgment rendered in the person's absence would be adequate; and

(4) whether the plaintiff would have an adequate remedy if the action were dismissed for nonjoinder.

(c) Pleading the Reasons for Nonjoinder. When asserting a claim for relief, a party must state:

(1) the name, if known, of any person who is required to be joined if feasible but is not joined; and

(2) the reasons for not joining that person.

(d) Exception for Class Actions. This rule is subject to Rule 23.

Rule 20. Permissive Joinder of Parties

(a) Persons Who May Join or Be Joined.

(1) ***Plaintiffs.*** Persons may join in one action as plaintiffs if:

(A) they assert any right to relief jointly, severally, or in the alternative with respect to or arising out of the same transaction, occurrence, or series of transactions or occurrences; and

(B) any question of law or fact common to all plaintiffs will arise in the action.

(2) ***Defendants.*** Persons — as well as a vessel, cargo, or other property subject to admiralty process in rem — may be joined in one action as defendants if:

(A) any right to relief is asserted against them jointly, severally, or in the alternative with respect to or arising out of the same transaction, occurrence, or series of transactions or occurrences; and

(B) any question of law or fact common to all defendants will arise in the action.

(3) ***Extent of Relief.*** Neither a plaintiff nor a defendant need be interested in obtaining or defending against all the relief demanded. The court may grant judgment to one or more plaintiffs according to their rights, and against one or more defendants according to their liabilities.

(b) Protective Measures. The court may issue orders — including an order for separate trials — to protect a party against embarrassment, delay, expense, or other prejudice that arises from including a person against whom the party asserts no claim and who asserts no claim against the party.

Rule 21. Misjoinder and Nonjoinder of Parties

Misjoinder of parties is not a ground for dismissing an action. On motion or on its own, the court may at any time, on just terms, add or drop a party. The court may also sever any claim against a party.

Rule 22. Interpleader

(a) Grounds.

(1) ***By a Plaintiff.*** Persons with claims that may expose a plaintiff to double or multiple liability may be joined as defendants and required to interplead. Joinder for interpleader is proper even though:

(A) the claims of the several claimants, or the titles on which their claims depend, lack a common origin or are adverse and independent rather than identical; or

(B) the plaintiff denies liability in whole or in part to any or all of the claimants.

(2) ***By a Defendant.*** A defendant exposed to similar liability may seek interpleader through a crossclaim or counterclaim.

(b) Relation to Other Rules and Statutes. This rule supplements — and does not limit — the joinder of parties allowed by Rule 20. The remedy this rule provides is in addition to — and does not supersede or limit — the remedy provided by 28 U.S.C. §§ 1335, 1397, and 2361. An action under those statutes must be conducted under these rules.

Rule 23. Class Actions

(a) Prerequisites. One or more members of a class may sue or be sued as representative parties on behalf of all members only if:

(1) the class is so numerous that joinder of all members is impracticable;

(2) there are questions of law or fact common to the class;

(3) the claims or defenses of the representative parties are typical of the claims or defenses of the class; and

(4) the representative parties will fairly and adequately protect the interests of the class.

(b) Types of Class Actions. A class action may be maintained if Rule 23(a) is satisfied and if:

(1) prosecuting separate actions by or against individual class members would create a risk of:

(A) inconsistent or varying adjudications with respect to individual class members that would establish incompatible standards of conduct for the party opposing the class; or

(B) adjudications with respect to individual class members that, as a practical matter, would be dispositive of the interests of the other members not parties to the individual adjudications or would substantially impair or impede their ability to protect their interests;

(2) the party opposing the class has acted or refused to act on grounds that apply generally to the class, so that final injunctive relief or corresponding declaratory relief is appropriate respecting the class as a whole; or

(3) the court finds that the questions of law or fact common to class members predominate over any questions affecting only individual members, and that a class action is superior to other available methods for fairly and efficiently adjudicating the controversy. The matters pertinent to these findings include:

(A) the class members' interests in individually controlling the prosecution or defense of separate actions;

(B) the extent and nature of any litigation concerning the controversy already begun by or against class members;

(C) the desirability or undesirability of concentrating the litigation of the claims in the particular forum; and

(D) the likely difficulties in managing a class action.

(c) Certification Order; Notice to Class Members; Judgment; Issues Classes; Subclasses.

(1) *Certification Order.*

(A) *Time to Issue.* At an early practicable time after a person sues or is sued as a class representative, the court must determine by order whether to certify the action as a class action.

(B) *Defining the Class; Appointing Class Counsel.* An order that certifies a class action must define the class and the class claims, issues, or defenses, and must appoint class counsel under Rule 23(g).

(C) *Altering or Amending the Order.* An order that grants or denies class certification may be altered or amended before final judgment.

(2) *Notice.*

(A) *For (b)(1) or (b)(2) Classes.* For any class certified under Rule 23(b)(1) or (b)(2), the court may direct appropriate notice to the class.

(B) *For (b)(3) Classes.* For any class certified under Rule 23(b)(3), the court must direct to class members the best notice that is practicable under the circumstances, including individual notice to all members who can be identified through reasonable effort. The notice must clearly and concisely state in plain, easily understood language:

(i) the nature of the action;

(ii) the definition of the class certified;

(iii) the class claims, issues, or defenses;

(iv) that a class member may enter an appearance through an attorney if the member so desires;

(v) that the court will exclude from the class any member who requests exclusion;

(vi) the time and manner for requesting exclusion; and

(vii) the binding effect of a class judgment on members under Rule 23(c)(3).

(3) *Judgment.* Whether or not favorable to the class, the judgment in a class action must:

(A) for any class certified under Rule 23(b)(1) or (b)(2), include and describe those whom the court finds to be class members; and

(B) for any class certified under Rule 23(b)(3), include and specify or describe those to whom the Rule 23(c)(2) notice was directed, who have not requested exclusion, and whom the court finds to be class members.

(4) ***Particular Issues.*** When appropriate, an action may be brought or maintained as a class action with respect to particular issues.

(5) ***Subclasses.*** When appropriate, a class may be divided into subclasses that are each treated as a class under this rule.

(d) Conducting the Action.

(1) ***In General.*** In conducting an action under this rule, the court may issue orders that:

(A) determine the course of proceedings or prescribe measures to prevent undue repetition or complication in presenting evidence or argument;

(B) require — to protect class members and fairly conduct the action — giving appropriate notice to some or all class members of:

(i) any step in the action;

(ii) the proposed extent of the judgment; or

(iii) the members' opportunity to signify whether they consider the representation fair and adequate, to intervene and present claims or defenses, or to otherwise come into the action;

(C) impose conditions on the representative parties or on intervenors;

(D) require that the pleadings be amended to eliminate allegations about representation of absent persons and that the action proceed accordingly; or

(E) deal with similar procedural matters.

(2) ***Combining and Amending Orders.*** An order under Rule 23(d)(1) may be altered or amended from time to time and may be combined with an order under Rule 16.

(e) Settlement, Voluntary Dismissal, or Compromise. The claims, issues, or defenses of a certified class may be settled, voluntarily dismissed, or compromised only with the court's approval. The following procedures apply to a proposed settlement, voluntary dismissal, or compromise:

(1) The court must direct notice in a reasonable manner to all class members who would be bound by the proposal.

(2) If the proposal would bind class members, the court may approve it only after a hearing and on finding that it is fair, reasonable, and adequate.

(3) The parties seeking approval must file a statement identifying any agreement made in connection with the proposal.

(4) If the class action was previously certified under Rule 23(b)(3), the court may refuse to approve a settlement unless it affords a new opportunity to request exclusion to individual class members who had an earlier opportunity to request exclusion but did not do so.

(5) Any class member may object to the proposal if it requires court approval under this subdivision (e); the objection may be withdrawn only with the court's approval.

(f) Appeals. A court of appeals may permit an appeal from an order granting or denying class-action certification under this rule if a petition for permission to appeal is filed with the circuit clerk within 10 days after the order is entered. An appeal does not stay proceedings in the district court unless the district judge or the court of appeals so orders.

(g) Class Counsel.

(1) ***Appointing Class Counsel.*** Unless a statute provides otherwise, a court that certifies a class must appoint class counsel. In appointing class counsel, the court:

(A) must consider:

(i) the work counsel has done in identifying or investigating potential claims in the action;

(ii) counsel's experience in handling class actions, other complex litigation, and the types of claims asserted in the action;

(iii) counsel's knowledge of the applicable law; and

(iv) the resources that counsel will commit to representing the class;

(B) may consider any other matter pertinent to counsel's ability to fairly and adequately represent the interests of the class;

(C) may order potential class counsel to provide information on any subject pertinent to the appointment and to propose terms for attorney's fees and nontaxable costs;

(D) may include in the appointing order provisions about the award of attorney's fees or nontaxable costs under Rule 23(h); and

(E) may make further orders in connection with the appointment.

(2) ***Standard for Appointing Class Counsel.*** When one applicant seeks appointment as class counsel, the court may appoint that applicant only if the applicant is adequate under Rule 23(g)(1) and (4). If more than one adequate applicant seeks appointment, the court must appoint the applicant best able to represent the interests of the class.

(3) ***Interim Counsel.*** The court may designate interim counsel to act on behalf of a putative class before determining whether to certify the action as a class action.

(4) ***Duty of Class Counsel.*** Class counsel must fairly and adequately represent the interests of the class.

(h) Attorney's Fees and Nontaxable Costs. In a certified class action, the court may award reasonable attorney's fees and nontaxable costs that are authorized by law or by the parties' agreement. The following procedures apply:

(1) A claim for an award must be made by motion under Rule 54(d)(2), subject to the provisions of this subdivision (h), at a time the court sets. Notice of the motion must be served on all parties and, for motions by class counsel, directed to class members in a reasonable manner.

(2) A class member, or a party from whom payment is sought, may object to the motion.

(3) The court may hold a hearing and must find the facts and state its legal conclusions under Rule 52(a).

(4) The court may refer issues related to the amount of the award to a special master or a magistrate judge, as provided in Rule 54(d)(2)(D).

Rule 23.1. Derivative Actions

(a) Prerequisites. This rule applies when one or more shareholders or members of a corporation or an unincorporated association bring a derivative action to enforce a right that the corporation or association may properly assert but has failed to enforce. The derivative action may not be maintained if it appears that the plaintiff does not fairly and adequately represent the interests of shareholders or members who are similarly situated in enforcing the right of the corporation or association.

(b) Pleading Requirements. The complaint must be verified and must:

(1) allege that the plaintiff was a shareholder or member at the time of the transaction complained of, or that the plaintiff's share or membership later devolved on it by operation of law;

(2) allege that the action is not a collusive one to confer jurisdiction that the court would otherwise lack; and

(3) state with particularity:

(A) any effort by the plaintiff to obtain the desired action from the directors or comparable authority and, if necessary, from the shareholders or members; and

(B) the reasons for not obtaining the action or not making the effort.

(c) Settlement, Dismissal, and Compromise. A derivative action may be settled, voluntarily dismissed, or compromised only with the court's approval. Notice of a proposed settlement, voluntary dismissal, or compromise must be given to shareholders or members in the manner that the court orders.

Rule 23.2. Actions Relating to Unincorporated Associations

This rule applies to an action brought by or against the members of an unincorporated association as a class by naming certain members as representative parties. The action may be maintained only if it appears that those parties will fairly and adequately protect the interests of the association and its members. In conducting the action, the court may issue any appropriate orders corresponding with those in Rule 23(d), and the procedure for settlement, voluntary dismissal, or compromise must correspond with the procedure in Rule 23(e).

Rule 24. Intervention

(a) Intervention of Right. On timely motion, the court must permit anyone to intervene who:

(1) is given an unconditional right to intervene by a federal statute; or

(2) claims an interest relating to the property or transaction that is the subject of the action, and is so situated that disposing of the action may as a practical matter impair or impede the movant's ability to protect its interest, unless existing parties adequately represent that interest.

(b) Permissive Intervention.

(1) ***In General.*** On timely motion, the court may permit anyone to intervene who:

(A) is given a conditional right to intervene by a federal statute; or

(B) has a claim or defense that shares with the main action a common question of law or fact.

(2) ***By a Government Officer or Agency.*** On timely motion, the court may permit a federal or state governmental officer or agency to intervene if a party's claim or defense is based on:

(A) a statute or executive order administered by the officer or agency; or

(B) any regulation, order, requirement, or agreement issued or made under the statute or executive order.

(3) ***Delay or Prejudice.*** In exercising its discretion, the court must consider whether the intervention will unduly delay or prejudice the adjudication of the original parties' rights.

(c) Notice and Pleading Required. A motion to intervene must be served on the parties as provided in Rule 5. The motion must state the grounds for intervention and be accompanied by a pleading that sets out the claim or defense for which intervention is sought.

Rule 25. Substitution of Parties

(a) Death.

(1) ***Substitution if the Claim Is Not Extinguished.*** If a party dies and the claim is not extinguished, the court may order substitution of the proper party. A motion for substitution may be made by any party or by the decedent's successor or representative. If the motion is not made within 90 days after service of a statement noting the death, the action by or against the decedent must be dismissed.

(2) ***Continuation Among the Remaining Parties.*** After a party's death, if the right sought to be enforced survives only to or against the remaining parties, the action does not abate, but proceeds in favor of or against the remaining parties. The death should be noted on the record.

(3) ***Service.*** A motion to substitute, together with a notice of hearing, must be served on the parties as provided in Rule 5 and on nonparties as provided in Rule 4. A statement noting death must be served in the same manner. Service may be made in any judicial district.

(b) Incompetency. If a party becomes incompetent, the court may, on motion, permit the action to be continued by or against the party's representative. The motion must be served as provided in Rule 25(a)(3).

(c) Transfer of Interest. If an interest is transferred, the action may be continued by or against the original party unless the court, on motion, orders the transferee to be substituted in the action or joined with the original party. The motion must be served as provided in Rule 25(a)(3).

(d) Public Officers; Death or Separation from Office. An action does not abate when a public officer who is a party in an official capacity dies, resigns, or otherwise ceases to hold office while the action is pending. The officer's successor is automatically substituted as a party. Later proceedings should be in the substituted party's name, but any misnomer not affecting the parties' substantial rights must be disregarded. The court may order substitution at any time, but the absence of such an order does not affect the substitution.

TITLE V. DISCLOSURES AND DISCOVERY

Rule 26. Duty to Disclose; General Provisions Governing Discovery

(a) Required Disclosures.

(1) ***Initial Disclosure.***

(A) *In General.* Except as exempted by Rule 26(a)(1)(B) or as otherwise stipulated or ordered by the court, a party must, without awaiting a discovery request, provide to the other parties:

(i) the name and, if known, the address and telephone number of each individual likely to have discoverable information — along with the subjects of that information — that the disclosing party may use to support its claims or defenses, unless the use would be solely for impeachment;

(ii) a copy — or a description by category and location — of all documents, electronically stored information, and tangible things that the disclosing party has in its possession, custody, or control and may use to support its claims or defenses, unless the use would be solely for impeachment;

(iii) a computation of each category of damages claimed by the disclosing party — who must also make available for inspection and copying as under Rule 34 the documents or other evidentiary material, unless privileged or protected from disclosure, on which each computation is based, including materials bearing on the nature and extent of injuries suffered; and

(iv) for inspection and copying as under Rule 34, any insurance agreement under which an insurance business may be liable to satisfy all or part of a possible judgment in the action or to indemnify or reimburse for payments made to satisfy the judgment.

(B) *Proceedings Exempt from Initial Disclosure.* The following proceedings are exempt from initial disclosure:

(i) an action for review on an administrative record;

(ii) a petition for habeas corpus or any other proceeding to challenge a criminal conviction or sentence;

(iii) an action brought without an attorney by a person in the custody of the United States, a state, or a state subdivision;

(iv) an action to enforce or quash an administrative summons or subpoena;

(v) an action by the United States to recover benefit payments;

(vi) an action by the United States to collect on a student loan guaranteed by the United States;

(vii) a proceeding ancillary to a proceeding in another court; and

(viii) an action to enforce an arbitration award.

(C) *Time for Initial Disclosures — In General.* A party must make the initial disclosures at or within 14 days after the parties' Rule 26(f) conference unless a different time is set by stipulation or court order, or unless a party objects during the conference that initial disclosures are not appropriate in this action and states the objection in the proposed discovery plan. In ruling on the objection, the court must determine what disclosures, if any, are to be made and must set the time for disclosure.

(D) *Time for Initial Disclosures — For Parties Served or Joined Later.* A party that is first served or otherwise joined after the Rule 26(f) conference must make the initial disclosures within 30 days after being served or joined, unless a different time is set by stipulation or court order.

(E) *Basis for Initial Disclosure; Unacceptable Excuses.* A party must make its initial disclosures based on the information then reasonably available to it. A party is not excused from making its disclosures because it has not fully investigated the case or because it challenges the sufficiency of another party's disclosures or because another party has not made its disclosures.

(2) *Disclosure of Expert Testimony.*

(A) *In General.* In addition to the disclosures required by Rule 26(a)(1), a party must disclose to the other parties the identity of any witness it may use at trial to present evidence under Federal Rule of Evidence 702, 703, or 705.

(B) *Written Report.* Unless otherwise stipulated or ordered by the court, this disclosure must be accompanied by a written report — prepared and signed by the witness — if the witness is one retained or specially employed to provide expert testimony in the case or one whose duties as the party's employee regularly involve giving expert testimony. The report must contain:

(i) a complete statement of all opinions the witness will express and the basis and reasons for them;

(ii) the data or other information considered by the witness in forming them;

(iii) any exhibits that will be used to summarize or support them;

(iv) the witness's qualifications, including a list of all publications authored in the previous ten years;

(v) a list of all other cases in which, during the previous four years, the witness testified as an expert at trial or by deposition; and

(vi) a statement of the compensation to be paid for the study and testimony in the case.

(C) *Time to Disclose Expert Testimony.* A party must make these disclosures at the times and in the sequence that the court orders. Absent a stipulation or a court order, the disclosures must be made:

(i) at least 90 days before the date set for trial or for the case to be ready for trial; or

(ii) if the evidence is intended solely to contradict or rebut evidence on the same subject matter identified by another party under Rule 26(a)(2)(B), within 30 days after the other party's disclosure.

(D) *Supplementing the Disclosure.* The parties must supplement these disclosures when required under Rule 26(e).

(3) ***Pretrial Disclosures.***

(A) *In General.* In addition to the disclosures required by Rule 26(a)(1) and (2), a party must provide to the other parties and promptly file the following information about the evidence that it may present at trial other than solely for impeachment:

(i) the name and, if not previously provided, the address and telephone number of each witness — separately identifying those the party expects to present and those it may call if the need arises;

(ii) the designation of those witnesses whose testimony the party expects to present by deposition and, if not taken stenographically, a transcript of the pertinent parts of the deposition; and

(iii) an identification of each document or other exhibit, including summaries of other evidence — separately identifying those items the party expects to offer and those it may offer if the need arises.

(B) *Time for Pretrial Disclosures; Objections.* Unless the court orders otherwise, these disclosures must be made at least 30 days before trial. Within 14 days after they are made, unless the court sets a different time, a party may serve and promptly file a list of the following objections: any objections to the use under Rule 32(a) of a deposition designated by another party under Rule 26(a)(3)(A)(ii); and any objection, together with the grounds for it, that may be made to the admissibility of materials identified under Rule 26(a)(3)(A)(iii). An objection not so made — except for one under Federal Rule of Evidence 402 or 403 — is waived unless excused by the court for good cause.

(4) ***Form of Disclosures.*** Unless the court orders otherwise, all disclosures under Rule 26(a) must be in writing, signed, and served.

(b) Discovery Scope and Limits.

(1) ***Scope in General.*** Unless otherwise limited by court order, the scope of discovery is as follows: Parties may obtain discovery regarding any nonprivileged matter that is relevant to any party's claim or defense — including the existence, description, nature, custody, condition, and location of any documents or other tangible things and the identity and location of persons who know of any discoverable matter. For good cause, the court may order discovery of any matter relevant to the subject matter involved in the action. Relevant information need not be admissible at the trial if the discovery appears reasonably calculated to lead to the discovery of admissible evidence. All discovery is subject to the limitations imposed by Rule 26(b)(2)(C).

(2) ***Limitations on Frequency and Extent.***

(A) *When Permitted.* By order, the court may alter the limits in these rules on the number of depositions and interrogatories or on the length of depositions under Rule 30. By order or local rule, the court may also limit the number of requests under Rule 36.

(B) *Specific Limitations on Electronically Stored Information.* A party need not provide discovery of electronically stored information from sources that the party identifies as not reasonably accessible because of undue burden or cost. On motion to compel discovery or for a protective order, the party from whom discovery is sought must show that the information is not reasonably accessible because of undue burden or cost. If that showing is made, the court may nonetheless order discovery from such sources if the requesting party shows good cause, considering the limitations of Rule 26(b)(2)(C). The court may specify conditions for the discovery.

(C) *When Required.* On motion or on its own, the court must limit the frequency or extent of discovery otherwise allowed by these rules or by local rule if it determines that:

(i) the discovery sought is unreasonably cumulative or duplicative, or can be obtained from some other source that is more convenient, less burdensome, or less expensive;

(ii) the party seeking discovery has had ample opportunity to obtain the information by discovery in the action; or

(iii) the burden or expense of the proposed discovery outweighs its likely benefit, considering the needs of the case, the amount in controversy, the parties' resources, the importance of the issues at stake in the action, and the importance of the discovery in resolving the issues.

(3) *Trial Preparation: Materials.*

(A) *Documents and Tangible Things.* Ordinarily, a party may not discover documents and tangible things that are prepared in anticipation of litigation or for trial by or for another party or its representative (including the other party's attorney, consultant, surety, indemnitor, insurer, or agent). But, subject to Rule 26(b)(4), those materials may be discovered if:

(i) they are otherwise discoverable under Rule 26(b)(1); and

(ii) the party shows that it has substantial need for the materials to prepare its case and cannot, without undue hardship, obtain their substantial equivalent by other means.

(B) *Protection Against Disclosure.* If the court orders discovery of those materials, it must protect against disclosure of the mental impressions, conclusions, opinions, or legal theories of a party's attorney or other representative concerning the litigation.

(C) *Previous Statement.* Any party or other person may, on request and without the required showing, obtain the person's own previous statement about the action or its subject matter. If the request is refused, the person may move for a court order, and Rule 37(a)(5) applies to the award of expenses. A previous statement is either:

(i) a written statement that the person has signed or otherwise adopted or approved; or

(ii) a contemporaneous stenographic, mechanical, electrical, or other recording — or a transcription of it — that recites substantially verbatim the person's oral statement.

(4) *Trial Preparation: Experts.*

(A) *Expert Who May Testify.* A party may depose any person who has been identified as an expert whose opinions may be presented at trial. If Rule 26(a)(2)(B) requires a report from the expert, the deposition may be conducted only after the report is provided.

(B) *Expert Employed Only for Trial Preparation.* Ordinarily, a party may not, by interrogatories or deposition, discover facts known or opinions held by an expert who has been retained or specially employed by another party in anticipation of litigation or to prepare for trial and who is not expected to be called as a witness at trial. But a party may do so only:

(i) as provided in Rule 35(b); or

(ii) on showing exceptional circumstances under which it is impracticable for the party to obtain facts or opinions on the same subject by other means.

(C) *Payment.* Unless manifest injustice would result, the court must require that the party seeking discovery:

(i) pay the expert a reasonable fee for time spent in responding to discovery under Rule 26(b)(4)(A) or (B); and

(ii) for discovery under (B), also pay the other party a fair portion of the fees and expenses it reasonably incurred in obtaining the expert's facts and opinions.

(5) ***Claiming Privilege or Protecting Trial-Preparation Materials.***

(A) *Information Withheld.* When a party withholds information otherwise discoverable by claiming that the information is privileged or subject to protection as trial-preparation material, the party must:

(i) expressly make the claim; and

(ii) describe the nature of the documents, communications, or tangible things not produced or disclosed — and do so in a manner that, without revealing information itself privileged or protected, will enable other parties to assess the claim.

(B) *Information Produced.* If information produced in discovery is subject to a claim of privilege or of protection as trial-preparation material, the party making the claim may notify any party that received the information of the claim and the basis for it. After being notified, a party must promptly return, sequester, or destroy the specified information and any copies it has; must not use or disclose the information until the claim is resolved; must take reasonable steps to retrieve the information if the party disclosed it before being notified; and may promptly present the information to the court under seal for a determination of the claim. The producing party must preserve the information until the claim is resolved.

(c) Protective Orders.

(1) ***In General.*** A party or any person from whom discovery is sought may move for a protective order in the court where the action is pending — or as an alternative on matters relating to a deposition, in the court for the district where the deposition will be taken. The motion must include a certification that the movant has in good faith conferred or attempted to confer with other affected parties in an effort to resolve the dispute without court action. The court may, for good cause, issue an order to protect a party or person from annoyance, embarrassment, oppression, or undue burden or expense, including one or more of the following:

(A) forbidding the disclosure or discovery;

(B) specifying terms, including time and place, for the disclosure or discovery;

(C) prescribing a discovery method other than the one selected by the party seeking discovery;

(D) forbidding inquiry into certain matters, or limiting the scope of disclosure or discovery to certain matters;

(E) designating the persons who may be present while the discovery is conducted;

(F) requiring that a deposition be sealed and opened only on court order;

(G) requiring that a trade secret or other confidential research, development, or commercial information not be revealed or be revealed only in a specified way; and

(H) requiring that the parties simultaneously file specified documents or information in sealed envelopes, to be opened as the court directs.

(2) *Ordering Discovery.* If a motion for a protective order is wholly or partly denied, the court may, on just terms, order that any party or person provide or permit discovery.

(3) *Awarding Expenses.* Rule 37(a)(5) applies to the award of expenses.

(d) Timing and Sequence of Discovery.

(1) *Timing.* A party may not seek discovery from any source before the parties have conferred as required by Rule 26(f), except in a proceeding exempted from initial disclosure under Rule 26(a)(1)(B), or when authorized by these rules, by stipulation, or by court order.

(2) *Sequence.* Unless, on motion, the court orders otherwise for the parties' and witnesses' convenience and in the interests of justice:

(A) methods of discovery may be used in any sequence; and

(B) discovery by one party does not require any other party to delay its discovery.

(e) Supplementing Disclosures and Responses.

(1) ***In General.*** A party who has made a disclosure under Rule 26(a) — or who has responded to an interrogatory, request for production, or request for admission — must supplement or correct its disclosure or response:

(A) in a timely manner if the party learns that in some material respect the disclosure or response is incomplete or incorrect, and if the additional or corrective information has not otherwise been made known to the other parties during the discovery process or in writing; or

(B) as ordered by the court.

(2) ***Expert Witness.*** For an expert whose report must be disclosed under Rule 26(a)(2)(B), the party's duty to supplement extends both to information included in the report and to information given during the expert's deposition. Any additions or changes to this information must be disclosed by the time the party's pretrial disclosures under Rule 26(a)(3) are due.

(f) Conference of the Parties; Planning for Discovery.

(1) ***Conference Timing.*** Except in a proceeding exempted from initial disclosure under Rule 26(a)(1)(B) or when the court orders otherwise, the parties must confer as soon as practicable — and in any event at least 21 days before a scheduling conference is to be held or a scheduling order is due under Rule 16(b).

(2) ***Conference Content; Parties' Responsibilities.*** In conferring, the parties must consider the nature and basis of their claims and defenses and the possibilities for promptly settling or resolving the case; make or arrange for the disclosures required by Rule 26(a)(1); discuss any issues about preserving discoverable information; and develop a proposed discovery plan. The attorneys of record and all unrepresented parties that have appeared in the case are jointly responsible for arranging the conference, for attempting in good faith to agree on the proposed discovery plan, and for submitting to the court within 14 days after the conference a written report outlining the plan. The court may order the parties or attorneys to attend the conference in person.

(3) ***Discovery Plan.*** A discovery plan must state the parties' views and proposals on:

(A) what changes should be made in the timing, form, or requirement for disclosures under Rule 26(a), including a statement of when initial disclosures were made or will be made;

(B) the subjects on which discovery may be needed, when discovery should be completed, and whether discovery should be conducted in phases or be limited to or focused on particular issues;

(C) any issues about disclosure or discovery of electronically stored information, including the form or forms in which it should be produced;

(D) any issues about claims of privilege or of protection as trial-preparation materials, including — if the parties agree on a procedure to assert these claims after production — whether to ask the court to include their agreement in an order;

(E) what changes should be made in the limitations on discovery imposed under these rules or by local rule, and what other limitations should be imposed; and

(F) any other orders that the court should issue under Rule 26(c) or under Rule 16(b) and (c).

(4) ***Expedited Schedule.*** If necessary to comply with its expedited schedule for Rule 16(b) conferences, a court may by local rule:

(A) require the parties' conference to occur less than 21 days before the scheduling conference is held or a scheduling order is due under Rule 16(b); and

(B) require the written report outlining the discovery plan to be filed less than 14 days after the parties' conference, or excuse the parties from submitting a written report and permit them to report orally on their discovery plan at the Rule 16(b) conference.

(g) Signing Disclosures and Discovery Requests, Responses, and Objections.

(1) ***Signature Required; Effect of Signature.*** Every disclosure under Rule 26(a)(1) or (a)(3) and every discovery request, response, or objection must be signed by at least one attorney of record in the attorney's own name — or by the party personally, if unrepresented — and must state the signer's address, e-mail address, and telephone number. By signing, an attorney or party certifies that to the best of the person's knowledge, information, and belief formed after a reasonable inquiry:

(A) with respect to a disclosure, it is complete and correct as of the time it is made; and

(B) with respect to a discovery request, response, or objection, it is:

(i) consistent with these rules and warranted by existing law or by a nonfrivolous argument for extending, modifying, or reversing existing law, or for establishing new law;

(ii) not interposed for any improper purpose, such as to harass, cause unnecessary delay, or needlessly increase the cost of litigation; and

(iii) neither unreasonable nor unduly burdensome or expensive, considering the needs of the case, prior discovery in the case, the amount in controversy, and the importance of the issues at stake in the action.

(2) ***Failure to Sign.*** Other parties have no duty to act on an unsigned disclosure, request, response, or objection until it is signed, and the court must strike it unless a signature is promptly supplied after the omission is called to the attorney's or party's attention.

(3) ***Sanction for Improper Certification.*** If a certification violates this rule without substantial justification, the court, on motion or on its own, must impose an appropriate sanction on the signer, the party on whose behalf the signer was acting, or both. The sanction may include an order to pay the reasonable expenses, including attorney's fees, caused by the violation.

Rule 27. Depositions to Perpetuate Testimony

(a) Before an Action Is Filed.

(1) ***Petition.*** A person who wants to perpetuate testimony about any matter cognizable in a United States court may file a verified petition in the district court for the district where any expected adverse party resides. The petition must ask for an order authorizing the petitioner to depose the named persons in order to perpetuate their testimony. The petition must be titled in the petitioner's name and must show:

(A) that the petitioner expects to be a party to an action cognizable in a United States court but cannot presently bring it or cause it to be brought;

(B) the subject matter of the expected action and the petitioner's interest;

(C) the facts that the petitioner wants to establish by the proposed testimony and the reasons to perpetuate it;

(D) the names or a description of the persons whom the petitioner expects to be adverse parties and their addresses, so far as known; and

(E) the name, address, and expected substance of the testimony of each deponent.

(2) ***Notice and Service.*** At least 20 days before the hearing date, the petitioner must serve each expected adverse party with a copy of the petition and a notice stating the time and place of the hearing. The notice may be served either inside or outside the district or state in the manner provided in Rule 4. If that service cannot be made with reasonable diligence on an expected adverse party, the court may order service by publication or otherwise. The court must appoint an attorney to represent persons not served in the manner provided in Rule 4 and to cross-examine the deponent if an unserved person is not otherwise represented. If any expected adverse party is a minor or is incompetent, Rule 17(c) applies.

(3) ***Order and Examination.*** If satisfied that perpetuating the testimony may prevent a failure or delay of justice, the court must issue an order that designates or describes the persons whose depositions may be taken, specifies the subject matter of the examinations, and states whether the depositions will be taken orally or by written interrogatories. The depositions may then be taken under these rules, and the court may issue orders like those authorized by Rules 34 and 35. A reference in these rules to the court where an action is pending means, for purposes of this rule, the court where the petition for the deposition was filed.

(4) ***Using the Deposition.*** A deposition to perpetuate testimony may be used under Rule 32(a) in any later-filed district-court action involving the same subject matter if the deposition either was taken under these rules or, although not so taken, would be admissible in evidence in the courts of the state where it was taken.

(b) Pending Appeal.

(1) ***In General.*** The court where a judgment has been rendered may, if an appeal has been taken or may still be taken, permit a party to depose witnesses to perpetuate their testimony for use in the event of further proceedings in that court.

(2) ***Motion.*** The party who wants to perpetuate testimony may move for leave to take the depositions, on the same notice and service as if the action were pending in the district court. The motion must show:

(A) the name, address, and expected substance of the testimony of each deponent; and

(B) the reasons for perpetuating the testimony.

(3) ***Court Order.*** If the court finds that perpetuating the testimony may prevent a failure or delay of justice, the court may permit the depositions to be taken and may issue orders like those authorized by Rules 34 and 35. The depositions may be taken and used as any other deposition taken in a pending district-court action.

(c) Perpetuation by an Action. This rule does not limit a court's power to entertain an action to perpetuate testimony.

Rule 28. Persons Before Whom Depositions May Be Taken

(a) Within the United States.

(1) ***In General.*** Within the United States or a territory or insular possession subject to United States jurisdiction, a deposition must be taken before:

(A) an officer authorized to administer oaths either by federal law or by the law in the place of examination; or

(B) a person appointed by the court where the action is pending to administer oaths and take testimony.

(2) ***Definition of "Officer."*** The term "officer" in Rules 30, 31, and 32 includes a person appointed by the court under this rule or designated by the parties under Rule 29(a).

(b) In a Foreign Country.

(1) ***In General.*** A deposition may be taken in a foreign country:

(A) under an applicable treaty or convention;

(B) under a letter of request, whether or not captioned a "letter rogatory";

(C) on notice, before a person authorized to administer oaths either by federal law or by the law in the place of examination; or

(D) before a person commissioned by the court to administer any necessary oath and take testimony.

(2) ***Issuing a Letter of Request or a Commission.*** A letter of request, a commission, or both may be issued:

(A) on appropriate terms after an application and notice of it; and

(B) without a showing that taking the deposition in another manner is impracticable or inconvenient.

(3) ***Form of a Request, Notice, or Commission.*** When a letter of request or any other device is used according to a treaty or convention, it must be captioned in the form prescribed by that treaty or convention. A letter of request may be addressed "To the Appropriate Authority in [name of country]." A deposition notice or a commission must designate by name or descriptive title the person before whom the deposition is to be taken.

(4) ***Letter of Request — Admitting Evidence.*** Evidence obtained in response to a letter of request need not be excluded merely because it is not a verbatim transcript, because the testimony was not taken under oath, or because of any similar departure from the requirements for depositions taken within the United States.

(c) Disqualification. A deposition must not be taken before a person who is any party's relative, employee, or attorney; who is related to or employed by any party's attorney; or who is financially interested in the action.

Rule 29. Stipulations About Discovery Procedure

Unless the court orders otherwise, the parties may stipulate that:

(a) a deposition may be taken before any person, at any time or place, on any notice, and in the manner specified — in which event it may be used in the same way as any other deposition; and

(b) other procedures governing or limiting discovery be modified — but a stipulation extending the time for any form of discovery must have court approval if it would interfere with the time set for completing discovery, for hearing a motion, or for trial.

Rule 30. Depositions by Oral Examination

(a) When a Deposition May Be Taken.

(1) ***Without Leave.*** A party may, by oral questions, depose any person, including a party, without leave of court except as provided in Rule 30(a)(2). The deponent's attendance may be compelled by subpoena under Rule 45.

(2) ***With Leave.*** A party must obtain leave of court, and the court must grant leave to the extent consistent with Rule 26(b)(2):

(A) if the parties have not stipulated to the deposition and:

(i) the deposition would result in more than 10 depositions being taken under this rule or Rule 31 by the plaintiffs, or by the defendants, or by the third-party defendants;

(ii) the deponent has already been deposed in the case; or

(iii) the party seeks to take the deposition before the time specified in Rule 26(d), unless the party certifies in the notice, with supporting facts, that the deponent is expected to leave the United States and be unavailable for examination in this country after that time; or

(B) if the deponent is confined in prison.

(b) Notice of the Deposition; Other Formal Requirements.

(1) ***Notice in General.*** A party who wants to depose a person by oral questions must give reasonable written notice to every other party. The notice must state the time and place of the deposition and, if known, the deponent's name and address. If the name is unknown, the notice must provide a general description sufficient to identify the person or the particular class or group to which the person belongs.

(2) ***Producing Documents.*** If a subpoena duces tecum is to be served on the deponent, the materials designated for production, as set out in the subpoena, must be listed in the notice or in an attachment. The notice to a party deponent may be accompanied by a request under Rule 34 to produce documents and tangible things at the deposition.

(3) ***Method of Recording.***

(A) *Method Stated in the Notice.* The party who notices the deposition must state in the notice the method for recording the testimony. Unless the court orders otherwise, testimony may be recorded by audio, audiovisual, or stenographic means. The noticing party bears the recording costs. Any party may arrange to transcribe a deposition.

(B) *Additional Method.* With prior notice to the deponent and other parties, any party may designate another method for recording the testimony in addition to that specified in the original notice. That party bears the expense of the additional record or transcript unless the court orders otherwise.

(4) ***By Remote Means.*** The parties may stipulate — or the court may on motion order — that a deposition be taken by telephone or other remote means. For the purpose of this rule and Rules 28(a), 37(a)(2), and 37(b)(1), the deposition takes place where the deponent answers the questions.

(5) ***Officer's Duties.***

(A) *Before the Deposition.* Unless the parties stipulate otherwise, a deposition must be conducted before an officer appointed or designated under Rule 28. The officer must begin the deposition with an on-the-record statement that includes:

(i) the officer's name and business address;

(ii) the date, time, and place of the deposition;

(iii) the deponent's name;

(iv) the officer's administration of the oath or affirmation to the deponent; and

(v) the identity of all persons present.

(B) *Conducting the Deposition; Avoiding Distortion.* If the deposition is recorded nonstenographically, the officer must repeat the items in Rule 30(b)(5)(A)(i)-(iii) at the beginning of each unit of the recording medium. The deponent's and attorneys' appearance or demeanor must not be distorted through recording techniques.

(C) *After the Deposition.* At the end of a deposition, the officer must state on the record that the deposition is complete and must set out any stipulations made by the attorneys about custody of the transcript or recording and of the exhibits, or about any other pertinent matters.

(6) ***Notice or Subpoena Directed to an Organization.*** In its notice or subpoena, a party may name as the deponent a public or private corporation, a partnership, an association, a governmental agency, or other entity and must describe with reasonable particularity the matters for examination. The named organization must then designate one or more officers, directors, or managing agents, or designate other persons who consent to testify on its behalf; and it may set out the matters on which each person designated will testify. A subpoena must advise a nonparty organization of its duty to make this designation. The persons designated must testify about information known or reasonably available to the organization. This paragraph (6) does not preclude a deposition by any other procedure allowed by these rules.

(c) Examination and Cross-Examination; Record of the Examination; Objections; Written Questions.

(1) ***Examination and Cross-Examination.*** The examination and cross-examination of a deponent proceed as they would at trial under the Federal Rules of Evidence, except Rules 103 and 615. After putting the deponent under oath or affirmation, the officer must record the testimony by the method designated under Rule 30(b)(3)(A). The testimony must be recorded by the officer personally or by a person acting in the presence and under the direction of the officer.

(2) *Objections.* An objection at the time of the examination — whether to evidence, to a party's conduct, to the officer's qualifications, to the manner of taking the deposition, or to any other aspect of the deposition — must be noted on the record, but the examination still proceeds; the testimony is taken subject to any objection. An objection must be stated concisely in a nonargumentative and nonsuggestive manner. A person may instruct a deponent not to answer only when necessary to preserve a privilege, to enforce a limitation ordered by the court, or to present a motion under Rule 30(d)(3).

(3) *Participating Through Written Questions.* Instead of participating in the oral examination, a party may serve written questions in a sealed envelope on the party noticing the deposition, who must deliver them to the officer. The officer must ask the deponent those questions and record the answers verbatim.

(d) Duration; Sanction; Motion to Terminate or Limit.

(1) *Duration.* Unless otherwise stipulated or ordered by the court, a deposition is limited to 1 day of 7 hours. The court must allow additional time consistent with Rule 26(b)(2) if needed to fairly examine the deponent or if the deponent, another person, or any other circumstance impedes or delays the examination.

(2) *Sanction.* The court may impose an appropriate sanction — including the reasonable expenses and attorney's fees incurred by any party — on a person who impedes, delays, or frustrates the fair examination of the deponent.

(3) *Motion to Terminate or Limit.*

(A) *Grounds.* At any time during a deposition, the deponent or a party may move to terminate or limit it on the ground that it is being conducted in bad faith or in a manner that unreasonably annoys, embarrasses, or oppresses the deponent or party. The motion may be filed in the court where the action is pending or the deposition is being taken. If the objecting deponent or party so demands, the deposition must be suspended for the time necessary to obtain an order.

(B) *Order.* The court may order that the deposition be terminated or may limit its scope and manner as provided in Rule 26(c). If terminated, the deposition may be resumed only by order of the court where the action is pending.

(C) *Award of Expenses.* Rule 37(a)(5) applies to the award of expenses.

(e) Review by the Witness; Changes.

(1) ***Review; Statement of Changes.*** On request by the deponent or a party before the deposition is completed, the deponent must be allowed 30 days after being notified by the officer that the transcript or recording is available in which:

(A) to review the transcript or recording; and

(B) if there are changes in form or substance, to sign a statement listing the changes and the reasons for making them.

(2) ***Changes Indicated in the Officer's Certificate.*** The officer must note in the certificate prescribed by Rule 30(f)(1) whether a review was requested and, if so, must attach any changes the deponent makes during the 30-day period.

(f) Certification and Delivery; Exhibits; Copies of the Transcript or Recording; Filing.

(1) ***Certification and Delivery.*** The officer must certify in writing that the witness was duly sworn and that the deposition accurately records the witness's testimony. The certificate must accompany the record of the deposition. Unless the court orders otherwise, the officer must seal the deposition in an envelope or package bearing the title of the action and marked "Deposition of [witness's name]" and must promptly send it to the attorney who arranged for the transcript or recording. The attorney must store it under conditions that will protect it against loss, destruction, tampering, or deterioration.

(2) ***Documents and Tangible Things.***

(A) *Originals and Copies.* Documents and tangible things produced for inspection during a deposition must, on a party's request, be marked for identification and attached to the deposition. Any party may inspect and copy them. But if the person who produced them wants to keep the originals, the person may:

(i) offer copies to be marked, attached to the deposition, and then used as originals — after giving all parties a fair opportunity to verify the copies by comparing them with the originals; or

(ii) give all parties a fair opportunity to inspect and copy the originals after they are marked — in which event the originals may be used as if attached to the deposition.

(B) *Order Regarding the Originals.* Any party may move for an order that the originals be attached to the deposition pending final disposition of the case.

(3) ***Copies of the Transcript or Recording.*** Unless otherwise stipulated or ordered by the court, the officer must retain the stenographic notes of a deposition taken stenographically or a copy of the recording of a deposition taken by another method. When paid reasonable charges, the officer must furnish a copy of the transcript or recording to any party or the deponent.

(4) ***Notice of Filing.*** A party who files the deposition must promptly notify all other parties of the filing.

(g) Failure to Attend a Deposition or Serve a Subpoena; Expenses. A party who, expecting a deposition to be taken, attends in person or by an attorney may recover reasonable expenses for attending, including attorney's fees, if the noticing party failed to:

(1) attend and proceed with the deposition; or

(2) serve a subpoena on a nonparty deponent, who consequently did not attend.

Rule 31. Depositions by Written Questions

(a) When a Deposition May Be Taken.

(1) ***Without Leave.*** A party may, by written questions, depose any person, including a party, without leave of court except as provided in Rule 31(a)(2). The deponent's attendance may be compelled by subpoena under Rule 45.

(2) ***With Leave.*** A party must obtain leave of court, and the court must grant leave to the extent consistent with Rule 26(b)(2):

(A) if the parties have not stipulated to the deposition and:

(i) the deposition would result in more than 10 depositions being taken under this rule or Rule 30 by the plaintiffs, or by the defendants, or by the third-party defendants;

(ii) the deponent has already been deposed in the case; or

(iii) the party seeks to take a deposition before the time specified in Rule 26(d); or

(B) if the deponent is confined in prison.

(3) ***Service; Required Notice.*** A party who wants to depose a person by written questions must serve them on every other party, with a notice stating, if known, the deponent's name and address. If the name is unknown, the notice must provide a general description sufficient to identify the person or the particular class or group to which the person belongs. The notice must also state the name or descriptive title and the address of the officer before whom the deposition will be taken.

(4) ***Questions Directed to an Organization.*** A public or private corporation, a partnership, an association, or a governmental agency may be deposed by written questions in accordance with Rule 30(b)(6).

(5) ***Questions from Other Parties.*** Any questions to the deponent from other parties must be served on all parties as follows: cross-questions, within 14 days after being served with the notice and direct questions; redirect questions, within 7 days after being served with cross-questions; and recross-questions, within 7 days after being served with redirect questions. The court may, for good cause, extend or shorten these times.

(b) Delivery to the Officer; Officer's Duties. The party who noticed the deposition must deliver to the officer a copy of all the questions served and of the notice. The officer must promptly proceed in the manner provided in Rule 30(c), (e), and (f) to:

(1) take the deponent's testimony in response to the questions;

(2) prepare and certify the deposition; and

(3) send it to the party, attaching a copy of the questions and of the notice.

(c) Notice of Completion or Filing.

(1) ***Completion.*** The party who noticed the deposition must notify all other parties when it is completed.

(2) ***Filing.*** A party who files the deposition must promptly notify all other parties of the filing.

Rule 32. Using Depositions in Court Proceedings

(a) Using Depositions.

(1) ***In General.*** At a hearing or trial, all or part of a deposition may be used against a party on these conditions:

(A) the party was present or represented at the taking of the deposition or had reasonable notice of it;

(B) it is used to the extent it would be admissible under the Federal Rules of Evidence if the deponent were present and testifying; and

(C) the use is allowed by Rule 32(a)(2) through (8).

(2) *Impeachment and Other Uses.* Any party may use a deposition to contradict or impeach the testimony given by the deponent as a witness, or for any other purpose allowed by the Federal Rules of Evidence.

(3) *Deposition of Party, Agent, or Designee.* An adverse party may use for any purpose the deposition of a party or anyone who, when deposed, was the party's officer, director, managing agent, or designee under Rule 30(b)(6) or 31(a)(4).

(4) *Unavailable Witness.* A party may use for any purpose the deposition of a witness, whether or not a party, if the court finds:

(A) that the witness is dead;

(B) that the witness is more than 100 miles from the place of hearing or trial or is outside the United States, unless it appears that the witness's absence was procured by the party offering the deposition;

(C) that the witness cannot attend or testify because of age, illness, infirmity, or imprisonment;

(D) that the party offering the deposition could not procure the witness's attendance by subpoena; or

(E) on motion and notice, that exceptional circumstances make it desirable — in the interest of justice and with due regard to the importance of live testimony in open court — to permit the deposition to be used.

(5) *Limitations on Use.*

(A) *Deposition Taken on Short Notice.* A deposition must not be used against a party who, having received less than 11 days' notice of the deposition, promptly moved for a protective order under Rule 26(c)(1)(B) requesting that it not be taken or be taken at a different time or place — and this motion was still pending when the deposition was taken.

(B) *Unavailable Deponent; Party Could Not Obtain an Attorney.* A deposition taken without leave of court under the unavailability provision of Rule 30(a)(2)(A)(iii) must not be used against a party who shows that, when served with the notice, it could not, despite diligent efforts, obtain an attorney to represent it at the deposition.

(6) *Using Part of a Deposition.* If a party offers in evidence only part of a deposition, an adverse party may require the offeror to introduce other parts that in fairness should be considered with the part introduced, and any party may itself introduce any other parts.

(7) *Substituting a Party.* Substituting a party under Rule 25 does not affect the right to use a deposition previously taken.

(8) *Deposition Taken in an Earlier Action.* A deposition lawfully taken and, if required, filed in any federal- or state-court action may be used in a later action involving the same subject matter between the same parties, or their representatives or successors in interest, to the same extent as if taken in the later action. A deposition previously taken may also be used as allowed by the Federal Rules of Evidence.

(b) Objections to Admissibility. Subject to Rules 28(b) and 32(d)(3), an objection may be made at a hearing or trial to the admission of any deposition testimony that would be inadmissible if the witness were present and testifying.

(c) Form of Presentation. Unless the court orders otherwise, a party must provide a transcript of any deposition testimony the party offers, but may provide the court with the testimony in nontranscript form as well. On any party's request, deposition testimony offered in a jury trial for any purpose other than impeachment must be presented in nontranscript form, if available, unless the court for good cause orders otherwise.

(d) Waiver of Objections.

(1) *To the Notice.* An objection to an error or irregularity in a deposition notice is waived unless promptly served in writing on the party giving the notice.

(2) *To the Officer's Qualification.* An objection based on disqualification of the officer before whom a deposition is to be taken is waived if not made:

(A) before the deposition begins; or

(B) promptly after the basis for disqualification becomes known or, with reasonable diligence, could have been known.

(3) *To the Taking of the Deposition.*

(A) *Objection to Competence, Relevance, or Materiality.* An objection to a deponent's competence — or to the competence, relevance, or materiality of testimony — is not waived by a failure to make the objection before or during the deposition, unless the ground for it might have been corrected at that time.

(B) *Objection to an Error or Irregularity.* An objection to an error or irregularity at an oral examination is waived if:

(i) it relates to the manner of taking the deposition, the form of a question or answer, the oath or affirmation, a party's conduct, or other matters that might have been corrected at that time; and

(ii) it is not timely made during the deposition.

(C) *Objection to a Written Question.* An objection to the form of a written question under Rule 31 is waived if not served in writing on the party submitting the question within the time for serving responsive questions or, if the question is a recross-question, within 5 days after being served with it.

(4) ***To Completing and Returning the Deposition.*** An objection to how the officer transcribed the testimony — or prepared, signed, certified, sealed, endorsed, sent, or otherwise dealt with the deposition — is waived unless a motion to suppress is made promptly after the error or irregularity becomes known or, with reasonable diligence, could have been known.

Rule 33. Interrogatories to Parties

(a) In General.

(1) ***Number.*** Unless otherwise stipulated or ordered by the court, a party may serve on any other party no more than 25 written interrogatories, including all discrete subparts. Leave to serve additional interrogatories may be granted to the extent consistent with Rule 26(b)(2).

(2) ***Scope.*** An interrogatory may relate to any matter that may be inquired into under Rule 26(b). An interrogatory is not objectionable merely because it asks for an opinion or contention that relates to fact or the application of law to fact, but the court may order that the interrogatory need not be answered until designated discovery is complete, or until a pretrial conference or some other time.

(b) Answers and Objections.

(1) ***Responding Party.*** The interrogatories must be answered:

(A) by the party to whom they are directed; or

(B) if that party is a public or private corporation, a partnership, an association, or a governmental agency, by any officer or agent, who must furnish the information available to the party.

(2) ***Time to Respond.*** The responding party must serve its answers and any objections within 30 days after being served with the interrogatories. A shorter or longer time may be stipulated to under Rule 29 or be ordered by the court.

(3) ***Answering Each Interrogatory.*** Each interrogatory must, to the extent it is not objected to, be answered separately and fully in writing under oath.

(4) ***Objections.*** The grounds for objecting to an interrogatory must be stated with specificity. Any ground not stated in a timely objection is waived unless the court, for good cause, excuses the failure.

(5) ***Signature.*** The person who makes the answers must sign them, and the attorney who objects must sign any objections.

(c) Use. An answer to an interrogatory may be used to the extent allowed by the Federal Rules of Evidence.

(d) Option to Produce Business Records. If the answer to an interrogatory may be determined by examining, auditing, compiling, abstracting, or summarizing a party's business records (including electronically stored information), and if the burden of deriving or ascertaining the answer will be substantially the same for either party, the responding party may answer by:

(1) specifying the records that must be reviewed, in sufficient detail to enable the interrogating party to locate and identify them as readily as the responding party could; and

(2) giving the interrogating party a reasonable opportunity to examine and audit the records and to make copies, compilations, abstracts, or summaries.

Rule 34. Producing Documents, Electronically Stored Information, and Tangible Things, or Entering onto Land, for Inspection and Other Purposes

(a) In General. A party may serve on any other party a request within the scope of Rule 26(b):

(1) to produce and permit the requesting party or its representative to inspect, copy, test, or sample the following items in the responding party's possession, custody, or control:

(A) any designated documents or electronically stored information — including writings, drawings, graphs, charts, photographs, sound recordings, images, and other data or data compilations — stored in any medium from which information can be obtained either directly or, if necessary, after translation by the responding party into a reasonably usable form; or

(B) any designated tangible things; or

(2) to permit entry onto designated land or other property possessed or controlled by the responding party, so that the requesting party may inspect, measure, survey, photograph, test, or sample the property or any designated object or operation on it.

(b) Procedure.

(1) ***Contents of the Request.*** The request:

(A) must describe with reasonable particularity each item or category of items to be inspected;

(B) must specify a reasonable time, place, and manner for the inspection and for performing the related acts; and

(C) may specify the form or forms in which electronically stored information is to be produced.

(2) ***Responses and Objections.***

(A) *Time to Respond.* The party to whom the request is directed must respond in writing within 30 days after being served. A shorter or longer time may be stipulated to under Rule 29 or be ordered by the court.

(B) *Responding to Each Item.* For each item or category, the response must either state that inspection and related activities will be permitted as requested or state an objection to the request, including the reasons.

(C) *Objections.* An objection to part of a request must specify the part and permit inspection of the rest.

(D) *Responding to a Request for Production of Electronically Stored Information.* The response may state an objection to a requested form for producing electronically stored information. If the responding party objects to a requested form — or if no form was specified in the request — the party must state the form or forms it intends to use.

(E) *Producing the Documents or Electronically Stored Information.* Unless otherwise stipulated or ordered by the court, these procedures apply to producing documents or electronically stored information:

(i) A party must produce documents as they are kept in the usual course of business or must organize and label them to correspond to the categories in the request;

(ii) If a request does not specify a form for producing electronically stored information, a party must produce it in a form or forms in which it is ordinarily maintained or in a reasonably usable form or forms; and

(iii) A party need not produce the same electronically stored information in more than one form.

(c) Nonparties. As provided in Rule 45, a nonparty may be compelled to produce documents and tangible things or to permit an inspection.

Rule 35. Physical and Mental Examinations

(a) Order for an Examination.

(1) ***In General.*** The court where the action is pending may order a party whose mental or physical condition — including blood group — is in controversy to submit to a physical or mental examination by a suitably licensed or certified examiner. The court has the same authority to order a party to produce for examination a person who is in its custody or under its legal control.

(2) ***Motion and Notice; Contents of the Order.*** The order:

(A) may be made only on motion for good cause and on notice to all parties and the person to be examined; and

(B) must specify the time, place, manner, conditions, and scope of the examination, as well as the person or persons who will perform it.

(b) Examiner's Report.

(1) ***Request by the Party or Person Examined.*** The party who moved for the examination must, on request, deliver to the requester a copy of the examiner's report, together with like reports of all earlier examinations of the same condition. The request may be made by the party against whom the examination order was issued or by the person examined.

(2) ***Contents.*** The examiner's report must be in writing and must set out in detail the examiner's findings, including diagnoses, conclusions, and the results of any tests.

(3) ***Request by the Moving Party.*** After delivering the reports, the party who moved for the examination may request — and is entitled to receive — from the party against whom the examination order was issued like reports of all earlier or later examinations of the same condition. But those reports need not be delivered by the party with custody or control of the person examined if the party shows that it could not obtain them.

(4) ***Waiver of Privilege.*** By requesting and obtaining the examiner's report, or by deposing the examiner, the party examined waives any privilege it may have — in that action or any other action involving the same controversy — concerning testimony about all examinations of the same condition.

(5) ***Failure to Deliver a Report.*** The court on motion may order — on just terms — that a party deliver the report of an examination. If the report is not provided, the court may exclude the examiner's testimony at trial.

(6) ***Scope.*** This subdivision (b) applies also to an examination made by the parties' agreement, unless the agreement states otherwise. This subdivision does not preclude obtaining an examiner's report or deposing an examiner under other rules.

Rule 36. Requests for Admission

(a) Scope and Procedure.

(1) ***Scope.*** A party may serve on any other party a written request to admit, for purposes of the pending action only, the truth of any matters within the scope of Rule 26(b)(1) relating to:

(A) facts, the application of law to fact, or opinions about either; and

(B) the genuineness of any described documents.

(2) ***Form; Copy of a Document.*** Each matter must be separately stated. A request to admit the genuineness of a document must be accompanied by a copy of the document unless it is, or has been, otherwise furnished or made available for inspection and copying.

(3) ***Time to Respond; Effect of Not Responding.*** A matter is admitted unless, within 30 days after being served, the party to whom the request is directed serves on the requesting party a written answer or objection addressed to the matter and signed by the party or its attorney. A shorter or longer time for responding may be stipulated to under Rule 29 or be ordered by the court.

(4) ***Answer.*** If a matter is not admitted, the answer must specifically deny it or state in detail why the answering party cannot truthfully admit or deny it. A denial must fairly respond to the substance of the matter; and when good faith requires that a party qualify an answer or deny only a part of a matter, the answer must specify the part admitted and qualify or deny the rest. The answering party may assert lack of knowledge or information as a reason for failing to admit or deny only if the party states that it has made reasonable inquiry and that the information it knows or can readily obtain is insufficient to enable it to admit or deny.

(5) ***Objections.*** The grounds for objecting to a request must be stated. A party must not object solely on the ground that the request presents a genuine issue for trial.

(6) ***Motion Regarding the Sufficiency of an Answer or Objection.*** The requesting party may move to determine the sufficiency of an answer or objection. Unless the court finds an objection justified, it must order that an answer be served. On finding that an answer does not comply with this rule, the court may order either that the matter is admitted or that an amended answer be served. The court may defer its final decision until a pretrial conference or a specified time before trial. Rule 37(a)(5) applies to an award of expenses.

(b) Effect of an Admission; Withdrawing or Amending It. A matter admitted under this rule is conclusively established unless the court, on motion, permits the admission to be withdrawn or amended. Subject to Rule 16(e), the court may permit withdrawal or amendment if it would promote the presentation of the merits of the action and if the court is not persuaded that it would prejudice the requesting party in maintaining or defending the action on the merits. An admission under this rule is not an admission for any other purpose and cannot be used against the party in any other proceeding.

Rule 37. Failure to Make Disclosures or to Cooperate in Discovery; Sanctions

(a) Motion for an Order Compelling Disclosure or Discovery.

(1) ***In General.*** On notice to other parties and all affected persons, a party may move for an order compelling disclosure or discovery. The motion must include a certification that the movant has in good faith conferred or attempted to confer with the person or party failing to make disclosure or discovery in an effort to obtain it without court action.

(2) ***Appropriate Court.*** A motion for an order to a party must be made in the court where the action is pending. A motion for an order to a nonparty must be made in the court where the discovery is or will be taken.

(3) ***Specific Motions.***

(A) *To Compel Disclosure.* If a party fails to make a disclosure required by Rule 26(a), any other party may move to compel disclosure and for appropriate sanctions.

(B) *To Compel a Discovery Response.* A party seeking discovery may move for an order compelling an answer, designation, production, or inspection. This motion may be made if:

(i) a deponent fails to answer a question asked under Rule 30 or 31;

(ii) a corporation or other entity fails to make a designation under Rule 30(b)(6) or 31(a)(4);

(iii) a party fails to answer an interrogatory submitted under Rule 33; or

(iv) a party fails to respond that inspection will be permitted — or fails to permit inspection — as requested under Rule 34.

(C) *Related to a Deposition.* When taking an oral deposition, the party asking a question may complete or adjourn the examination before moving for an order.

(4) ***Evasive or Incomplete Disclosure, Answer, or Response.*** For purposes of this subdivision (a), an evasive or incomplete disclosure, answer, or response must be treated as a failure to disclose, answer, or respond.

(5) ***Payment of Expenses; Protective Orders.***

(A) *If the Motion Is Granted (or Disclosure or Discovery Is Provided After Filing).* If the motion is granted — or if the disclosure or requested discovery is provided after the motion was filed — the court must, after giving an opportunity to be heard, require the party or deponent whose conduct necessitated the motion, the party or attorney advising that conduct, or both to pay the movant's reasonable expenses incurred in making the motion, including attorney's fees. But the court must not order this payment if:

(i) the movant filed the motion before attempting in good faith to obtain the disclosure or discovery without court action;

(ii) the opposing party's nondisclosure, response, or objection was substantially justified; or

(iii) other circumstances make an award of expenses unjust.

(B) *If the Motion Is Denied.* If the motion is denied, the court may issue any protective order authorized under Rule 26(c) and must, after giving an opportunity to be heard, require the movant, the attorney filing the motion, or both to pay the party or deponent who opposed the motion its reasonable expenses incurred in opposing the motion, including attorney's fees. But the court must not order this payment if the motion was substantially justified or other circumstances make an award of expenses unjust.

(C) *If the Motion Is Granted in Part and Denied in Part.* If the motion is granted in part and denied in part, the court may issue any protective order authorized under Rule 26(c) and may, after giving an opportunity to be heard, apportion the reasonable expenses for the motion.

(b) Failure to Comply with a Court Order.

(1) ***Sanctions in the District Where the Deposition Is Taken.*** If the court where the discovery is taken orders a deponent to be sworn or to answer a question and the deponent fails to obey, the failure may be treated as contempt of court.

(2) ***Sanctions in the District Where the Action Is Pending.***

(A) *For Not Obeying a Discovery Order.* If a party or a party's officer, director, or managing agent — or a witness designated under Rule 30(b)(6) or 31(a)(4) — fails to obey an order to provide or permit discovery, including an order under Rule 26(f), 35, or 37(a), the court where the action is pending may issue further just orders. They may include the following:

(i) directing that the matters embraced in the order or other designated facts be taken as established for purposes of the action, as the prevailing party claims;

(ii) prohibiting the disobedient party from supporting or opposing designated claims or defenses, or from introducing designated matters in evidence;

(iii) striking pleadings in whole or in part;

(iv) staying further proceedings until the order is obeyed;

(v) dismissing the action or proceeding in whole or in part;

(vi) rendering a default judgment against the disobedient party; or

(vii) treating as contempt of court the failure to obey any order except an order to submit to a physical or mental examination.

(B) *For Not Producing a Person for Examination.* If a party fails to comply with an order under Rule 35(a) requiring it to produce another person for examination, the court may issue any of the orders listed in Rule 37(b)(2)(A)(i)-(vi), unless the disobedient party shows that it cannot produce the other person.

(C) *Payment of Expenses.* Instead of or in addition to the orders above, the court must order the disobedient party, the attorney advising that party, or both to pay the reasonable expenses, including attorney's fees, caused by the failure, unless the failure was substantially justified or other circumstances make an award of expenses unjust.

(c) Failure to Disclose, to Supplement an Earlier Response, or to Admit.

(1) ***Failure to Disclose or Supplement.*** If a party fails to provide information or identify a witness as required by Rule 26(a) or (e), the party is not allowed to use that information or witness to supply evidence on a motion, at a hearing, or at a trial, unless the failure was substantially justified or is harmless. In addition to or instead of this sanction, the court, on motion and after giving an opportunity to be heard:

(A) may order payment of the reasonable expenses, including attorney's fees, caused by the failure;

(B) may inform the jury of the party's failure; and

(C) may impose other appropriate sanctions, including any of the orders listed in Rule 37(b)(2)(A)(i)-(vi).

(2) ***Failure to Admit.*** If a party fails to admit what is requested under Rule 36 and if the requesting party later proves a document to be genuine or the matter true, the requesting party may move that the party who failed to admit pay the reasonable expenses, including attorney's fees, incurred in making that proof. The court must so order unless:

(A) the request was held objectionable under Rule 36(a);

(B) the admission sought was of no substantial importance;

(C) the party failing to admit had a reasonable ground to believe that it might prevail on the matter; or

(D) there was other good reason for the failure to admit.

(d) Party's Failure to Attend Its Own Deposition, Serve Answers to Interrogatories, or Respond to a Request for Inspection.

(1) ***In General.***

(A) *Motion; Grounds for Sanctions.* The court where the action is pending may, on motion, order sanctions if:

(i) a party or a party's officer, director, or managing agent — or a person designated under Rule 30(b)(6) or 31(a)(4) — fails, after being served with proper notice, to appear for that person's deposition; or

(ii) a party, after being properly served with interrogatories under Rule 33 or a request for inspection under Rule 34, fails to serve its answers, objections, or written response.

(B) *Certification.* A motion for sanctions for failing to answer or respond must include a certification that the movant has in good faith conferred or attempted to confer with the party failing to act in an effort to obtain the answer or response without court action.

(2) ***Unacceptable Excuse for Failing to Act.*** A failure described in Rule 37(d)(1)(A) is not excused on the ground that the discovery sought was objectionable, unless the party failing to act has a pending motion for a protective order under Rule 26(c).

(3) ***Types of Sanctions.*** Sanctions may include any of the orders listed in Rule 37(b)(2)(A)(i)-(vi). Instead of or in addition to these sanctions, the court must require the party failing to act, the attorney advising that party, or both to pay the reasonable expenses, including attorney's fees, caused by the failure, unless the failure was substantially justified or other circumstances make an award of expenses unjust.

(e) Failure to Provide Electronically Stored Information. Absent exceptional circumstances, a court may not impose sanctions under these rules on a party for failing to provide electronically stored information lost as a result of the routine, good-faith operation of an electronic information system.

(f) Failure to Participate in Framing a Discovery Plan. If a party or its attorney fails to participate in good faith in developing and submitting a proposed discovery plan as required by Rule 26(f), the court may, after giving an opportunity to be heard, require that party or attorney to pay to any other party the reasonable expenses, including attorney's fees, caused by the failure.

TITLE VI. TRIALS

Rule 38. Right to a Jury Trial; Demand

(a) Right Preserved. The right of trial by jury as declared by the Seventh Amendment to the Constitution — or as provided by a federal statute — is preserved to the parties inviolate.

(b) Demand. On any issue triable of right by a jury, a party may demand a jury trial by:

(1) serving the other parties with a written demand — which may be included in a pleading — no later than 10 days after the last pleading directed to the issue is served; and

(2) filing the demand in accordance with Rule 5(d).

(c) Specifying Issues. In its demand, a party may specify the issues that it wishes to have tried by a jury; otherwise, it is considered to have demanded a jury trial on all the issues so triable. If the party has demanded a jury trial on only some issues, any other party may — within 10 days after being served with the demand or within a shorter time ordered by the court — serve a demand for a jury trial on any other or all factual issues triable by jury.

(d) Waiver; Withdrawal. A party waives a jury trial unless its demand is properly served and filed. A proper demand may be withdrawn only if the parties consent.

(e) Admiralty and Maritime Claims. These rules do not create a right to a jury trial on issues in a claim that is an admiralty or maritime claim under Rule 9(h).

Rule 39. Trial by Jury or by the Court

(a) When a Demand Is Made. When a jury trial has been demanded under Rule 38, the action must be designated on the docket as a jury action. The trial on all issues so demanded must be by jury unless:

(1) the parties or their attorneys file a stipulation to a nonjury trial or so stipulate on the record; or

(2) the court, on motion or on its own, finds that on some or all of those issues there is no federal right to a jury trial.

(b) When No Demand Is Made. Issues on which a jury trial is not properly demanded are to be tried by the court. But the court may, on motion, order a jury trial on any issue for which a jury might have been demanded.

(c) Advisory Jury; Jury Trial by Consent. In an action not triable of right by a jury, the court, on motion or on its own:

(1) may try any issue with an advisory jury; or

(2) may, with the parties' consent, try any issue by a jury whose verdict has the same effect as if a jury trial had been a matter of right, unless the action is against the United States and a federal statute provides for a nonjury trial.

Rule 40. Scheduling Cases for Trial

Each court must provide by rule for scheduling trials. The court must give priority to actions entitled to priority by a federal statute.

Rule 41. Dismissal of Actions

(a) Voluntary Dismissal.

(1) *By the Plaintiff.*

(A) *Without a Court Order.* Subject to Rules 23(e), 23.1(c), 23.2, and 66 and any applicable federal statute, the plaintiff may dismiss an action without a court order by filing:

(i) a notice of dismissal before the opposing party serves either an answer or a motion for summary judgment; or

(ii) a stipulation of dismissal signed by all parties who have appeared.

(B) *Effect.* Unless the notice or stipulation states otherwise, the dismissal is without prejudice. But if the plaintiff previously dismissed any federal- or state-court action based on or including the same claim, a notice of dismissal operates as an adjudication on the merits.

(2) *By Court Order; Effect.* Except as provided in Rule 41(a)(1), an action may be dismissed at the plaintiff's request only by court order, on terms that the court considers proper. If a defendant has pleaded a counterclaim before being served with the plaintiff's motion to dismiss, the action may be dismissed over the defendant's objection only if the counterclaim can remain pending for independent adjudication. Unless the order states otherwise, a dismissal under this paragraph (2) is without prejudice.

(b) Involuntary Dismissal; Effect. If the plaintiff fails to prosecute or to comply with these rules or a court order, a defendant may move to dismiss the action or any claim against it. Unless the dismissal order states otherwise, a dismissal under this subdivision (b) and any dismissal not under this rule — except one for lack of jurisdiction, improper venue, or failure to join a party under Rule 19 — operates as an adjudication on the merits.

(c) Dismissing a Counterclaim, Crossclaim, or Third-Party Claim. This rule applies to a dismissal of any counterclaim, crossclaim, or third-party claim. A claimant's voluntary dismissal under Rule 41(a)(1)(A)(i) must be made:

(1) before a responsive pleading is served; or

(2) if there is no responsive pleading, before evidence is introduced at a hearing or trial.

(d) Costs of a Previously Dismissed Action. If a plaintiff who previously dismissed an action in any court files an action based on or including the same claim against the same defendant, the court:

(1) may order the plaintiff to pay all or part of the costs of that previous action; and

(2) may stay the proceedings until the plaintiff has complied.

Rule 42. Consolidation; Separate Trials

(a) Consolidation. If actions before the court involve a common question of law or fact, the court may:

(1) join for hearing or trial any or all matters at issue in the actions;

(2) consolidate the actions; or

(3) issue any other orders to avoid unnecessary cost or delay.

(b) Separate Trials. For convenience, to avoid prejudice, or to expedite and economize, the court may order a separate trial of one or more separate issues, claims, crossclaims, counterclaims, or third-party claims. When ordering a separate trial, the court must preserve any federal right to a jury trial.

Rule 43. Taking Testimony

(a) In Open Court. At trial, the witnesses' testimony must be taken in open court unless a federal statute, the Federal Rules of Evidence, these rules, or other rules adopted by the Supreme Court provide otherwise. For good cause in compelling circumstances and with appropriate safeguards, the court may permit testimony in open court by contemporaneous transmission from a different location.

(b) Affirmation Instead of an Oath. When these rules require an oath, a solemn affirmation suffices.

(c) Evidence on a Motion. When a motion relies on facts outside the record, the court may hear the matter on affidavits or may hear it wholly or partly on oral testimony or on depositions.

(d) Interpreter. The court may appoint an interpreter of its choosing; fix reasonable compensation to be paid from funds provided by law or by one or more parties; and tax the compensation as costs.

Rule 44. Proving an Official Record

(a) Means of Proving.

(1) *Domestic Record.* Each of the following evidences an official record — or an entry in it — that is otherwise admissible and is kept within the United States, any state, district, or commonwealth, or any territory subject to the administrative or judicial jurisdiction of the United States:

(A) an official publication of the record; or

(B) a copy attested by the officer with legal custody of the record — or by the officer's deputy — and accompanied by a certificate that the officer has custody. The certificate must be made under seal:

(i) by a judge of a court of record in the district or political subdivision where the record is kept; or

(ii) by any public officer with a seal of office and with official duties in the district or political subdivision where the record is kept.

(2) *Foreign Record.*

(A) *In General.* Each of the following evidences a foreign official record — or an entry in it — that is otherwise admissible:

(i) an official publication of the record; or

(ii) the record — or a copy — that is attested by an authorized person and is accompanied either by a final certification of genuineness or by a certification under a treaty or convention to which the United States and the country where the record is located are parties.

(B) *Final Certification of Genuineness.* A final certification must certify the genuineness of the signature and official position of the attester or of any foreign official whose certificate of genuineness relates to the attestation or is in a chain of certificates of genuineness relating to the attestation. A final certification may be made by a secretary of a United States embassy or legation; by a consul general, vice consul, or consular agent of the United States; or by a diplomatic or consular official of the foreign country assigned or accredited to the United States.

(C) *Other Means of Proof.* If all parties have had a reasonable opportunity to investigate a foreign record's authenticity and accuracy, the court may, for good cause, either:

(i) admit an attested copy without final certification; or

(ii) permit the record to be evidenced by an attested summary with or without a final certification.

(b) Lack of a Record. A written statement that a diligent search of designated records revealed no record or entry of a specified tenor is admissible as evidence that the records contain no such record or entry. For domestic records, the statement must be authenticated under Rule 44(a)(1). For foreign records, the statement must comply with (a)(2)(C)(ii).

(c) Other Proof. A party may prove an official record — or an entry or lack of an entry in it — by any other method authorized by law.

Rule 44.1. Determining Foreign Law

A party who intends to raise an issue about a foreign country's law must give notice by a pleading or other writing. In determining foreign law, the court may consider any relevant material or source, including testimony, whether or not submitted by a party or admissible under the Federal Rules of Evidence. The court's determination must be treated as a ruling on a question of law.

Rule 45. Subpoena

(a) In General.

(1) ***Form and Contents.***

(A) *Requirements — In General.* Every subpoena must:

(i) state the court from which it issued;

(ii) state the title of the action, the court in which it is pending, and its civil-action number;

(iii) command each person to whom it is directed to do the following at a specified time and place: attend and testify; produce designated documents, electronically stored information, or tangible things in that person's possession, custody, or control; or permit the inspection of premises; and

(iv) set out the text of Rule 45(c) and (d).

(B) *Command to Attend a Deposition — Notice of the Recording Method.* A subpoena commanding attendance at a deposition must state the method for recording the testimony.

(C) *Combining or Separating a Command to Produce or to Permit Inspection; Specifying the Form for Electronically Stored Information.* A command to produce documents, electronically stored information, or tangible things or to permit the inspection of premises may be included in a subpoena commanding attendance at a deposition, hearing, or trial, or may be set out in a separate subpoena. A subpoena may specify the form or forms in which electronically stored information is to be produced.

(D) *Command to Produce; Included Obligations.* A command in a subpoena to produce documents, electronically stored information, or tangible things requires the responding party to permit inspection, copying, testing, or sampling of the materials.

(2) ***Issued from Which Court.*** A subpoena must issue as follows:

(A) for attendance at a hearing or trial, from the court for the district where the hearing or trial is to be held;

(B) for attendance at a deposition, from the court for the district where the deposition is to be taken; and

(C) for production or inspection, if separate from a subpoena commanding a person's attendance, from the court for the district where the production or inspection is to be made.

(3) ***Issued by Whom.*** The clerk must issue a subpoena, signed but otherwise in blank, to a party who requests it. That party must complete it before service. An attorney also may issue and sign a subpoena as an officer of:

(A) a court in which the attorney is authorized to practice; or

(B) a court for a district where a deposition is to be taken or production is to be made, if the attorney is authorized to practice in the court where the action is pending.

(b) Service.

(1) ***By Whom; Tendering Fees; Serving a Copy of Certain Subpoenas.*** Any person who is at least 18 years old and not a party may serve a subpoena. Serving a subpoena requires delivering a copy to the named person and, if the subpoena requires that person's attendance, tendering the fees for 1 day's attendance and the mileage allowed by law. Fees and mileage need not be tendered when the subpoena issues on behalf of the United States or any of its officers or agencies. If the subpoena commands the production of documents, electronically stored information, or tangible things or the inspection of premises before trial, then before it is served, a notice must be served on each party.

(2) ***Service in the United States.*** Subject to Rule 45(c)(3)(A)(ii), a subpoena may be served at any place:

(A) within the district of the issuing court;

(B) outside that district but within 100 miles of the place specified for the deposition, hearing, trial, production, or inspection;

(C) within the state of the issuing court if a state statute or court rule allows service at that place of a subpoena issued by a state court of general jurisdiction sitting in the place specified for the deposition, hearing, trial, production, or inspection; or

(D) that the court authorizes on motion and for good cause, if a federal statute so provides.

(3) ***Service in a Foreign Country.*** 28 U.S.C. § 1783 governs issuing and serving a subpoena directed to a United States national or resident who is in a foreign country.

(4) ***Proof of Service.*** Proving service, when necessary, requires filing with the issuing court a statement showing the date and manner of service and the names of the persons served. The statement must be certified by the server.

(c) Protecting a Person Subject to a Subpoena.

(1) ***Avoiding Undue Burden or Expense; Sanctions.*** A party or attorney responsible for issuing and serving a subpoena must take reasonable steps to avoid imposing undue burden or expense on a person subject to the subpoena. The issuing court must enforce this duty and impose an appropriate sanction — which may include lost earnings and reasonable attorney's fees — on a party or attorney who fails to comply.

(2) ***Command to Produce Materials or Permit Inspection.***

(A) *Appearance Not Required.* A person commanded to produce documents, electronically stored information, or tangible things, or to permit the inspection of premises, need not appear in person at the place of production or inspection unless also commanded to appear for a deposition, hearing, or trial.

(B) *Objections.* A person commanded to produce documents or tangible things or to permit inspection may serve on the party or attorney designated in the subpoena a written objection to inspecting, copying, testing or sampling any or all of the materials or to inspecting the premises — or to producing electronically stored information in the form or forms requested. The objection must be served before the earlier of the time specified for compliance or 14 days after the subpoena is served. If an objection is made, the following rules apply:

(i) At any time, on notice to the commanded person, the serving party may move the issuing court for an order compelling production or inspection.

(ii) These acts may be required only as directed in the order, and the order must protect a person who is neither a party nor a party's officer from significant expense resulting from compliance.

(3) ***Quashing or Modifying a Subpoena.***

(A) *When Required.* On timely motion, the issuing court must quash or modify a subpoena that:

(i) fails to allow a reasonable time to comply;

(ii) requires a person who is neither a party nor a party's officer to travel more than 100 miles from where that person resides, is employed, or regularly transacts business in person — except that, subject to Rule 45(c)(3)(B)(iii), the person may be commanded to attend a trial by traveling from any such place within the state where the trial is held;

(iii) requires disclosure of privileged or other protected matter, if no exception or waiver applies; or

(iv) subjects a person to undue burden.

(B) *When Permitted.* To protect a person subject to or affected by a subpoena, the issuing court may, on motion, quash or modify the subpoena if it requires:

(i) disclosing a trade secret or other confidential research, development, or commercial information;

(ii) disclosing an unretained expert's opinion or information that does not describe specific occurrences in dispute and results from the expert's study that was not requested by a party; or

(iii) a person who is neither a party nor a party's officer to incur substantial expense to travel more than 100 miles to attend trial.

(C) *Specifying Conditions as an Alternative.* In the circumstances described in Rule 45(c)(3)(B), the court may, instead of quashing or modifying a subpoena, order appearance or production under specified conditions if the serving party:

(i) shows a substantial need for the testimony or material that cannot be otherwise met without undue hardship; and

(ii) ensures that the subpoenaed person will be reasonably compensated.

(d) Duties in Responding to a Subpoena.

(1) ***Producing Documents or Electronically Stored Information.*** These procedures apply to producing documents or electronically stored information:

(A) *Documents.* A person responding to a subpoena to produce documents must produce them as they are kept in the ordinary course of business or must organize and label them to correspond to the categories in the demand.

(B) *Form for Producing Electronically Stored Information Not Specified.* If a subpoena does not specify a form for producing electronically stored information, the person responding must produce it in a form or forms in which it is ordinarily maintained or in a reasonably usable form or forms.

(C) *Electronically Stored Information Produced in Only One Form.* The person responding need not produce the same electronically stored information in more than one form.

(D) *Inaccessible Electronically Stored Information.* The person responding need not provide discovery of electronically stored information from sources that the person identifies as not reasonably accessible because of undue burden or cost. On motion to compel discovery or for a protective order, the person responding must show that the information is not reasonably accessible because of undue burden or cost. If that showing is made, the court may nonetheless order discovery from such sources if the requesting party shows good cause, considering the limitations of Rule 26(b)(2)(C). The court may specify conditions for the discovery.

(2) ***Claiming Privilege or Protection.***

(A) *Information Withheld.* A person withholding subpoenaed information under a claim that it is privileged or subject to protection as trial-preparation material must:

(i) expressly make the claim; and

(ii) describe the nature of the withheld documents, communications, or tangible things in a manner that, without revealing information itself privileged or protected, will enable the parties to assess the claim.

(B) *Information Produced.* If information produced in response to a subpoena is subject to a claim of privilege or of protection as trial-preparation material, the person making the claim may notify any party that received the information of the claim and the basis for it. After being notified, a party must promptly return, sequester, or destroythe specified information and any copies it has; must not use or disclose the information until the claim is resolved; must take reasonable steps to retrieve the information if the party disclosed it before being notified; and may promptly present the information to the court under seal for a determination of the claim. The person who produced the information must preserve the information until the claim is resolved.

(e) Contempt. The issuing court may hold in contempt a person who, having been served, fails without adequate excuse to obey the subpoena. A nonparty's failure to obey must be excused if the subpoena purports to require the nonparty to attend or produce at a place outside the limits of Rule 45(c)(3)(A)(ii).

Rule 46. Objecting to a Ruling or Order

A formal exception to a ruling or order is unnecessary. When the ruling or order is requested or made, a party need only state the action that it wants the court to take or objects to, along with the grounds for the request or objection. Failing to object does not prejudice a party who had no opportunity to do so when the ruling or order was made.

Rule 47. Selecting Jurors

(a) Examining Jurors. The court may permit the parties or their attorneys to examine prospective jurors or may itself do so. If the court examines the jurors, it must permit the parties or their attorneys to make any further inquiry it considers proper, or must itself ask any of their additional questions it considers proper.

(b) Peremptory Challenges. The court must allow the number of peremptory challenges provided by 28 U.S.C. § 1870.

(c) Excusing a Juror. During trial or deliberation, the court may excuse a juror for good cause.

Rule 48. Number of Jurors; Verdict

A jury must initially have at least 6 and no more than 12 members, and each juror must participate in the verdict unless excused under Rule 47(c). Unless the parties stipulate otherwise, the verdict must be unanimous and be returned by a jury of at least 6 members.

Rule 49. Special Verdict; General Verdict and Questions

(a) Special Verdict.

(1) *In General.* The court may require a jury to return only a special verdict in the form of a special written finding on each issue of fact. The court may do so by:

(A) submitting written questions susceptible of a categorical or other brief answer;

(B) submitting written forms of the special findings that might properly be made under the pleadings and evidence; or

(C) using any other method that the court considers appropriate.

(2) *Instructions.* The court must give the instructions and explanations necessary to enable the jury to make its findings on each submitted issue.

(3) *Issues Not Submitted.* A party waives the right to a jury trial on any issue of fact raised by the pleadings or evidence but not submitted to the jury unless, before the jury retires, the party demands its submission to the jury. If the party does not demand submission, the court may make a finding on the issue. If the court makes no finding, it is considered to have made a finding consistent with its judgment on the special verdict.

(b) General Verdict with Answers to Written Questions.

(1) *In General.* The court may submit to the jury forms for a general verdict, together with written questions on one or more issues of fact that the jury must decide. The court must give the instructions and explanations necessary to enable the jury to render a general verdict and answer the questions in writing, and must direct the jury to do both.

(2) ***Verdict and Answers Consistent.*** When the general verdict and the answers are consistent, the court must approve, for entry under Rule 58, an appropriate judgment on the verdict and answers.

(3) ***Answers Inconsistent with the Verdict.*** When the answers are consistent with each other but one or more is inconsistent with the general verdict, the court may:

(A) approve, for entry under Rule 58, an appropriate judgment according to the answers, notwithstanding the general verdict;

(B) direct the jury to further consider its answers and verdict; or

(C) order a new trial.

(4) ***Answers Inconsistent with Each Other and the Verdict.*** When the answers are inconsistent with each other and one or more is also inconsistent with the general verdict, judgment must not be entered; instead, the court must direct the jury to further consider its answers and verdict, or must order a new trial.

Rule 50. Judgment as a Matter of Law in a Jury Trial; Related Motion for a New Trial; Conditional Ruling

(a) Judgment as a Matter of Law.

(1) ***In General.*** If a party has been fully heard on an issue during a jury trial and the court finds that a reasonable jury would not have a legally sufficient evidentiary basis to find for the party on that issue, the court may:

(A) resolve the issue against the party; and

(B) grant a motion for judgment as a matter of law against the party on a claim or defense that, under the controlling law, can be maintained or defeated only with a favorable finding on that issue.

(2) ***Motion.*** A motion for judgment as a matter of law may be made at any time before the case is submitted to the jury. The motion must specify the judgment sought and the law and facts that entitle the movant to the judgment.

(b) Renewing the Motion After Trial; Alternative Motion for a New Trial. If the court does not grant a motion for judgment as a matter of law made under Rule 50(a), the court is considered to have submitted the action to the jury subject to the court's later deciding the legal questions raised by the motion. No later than 10 days after the entry of judgment — or if the motion addresses a jury issue not decided by a verdict, no later than 10 days after the jury was discharged — the movant may file a renewed motion for judgment as a matter of law and may include an alternative or joint request for a new trial under Rule 59. In ruling on the renewed motion, the court may:

(1) allow judgment on the verdict, if the jury returned a verdict;

(2) order a new trial; or

(3) direct the entry of judgment as a matter of law.

(c) Granting the Renewed Motion; Conditional Ruling on a Motion for a New Trial.

(1) ***In General.*** If the court grants a renewed motion for judgment as a matter of law, it must also conditionally rule on any motion for a new trial by determining whether a new trial should be granted if the judgment is later vacated or reversed. The court must state the grounds for conditionally granting or denying the motion for a new trial.

(2) ***Effect of a Conditional Ruling.*** Conditionally granting the motion for a new trial does not affect the judgment's finality; if the judgment is reversed, the new trial must proceed unless the appellate court orders otherwise. If the motion for a new trial is conditionally denied, the appellee may assert error in that denial; if the judgment is reversed, the case must proceed as the appellate court orders.

(d) Time for a Losing Party's New-Trial Motion. Any motion for a new trial under Rule 59 by a party against whom judgment as a matter of law is rendered must be filed no later than 10 days after the entry of the judgment.

(e) Denying the Motion for Judgment as a Matter of Law; Reversal on Appeal. If the court denies the motion for judgment as a matter of law, the prevailing party may, as appellee, assert grounds entitling it to a new trial should the appellate court conclude that the trial court erred in denying the motion. If the appellate court reverses the judgment, it may order a new trial, direct the trial court to determine whether a new trial should be granted, or direct the entry of judgment.

Rule 51. Instructions to the Jury; Objections; Preserving a Claim of Error

(a) Requests.

(1) ***Before or at the Close of the Evidence.*** At the close of the evidence or at any earlier reasonable time that the court orders, a party may file and furnish to every other party written requests for the jury instructions it wants the court to give.

(2) ***After the Close of the Evidence.*** After the close of the evidence, a party may:

(A) file requests for instructions on issues that could not reasonably have been anticipated by an earlier time that the court set for requests; and

(B) with the court's permission, file untimely requests for instructions on any issue.

(b) Instructions. The court:

(1) must inform the parties of its proposed instructions and proposed action on the requests before instructing the jury and before final jury arguments;

(2) must give the parties an opportunity to object on the record and out of the jury's hearing before the instructions and arguments are delivered; and

(3) may instruct the jury at any time before the jury is discharged.

(c) Objections.

(1) ***How to Make.*** A party who objects to an instruction or the failure to give an instruction must do so on the record, stating distinctly the matter objected to and the grounds for the objection.

(2) ***When to Make.*** An objection is timely if:

(A) a party objects at the opportunity provided under Rule 51(b)(2); or

(B) a party was not informed of an instruction or action on a request before that opportunity to object, and the party objects promptly after learning that the instruction or request will be, or has been, given or refused.

(d) Assigning Error; Plain Error.

(1) ***Assigning Error.*** A party may assign as error:

(A) an error in an instruction actually given, if that party properly objected; or

(B) a failure to give an instruction, if that party properly requested it and — unless the court rejected the request in a definitive ruling on the record — also properly objected.

(2) ***Plain Error.*** A court may consider a plain error in the instructions that has not been preserved as required by Rule 51(d)(1) if the error affects substantial rights.

Rule 52. Findings and Conclusions by the Court; Judgment on Partial Findings

(a) Findings and Conclusions.

(1) ***In General.*** In an action tried on the facts without a jury or with an advisory jury, the court must find the facts specially and state its conclusions of law separately. The findings and conclusions may be stated on the record after the close of the evidence or may appear in an opinion or a memorandum of decision filed by the court. Judgment must be entered under Rule 58.

(2) ***For an Interlocutory Injunction.*** In granting or refusing an interlocutory injunction, the court must similarly state the findings and conclusions that support its action.

(3) ***For a Motion.*** The court is not required to state findings or conclusions when ruling on a motion under Rule 12 or 56 or, unless these rules provide otherwise, on any other motion.

(4) ***Effect of a Master's Findings.*** A master's findings, to the extent adopted by the court, must be considered the court's findings.

(5) ***Questioning the Evidentiary Support.*** A party may later question the sufficiency of the evidence supporting the findings, whether or not the party requested findings, objected to them, moved to amend them, or moved for partial findings.

(6) ***Setting Aside the Findings.*** Findings of fact, whether based on oral or other evidence, must not be set aside unless clearly erroneous, and the reviewing court must give due regard to the trial court's opportunity to judge the witnesses' credibility.

(b) Amended or Additional Findings. On a party's motion filed no later than 10 days after the entry of judgment, the court may amend its findings — or make additional findings — and may amend the judgment accordingly. The motion may accompany a motion for a new trial under Rule 59.

(c) Judgment on Partial Findings. If a party has been fully heard on an issue during a nonjury trial and the court finds against the party on that issue, the court may enter judgment against the party on a claim or defense that, under the controlling law, can be maintained or defeated only with a favorable finding on that issue. The court may, however, decline to render any judgment until the close of the evidence. A judgment on partial findings must be supported by findings of fact and conclusions of law as required by Rule 52(a).

Rule 53. Masters

(a) Appointment.

(1) ***Scope.*** Unless a statute provides otherwise, a court may appoint a master only to:

(A) perform duties consented to by the parties;

(B) hold trial proceedings and make or recommend findings of fact on issues to be decided without a jury if appointment is warranted by:

(i) some exceptional condition; or

(ii) the need to perform an accounting or resolve a difficult computation of damages; or

(C) address pretrial and posttrial matters that cannot be effectively and timely addressed by an available district judge or magistrate judge of the district.

(2) ***Disqualification.*** A master must not have a relationship to the parties, attorneys, action, or court that would require disqualification of a judge under 28 U.S.C. § 455, unless the parties, with the court's approval, consent to the appointment after the master discloses any potential grounds for disqualification.

(3) ***Possible Expense or Delay.*** In appointing a master, the court must consider the fairness of imposing the likely expenses on the parties and must protect against unreasonable expense or delay.

(b) Order Appointing a Master.

(1) ***Notice.*** Before appointing a master, the court must give the parties notice and an opportunity to be heard. Any party may suggest candidates for appointment.

(2) ***Contents.*** The appointing order must direct the master to proceed with all reasonable diligence and must state:

(A) the master's duties, including any investigation or enforcement duties, and any limits on the master's authority under Rule 53(c);

(B) the circumstances, if any, in which the master may communicate ex parte with the court or a party;

(C) the nature of the materials to be preserved and filed as the record of the master's activities;

(D) the time limits, method of filing the record, other procedures, and standards for reviewing the master's orders, findings, and recommendations; and

(E) the basis, terms, and procedure for fixing the master's compensation under Rule 53(g).

(3) ***Issuing.*** The court may issue the order only after:

(A) the master files an affidavit disclosing whether there is any ground for disqualification under 28 U.S.C. § 455; and

(B) if a ground is disclosed, the parties, with the court's approval, waive the disqualification.

(4) ***Amending.*** The order may be amended at any time after notice to the parties and an opportunity to be heard.

(c) Master's Authority.

(1) ***In General.*** Unless the appointing order directs otherwise, a master may:

(A) regulate all proceedings;

(B) take all appropriate measures to perform the assigned duties fairly and efficiently; and

(C) if conducting an evidentiary hearing, exercise the appointing court's power to compel, take, and record evidence.

(2) ***Sanctions.*** The master may by order impose on a party any noncontempt sanction provided by Rule 37 or 45, and may recommend a contempt sanction against a party and sanctions against a nonparty.

(d) Master's Orders. A master who issues an order must file it and promptly serve a copy on each party. The clerk must enter the order on the docket.

(e) Master's Reports. A master must report to the court as required by the appointing order. The master must file the report and promptly serve a copy on each party, unless the court orders otherwise.

(f) Action on the Master's Order, Report, or Recommendations.

(1) ***Opportunity for a Hearing; Action in General.*** In acting on a master's order, report, or recommendations, the court must give the parties notice and an opportunity to be heard; may receive evidence; and may adopt or affirm, modify, wholly or partly reject or reverse, or resubmit to the master with instructions.

(2) ***Time to Object or Move to Adopt or Modify.*** A party may file objections to — or a motion to adopt or modify — the master's order, report, or recommendations no later than 20 days after a copy is served, unless the court sets a different time.

(3) ***Reviewing Factual Findings.*** The court must decide de novo all objections to findings of fact made or recommended by a master, unless the parties, with the court's approval, stipulate that:

(A) the findings will be reviewed for clear error; or

(B) the findings of a master appointed under Rule 53(a)(1)(A) or (C) will be final.

(4) ***Reviewing Legal Conclusions.*** The court must decide de novo all objections to conclusions of law made or recommended by a master.

(5) ***Reviewing Procedural Matters.*** Unless the appointing order establishes a different standard of review, the court may set aside a master's ruling on a procedural matter only for an abuse of discretion.

(g) Compensation.

(1) ***Fixing Compensation.*** Before or after judgment, the court must fix the master's compensation on the basis and terms stated in the appointing order, but the court may set a new basis and terms after giving notice and an opportunity to be heard.

(2) ***Payment.*** The compensation must be paid either:

(A) by a party or parties; or

(B) from a fund or subject matter of the action within the court's control.

(3) ***Allocating Payment.*** The court must allocate payment among the parties after considering the nature and amount of the controversy, the parties' means, and the extent to which any party is more responsible than other parties for the reference to a master. An interim allocation may be amended to reflect a decision on the merits.

(h) Appointing a Magistrate Judge. A magistrate judge is subject to this rule only when the order referring a matter to the magistrate judge states that the reference is made under this rule.

TITLE VII. JUDGMENT

Rule 54. Judgment; Costs

(a) Definition; Form. "Judgment" as used in these rules includes a decree and any order from which an appeal lies. A judgment should not include recitals of pleadings, a master's report, or a record of prior proceedings.

(b) Judgment on Multiple Claims or Involving Multiple Parties. When an action presents more than one claim for relief — whether as a claim, counterclaim, crossclaim, or third-party claim — or when multiple parties are involved, the court may direct entry of a final judgment as to one or more, but fewer than all, claims or parties only if the court expressly determines that there is no just reason for delay. Otherwise, any order or other decision, however designated, that adjudicates fewer than all the claims or the rights and liabilities of fewer than all the parties does not end the action as to any of the claims or parties and may be revised at any time before the entry of a judgment adjudicating all the claims and all the parties' rights and liabilities.

(c) Demand for Judgment; Relief to Be Granted. A default judgment must not differ in kind from, or exceed in amount, what is demanded in the pleadings. Every other final judgment should grant the relief to which each party is entitled, even if the party has not demanded that relief in its pleadings.

(d) Costs; Attorney's Fees.

(1) ***Costs Other Than Attorney's Fees.*** Unless a federal statute, these rules, or a court order provides otherwise, costs — other than attorney's fees — should be allowed to the prevailing party. But costs against the United States, its officers, and its agencies may be imposed only to the extent allowed by law. The clerk may tax costs on 1 day's notice. On motion served within the next 5 days, the court may review the clerk's action.

(2) ***Attorney's Fees.***

(A) *Claim to Be by Motion.* A claim for attorney's fees and related nontaxable expenses must be made by motion unless the substantive law requires those fees to be proved at trial as an element of damages.

(B) *Timing and Contents of the Motion.* Unless a statute or a court order provides otherwise, the motion must:

(i) be filed no later than 14 days after the entry of judgment;

(ii) specify the judgment and the statute, rule, or other grounds entitling the movant to the award;

(iii) state the amount sought or provide a fair estimate of it; and

(iv) disclose, if the court so orders, the terms of any agreement about fees for the services for which the claim is made.

(C) *Proceedings.* Subject to Rule 23(h), the court must, on a party's request, give an opportunity for adversary submissions on the motion in accordance with Rule 43(c) or 78. The court may decide issues of liability for fees before receiving submissions on the value of services. The court must find the facts and state its conclusions of law as provided in Rule 52(a).

(D) *Special Procedures by Local Rule; Reference to a Master or a Magistrate Judge.* By local rule, the court may establish special procedures to resolve fee-related issues without extensive evidentiary hearings. Also, the court may refer issues concerning the value of services to a special master under Rule 53 without regard to the limitations of Rule 53(a)(1), and may refer a motion for attorney's fees to a magistrate judge under Rule 72(b) as if it were a dispositive pretrial matter.

(E) *Exceptions.* Subparagraphs (A)-(D) do not apply to claims for fees and expenses as sanctions for violating these rules or as sanctions under 28 U.S.C. § 1927.

Rule 55. Default; Default Judgment

(a) Entering a Default. When a party against whom a judgment for affirmative relief is sought has failed to plead or otherwise defend, and that failure is shown by affidavit or otherwise, the clerk must enter the party's default.

(b) Entering a Default Judgment.

(1) ***By the Clerk.*** If the plaintiff's claim is for a sum certain or a sum that can be made certain by computation, the clerk — on the plaintiff's request, with an affidavit showing the amount due — must enter judgment for that amount and costs against a defendant who has been defaulted for not appearing and who is neither a minor nor an incompetent person.

(2) ***By the Court.*** In all other cases, the party must apply to the court for a default judgment. A default judgment may be entered against a minor or incompetent person only if represented by a general guardian, conservator, or other like fiduciary who has appeared. If the party against whom a default judgment is sought has appeared personally or by a representative, that party or its representative must be served with written notice of the application at least 3 days before the hearing. The court may conduct hearings or make referrals — preserving any federal statutory right to a jury trial — when, to enter or effectuate judgment, it needs to:

(A) conduct an accounting;

(B) determine the amount of damages;

(C) establish the truth of any allegation by evidence; or

(D) investigate any other matter.

(c) Setting Aside a Default or a Default Judgment. The court may set aside an entry of default for good cause, and it may set aside a default judgment under Rule 60(b).

(d) Judgment Against the United States. A default judgment may be entered against the United States, its officers, or its agencies only if the claimant establishes a claim or right to relief by evidence that satisfies the court.

Rule 56. Summary Judgment

(a) By a Claiming Party. A party claiming relief may move, with or without supporting affidavits, for summary judgment on all or part of the claim. The motion may be filed at any time after:

(1) 20 days have passed from commencement of the action; or

(2) the opposing party serves a motion for summary judgment.

(b) By a Defending Party. A party against whom relief is sought may move at any time, with or without supporting affidavits, for summary judgment on all or part of the claim.

(c) Serving the Motion; Proceedings. The motion must be served at least 10 days before the day set for the hearing. An opposing party may serve opposing affidavits before the hearing day. The judgment sought should be rendered if the pleadings, the discovery and disclosure materials on file, and any affidavits show that there is no genuine issue as to any material fact and that the movant is entitled to judgment as a matter of law.

(d) Case Not Fully Adjudicated on the Motion.

(1) ***Establishing Facts.*** If summary judgment is not rendered on the whole action, the court should, to the extent practicable, determine what material facts are not genuinely at issue. The court should so determine by examining the pleadings and evidence before it and by interrogating the attorneys. It should then issue an order specifying what facts — including items of damages or other relief — are not genuinely at issue. The facts so specified must be treated as established in the action.

(2) ***Establishing Liability.*** An interlocutory summary judgment may be rendered on liability alone, even if there is a genuine issue on the amount of damages.

(e) Affidavits; Further Testimony.

(1) ***In General.*** A supporting or opposing affidavit must be made on personal knowledge, set out facts that would be admissible in evidence, and show that the affiant is competent to testify on the matters stated. If a paper or part of a paper is referred to in an affidavit, a sworn or certified copy must be attached to or served with the affidavit. The court may permit an affidavit to be supplemented or opposed by depositions, answers to interrogatories, or additional affidavits.

(2) ***Opposing Party's Obligation to Respond.*** When a motion for summary judgment is properly made and supported, an opposing party may not rely merely on allegations or denials in its own pleading; rather, its response must — by affidavits or as otherwise provided in this rule — set out specific facts showing a genuine issue for trial. If the opposing party does not so respond, summary judgment should, if appropriate, be entered against that party.

(f) When Affidavits Are Unavailable. If a party opposing the motion shows by affidavit that, for specified reasons, it cannot present facts essential to justify its opposition, the court may:

(1) deny the motion;

(2) order a continuance to enable affidavits to be obtained, depositions to be taken, or other discovery to be undertaken; or

(3) issue any other just order.

(g) Affidavit Submitted in Bad Faith. If satisfied that an affidavit under this rule is submitted in bad faith or solely for delay, the court must order the submitting party to pay the other party the reasonable expenses, including attorney's fees, it incurred as a result. An offending party or attorney may also be held in contempt.

Rule 57. Declaratory Judgment

These rules govern the procedure for obtaining a declaratory judgment under 28 U.S.C. § 2201. Rules 38 and 39 govern a demand for a jury trial. The existence of another adequate remedy does not preclude a declaratory judgment that is otherwise appropriate. The court may order a speedy hearing of a declaratory-judgment action.

Rule 58. Entering Judgment

(a) Separate Document. Every judgment and amended judgment must be set out in a separate document, but a separate document is not required for an order disposing of a motion:

(1) for judgment under Rule 50(b);

(2) to amend or make additional findings under Rule 52(b);

(3) for attorney's fees under Rule 54;

(4) for a new trial, or to alter or amend the judgment, under Rule 59; or

(5) for relief under Rule 60.

(b) Entering Judgment.

(1) ***Without the Court's Direction.*** Subject to Rule 54(b) and unless the court orders otherwise, the clerk must, without awaiting the court's direction, promptly prepare, sign, and enter the judgment when:

(A) the jury returns a general verdict;

(B) the court awards only costs or a sum certain; or

(C) the court denies all relief.

(2) ***Court's Approval Required.*** Subject to Rule 54(b), the court must promptly approve the form of the judgment, which the clerk must promptly enter, when:

(A) the jury returns a special verdict or a general verdict with answers to written questions; or

(B) the court grants other relief not described in this subdivision (b).

(c) Time of Entry. For purposes of these rules, judgment is entered at the following times:

(1) if a separate document is not required, when the judgment is entered in the civil docket under Rule 79(a); or

(2) if a separate document is required, when the judgment is entered in the civil docket under Rule 79(a) and the earlier of these events occurs:

(A) it is set out in a separate document; or

(B) 150 days have run from the entry in the civil docket.

(d) Request for Entry. A party may request that judgment be set out in a separate document as required by Rule 58(a).

(e) Cost or Fee Awards. Ordinarily, the entry of judgment may not be delayed, nor the time for appeal extended, in order to tax costs or award fees. But if a timely motion for attorney's fees is made under Rule 54(d)(2), the court may act before a notice of appeal has been filed and become effective to order that the motion have the same effect under Federal Rule of Appellate Procedure 4(a)(4) as a timely motion under Rule 59.

Rule 59. New Trial; Altering or Amending a Judgment

(a) In General.

(1) ***Grounds for New Trial.*** The court may, on motion, grant a new trial on all or some of the issues — and to any party — as follows:

(A) after a jury trial, for any reason for which a new trial has heretofore been granted in an action at law in federal court; or

(B) after a nonjury trial, for any reason for which a rehearing has heretofore been granted in a suit in equity in federal court.

(2) ***Further Action After a Nonjury Trial.*** After a nonjury trial, the court may, on motion for a new trial, open the judgment if one has been entered, take additional testimony, amend findings of fact and conclusions of law or make new ones, and direct the entry of a new judgment.

(b) Time to File a Motion for a New Trial. A motion for a new trial must be filed no later than 10 days after the entry of judgment.

(c) Time to Serve Affidavits. When a motion for a new trial is based on affidavits, they must be filed with the motion. The opposing party has 10 days after being served to file opposing affidavits; but that period may be extended for up to 20 days, either by the court for good cause or by the parties' stipulation. The court may permit reply affidavits.

(d) New Trial on the Court's Initiative or for Reasons Not in the Motion. No later than 10 days after the entry of judgment, the court, on its own, may order a new trial for any reason that would justify granting one on a party's motion. After giving the parties notice and an opportunity to be heard, the court may grant a timely motion for a new trial for a reason not stated in the motion. In either event, the court must specify the reasons in its order.

(e) Motion to Alter or Amend a Judgment. A motion to alter or amend a judgment must be filed no later than 10 days after the entry of the judgment.

Rule 60. Relief from a Judgment or Order

(a) Corrections Based on Clerical Mistakes; Oversights and Omissions. The court may correct a clerical mistake or a mistake arising from oversight or omission whenever one is found in a judgment, order, or other part of the record. The court may do so on motion or on its own, with or without notice. But after an appeal has been docketed in the appellate court and while it is pending, such a mistake may be corrected only with the appellate court's leave.

(b) Grounds for Relief from a Final Judgment, Order, or Proceeding. On motion and just terms, the court may relieve a party or its legal representative from a final judgment, order, or proceeding for the following reasons:

(1) mistake, inadvertence, surprise, or excusable neglect;

(2) newly discovered evidence that, with reasonable diligence, could not have been discovered in time to move for a new trial under Rule 59(b);

(3) fraud (whether previously called intrinsic or extrinsic), misrepresentation, or misconduct by an opposing party;

(4) the judgment is void;

(5) the judgment has been satisfied, released or discharged; it is based on an earlier judgment that has been reversed or vacated; or applying it prospectively is no longer equitable; or

(6) any other reason that justifies relief.

(c) Timing and Effect of the Motion.

(1) *Timing.* A motion under Rule 60(b) must be made within a reasonable time — and for reasons (1), (2), and (3) no more than a year after the entry of the judgment or order or the date of the proceeding.

(2) *Effect on Finality.* The motion does not affect the judgment's finality or suspend its operation.

(d) Other Powers to Grant Relief. This rule does not limit a court's power to:

(1) entertain an independent action to relieve a party from a judgment, order, or proceeding;

(2) grant relief under 28 U.S.C. § 1655 to a defendant who was not personally notified of the action; or

(3) set aside a judgment for fraud on the court.

(e) Bills and Writs Abolished. The following are abolished: bills of review, bills in the nature of bills of review, and writs of coram nobis, coram vobis, and audita querela.

Rule 61. Harmless Error

Unless justice requires otherwise, no error in admitting or excluding evidence — or any other error by the court or a party — is ground for granting a new trial, for setting aside a verdict, or for vacating, modifying, or otherwise disturbing a judgment or order. At every stage of the proceeding, the court must disregard all errors and defects that do not affect any party's substantial rights.

Rule 62. Stay of Proceedings to Enforce a Judgment

(a) Automatic Stay; Exceptions for Injunctions, Receiverships, and Patent Accountings. Except as stated in this rule, no execution may issue on a judgment, nor may proceedings be taken to enforce it, until 10 days have passed after its entry. But unless the court orders otherwise, the following are not stayed after being entered, even if an appeal is taken:

(1) an interlocutory or final judgment in an action for an injunction or a receivership; or

(2) a judgment or order that directs an accounting in an action for patent infringement.

(b) Stay Pending the Disposition of a Motion. On appropriate terms for the opposing party's security, the court may stay the execution of a judgment — or any proceedings to enforce it — pending disposition of any of the following motions:

(1) under Rule 50, for judgment as a matter of law;

(2) under Rule 52(b), to amend the findings or for additional findings;

(3) under Rule 59, for a new trial or to alter or amend a judgment; or

(4) under Rule 60, for relief from a judgment or order.

(c) Injunction Pending an Appeal. While an appeal is pending from an interlocutory order or final judgment that grants, dissolves, or denies an injunction, the court may suspend, modify, restore, or grant an injunction on terms for bond or other terms that secure the opposing party's rights. If the judgment appealed from is rendered by a statutory three-judge district court, the order must be made either:

(1) by that court sitting in open session; or

(2) by the assent of all its judges, as evidenced by their signatures.

(d) Stay with Bond on Appeal. If an appeal is taken, the appellant may obtain a stay by supersedeas bond, except in an action described in Rule 62(a)(1) or (2). The bond may be given upon or after filing the notice of appeal or after obtaining the order allowing the appeal. The stay takes effect when the court approves the bond.

(e) Stay Without Bond on an Appeal by the United States, Its Officers, or Its Agencies. The court must not require a bond, obligation, or other security from the appellant when granting a stay on an appeal by the United States, its officers, or its agencies or on an appeal directed by a department of the federal government.

(f) Stay in Favor of a Judgment Debtor Under State Law. If a judgment is a lien on the judgment debtor's property under the law of the state where the court is located, the judgment debtor is entitled to the same stay of execution the state court would give.

(g) Appellate Court's Power Not Limited. This rule does not limit the power of the appellate court or one of its judges or justices:

(1) to stay proceedings — or suspend, modify, restore, or grant an injunction — while an appeal is pending; or

(2) to issue an order to preserve the status quo or the effectiveness of the judgment to be entered.

(h) Stay with Multiple Claims or Parties. A court may stay the enforcement of a final judgment entered under Rule 54(b) until it enters a later judgment or judgments, and may prescribe terms necessary to secure the benefit of the stayed judgment for the party in whose favor it was entered.

Rule 63. Judge's Inability to Proceed

If a judge conducting a hearing or trial is unable to proceed, any other judge may proceed upon certifying familiarity with the record and determining that the case may be completed without prejudice to the parties. In a hearing or a nonjury trial, the successor judge must, at a party's request, recall any witness whose testimony is material and disputed and who is available to testify again without undue burden. The successor judge may also recall any other witness.

TITLE VIII. PROVISIONAL AND FINAL REMEDIES

Rule 64. Seizing a Person or Property

(a) Remedies Under State Law — In General. At the commencement of and throughout an action, every remedy is available that, under the law of the state where the court is located, provides for seizing a person or property to secure satisfaction of the potential judgment. But a federal statute governs to the extent it applies.

(b) Specific Kinds of Remedies. The remedies available under this rule include the following — however designated and regardless of whether state procedure requires an independent action:

- arrest;
- attachment;
- garnishment;
- replevin;
- sequestration; and
- other corresponding or equivalent remedies.

Rule 65. Injunctions and Restraining Orders

(a) Preliminary Injunction.

(1) ***Notice.*** The court may issue a preliminary injunction only on notice to the adverse party.

(2) ***Consolidating the Hearing with the Trial on the Merits.*** Before or after beginning the hearing on a motion for a preliminary injunction, the court may advance the trial on the merits and consolidate it with the hearing. Even when consolidation is not ordered, evidence that is received on the motion and that would be admissible at trial becomes part of the trial record and need not be repeated at trial. But the court must preserve any party's right to a jury trial.

(b) Temporary Restraining Order.

(1) *Issuing Without Notice.* The court may issue a temporary restraining order without written or oral notice to the adverse party or its attorney only if:

(A) specific facts in an affidavit or a verified complaint clearly show that immediate and irreparable injury, loss, or damage will result to the movant before the adverse party can be heard in opposition; and

(B) the movant's attorney certifies in writing any efforts made to give notice and the reasons why it should not be required.

(2) *Contents; Expiration.* Every temporary restraining order issued without notice must state the date and hour it was issued; describe the injury and state why it is irreparable; state why the order was issued without notice; and be promptly filed in the clerk's office and entered in the record. The order expires at the time after entry — not to exceed 10 days — that the court sets, unless before that time the court, for good cause, extends it for a like period or the adverse party consents to a longer extension. The reasons for an extension must be entered in the record.

(3) *Expediting the Preliminary-Injunction Hearing.* If the order is issued without notice, the motion for a preliminary injunction must be set for hearing at the earliest possible time, taking precedence over all other matters except hearings on older matters of the same character. At the hearing, the party who obtained the order must proceed with the motion; if the party does not, the court must dissolve the order.

(4) *Motion to Dissolve.* On 2 days' notice to the party who obtained the order without notice — or on shorter notice set by the court — the adverse party may appear and move to dissolve or modify the order. The court must then hear and decide the motion as promptly as justice requires.

(c) Security. The court may issue a preliminary injunction or a temporary restraining order only if the movant gives security in an amount that the court considers proper to pay the costs and damages sustained by any party found to have been wrongfully enjoined or restrained. The United States, its officers, and its agencies are not required to give security.

(d) Contents and Scope of Every Injunction and Restraining Order.

(1) *Contents.* Every order granting an injunction and every restraining order must:

(A) state the reasons why it issued;

(B) state its terms specifically; and

(C) describe in reasonable detail — and not by referring to the complaint or other document — the act or acts restrained or required.

(2) ***Persons Bound.*** The order binds only the following who receive actual notice of it by personal service or otherwise:

(A) the parties;

(B) the parties' officers, agents, servants, employees, and attorneys; and

(C) other persons who are in active concert or participation with anyone described in Rule 65(d)(2)(A) or (B).

(e) Other Laws Not Modified. These rules do not modify the following:

(1) any federal statute relating to temporary restraining orders or preliminary injunctions in actions affecting employer and employee;

(2) 28 U.S.C. § 2361, which relates to preliminary injunctions in actions of interpleader or in the nature of interpleader; or

(3) 28 U.S.C. § 2284, which relates to actions that must be heard and decided by a three-judge district court.

(f) Copyright Impoundment. This rule applies to copyright-impoundment proceedings.

Rule 65.1. Proceedings Against a Surety

Whenever these rules (including the Supplemental Rules for Admiralty or Maritime Claims and Asset Forfeiture Actions) require or allow a party to give security, and security is given through a bond or other undertaking with one or more sureties, each surety submits to the court's jurisdiction and irrevocably appoints the court clerk as its agent for receiving service of any papers that affect its liability on the bond or undertaking. The surety's liability may be enforced on motion without an independent action. The motion and any notice that the court orders may be served on the court clerk, who must promptly mail a copy of each to every surety whose address is known.

Rule 66. Receivers

These rules govern an action in which the appointment of a receiver is sought or a receiver sues or is sued. But the practice in administering an estate by a receiver or a similar court-appointed officer must accord with the historical practice in federal courts or with a local rule. An action in which a receiver has been appointed may be dismissed only by court order.

Rule 67. Deposit into Court

(a) Depositing Property. If any part of the relief sought is a money judgment or the disposition of a sum of money or some other deliverable thing, a party — on notice to every other party and by leave of court — may deposit with the court all or part of the money or thing, whether or not that party claims any of it. The depositing party must deliver to the clerk a copy of the order permitting deposit.

(b) Investing and Withdrawing Funds. Money paid into court under this rule must be deposited and withdrawn in accordance with 28 U.S.C. §§ 2041 and 2042 and any like statute. The money must be deposited in an interest-bearing account or invested in a court-approved, interest-bearing instrument.

Rule 68. Offer of Judgment

(a) Making an Offer; Judgment on an Accepted Offer. More than 10 days before the trial begins, a party defending against a claim may serve on an opposing party an offer to allow judgment on specified terms, with the costs then accrued. If, within 10 days after being served, the opposing party serves written notice accepting the offer, either party may then file the offer and notice of acceptance, plus proof of service. The clerk must then enter judgment.

(b) Unaccepted Offer. An unaccepted offer is considered withdrawn, but it does not preclude a later offer. Evidence of an unaccepted offer is not admissible except in a proceeding to determine costs.

(c) Offer After Liability Is Determined. When one party's liability to another has been determined but the extent of liability remains to be determined by further proceedings, the party held liable may make an offer of judgment. It must be served within a reasonable time — but at least 10 days — before a hearing to determine the extent of liability.

(d) Paying Costs After an Unaccepted Offer. If the judgment that the offeree finally obtains is not more favorable than the unaccepted offer, the offeree must pay the costs incurred after the offer was made.

Rule 69. Execution

(a) In General.

(1) ***Money Judgment; Applicable Procedure.*** A money judgment is enforced by a writ of execution, unless the court directs otherwise. The procedure on execution — and in proceedings supplementary to and in aid of judgment or execution — must accord with the procedure of the state where the court is located, but a federal statute governs to the extent it applies.

(2) ***Obtaining Discovery.*** In aid of the judgment or execution, the judgment creditor or a successor in interest whose interest appears of record may obtain discovery from any person — including the judgment debtor — as provided in these rules or by the procedure of the state where the court is located.

(b) Against Certain Public Officers. When a judgment has been entered against a revenue officer in the circumstances stated in 28 U.S.C. § 2006, or against an officer of Congress in the circumstances stated in 2 U.S.C. § 118, the judgment must be satisfied as those statutes provide.

Rule 70. Enforcing a Judgment for a Specific Act

(a) Party's Failure to Act; Ordering Another to Act. If a judgment requires a party to convey land, to deliver a deed or other document, or to perform any other specific act and the party fails to comply within the time specified, the court may order the act to be done — at the disobedient party's expense — by another person appointed by the court. When done, the act has the same effect as if done by the party.

(b) Vesting Title. If the real or personal property is within the district, the court — instead of ordering a conveyance — may enter a judgment divesting any party's title and vesting it in others. That judgment has the effect of a legally executed conveyance.

(c) Obtaining a Writ of Attachment or Sequestration. On application by a party entitled to performance of an act, the clerk must issue a writ of attachment or sequestration against the disobedient party's property to compel obedience.

(d) Obtaining a Writ of Execution or Assistance. On application by a party who obtains a judgment or order for possession, the clerk must issue a writ of execution or assistance.

(e) Holding in Contempt. The court may also hold the disobedient party in contempt.

Rule 71. Enforcing Relief For or Against a Nonparty

When an order grants relief for a nonparty or may be enforced against a nonparty, the procedure for enforcing the order is the same as for a party.

TITLE IX. SPECIAL PROCEEDINGS

Rule 71.1. Condemning Real or Personal Property

(a) Applicability of Other Rules. These rules govern proceedings to condemn real and personal property by eminent domain, except as this rule provides otherwise.

(b) Joinder of Properties. The plaintiff may join separate pieces of property in a single action, no matter whether they are owned by the same persons or sought for the same use.

(c) Complaint.

(1) ***Caption.*** The complaint must contain a caption as provided in Rule 10(a). The plaintiff must, however, name as defendants both the property — designated generally by kind, quantity, and location — and at least one owner of some part of or interest in the property.

(2) ***Contents.*** The complaint must contain a short and plain statement of the following:

(A) the authority for the taking;

(B) the uses for which the property is to be taken;

(C) a description sufficient to identify the property;

(D) the interests to be acquired; and

(E) for each piece of property, a designation of each defendant who has been joined as an owner or owner of an interest in it.

(3) ***Parties.*** When the action commences, the plaintiff need join as defendants only those persons who have or claim an interest in the property and whose names are then known. But before any hearing on compensation, the plaintiff must add as defendants all those persons who have or claim an interest and whose names have become known or can be found by a reasonably diligent search of the records, considering both the property's character and value and the interests to be acquired. All others may be made defendants under the designation "Unknown Owners."

(4) ***Procedure.*** Notice must be served on all defendants as provided in Rule 71.1(d), whether they were named as defendants when the action commenced or were added later. A defendant may answer as provided in Rule 71.1(e). The court, meanwhile, may order any distribution of a deposit that the facts warrant.

(5) ***Filing; Additional Copies.*** In addition to filing the complaint, the plaintiff must give the clerk at least one copy for the defendants' use and additional copies at the request of the clerk or a defendant.

(d) Process.

(1) ***Delivering Notice to the Clerk.*** On filing a complaint, the plaintiff must promptly deliver to the clerk joint or several notices directed to the named defendants. When adding defendants, the plaintiff must deliver to the clerk additional notices directed to the new defendants.

(2) ***Contents of the Notice.***

(A) *Main Contents.* Each notice must name the court, the title of the action, and the defendant to whom it is directed. It must describe the property sufficiently to identify it, but need not describe any property other than that to be taken from the named defendant. The notice must also state:

(i) that the action is to condemn property;

(ii) the interest to be taken;

(iii) the authority for the taking;

(iv) the uses for which the property is to be taken;

(v) that the defendant may serve an answer on the plaintiff's attorney within 20 days after being served with the notice;

(vi) that the failure to so serve an answer constitutes consent to the taking and to the court's authority to proceed with the action and fix the compensation; and

(vii) that a defendant who does not serve an answer may file a notice of appearance.

(B) *Conclusion.* The notice must conclude with the name, telephone number, and e-mail address of the plaintiff's attorney and an address within the district in which the action is brought where the attorney may be served.

(3) ***Serving the Notice.***

(A) *Personal Service.* When a defendant whose address is known resides within the United States or a territory subject to the administrative or judicial jurisdiction of the United States, personal service of the notice (without a copy of the complaint) must be made in accordance with Rule 4.

(B) *Service by Publication.*

(i) A defendant may be served by publication only when the plaintiff's attorney files a certificate stating that the attorney believes the defendant cannot be personally served, because after diligent inquiry within the state where the complaint is filed, the defendant's place of residence is still unknown or, if known, that it is beyond the territorial limits of personal service. Service is then made by publishing the notice — once a week for at least three successive weeks — in a newspaper published in the county where the property is located or, if there is no such newspaper, in a newspaper with general circulation where the property is located. Before the last publication, a copy of the notice must also be mailed to every defendant who cannot be personally served but whose place of residence is then known. Unknown owners may be served by publication in the same manner by a notice addressed to "Unknown Owners."

(ii) Service by publication is complete on the date of the last publication. The plaintiff's attorney must prove publication and mailing by a certificate, attach a printed copy of the published notice, and mark on the copy the newspaper's name and the dates of publication.

(4) ***Effect of Delivery and Service.*** Delivering the notice to the clerk and serving it have the same effect as serving a summons under Rule 4.

(5) ***Proof of Service; Amending the Proof or Notice.*** Rule 4(l) governs proof of service. The court may permit the proof or the notice to be amended.

(e) Appearance or Answer.

(1) ***Notice of Appearance.*** A defendant that has no objection or defense to the taking of its property may serve a notice of appearance designating the property in which it claims an interest. The defendant must then be given notice of all later proceedings affecting the defendant.

(2) ***Answer.*** A defendant that has an objection or defense to the taking must serve an answer within 20 days after being served with the notice. The answer must:

(A) identify the property in which the defendant claims an interest;

(B) state the nature and extent of the interest; and

(C) state all the defendant's objections and defenses to the taking.

(3) ***Waiver of Other Objections and Defenses; Evidence on Compensation.*** A defendant waives all objections and defenses not stated in its answer. No other pleading or motion asserting an additional objection or defense is allowed. But at the trial on compensation, a defendant — whether or not it has previously appeared or answered — may present evidence on the amount of compensation to be paid and may share in the award.

(f) Amending Pleadings. Without leave of court, the plaintiff may — as often as it wants — amend the complaint at any time before the trial on compensation. But no amendment may be made if it would result in a dismissal inconsistent with Rule 71.1(i)(1) or (2). The plaintiff need not serve a copy of an amendment, but must serve notice of the filing, as provided in Rule 5(b), on every affected party who has appeared and, as provided in Rule 71.1(d), on every affected party who has not appeared. In addition, the plaintiff must give the clerk at least one copy of each amendment for the defendants' use, and additional copies at the request of the clerk or a defendant. A defendant may appear or answer in the time and manner and with the same effect as provided in Rule 71.1(e).

(g) Substituting Parties. If a defendant dies, becomes incompetent, or transfers an interest after being joined, the court may, on motion and notice of hearing, order that the proper party be substituted. Service of the motion and notice on a nonparty must be made as provided in Rule 71.1(d)(3).

(h) Trial of the Issues.

(1) ***Issues Other Than Compensation; Compensation.*** In an action involving eminent domain under federal law, the court tries all issues, including compensation, except when compensation must be determined:

(A) by any tribunal specially constituted by a federal statute to determine compensation; or

(B) if there is no such tribunal, by a jury when a party demands one within the time to answer or within any additional time the court sets, unless the court appoints a commission.

(2) ***Appointing a Commission; Commission's Powers and Report.***

(A) *Reasons for Appointing.* If a party has demanded a jury, the court may instead appoint a three-person commission to determine compensation because of the character, location, or quantity of the property to be condemned or for other just reasons.

(B) *Alternate Commissioners.* The court may appoint up to two additional persons to serve as alternate commissioners to hear the case and replace commissioners who, before a decision is filed, the court finds unable or disqualified to perform their duties. Once the commission renders its final decision, the court must discharge any alternate who has not replaced a commissioner.

(C) *Examining the Prospective Commissioners.* Before making its appointments, the court must advise the parties of the identity and qualifications of each prospective commissioner and alternate, and may permit the parties to examine them. The parties may not suggest appointees, but for good cause may object to a prospective commissioner or alternate.

(D) *Commission's Powers and Report.* A commission has the powers of a master under Rule 53(c). Its action and report are determined by a majority. Rule 53(d), (e), and (f) apply to its action and report.

(i) Dismissal of the Action or a Defendant.

(1) ***Dismissing the Action.***

(A) *By the Plaintiff.* If no compensation hearing on a piece of property has begun, and if the plaintiff has not acquired title or a lesser interest or taken possession, the plaintiff may, without a court order, dismiss the action as to that property by filing a notice of dismissal briefly describing the property.

(B) *By Stipulation.* Before a judgment is entered vesting the plaintiff with title or a lesser interest in or possession of property, the plaintiff and affected defendants may, without a court order, dismiss the action in whole or in part by filing a stipulation of dismissal. And if the parties so stipulate, the court may vacate a judgment already entered.

(C) *By Court Order.* At any time before compensation has been determined and paid, the court may, after a motion and hearing, dismiss the action as to a piece of property. But if the plaintiff has already taken title, a lesser interest, or possession as to any part of it, the court must award compensation for the title, lesser interest, or possession taken.

(2) ***Dismissing a Defendant.*** The court may at any time dismiss a defendant who was unnecessarily or improperly joined.

(3) ***Effect.*** A dismissal is without prejudice unless otherwise stated in the notice, stipulation, or court order.

(j) Deposit and Its Distribution.

(1) ***Deposit.*** The plaintiff must deposit with the court any money required by law as a condition to the exercise of eminent domain and may make a deposit when allowed by statute.

(2) ***Distribution; Adjusting Distribution.*** After a deposit, the court and attorneys must expedite the proceedings so as to distribute the deposit and to determine and pay compensation. If the compensation finally awarded to a defendant exceeds the amount distributed to that defendant, the court must enter judgment against the plaintiff for the deficiency. If the compensation awarded to a defendant is less than the amount distributed to that defendant, the court must enter judgment against that defendant for the overpayment.

(k) Condemnation Under a State's Power of Eminent Domain. This rule governs an action involving eminent domain under state law. But if state law provides for trying an issue by jury — or for trying the issue of compensation by jury or commission or both — that law governs.

(l) Costs. Costs are not subject to Rule 54(d).

Rule 72. Magistrate Judges: Pretrial Order

(a) Nondispositive Matters. When a pretrial matter not dispositive of a party's claim or defense is referred to a magistrate judge to hear and decide, the magistrate judge must promptly conduct the required proceedings and, when appropriate, issue a written order stating the decision. A party may serve and file objections to the order within 10 days after being served with a copy. A party may not assign as error a defect in the order not timely objected to. The district judge in the case must consider timely objections and modify or set aside any part of the order that is clearly erroneous or is contrary to law.

(b) Dispositive Motions and Prisoner Petitions.

(1) ***Findings and Recommendations.*** A magistrate judge must promptly conduct the required proceedings when assigned, without the parties' consent, to hear a pretrial matter dispositive of a claim or defense or a prisoner petition challenging the conditions of confinement. A record must be made of all evidentiary proceedings and may, at the magistrate judge's discretion, be made of any other proceedings. The magistrate judge must enter a recommended disposition, including, if appropriate, proposed findings of fact. The clerk must promptly mail a copy to each party.

(2) ***Objections.*** Within 10 days after being served with a copy of the recommended disposition, a party may serve and file specific written objections to the proposed findings and recommendations. A party may respond to another party's objections within 10 days after being served with a copy. Unless the district judge orders otherwise, the objecting party must promptly arrange for transcribing the record, or whatever portions of it the parties agree to or the magistrate judge considers sufficient.

(3) ***Resolving Objections.*** The district judge must determine de novo any part of the magistrate judge's disposition that has been properly objected to. The district judge may accept, reject, or modify the recommended disposition; receive further evidence; or return the matter to the magistrate judge with instructions.

Rule 73. Magistrate Judges: Trial by Consent; Appeal

(a) Trial by Consent. When authorized under 28 U.S.C. § 636(c), a magistrate judge may, if all parties consent, conduct a civil action or proceeding, including a jury or nonjury trial. A record must be made in accordance with 28 U.S.C. § 636(c)(5).

(b) Consent Procedure.

(1) ***In General.*** When a magistrate judge has been designated to conduct civil actions or proceedings, the clerk must give the parties written notice of their opportunity to consent under 28 U.S.C. § 636(c). To signify their consent, the parties must jointly or separately file a statement consenting to the referral. A district judge or magistrate judge may be informed of a party's response to the clerk's notice only if all parties have consented to the referral.

(2) ***Reminding the Parties About Consenting.*** A district judge, magistrate judge, or other court official may remind the parties of the magistrate judge's availability, but must also advise them that they are free to withhold consent without adverse substantive consequences.

(3) *Vacating a Referral.* On its own for good cause — or when a party shows extraordinary circumstances — the district judge may vacate a referral to a magistrate judge under this rule.

(c) Appealing a Judgment. In accordance with 28 U.S.C. § 636(c)(3), an appeal from a judgment entered at a magistrate judge's direction may be taken to the court of appeals as would any other appeal from a district-court judgment.

Rule 74. [Abrogated.]

Rule 75. [Abrogated.]

Rule 76. [Abrogated.]

TITLE X. DISTRICT COURTS AND CLERKS: CONDUCTING BUSINESS; ISSUING ORDERS

Rule 77. Conducting Business; Clerk's Authority; Notice of an Order or Judgment

(a) When Court Is Open. Every district court is considered always open for filing any paper, issuing and returning process, making a motion, or entering an order.

(b) Place for Trial and Other Proceedings. Every trial on the merits must be conducted in open court and, so far as convenient, in a regular courtroom. Any other act or proceeding may be done or conducted by a judge in chambers, without the attendance of the clerk or other court official, and anywhere inside or outside the district. But no hearing — other than one ex parte — may be conducted outside the district unless all the affected parties consent.

(c) Clerk's Office Hours; Clerk's Orders.

(1) *Hours.* The clerk's office — with a clerk or deputy on duty — must be open during business hours every day except Saturdays, Sundays, and legal holidays. But a court may, by local rule or order, require that the office be open for specified hours on Saturday or a particular legal holiday other than one listed in Rule 6(a)(4)(A).

(2) *Orders.* Subject to the court's power to suspend, alter, or rescind the clerk's action for good cause, the clerk may:

(A) issue process;

(B) enter a default;

(C) enter a default judgment under Rule 55(b)(1); and

(D) act on any other matter that does not require the court's action.

(d) Serving Notice of an Order or Judgment.

(1) *Service.* Immediately after entering an order or judgment, the clerk must serve notice of the entry, as provided in Rule 5(b), on each party who is not in default for failing to appear. The clerk must record the service on the docket. A party also may serve notice of the entry as provided in Rule 5(b).

(2) *Time to Appeal Not Affected by Lack of Notice.* Lack of notice of the entry does not affect the time for appeal or relieve — or authorize the court to relieve — a party for failing to appeal within the time allowed, except as allowed by Federal Rule of Appellate Procedure (4)(a).

Rule 78. Hearing Motions; Submission on Briefs

(a) Providing a Regular Schedule for Oral Hearings. A court may establish regular times and places for oral hearings on motions.

(b) Providing for Submission on Briefs. By rule or order, the court may provide for submitting and determining motions on briefs, without oral hearings.

Rule 79. Records Kept by the Clerk

(a) Civil Docket.

(1) *In General.* The clerk must keep a record known as the "civil docket" in the form and manner prescribed by the Director of the Administrative Office of the United States Courts with the approval of the Judicial Conference of the United States. The clerk must enter each civil action in the docket. Actions must be assigned consecutive file numbers, which must be noted in the docket where the first entry of the action is made.

(2) *Items to be Entered.* The following items must be marked with the file number and entered chronologically in the docket:

(A) papers filed with the clerk;

(B) process issued, and proofs of service or other returns showing execution; and

(C) appearances, orders, verdicts, and judgments.

(3) ***Contents of Entries; Jury Trial Demanded.*** Each entry must briefly show the nature of the paper filed or writ issued, the substance of each proof of service or other return, and the substance and date of entry of each order and judgment. When a jury trial has been properly demanded or ordered, the clerk must enter the word "jury" in the docket.

(b) Civil Judgments and Orders. The clerk must keep a copy of every final judgment and appealable order; of every order affecting title to or a lien on real or personal property; and of any other order that the court directs to be kept. The clerk must keep these in the form and manner prescribed by the Director of the Administrative Office of the United States Courts with the approval of the Judicial Conference of the United States.

(c) Indexes; Calendars. Under the court's direction, the clerk must:

(1) keep indexes of the docket and of the judgments and orders described in Rule 79(b); and

(2) prepare calendars of all actions ready for trial, distinguishing jury trials from nonjury trials.

(d) Other Records. The clerk must keep any other records required by the Director of the Administrative Office of the United States Courts with the approval of the Judicial Conference of the United States.

Rule 80. Stenographic Transcript as Evidence

If stenographically reported testimony at a hearing or trial is admissible in evidence at a later trial, the testimony may be proved by a transcript certified by the person who reported it.

TITLE XI. GENERAL PROVISIONS

Rule 81. Applicability of the Rules in General; Removed Actions

(a) Applicability to Particular Proceedings.

(1) ***Prize Proceedings.*** These rules do not apply to prize proceedings in admiralty governed by 10 U.S.C. §§ 7651–7681.

(2) ***Bankruptcy.*** These rules apply to bankruptcy proceedings to the extent provided by the Federal Rules of Bankruptcy Procedure.

(3) ***Citizenship.*** These rules apply to proceedings for admission to citizenship to the extent that the practice in those proceedings is not specified in federal statutes and has previously conformed to the practice in civil actions. The provisions of 8 U.S.C. § 1451 for service by publication and for answer apply in proceedings to cancel citizenship certificates.

(4) ***Special Writs.*** These rules apply to proceedings for habeas corpus and for quo warranto to the extent that the practice in those proceedings:

(A) is not specified in a federal statute, the Rules Governing Section 2254 Cases, or the Rules Governing Section 2255 Cases; and

(B) has previously conformed to the practice in civil actions.

(5) ***Proceedings Involving a Subpoena.*** These rules apply to proceedings to compel testimony or the production of documents through a subpoena issued by a United States officer or agency under a federal statute, except as otherwise provided by statute, by local rule, or by court order in the proceedings.

(6) ***Other Proceedings.*** These rules, to the extent applicable, govern proceedings under the following laws, except as these laws provide other procedures:

(A) 7 U.S.C. §§ 292, 499g(c), for reviewing an order of the Secretary of Agriculture;

(B) 9 U.S.C., relating to arbitration;

(C) 15 U.S.C. § 522, for reviewing an order of the Secretary of the Interior;

(D) 15 U.S.C. § 715d(c), for reviewing an order denying a certificate of clearance;

(E) 29 U.S.C. §§ 159, 160, for enforcing an order of the National Labor Relations Board;

(F) 33 U.S.C. §§ 918, 921, for enforcing or reviewing a compensation order under the Longshore and Harbor Workers' Compensation Act; and

(G) 45 U.S.C. § 159, for reviewing an arbitration award in a railway-labor dispute.

(b) Scire Facias and Mandamus. The writs of scire facias and mandamus are abolished. Relief previously available through them may be obtained by appropriate action or motion under these rules.

(c) Removed Actions.

(1) *Applicability.* These rules apply to a civil action after it is removed from a state court.

(2) *Further Pleading.* After removal, repleading is unnecessary unless the court orders it. A defendant who did not answer before removal must answer or present other defenses or objections under these rules within the longest of these periods:

(A) 20 days after receiving — through service or otherwise — a copy of the initial pleading stating the claim for relief;

(B) 20 days after being served with the summons for an initial pleading on file at the time of service; or

(C) 5 days after the notice of removal is filed.

(3) *Demand for a Jury Trial.*

(A) *As Affected by State Law.* A party who, before removal, expressly demanded a jury trial in accordance with state law need not renew the demand after removal. If the state law did not require an express demand for a jury trial, a party need not make one after removal unless the court orders the parties to do so within a specified time. The court must so order at a party's request and may so order on its own. A party who fails to make a demand when so ordered waives a jury trial.

(B) *Under Rule 38.* If all necessary pleadings have been served at the time of removal, a party entitled to a jury trial under Rule 38 must be given one if the party serves a demand within 10 days after:

(i) it files a notice of removal; or

(ii) it is served with a notice of removal filed by another party.

(d) Law Applicable.

(1) *State Law.* When these rules refer to state law, the term "law" includes the state's statutes and the state's judicial decisions.

(2) *District of Columbia.* The term "state" includes, where appropriate, the District of Columbia. When these rules provide for state law to apply, in the District Court for the District of Columbia:

(A) the law applied in the District governs; and

(B) the term "federal statute" includes any Act of Congress that applies locally to the District.

Rule 82. Jurisdiction and Venue Unaffected

These rules do not extend or limit the jurisdiction of the district courts or the venue of actions in those courts. An admiralty or maritime claim under Rule 9(h) is not a civil action for purposes of 28 U.S.C. §§ 1391-1392.

Rule 83. Rules by District Courts; Judge's Directives

(a) Local Rules.

(1) ***In General.*** After giving public notice and an opportunity for comment, a district court, acting by a majority of its district judges, may adopt and amend rules governing its practice. A local rule must be consistent with — but not duplicate — federal statutes and rules adopted under 28 U.S.C. §§ 2072 and 2075, and must conform to any uniform numbering system prescribed by the Judicial Conference of the United States. A local rule takes effect on the date specified by the district court and remains in effect unless amended by the court or abrogated by the judicial council of the circuit. Copies of rules and amendments must, on their adoption, be furnished to the judicial council and the Administrative Office of the United States Courts and be made available to the public.

(2) ***Requirement of Form.*** A local rule imposing a requirement of form must not be enforced in a way that causes a party to lose any right because of a nonwillful failure to comply.

(b) Procedure When There Is No Controlling Law. A judge may regulate practice in any manner consistent with federal law, rules adopted under 28 U.S.C. §§ 2072 and 2075, and the district's local rules. No sanction or other disadvantage may be imposed for noncompliance with any requirement not in federal law, federal rules, or the local rules unless the alleged violator has been furnished in the particular case with actual notice of the requirement.

Rule 84. Forms

The forms in the Appendix suffice under these rules and illustrate the simplicity and brevity that these rules contemplate.

Rule 85. Title

These rules may be cited as the Federal Rules of Civil Procedure.

Rule 86. Effective Dates

(a) In General. These rules and any amendments take effect at the time specified by the Supreme Court, subject to 28 U.S.C. § 2074. They govern:

(1) proceedings in an action commenced after their effective date; and

(2) proceedings after that date in an action then pending unless:

(A) the Supreme Court specifies otherwise; or

(B) the court determines that applying them in a particular action would be infeasible or work an injustice.

(b) December 1, 2007 Amendments. If any provision in Rules 1-5.1, 6-73, or 77-86 conflicts with another law, priority in time for the purpose of 28 U.S.C. § 2072(b) is not affected by the amendments taking effect on December 1, 2007.

* * * * * * *

APPENDIX OF FORMS

Form 1. Caption. *(Use on every summons, complaint, answer, motion, or other document.)*

United States District Court
for the
__________District of __________

A B, Plaintiff	)	
	)	
v.	)	
	)	**Civil Action No. ________**
C D, Defendant	)	
	)	
v.	)	
	)	
E F, Third-Party Defendant	)	
(Use if needed.)	)	

(Name of Document)

Form 2. Date, Signature, Address, E-mail Address, and Telephone Number. *(Use at the conclusion of pleadings and other papers that require a signature.)*

Date ________________

____
(Signature of the attorney or unrepresented party)

____
(Printed name)

____
(Address)

____
(E-mail address)

____
(Telephone number)

Form 3. Summons.

(Caption — See Form 1.)

To *name the defendant*:

A lawsuit has been filed against you.

Within 20 days after service of this summons on you (not counting the day you received it), you must serve on the plaintiff an answer to the attached complaint or a motion under Rule 12 of the Federal Rules of Civil Procedure. The answer or motion must be served on the plaintiff's attorney, ____________, whose address is ____________. If you fail to do so, judgment by default will be entered against you for the relief demanded in the complaint. You also must file your answer or motion with the court.

Date ________________ ________________
Clerk of Court

(Court Seal)

(Use 60 days if the defendant is the United States or a United States agency, or is an officer or employee of the United States allowed 60 days by Rule 12(a)(3).)

Form 4. Summons on a Third-Party Complaint.

(Caption — See Form 1.)

To *name the third-party defendant*:

A lawsuit has been filed against defendant ____________, who as third-party plaintiff is making this claim against you to pay part or all of what [he] may owe to the plaintiff ____________.

Within 20 days after service of this summons on you (not counting the day you received it), you must serve on the plaintiff and on the defendant an answer to the attached third-party complaint or a motion under Rule 12 of the Federal Rules of Civil Procedure. The answer or motion must be served on the defendant's attorney, ____________, whose address is ____________, and also on the plaintiff's attorney, ____________, whose address is, ____________. If you fail to do so, judgment by default will be entered against you for the relief demanded in the third-party complaint. You also must file the answer or motion with the court and serve it on any other parties.

A copy of the plaintiff's complaint is also attached. You may — but are not required to — respond to it.

Date ________________

____
Clerk of Court

(Court Seal)

Form 5. Notice of a Lawsuit and Request to Waive Service of a Summons.

(Caption — See Form 1.)

To (*name the defendant — or if the defendant is a corporation, partnership, or association name an officer or agent authorized to receive service)*:

Why are you getting this?

A lawsuit has been filed against you, or the entity you represent, in this court under the number shown above. A copy of the complaint is attached.

This is not a summons, or an official notice from the court. It is a request that, to avoid expenses, you waive formal service of a summons by signing and returning the enclosed waiver. To avoid these expenses, you must return the signed waiver within (*give at least 30 days or at least 60 days if the defendant is outside any judicial district of the United States*) from the date shown below, which is the date this notice was sent. Two copies of the waiver form are enclosed, along with a stamped, self-addressed envelope or other prepaid means for returning one copy. You may keep the other copy.

What happens next?

If you return the signed waiver, I will file it with the court. The action will then proceed as if you had been served on the date the waiver is filed, but no summons will be served on you and you will have 60 days from the date this notice is sent (see the date below) to answer the complaint (or 90 days if this notice is sent to you outside any judicial district of the United States).

If you do not return the signed waiver within the time indicated, I will arrange to have the summons and complaint served on you. And I will ask the court to require you, or the entity you represent, to pay the expenses of making service.

Please read the enclosed statement about the duty to avoid unnecessary expenses.

I certify that this request is being sent to you on the date below.

(Date and sign — See Form 2.)

Form 6. Waiver of the Service of Summons.

(Caption — See Form 1.)

To *name the plaintiff's attorney or the unrepresented plaintiff*:

I have received your request to waive service of a summons in this action along with a copy of the complaint, two copies of this waiver form, and a prepaid means of returning one signed copy of the form to you.

I, or the entity I represent, agree to save the expense of serving a summons and complaint in this case.

I understand that I, or the entity I represent, will keep all defenses or objections to the lawsuit, the court's jurisdiction, and the venue of the action, but that I waive any objections to the absence of a summons or of service.

I also understand that I, or the entity I represent, must file and serve an answer or a motion under Rule 12 within 60 days from ______________, the date when this request was sent (or 90 days if it was sent outside the United States). If I fail to do so, a default judgment will be entered against me or the entity I represent.

(Date and sign — See Form 2.)

(Attach the following to Form 6.)

Duty to Avoid Unnecessary Expenses of Serving a Summons

Rule 4 of the Federal Rules of Civil Procedure requires certain defendants to cooperate in saving unnecessary expenses of serving a summons and complaint. A defendant who is located in the United States and who fails to return a signed waiver of service requested by a plaintiff located in the United States will be required to pay the expenses of service, unless the defendant shows good cause for the failure.

"Good cause" does *not* include a belief that the lawsuit is groundless, or that it has been brought in an improper venue, or that the court has no jurisdiction over this matter or over the defendant or the defendant's property.

If the waiver is signed and returned, you can still make these and all other defenses and objections, but you cannot object to the absence of a summons or of service.

If you waive service, then you must, within the time specified on the waiver form, serve an answer or a motion under Rule 12 on the plaintiff and file a copy with the court. By signing and returning the waiver form, you are allowed more time to respond than if a summons had been served.

Form 7. Statement of Jurisdiction.

a. (*For diversity-of-citizenship jurisdiction.*) The plaintiff is [a citizen of *Michigan*] [a corporation incorporated under the laws of *Michigan* with its principal place of business in *Michigan*]. The defendant is [a citizen of *New York*] [a corporation incorporated under the laws of *New York* with its principal place of business in *New York*]. The amount in controversy, without interest and costs, exceeds the sum or value specified by 28 U.S.C. § 1332.

b. (*For federal-question jurisdiction.*) This action arises under [the United States Constitution, *specify the article or amendment and the section*] [a United States treaty *specify*] [a federal statute, ___U.S.C. § ___].

c. (*For a claim in the admiralty or maritime jurisdiction.*) This is a case of admiralty or maritime jurisdiction. (*To invoke admiralty status under Rule 9(h) use the following:* This is an admiralty or maritime claim within the meaning of Rule 9(h).)

Form 8. Statement of Reasons for Omitting a Party. (*If a person who ought to be made a party under Rule 19(a) is not named, include this statement in accordance with Rule 19(c).*)

This complaint does not join as a party *name* who [is not subject to this court's personal jurisdiction] [cannot be made a party without depriving this court of subject-matter jurisdiction] because *state the reason.*

Form 9. Statement Noting a Party's Death.

(Caption — See Form 1.)

In accordance with Rule 25(a) *name the person,* who is [a party to this action] [a representative of or successor to the deceased party] notes the death during the pendency of this action of *name*, [*describe as party* in this action].

(Date and sign — See Form 2.)

Form 10. Complaint to Recover a Sum Certain.

(Caption — See Form 1.)

1. (Statement of Jurisdiction — See Form 7.)

(*Use one or more of the following as appropriate and include a demand for judgment.*)

(*a*) *On a Promissory Note*

2. On __*date*__, the defendant executed and delivered a note promising to pay the plaintiff on _*date*_ the sum of $ _______ with interest at the rate of ___ percent. A copy of the note [is attached as Exhibit A] [is summarized as follows: ________________.]

3. The defendant has not paid the amount owed.

(*b*) *On an Account*

2. The defendant owes the plaintiff $ _______ according to the account set out in Exhibit A.

(*c*) *For Goods Sold and Delivered*

2. The defendant owes the plaintiff $ _______ for goods sold and delivered by the plaintiff to the defendant from _*date*_ to _*date*_.

(*d*) *For Money Lent*

2. The defendant owes the plaintiff $ _______ for money lent by the plaintiff to the defendant on _*date*_.

(*e*) *For Money Paid by Mistake*

2. The defendant owes the plaintiff $ _______ for money paid by mistake to the defendant on _*date*_ under these circumstances: *describe with particularity in accordance with Rule 9(b).*

(*f*) *For Money Had and Received*

2. The defendant owes the plaintiff $ _______ for money that was received from _*name*_ on _*date*_ to be paid by the defendant to the plaintiff.

Demand for Judgment

Therefore, the plaintiff demands judgment against the defendant for $ _______, plus interest and costs.

(Date and sign — See Form 2.)

Form 11. Complaint for Negligence.

(Caption — See Form 1.)

1 (Statement of Jurisdiction — See Form 7.)

2. On _date_, at _place_, the defendant negligently drove a motor vehicle against the plaintiff.

3. As a result, the plaintiff was physically injured, lost wages or income, suffered physical and mental pain, and incurred medical expenses of $ _______.

Therefore, the plaintiff demands judgment against the defendant for $ _______, plus costs.

(Date and sign — See Form 2).

Form 12. Complaint for Negligence When the Plaintiff Does Not Know Who Is Responsible.

(Caption — See Form 1.)

1. (Statement of Jurisdiction — See Form 7.)

2. On _date_, at _place_, defendant _name_ or defendant _name_ or both of them willfully or recklessly or negligently drove, or caused to be driven, a motor vehicle against the plaintiff.

3. As a result, the plaintiff was physically injured, lost wages or income, suffered mental and physical pain, and incurred medical expenses of $ _______.

Therefore, the plaintiff demands judgment against one or both defendants for $ _______, plus costs.

(Date and sign — See Form 2.)

Form 13. Complaint for Negligence Under the Federal Employers' Liability Act.

(Caption — See Form 1.)

1. (Statement of Jurisdiction — See Form 7.)

2. At the times below, the defendant owned and operated in interstate commerce a railroad line that passed through a tunnel located at _____________.

3. On date, the plaintiff was working to repair and enlarge the tunnel to make it convenient and safe for use in interstate commerce.

4. During this work, the defendant, as the employer, negligently put the plaintiff to work in a section of the tunnel that the defendant had left unprotected and unsupported.

5. The defendant's negligence caused the plaintiff to be injured by a rock that fell from an unsupported portion of the tunnel.

6. As a result, the plaintiff was physically injured, lost wages or income, suffered mental and physical pain, and incurred medical expenses of $ ________.

Therefore, the plaintiff demands judgment against the defendant for $ ________, and costs.

(Date and sign — See Form 2.)

Form 14. Complaint for Damages Under the Merchant Marine Act.

(Caption — See Form 1.)

1. (Statement of Jurisdiction — See Form 7.)

2. At the times below, the defendant owned and operated the vessel *name* and used it to transport cargo for hire by water in interstate and foreign commerce.

3. On *date*, at *place*, the defendant hired the plaintiff under seamen's articles of customary form for a voyage from ______________ to ______________ and return at a wage of $ ________ a month and found, which is equal to a shore worker's wage of $ ________ a month.

4. On *date*, the vessel was at sea on the return voyage. (*Describe the weather and the condition of the vessel.*)

5. (*Describe as in Form 11 the defendant's negligent conduct.*)

6. As a result of the defendant's negligent conduct and the unseaworthiness of the vessel, the plaintiff was physically injured, has been incapable of any gainful activity, suffered mental and physical pain, and has incurred medical expenses of $ ________.

Therefore, the plaintiff demands judgment against the defendant for $ ________, plus costs.

(Date and sign — See Form 2.)

Form 15. Complaint for the Conversion of Property.

(Caption — See Form 1.)

1. (Statement of Jurisdiction — See Form 7.)

2. On ___*date*___, at ___*place*___, the defendant converted to the defendant's own use property owned by the plaintiff. The property converted consists of ___*describe*___.

3. The property is worth $ ________.

Therefore, the plaintiff demands judgment against the defendant for $ ________, plus costs.

(Date and sign — See Form 2.)

Form 16. Third-Party Complaint.

(Caption — See Form 1.)

1. Plaintiff ___*name*___ has filed against defendant ___*name*___ a complaint, a copy of which is attached.

2. (*State grounds entitling* *defendant's name* *to recover from* *third-party defendant's name* *for (all or an identified share) of any judgment for* *plaintiff's name* *against* *defendant's name*.)

Therefore, the defendant demands judgment against *third-party defendant's name* for *all or an identified share* of sums that may be adjudged against the defendant in the plaintiff's favor.

(Date and sign — See Form 2.)

Form 17. Complaint for Specific Performance of a Contract to Convey Land.

(Caption — See Form 1.)

1. (Statement of Jurisdiction — See Form 7.)

2. On ___*date*___, the parties agreed to the contract [attached as Exhibit A][summarize the contract].

3. As agreed, the plaintiff tendered the purchase price and requested a conveyance of the land, but the defendant refused to accept the money or make a conveyance.

4. The plaintiff now offers to pay the purchase price.

Therefore, the plaintiff demands that:

(a) the defendant be required to specifically perform the agreement and pay damages of $ _______, plus interest and costs, or

(b) if specific performance is not ordered, the defendant be required to pay damages of $ _______, plus interest and costs.

(Date and sign — See Form 2.)

Form 18. Complaint for Patent Infringement.

(Caption — See Form 1.)

1. (Statement of Jurisdiction — See Form 7.)

2. On _date_, United States Letters Patent No. _______ were issued to the plaintiff for an invention in an _electric motor_. The plaintiff owned the patent throughout the period of the defendant's infringing acts and still owns the patent.

3. The defendant has infringed and is still infringing the Letters Patent by making, selling, and using _electric motors_ that embody the patented invention, and the defendant will continue to do so unless enjoined by this court.

4. The plaintiff has complied with the statutory requirement of placing a notice of the Letters Patent on all _electric motors_ it manufactures and sells and has given the defendant written notice of the infringement.

Therefore, the plaintiff demands:

(a) a preliminary and final injunction against the continuing infringement;

(b) an accounting for damages; and

(c) interest and costs.

(Date and sign — See Form 2.)

Form 19. Complaint for Copyright Infringement and Unfair Competition.

(Caption — See Form 1.)

1. (Statement of Jurisdiction — See Form 7.)

2. Before _date_, the plaintiff, a United States citizen, wrote a book entitled ____________.

3. The book is an original work that may be copyrighted under United States law. A copy of the book is attached as Exhibit A.

4. Between _date_ and _date_, the plaintiff applied to the copyright office and received a certificate of registration dated _______ and identified as _date, class, number_.

5. Since _date_, the plaintiff has either published or licensed for publication all copies of the book in compliance with the copyright laws and has remained the sole owner of the copyright.

6. After the copyright was issued, the defendant infringed the copyright by publishing and selling a book entitled ____________, which was copied largely from the plaintiff's book. A copy of the defendant's book is attached as Exhibit B.

7. The plaintiff has notified the defendant in writing of the infringement.

8. The defendant continues to infringe the copyright by continuing to publish and sell the infringing book in violation of the copyright, and further has engaged in unfair trade practices and unfair competition in connection with its publication and sale of the infringing book, thus causing irreparable damage.

Therefore, the plaintiff demands that:

(a) until this case is decided the defendant and the defendant's agents be enjoined from disposing of any copies of the defendant's book by sale or otherwise;

(b) the defendant account for and pay as damages to the plaintiff all profits and advantages gained from unfair trade practices and unfair competition in selling the defendant's book, and all profits and advantages gained from infringing the plaintiff's copyright (but no less than the statutory minimum);

(c) the defendant deliver for impoundment all copies of the book in the defendant's possession or control and deliver for destruction all infringing copies and all plates, molds, and other materials for making infringing copies;

(d) the defendant pay the plaintiff interest, costs, and reasonable attorney's fees; and

(e) the plaintiff be awarded any other just relief.

(Date and sign — See Form 2.)

Form 20. Complaint for Interpleader and Declaratory Relief.

(Caption — See Form 1.)

1. (Statement of Jurisdiction — See Form 7.)

2. On *date*, the plaintiff issued a life insurance policy on the life of *name* with *name* as the named beneficiary.

3. As a condition for keeping the policy in force, the policy required payment of a premium during the first year and then annually.

4. The premium due on *date* was never paid, and the policy lapsed after that date.

5. On *date*, after the policy had lapsed, both the insured and the named beneficiary died in an automobile collision.

6. Defendant *name* claims to be the beneficiary in place of *name* and has filed a claim to be paid the policy's full amount.

7. The other two defendants are representatives of the deceased persons' estates. Each defendant has filed a claim on behalf of each estate to receive payment of the policy's full amount.

8. If the policy was in force at the time of death, the plaintiff is in doubt about who should be paid.

Therefore, the plaintiff demands that:

(a) each defendant be restrained from commencing any action against the plaintiff on the policy;

(b) a judgment be entered that no defendant is entitled to the proceeds of the policy or any part of it, but if the court determines that the policy was in effect at the time of the insured's death, that the defendants be required to interplead and settle among themselves their rights to the proceeds, and that the plaintiff be discharged from all liability except to the defendant determined to be entitled to the proceeds; and

(c) the plaintiff recover its costs.

(Date and sign — See Form 2.)

Form 21. Complaint on a Claim for a Debt and to Set Aside a Fraudulent Conveyance Under Rule 18(b).

(Caption — See Form 1.)

1. (Statement of Jurisdiction — See Form 7.)

2. On _date_, defendant _name_ signed a note promising to pay to the plaintiff on _date_ the sum of $ _______ with interest at the rate of ___ percent. [The pleader may, but need not, attach a copy or plead the note verbatim.]

3. Defendant _name_ owes the plaintiff the amount of the note and interest.

4. On _date_, defendant _name_ conveyed all defendant's real and personal property _if less than all, describe it fully_ to defendant _name_ for the purpose of defrauding the plaintiff and hindering or delaying the collection of the debt.

Therefore, the plaintiff demands that:

(a) judgment for $ _______, plus costs, be entered against defendant(s) _name(s)_; and

(b) the conveyance to defendant _name_ be declared void and any judgment granted be made a lien on the property.

(Date and sign — See Form 2.)

Form 30. Answer Presenting Defenses Under Rule 12(b).

(Caption — See Form 1.)

Responding to Allegations in the Complaint

1. Defendant admits the allegations in paragraphs _______.

2. Defendant lacks knowledge or information sufficient to form a belief about the truth of the allegations in paragraphs _______.

3. Defendant admits _identify part of the allegation_ in paragraph _______ and denies or lacks knowledge or information sufficient to form a belief about the truth of the rest of the paragraph.

Failure to State a Claim

4. The complaint fails to state a claim upon which relief can be granted.

Failure to Join a Required Party

5. If there is a debt, it is owed jointly by the defendant and _name_ who is a citizen of _______. This person can be made a party without depriving this court of jurisdiction over the existing parties.

Affirmative Defense — Statute of Limitations

6. The plaintiff's claim is barred by the statute of limitations because it arose more than ___ years before this action was commenced.

Counterclaim

7. *(Set forth any counterclaim in the same way a claim is pleaded in a complaint. Include a further statement of jurisdiction if needed.)*

Crossclaim

8. *(Set forth a crossclaim against a coparty in the same way a claim is pleaded in a complaint. Include a further statement of jurisdiction if needed.)*

(Date and sign — See Form 2.)

Form 31. Answer to a Complaint for Money Had and Received with a Counterclaim for Interpleader.

(Caption — See Form 1.)

Response to the Allegations in the Complaint

(See Form 30.)

Counterclaim for Interpleader

1. The defendant received from ___*name*___ a deposit of $ _______.

2. The plaintiff demands payment of the deposit because of a purported assignment from ___*name*___, who has notified the defendant that the assignment is not valid and who continues to hold the defendant responsible for the deposit.

Therefore, the defendant demands that:

(a) ___*name*___ be made a party to this action;

(b) the plaintiff and ___*name*___ be required to interplead their respective claims;

(c) the court decide whether the plaintiff or ___*name*___ or either of them is entitled to the deposit and discharge the defendant of any liability except to the person entitled to the deposit; and

(d) the defendant recover costs and attorney's fees.

(Date and sign — See Form 2.)

Form 40. Motion to Dismiss Under Rule 12(b) for Lack of Jurisdiction, Improper Venue, Insufficient Service of Process, or Failure to State a Claim.

(Caption — See Form 1.)

The defendant moves to dismiss the action because:

1. the amount in controversy is less than the sum or value specified by 28 U.S.C. § 1332;

2. the defendant is not subject to the personal jurisdiction of this court;

3. venue is improper (this defendant does not reside in this district and no part of the events or omissions giving rise to the claim occurred in the district);

4. the defendant has not been properly served, as shown by the attached affidavits of ______________; or

5. the complaint fails to state a claim upon which relief can be granted.

(Date and sign — See Form 2.)

Form 41. Motion to Bring in a Third-Party Defendant.

(Caption — See Form 1.)

The defendant, as third-party plaintiff, moves for leave to serve on *name* a summons and third-party complaint, copies of which are attached.

(Date and sign — See Form 2.)

Form 42. Motion to Intervene as a Defendant Under Rule 24.

(Caption — See Form 1.)

1. *name* moves for leave to intervene as a defendant in this action and to file the attached answer.

(*State grounds under Rule 24(a) or (b).*)

2. The plaintiff alleges patent infringement. We manufacture and sell to the defendant the articles involved, and we have a defense to the plaintiff's claim.

3. Our defense presents questions of law and fact that are common to this action.

(Date and sign — See Form 2.)

[An Intervener's Answer must be attached. See Form 30.]

Form 50. Request to Produce Documents and Tangible Things, or to Enter onto Land Under Rule 34.

(Caption — See Form 1.)

The plaintiff _name_ requests that the defendant _name_ respond within ___ days to the following requests:

1. To produce and permit the plaintiff to inspect and copy and to test or sample the following documents, including electronically stored information:

(Describe each document and the electronically stored information, either individually or by category.)

(State the time, place, and manner of the inspection and any related acts.)

2. To produce and permit the plaintiff to inspect and copy — and to test or sample — the following tangible things:

(Describe each thing, either individually or by category.)

(State the time, place, and manner of the inspection and any related acts.)

3. To permit the plaintiff to enter onto the following land to inspect, photograph, test, or sample the property or an object or operation on the property.

(Describe the property and each object or operation.)

(State the time and manner of the inspection and any related acts.)

(Date and sign — See Form 2.)

Form 51. Request for Admissions Under Rule 36.

(Caption — See Form 1.)

The plaintiff _name_ asks the defendant _name_ to respond within 30 days to these requests by admitting, for purposes of this action only and subject to objections to admissibility at trial:

1. The genuineness of the following documents, copies of which [are attached] [are or have been furnished or made available for inspection and copying].

(List each document.)

2. The truth of each of the following statements:

(List each statement.)

(Date and sign — See Form 2.)

Form 52. Report of the Parties' Planning Meeting.

(Caption — See Form 1.)

1. The following persons participated in a Rule 26(f) conference on *date* by *state the method of conferring*:

(*e.g., name* representing the plaintiff.)

2. Initial Disclosures. The parties [have completed] [will complete by *date*] the initial disclosures required by Rule 26(a)(1).

3. Discovery Plan. The parties propose this discovery plan:

(*Use separate paragraphs or subparagraphs if the parties disagree.*)

(a) Discovery will be needed on these subjects: (*describe.*)

(b) (Dates for commencing and completing discovery, including discovery to be commenced or completed before other discovery.)

(c) (Maximum number of interrogatories by each party to another party, along with the dates the answers are due.)

(d) (Maximum number of requests for admission, along with the dates responses are due.)

(e) (Maximum number of depositions by each party.)

(f) (Limits on the length of depositions, in hours.)

(g) (Dates for exchanging reports of expert witnesses.)

(h) (Dates for supplementations under Rule 26(e).)

4. Other Items:

(a) (A date if the parties ask to meet with the court before a scheduling order.)

(b) (Requested dates for pretrial conferences.)

(c) (Final dates for the plaintiff to amend pleadings or to join parties.)

(d) (Final dates for the defendant to amend pleadings or to join parties.)

(e) (Final dates to file dispositive motions.)

(f) (State the prospects for settlement.)

(g) (Identify any alternative dispute resolution procedure that may enhance settlement prospects.)

(h) (Final dates for submitting Rule 26(a)(3) witness lists, designations of witnesses whose testimony will be presented by deposition, and exhibit lists.)

(i) (Final dates to file objections under Rule 26(a)(3).)

(j) (Suggested trial date and estimate of trial length.)

(k) (Other matters.)

(Date and sign — See Form 2.)

Form 60. Notice of Condemnation.

(Caption — See Form 1.)

To *name the defendant*.

1. A complaint in condemnation has been filed in the United States District Court for the ________ District of ________, to take property to use for *purpose*. The interest to be taken is *describe*. The court is located in the United States courthouse at this address: ____________.

2. The property to be taken is described below. You have or claim an interest in it.

(Describe the property.)

3. The authority for taking this property is *cite*.

4. If you want to object or present any defense to the taking you must serve an answer on the plaintiff's attorney within 20 days [after being served with this notice] [from (insert the date of the last publication of notice)]. Send your answer to this address: ____________.

5. Your answer must identify the property in which you claim an interest, state the nature and extent of that interest, and state all your objections and defenses to the taking. Objections and defenses not presented are waived.

6. If you fail to answer you consent to the taking and the court will enter a judgment that takes your described property interest.

7. Instead of answering, you may serve on the plaintiff's attorney a notice of appearance that designates the property in which you claim an interest. After you do that, you will receive a notice of any proceedings that affect you. Whether or not you have previously appeared or answered,

you may present evidence at a trial to determine compensation for the property and share in the overall award.

(Date and sign — See Form 2.)

Form 61. Complaint for Condemnation.

(Caption — See Form 1; name as defendants
the property and at least one owner.)

1. (Statement of Jurisdiction — See Form 7.)

2. This is an action to take property under the power of eminent domain and to determine just compensation to be paid to the owners and parties in interest.

3. The authority for the taking is _______.

4. The property is to be used for _____________.

5. The property to be taken is (*describe in enough detail for identification — or attach the description and state "is described in Exhibit A, attached."*)

6. The interest to be acquired is _____________.

7. The persons known to the plaintiff to have or claim an interest in the property are: _____________. *(For each person include the interest claimed.)*

8. There may be other persons who have or claim an interest in the property and whose names could not be found after a reasonably diligent search. They are made parties under the designation "Unknown Owners."

Therefore, the plaintiff demands judgment:

(a) condemning the property;

(b) determining and awarding just compensation; and

(c) granting any other lawful and proper relief.

(Date and sign — See Form 2.)

Form 70. Judgment on a Jury Verdict.

(Caption — See Form 1.)

This action was tried by a jury with Judge ________ presiding, and the jury has rendered a verdict.

It is ordered that:

[the plaintiff _name_ recover from the defendant _name_ the amount of $ _______ with interest at the rate of ___%, along with costs.]

[the plaintiff recover nothing, the action be dismissed on the merits, and the defendant _name_ recover costs from the plaintiff _name_.]

Date _______________ _______________
Clerk of Court

Form 71. Judgment by the Court without a Jury.

(Caption — See Form 1.)

This action was tried by Judge _______ without a jury and the following decision was reached:

It is ordered that [the plaintiff _name_ recover from the defendant _name_ the amount of $ _______, with prejudgment interest at the rate of ___%, postjudgment interest at the rate of ___%, along with costs.] [the plaintiff recover nothing, the action be dismissed on the merits, and the defendant _name_ recover costs from the plaintiff _name_.]

Date _______________ _______________
Clerk of Court

Form 80. Notice of a Magistrate Judge's Availability.

1. A magistrate judge is available under title 28 U.S.C. § 636(c) to conduct the proceedings in this case, including a jury or nonjury trial and the entry of final judgment. But a magistrate judge can be assigned only if all parties voluntarily consent.

2. You may withhold your consent without adverse substantive consequences. The identity of any party consenting or withholding consent will not be disclosed to the judge to whom the case is assigned or to any magistrate judge.

3. If a magistrate judge does hear your case, you may appeal directly to a United States court of appeals as you would if a district judge heard it.

A form called *Consent to an Assignment to a United States Magistrate Judge* is available from the court clerk's office.

Form 81. Consent to an Assignment to a Magistrate Judge.

(Caption — See Form 1.)

I voluntarily consent to have a United States magistrate judge conduct all further proceedings in this case, including a trial, and order the entry of final judgment. (Return this form to the court clerk — not to a judge or magistrate judge.)

Date ________________ ____________________

Signature of the Party

Form 82. Order of Assignment to a Magistrate Judge.

(Caption — See Form 1.)

With the parties' consent it is ordered that this case be assigned to United States Magistrate Judge _______ of this district to conduct all proceedings and enter final judgment in accordance with 28 U.S.C. § 636(c).

Date ________________ ____________________

United States District Judge